CHILD LANGUAGE
A BOOK OF READINGS

PRENTICE-HALL INTERNATIONAL, INC., London
PRENTICE-HALL OF AUSTRALIA, PTY. LTD., Sydney
PRENTICE-HALL OF CANADA, LTD., Toronto
PRENTICE-HALL OF INDIA PRIVATE LIMITED, New Delhi
PRENTICE-HALL OF JAPAN, INC., Tokyo

CHILD LANGUAGE

A BOOK OF READINGS

Edited by

Aaron Bar-Adon
University of Texas

Werner F. Leopold
Northwestern University

PRENTICE-HALL, INC., ENGLEWOOD CLIFFS, NEW JERSEY

© 1971 by *PRENTICE-HALL, INC., ENGLEWOOD CLIFFS, NEW JERSEY*

13–130765–7

Library of Congress Catalog Card Number: 74–87264

Printed in the United States of America

Current Printing (last number):

10 9 8 7 6 5 4 3 2 1

To
Zipporah
&
Marguerite

CONTENTS

INTRODUCTION〜〜〜〜〜〜〜〜〜

There has been a growing interest in the study of child language on the part of linguists and psychologists (psycholinguists), as well as of educators and representatives in other fields.

The literature on child language is by now quite rich, although it is a relatively new field, and its treatment, from a linguistic point of view, is fairly recent.

This book is an attempt to help the student of child language, especially the beginning student, whether graduate or undergraduate, find his way to some of the high points of American and international research, such as French, German, Hebrew, Polish, and Russian.

The selections in this reader are intended to introduce him to various fields of child language and to different theories and research methods, both psychological and linguistic, as well as to various stages in the history of child language research. Naturally, special attention has been given to contemporary and even most recent research on all facets of child language: phonology, morphology, syntax, semantics, as well as to the study of first language acquisition within a generative-transformational theory of language and the search for linguistic universals.

The bulk of the work on this volume was done in 1965–1967, but a number of selections were added during the final editing stage in 1967 and 1968. Some of the studies are still in print in their original form.

The selections are chosen from the contributions of linguists, psychologists, and representatives of related fields and reflect the development of the study of child language from the 19th (even 18th) century to the present day. Moreover, the *chronological* arrangement of the selections will enable the student to see this development. The titles of the selections are usually indicative by themselves of the topics and areas—e.g., syntax, phonology, and general linguistic or psycholinguistic theory, thus making further classification quite redundant.

To choose from the vast number of studies published in recent times was difficult and, to a certain extent, arbitrary. Each contribution is considered significant in one way or another, and the editors regret that many important studies had to be omitted because of space limitations. A greater number of valuable publications was probably passed over than was included. It would be easy to fill another volume without lowering quality.

One handicap of a reader is the unavoidably severe limitation of length. For practical reasons, articles were found to be more suitable for inclusion than chapters of books, and short articles usually had to be preferred over long ones. Occasionally, however, extracts from, or abstracts of, longer publications were resorted to.

Most of the selections concern children of preschool age, but a few interesting studies of school-age children are included.

Of course, this reader is not meant to be a complete course in child language but, rather, is designed to attract the reader and to stimulate him to further study this exciting field. For the convenience of the student, introductions were added to each selection to give him an idea about the backgrounds of the authors and their works and the problems encountered, and sometimes a summary was included. References were also added in many cases to direct him to further work.

In order to accommodate the curious reader, we have added a section of annotated bibliographies and other reference lists, as well as another section of reviews on the study of child language, from either the historical or the thematic point of view. These reviews usually include comprehensive reference lists, hence some overlap between these two sections. We expect the serious student to use the references to deepen his mastery of the field.

We wish to express our gratitude to all the contributors and publishers for their kind cooperation.

We should also like to thank Winifred P. Lehmann, James H. Sledd, Roger Brown, and Ursula Bellugi-Klima for their advice and encouragement at various stages of the work, as well as the University of Texas at Austin for secretarial assistance and Mary T. Willenborg for her assistance in preparing most of the manuscript for the printers.

ON THE STUDY OF CHILD LANGUAGE

The first paper, "The Study of Child Language and Infant Bilingualism" by Werner F. Leopold, is a brief review of this area from the middle of the nineteenth century to the middle of this century. It serves as an introduction to this entire volume.

For supplementary work, we refer the reader to several reviews and summaries of research in this field arranged chronologically:

McCarthy, Dorothea, "Language Development in Children," in *Manual of Child Psychology*, ed. L. Carmichael, pp. 476–581. New York, London: John Wiley & Sons, Inc., 1946. Second edition, New York, 1954, pp. 492–630.

Brown, Roger, *Words and Things*. New York: The Free Press, 1956.

Leopold, W. F., "Roman Jakobson and the Study of Child Language," in *For Roman Jakobson*, ed. M. Halle et al., pp. 285–88. The Hague: Mouton Publishers, 1956.

Brown, R. W., and J. Berko, "Psycholinguistic Research Methods," in *Handbook of Research Methods in Child Development*, ed. P. H. Mussen, pp. 515–17. New York: John Wiley & Sons, Inc., 1960.

Carroll, J. B., "Language Development in Children," in *Encyclopedia of Educational Research* (3rd ed.), ed. Chester W. Harris, pp. 744–52. New York: The Macmillan Co., 1960. Reprinted in our reader.

Ervin, S., and W. Miller, "Language Development," in *Child Psychology*, ed. H. W. Stevenson, Part I. Chicago: University of Chicago Press, 1963. Sixty-second Yearbook of the National Society for the Study of Education.

Carroll, J. B., *Language and Thought*, p. 118. Englewood Cliffs, N. J.: Prentice-Hall, Inc. 1964.

Ervin-Tripp, S. M., "Language Development," in *Review of Child Development Research*, ed. M. Hoffman and L. Hoffman, Vol. 2, pp. 55–105. Ann Arbor: The University of Michigan Press, 1966.

Braine, Martin D. S., "The Acquisition of Language in Infant and Child," in *The Learning of* Language, ed. Carroll Reed, forthcoming.

McNeill, David, "The Development of Language," in Carmichael, ed., *Manual of Child Psychology*, ed. P. A. Mussen, forthcoming.

For Russian child language research, see Dan Slobin's papers:

"Grammatical Development in Russian-speaking Children," in *The Development of Language Functions*, ed. K. F. Riegel, pp. 93–100. Ann Arbor: University of Michigan Center for Human Growth and Development, Language Development Program, Report No. 8, 1965. See Chapter 53 in this volume.

"The Acquisition of Russian as a Native Language," in *The Genesis of Language*, ed. F. Smith and G. A. Miller, pp. 129–48. Cambridge, Mass.: The M. I. T. Press, 1966.

For German child language study, consult:

Stern, W. C., *Die Kindersprache* (4th ed.). Leipzig: Barth, 1928.

Leopold, W. F., "Die Kindersprache," *Phonetica*, IV, No. 4 (1959), 191–214.

Kainz, F. *Sprachentwicklung im Kindes und Jugendalter*. Munich: Reinhardt, 1964.

The following bibliographies will also be of help:

I

Dale, E., and D. Reichert, *Bibliography of Vocabulary Studies*. Columbus: Ohio State University Press, 1949. Second edition by E. Dale, p. 174, 1957.

Leopold, Werner F., *Bibliography of Child Language*, p. 115. Evanston, Ill.: Northwestern University Press, 1952.

———, "Die Kindersprache." See above.

McCarthy, Dorothea, "Language Development in Children." See above.

Sableski, Julia A., "A Selective Annotated Bibliography on Child Language," *The Linguistic Reporter*, VII, No. 2 (April 1965), 4–6. Twenty-eight items.

II

Ervin, Susan, "Publications on Psycholinguistics," *International Journal of American Linguistics*, XXX, No. 1 (January 1964), 90–93.

———, "Publications on Psycholinguistics," *International Journal of American Linguistics*, XXX, No. 2 (April 1964), 184–93.

III

Extensive bibliographies are also included in:

Bar-Adon, Aaron, *Children's Hebrew in Israel*, Vol. 1, pp. 41–43. Jerusalem, 1959. In Hebrew, with particular references to Hebrew child language.

McNeill, David, "The Development of Language." See above.

——, "Developmental Psycholinguistics," in *The Genesis of Language*, ed. F. Smith and G. A. Miller, pp. 82–84. Cambridge, Mass.: The M. I. T. Press, 1966.

Slobin, Dan I., "The Acquisition of Russian as a Native Language," in *The Genesis of Language*, ed. Frank Smith and George Miller, pp. 146–48. Cambridge, Mass.: The M. I. T. Press, 1966.

TOPICAL TABLE OF CONTENTS

Since the readings are arranged according to the chronological order of their publication, we are adding here a Topical Table of Contents to supplement the main Table of Contents for easier reference.

Instead of copying the full titles again, we will refer to the readings by the sequential numbers only. Readings that relate to several topics may appear in more than one listing.

CHILD LANGUAGE
A BOOK OF READINGS

WERNER F. LEOPOLD

1 This article, which gives a concise survey of the study of child language until 1946, was published in 1948 at the time that Leopold's four-volume study of *Speech Development of a Bilingual Child* was about to be completed. The first volume covering "Vocabulary Growth in the First Two Years" appeared in 1939 (Evanston: Northwestern University Press). The second volume on "Sound-Learning in the First Two Years" appeared in 1947, and the third volume on "Grammar and General Problems in the First Two Years" appeared in 1949, and in the same year his fourth volume also appeared, which constitutes a "Diary From Age Two." A summary of this work is included in Leopold's "Patterning in Children's Language Learning" (*Language Learning*, 1953–54), which is included in this reader in lieu of a selection from that comprehensive work. One of the by-products of Leopold's work was the *Bibliography of Child Language* (Evanston: Northwestern University Press, 1952), which is cited among the bibliographies in the Introduction.

One might say that this paper convinced American linguists that Child Language is a worthwhile and respectable field for research. The term "child language," which is now generally used in place of the earlier terms "children's language" or "children's speech," was launched in this paper.

For supplementary work on the study of child language see the Introduction.

A. B. A.

THE STUDY OF CHILD LANGUAGE AND INFANT BILINGUALISM

Child language and infant bilingualism[1] have so far only received marginal consideration from most linguistic scholars. The linguistic literature contains frequent references to children's language learning; but most of these references are casual side-glances designed to support a point which the author wishes to make. On closer inspection they often prove to be based on very superficial observation, to be rooted in untested traditional impressions, and to clash with the findings of those who have really studied child language. Marcel Cohen complains rightly[2] that those who mention child language indulge too often in speculative interpretations and sweeping generalizations instead of taking the trouble to investigate child language.

For example, one finds again and again the assumption that *mama* is one of the first words spoken by infants. Kretschmer, Trombetti, Royen,[3] and many others mention the 'fact' and draw their own far-reaching conclusions from it. It is true, of course, that children say *mama* early and frequently. I suspect that it is the frequency of its use which leads superficial observers into chronological illusions. *Mama* is frequent and early, but by no means always among the first words. *Papa* is usually earlier. It appears far more commonly as the first meaningful word than does *mama*.[4]

'Meaningful' is an important qualification. Although not usually the first, [ma ma] is

Reprinted from Word *4.1–17 (1948) by permission of the Linguistic Circle of New York, Inc.*

[1] This paper was presented in abridged form before the Germanic section of the Modern Language Association in Chicago, 1945, and at the summer meeting of the Linguistic Society at Ann Arbor, 1947.

[2] *Bulletin de la Société de Linguistique de Paris*, XXXVII (1936), 19.

[3] Kretschmer cited and quoted by Alfredo Trombetti, *Elementi di glottologia* (Bologna, 1923) 231 and by G. Royen, *Die nominalen Klassifikationssysteme in den Sprachen der Erde* (Vienna: Mödling, 1929), 785.

[4] P. Schäfer, "Die kindliche Entwicklungsstufe des reinen Sprachverständnisses nach ihrer Abgrenzung," *Zeitschrift für pädagogische Psychologie*, XXII (1921), 319.

an early babbling syllable. It is natural that fond mothers, waiting for the traditional word, joyfully interpret it as a reference to themselves; but dispassionate scholars should not follow them into the trap. Unprejudiced observers find that these babbling syllables have at first no meaning at all, are mere muscle exercises. Then, very commonly, the meaning of food becomes attached to them. The word *mjamjam*, sometimes used by older children in the sense of 'it tastes good,' is nothing but a phonetic variant of the babbling word with the meaning of food.

Eventually, of course, *mama* comes to be filled with the conventional meaning. The teaching endeavors of the parents and their persistent misinterpretation of the child's intentions are entirely responsible for this semantic development. Often this takes many months. In the case which I studied,[5] not even the phonetic combination [mama] occurred in the babbling stage until the end of the tenth month; [baba] was fully two and a half months earlier. For one whole month [mama] was said without any meaning. Then it slowly developed the meaning 'food,' together with such variants as [m:] and [mjamjam]. The standard reference of the word *mama* was not understood by the child until the very end of the first year, half a month later than that of *papa*, and even then the little girl did not say it herself with this meaning. At the end of the thirteenth month the child said [*pa-pa*] with the standard meaning. One month later I tried to teach her to say *mama*, but with all good will she was unable to say the combination intentionally. She said [m:papa], and another month later [baba] actually meant 'mama' as well as 'papa.' Finally, at the beginning of the sixteenth month, the child was taught by her mother to say *mama* with the traditional meaning, and then the word became established quickly and was used frequently and correctly. But that was two and a half months after the learning of *papa* with meaning. *Mama* was preceded by six other designations of persons, including the general term *baby*, which was used for all children. Even the part-time maid was named

earlier than the mother.[6] The explanation undoubtedly is not that the mother was less important for the child than the father and other persons. On the contrary, the mother's place in the child's world was so central that specific naming was not needed at first.

This is a sample of how exact, unprejudiced records can correct the picture obtained by the vague impressions of casual observers. In the literature of child language there are many studies which do not avoid the pitfalls to which fond mothers are exposed. In fact, many of the authors are fond mothers and fathers. Some are amateurs; more are scholars; but few are linguistic scholars, and it takes the best techniques of a linguistic scholar to guard against misinterpretations. Certainly there is no reason for linguists themselves to commit the same mistakes if they will take more of a first-hand interest in child language. Few have done so up to now.

Most of the many articles and books on child language have been produced, not by linguists, but by psychologists and educators, who deserve credit for having seen the importance of the study of child language and for having pursued it energetically. Scholars in other fields have made contributions, but linguistic scholars, who ought to be most competent, have lagged behind.

The exact study of child language began in Germany in the middle of the nineteenth century under the impetus of the philosophy of Herbart. There were forerunners. Tiedemann, a professor of philosophy at the University of Marburg, had published a set of observations in 1787. They were significant enough to be republished a hundred years later in German, French, and English.[7]

---

[5] W. F. Leopold, *Speech Development of a Bilingual Child*, vol. I, *Vocabulary Growth in the First Two Years* (1939); vol. II, *Sound-Learning in the First Two Years* (Evanston: Northwestern University Studies in the Humanities, 1947), nos. 6 and 11. Volumes III and IV [published 1949].

[6] Cp. my I, 42 f., 101 f., 170.

[7] Dietrich Tiedemann, *Beobachtungen über die Entwicklung der Seelenfähigkeiten bei Kindern*. New eidtion by Ufer (Altenburg, 1897); cf. A. Jakobstötter, *Die Psychologie Dietrich Tiedemanns*, dissertation (Erlangen, 1898). "Observations sur le développement des facultés de l'âme chez les enfants" (trans. H. Michelant), *Journal Général de l'Instruction Publique* (1863), 251, 291, 309, 319; Bernard Perez, *Thierry Tiedemann et la science de l'enfant* (Paris, 1881). *Tiedemann's Record of Infant-Life*; an English version of the French translation and commentary by Bernard Perez, with notes, by F. L. Solden (1877; Syracuse, N. Y., 1890); cf. C. Murchison and S. Langer, Tiedemann's observations on the development of the mental faculties of children, *Pedagogical Seminary*, XXXIV (1927), 205–30.

The educational theorist Schwarz had included a noteworthy treatment of child language in his great work on pedagogy (1802).[8] Feldmann (1838) had given incidental statistics on the first words of 33 children.[9]

But research really got under way with the pioneer work of Herbart's follower Sigismund,[10] who inspired many later writers. Sigismund was a physician and some of his first followers were also physicians, who used a physiological approach: Kussmaul, Vierordt.[11] The physician Löbisch[12] had used the same approach before Sigismund; the Russian Sikorsky continued to use it later.[13]

One of the most remarkable early summaries is that of Franke.[14] His physiological approach led him to a brilliant, searching phonetic and even phonemic analysis of children's sound learning. His results are not always correct; there are linguistic weaknesses; his belief in hereditary features of sound mastery is objectionable; his preoccupation with the parallelism between the language learning of children and that of mankind, while interesting and not fruitless, is not entirely wholesome; but after all is said, his study remains a significant one.

With Herbart's follower Strümpell,[15] an educator, research swung back into psychological channels, as charted by Sigismund.

The Herbart school in Germany received succor from England through Darwin and his followers. Evolutionism led to the recording of consecutive, systematic observations. Darwin[16] himself made such observations in 1840, although they were not published until 1877. A few years earlier, the French philosopher Taine[17] had published his data, collected around 1870. Both these studies were brief and sketchy, but the way was paved for more comprehensive genetic investigations.

Other representatives of the biological and evolutionary approach were Romanes and Baldwin. Romanes,[18] the English biologist, friend of Darwin, to be sure has only general statements on child language, which interested him as a link between animal speech and human language. He has the merit of recognizing that evolutionism had been practically applied in comparative linguistics before it had been clearly formulated in natural science.[19] Baldwin, an American, also used child language only occasionally

---

[8] Friedrich Heinrich Christian Schwarz, *Erziehungslehre* (Leipzig, 1802–13, 4 vols.; second ed. 1829–30, 3 vols.); cf. Friedrich Richter, *Die Entwicklung der psychologischen Kindersprachforschung* (Münster, 1927) p. 8 f.

[9] Heinrich Feldmann, *De statu normali functionum corporis humani* dissertation (Bonn, 1833); cf. Preyer see note 27) II, 248 f.

[10] Berthold Sigismund, *Kind und Welt* (Braunschweig, 1856; new ed. by Chr. Ufer, Braunschweig, 1897; by Karl Markscheffel, Langensalza, 1900).

[11] Adolf Kussmaul, *Untersuchungen über das Seelenleben des neugeborenen Menschen* (1859, third ed., 1896); *Die Störungen der Sprache* (1877, fourth ed., 1910). Karl von Vierordt, Die Sprache des Kindes, *Deutsche Revue*, III (1879), 29–46; Sprechen, Gerhardt's *Handbuch der Kinderkrankheiten*, I (1881), 454–57.

[12] J. E. Löbisch, *Entwickelungsgeschichte der Seele des Kindes* (Wien, 1851, 1854).

[13] I. A. Sikorsky, Du développement du langage chez les enfants, *Archives de Neurologie* 1883 and 1884; *Die Seele des Kindes* (Leipzig, 1902; second ed, 1908); cf. also Hermann Gutzmann, *Des Kindes Sprache und Sprachfehler* (Leipzig, 1894; second ed., 1931), a good, practical, popular handbook for speech hygiene, written by a professor of medicine who was an expert physiological phonetician. Otherwise, I consider matters of speech pathology and therapeutics outside the scope of my survey. For bibliography concerning aphasia, see Jakobson's book of 1941 (note 79) and the references given there on p. 78, note 1. Jakobson also includes works in Slavic languages and refers, in the same note, to sources for Slavic and Japanese bibliography. The present paper only covers contributions written in Germanic and Romance languages.

[14] Carl Franke, "Sprachentwicklung der Kinder und der Menschheit," W. Rein's *Encyclopädisches Handbuch der Pädagogik*, VI (1899), 751–94; VIII, 742–90 (second ed., 1908); cp. "Über die erste Lautstufe der Kinder," *Anthropos*, VII (1912), 663–76. According to Stern (see note 51) 7 note 1, Franke was a linguist.

[15] Ludwig Strümpell, *Pscyhologische Pädagogik* (Leipzig, 1880); appendix 352–68: "Notizen über die geistige Entwickelung eines weiblichen Kindes während der ersten zwei Lebensjahre."

[16] Charles Darwin, "A biographical sketch of an infant," *Mind*, II (1877) 285–94; German translation: *Kosmos*, I (1877) and *Gesammelte kleinere Schriften*, II (1886), 145 ff.

[17] H. Taine, De l'acquisition du langage chez des enfants et dans l'espèce humaine, *De l'intelligence* (Paris, 1870; twelfth ed., 1912), I, 357 ff.; German translation, *Der Verstand*, I (1880) 283 ff.; cp. M. Taine, "On the Acquisition of Language by Children," *Mind*, II (1871), 252–59; "Note sur l'acquisition du langage chez les enfants et les peuples primitifs," *Revue Philosophique*, I (1876), 3–23.

[18] G. J. Romanes, *Mental Evolution in Man* (London, 1888; New York, 1889); *L'évolution mentale chez l'homme* (Paris, 1891); *Die geistige Entwicklung beim Menschen* (Leipzig, 1893).

[19] Romanes, p. 240 (English edition).

as a stepping-stone to larger purposes.[20] Both have therefore only a marginal position in the history of child-language research as active workers; but both emphasized the crucial place of child language in the investigation of the human mind and of language, and did much to give prestige to the genetic method. Besides, Baldwin's principle of the 'circular reaction' in the speaking process became a fruitful theory, which was carried over into the study of child language by his student, the psychologist Allport,[21] and by the linguist Bloomfield,[22] both representatives of behaviorism.

The first great systematic studies were those of Perez[23] in France (1878) and Preyer[24] in Germany (1882). The latter especially had a profound and lasting effect on subsequent research. Preyer was a physiologist at Jena, but his approach is not physiological. He was inspired by Sigismund. His book comprises all phases of the mental development of the child as disclosed by a minute study of his own son. Almost a whole volume is devoted to the topic 'Learning to speak,' and 90 pages contain a most careful chronological record of the beginnings of speech during the first three years. Much of Preyer's theorizing lent itself to violent attacks, which did not fail to come forth,[25] but the factual

record retains its value to the present day.[26]

A little earlier, in 1877, an American scholar, Holden, professor of astronomy at the University of Wisconsin, had published a brief record.[27] This painstaking study deserves credit as a pioneer effort; but it has serious defects, especially in phonetics. The author acknowledges, modestly enough, the difficulties of research in a field to which he is unaccustomed. Some workers in America[28] followed his method, with all its defects, for more than four decades, much longer than the progress in research warranted.

One of the most fruitful early investigations is that of the German philosopher Schultze (1880).[29] He postulated the 'principle of the least effort' for the sequence of children's sound learning. This controversial principle has remained a pivotal point of discussion to the present day. As such it has the merit of having stimulated thinking about the essentials of sound learning and of having provided a common point of departure for many opinions. The controversy is not yet decided and continues to revolve around his tenet. He himself was conscious of having generalized on the basis of insufficient individual record material.

In 1893 the French educator Compayré included in his book on the development of the child,[30] most of which is a psychological summary, a lucid and sane general chapter (XI) on the child's language learning. The treatment is second-hand; Preyer, Romanes,

---

[20] James Mark Baldwin, *Mental Development in the Child and in the Race* (New York, 1895; third ed. 1906); *Le développement mental chez l'enfant et dans la race* (Paris, 1897); *Die Entwicklung des Geistes beim Kinde und bei der Rasse* (Berlin, 1898); cf. Richter (see note 10) 29, 84 f.

[21] F. H. Allport, *Social Psychology* (New York [1924]); cp. M. M. Lewis (see note 58) 59, 79.

[22] Leonard Bloomfield, *Language* (New York, 1933), pp. 29–31, 512.

[23] Bernard Perez, *La psychologie de l'enfant; les trois premières années* (Paris, 1878; seventh ed. 1911); *The First Three Years of Childhood* (London, 1885; Chicago, 1885; Syracuse N. Y., 1889); continuations of the study (Paris, 1886 and 1888); cp. his account of Tiedemann (note 7).

[24] W. Preyer, *Die Seele des Kindes* (Leipzig, 1882; ninth ed., 1923); *The Mind of the Child* (New York, 1888–1890; 2 vols.); *L'âme de l'enfant*, traduit de l'anglais (Paris, 1887); other editions and extracts in German and English. My references are to the English edition, second volume (1890).

[25] For example from Ament, Meumann, Idelberger.

[26] Cf. Karl Bühler (see note 54), fifth ed, p. 52 f.

[27] E. S. Holden, "On the Vocabularies of Children under Two Years of Age," *Transactions American Philological Association*, VIII (1877), 58–68; summarized by Preyer, II, 252–55 (English edition), who includes several other published and unpublished records in his book.

[28] For example N. R. Heilig, "A Child's Vocabulary," *Pedagogical Seminary*, XX (1913), 1–16; W. G. Bateman, "A Child's Progress in Speech," *Journal of Educational Psychology*, V (1914), 307–20; "Two Children's Progress in Speech," same journal, VI (1915), 475–93; C. L. and B. I. Hull, "Parallel Learning Curves of an Infant in Vocabulary and in Voluntary Control of the Bladder," *Pedagogical Seminary*, XXVI (1919), 272–83.

[29] Fritz Schultze, *Die Sprache des Kindes* (Leipzig, 1880).

[30] G. Compayré, *L'évolution intellectuelle et morale de l'enfant* (Paris, 1893).

Egger,[31] Darwin, Pollock[32] are his authorities; but he was considered the leader in the field of child psychology in France at the turn of the century,[33] and his book was translated into English, German, and Spanish.[34] On account of its influence as well as its quality it cannot be passed over in silence.

Toward the end of the century the psychologists took over in earnest. The inspiration came from Germany once more. The Englishman Sully, trained in German universities, published his *Studies of Childhood*[35] in 1896 and included in them his observations of the language of a boy. They dated back to 1880, two years before the publication of Preyer's work, which he used with admiration for the later redaction. Although phonetically crude, the book gives a good general picture of child language and is one of the best summarizing works in the field. It passes the linguist's judgment more successfully than many later publications.

A far-reaching influence was exerted by the great German psychologist Wundt,[36]

who, inspired by Sigismund,[37] paid serious attention to the study of child language. A direct line leads from him to the German scholar Meumann and the latter's student Idelberger[38] as well as to the influential American psychologist Stanley Hall,[39] who inspired a whole school of American students of child language, represented by such names as Tracy, Dewey,[40] Lukens, Chamberlain.[41]

The Canadian Tracy, in his *Psychology of Childhood* (1893),[42] gave in one chapter a summary of previous child-language studies, with no observations of his own. The book, now antiquated, commanded attention for a long time. It presented a good general picture of child language and dealt especially with phonetic aspects, although not with full adequacy.

In 1899 a young German philosopher, Ament, interrupted the stream of psychologists' studies with an enthusiastic and ambitious book on the speaking and thinking of children,[43] based on direct and second-hand observations. He considered briefly all aspects of the grammar of child language. The book was attacked[44] and vindicated[45] in turn by later students. It retains at least historical

[31] Emile Egger, *Observations et réflexions sur le développement de l'intelligence et du langage chez les enfants* (Paris, 1879; fifth ed., 1887); *Beobachtungen und Betrachtungen über die Entwicklung der Intelligenz und der Sprache bei Kindern* (Leipzig, 1903).

[32] F. Pollock, "An Infant's Progress in Language," *Mind*, III (1878), 392–40. Pollock, a jurist, took notes on the linguistic development of a girl during her first 23 months, following the example of Darwin and Taine, at first for his own amusement. Although he has 'no pretensions to skill in phonetics,' he uses at least a consistent phonetic notation. His account is very incomplete and phonetically not satisfactory, but it is sober and deserves attention as a good early contribution.

[33] Cp. Richter (see note 8) p. 88.

[34] *The Intellectual and Moral Development of the Child* (New York, 1896–1902; 2 vols.). *Die Entwicklung der Kindesseele*, translated from the second French edition (Altenburg, 1900; second ed., 1924). *La evolución intelectual y moral del niño* (Madrid, 1905).

[35] James Sully, *Studies of Childhood* (New York and London, 1896; reissue, 1900; new editions, 1903, 1908); *Untersuchungen über die Kindheit* (Leipzig, 1897; second ed., 1904); *Etudes sur l'enfance* (Paris, 1898).

[36] Wilhelm Wundt, *Grundzüge der physiologischen Psychologie* (1874; fourth ed., 1893; 2 vols.); "Die Sprache und das Denken," *Essays* (Leipzig, 1885; second ed., 1906), pp. 269–317.

[37] Cf. Richter (see note 8), p. 15.

[38] H. A. Idelberger, *Hauptprobleme der kinderlichen Sprachentwicklung, nach eigenen Beobachtungen behandelt* (Zürich dissertation, Berlin, n. d, [1903 ?]), also *Zeitschrift für pädagogische Psychologie* V (1903–4), 241–97; 425–56.

[39] G. Stanley Hall, "The Contents of Children's Minds on Entering School," and "Notes on the Study of Infants," *Pedagogical Seminary*, I (1891), 127–38 and 139–73. Language incidentally.

[40] John Dewey, "The Psychology of Infant Language," *Psychological Review* I (1894), 63–66. Observations inspired by Tracy and Romanes.

[41] Alexander Francis Chamberlain, *The Child* (London, 1900; New York, 1901); "Notes on Indian Child Language," *American Anthropologist*, III (1890), 237–41; (1893), 321 f. Preterite-Forms, etc., in the Language of English-Speaking Children," *Modern Language Notes*, XXI (1906), 42–44; id. and Isabel C. Chamberlain, "Studies of a Child," *Pedagogical Seminary*, XI (1904), 264–91, 452–83; XII (1905), 427–53; XVI (1909), 64–103.

[42] Frederick Tracy, *The Psychology of Childhood* (Boston, 1893; seventh ed., 1909); *Psychologie der Kindheit* (Leipzig, 1899; fourth ed., 1912).

[43] Wilhelm Ament, *Die Entwicklung von Sprechen und Denken beim Kinde* (Leipzig, 1899; reprint, 1912).

[44] By Meumann and by Lindner, for example.

[45] By Karl Bühler.

importance. Ament gave a complete survey of the history of child-language research from Herodotus on. His book summarizes and terminates the 'intellectualistic' approach.[46]

Wundt made his most significant contribution in 1900 in the first volume of his *Völkerpsychologie*, a part of which is devoted to a detailed study of the sounds of children.[47] As in all of his work on language, Wundt's importance lies less in his psychological theories, which are debatable, than in the array of facts which he presents.

A few years later his student Meumann[48] created a stir in child-language research by attacking the one-sided intellectual interpretation of children's speech. He laid the stress on the emotional and voluntaristic urges operating in it. Although he did not go too far in the new direction, a violent discussion ensued, which helped to put the thinking about child language on a broader base.

One of his critics was Lindner, a normal-school teacher in Saxony, who had assiduously studied child language since 1882 and was thus one of the pioneers contemporaneous with Preyer. His records,[49] like all exact individual case studies,[50] retain their usefulness, as source materials, much longer than speculative publications.

The work of the psychologists reached a summit in 1907 with the publication of the comprehensive study *Die Kindersprache* by

Clara and William Stern,[51] which, brought up to date in the fourth edition, stands today as the most authoritative book on child language. It contains the first-hand observations of the authors and epitomizes the results of the international literature in a systematic manner. The approach is psychological, but an earnest attempt is made to digest the linguistic literature as well. The weakest point is phonetics, which is consciously neglected. The first two years, in which the latter is of paramount importance, receive only slight consideration.[52] In the same year there appeared in English the sensible survey of O'Shea.[53]

Of later contributions by psychologists, the books of Karl Bühler (1918)[54] and Charlotte Bühler (1928),[55] both native Germans, who later taught in Vienna and eventually came to the U.S., must be mentioned. The Frenchman Guillaume presented a book and several articles (1925–27).[56] His psychology is untechnical and his grammatical approach is

[46] Cp. Stern (see note 51) p. 5.

[47] Wilhelm Wundt, *Völkerpsychologie*, vol. I, *Die Sprache*, part 1 (Leipzig, 1900; third ed., 1911) pp. 284–319 (fourth ed., 1921).

[48] E. Meumann, Die Entstehung der ersten Wortbedeutungen beim Kinde, Wundt's *Philosophische Studien*, XX (1902), 152–214; also separately (Leipzig, 1902; second ed., 1908); *Die Sprache des Kindes* (Zürich, 1903).

[49] Gustav Lindner, "Beobachtungen und Bemerkungen über die Entwicklung der Sprache des Kindes," *Kosmos*, VI (1882), 321–42, 430–41; "Zum Studium der Kindersprache," *Kosmos*, IX (1885), 161–73, 241–59; *Aus dem Naturgarten der Kindersprache* (Leipzig, 1898; material collected, 1883–7); "Neuere Forschungen und Anschauungen über die Sprache des Kindes," *Zeitschrift für pädagogische Psychologie*, VII (1906), 377–92.

[50] McCarthy calls such studies 'biographic.' However, the aspect of growth and development, which would seem to be implied in 'biographic,' is often missing.

[51] Clara und William Stern, *Die Kindersprache* (Leipzig, 1907; fourth ed., 1928). First edition reviewed by A. Meillet, *Bulletin de la Societé de linguistic de Paris*, XVI, 65–67.

[52] Recently the attention of investigators has turned more and more to the early formative phase of language learning. Gesell and Thompson (A. Gesell and H. Thompson, *Infant Behavior*, [New York, 1934]) pp. 234, 245, as quoted by McCarthy (see note 66) p. 488, complained: 'In spite of voluminous literature on the subject of children's speech, the ontogenesis of language in the first year of life has had relatively little systematic attention.' E. Dewey, *Infant Behavior* (New York, 1935) p. 252, quoted by McCarthy, p. 493, speaking about sound learning, said: 'Before the question can be decided we must have more exact, complex, and phonetically correct records of all sounds made by infants, from the time of birth to the appearance of speech.' Partial answers to these demands are, among others, Grègoire's book of 1937 (see note 78) and my own volumes of 1939 ff. (see note 5).

[53] M. V. O'Shea, *Linguistic Development and Education* (New York and London, 1907).

[54] Karl Bühler, *Die geistige Entwicklung des Kindes* (Jena, 1918; fifth ed., 1929; sixth ed., 1930); *The Mental Development of the Child* (London and New York, 1930).

[55] Charlotte Bühler, *Kindheit und Jugend* (Leipzig, 1928; third ed., 1931).

[56] Paul Guillaume, *L'imitation chez l'enfant* (Paris, 1925); "Les débuts de la phrase dans le langage de l'enfant," *Journal de Psychologie*, XXIV (1927), 1–25; "Le développement des éléments formels dans le langage de l'enfant," XXIV, 203–29.

sensible and satisfactory. The articles specialize in child syntax and morphology. They are important although they deal mostly with principles; illustrations from the author's own observations are used sparsely. Delacroix, a French psychologist with a special interest in the psychology of language, wrote several studies, from 1924 to 1934, in which he paid attention to child language.[57] Although he does not register details, his general discussions, which are clear, simple, sensible and to the point, are of great value. *Infant Speech* (1936) by the English educator Lewis[58] is a notable work, rich in first- and second-hand materials, particularly concerning the second year, and circumspect in its fine psychological explanations of speech development within the frame of the total development; but it lacks the broadened linguistic outlook of Stern, although it is superior to the latter's work in phonetics and attention to the beginnings of speaking.

These boulders in the history of psychological and educational research in child language are imbedded in a broad stream of smaller studies, mostly articles in educational and psychological journals. With more or less competence, many observations made on individual children were reported, usually with emphasis on one or the other aspect of language learning. An enormous number of them dealt with the acquisition of vocabulary, with much counting of words at certain ages, which has proven rather barren for the progress of research. Most of these studies neglect exact phonetic description, although the first two years of speaking cannot be studied adequately without it. Child forms in popular spelling do not give a clear impression of the child's pronunciation, especially in English, and American observers were the chief contributors to the flood of such studies. Besides, these studies do not usually pay much attention to the gradual growth of the child's language, which is much more impor-

tant than cross sections at certain stages. The interest was laudable and usable results were obtained, but the aggregate achievement is not very impressive.[59]

One of the more significant early contributions is that of Lukens,[60] a student of Stanley Hall and therefore ultimately of the Wundt School; but it too has grave linguistic defects.

The Belgian educator Decroly[61] attempted a summary of what was known in a small book (1933), leaning heavily on Stern and others and hardly leading beyond them. The German psychologist Friedrich Richter [see note 8] gave the only complete account of the history of child-language research from Aristotle to Stern in 1927; this dissertation is an indispensable tool.

A methodological contribution of educational research since the twenties is the group test administered to many children at different ages. Dorothea McCarthy,[62] Madorah Smith,[63] Beth Wellman,[64] Harold M. Williams,[65] all Americans, are some significant names in this line of endeavor. Group results are interesting as a corrective to accidental conditions prevailing in individual records. The results are often presented in intricate statistical analyses, with graphs and charts. With this method everything depends on the

---

[57] Henri Delacroix, "L'activité linguistique de l'enfant," *Journal de Psychologie*, XXI (1924), 4–17; *Le langage et la pensée* (Paris, 1924); revised ed. 1930, (especially Livre III, chap. 1); *L'enfant et le langage* (Paris, 1934); also, "Le développement du langage chez l'individu," in Georges Dumas, *Traité de psychologie* (Paris, 1924), II, 166–73.

[58] M. M. Lewis, *Infant Speech* (London, 1936).

[59] Cp. National Society for the Study of Education, 28th yearbook (Bloomington, Ill., 1929) p. 566: 'In spite of the fact that the number of published articles dealing with language development is relatively large, the knowledge of the subject is still comparatively meager'; p. 568: 'There is need for studies of growth by means of systematic records on the same children from birth through the preschool period.'

[60] H. T. Lukens, "Preliminary report on the learning of language," *Pedagogical Seminary*, III (1894), 424–60.

[61] Ov. Decroly, *Comment l'enfant arrive à parler*, no place or date (Brussels, 1933).

[62] Of many publications I mention one: Dorothea A. McCarthy, *The Language of the Preschool Child*, Minneapolis [1930]; cf. note 66.

[63] Of many publications, several of them involving bilingualism, I mention one: Madorah E. Smith, *An Investigation of the Development of the Sentence and the Extent of Vocabulary in Young Children*, Iowa City [1926].

[64] Beth L. Wellman and others, *Speech Sounds of Young Children* (Iowa City, 1931).

[65] Harold M. Williams, "A Qualitative Analysis of the Erroneous Speech Sound Substitutions of Preschool Children, *University of Iowa Studies in Child Welfare* 13, no. 2 (Iowa City, 1937) and other papers.

formulation of the linguistic problems covered by the figures, and the linguist is not always satisfied with it. Studies of this type are often distinguished by succinctness and rigorous method, worthy of imitation. But the linguistic scholar looking for assistance in his work cannot help feeling at times that the results achieved are not commensurate with the excellent method used. As far as phonetic problems are concerned, recent educational studies have wisely turned to phonetic transcription; IPA symbols are usually employed.

The results of group studies (or cross sections) are now available in a convenient and competent summary by McCarthy.[66]

So far, no linguistic scholars have been mentioned. I have stated that linguists have not paid as much attention to child language as they should and that they lag behind psychologists and pedagogs.[67] However, some of the best investigations have come from linguists, even though most of them come rather late in the history of research.

Schleicher, the famous Indo-Europeanist, published a note on child language in 1861.[68]

The French classical scholar Egger, in 1879, was the first who tried to explain sound substitutions by citing ancient and modern parallels.[31] In the course of sensible generalities he reported observations made on his children and grandchildren. The study had been presented as a lecture as early as 1871.

Humphreys, a professor of Greek at Vanderbilt University and therefore also a linguist in a sense, published a brief contribution in 1880.[69] His chief interest was vocabulary, but he also paid attention to sounds and gave a table of substitutions, unique for his time, for a girl two years old.

The French linguist Deville wrote an extensive article in continuations (1890–91), in which he recorded the speech development of his daughter to the age of two, month by month and topic by topic, sounds and words.[70] He confined himself to reporting the case, avoiding generalizations. Though concise, the study is ample enough to give a satisfying description of the infant's speech, and the element of gradual development is not completely neglected. Sounds are described adequately, although Deville does not choose to examine principles of sound substitution. His study remains a valuable primary source and one of the best studies of child language after nearly 60 years, because he had the wisdom to confine his endeavor to a restricted, well-defined job and to do that job thoroughly.

All other linguistic investigations belong to the present century. The Frenchman Grammont, well known to linguistic scholars because of his thorough studies of assimilation and related phenomena, studied child language from the same points of view in 1902.[71] His article is satisfactory only as far as these phenomena are concerned; but he fully appreciated the fruitfulness of child-language studies for linguistics and called for exact investigation of the relationship between the standard language and the child's transformations of it in sounds and lexical items.

The Bulgarian professor Gheorgov contributed careful records of the language learning of his two sons in 1905 and 1908.[72]

---

[66] Dorothea McCarthy, "Language Development in Children," in Leonard Carmichael, ed., *Manual of Child Psychology* (New York and London, 1946), pp. 476–581. The psychologists have by now accorded the study of child language an important position in the field of child development.

[67] This was already the complaint of Ament (pp. 11, 26) in 1899. He demanded a field of child linguistics separate from child psychology. Cf. Stern (p. 6, with footnote) in 1907 and 1927.

[68] August Schleicher, "Einige beobachtungen an kindern," *Beiträge zur vergleichenden Sprachforschung*, II (1861), 497 f.; supplement, IV (1865), 128.

[69] M. W. Humphreys, "A Contribution to Infantile Linguistic (!)," *Transactions of the American Philological Association*, XI (1880), 5–17.

[70] Gabriel Deville, "Notes sur le développement du langage," *Revue de Linguistique et de Philologie Comparée*, XXIII (1890), 330–43; XXIV (1891), 10–42, 128–43, 242–57, 300–20.

[71] Maurice Grammont, "Observations sur le langage des enfants," *Mélanges linguistiques offerts à M. Antoine Meillet* (Paris, 1902), pp. 61–82.

[72] I. A. Gheorgov, "Die ersten Anfänge des sprachlichen Ausdrucks für das Selbstbewusstsein bei Kindern," *Archiv für die gesamte Psychologie*, V (1905), 329–404; also in *Sammlung von Abhandlungen zur psychologischen Pädagogik*, ed. E. Meumann, vol. II, no. 1 (Leipzig, 1905); "Ein Beitrag zur grammatischen Entwicklung der Kindersprache," same journal, XI (1908), 242–432; also separately (Leipzig, 1908); cf. further: "Le développement du langage chez l'enfant, Premier congrès international de pédologie tenu a Bruxelles . . . 1911, *Rapports* vol. II (Ghent, 1912).

He published his long, exhaustive articles in a psychological journal, but his orientation is lingusitic. In fact, his interest is almost exclusively devoted to the morphology of child language, which nobody has treated more fully.

The well-known German Indo-Europeanist Meringer, who liked to explore less-traveled side-avenues of linguistics, published something about child language in 1906.[73] In spite of occasional glimpses of methodological insight he tried to cover too much ground; his observations go from birth to age seven. The linguistic biographies of five children are sketchy and not so satisfactory as we should like the contribution of a competent linguist to be.

The Dane Jespersen, another scholar who did not confine himself to the traditional paths of linguistics, published a comparison of the speech of adults and children in 1916 and incorporated the results in his book *Language* (1922)[74] as one of its four chapters. This is the only introduction to linguistics which accords major consideration to child language. It gives an excellent, lively discussion of general principles involved in language learning.

The Frenchman O. Bloch, in a series of articles from 1913 to 1924, analyzed the language learning of his three children and some others while they were growing up.[75] The articles are devoted to various aspects of language learning, sounds and syntax being given most attention. These articles are among the most valuable publications in the field.

The oustanding French linguist Marcel

Cohen wrote several brief articles between 1925 and 1933, in which he gave fragmentary data, from his own observation, concerning selected grammatical phenomena.[76] One of them is devoted to the principles of growth in child language. He tries to find in child language confirmations for principles of general linguistics. His contributions are not of major importance; but it is reassuring to find a leading linguistic scholar who recognizes the interest which child-language study holds for linguistics. His merit is that he is not satisfied with unreliable generalizations, but sees the need for detailed factual investigations.

Bloomfield, in his book *Language* (1933)[77] makes scant mention of child language and is very critical of previous studies; but he appreciates the importance of the infantile language-learning process and the need for exact and competent study of it.

The Belgian Grégoire published an article in 1933 and a book in 1937, in which he subjected the language of his two sons during the first two years to minute phonetic and psychological analysis in chronological arrangement.[78] He uses IPA transcription. The children were late speakers. The study is therefore mostly concerned with the babbling stage, which had never before been examined with such meticulous care. With more contributions of this kind, on a sound linguistic basis, we may hope eventually to make real headway in the study of child language.

A decisive step forward was made by the

---

[73] Rudolf Meringer, *Aus dem Leben der Sprache. Versprechen. Kindersprache. Nachahmungstrieb.* Festschrift University of Graz, 1906 (Berlin, 1908), pp. 113–20, 145–230.

[74] Otto Jespersen, *Nutidssprog hos børn og voxne* (Copenhagen, 1916); also *Børnesprog* (1923); *Sproget: barnet, kvinden, slægten* (1941). Otto Jespersen, *Language; Its Nature, Development, and Origin* (London and New York, 1922).

[75] Oscar Bloch, "Notes sur le langage de l'enfant," *Mémoires de la Société de Linguistique de Paris*, XVIII (1913), 37–59; "Les premiers stades du langage de l'enfant," *Journal de Psychologie*, XVIII (1921), 693–712; "Langage d'action dans les premiers stades du langage de l'enfant, same journal XX (1923), 670–2; "La phrase dans le langage de l'enfant, same journal, XXI (1924), 18–43.

[76] Marcel Cohen, "Sur les langages successifs de l'enfant," *Mélanges linguistiques . . . J. Vendryes.* (Paris, 1925) pp. 109–27; "A propos de la troisième personne du féminin au pluriel en francais," *Bulletin de la Société de Linguistique de Paris*, XXVII (1927), 201–8; "Observations sur les dernières persistances du langage enfantin," *Journal de Psychologie*, XXX (1933), 390–99.

[77] Leonard Bloomfield, *Language* (New York, 1933).

[78] A. Grégoire, "L'apprentissage de la parole pendant les deux premières années de l'enfance," *Journal de Psychologie*, XXX (1933), 375–89. Antoine Grégoire, *L'apprentissage du langage; les deux premières années* (Liège-Paris, 1937); a second volume appeared in 1947. The book was hailed enthusiastically by the reviewer Adolf Busemann, in *Zeitschrift für Psychologie*, CXLVI (1939), 189 f., as a new beginning in child-language research.

Russian-American linguist Jakobson,[79] formerly of Brno and Oslo, now of Columbia University, in 1939 and 1941. He applied to child language the new methodological insight of phonemics; Jakobson is one of the originators of this method. The fruitful new approach disregards the accidental individual differences in the sequence of sound learning and investigates instead the phonemic contrasts which dominate this sequence. With this method it is possible to overcome the deadlock at which the study of child language, with its apparently irreconcilable divergent results, seemed to have arrived. Jakobson's study shows that we have still not enough linguistically exact investigations of individual cases. In details Jakobson's theory is open to corrections; but as a whole it furnishes the tool for progress.

The first fruit of the new approach is an article by Velten[80] of Indiana University (1943), in which the very slow language learning of his daughter is analyzed phonemically with Jakobson's method, slightly modified. The title of the paper recognizes the possibility of extending the principle of contrast to the learning of vocabulary; but because the child's speech was rather undeveloped by age two, the results along this new line are scanty.

My own volumes on child language [see note 5] aim at a systematic examination of the language learning of the first two years from every aspect of linguistics: vocabulary, sounds, morphology, syntax, meaning, etc. The speech of my two daughters is analyzed with a degree of completeness and detail not attempted before, and coordinated in footnotes with the results of other investigators, both linguists and nonlinguists. The fourth volume deals with the later years in diary form.

Enough recognized linguists have expressed their interest in the study of child language to prove that this field does not deserve the neglect which on the whole has been its fate up to now. This should be obvious on purely theoretical grounds. We have studied language and languages of every conceivable type, standard languages, dialects, languages not written, languages of special groups, with ever varying methods, throwing light into every nook and cranny of the speaking activity. Why should just child language, which is incontestably a province of language, be outside the pale of linguistic inquiry?

The study of child language is closely linked with the traditional approaches of descriptive and historical linguistics. Bloomfield characterizes infantile language learning as a 'slow-motion picture of ordinary processes of speech.'[81] Grammont says: 'Toutes les modifications fonétiques, morfologiques ou syntaxiques qui caractérisent la vie des langues apparaissent dans le parler des enfants.'[82] Language learning never ends. 'Every speaker is constantly adapting his speech-habits to those of his interlocutors,' says Bloomfield of adult speakers; 'he gives up forms he has been using, adopts new ones' etc.[83] There is no better language situation to study such adaptations than child language. There the changes take place much more noticeably and rapidly, the child's constant endeavor being to conform to the speech of his surroundings. Bloomfield again says: 'To the end of his life, the speaker keeps on doing the very things which make up infantile language-learning.'[84] The gradual development of a phonemic system and of phonetic refinements; the building-up of a syntax, from crude beginnings to the expression of the finest shades of thought, will, and feeling; the evolution of morphological devices, from complete absence to faithful imitation of the standard; the principles of word-formation; the constant modifications of meaning, with extensions, restrictions, and transfer; the

---

[79] Roman Jakobson, "Le développement du langage enfantin et les cohérences correspondantes dans les langues du monde," Cinquième Congrès International des Linguistes, Résumés des communications (Bruges, 1939); Kindersprache, Aphasie und allgemeine Lautgesetze (Uppsala, 1941).

[80] H. V. Velten, "The Growth of Phonemic and Lexical Patterns in Infant Language," Language, XIX (1943), 281–92.

[81] Bloomfield, p. 46. Child language shares with slow-motion pictures the accessibility to minute observation. As far as the rate of progress is concerned, child language is rather a fast-motion picture of linguistic development.

[82] Grammont (see note 71), p. 61.

[83] Bloomfield, p. 326, 328.

[84] Bloomfield, p. 46.

growth of vocabulary with all its phonetic and semantic difficulties; in short, every pattern of grammar, every process of language shows up in child language in a nascent state, in coarser, more tangible shapes, compressed into a much shorter time and therefore more accessible to observation.

The only field in which caution is necessary is the comparison with theories about the origin of language. A child's learning to imitate a fully developed standard language is quite different from man's original learning to speak without a model. Yet even in this respect the study of infantile learning should be helpful.[85] As Guillaume has pointed out,[86] historical linguistics does not lead back to pregrammatical stages. Child language does.[87]

The study of child language is definitely a concern of general linguistics. Even if it should lead to no new knowledge concerning the speaking process, it throws new light on many known principles. The polarity between conservative and progressive impulses in language dominates all of child language. The goal is as conservative as it could be: the child strives to learn the language exactly as his environment speaks it, and nursery usage is more conservative than any other domain of language.[88] Yet, in the process of learning the child utilizes the limited material acquired with supreme disregard for established practices, striking wildly out of bounds in every direction, but in the same manner as adults do with less freedom of action.

The chief reason why linguistic scholars have not often carried out exact studies of child language is the enormous difficulty of such projects and the patience and sustained effort necessary for seeing them through. Such studies cannot be made in a few months of concentrated work, and their yield is not spectacular enough to satisfy the ambitious scholar. Enough well-known linguists have expressed their interest in such studies and recognized the importance of child language for linguistics to justify a call for further competent aid in the cultivating of this field. Scholars who do not care to make a detailed study could still make valuable contributions by observing the phonemic development or some other partial linguistic phase and publishing their results in brief summaries.

As far as infant bilingualism, which is involved in my own study, is concerned, the situation is even less satisfactory. Surprisingly little has been written about any phase of bilingualism.

There are a number of studies from countries and districts in which a bilingual condition exists as a practical problem: Alsace-Lorraine, Luxemburg, Belgium, Switzerland, Wales, South Africa, India, the southwest and the big cities of the U. S.[89] They were

---

[85] Cp. Hermann Paul, *Prinzipien der Sprachgeschichte* (Halle, fifth ed., 1920) p. 187; Stern, p. 7.

[86] Guillaume, Les débuts de la phrase (see note 56), 1.

[87] Perhaps the chief exponent of the attempt to utilize the language learning of small children for speculations about the language learning of mankind is Carl Franke (1899; see note 14). Hermann Gutzmann (ep. note 13) compares the learning of children and primitive peoples in "Die Sprachlaute des Kindes und der Naturvölker," *Zeitschrift für pädagogische Psychologie*, I (1899), 28–40; he also deals with ontogenetic and phylogenetic parallelism.

[88] In Tiedemann's observations of 1787 (note 7) one finds the same little tricks of linguistic training as are still standard practice in German nurseries. American nursery rimes cling to the words and situations of the rural England of long ago, although both have largely become meaningless for modern city children.

[89] For example: D. J. Saer, F. Smith, and J. Hughes, *The Bilingual Problem ... Wales* (Aberystwyth, 1924); C. H. Schmidt, *The Language Medium Question* (Pretoria, 1926); Michael West, *Bilingualism (... Bengal)* (Calcutta, 1926); S. S. Laurie, *Lectures on Language and Linguistic Method in the School* (Edinburgh, third ed., 1899); Frank Smith, "Bilingualism and Mental Development," *British Journal of Psychology*, XIII (1923), 271–82; "Conférence internationale sur le bilinguisme (1928)," *Le bilinguisme et l'éducation* (Geneva and Luxemburg 1929; also Spanish ed., Bilbao, Madrid, and Barcelona, 1932); Moses N. H. Hoffman, *The Measurement of Bilingual Background* (New York, 1934); Herschel T. Manuel, *The Education of Mexican- and Spanish-Speaking Children in Texas* (Austin, 1930); Klonda Lynn, "Bilingualism in the Southwest," *Quarterly Journal of Speech*, XXXI (1945), 175–80; (Arizona); Joseph G. Yoshioka, "A Study of Bilingualism," *Pedagogical Seminary*, XXXVI (1929), 473–9; (Japanese in California); P. M. Symonds, "The Effect of Attendance at Chinese Language Schools on Ability with the English Language," *Journal of Applied Psychology*, VIII (1924), 411–23, (Hawaii); William A. Stark, "The Effect of Bilingualism on General Intelligence ... Dublin Primary Schools" (thesis, Glasgow, 1939; outline in) *British Journal of Educational Psychology*, X (1940) 78 f.; Wilhelm Henss, "Das Problem der

written by educators, school teachers who had to struggle with language difficulties in schools in which instruction was given in the dominant language to children who had grown up with another language. Usually they believe that bilingualism influences the development of a child unfavorably; but many of them have a pedagogical ax to grind.[90] Often they plead for more consideration for the mother tongue in the school.

Bilingualism of school children who learn one language after another is however a matter quite different from the simultaneous learning of two languages by smaller children. I know of only three books on this topic. The classical study is that of Ronjat, which describes the French-German bilingualism of his son during the first three or four years of his life.[91] It presents the most nearly ideal case of bilingualism, the child learning to use both languages with equal facility and continuing to use both in later life. The study was guided by Grammont and inspired by other leading linguists. It is linguistically sound and phonetically careful. It presents systematically the total linguistic development from the point of view of bilingualism.

Somewhat less satisfactory is the book of Pavlovitch, which describes the French-Serbian bilingualism of his son during the first two years.[92] The author had thorough

linguistic training in Serbia and France and availed himself of the counsel of Meillet and Ernault. The systematic presentation, linguistically oriented, is generally sound. But the second language, French, enters the picture rather late. The phonetic treatment, which is of paramount importance for the second year, is not fully satisfactory. In addition to his own observations, he tried to summarize child language in general; the attempt was premature.

Geissler,[93] who lived among the Germans in Belgrade, published in 1938 a thorough study of the bilingualism of German children in foreign surroundings. Up to the present this work must be considered *the* book on child bilingualism in general. Geissler analyzes the bilingualism of small children, of school children, and of adolescents in separate chapters, taking differences of individual character and types of bilingual situations into account with excellent method. Geissler is not a linguist, and his pronouncements on language in general and child language in particular contain too many vague generalities. But apart from Ronjat's case study, his is the only book which treats the entire linguistic development of children from the point of view of bilingualism.

This is all that I have found on the bilingualism of small children.[94] Some articles on child language include a limited amount of foreign vocabulary.[95]

Yet, many linguistic scholars have recognized the importance of the study of bilingualism for their science and deplored the neglect of it. Meillet calls specifically for investigation of infant bilingualism.[96] The substratum hypothesis runs through the

---

Zwei- und Mehrsprachigkeit und seine Bedeutung für den Unterricht ... ," *Zeitschrift für Pädagogische Psychologie*, XXVIII (1927), 393–414, (Holland); Pierre Bovet, "Les problèmes scolaires posés par le bilinguisme," *Schweizer Erziehungsrundschau* (1935), 254; B. Baier, *Die Sprachenfrage im Volksschulwesen Elsass-Lothringens* (Frankfurt, 1928).

[90] The judicious studies of Seth Arsenian, an American psychologist, favor bilingualism: *Bilingualism and Mental Development* (New York, 1937); "Bilingualism in the Post-War World," *Psychological Bulletin*, XLII (1945), 65–86; R. Pintner and Arsenian, "The Relation of Bilingualism to Verbal Intelligence and School Adjustment," *Journal of Educational Research*, XXXI (1937), 255–63. Prejudices against bilingualism are attacked by N. Braunshausen, *Le bilinguisme* ... (Cahiers de la Centrale du P.E.S. de Belgique 7, 1933).

[91] Jules Ronjat, *Le développement du langage observé chez un enfant bilingue* (Paris, 1913); cp. supplementary report of 1923 in Michael West, *Bilingualism*, p. 59, note 2.

[92] Milivoie Pavlovitch, *Le langage enfantin; acquisition du serbe et du français par un enfant serbe* (Paris, 1920).

[93] Heinrich Geissler, *Zweisprachigkeit deutscher Kinder im Ausland* (Stuttgart, 1938).

[94] William Stern, "Uber Zweisprachigkeit in der frühen Kindheit," *Zeitschrift für angewandte Psychologie*, XXX (1928), 168–72, expresses surprise that bilingualism of small children has not been studied more.

[95] For instance: W. G. Bateman, "A Child's Progress in Speech with Detailed Vocabularies," *Journal of Educational Psychology*, V (1914), 307–20, (Chinese); Mildren Langenbeck, "A Study of a Five-Year-Old Child," *Pedagogical Seminary*, XX (1915), 65–88, (German); Velten (see note 80; French, Norwegian).

[96] *Bulletin de la Société de Linguistique de Paris* 16. LXVI.

entire linguistic literature as a more or less mystic explanation of puzzling phenomena in language.[97] Yet nothing useful can come from speculative thinking until the effect of bilingualism has been studied in tangible case histories.

America offers countless opportunities for observing infant bilingualism in the making. Children in immigrant families and in the Spanish-speaking southwest often grow up with two languages. Most of the parents do not have the equipment to study the problem. Even in cultured families, including those of university professors, the training of the parents is rarely a linguistic one, because linguistics unfortunately has not yet become a necessary ingredient of general culture. In

the much reduced number of remaining cases, where both a bilingual situation and linguistic competence are present, either the interest in the problem or the patience to carry out such a project is usually wanting. I know myself of several cases in which enthusiasm for such a study was kindled by my own work; but the energy flagged when the difficulty of the project became evident. I appeal to the few who are capable of carrying out such an investigation to add sorely needed case histories of infant bilingualism[98] and infant language to the available material, as indispensable spade work for the higher purposes of linguistics.

---

[97] Cp. Bloomfield, p. 386.

[98] The paucity of records dealing with child bilingualism is deplored by McCarthy in her summary of 1946 (see note 66) pp. 566 and 568.

DIETRICH TIEDEMANN

2 The history of child-language research begins at the end of the eighteenth century with the careful day by day record of the Marburg philosopher Tiedemann, who observed the psychological development of his son Friedrich (who later became a famous anatomist) from birth, carefully and in detail. He published his study in 1787 under the title, "Über die Entwickelung der Seelenfähigkeiten bei Kindern," in the *Hessische Beiträge zur Gelehrsamkeit und Kunst*. This record was so remarkable that it was republished in German, French, and English for almost a century and a half. Most of it is concerned with psychological observations, in agreement with the title, but in the second half many observations of speech learning are included. These are here excerpted from Suzanne Langer's translation published in the *Pedagogical Seminary*, XXXIV (1927), 205–30: Carl Murchison and Suzanne Langer, "Tiedemann's Observations on . . . Children."

The boy was born August 23, 1781. Tiedemann's first observation on his speaking development is dated February 10, 1782.

W. F. L.

OBSERVATIONS ON THE DEVELOPMENT OF THE MENTAL FACULTIES OF CHILDREN

Translated by Carl Murchison and Susanne K. Langer, reprinted from Carl Murchison and Susanne K. Langer, "Tiedemann's Observations on the Development of the Mental Faculties of Children," The

. . . On February 10th he showed the first signs of surprise and approval; so far his only expressions of pain, anger, impatience, and pleasure had been crying, writhing, laughing. Now, when he saw something new and delightful, he greeted it with the exclama-

---

Pedagogical Seminary and Journal of Genetic Psychology 34.205–230 (1927), *by permission of The Journal Press.*

tion "ach!"[1]—the natural sign of admiration. So he could clearly recognize what was new and had a distinct sensation of the novelty. At this time he also commenced to make use of his feet for walking. Whenever he was put upon his feet he gave evidence of joy.... Differences of speaking tone, characteristic of different emotions, especially of disapproval and satisfaction, he had learned to comprehend, for he let himself be silenced by threats.

After all manner of exercise in the production of tones, and after the acquisition of some skill in using the speech organs variously, he commenced, on the 14th of March, to articulate consciously and to repeat sounds. His mother said to him the syllable "Ma"; he gazed attentively at her mouth, and attempted to imitate the syllable. Furthermore, it was observed that when he heard a word easy of pronunciation, his lips would move as he softly repeated it to himself.

On April 27th he showed marked evidence of attachment to certain persons, and recognition of them, for he wept when his nurse or his mother was chastised. Also one could see him now perform the most difficult of all the associations of the ideas, that which animals rarely attain, and never of their impulse—the connection of an idea with its verbal symbol. When he was asked, where is this or that common and familiar object he would point it out with his finger. So he had clear conceptions not only of such objects, but also of articulate sounds, and knew furthermore that these sounds designated those objects or images, i.e., he had associated these very diverse ideas. Therefore, one may safely assume that the higher mental faculties, judgment and comparison, had already commenced to function, and had distinguished ideas that were really very similar. In the case of articulation this power of comparison is particularly necessary. It is well known that the words of a foreign language seem to us at first to be all alike and in no wise distinguishable. ...

Visible signs of reflection and of the ability to differentiate appeared on May 13th. Whenever he met with anything novel or strange he would point his finger at it to call other people's attention to it, and employed

the sound, "ha! ha!" That the pointing as well as the exclamation was addressed to others is apparent from the fact that he was satisfied as soon as people signified that they also had taken note. One may gather from this how deep in human nature lies the desire to reveal themselves to others, and to feel their participation in anything that strikes our interest. ... A few sounds he could already imitate recognizably, without, however, associating them at once with their proper ideas. Certain names of very familiar objects he understood perfectly, so that even in their absence he had the image of them in mind and looked around in order to point them out. Now he learned also to comprehend a few sentences; on the 14th he knew already what was meant by: "Make a bow," "Swat the fly," which he always accompanied by the appropriate motions. ...

A few words he pronounced clearly on November 27th and knew also their meanings exactly; these were "Papa" and "Mama," though he did not use them to call persons, but merely by accident, without intending to say anything thereby. So it appears that words awakened in him their proper images and ideas, but not conversely, images of objects and desire of them, any concept of the corresponding word; presumably because children begin by learning words more for the sake of understanding the intention of others than in order to impart their own—just as adults, in learning a foreign language, will sooner translate the words thereof into their mother tongue than to give expression through the medium of the new language. Only a few simple sounds were significantly used by the boy, such as "ha! ha!" when something strange met his eyes, likewise a few expressions of displeasure and negation. The sound "ha!" seems indeed to be the natural expression of reflection and of surprise. It originates in a sudden expulsion of the breath which has been withheld, and the breath is stopped when by the sudden occurrence of some novelty the train of thought is hemmed and suddenly deflected into a new channel. Since the speech organs were not yet sufficiently trained to produce all sorts of articulation, especially long and compound words, he usually denoted the corresponding objects by gestures. On November 29th one could

---

[1] [English "ah!"—Transl. Note.]

observe a signification of this sort that indicated a certain amount of complexity in his ideas, and spoke of some amount of original composition on his part. He had been taught to reply to the question, "How big (*grand*) are you?", by lifting up his hands; now he was required to say the word "*grand-mama*," and as the word "grand" was too difficult for him to pronounce, he lifted up his hands and at the same time said "mama."
. . .

On December 26th he showed evident pleasure if any one laughed at his antics or praised them; indeed, he sought to invite laughter by all sorts of gestures and postures, as he could already walk without assistance. Now also he clearly showed an impulse to imitation, as he had his body and his speech organs fairly under control. Thus he imitated all sorts of sounds, the bell, for instance, when it rang. Also he learned to pronounce certain words significantly, especially "take, take," when he wanted to be picked up or taken from his chair. One could now discover distinct signs of memory, but only through present sensation, not through mere ideas. If he had been several times in a certain place and then beheld the scene from afar, he would point to it with his finger. As he still lacked verbal expression, his ideas could as yet have no free course independent of sensations, and therefore the past could not return to his consciousness without sensuous assistance.
. . .

. . . The boy's mania for imitation extended further and further. Besides a few sounds which he imitated, he attempted also to imitate conversations, to which end he produced a profusion of incomprehensible sounds. Imitation always begins with the most external aspect of things, because this most easily impresses the senses; also he had undoubtedly some conception of the purpose of speech, as he accompanied the senseless sounds with gestures that gave them meaning. If, for example, he wanted to be placed somewhere where he could not betake himself he would point out the spot with his finger and accompany this with a string of half-articulated sounds. . . . He understood a variety of phrases such as: "fetch that," "leave that alone," "put it over there," and so forth; but he made no use of them as yet to demand

anything of other people, partly because his speech organs were not yet pliable and controlled enough, partly also because, although the transition from things to words was established through habit, the converse was not yet the case. . . .

He now made considerable progress in talking; on the 8th of March, at the sight of an object, he would repeat its name if he had frequently heard it, but he still found it hard to pronounce words of several syllables. Of these he usually said only the end syllables or the syllable that was chiefly accented, because this appealed most readily to his ear. The consonants z, sch, w, st, sp, as also the diphthongs he could not well pronounce; p, t, and k he found the easiest. The former consonants, by reason of their compoundness require in part a greater pliability of the speech organs and in part a more refined and practiced ear for their apprehension; the same is true of the double vowels. . . .

On the 27th of March he could already pronounce words of two syllables, and knew almost all the external parts of his body, which he pointed out correctly when their names were mentioned to him; also most of the objects in the room were known to him by name. Now began the purposive use of speech, and the words were linked directly with their meanings so that the idea of a thing immediately suggested its name. If the boy desired anything, he would call it by its name, howbeit this was true of only a very few objects as yet. To combine several words in a sentence was still beyond his power. But even this he was secretly practicing, for on June 3rd he succeeded in saying short sentences, consisting of a noun and a verb, though without correct grammatical form. Instead of the imperative he always employed the infinitive, and used the nominative in place of all other cases; the article was omitted altogether. The nominative he had most frequently heard when things were named for him; the sense of the other case endings was not clear to him as yet. Add to this the fact that these are often slurred over in pronunciation. The infinitive we use most frequently, since the other tenses are often expressed in our dialect by this form together with the permutation of other words; so he had been primarily impressed by it. Probably this incorrectness of speech has its source in the peculiarities of our language. . . .

His faculty of memory had received considerable practice. On July 20th he came to a spot in the house where four weeks ago he had been punished for defiling the place; and immediately he said, without further incentive, that whoever dirtied the room would receive a spanking—not, indeed, in completely articulate words, but plainly enough to convey his meaning. . . .

On July 24th he heard some ducks screaming without being able to see them, and at once he remarked, "Ducks," though he had rarely seen or heard them before. Here then the cry of the bird was already linked with the image thereof, and the image with the word. This presupposes not only association, but also reflection, which determines that the two impressions of hearing and sight respectively are caused by the same object and therefore must be conceived together. Ideas once associated became more and more surely linked, so that they would not separate even after several months. On the 26th of July he saw some potatoes, which he had not seen for several months, but had previously eaten with pleasure, and he immediately said, "Potatoes." By this and by the increase of his vocabulary his series of association now became more independent of external impressions and it became apparent that in his little brain several ideas were already spontaneously awakened and linked in sequences. The boy had heard people tell how a girl had been slain by lightning; the expression of the story tellers had impressed him deeply, so that upon a later occasion he tried with fragmentary words and gestures to reproduce the tale, though this could not be understood by any one save those who had been present at the previous telling.

On the 30th of July he finally succeeded in uttering complete, though short sentences, for example: *There he stands. There he lies.* . . .

With increasing practice in speaking and the acquisition of various words, his ideas were subjected more and more to the caprice and desires of his soul, so that more and longer series of them could be spontaneously aroused, and chains of thought be carried through. By this means the faculties which deal with and develop the ideas gained practice, especially the faculty of imagination. On the 29th of October the boy took several chopped-off stalks of white cabbage, and let them represent different persons who called upon each other. Thus without particular incentive, the images were here recalled of persons visiting each other, and these images were transferred to the cabbage stalks, so that the latter represented the former. So the first phase of imagination seems to be that familiar characters are transferred to unfamiliar objects. At the same time this entails a voluntary and autonomous association of ideas, the first source of all language, in fact, of any symbolic expression. Never has anything of the sort been observed in animals, never, amongst their images and ideas, any autonomous association of ideas; so the reason why animals have no speech does seem to lie deeper than in the mere lack of adroitness of the speech organs.

Now, moreover, appeared the faculty of thought, and the search for a satisfactory reason. On the morning of the 13th of November the boy looked out of the window and saw a bright cloud in the sky; in this connection he remembered a rainbow he had seen several weeks before, and he immediately formed the judgment, "I see a rainbow." The relation of similarity is probably the first source of judgment, because similarity calls up absent images and thus stimulates comparison between present sensations and objects previously known. When he was told that this was not a rainbow, he promptly replied, "The rainbow is asleep just now." Very probably he wanted thereby to give himself some reason why this could not be the rainbow; thus his faculty of thought was already in search of reasons for his judgments. . . .

Another and similar example was observed the same way. I held my watch to his ear; when he had listened for a while to its beat, he said that Fripon (a little dog in the house) was imprisoned therein. Thus he presupposed that the movement and sound must originate in a living creature, a proposition which almost all uncivilized races accept, and which is based on that same anthropomorphism which lets us conceive all moving objects as like to us or to the animals, that is to say, as endowed with life. This much is clear from these examples: that this opinion of untutored nations springs from the conceptions of an intellect not yet integrated nor led by experience. This is also borne out by a judgment the boy passed on April 2nd. In the evening, when he no longer saw the sun in the sky, he said, "The sun has gone to bed; tomorrow he will get up again, drink his tea and eat his bread and butter." All these opinions originated purely in his own deliberations; no one had told him this sort of thing before, so that he might have been adopting foreign notions. Also the variety of the occasions shows that nothing learned or repeated, but only the product of his own thinking was involved.

His self-estimation now began to develop more fully, and to grow into real desire for appreciation, so that the boy now took consideration of the praise and blame of others, without distinction. On February 14th, 1784, he said, when he thought he had acted very cleverly: "People will say, 'That is a nice little boy.' " If he was naughty and was told, "The neighbor sees you," he would desist at once.

This is as far as my observations go. Other business prevented me from their continuation. I greatly desire that others may make similar ones; it will then be possible to determine various things by comparison, and that important branch of psychology, too little exploited as yet, which studies the development of human faculties—the foundation of pedagogy—will make appreciable progress thereby.

BERTHOLD SIGISMUND

3 The modern study of child language, with exact recording of observations, began in Germany and Austria in the middle of the nineteenth century. Several of the early observers were physiologists: Löbisch (1851), Sigismund (1856), Kussmaul (1859), Vierordt (1879), and Sikorsky (1883). Sigismund is representative of this group; his study, *Kind und Welt* (Brunswick, 1856), was considered remarkable enough to be reissued in new editions in 1897 and 1900. An abstract of his work is reproduced here as prepared by Preyer in an appendix to his classical study in which he reports earlier research in the field. The translation is that of H. W. Brown in the English edition of Preyer's *The Mind of the Child* (New York, 1889).

W. F. L.

ABSTRACT by William Preyer of KIND UND WELT

Among the earlier as among the later statements concerning the acquirement of speech, there are several that have been put forth by writers on the subject without a sufficient basis of observed facts. Not only Buffon, but also Taine and his successors, have, from a few individual cases, deduced general propositions which are not of general application.

Translated by H. W. Brown, reprinted from William Preyer, The Mind of the Child (*New York: Appleton-Century-Crofts, 1889*), 2.221–223.

Good observations were first supplied in Germany by Berthold Sigismund in his pamphlet, "Kind und Welt" ("The Child and the World") (1856); but his observations were scanty.

He noted, as the first articulate sounds made by a child from Thüringen (Rudolstadt), *ma, ba, bu, appa, ange, anne, brrr, arrr:* these were made about the middle of the first three months.

Sigismund is of the opinion that this first lisping, or babbling, consists in the production of syllables with only two sounds, of which the consonant is most often the first; that the first consonants distinctly pronounced are labials; that the lips, brought into activity by sucking, are the first organs of articulation; but this conjecture lacks general confirmation.

In the second three months (in the case of one child in the twenty-third week, with other healthy children considerably earlier) were heard, for the first time, the loud and high *crowing* sounds, uttered by the child spontaneously, jubilantly, with lively movements of the limbs that showed the waxing power of the muscles: the child seemed to take pleasure in making the sounds. The utterance of syllables, on the other hand, is at this period often discontinued for weeks at a time.

In the third quarter of the first year, the lisping or stammering was more frequent. New sounds were added: *bä, fbu, fu;* and the following were among those that were repeated without cessation, *bäbäbä, dädädä;* also *adad, eded.*

In the next three months the child manifested his satisfaction in any object by the independent sound *ei, ei.* The first imitations of sounds, proved to be such, were made after the age of eleven months. But it is more significant, for our comprehension of the process of learning to speak, that long before the boy tried to imitate words, or gestures, viz., at the age of nine months, he distinguished accurately the words "father, mother, light, window, moon, lane"; for he looked, or pointed, at the object designated, as soon as one of these words was spoken.

And when, finally, imitation began, musical tones, e.g., F, C, were imitated sooner than the spoken sounds, although the former were an octave higher. And the *ei, ei,* was repeated in pretty nearly the same tone or accent in which it had been pronounced for the child. Sneezing was not imitated till after fourteen months. The first word imitated by the child of his own accord (after fourteen months) was the cry "Neuback" (fresh-bake), as it resounded from the street; it was given

back by the child, unsolicited, as *ei-a.* As late as the sixteenth month he replied to the word *papa,* just as he did to the word *Ida,* only with *atta;* yet he had in the mean time learned to understand "lantern, piano, stove, bird, ninepin, pot"—in all, more than twenty words—and to indicate by a look the objects named; he had also learned to make the new imperfect sounds *pujéh, pujéh, tupe tupe téh, ämmäm, atta, ho.*

In the seventeenth month came in place of these sounds the babbled syllables *mäm, mam, mad-am, a-dam, das;* in the case of other children, syllables different from these. Children often say several syllables in quick succession, "then suddenly stop as if they were thinking of something new—actually strain, as if they must exert themselves to bring their organs to utterance, until at last a new sound issues, and then this is repeated like the clack of a mill." Along with this appears the frequent doubling of syllables, as in *papa, mama.*

The boy, at twenty months, told his father the following, with pretty long pauses and animated gestures: *atten—beene—titten—bach—einc—puff—anna,* i.e., "Wir waren im Garten, haben Beeren und Kirschen gegessen, und in den Bach Steine geworfen; dann kam Anna" (we were in the garden, ate berries and cherries, and threw stones into the brook; then Anna came).

The observations of Sigismund are remarkable for their objectivity, their clearness of exposition, and their accuracy, and they agree with mine, as may easily be seen, in many respects perfectly. Unfortunately, this excellent observer (long since deceased) did not finish his work. The first part only has appeared. Moreover, the statements as to the date of the first imitations . . . are not wholly in accord with one another.

AUGUST SCHLEICHER ⁓⁓⁓⁓⁓⁓⁓⁓⁓⁓⁓⁓⁓

4 The first linguist who published observations on children's language learning was Schleicher, whose name is one of the most famous in the history of linguistic research. He took time out from his work on the history of Indo-European languages to assemble casual but expert observations of the speech development of his own children. They were published in *Beiträge zur vergleichenden Sprachforschung*, II (1861), 497–98, with a supplement in the same journal, IV (1865), 128.

Noteworthy is the phonetic soundness of the observations made at a time when the science of phonetics was barely getting under way with the work of pioneers like Brücke and had not yet acquired its modern name.

Schleicher challenged other scholars to contribute their observations of child language. A few years later the suggestion bore fruit. Jan Baudouin de Courtenay, also a well-known scholar in historical linguistics and at the same time a forerunner of descriptive linguistics, published, under the same title and in the same journal, VI (1870), 215–20, in German, somewhat fuller and more systematic observations of Polish child language. (His article is not included here.)

W. F. L.

SOME OBSERVATIONS MADE ON CHILDREN (1861–62)

(1) The change of k and g into t and d in the pronunciation of children is familiar. Before my oldest boy, who had earlier pronounced an actual t for k, learned to pronounce a pure k, he produced a palatal c (that sound which strikes the ear sometimes as kj, sometimes as tj). In some words I think I have observed this very exactly and reliably, e.g. in *kamm, komm*, which he pronounced at first as *tamm, tomm* (or rather, more exactly, in the Franconian-Thuringian manner, as *damm, domm*), later as *camm, comm* and eventually with pure k. He also sometimes changed gutturals into labials, e.g. in *schnapen* for *Schnaken, schimpen* for *Schinken*. The same sound changes of the gutturals in individual Indo-European languages are well known. There was no trace in my boy's speech of the familiar intermediate stage *kv*.

(2) The same boy pronounced long ā as *au* almost regularly, e.g. *hofraud* (*Hofrad* he calls the wheelbarrow which is usually kept

Reprinted from Beiträge zur Vergleichenden Sprachforschung *2.497–498 (1861), Supplement 4.128 (1862).*

in the courtyard!), *salaut, gesaugt* ('dictum') and so forth. It is known that the same change of ā takes place in Norse (written ā is pronounced *au*).

(3) He regularly changed the combination *schw* into f, thus *fizt* (schwitzt), *fanz* (Schwanz), *farz* (schwarz), and so forth. This sound change is brought about by mutual assimilation of the spirants to each other, ś (sch) taking on labial quality from the following w and becoming f, and w making itself more similar to the preceding ś by becoming a surd and also dental-labial spirant (f). In the same manner Old Bulg. *chv* becomes Modern Bulg. *f*, e.g. Old Bulg. *chvala*, Mod. Bulg, *fala* ('laus, gloria').

(4) My little girl, now 1¾ years old, sometimes allows the terminal sound of a syllable to have an assimilating effect on the initial sound of the same syllable (Schiefner has discussed this phenomenon), e.g. in *nanke* for *danke, mauf* for *nauf* (*hinauf*) (she also says *lā* for *ja*).

(5) Two words are fused into one (as is done purposely in thieves' jargons). Thus my Erhart produced from *blenden* and *glänzen* a *blänzen*: "die Sonne *blänzt* mir" for "*blendet* mich"; my little Emma made "nütze" out of "Netz" and "Mütze."

(6)   The power of analogy was evident in the first speaking exercises of my children. At a time when I hardly considered it possible that a child had absorbed enough language to identify a formation as the usual one, forms like *gegebt, getūt, geschreibt*, etc. for *gegeben, getan, geschrieben*, were already produced. . . .

Perhaps these superficial notes will induce one or the other linguist to use materials at his disposal for further observations, which are not without interest for our field, especially for sound physiology. Incidentally, not all children are equally suitable for such observations. At least that is what I feel in the case of my Ernst, now almost three years old, who uses, for example, for k before vowels a sound which is scarcely audible, much less accurately definable.

of the mouth than we do, something like Brücke's s. This is a spirant (sibilant) during the pronunciation of which the tongue remains approximately in the same position which it takes for i or e, except that the tip of the tongue touches the top. Words like *mich, dich, licht, reich*, etc. sound like *miç, diç, liçt, leiç* (concerning 1 = r, see below).

The same child transforms initial s and *sch* into a dark, faintly articulated d (t is not used in this region, it occurs only exceptionally), e.g. *im dommer deint die donne dēr dön*. Since the same language artist also changes g and k and, of course, t into d, she pronounces no fewer than six different sounds of our language (k, g, t, d, s, sch) in one and the same way.

Terminal and medial r before and after consonants is suppressed, but replaced by l before vowels; thus *reich* is spoken as *leiç*, *richtig* as *liçdiç* etc.

SUPPLEMENT

After palatal vowels my little girl, now almost three years old, speaks *ch* farther in the front

HIPPOLYTE TAINE

The famous philosopher, psychologist, and historian Taine is among the early students of child language. His charmingly written report is here reproduced in full in the smooth translation (anonymous) printed in the second volume of the English journal *Mind*. It is pleasing to get a glimpse of the home life of a great man fondly observing the language learning of his little girl. The observations, although limited in scope, are presented with the exactness and careful attention to detail which characterize the true scholar. It is amusing to see that Taine, who is known for his positivistic emphasis on the influences beyond the individual's control, attributes unlimited independence, originality, and "invention" to the child. His factual observations remain of interest even today.

W. F. L.

ACQUISITION OF LANGUAGE BY CHILDREN

The following observations were made from time to time and written down on the spot. The subject of them was a little girl whose

Reprinted from Mind 2.252–259 (1877) *by permission of* Mind.

development was ordinary, neither precocious nor slow.

From the first hour, probably by reflex action, she cried incessantly, kicked about, and moved all her limbs and perhaps all her muscles. In the first week, no doubt also by reflex action, she moved her fingers and even grasped for some time one's forefinger when given her. About the third month she begins to feel with her hands and to stretch out her arms, but she cannot yet direct her hand, she touches and moves at random; she tries the movements of her arms and the tactile and muscular sensations which follow from them; nothing more. In my opinion it is out of this enormous number of movements, constantly essayed, that there will be evolved by gradual selection the intentional movements having an object and attaining it. In the last fortnight (at two and a half months) I make sure of one that is evidently acquired; hearing her grandmother's voice she turns her head to the side from which it comes.

There is the same spontaneous apprenticeship for cries as for movements. The progress of the vocal organ goes on just like that of the limbs; the child learns to emit such or such a sound as it learns to turn its head or its eyes, that is to say by gropings and constant attempts.

At about three and a half months, in the country, she was put on a carpet in the garden; there lying on her back or stomach, for hours together, she kept moving about her four limbs and uttering a number of cries and different exclamations, but vowels only, no consonants; this continued for several months.

By degrees consonants were added to the vowels and the exclamations became more and more articulate. It all ended in a sort of very distinct twittering, which would last a quarter of an hour at a time and be repeated ten times a day. The sounds (both vowels and consonants), at first very vague and difficult to catch, approached more and more nearly to those that we pronounce, and the series of simple cries came almost to resemble a foreign language that we could not understand. She takes delight in her twitter like a bird, she seems to smile with joy over it, but as yet it is only the twittering of a bird, for she attaches no meaning to the sounds she utters. She has learned only the materials of language. (Twelve months.)

She has acquired the greater part quite by herself, the rest thanks to the help of others and by imitation. She first made the sound *mm* spontaneously by blowing noisily with closed lips. This amused her and was a discovery to her. In the same way she made another sound, *kraaau*, pronounced from the throat in deep gutturals; this was her own invention, accidental and fleeting. The two noises were repeated before her several times; she listened attentively and then came to make them immediately she heard them. In the same way with the sound *papapapa*, which she said several times by chance and of her own accord, which was then repeated to her a hundred times to fix it in her memory, and which in the end she said voluntarily, with a sure and easy execution, (always without understanding its meaning) as if it were a mere sound that she liked to make. In short, example and education were only of use in calling her attention to the sounds that she had already found out for herself, in calling forth their repetition and perfection, in directing her preference to them and in making them emerge and survive amid the crowd of similar sounds. But all initiative belongs to her. The same is true of her gestures. For many months she has spontaneously attempted all kinds of movements of the arms, the bending of the hand over the wrist, the bringing together of the hands, etc. Then after being shown the way and with repeated trials she has learned to clap her hands to the sound *bravo*, and to turn her open hands regularly to the strain *au bois Joliette*, etc. Example, instruction, and education are only directing channels; the source is higher.

To be sure of this it is enough to listen for a while to her twitter. Its flexibility is surprising; I am persuaded that all the shades of emotion, wonder, joy, wilfulness, and sadness are expressed by differences of tone; in this she equals or even surpasses a grown up person. If I compare her to animals, even to those most gifted in this respect (dog, parrot, singing birds), I find that with a less extended gamut of sounds she far surpasses them in the delicacy and abundance of her expressive intonations. Delicacy of impressions and delicacy of expressions are in fact the distinctive characteristic of man among animals and, as I have shown (*De l'Intelligence*, I. b. i.), are the source in him of language and of general ideas; he is among them what a great and fine poet, Heine or Shakespeare, would be among workmen and peasants; in a word, man is sensible of innumerable shades, or rather of a whole order of shades which escape them. The same thing is seen besides in the kind and degree of his curiosity. Any one may observe that from the fifth or sixth month children employ their whole time for two years and more in making physical experiments. No animal, not even the cat or dog, makes this constant study of all bodies within its reach; all day long the child of whom I speak (at twelve months) touches, feels, turns round, lets drop, tastes, and experiments upon everything she gets hold of; whatever it may be, ball, doll, coral, or plaything, when once it is sufficiently known she throws it aside, it is no longer new, she has nothing to learn from it and has no further interest in it. It is pure curiosity; physical need, greediness, count for nothing in the case; it seems as if already in her little brain every group of perceptions was tending to complete itself, as in that of a child who makes use of language.

As yet she attaches no meaning to any word she utters, but there are two or three words to which she attaches meaning when she hears them. She sees her grandfather every day, and a chalk portrait of him, much smaller than life but a very good likeness, has been often shown her. From about ten months when asked "Where is grandfather?" she turns to this portrait and laughs. Before the portrait of her grandmother, not so good a likeness, she makes no such gesture and gives no sign of intelligence. From eleven months when asked "Where is mama?" she turns towards her mother, and she does the same for her father. I should not venture to say that these three actions surpass the intelligence of animals. A little dog here understands as well when it hears the word *sugar;* it comes from the other end of the garden to get a bit. There is nothing more in this than an association, for the dog between a sound and some sensation of taste, for the child between a sound and the form of an individual face perceived; the object denoted by the sound has not as yet a general character. However I believe that the step was made at twelve months; here is a fact decisive in my opinion. This winter she was carried every day to her grandmother's, who often showed her a painted copy of a picture by Luini of the infant Jesus naked, saying at the same time "There's *bébé.*" A week ago in another room when she was asked "Where's *bébé*" meaning herself, she turned at once to the pictures and

engravings that happened to be there. *Bébé* has then a general signification for her, namely whatever she thinks is common to all pictures and engravings of figures and landscapes, that is to say, if I am not mistaken, *something variegated in a shining frame.* In fact it is clear that the objects painted or drawn in the frame are as Greek to her; on the other hand, the bright square inclosing any representation must have struck her. This is her first general word. The meaning that she gives it is not what we give it, but it is only the better fitted for showing the original work of infantile intelligence. For if we supplied the word, we did not supply the meaning; the general character which we wished to make the child catch is not that which she has chosen. She has caught another suited to her mental state for which we have no precise word.

Fourteen months and three weeks. The acquisitions of the last six weeks have been considerable; she understands several other words besides *bébé,* and there are five or six that she uses attaching meaning to them. To the simple warbling which was nothing but a succession of vocal gestures, the beginnings of intentional and determinate language have succeeded. The principal words she at present utters are *papa, mama, tété* (nurse), *oua-oua* (dog), *koko* (chicken), *dada* (horse or carriage), *mia* (puss, cat), *kaka,* and *tem;* the two first were *papa* and *tem,* this last word very curious and worth the attention of the observer.

Papa was pronounced for more than a fortnight unintentionally and without meaning, as a mere twitter, an easy and amusing articulation. It was later that the association between the word and the image or perception of the object was fixed, that the image or perception of her father called to her lips the sound *papa,* that the word uttered by another definitely and regularly called up in her the remembrance, image, expectation of, and search for her father. There was an insensible transition from the one state to the other, which it is difficult to unravel. The first state still returns at certain times though the second is established; she still sometimes plays with the sound though she understands its meaning. This is easily seen in her later words, for instance in the word *kaka.* To the great displeasure of her mother she still often repeats this ten times in succession, without purpose or meaning, as an interesting vocal gesture and to exercise a new faculty; but she often also says it with a purpose when there is occasion. Further it is plain that she has changed or enlarged its meaning as with the word *bébé;* for instance yesterday in the garden seeing two little wet places left by the watering pot on the gravel she said her word with an evident meaning; she meant by it *whatever wets.*

She makes imitative sounds with great ease. She has seen and heard chickens and repeats *koko* much more exactly than we can do, with the guttural intonation of the creatures themselves. This is only a faculty of the throat: there is another much more striking, which is the specially human gift and which shows itself in twenty ways, I mean the aptitude for seizing analogies—the source of general ideas and of language. She was shown birds two inches long, painted red and blue on the walls of a room, and was told once "There are *kokos.*" She was at once sensible of the resemblance and for half a day her great pleasure was to be carried along the walls of the room crying out *koko!* with joy at each fresh bird. No dog or parrot would have done as much; in my opinion we come here upon the essence of language. Other analogies are seized with the same ease. She was in the habit of seeing a little black dog belonging to the house which often barks, and it was to it that she first learnt to apply the word *oua-oua.* Very quickly and with very little help she applied it to dogs of all shapes and kinds that she saw in the streets and then, what is still more remarkable, to the bronze dogs near the staircase. Better still, the day before yesterday when she saw a goat a month old that bleated, she said *oua-oua,* calling it by the name of the dog which is most like it in form and not by that of the horse which is too big or of the cat which has quite a different gait.[1] This is the distinctive trait of man; two successive impressions, though very unlike, yet leave a common residue which is a distinct impres-

sion, solicitation, impulse, of which the final effect is some expression invented or suggested, that is to say, some gesture, cry, articulation, name.

I now come to the word *tem,* one of the most remarkable and one of the first she uttered. All the others were probably attributives[2] and those who heard them had no difficulty in understanding them; this is probably a demonstrative word; and as there was no other into which it could be translated, it took several weeks to make out its meaning.

At first and for more than a fortnight the child uttered the word *tem* as she did the word *papa* without giving it a precise meaning, like a simple twitter. She made a dental articulation ending with a labial articulation and was amused by it. Little by little she associated this word with a distinct intention; it now signifies for her *give, take, look;* in fact, she says it very decidedly several times together in an urgent fashion, sometimes that she may have some new object that she sees, sometimes to get us to take it, sometimes to draw attention to herself. All these meanings are mixed up in the word *tem.* Perhaps it comes from the word *tiens* that is often used to her and with something of the same meaning. But it seems to me rather a word that she has created spontaneously, a sympathetic articulation that she herself has found in harmony with all fixed and distinct intention, and which consequently is associated with her principal fixed and distinct intentions, which at present are desires to take, to have, to make others take, to look, to make others look. In this case it is a *natural vocal gesture,* not learned, and at the same time imperative and demonstrative, since it expresses both command and the presence of the object to which the command refers; the dental *t* and the labial *m* united in a short, dry, and quickly stifled sound, correspond very well, without convention and by their nature alone, to this start of attention, to this sharp and decided outbreak of volition. This origin is the more probable that other and later words, of which we shall presently speak, are evi-

---

[1] "When the Romans first saw elephants they called them Lucanian oxen. In the same way savage tribes have called horses on seeing them for the first time 'large pigs'." (*Lectures on Mr. Darwin's Philosophy of Language* by Max Müller, p. 48 [1873]).

[2] Max Müller, *Lectures on the Science of Language,* 6th ed., I, 309. The roots of a language are 400 or 500 in number, and are divided into two groups, the attributive and the demonstrative.

dently the work not of imitation but of invention.[3]

From the 15th to the 17th month. Great progress. She has learnt to walk and even to run, and is firm on her little legs. We see her gaining ideas every day and she understands many phrases, for instance: "bring the ball," "come on papa's knee," "go down," "come here," etc. She begins to distinguish the tone of displeasure from that of satisfaction, and leaves off doing what is forbidden her with a grave face and voice; she often wants to be kissed, holding up her face and saying in a coaxing voice *papa* or *mama*—but she has learnt or invented very few new words. The chief are *Pa* (Paul), *Babert* (Gilbert), *bébé* (baby), *bééé* (goat), *cola* (chocolate), *oua-oua* (anything good to eat), *ham* (eat, I want to eat). There are a good many others that she understands but cannot say, for instance *grand-père* and *grand-mère*, her vocal organs having been too little exercised to produce all the sounds that she knows, and to which she attaches meaning.

Cola (chocolate) is one of the first sweet-meats that was given her and it is the one she likes best. She went every day to her grandmother's who would give her a lozenge. She knows the box very well and keeps on pointing to it to have it opened. Of herself and without or rather in spite of us she has extended the meaning of the word and applies it now to anything sweet; she says *cola* when sugar, tart, a grape, a peach, or a fig is given her.[4] We have already had several examples of this spontaneous generalization; it was easy in this instance, for the tastes of chocolate, of the grape, of the peach, etc. agree in this, that being all pleasant they provoke the same desire, that of experiencing once more the agreeable sensation. So distinct a desire or impulse easily leads to a

movement of the head, a gesture of the hand, an expression, and consequently to a word.

Bébé. We have seen the strange signification that she at first gave to this word; little by little she came nearer to the usual meaning. Other children were pointed out to her as *bébés*, and she was herself called by the name and now answers to it. Further, when put down before a very low mirror and shown her face reflected in it, she was told "that's *bébé*," and she now goes alone to the mirror and says *bébé*, laughing when she sees herself. Starting from this she has extended the meaning of the word, and calls *bébés* all little figures, for instance, some half-size plaster statues which are on the staircase, and the figures of men and women in small pictures and prints. Once more, education produced an unexpected effect on her; the general character grasped by the child is not that which we intended; we taught her the sound, she has invented the sense.

Ham (eat, I want to eat). Here both sound and sense were invented. The sound was first heard in her fourteenth month. For several weeks I thought it no more than one of her warblings, but at last I found that it was always produced without fail in presence of food. The child now never omits to make it when she is hungry or thirsty, all the more that she sees that we understand it, and that by this articulation she gets something to eat or drink. On listening attentively and attempting to reproduce it, we perceive that it is the *natural vocal gesture* of a person snapping up anything; it begins with a guttural aspirate like a bark, and ends with the closing of the lips as if food were seized and swallowed. A man among savages would do just the same, if with tied hands and solely dependent for expression upon his vocal organs he wished to say that he wanted food. Little by little the intensity and peculiarity of the original pronunciation were lessened; we had repeated her word but in a milder form; consequently she left off making so much of the guttural and labial parts, and the intermediate vowel came to the front; instead of *Hamm* she says *am*, and now we generally use the word as she does. Originality and invention are so strong in a child that if it learns our language from us, we learn its from the child.

Oua-oua. It is only for the last three weeks

---

[3] A neighbor's little boy had at twenty months a vocabulary of seven words, and among them the words *ça y est*, somewhat analogous to *tem*, and like it untranslatable into our language, for he used it to say *there, I have it, it's done, he has come*, and meant by it the completion of any action or effect.

[4] In the same way the above-mentioned little boy of twenty months used the word *téterre* (*pomme de terre*) to designate potatoes, meat, beans, almost everything good to eat except milk, which he called *lolo*. Perhaps to him *téterre* meant everything solid or half solid that is good to eat.

(the end of her sixteenth month), that she has used this word in the sense of something good to eat. It was some time before we understood it, for she has long used it and still uses it besides in the sense of dog. A barking in the street never fails to call forth this word in the sense of dog, uttered with the lively joy of a discovery. In the new sense the sound has oscillated between *va-va* and *oua-oua*. Very likely the sound that I write *oua-oua* is double to her according to the double meaning she attaches to it, but my ear cannot catch the difference; the senses of children, much less blunted than ours, perceive delicate shades that we no longer distinguish. In any case, on seeing at table a dish she wishes for, she says *oua-oua* several times in succession, and she uses the same word when, having eaten some of it, she wishes for more, but it is always in presence of a dish and to point out something eatable. By this the word is distinguished from *am* which she only uses to make known her want of food, without specifying any particular thing. Thus, when in the garden she hears the dinner bell she says *am* and not *oua-oua;* on the other hand, at table before a cutlet she says *oua-oua* much oftener than *am*.

For the last two months, on the other hand, she has left off using the word *tem* (give, take, look) of which I spoke above, and I do not think she has replaced it by another. This is no doubt because we did not choose to learn it, for it did not correspond to any one of our ideas, but combined three that are quite distinct; we did not use it with her and therefore she left off using it herself.

On summing up the facts I have just related we arrive at the following conclusions, which observers should test by observations made on other children.

At first a child cries and uses its vocal organ, in the same way as its limbs, spontaneously and by reflex action. Spontaneously and from mere pleasure of action it then uses its vocal organ in the same way as its limbs, and acquires the complete use of it by trial and error. From inarticulate it thus passes to articulate sounds. The variety of intonations that it acquires shows in it a superior delicacy of impression and expression. By this delicacy it is capable of general ideas. We only help it to catch them by the suggestion of our words. It attaches to them ideas that we do not expect and spontaneously generalizes outside and beyond our *cadres*. At times it invents not only the meaning of the word, but the word itself. Several vocabularies may succeed one another in its mind by the obliteration of old words, replaced by new ones. Many meanings may be given in succession to the same word which remains unchanged. Many of the words invented are natural vocal gestures. In short, it learns a ready-made language as a true musician learns counterpoint or a true poet prosody; it is an original genius adapting itself to a form constructed bit by bit by a succession of original geniuses; if language were wanting, the child would recover it little by little or would discover an equivalent.

These observations were interrupated by the calamities of the year 1870. The following notes may help to determine the mental state of a child; in many respects it is that of primitive peoples at the poetical and mythological stage. A jet of water, that the child saw under the windows for three months, threw her every day into new transports of joy, as did also the river under a bridge; it was evident that sparkling running water seemed to her to be of extraordinary beauty. "*L'eau!*" she goes on exclaiming (twenty months). A little later (two and a half years) she was very much struck by the sight of the moon. She wanted to see it every evening; when she saw it through the windowpanes there were cries of joy; when she walked it seemed to her that it walked too, and this discovery charmed her. As the moon according to the hour appeared in different places, now in front of the house now behind it, she cried out "Another moon, another moon!" One evening (three years) on inquiring for the moon and being told that it had set (*que'elle est allée se coucher*) she replies "But where's the moon's *bonne*?" All this closely resembles the emotions and conjectures of primitive peoples, their lively and deep admiration for great natural objects, the power that analogy, language, and metaphor exercise over them, leading them to solar and lunar myths, etc. If we admit that such a state of mind was universal at any time, we could at once divine the worship and legends that would be formed. They would be those of the *Vedas,* of the *Edda,* and even of Homer.

If we speak to her of an object at a little distance but that she can clearly represent to herself from having seen either it or others like it, her first question always is "What does it say?"—"What does the rabbit say?"—"What does the bird say?"—"What does the horse say?"—"What does the big tree say?" Animal or tree, she immediately treats it as a person and wants to know its thoughts and words; that is what she cares about; by a spontaneous induction she imagines it like herself, like us; she humanizes it. This disposition is found among primitive peoples, the more strong the more primitive they are; in the *Edda,* especially in the *Mabinogion,* animals have also the gift of speech; the eagle, the stag, and the salmon are old and experienced sages, who remember bygone events and instruct man.[5]

It takes much time and many steps for a child to arrive at ideas which to us seem simple. When her dolls had their heads broken she was told that they were dead. One day her grandmother said to her, "I am old, I shall not be always with you, I shall die." "Then shall you have your head broken?" She repeated this idea several times and still (three years and a month) with her 'to be dead' is to have the head broken. The day before

yesterday a magpie killed by the gardener was hung by one foot at the end of a stick, like a fan; she was told that the magpie was dead and she wished to see it. "What is the magpie doing?" "It is doing nothing, it can't move, it is dead." "Ah!" For the first time the idea of final immobility entered her head. Suppose a people to stop short at this idea and not to define death otherwise; the other world would be to it the *scheol* of the Hebrews, the place where the immoveable dead live a vague, almost extinct life. *Yesterday* means to her *in the past,* and *tomorrow—in the future,* neither of these words denoting to her mind a precise day in relation to today, either preceding or following it. This is another example of too extended a meaning, which must be narrowed. There is hardly a word used by children which has not to undergo this operation. Like primitive peoples they are inclined to general and wide ideas; linguists tell us that such is the character of roots and consequently of the first conceptions as they are found in the most ancient documents, especially in the *Rig-Veda.*

Speaking generally, the child presents in a passing state the mental characteristics that are found in a fixed state in primitive civilizations, very much as the human embryo presents in a passing state the physical characteristics that are found in a fixed state in the classes of inferior animals.

---

[5] Similarly she says, "My carriage *won't* go, it is *naughty.*"

CHARLES DARWIN〜〜〜〜〜〜〜〜〜〜〜〜〜〜〜〜

Taine's observations of child language caused Darwin to publish in the same journal his own observations made on one of his children, a boy, thirty-seven years earlier, with side-glances at his other "infants."

Darwin's observations are of interest because of his importance in the history of science. But he did not focus his attention on language learning as much as Taine had done. He reports about the total psychological development of the boy, topically arranged under the headings anger, fear, pleasurable sensations, affection, association of ideas, reason, etc., moral sense, unconsciousness, shyness. At the end he turns to means of communication. Only these few pages are reprinted here.

W. F. L.

A BIOGRAPHICAL SKETCH OF AN INFANT

M. Taine's very interesting account of the mental development of an infant, translated in the last number of *Minde* (p. 252), has led me to look over a diary which I kept thirty-seven years ago with respect to one of my own infants. I had excellent opportunities for close observation, and wrote down at once whatever was observed. My chief object was expression, and my notes were used in my book on this subject; but as I attended to some other points, my observations may possibly possess some little interest in comparison with those by M. Taine, and with others which hereafter no doubt will be made. I feel sure, from what I have seen with my own infants, that the period of development of the several faculties will be found to differ considerably in different infants. . . .

Means of communication. The noise of crying or rather of squalling, as no tears are shed for a long time, is of course uttered in an instinctive manner, but serves to show that there is suffering. After a time the sound differs according to the cause, such as hunger or pain. This was noticed when this infant was eleven weeks old, and I believe at an earlier age in another infant. Moreover, he appeared soon to learn to begin crying voluntarily, or to wrinkle his face in the manner proper to the occasion, so as to show that he wanted something. When 46 days old, he first made little noises without any meaning to please himself, and these soon became varied. An incipient laugh was observed on the 113th day, but much earlier in another infant. At this date I thought, as already remarked, that he began to try to imitate sounds, as he certainly did at a considerably later period. When five and a half months old, he uttered an articulate sound "da" but without any meaning attached to it. When a little over a year old, he used gestures to explain his wishes; to give a simple instance, he picked up a bit of paper and giving it to

me pointed to the fire, as he had often seen and liked to see paper burnt. At exactly the age of a year, he made the great step of inventing a word for food, namely, *mum*, but what led him to it I did not discover. And now instead of begining to cry when he was hungry, he used this word in a demonstrative manner or as a verb, implying "Give me food." This word therefore corresponds with *ham* as used by M. Taine's infant at the later age of 14 months. But he also used *mum* as a substantive of wide signification; thus he called sugar *shu-mum*, and a little later after he had learned the word "black," he called liquorice *black-shu-mum*,—black-sugar-food.

I was particularly struck with the fact that when asking for food by the word *mum* he gave to it (I will copy the words written down at the time) "a most strongly marked interrogatory sound at the end." He also gave to "Ah," which he chiefly used at first when recognizing any person or his own image in a mirror, an exclamatory sound, such as we employ when surprised. I remark in my notes that the use of these intonations seemed to have arisen instinctively, and I regret that more observations were not made on this subject. I record, however, in my notes that at a rather later period, when between 18 and 21 months old, he modulated his voice in refusing peremptorily to do anything by a defiant whine, so as to express "That I won't"; and again his humph of assent expressed "Yes, to be sure." M. Taine also insists storngly on the highly expressive tones of the sounds made by his infant before she had learnt to speak. The interrogatory sound which my child gave to the word *mum* when asking for food is especially curious; for if anyone will use a single word or a short sentence in this manner, he will find that the musical pitch of his voice rises considerably at the close. I did not then see that this fáct bears on the view which I have elsewhere maintained that before man used articulate language, he uttered notes in a true musical scale as does the anthropoid ape Hylobates.

Finally, the wants of an infant are at first made intelligible by instinctive cries, which after a time are modified in part unconsciously, and in part, as I believe, voluntarily as a means of communication,—by the

Reprinted from Mind 2.285, 292–294 (1877) *by permission of* Mind.

unconscious expression of the features,—by gestures and in a marked manner by different intonations,—lastly by words of a general nature invented by himself, then of a more precise nature imitated from those which he hears; and these latter are acquired at a wonderfully quick rate. . . . Before he was a year old, he understood intonations and gestures, as well as several words and short sentences. He understood one word, namely, his nurse's name, exactly five months before he invented his first word *mum;* and this is what might have been expected, as we know that the lower animals easily learn to understand spoken words.

FRITZ SCHULTZE

7 Among the early specialized child-language studies is the little book published by Fritz Schultze, Professor of Philosophy and Pedagogy in Dresden, under the title *Die Sprache des Kindes* (Leipzig, 1880), 44 pp. It came to occupy a pivotal position in early child-language research for decades. To explain the sequence of sound acquisition Schultze applied the much debated principle of least effort, which served as a common denominator for later studies of child language. He tested the hypothesis by his own observations and the few published records available at his time. Although not a phonetician, he had good phonetic judgment. His explanations, on an articulatory basis, foreshadow phonemic principles.

Samples are given here in English translation, but to do it justice the little book ought to be studied as a whole.

W. F. L.

THE SPEECH OF THE CHILD

. . . We now turn to the description of speech development in the speaking period proper and first raise the question in which sequence the child gradually masters the phonetic elements of the language, vowels and consonants. Here I believe I can, on the foundation of my observations, state the following basic law: that the speech sounds are produced by children in an order which begins with the sounds articulated with the least physiological effort, gradually proceeds to the speech sounds produced with greater effort, and ends with the sounds which require the greatest effort for their production.[1]

By physiological effort is meant the amount of nerve and muscle energy needed to bring about the position of the speech organs necessary for the production of a speech sound. This law has to do with vowels as well as consonants. Let us look first at the learning of vowels. . . .

In which sequence do the vowels gradually emerge in child language? My observations agree well with those of Sigismund.[2] They show as the first vowel Ä, which is already heard in crying; as the second, A [all vowels

---

Reprinted in translation by the editors from Fritz Schultze, Die Sprache des Kindes; eine Anregung zur Erforschung des Gegenstandes (*Leipzig: Günter, 1880*), *pp. 44–46.*

[1] Even though I should like to claim general validity for this axiom, at least hypothetically, it does not state that the sequence of speech sounds is one and the same for the children of all peoples and tribes. On the contrary, this would fail to recognize the important role which heredity doubtless plays in the acquisition and production of speech sounds on the part of the child. . . .

[2] "Tagebuch eines Vates" (Diary of a Father), p. 112: "The basic vowels of our German language, a, i, u, have likewise been heard from her by the age of eight months, but not yet the more subdued secondary vowels, e and o. . . ."

of course with their German values], which appears already in very pure form in babbling; next follows U; O appears later than U. The reason is probably the following: in the series A–O–U, the extremes are A and U because the lips and tongue are least removed from their position of rest in the case of A, most in the case of U. In this regard O occupies a midway position. With a running start, so to speak, the child seems to succeed more easily in achieving the U position, which is the extreme opposite of the A position, than contriving in an exact manner the delicate middle position of the O. The latter apparently requires a more practiced and experienced feeling of accomodation and innervation, as in general coarser contrasts are perceived more easily than the intermediate, more delicate transitions.

E, I, Ö, Ü all appear later than the vowels just named (Ä, A, U, O). This is not surprising since for all of them the physiological effort needed is very great: the front part of the tongue must be raised considerably, and for Ö and Ü a difficult lip adjustment must be made in addition. The difficulty increases in the series by one degree for each successive vowel; as a result E is the first of them to be produced, while I appears very late. Ö and especially Ü are exceedingly difficult for the child, who replaces them always by E and I, in spite of all efforts to teach the correct

pronunciation; thus they say *schen* in place of *schön*, *iber* in place of *über*, as is done in many German dialects.

When we said that E also appears later than Ä, A, U, O we meant the long E which we pronounce in *See*, *geh*, etc. For the sound *hähähä*, which the child produces already in the babbling stage, contains a real *ä*, which is ejected by the child, because of the faintness of the expiration, with a very short breath, as it were as an eighth note rather than a whole note. . . . Thus as far as my observations go, the vowels appear in the following sequence successively in the developmental process of the child's speaking: Ä, A, U, O, E, I, Ö, Ü, a series in which the physiological effort increases gradually. In my observations the diphthongs follow each other in this order: first EI (very early, earlier than E and I), then AU (at first replaced by A), last EU and ÄU, for which the child at first substitutes EI. . . .

In which order does the child learn to pronounce the consonants? Here, too, my observations have revealed to me the law stated above as a hypothesis, according to which the child learns to produce the sounds in a sequence of steps which rise from the sounds requiring the least physiological effort to those entailing greater efforts. [Details on consonants follow in Schultze's study.]

WILLIAM PREYER

8 The German physiologist Preyer was born in England, but he did not use his English name in full in his publications.

In addition to many books in his special field he published a number of careful studies of children and is sometimes considered the founder of child psychology. *Die Seele des Kindes* (1882; English translations 1888–1889), a thorough study of child psychology, included a detailed account of his son's speech development during the first 1000 days. This great record became the model for many later ones. The factual report in chronological order retains its importance to the present day, whereas his theories were the center of debate from the beginning. His chief interest was to demonstrate that the child forms concepts without language.

Since a brief extract from the factual record would not do justice to his work, a theoretical passage dealing with concepts is presented here in the English translation which is found in Emma Marwedel's book *Conscious Motherhood* (Boston, 1889).

The selection mentions Romanes and Lindner. Romanes was an English biologist and evolutionist, and an intimate friend of Darwin. In his work, *Mental Evolution in Man* (1888), he took an interest in child language as a link between animal speech and human language. He recognized that comparative linguistics had grasped and applied the theory of evolution earlier than natural science. Lindner, a German normal-school teacher, was the author of another remarkable early record of child language, *Aus dem Naturgarten der Kindersprache* (1888), but when Preyer wrote, he had only published observations about his first child, "Beobachtungen und Bemerkungen über die Entwicklung der Sprache des Kindes" (1882), also a detailed record, one of very few which existed at the time.

W. F. L.

HISTORY OF THE DEVELOPMENT OF SPEECH

At this stage of its intellectual development, the child is superior to a very intelligent animal; not on account of its knowledge of speech, which it shares with the more intelligent portion of the brute creation, but because it already forms much more numerous and complex ideas. The period during which a strong, healthy child is on the same mental plane with animals closes, certainly, by the end of its first year. And long before this it has gained, though its inborn *sensations* of pleasure and pain, more or less accurate *concepts* in, at least, one department, that of food. This is probably the first notion which the infant obtains; and Romanes is correct in saying that the *idea* of food arises within us as a result of hunger, quite independently of speech.

Whoever has conscientiously watched the intellectual development of infants must be convinced that the formation of concepts does not go hand in hand with the acquisition of words, but is a necessary condition to the understanding of the first words that are to be learned. Long before the child understands a single word, before it consistently uses a syllable in a definite sense, it already has a number of concepts which it expresses by looks, gestures, and cries. The association of touched and seen objects with impres-

Reprinted from Emma Marwedel, Conscious Motherhood (*Boston: D. C. Heath & Company, 1889*), *518–522, a condensed translation from Preyer's* Die Seele des Kindes (*Leipzig: 1882*).

sions of taste is probably the first source of ideas. The *alalic* (nonarticulating) toothless child has a lively interest in bottles, and when it sees a bottle filled with any white, opaque fluid (*e. g.*, water of lead), it cries and stretches out its arms for it, thinking it is a bottle of milk, as my child did in its thirty-first week. An empty bottle, or one containing water, is not nearly so attractive; that is, the concept of food arises at the sight of a bottle with definite contents, without any words whatever being understood or even uttered. The formation of ideas and concepts is thus shown to be independent of words.

It is not impossible that the making of concepts should continue after a total loss of verbal memory (as in the case of Lordat); but, nevertheless, it is certain that ideas of a higher order can only be formed by one who has completely mastered the art of speech. Intelligent mute children are acquainted with much more numerous and complicated concepts, but not many more of the higher abstractions than very intelligent animals, and adults whose vocabulary is small have no stronger power of abstraction than children. The latter learn abstract words more slowly than concrete ones, but retain them longer; for, when the memory fails, proper names and designations of concrete objects are first forgotten.

At all events, the intelligent mute child, even without knowledge of words, can form abstractions of a lower order. When Sigismund showed his little son, less than a year old, a stuffed woodcock, and, pointing to it, said, "Bird," the child, who could not speak a word, looked instantly toward another part of the room where a stuffed owl stood. The idea was already formed here. But how little specialized the first ideas are which are independent of food we can see from the fact that with Lindner's child (in the tenth month), "up" meant also "down," and "warm," also "cold." If these instances, which are by no means uncommon, are not due to a failure to differentiate the ideas, "then," as Lindner says, "the child already has an instinctive feeling that antitheses are only the extremes of one and the same series of ideas."

Before the newborn babe is able to seek the pleasurable and avoid the painful, it expresses its feelings and needs by monotonous cries. These gradually vary, so that we are able to distinguish certain sounds as indicative of pleasure and pain. Then come spontaneously uttered syllables, and not until long after, the imitation of natural sounds. The imperfect utterance of these gives the effect of new terms, and since the child also uses familiar words in a new sense, his dialect gains an original aspect, and is called "baby talk." But it is important to remember that feelings and concepts do not now arise for the first time; they have simply reached their first articulate expression.

In adults new concepts generate new words, while with the mute child they only excite new cries and motions of the face and muscles. Many conditions are often expressed by the same cry, just as a person affected with aphasia will often denote every mental state by one and the same word. Even when a person is fully master of his language, the words at his disposal are not always adequate to express his ideas, as when he desires to give a description of a cloud, or of a pain he is suffering. The idea is clear, but the words are insufficient. The bulk of philosophical and theological literature is due to the fact that different persons do not attach the same idea to the same word. If an idea is especially difficult to express clearly in words, e.g., "die," it is designated by many different terms, which increase the confusion. But words are absolutely necessary for the clear conception of higher ideas and their accurate transfer to other persons; hence, it is impor-

tant to know how the child learns first to utter and then to employ words.

We must note that it appears quite immaterial what syllables and words are employed to first designate the childish concepts. We can teach the child false terms, but it will use them loyally. If we should teach it later on that "twice three are five," it would only give the name of "five" to what is really six, and soon adopt the current phraseology.

For the first articulate expression of concepts, some of those easily uttered syllables are employed which have been previously uttered by the child without consciousness or aim; the meaning is introduced into them wholly by the parents or nurse. Such syllables are *pa* and *ma*, with their reduplications, *papa*, *mamma*, as appellations of the parents. The sense of these syllables varies more or less in different dialects, while in some languages the *ma* sound designates the father, and the *pa* or *ba* sound the mother. Similarly, the syllable "tata" is sometimes employed to denote the parents or grandparents, but often in the sense of "good by," "gone."

At this period the child has a strong inclination to mechanically repeat all sorts of sounds, syllables, and words, just as it imitates gestures. The ear assists this operation, but is not indispensable to it, since even those born deaf learn to speak by imitating the motions of the tongue and lips. This they often do better than the infant which can hear, since the latter depends very largely upon the sound. I have always found that it was very difficult for a child to imitate a position of the mouth which was not accompanied by the corresponding sound; while if the acoustic effect was added, the task was easily accomplished. Accordingly, the connection between the ear and the center of speech must be freer than that between the eye and the center of speech. In the case of the child which does not yet talk, but which can repeat syllables correctly and begin to connect them with primitive concepts, the act of imitation takes longer than with the normal adult, although the nerve lines in the brain are both absolutely and relatively shorter.

9 The Canadian Tracy was, like Dewey, a student of Stanley Hall who had studied in Germany for years, worked with Wundt, and introduced his methods into the United States. Tracy's book on child psychology exerted a considerable influence. One chapter deals with child language and presents a good general treatment on the basis of published and unpublished records, at second hand. The survey is scanty and must be considered antiquated by now, but it commanded much attention in its time.

Tracy reports the first two years in four sections of six months each. The first of these is reprinted here to give an idea of his method. It will be noticed that Tracy, like many students of child language, does not recognize that cooing and babbling are stages of language learning which are completely different in character.

W. F. L.

FIRST SIX MONTHS

"In Thuringia," says Sigismund, "they call the first three months 'das dumme Vierteljahr,' " and during the second three months, according to Schultze, no advance is made on the first. It might seem, then, that in this first half-year there is nothing worthy of our attention in the matter of language. This, however, is very far from being the case, for in this period a most important apprenticeship is going on. The little child, even in the cradle, and before he is able to raise himself to a sitting posture, is receiving impressions every waking moment from the environment; is hearing the words, seeing the gestures, and noting—in a manner perhaps not purely involuntary—the intonations of those around him; and out of this material he afterwards builds up his own vocabulary. Not only so, but during this period, that peculiarly charming infantile babble (which Ploss calls "das Lallen") begins, which, though only an "awkward twittering," yet contains in rudimentary form nearly all the sounds which afterwards, by combination, yield the potent instrument of speech. A wonderful variety of sounds, some of which afterwards give the child difficulty when he tries to produce them, are now produced automatically,

Reprinted from Frederick Tracy, The Psychology of Childhood, 7th ed. (*Boston: D. C. Heath & Company, 1909*), *128–131.*

by a purely impulsive exercise of the vocal muscles; in the same way as the child at this age performs automatically many eye movements, which afterwards become difficult, or even impossible. M. Taine thinks that "all shades of emotion, wonder, joy, wilfulness, and sadness" are at this time expressed by differences of tone, equalling or even surpassing the adult.

The child's first act is to cry. This cry has been variously interpreted. Semmig calls it "the triumphant song of everlasting life," and describes it as "heavenly music"— *himmlische Musik;* Kant said it was a cry of wrath, and others have spoken of it as a sorrowful wail on entering this world of sin; or as the foreboding of the pains and sorrows of life. It seems more scientific, though less poetic, to accept the explanation of the "unembarrassed naturalist," who sees in it nothing more nor less than the expression of the painfulness of the first breathing—the rush of cold air upon the lungs.

A more important point is the relation of this first vocal utterance to the speech that is to follow. The cry at first is merely an automatic or reflex "squall," without expressive modulation or distinctive timbre; the same cry serves to express all sorts of feelings. But very soon it becomes differentiated and assumes various shadings to express various mental states. This differentiation begins at different times in different children. A girl only fifteen days old expressed her desire to be fed by a particular sort of cry. In another case, the cry had ceased to be a mere squall by the end of the first month. In another, the feelings of hunger, cold, pain, joy, and desire were expressed by different sounds before the end of the fifth week. Others report the transition from the "cry" to the "voice," involving cooperation of the mouth and tongue, at different times, but all within the first three months.

These cries are variously described. According to one, "the cry of pain is generally longer continued than the cry of fear." Another speaks of the cry of fear as "short and explosive," while hunger is expressed by a long drawn out wail. Another child at two months expressed pleasure and pain by different forms of the vowel *a*. Sigismund's boy, in his sixth month, expressed pleasure by a peculiar crowing shout, accompanied by kicking and prancing.

The next step is taken when these cries and babblings assume an articulate character. The alphabetic sounds begin to be heard. Of these, the vowels usually precede the consonants; and of the vowels, *a* with its various shadings is generally the first to appear.[1] In one case

---

[1] It is necessary at this point to adopt a system of diacritical marks, as in all that follows the child's pronunciation is of great importance. We shall, therefore, adopt the following system, and shall take the liberty of changing, wherever necessary, the spelling of the recorded observations, for the sake of uniformity:

a as in *calm*.
ă as in *fat*.
ā as in *fate*.
â as in *awl*.
ä (German *a* umlaut).
e as in *pet*.
ē or *ee* as in *eat*, *feet*, etc.
i as in *pit*.
ī as in *ice*.
o as in *pot*.
ō as in *old*.
ö (German *o* umlaut).
oo as in *food*.
ŏŏ as in *foot*.
u as in *up*.
ū as in *use*.
ü (German *u* umlaut).

Some changes will also be made in the use of consonants. For example, such words as *corner*, *chorus*, *coffee*, etc., will be spelled with a *k*; words like *cigar*, *center*, etc., with an *s*; and in such words as *write*, the silent *w* will be omitted. Other changes will be indicated as they are made.

the following series was developed: *ë-a-u*. In another, the sound of *a-a*, as an expression of joy, was heard in the tenth week. According to Löbisch, the vowels developed in this order: *a-e-o-u-i*. One child began with *a*, and then proceeded to *ai-ā-au-â*, while the pure sound of *ō* was late in appearing. In another case all the vowels were heard in the first five months, *ä* being the most frequently employed; and in another, the primitive *a* (of which the child's first cries largely consisted) became differentiated into the various vowel sounds during the first month. Preyer reports the use of the vowel-sounds in the following order: *uä-ao-ai-uao-ä-o-ö-ū-e-ä-i-ū*; and Sigismund in the following: *a-ä-u-ei-o-i-ö-ü-äu-au*.

Long before the sixth month, the primitive vowels are combined with one another (as we see) and with consonants, to produce the first syllabic utterances. These first syllables are, for the most part, mechanical. In a great many of the cases under consideration, the first consonants to make their appearance are the labials, *b-p-m*, and these are almost always initial at first, and not final. The easy consonant *m*, combined in this way with the easy vowel *a*, yields the familiar combination *ma*, which, by spontaneous reduplication, becomes *mama*. In a similar manner, *papa*, *baba* (afterwards *baby*) and the like are constructed. The labials are not always, however, the first consonantal sounds uttered. Sometimes the gutturals (*g* or *k*) precede them; and the two consonants which are usually the last to appear (viz., *r* and *l*) are used by some children quite early. In the case of the boy A., the first sounds were guttural, *gg*, though the earliest combination was *mam-mam*, used in crying. At five months "he dropped the throat sounds almost entirely, and began the shrill enunciation of vowels"; and at six months he lowered his voice and began to use lip sounds, simultaneously with the cutting of his first teeth. In another case, *m* appeared as the first consonant in the second month and was followed by *b-d-n-r*, occasionally *g* and *h*, and very rarely *k;* the first syllables were *pa-ma-ta-na*. Löbisch observed the consonants in this order: *m-(w)-b-p-d-t-l-n-s-r;* Sigismund in this: *b-m-n-d-s-g-w-f-ch-k-l-r-sch;* and Dr. Brown in this: *b-p-f-r-m-g-k-h-t-d-l-n*. In some cases nearly all syllables have been correctly pronounced during the first half-year; while in others progress is much slower, very few syllables being certainly mastered before the ninth month.

We may sometimes observe here also the beginnings of vocal imitation. The boy A. was observed to "watch attentively the lip movements of his attendants"; and other observers have remarked, from about the fourth month, "a curious mimicry of conversation, imitating especially the *cadences*, so that persons in the adjoining room would think conversation was going on." The same thing was observed in A. a little later.

JOHN DEWEY

10 Among the early American child-language studies is the following article by John Dewey which has historical importance because of his enormous, long-lasting influence on the educational world. While the method of establishing statistics for the parts of speech in children's language, in which he follows Tracy, must be considered antiquated, he presents some sensible comments and some interesting observations. It can be assumed that the article contributed impetus to the study of child language by psychologists and educators.

W. F. L.

THE PSYCHOLOGY OF INFANT LANGUAGE

In his interesting and valuable article on *The Language of Childhood*,[1] Mr. Tracy undertakes, upon a basis of 5400 words used by at least twenty different children, to determine the relative frequency of the various parts of speech. Before making some remarks, I wish first to submit my own mite for the further use of students. A refers to a boy; B to a girl, 20 months younger.[2]

A AT 19 MOS. OLD

Parts of Speech		Per cent
Nouns	68	60
Verbs	24	21
Adjectives	13	11
Adverbs	4	3
Interjections	6	5
Total	115	100

Pronouns, prepositions, conjunctions, none.

B[3] AT 18 MOS. OLD

Parts of Speech		Per cent
Nouns	76	53
Verbs	40	28
Adjectives	2	1
Adverbs	9	6
Interjections	7	5
Pronouns	8	6
Conjunctions	2	1
Total	144	100

Prepositions, none.

For purposes of comparison, I append the per cents reached by Mr. Tracy by averaging all his results:

Reprinted from Psychological Review *1.63–66 (1894), published by the American Psychological Association.*

[1] *American Journal of Psychology* vol. VI., No. i, reprinted in *The Psychology of Childhood* (Boston: Heath & Company, 1893).

[2] The presence of other children in the family should always, I think, form part of the data with reference to a child's vocabulary. At least, it is one of the old wives' saws on this matter that the presence of other children both hastens and extends a vocabulary.

[3] A's vocabulary was kept continuously; B's vocabulary was taken from words actually used within a period of five or six days; a number of words contained in her vocabulary four months previously do not appear at all.

Nouns	60
Verbs	20
Adjectives	9
Adverbs	5
Pronouns	2
Prepositions	2
Interjections	1.7
Conjunctions	0.3
	100.0

I wish to remark (1) concerning the relative frequency of verbs, and (2) concerning the different rates of distribution in different children:

(1) Mr. Tracy notes that since the relative frequency of verbs in the language is but 11 per cent, the child, *comparatively* speaking, uses verbs with 1.81 the ease with which he uses nouns, and makes some judicious remarks concerning the prevalence of concepts of activity in the child mind. I think he could make his case much stronger. Mr. Tracy, I take it, has classified his words according to the sense which they have to an adult, and I have followed that principle in my own table.[4] In a sense, however, this is as artificial as Mr. Tracy notes that it is to put knife under *k* instead of under *n*, because *we spell* it with a *k*. The psychological classification is to class the word according to what it means to a child, not to an adult with his grammatical forms all differentiated.

Such a classification would in all probability increase immensely the percentage of verbs. It is true that such a method demands much more care in observation, and opens the way to the very variable error of interpretation; but the greater certainty of the method followed above is after all only seeming—it does not express the *child's* vocabulary, but our interpretation of it according to a fixed but highly conventional standard. It is out of the question to redistribute the language of A and B, given above; but I subjoin the vocabulary of a child in his twelfth month where contemporaneous observation makes me

reasonably sure of what the child means:

See there; bye-bye; bottle; papa; mamma; grandma; Freddy; burn; fall; water; down; door; no, no; stop; thank you; boo (peek-a-boo); daw (used when he sees anything which he wants given to him)—17 in all.

Of the above, only the four proper nouns are, psychologically speaking, names of objects. Water is a verb as well as a noun; door is *always* accompanied by gestures of reaching, and an attempt to swing the door back and fro; 'daw' is apparently a request, an expression of expectation of something good to eat and the name of a thing all together; bottle certainly has adjectival and verbal implications as well as nominal. At present I should regard it as a complex, 'nominal-adjectival-verbal,' the emphasis being on the noun, while six weeks previously it was, say, 'verbal-adjectival-nominal.' 'Stop'; 'no, no'; 'burn'; 'see there,' etc., are equally interjections and verbs. 'Thank you' is at times a request for something, and is almost invariably said when giving an article to any one else. We have then a graded and continuous series, so far as *sense* is concerned, the proper names (23 per cent) at one end, and the interjectional forms 'no, no,' 'peek-a-boo,' at the other. These have a verbal coloring, however. Between these classes are a nominal-adjectival-verbal-interjectional complex, the verbal-interjectional meaning prevailing on the whole, the adjectival in all cases subordinate.[5] The tendency to apply the same term to a large number of objects ('ball' to ball, orange, moon, lampglobe, etc.) can be understood, I think, only if we keep in mind the extent to which the formal noun, 'ball,' has really an active sense. 'Ball' is 'to throw' just as much as it is the round thing. I do

---

[4] Phrases like 'all light,' 'all dark,' 'all gone,' 'out' (for 'go out'), etc., I have treated as verbs. It is obvious that they might be considered either as interjections or as adjectives. The relatively larger per cent of verbs in my table may be due to this classification.

[5] The fact that interjections fail so late, as a rule, in aphasia, taken with the highly immediate and emotional character of child life, indicates the defective character of a method of classification which reduces the percentage of interjections to 1.7. The philologist's objections to making interjections a primitive form of speech, however sound grammatically, seem to me to rest upon attaching a limited, technical sense to the concept *interjection*, which is without ground psychologically. In the infant mind (whether race or child) the emotional state and the tendency to react aroused by an object *must*, I should say, be fused, and both precede any clear recognition of the 'object' as such, or of any objective quality.

not believe that the child either confuses the moon with his ball, or abstracts the roundness of it; the roundness suggests to him something which he has thrown, so that the moon is something to throw—if he could only get hold of it.

What I would suggest, then, along the line of a study of the distribution of vocabulary into parts of speech is such observation and record as would note carefully the original sense to the child of his words, and the gradual *differentiation* of the original protoplasmic verbal-nominal-interjectional form (as it seems to me), until words assume their present rigidity.

(2) No one can examine the statistics given without being struck by the great differences in different children. F, in Mr. Tracy's tables, has 15 per cent interjections; while K, with a vocabulary of 250 words, has none at all. F has 11 per cent adverbs; while K has but 2 per cent; in my own table, A has 4, while B has 9 per cent. So in my two, A has 11 per cent adjectives; B, 1 per cent; while Mr.

Tracy's vary from a maximum of 13 to a minimum of 3 per cent. I believe the tendency in all psychological investigation, at present, is to attempt to get a *uniform* mathematical statement, eliminating individual differences; for pedagogical and ethical purposes, at least, it is these differences which are, finally, most important. And on strictly psychological grounds the varying ratio of adverbs and pronouns on one side and nouns and adjectives on the other must denote a very different psychological attitude—different methods of attaching interest and distributing attention. Observation of different mental traits as connected with these linguistic differences would not only add to the *terra incognita*, individual psychology (and it would seem that all psychology must be finally individual), but throw great light upon the psychology of language. How vague and formal at present our answers, for example, when we are asked to what psychological state and need an adverb corresponds!

JAMES SULLY

Sully, professor of "philosophy" in London, actually a psychologist, wrote one of the best and most readable early works on child psychology: *Studies of Childhood* (1896). It includes two long chapters dealing with child language. Sully's collection goes back to 1880, two years before the publication of Preyer's great work, which Sully knew, admired, and followed in method. He is a careful observer and gives a good general picture of child language.

The following sample is taken from Sully's smaller book, *Children's Ways* (1897), in which he presents a selection from his larger work. The pages are taken from chapter III, "Attacking our Language." The treatment is anecdotal, but his sensible approach to child language can be appreciated in the sample.

W. F. L.

ATTACKING OUR LANGUAGE

The first difficulty which our little linguist has to encounter is the mechanical one of reproducing, with a recognizable measure of approximation, our verbal sounds. What a

Reprinted from James Sully, Children's Ways (*New York: Appleton-Century-Crofts, 1897*), 30–37.

very rough approximation it is at first, all mothers know. When, for example, a child expects you to translate his sound "koppa" into "Tommy," or "pots" into "hippopotamus," it will be acknowledged that he is making heavy demands. Yet though he causes us difficulties in this way he does so because he finds himself in difficulties. His articulatory organ cannot master the terrible words we put in his way, and he is driven to these short cuts and other makeshifts.

THE NAMER OF THINGS

Leaving now the problem of getting over the mechanical difficulties of our speech, let us see what the little explorer has to do when trying to use verbal sounds with their right meanings. Here, too, we shall find that huge difficulties beset his path, and that his arrival at the goal proves him to have been in his way as valiant and hard-working as an African explorer.

One feature of the early tussle with our language is curious and often quaintly pretty. Having at first but few names, the little experimenter makes the most of these by extending them in new and surprising directions. The extension of names to new objects on the ground of some perceived likeness has been touched on above; and many other examples might be given. Thus when one child first saw a star and wanted to name it he called it, as if by a poetic metaphor, an "eye." In like manner the name "pin" was extended by another child to a crumb just picked up, a fly, and a caterpillar, and seemed to mean something little to be taken between the fingers. The same child used the sound "'at" (hat) for anything put on the head, including a hairbrush. Similarly children often extend the names "Mamma, baby" to express any contrast of size, as when a small coin was called by an American child a "baby dollar."

In this extension of language by the child we find not merely a tendency to move along lines of analogy, as in the above instances, but to go from a thing to its accompaniments by way of what the psychologist calls association. This is illustrated by the case of Darwin's grandchild, who after learning to use the common children's name for duck, "quack," proceeded to call a sheet of water "quack." In like manner a little girl called the gas lamp "pop" from the sound produced when lighting it, and then carried over the name "pop" to the stool on which the maid stood when proceeding to light it.

There is another curious way in which children are driven by the slenderness of their verbal resources to "extend" the names they

learn. They will often employ a word which indicates some relation to express what may be called the inverted relation. For example, like the unschooled yokel they will sometimes make the word "learn" do duty for "teach" also. In one case "spend" was made to express "cost." It was a somewhat similar inversion when a little girl called her parasol blown about by the wind "a windy parasol," and a stone that made her hand sore "a very sore stone.". . .

THE SENTENCE-BUILDER

It is an interesting moment when the young linguist tries his hand at putting words together in sentences. As is pretty well known, a child has for some time to try to make known his thoughts and wishes by single vocables, such as "mamma," "milk," "puss," "up," and so forth. Each of these words serves in the first baby language for a variety of sentences. Thus "Puss!" means sometimes "Puss is doing something," at other times "I want puss," and so forth. But somewhere about the age of one year nine months the child makes bold to essay a more explicit and definite form of statement.

The construction of sentences proceeds in a cautious manner. At first the structure is of the simplest, two words being placed one after the other, in what is called apposition, as in the couple, "Big bir" (big bird), "Papa no" (papa's nose), and the like.

Later on longer sentences are attempted of a similar pattern; and it is truly wonderful how much the child manages to express in this rude fashion without any aid from those valuable auxiliaries, prepositions, and the like. For example, one boy when in his twentieth month gave this elaborate order to his father, "Dada toe toe ba," that is, "Dada is to go and put his toes in the bath."

Quaint inversions of our order not infrequently occur in this early sentence making. Thus one child used the form, "Out-pull-baby 'pecs," meaning in our language, "Baby pulls (or will pull) ou the spectacles." Sometimes the order reminds us still more closely of the idiom of foreign languages, as when a little girl said: "How Babba (baby, *i.e.*, herself) does feed nicely!"

Another curious feature of children's first

style of composition is the fondness for antithesis. A little boy used when wishing to express his approval of something, say a dog, to use the form, "This a nice bow-wow, not nasty bow-bow." Similarly a little girl said, "Boo (the name of her cat) dot (got) tail; poor Babba (baby) dot no tail," proceeding to search for a tail under her skirts.

In the first attempts to fit our words together dreadful slips are apt to occur. The way in which children are wont to violate the rules of grammar when using verbs, as in saying "eated" for "ate," "scram" for "screamed," "be'd" for "was," and so on, is well known, and there are many excuses to be found for these very natural errors. . . .

THE INTERPRETER OF WORDS

There is one part of this task of mastering our language which deserves especial notice, *viz.*, the puzzling out of the meanings we put, or try to put, into our words.

Many good stories of children show that they have a way of sadly misunderstanding our words. This arises often from the ignorance of the child and the narrowness of his experience, as when a Sunday school scholar understood the story of the good Samaritan to mean that a gentleman came and poured some paraffin (*i.e.*, oil) over the poor man. By a child's mind what we call accidentals often get taken to be the real meaning. A boy and a girl, twins, had been dressed alike. Later on the boy was put into a "suit." A lady asked the girl about this time whether they were not the twins, when she replied, "No, we *used* to be." "Twin" was inseparably associated in her mind with the similarity in dress.

It should be remembered, too, that we greatly add to the difficulties of the small student of our language by reason of the ambiguities of our expressions, and of our short and elliptical modes of speaking. It was a quite natural misconception when an American child, noting that children were "half price" at a certain show, wanted his mother to get a baby now that they were cheap. Many another child besides Jean Ingelow has been saddened at being told by her father or other grown-up who was dancing her on his knee that he must put her down as he "had a bone in his leg." Much misapprehension arises, too from our figurative use of language, which the little listener is apt to interpret in a very literal way, as when a small boy indignantly resented the statement of his mother who was driving him behind a rather skittish pony, "Pony has lost his head."

Children are desirous of understanding us and make brave efforts to put meanings into our words, sometimes falling comically short of the mark. A little fellow of two who had been called "fat" by his nurse when given his bath, afterwards proceeded to call his father "fat" when he saw him taking his bath. "Fat" had by a natural misconception taken on the meaning of "naked." It was a simple movement of childish thought when a little schoolgirl answered the question of the Inspector, "What is an average?" by saying, "What the hen lays eggs on." She had heard her mother say, "The hen lays so many eggs 'on the average' every week," and had no doubt imagined a little myth about this average.

12 Ament's book, *Die Entwicklung von Sprechen und Denken beim Kinde* (Leipzig, 1899; reprint, 1912) is one of the classics of child-language study. The young philosopher used published records and his own observations of the speech of his four (later five) young cousins to devise a brief but complete grammar of child language. Two of the cousins are mentioned in the following selection which shows the earnest endeavor to explain the sounds of child language by psychological and linguistic principles. His arguments are still largely valid, although he did not achieve the insights of later structural linguistics (Jakobson) and more recent work. Haeckel's biogenetic law of ontophylogenetic parallelism, which was frequently debated in child language studies of the period, is alluded to in the passage.

The records which Ament mentions in this extract deal with sound substitutions. Humphreys was a professor of Greek at Vanderbilt University. He published a brief but good pioneer study of the speech of a two-year-old child, with a list of consonant substitutions (1880). Sully's valuable book, *Studies of Childhood* (1896), from which the preceding selection has been taken, was new when Ament wrote. Kathleen C. Moore collected good observations from the first two years of her boy but published them in a too condensed form (1896). Oltuszewski's book on the first three years of a Polish child (1897), like Sully's one of the many studies strongly influenced by Preyer, is also concerned with the sequence of sound acquisition.

W. F. L.

From ENTWICKLUNG VON SPRECHEN UND DENKEN BEIM KINDE

The difficulties of method are great and require the closest examination so as to avoid confusion between similar products of different causes. In this respect the literature is full of mistakes, which unfortunately are mostly beyond control today. The significance of the English sound substitutions of Humphreys and Sully (those of Moore I have not even included) as well as the Polish ones of Oltuszewski is considerably diminished by the fact that these scholars have not separated pure sound substitutions from other phenomena. Humphreys escapes my direct appraisal because of a lack of examples. Sully and Oltuszewski however give examples and

make it possible to trace their errors. Unfortunately neither of them says if further examples beyond these were available.

The most important complications which have come to my attention in the course of my investigations are the following:

(1) By means of prolepsis and metalepsis, sounds often replace others, which does not simply amount to sound substitution. As long as further examples are missing it is wrong to conclude from *bambe* (lamp), as Sully does,[1] or from *goga* (*droga*), as Oltuszewski does,[2] that *l* is changed into *b* or *d* into *g*. Pure sound substitutions of this type have not been observed in any of the three languages compared; therefore I have left both instances out of account. Still greater difficulties are caused by the fact that not only identical but also related sounds can be anticipated or linger. Since these phenomena can concern not only sounds in the same word but also in adjoining words, it is possible that

---

Reprinted in translation by the editors from Wilhelm Ament, Entwicklung von Sprechen und Denken beim Kinde (*Leipzig, 1899; reprinted 1912*), 70–72, *by permission of C. C. Buchners Verlag.*

---

[1] *Studies of Childhood*, German edition, p. 141.
[2] *Die Entwicklung der Sprache beim Kinde*, p. 35.

many of the cases that I have included in the phonology as pure sound substitutions are to be considered under this aspect and eliminated there. This will have to be clarified by future investigations.

(2) A blending of phenomena is contained, for example, in Irma's *kalerne* (*Laterne*, 'lantern'), 1086th day. The child converted *t* into *k* and performed a metathesis with them.

(3) In unstressed terminal syllables the vowel is often replaced by a diminutive *-i*, which must of course not be taken for a sound change, for example Louise's *mómi* (*Mama*), *ádi* (*adieu*).

(4) When of two consonants one is omitted and the other replaced, it is often doubtful which is omitted and which replaced, as for example when Louise makes *fei* out of *zwei* ('two') Here, only a comparison with the replacement and omission of such sounds in other cases can lead to the correct appraisal.

(5) One of the most diffcult complications arises as the child reaches the age when he attempts to give a meaning to unfamiliar words by means of etymology. When Irma at this stage forms *eifer* (*Eiter*, 'pus') on the 1629th day, only the exact observation of the word formation with the aid of etymology can forestall the error of seeing a sound law in this formation.

In general the following transformations can be distinguished:

1. Transformations which are parallel to phenomena in adult language.
2. Transformations which have no parallel in adult language.

In looking over the phenomena of word transformation the linguist finds old friends everywhere, in elision, infixation, substitution, displacement, metathesis, prolepsis, metalepsis of sound and syllables. The first group of transformations prevails to such an extent that the second can make a showing only in a few phenomena, such as diminutive endings. This shows very clearly the ontogenetic recapitulation of phylogenetic development.

The transformation of a word is not always finished with the first form. Often words undergo a continuous sound change in the course of months, just as the words of a developed language are constantly transformed in the course of thousands of years. The very first word of Louise demonstrates such a continuous change of a word, which is very interesting furthermore because a semantic change is intimately connected with it:

> *mammmamm*
> = sound, food, beverage, interjection, persons

> *momi*
> = mother

> *máma*
> = initially mother, aunt; later only mother.

CARL FRANKE

13 One of the most brilliant early summaries of the international literature of child language, combined with his own observations, was contributed by Professor Carl Franke of Löbau (Saxony) to Rein's *Handbuch der Pädagogik* (1899; second ed., 1908), vol. VIII, 742–90. The first part of the article deals with children's learning to speak; the second draws a parallel with the development of language in prehistoric mankind, a favorite concern of Franke's, who published, in addition, many studies of the German language and German dialects.

In 1907 the epoch-making monograph of Clara and William Stern appeared. Thereupon Franke reexamined his own studies and compared his results with those of Stern, in an article, "Über die erste Lautstufe der Kinder," *Anthropos*, VII (1912), 663–76. The following excerpts, in English translation, are from this article. After having reported about the first spoken words in the international literature he draws tentative conclusions (Vermutungen) with which these excerpts start. (Most of the earlier studies he refers to can be found in W. F. Leopold's *Bibliography of Child Language*, [1952].)

W. F. L.

ÜBER DIE ERSTE LAUTSTUFE DER KINDER

At first most French, German, and English children learning to speak produce exclusively pure vocalic and one-consonantal forms for some time—for almost half a year in the case of French children, about three months in the case of German and English (presumably Germanic in general) children. Those German and English children who have forms with two or even three consonants as early as the first three months of speaking are definitely in the minority during this period, in fact for some time longer. With Slavic children formations with two consonants appear either at once at the beginning of speaking or very soon thereafter, but these formations remain in the minority for most of them for about three months.

Nor is it justified to assume that the children form their first words with one consonant because they cannot yet pronounce most consonants. The lip sounds *m*, *b*, and *p* are probably the easiest. Eight of the children, whose linguistic beginnings are reviewed by Stern, produced word forms with *m* and vowels as early as the first months of speaking, five in the first three months. Forms with *b* or *p* and vowels were used by five children in the first month, by six in the first three months of speaking. As early as 1528 Cuspinianus wrote in his work, *Austria:* "When the children begin to speak they say *pepp mem* when they want something to eat." Wackernagel states: "Our children call *memm* when they want something to drink." But all these children have, in the first period of speaking, no word forms as yet which contain both *m* and *b* or *p*. Günther Stern transformed *bim* into *bä* as late as 1; 11 [first year; eleventh month]; Hilde Stern simplified *bums* to *bu* or *buä* by 0; 11 and *Baum* to *mamau* as late as 1; 5, whereas my older son said *bau* for it by

1; 9 and Lindner's child said *maum*. This example is very convincing because the three children show individual differences in the way they imitate the word *Baum* ('tree'), but none retains both *b* and *m*. The only one who does is Stumpf's son at 0; 9½, in one word, *papn-mapn*, but his speech development is very exceptional in other respects, too. . . .

Apparently children in the first speaking period have no difficulty articulating at least *m*, *b* or *p*, *n*, *d* or *t*. The difficulty lies only in the change of place or manner of articulation of consonants in one word. I consider this the most characteristic feature of the first sound stage. Even if one or the other consonant were still too difficult for a child, he could substitute another which is easier for him, as he does in words which contain a single consonant that is still too hard for him then and in later sound stages. Thus Shinn's niece had at the age of one *my* for *by;* my older son had *ab* for *Affe* ('monkey') in the first month of speaking (1; 9¾); Günther Stern spoke *papao* at 1; 10 and the Lange twins spoke *tata* for *Kakao* ('cocoa'). . . .

Concerning the dropping of sounds by children, Stern stated the rule: "Initial and terminal consonants are omitted most frequently; next those that are elements of a consonant cluster." I formulate this rule for the first sound stage more narrowly and exactly. At this stage the child omits, in a word with different consonants, all except one, and this he sometimes substitutes for those he omits. Of the different consonants in a word, the most stable is the medial, next the initial, last the terminal. In short: at this stage the children favor the types vowel-consonant-vowel and consonant-vowel. But which consonants of a word are dropped at the first sound stage depends on many things: (1) on their position, as has been stated; (2) on their greater or lesser difficulty; (3) on the number of syllables; and (4) on the stress. Stern also declared that long words and unstressed syllables are especially subject to mutilation. . . .

Reprinted in translation by the editors from Anthropos 7.663–676 (1912) *by permission of* Anthropos.

As it is more difficult for speakers of Romance languages than for speakers of Germanic languages to learn a foreign language, but less difficult for Slavs, the easier one-consonant sound stage is more sharply defined with French children, and less sharply with Slavic than with Germnic children. These national differences caution us against extending our results to non-Indo-European children without further investigation.

TABLE 1: One-syllable and one-consonant word forms of the first sound stage.

Child	Year; month	(Cons.–Cons.– Vow.) vow.	×2	Vow.– cons.
Ament's niece	0;11¹/₂–1;3	1	—	—
Deville	0;10–1;3	1	6	—
Eva Stern	0;9–0;11	—	2	—
Hilde Stern	0;10¹/₂–1;3¹/₂	3	7	—
Gunther Stern	0;9–1;¹/₂	1	4	—
My oldest son	1;9–1;9³/₄	10	7	2
Gheorgov I	1;1¹/₂–1;3¹/₂	4	—	—
Gheorgov II	1;2–1;5¹/₂	2	—	—
Idelberger	0;8–1;3	—	5	—
Lange twins	1;9–2	1	2	—
Lindner's son	1;1¹/₂–1;3¹/₂	1	1	—
Lindner's daughter	0;9¹/₂	—	2	1
Major	1–1;2¹/₂	2	—	1
Oltuscewski	1–1;2	4	4	—
Schneider's daughter F	0;10–0;11¹/₂	1	—	—
Schneider's daughter S	0;10–0;11¹/₂	1	1	—
Preyer	0;11–1;7	1	2	—
Shinn's niece	0;10–1	3	2	—
Strümpell's daughter	10¹/₂	—	1	—
Stumpf's son	0;9¹/₂–1;3	1	1	—
Tögel's son	1;2–1;3	1	3	—
Volz' son	0;10–0;11	—	2	—
Total		38	52	4

Since the Germanic and especially the Slavic languages, are among those richest in consonants, the child's first sound stage seems shortened and its half-year duration, in the case of Romance children, comes closer to the original situation. The stage of the sentence word or one-word sentence has about the same duration, that is the time during which the child does not yet combine the individual words into a sentence. It is therefore probable that the first sound stage originally coincided with the period of the one-word sentence. Although no language group now speaks only in one-word sentences, it is assumed that primitive man once did so. In my opinion it is likewise to be assumed that his one-word sentences contained only one single consonant each, or, that he formed not only sentences but words like a child beginning to speak. Undoubtedly these primitive men lived during the glacial period or the diluvium, possibly even earlier than Neanderthal man.

In conclusion I emphasize that I definitely subordinate the division by sound stages to the division by sentence stages which Stern advocated. Therefore I formulate the rule as follows: Romance children remain on the first sound stage during almost the whole period of the one-word sentence; Germanic children approximately during the first half of it; Slavic children a still shorter time. With H. Paul, I consider the progress of man from the one-word sentence to sentences of several words the most important step in the development of language, and van Ginneken's division of languages by type of sentence structure has great appeal for me. That I deal more with the physiological aspect of linguistic development than the psychological is merely the consequence of my training. I do not wish to contest Stern's results but to supplement them.

WILHELM WUNDT

14 Wundt, Professor of Philosophy and Psychology at the University of Leipzig, is considered the founder of modern experimental psychology. His influence in Germany, Europe, and the United States was very great and long lasting. He took an interest in child language from 1875 to obtain access to the problem of the origin of language by direct observation. Later he made his studies a part of his great ten-volume work, *Völkerpsychologie* (1900). Volume I is concerned with language; chapter 3 deals with speech sounds, and the second part of the chapter is devoted to the speech sounds of children. The following pages are a translation of the subchapter "Exchanges and Mutilations of Sounds in Child Language" (third ed., 1911).

W. F. L.

EXCHANGES AND MUTILATIONS OF SOUNDS IN CHILD LANGUAGE

The peculiarities of child language considered so far are the result of relations with the environment, the latter having generally more effect than the child. The situation is quite different with regard to a last set of phenomena which originate almost exclusively in the speaking child himself; these are the exchanges and "multilations" of sounds. They are the phenomena of longest duration, their last vestiges being noticeable as a rule when the language has been completely acquired in other respects.

The prevailing opinion is that all these sound changes are caused by the inability of the child to produce certain sounds. The child is said to regularly substitute an easier sound for the more difficult one. Fritz Schultze tried to reduce the principle of this substitution to a rule. According to him the child replaces the unpronounceable sound by one most closely related to it which can be articulated with less physiological difficulty, and if he cannot master that one, he omits it entirely. (Fritz Schultze, *Die Sprache des Kindes* [1880], p. 34 ff.) Other observers have partly accepted, partly opposed this rule. On the whole, however, not the principle as

Reprinted in translation by the editors from Völker- psychologie (*1900; 3rd ed., 1911*), *1.314–319.*

such, but only the rule connected with it has been criticized (especially by Preyer, *Seele des Kindes*, third ed. pp. 346, 434, and by W. Ament, *Die Entwicklung von Sprechen und Denken*, etc., pp. 65 ff.) I am inclined, on the contrary, to grant a certain validity to the rule postulated by Schultze that, in the sound transformations of the child, the point of closure is moved from back to front, from the guttural and palatal to the labial and dental articulations. On the other hand I do not think it is possible to maintain the rather generally accepted principle that the child substitutes other sounds wherever the required ones are impossible or difficult for him. It seems to me this assumption is invalidated simply by the fact that the child is usually in full possession of all the articulations which are needed for the various sound formations from the beginning of his imitative speech movements, and uses them constantly in the emotive sounds which precede real speech. Furthermore the same sounds are avoided in certain words and used in others at the same time. The same child who calls the *Kind* "Tind" and the *Pfeife* "Peipe" may pronounce the word *Gasse* as "Gack" and *Vater* as "Faata." The reason for these transformations is not the inability to produce these sounds at all; they must depend on other conditions. As a matter of fact observation of the child and a closer look at the sound transformations which take place yield two conditions which make it quite understandable that more or less radical changes must take place in the imitation of sounds, although the child is capable of producing the required sounds. The first of these conditions is the imperfect acoustic and optic apperception of the sounds and sound movements. The second is the contact effect of sounds which plays a part in coherent speech and is greatly increased in children's speech.

In the first place the learning of imitative articulatory movements is not only determined by the sounds being heard, but also decisively by the sound movements being seen. That is why children born blind begin imitative speech much later than those with sight, and in most cases of so-called "Hörstummheit," in which speech does not develop in spite of ability to hear and apparently adequate intelligence, defects of vision at least contribute to the situation. (A. Liebmann, *Vorlesungen über Sprachstörungen*, no. 3: "Hörstummheit," 1898, p. 16.) For children's speech defects and speech impediments in general, see H. Gutzmann, *Des Kindes Sprache und Sprachfehler*, (1894); *Sprachentwicklung des Kindes und ihre Hemmungen* (1902).) Such defects of vision, to be sure, impede the imitation of words for an additional reason: they prevent the association between word, gesture, and thing. But an important aspect of this impeding influence must be sought in the fact that the impulse given by seeing the articulatory movements is missing. For just in the first stage of word formation, especially in the so-called echolalia, one observes that the child attentively reads the word from the lips of the speaker before repeating it. He thus imitates at the same time the acoustic and the optic impression of the word, predominantly the latter at first, since the articulatory movement seen produces a far stronger impulse for imitation than the sound heard. This directly explains the strong preponderance of labial and dental sounds in child language: the child imitates above all the components of sound movements which are accessible to his vision. The inexactness of the auditory perception is secondary, but it is partially responsible for the child persevering for a long time in his faulty articulations. In this regard the child merely does in increased measure what we can continually observe also in the speech of

adults imitating sounds which are unfamiliar to their organs of speech. Our habitual word concepts are combinations of sound perceptions and articulatory perceptions. The word impressions are apperceived with relative faithfulness only when they coincide with the corresponding sound sensations of earlier identical impressions and become associated simultaneously and directly with the articulations required for them. That is why we can hear quite correctly only those speech sounds which we can also produce correctly ourselves. He who confuses the lingual *r* with the guttural, or voiceless sounds with voiced, usually misses the differences also when hearing the sounds. The same is true in acquiring a foreign language, which is for this reason always remodeled according to the familiar sounds of the native language. For the child, all these associations of sound and articulatory sensations are still unformed, and at the start, assimilated word structures are not yet known to him, or known only in modified shape. It is therefore a matter of course that the speech sounds with which he imitates the imperfectly heard and seen sounds come to agree with the speech of the environment only very gradually.

In addition to the modifications to which the individual sound as such is exposed, there is a second element which has a decisive influence on the phonetic form: the contact effects of the sounds which occur because of their being combined into compound word structure, and which follow the same laws of general validity that we find operating everywhere in language. Child language is subjected to them not only more strongly but also prevailingly in a different direction. All these effects, known by the designation of "progressive and regressive assmiliations and dissimilations,". . . are to be interpreted as psychophysical processes caused by associations of sound concepts and at the same time by mechanical conditions of articulatory movements. They increase with the speed of the discourse, but decrease with growing practice in articulatory movements and the conceptual movements which go parallel with them.

The child has of course very little practice of this kind and the conceptual movement is slower compared with normal consciousness. That explains why the language of the child is replete with these contact effects by which sounds are assimilated to, or by dissimilation separated from each other or suppressed completely. The slower conceptual movement of the child explains particularly the other fact that progressive assimilations are far more numerous in child language. From a large number of observations of this kind I can cite only very few regressive assimilations; they are mostly examples in which the trend of independent sound exchange favors the modification anyway. Thus *wott* for "fort", *Däthe* for "Käthe," *Nanone* for "Kanone." In contrast to these examples there is a large number of progressive assimilations, partly by themselves, partly combined with sound exchanges and dissimilations, for example, *Nana* for "Nase," *Tata* for "Tante," *Munn* for "Mund," *Nann* for "Nacht," *Gag* for "Kleid," *Guga* for "Kuchen," *Dedde* for "Decke," *Bebe* for "Besen," *Bübü* for "Bücher," *Bibbe* for "Bitte," *Joj* for "Schoß," *Auau* for "Auge," *Mormor* for "Morgen,"

Dodonana for "Promenade," etc. The assimilations are, as can be seen, sometimes consonantal, sometimes vocalic, most commonly both simultaneously, dissimilations playing a part in some cases. Incidentally the latter occur occasionally by themselves, especially when consonants come together: thus in *Faata* for "Vater," *Aam* for "Arm," *Baat* for "Bart." This preponderance of progressive assimilation is noteworthy because in all cultural languages of Indo-European and Semitic provenience, the opposite, regressive form of assimilation prevails, whereas in other languages, for example, in the Ural-Altaic, progressive assimilation, primarily vocalic, is dominant, as in child language. . . . Here they needed emphasizing as the elements which, more than others, have an effect on the sound deviations of child language. At the same time the above examples show how much these phenomena favor the sound repetitions which are characteristic of child language. The preceding syllable having an assimilating effect on the following one automatically results in a sound repetition.

WILLIAM STERN〜〜〜〜〜〜〜〜〜〜〜〜〜〜〜〜〜〜〜〜〜〜

15 Clara and William Stern's work *Kindersprache* (1907; fourth ed., 1928) is one of the classics of child language study. (Footnotes in the following selection refer to it as *Children's Speech*—misleadingly, because the work has not been translated into English. The term dhild language, now generally accepted, did not come into use until after 1939.) For serious studies this work must be used, but its value is in the details of three children's language-learning. It is difficult to make suitable selections from it.

The following presents instead part of Stern's own summary included as Part 3 in *Psychologie der frühen Kindheit* (1914; eighth ed., 1965, with a preface by his son Günther, the same who is mentioned repeatedly in the following passage). The translation is that of Anna Barwell (with a few minor corrections) in the English edition, *Psychology of Early Childhood* (London and New York, 1924), pp. 164–75. The passage is reprinted from the 1930 edition by permission. The English version translates the children's mutilated German words fairly skillfully into mutilated English words, which makes them easier to digest for the English reader; but in this form they are of course not authentic source material. The numerous references to earlier literature can be checked in the *Bibliography of Child Language* (1952) by W. F. Leopold.

Cooing and babbling are not distinguished in Stern's studies. Kaczmarek is superior in this regard. Stern pays only minor attention to the learning of sounds and to the beginnings of language acquisition, a stage of crucial importance for child phonetics. For the later stages of language-learning, the book which he wrote with his wife is of paramount importance. The reader is urged to read the latter.

W. F. L.

THE CHIEF PERIODS OF FURTHER SPEECH DEVELOPMENT

1. LEAVING THE FIRST STAGE BEHIND

That first period of unconscious speech for particular occasions. . . , as a rule, lasts for six months or a little more, without showing any very special progress within its own limits.

But then a decisive turn takes place once more in the development of speech with the *awakening of a faint consciousness of the meaning of speech and the will to achieve it.*[1]

If, up till then, sound forms have only been used here and there to express experiences, connected with them by some association of perception or emotion, now the discovery is made that there are in addition to those, other sound forms of distinguishing (symbolic) value viz., a sign belonging to every object as a designation in speech concerning it, that is, that *every thing has a name.*

This change has two evident symptoms:

1. In the child's suddenly awakened enquiry as to names of things.
2. In the increase—often proceeding by leaps and bounds—of vocabulary, especially in important words.

Both changes may be active in varying degree, and do not necessarily occur at exactly the same time, since the words acquired by constant inquiry may lie hidden in the child's consciousness for a more or less lengthy time before they are used.

As Hilde was about 1; 6 we noticed a period when the question "*isn't that?*" or the demonstrative *that! that!* entirely usurped all her speech and thoughts in its demand for the

names of all actual things and pictures of them, and at the same time her vocabulary increased rapidly. Gunther (1; 7) began his unwearied search for names with the question *that? that?* but, in his case, several months passed before he used what he had learned in his ordinary speech. The record of Scupin's son (1; 10) reads: "His joy in naming things is great. Today he stood in the middle of the room and said as he pointed to the several things: *lamp, the cupboard, the bassy* (basket)."

The occurrence just described must now doubtless be considered as a *mental* act of the child's in the real sense of the word. The insight into the relation between sign and import which the child gains here is something fundamentally different from the simple dealing with perceptions and their associations[2] And the demand that some name must belong to every object, whatever

---

[2] Where speech development takes place under nonnormal circumstances, this moment of discovery sometimes makes its appearance with especial distinctness. For this reason the description is instructive which Miss Sullivan, Helen Keller's teacher, gave of the corresponding event. This child, deprived of both higher senses, grew up without speech to the age of seven years. At last Miss S. succeeded by touches on the palm of the hand in teaching her the finger alphabet; next, Helen acquired a few finger symbols by association with objects touched at the same time, but without having any idea of the symbolic meaning of the finger signs. At the beginning of the second month of instruction, the following occurrence took place (taken from Miss Sullivan's own report): "We went to the pump, where I let Helen hold the cup under the spout while I pumped. As the cold water poured out and filled the cup, I spelt 'water' on her empty hand. The word, immediately following the sensation of the cold water rushing over her hand, seemed to take her aback. She dropped the cup and stood rooted to the ground. Quite a new light passed over her features. She spelt the word water several times, then crouching down touched the ground and asked its name, and in the same way pointed to the pump and the grating, then turning round suddenly she asked my name. All the way home she was most excited, and inquired the name of everything she touched, so that in the course of a few hours she had embodied thirty new words in her vocabulary" (cf. W. Stern: VI).

Translated by Anna Berwell, reprinted from William Stern, Psychology of Early Childhood (*London: George Allen and Unwin Ltd., 1924; 2nd ed., 1930*), *164–175, by permission of the publisher.*
[1] *Children's Speech*, pp. 190 ff.

its nature, we may consider as a real—perhaps the child's first—general thought.[3]

But of course the distinctive diffuse nature of the child's mentality must still be borne in mind. It is true that at this point words become "names" or symbols of things, but that does not mean that they immediately acquire nothing but a demonstrative and purely conventional relationship to the object designated [like any chance word or a chemical formula in adult speech]. On the contrary, the name has at once a much more original and primitive connection with the thing named; it becomes actually a quality of the object and also an expression of it as well. The thing itself gains from the fact that it can be named, an increase in stability and permanence, and the name from its firm anchorage in the structure of the thing takes on some touch of its physiognomy; it sounds as the thing looks or moves or feels to the touch—a species of sound painting which now appears side by side with the natural utterance. (See above.)

Frequent use is made of the instance of Stumpf's son . . . , who as a small child had invented the name of *marage* for a brick and gave his reason for this when 17 years old as follows: "The brick looked just the same as the word sounds." This peculiar double function of the name as being on the one hand a designation for the thing, on the other an expressive part of its very self, is found in all primitive vocal thought and involves that magic of speech which is quite evident in uncivilized peoples, children, and in certain pathological psychic conditions, and indeed is never quite lost even amongst normal and educated human beings.[4]

About the same time (1; 6 to 1; 9), as regards syntax, the first period comes to an end; the sole dominance of the one-word sentence ceases, the child becomes capable of connecting several words to express one thought.[5] Here, too, understanding is generally in advance of power of expression.

Hilde (1; 4) could already obey the suggestion, "Touch your nose with your foot," and connected the two perceptions of nose and foot quite correctly; but not till 1; 5 did she utter her first sentence of more than one word: *there, see wow-wow*, and at 1; 7 the still more impressive one: *all, all milk!* (the milk is all gone).[6]

It is true these word collections were not all so fluently spoken as are our sentences; their characteristic rather was a jerky utterance (often interspersed by pauses) of the isolated words; in such case it is really more a question of a short chain of one-word sentences as: *Hilde—cocoa* (come Hilda, the cocoa is here), *ater—dolly* (father look, I have a dolly). It is only by degrees that such loose juxtapositions pass into the firm union of a really coherent sentence.

2. THE SECOND PERIOD OF SPEECH

Once the first period is over, rapid development generally begins; within a short time events follow so rapidly that we must confine ourselves to a consideration of the most important stages.

To show the quickness of the progress, we will first mention that girls at 2 years, boys at 2; 6 have a speaking vocabulary of about three hundred words.[7] In respect of constitution, this vocabulary is naturally of "paidocentric" tendency, i.e. it is grouped round the middle point of the child's interests, and the circumference of this circle gradually becomes wider and wider. In the first stages the exclusive material for the child's speech are words belonging to the most noticeable impressions of the immediate environment, such as parents, nurse, toys, animals, clothing,

---

[3] In *Children's Speech*, pp. 124 ff., the general growth of speech in childhood is shown to develop from three roots, viz., the expressive, the social, and the intentional. The first two become manifest in the earliest beginnings of speech—as we have already shown in this book, but intentional speech activity (the designation of an ideal) is not possible until after this first general thought.

[4] Cf. particularly Heinz Werner, Einführung in die Entwichlungs psychologie (Leipzig, 1926), II, pp. 183 ff. and elsewhere, also K. Koffka, Die Grundlagen der psychilschen Entwicklung, 2nd ed. (Osterwieck, 1925), p. 244.

[5] *Children's Speech*, pp. 199 ff.

[6] Our own son was a remarkable exception. Although in other ways he learned to speak with more difficulty than his sisters, at 1; 2 he connected his scanty words in sentences of more than one word: *moo hear?—do you* hear the cow lowing? *There is papa, see !*

[7] *Children's Speech*, pp. 226–28.

and food, then sounds and movements as well as activities that attract the child's attention. Within this vocabulary the division into kinds of words now becomes clear; the interjectional kinds of expression, which in the first period were almost masters of the field, fall now more and more into the background, whilst expressions of objective import come to the fore in an easily marked sequence.

The necessity of learning names is confined at first to persons and things; so that at first (1; 3 to 1; 6) the vocabulary consists, with the exception of interjections, almost entirely of nouns. A few months later these are joined fairly suddenly by verbs in considerable numbers, whilst at the same time the store of substantives keeps on growing; it is not until a third stage that adjectives are added as well as the finer framework of language, prepositions, adverbs, numerals, etc.[8]

A later section deals with the significance of the three stages thus arising: "Substance," "Action," "Relation and Attribute Stage," for the child's thought development[9] we will now only consider these relations by means of a few statistics. The vocabulary of a normal girl shows roughly the following divisions— interjections not being considered: At 1; 3 substantives 100 per cent; 1; 8 78 per cent substantives, 22 per cent verbs; 1; 11 63 per cent substantives, 23 per cent verbs, 24 per cent other classes of words.

But, after all, single words form only the raw material; the decisive step comes with the way in which they are used in the building up of speech. Here there are two outstanding points: the change of words by inflection, and their union by syntax.

3. THE THIRD PERIOD OF SPEECH

For a year the words that the child uses are fixed forms only, at 2; 0 they begin to live, to bend, to move.[10] This, too, we have to look upon as the beginning of an important new period in speech development, the third. The child of educated classes here already reches a stage which has never been attained by many fully developed adult languages, for the study of language reveals many so-called uninflected languages that can only express all more delicate shades of meaning by the juxtaposition of unchanging words. How much higher than these is a language which, by a slight modification, makes the same word express singular or plural, changes an action from the present to the past or future by adding a prefix and an affix, or expresses a quality in a greater or less degree by forms of comparison. Here the single word is no longer an isolated island, but the central sun whose rays represent the most delicate divergencies and relations of the main idea. The two-year-old child begins to acquire all this in the different forms of inflection (declension, conjugation, comparison) fairly simultaneously, so that, in reality, we are dealing with united psychic progress along the whole line.

It is true this fresh stage of development lasts some years; and four and five-year-old children often have a hard struggle with certain shades of inflection. As a whole, the regular, less inflected forms are more easily mastered than the more irregular and more strongly inflected, hence the frequent substitution of wrong forms of the first type for those of the last (drinked for drunk, badder for worse).

As to syntax, the end of the second year generally brings with it considerable development of sentences of more than one word.[11] Three, four, and more words are put together now to express one thought, not at first, of course, in the form of a fluent sentence, but as a jerky series of several short, little sentences. The same process, therefore, is repeated as in two-word sentences; the united structural form of a sentence only develops by degrees from elements but loosely knit together.

Thus Hilde (1; 10) expressed a wish that her mother should fetch pictures out of the back room as follows: Mama—wanty pickies —room—wanty pickies—back—dada, mama fetch.

The loose links of the original chain of words often produce an order of words in the sentence differing from the normal.[12] As the ideas bubble up into the little head, out rattle

---

[8] Ibid., pp. 344 ff.
[9] Chap. XXVII, 2.
[10] Children's Speech, p. 247, and Chap. XV.

[11] Ibid., pp. 202 ff.
[12] Children's Speech, pp. 217 ff.

words, however wrong their order may be. Certainly the very strangeness of position often makes for impressiveness. Sometimes the word most emphasized by the child comes full tilt at the very beginning; sometimes, on the other hand, the important word is used all alone as a special one-word sentence at the very end (this is specially the case for negation).

Gunther once at dinner pushed his high chair to a fresh place with the words: *A Gunther a father sit* (meaning probably, today Gunther wants to sit for once by father). When his mother asked: "Not by mother?" the answer came: *Yesterday a mumsey sitting a Gunter.*

Affix of negation: Idelberger's son (already 1; 6), *mama beat, no!*—mama must not beat. Stumpf's son (German boy): *ich haja kokadach mach olol kap—näh.* This very strange sentence in ordinary German runs: "Ich (hab) ein schönes Schokoladenhaus; das macht Rudolf kaputt—nein!" I (have) a fine chocolate house; that Rudolf break—no!

But sometimes it is all confusion, and the mood of the moment decides now this position and, a second later, another; notice the negation in the following chain sentence of our son's: *Gunther also a not make, Hilde also not a make—father also a make, no—no.*

With regard to meaning, the variety of sentences increases with astonishing speed. Although interjectional sentences containing an expression of will or emotion are still in the majority throughout childhood, yet statement sentences continually tend to take a more important place, and they refer not only to the present (as giving an account of what is to be seen in a picture), but also to experiences and impressions which have lately taken place, and to end with, they are questions.[13] In addition to those questions, mentioned earlier, as to the names of things (*isna that?* or something similar), we soon find questions as to the whereabouts of anything lost. Hilde (1; 9), *apple where?* Gunther (2; 8), *a, hat?* (*where is the hat?*); also questions to ascertain something (*may I eat these?*), and lastly, even questions of sympathy (*are you tired?*), said by Eva when she saw someone yawn. In these questions we

often notice that the word of interrogation is discarded, or, to speak more exactly, has not yet crossed the threshold of speech. But the other words, the intonation and the situation, are sufficient to make the sense quite clear. Some other types of questions on a higher level intellectually are not developed before the fourth stage.

4. THE FOURTH PERIOD OF SPEECH

The beginning of this period is formed by the appearance of subordinate sentences.

Like inflection, hypotaxis (the subordination of one sentence to another) is a form of speech completely wanting in many languages that can only express the dependent relation of thoughts by placing sentences side by side (parataxis). The child of European civilization passes this stage in about two and a half years,[14] and thereby proves that he has grasped not only logical thought relation but its word representation in principal and subordinate sentences.

Thus Hilde (2; 2) could already express cause and result, but only in parataxis; *porridge iid not here, can't twirly, twirly* (spin). Not for another whole year was she able to show the same relation by a causal subordinate clause: *you rub your hands, because it is so cold.*

Just as in interrrogatory sentences, the introductory particle may for a long time be omitted, so too in subordinate clauses conjunctions, relative pronouns, etc., that is, exactly the part of speech that determines (for the grammarian) the character of the subordinate sentence. Yet the clause in children's speech is unmistakable for the listener, even if the written form alone leaves the reader in doubt. When Gunther (2; 6) uttered the setence, *mother say, builded has Gunther,* his intonation explained that he meant to say: "I want to tell mother what

---

[13] *Ibid.*, pp. 212 ff.

[14] Many children even earlier. Thus our daughter Eva at 2; 0 uttered sentences such as: *look where glove is; daddy say if he can drink coffee.* Another girl of our acquaintance who had not begun to speak till very late (2; 0) then made such quick progress that at the age of 2; 7 she had got as far as subordinate sentences, e.g. *Shop we buyed thing, was funny man* (= in the shop where we bought something, there was a funny man).

Gunther has built," but not: "I want to tell mother Gunther has been building." For this reason the beginning of the period of subordinate clauses must not be fixed as only when the appropriate particles are really heard, for the stage of hidden knowledge of those words may often last for several months.

The following anthology of subordinate sentences which we recorded of Hilde (about 3; 0) shows how quickly hypotaxis gorws when once it is grasped by the child:

"*I will look in the kitchen and ask if she is coming here* (indirect question); *will whip the doll till it hurts her* (temporal clause); *that moves so today because it is broken* (causal clause); *you'll get no bread and butter if you're so nanghly* (conditional clause); *you must take away the beds so that I can get out* (clause of purpose); *dolly has disturbed me, so that I could not sleep* (consecutive clause)."

Nevertheless, many specially difficult constructions in subordination of clauses continue to be, for some considerable time yet, beyond the child's power; e.g., the hypothetical conditional clause with the subjunctive verbal forms—probably the most difficult of these clauses[15]—has only been mastered by our children at 4; 6.

Gunther (4; 8), of a friend who had undergone an operation: *If he were* (not) *cut at once, then he had died.*

With the mastery of such difficulties the period of children's speech, as such, may be considered as brought to an end.

The fourth period of speech development is characterized by two other facts.

The child for the second time comes into an *age of questions*,[16] now, however, concerned with something higher—the time question *when*, the causal question *why*. But too high a value must not be set upon these questions. The earliest "when" and "why" questions are, for the main part, not the expression of unmixed desire for knowledge on the child's part, but are most intimatcly connected with his small ego and its practical needs; for this reason the first "why" meets

the parents' ears in the annoyed expression, *why not, then?* if some wish of the child's is forbidden or withheld. And *"when?"* the child asks to find out when the earnestly desired meal time is to come at last.

Our son's (2; 11) first *when* was also extremely utilitarian. As he saw his elders biting the meat from fowl bones he asked: "*A shall we nibble? a are big, we can nibble* (the first *a* = when, the second = if we).

But besides such questions there are others from pure desire to know; not concerned with finding the justification of commands, but rather the reason of facts the child has observed.

At 2; 10 Gunther already asks: "*Tray so hot—why then?*" Hilde 3; 7 had so violent an attack of asking causal questions that sometimes she made a whole chain of them, each reason producing another inquiry as to *its* reason.

Thus about this time the following conversation—taken down literally in shorthand—took place as the child saw a whale in her picture-book:

Child's Questions	*Mother's Answers*
What is he eating?	Fish.
Why does he eat fish?	Because he is hungry.
Why doesn't he eat rolls?	Because we don't give him any.
Why don't we give him any?	Because bakers only make rolls for people.
Why not for fishes?	Because they haven't enough flour.
Why then haven't they enough?	Because not enough corn is grown. You know, don't you, that flour is made out of corn?
Oh, I see.	

The little Anna, who forms the subject of Elsa Köhler's report, at the age of 3; 2 constantly asks *why*, but curiously enough only as regards other human beings. *Why will she be pleased?* (when hearing a fairy tale repeated); *the wicked stepmother was dreadfully jealous, why?*" I never hear that questioning why in any other connection. Either she knows the reason, as is evident in her treatment of the matter, or she accepts the inex-

---

[15] TRANSLATOR'S NOTE.—Since, with very few exceptions, subjunctive verbal forms in English have given way to the use of auxiliaries, this statement loses much of its force when translated into English.

[16] *Childre's Speech*, p. 214.

plicable with the silent attitude that is one of her characteristics."

Another characteristic of the fourth period, i.e. the making of new words, is not of such common occurrence as the peculiarity just mentioned; it is very marked in many children but scarcely existent in others. It shows itself by an arbitrary enrichment of vocabulary in the form of derivatives and of compound words (of their own making). The child, as a rule, exercises his activity as speech creator quite unconsciously; his creations take their place just as naturally as all the other words which he has heard from those around him. Sometimes the child evinces a wonderfully fine feeling for language; in other cases, though, we find grotesque and impossible turns of expression. In many children these new creations reach a fairly high number; in our two older children, up to the end of the fifth year, we noticed respectively forty and fifty new compound words, and twenty of their own derivatives. The majority have but a momentary span of life, but many are persisted in for some time.

The compound words[17] are the simpler forms, because in this case only the expressions for two distinctive features in the object spoken of are joined together. From our son's third year we may mention: *milkapple-jam*—an imaginary dish; *fire-box*—a fireproof casserole over a spirit stove; *children-rubbish-box*—a chest for toys, etc.; *holeplate*—saucer with perforated rim. From Hilde's fourth year: *child-soldier*—an officer, looking short in the distance; *hariflame*—stray curls.

Children show themselves very ingenious in the use of such aids to the expression of more delicate color shades; amongst others, we notice *darkwhite, halfblue, greyred*. Compounds, too, are often formed in designation of occupations: *breadman* (baker), *beerboy* (the refreshment boy at railway stations), *lightman* (lamplighter). But the results of the other kind of word formation, derivatives, are specially used for names of callings:[18] children who have often heard such designations as painter, carrier, etc., in like manner make *machiner*, *muffiner* (muffin-seller), *coaler* (coal-heaver). Other groups of derivatives referring to

objects: *the reading* (printed matter), *the smoke* (cigar, used by many children); for qualities: *raggy* (torn), *porridgey* (porridge-stained); for conditions: *splashiness* (result of splashing water), *funniness*, etc.

5. OUTLINE OF SPEECH DEVELOPMENT IN CHILDHOOD

From the fourth to the fifth year we may look upon the child's speech development as mainly finished. Not that children's speech has, by then, already reached the stage of ordinary adult speech; it never does that at any period throughout childhood. Every one of the later cevelopment periods has rather its own special features; the eight-year-old does not speak like the eleven-year-old, nor like the fourteen-year-old, nor any of them like adults.[19] But, in any case, these later developments are incomparably less than those we have already discussed. The psychological law that every psychic function has its chief period of development is also true of speech, and this chief period is clearly marked between the first and fourth or fifth year of life.

We will now try to summarize the above considerations in a systematized plan; at the same time expressly stating that this must not be looked upon as a firm rule applicable to all, but only an attempt to give certain formulæ for the most generally prevalent tendencies in the development of early speech.

It will probably be found that each individual development will differ more or less from this outline, not only in details as to time, but even as regards stages reached within given periods; yet I think the outline has a certain value as a general guide.

Preliminary. First year. Babble. Imitation of sound forms, first understanding of requests made to the child.

First Period. About 1–1; 6. The child has mastered a few sounds used with special meanings, which must be considered sentences of one word. Speech elements so far show no understanding of grammar or ideas (concep-

---

[17] *Children's Speech*, Chap. XXII.
[18] *Ibid.*, Chap, XXIII.

[19] Berthold Otto has made well-known attempts to record such peculiarities in language at special ages, so that magazines intended for any age may be written in its particular style (which I, in passing, consider educationally wrong in principle).

tions) and their significance, no differentiation as yet between the objective and what touches will and emotion. In sound they are still near to babble—the natural symbols; word pictures and active sound expressions are most prevalent.

Second Period. About 1; 6–2; 0. Awakening of the consciousness of the object of speech (that everything has a name) and the will to master it. The vocabulary suddenly shows great increase; questions appear as to the names of things. About the same time the stage of "one-word sentences" is left behind; two, soon several, words are combined, first hesitatingly, then more and more fluently, in a complete sentence. Vocabulary contents are increased first by nouns, then by a large addition of verbs, and lastly by qualifying words and those expressing relation. Stages of substance, action, relation, and distinction.

Third Period. About 2–2; 6. Complete mastery of uninflected speech. The child learns to express the finer shades of ideas by modifications of words, and about the same time different forms of inflection (conjugation, declension, comparison) begin to develop. Sentence formation, although still in paratactic form (simple sentence), is very varied. Series of sentences—exclamations, descriptions (statements), questions—are formed. Questions refer to names of things, where, what information, etc.

Fourth Period. About 2; 6 and on. The purely paratactic sentence formation is left behind. The child learns to express varying order of thoughts (principal and subordinate) by hypotaxis, and there is rapid growth of the different kinds of subordinate clauses; although the finer differentiation of particles and the mastery of the harder verb forms (e.g., the conjunctive or subjunctive) may yet require a considerable time to learn. The child's questions begin to extend to time and, above all, to the causal relations (*why*). Tendency to independent word formation in compounds and derivatives.

KARL BÜHLER

16 The psychologist Karl Bühler of Vienna (who later lived in the U.S.) distinguished himself both in child psychology and in linguistic theory. He follows Marty and Husserl and disagrees with Wundt in the psychological approach to the theory of language.

The following remarkably perspicacious selection is translated by permission from "Vom Wesen der Syntax," his contribution to *Idealistische Neuphilologie, Festschrift für Karl Vossler* (Heidelberg, 1922), pp, 77–83. He is strongly interested in the role of intonation in the developing syntax of child language and of language in general. He mentions Hermann Paul, one of the most famous linguists of the turn of the century, whose *Prinzipien der Sprachgeschichte* (1880, reissued often to this day and translated into English) remains one of the most important theoretical works of historical linguistics. Some of Bühler's demands contained in the following excerpt have in the meantime been met by linguistic students of child language.

W. F. L.

VOM WESEN DER SYNTAX

It is possible to imagine a state of human language in which conditions are basically the same as in the signaling system at sea, where every meaningful sign serves an independent, self-contained language purpose and is therefore a sentence, under certain

Reprinted in translation by the editors from Idealistische Neuphilologie, Festschrift für Karl Vossler

(*Heidelberg: Carl Winter Universitäts Verlag, 1922*), *54–84, by permission of Charlotte Bühler.*

circumstances even functioning as a complex sentence. This situation can actually be observed in child language. About the turn from the first to the second year of life and far into the second, after having begun to use sound structures meaningfully, the child statisfies all his speaking needs in each case by a single, self-contained phonetic utterance which reveals no semantic analysis. By no device of drill can he be induced to pronounce more than one (say, two) of the well-known sound complexes like *mamam, papa, hoppa, dada*, etc. in rapid sequence—in one breath, as the saying goes. Nor can he be made to produce any other kind of language utterance which might give the impression of being phonetically subdivided. All of a sudden, utterances of two or more words appear spontaneously, without assistance from the adults. The transition from one stage of development to the next is often so sudden that it can be dated by day or hour. The general intellectual progress which is involved will not be explored here. I choose this point of departure only in order to undermine a widespread prejudice which is bolstered by the authority of W. Wundt. What should linguistic theory learn from the nursery? The child simply learns gradually the ready-made language of the environment, grows into it, or whatever you wish to call it. His procedure is not essentially different from that of, say, an ape who "learns by imitation" from his human master how to put on and take off shoes. As can be seen in his play the small child is a veritable ape, that is, an imitator. The fact that he adopts even the most subtle dialectal peculiarities of the speech of his environment proves after all, clearly and distinctly, that he lacks any faculty of creating language himself. "All this goes to show that the child's language is a product of the child's environment in which the child is basically only a passive participant."[1]

That is correct in about the same sense and to the same extent as calling the average human being the product of his environment, which of course does not prevent him from undergoing developments which are caused by the inner urges of human nature.

---

[1] W. Wundt, *Die Sprache* I, 2nd Ed., 1904, p. 301.

"Basically passive"—as the pebble is shaped in the brook—this certainly does not adequately describe the processes in the language of the child. Nor does the parallel with the parrot trained to speak a few words, or with the hunting dog who learns to execute suitable reactions to many spoken commands. The speaking adult, to be sure, begins to be the constant object of imitation for the child as early as the second half of the first year of life. One cannot imagine what would become of the initially quite spontaneous but meaningless babbling of the child without this continuous stimulus from the outside. But all this is easily reconciled with the by now completely established fact that the great process of the natural acquisition of language follows a strict pattern of inner development. True, the progress goes faster in one individual, slower in another, for outer and inner reasons. As early as the third year of life the fastest are ahead of the slowest by many months. The same holds true for the "breadth" and "precision" of the acquisition. But all that has nothing to do with what ought to interest linguists more than anything else: a development which goes by stages that are already clearly discernible, and that follow each other with scientific regularity.

To outline the origin of syntactic speech further: there is a phase of syntax without inflection, which can as a rule be observed in clear form for several months, until all at once, in consequence of an inner progress, the use of inflections begins with modifications of all types (comparison, declension, conjugation) approximately at the same time. Before that time the constructions of the child are—one is tempted to say—Chinese: *ich olol hoto wapa = ich (mein) Rudolph Pferd um,* 'Rudolph has toppled my horse'; *fallen tul bein anna ans = fallen Stuhl Bein Anna Hans,* which means that he himself (Hans) has fallen and hurt himself on the leg of Anna's chair. A few months earlier, at the stage of the one-word sentence, the child would have produced on such occasions only one single sentence word, perhaps *hoto*, to which the mishap had occurred, or *wapa*, pointing to the mishap itself, or *olol*, to the culprit. At this earlier period it would have been possible, although not probable, that the child would have produced the three words in three starts, one after the other, if indeed they were in his vocabulary at all. I said not probable; observation teaches us that in such repetitions of speaking generated by the same situation (an occurrence which is very common in itself) the track once followed is used again and again; the same word is repeated over and over. The other procedure presupposes a higher achievement, namely a threefold conception or, more accurately, condensation (*Zuspitzung*) of the same situation; and once this becomes possible, the genuine several-word sentences are bound to emerge soon. With that the chief element of progress has been singled out, namely the appearance of (metaphorically expressed) several points, centers, foci, aspects of conception, or whatever you want to call it, in the mastering of the same situation by the conscious mind. When this happens, a second requirement will easily be met, namely that each of these manners of conception reproduce a word which corresponds to it. In neat succession this works without a hitch. If I see it correctly, it is more difficult for the little ones to prepare several units of motion (words) in the speech center of the brain more or less simultaneously, an essentially physiological achievement. This is the third condition for the development of the genuine several-word sentence uttered in one breath. For comparison consider piano playing from notes—how the beginner perceives each note by itself and translates it into finger motion, while the practiced player grasps larger complexes at the same time and subjects them to an orderly motor transformation.

Let this suffice for the transition from the one-word stage to that of several words, or from asyntactic to syntactic speech. We do not yet know the rules governing syntactic constructions without inflection. It is quite possible that the field is largely dominated by chance, that is to say, the sequence of words is determined by emotion, impressions, and the constellation of reproduction tendencies of the moment, in free interaction untrammeled by tradition or convention. But for the purposes of linguistic theory it would be of great interest to record such a pure incipient case in exact detail. In my opinion comparative linguists ought to look seriously into

these matters so that they may be subjected to expert and exact investigation. Perhaps linguistic theory ought to take a still greater interest in the second transition, in the development of inflected language out of the state of syntax without inflection. If anywhere, we find in child language the opportunity to establish directly and as a nonhypothetic fact that for some inner reasons the one precedes the other, that inflections represent a younger stage of language development. Nobody ought to be misled by the objection that the child merely imitates what he hears in his setting. Of course the child imitates. The question is why the adoption of what is heard constantly and uniformly takes place in a strangely regular sequence, in layers, so to speak. We are reasonably well informed about the appearance of inflected forms in the language of the child; I do not intend to take up this final act of the ontogenesis of syntax in this place.

But we have not yet reached the end of either the problems or the possibilities of investigation of child language. What about the musical devices of syntax? What melodious speaking is and all that can be done with the musical modifications of language— I must say that, for myself I have nowhere received such a deep impression and such a clear (for the time being, I regret to say, merely intuitive) appreciation of the far-reaching power of these matters as through the observation of children. In the sentences of adults we distinguish the traditional melodies of commands, questions, and statements, and a few other kinds. We know how to discriminate between the emotional (excitement, compassion, scorn, etc.), affected, rhetorical, clerical, intimate (flirting and teasing), and plain manners of speaking in dozens of shades and degrees. Certainly; but this abundance comes into play only in exceptional situations far removed from the average and from the even pace of everyday moods and speaking situations. Furthermore, only in the superheated atmosphere of the most lively emotional dialogue does grammar commonly melt down to the point that parts of speech mean nothing any more, words hardly anything, and the musical element everything. This however is the normal condition of child language before there is any grammar in it at all, and long afterwards whenever there is the slightest incentive for emotional speech. To begin with the simplest matters: one ought to record phonographically the same word, say *papa* or *heiss* ('hot') or *Stuhl* ('chair') or *lade* (*Schokolade*, 'chocolate') or some other word, of the same child in varied speech situations so as to have them together for exact and repeatable comparison. This alone I think would yield some insights which would be important for the theory of syntax; for example, the apparently simple statements of the one-word sentence are transformed by musical means into a sentence. The use of musical devices in the several-word sentence would of course reveal more. One should not assume that the result can be predicted summarily, that the child unavoidably imitates this use, too, from adult speech and that everything in it is to be considered as learned, as introduced from the outside. That certainly does not do justice to the process. All natural, primitive gestures contain a strong instinctive, innate nucleus, and according to my experience the musical modifications of speaking are in the same category. One example: it struck me how early an exactly and continuously observed child used the familiar, strange melody of the coaxing, suggesting childish request. Sustained on one tone with an extremely low, very soft voice, without rise or fall during the utterance or at its end, perhaps at a somewhat reduced speed, little requests were made as early as the second year, when the child was hardly able to walk and did not yet speak with inflected words—requests which had perhaps in the child's expectation little chance of being fulfilled, for example, *papa strasse gehen* ('Papa go street') and others. Where does the child get this coaxing melody? My own speech sounds very affected when I imitate it. I have found it in other children and suspect that it is an early common property of child language. Is it learned and exaggerated in imitation as happens otherwise with children? I cannot believe it. Child language has far too many musical shades, far more than children's songs which the child has learned and already mastered, although they are of course imitated very crudely for a long time.

To summarize: in ontogenesis the musical modulations of speech from the beginning present a wealth of expressive possibilities. If the sound structures of the first words which are phonetically invariable on the whole, serve to make statements (*Nennfunktion, Darstellung*), then the musical forms shape such statements (*Nennungen*) into sentences. The child's word *tul* makes the same statement as our *Stuhl* ('chair'), but the musical shade which is given to it reveals, along with gestures and the situation as a whole, what is the matter with the chair. If one wishes to call this interaction of purpose and means "syntactic" in the total meaning (*Gesamtsinn*), i.e. in the total purpose of speech, which I consider justified in view of exclamations like "Fire!" or shouted addresses like "John!", then the point of origin of syntax has ben demonstrated in ontogenesis. To say it once more with other words: at the moment and to the extent that the specific innovation of human speech, the function of making statements, takes hold of the sound structures which have already reached a relatively stable phonetic form (*mamam*, for example, no longer being used for any kind of desire but only for those connected with the mother's person)—at that moment and to that extent, the conditions for the most primitive syntaxes (*Syntaxen*) have come into being. The phonetic sound complex makes a statement; the musical element, in combination with gestures and the situation, reveals in what way the stated fact fills the child's soul, and triggers in the understanding adult what is to be done to or with the object stated. That is the syntax of the one-word sentence, which satisfies all the child's (primitive) speaking needs for about one year.

The several-word sentence devoid of inflection, which prevails at the next stage for about three to six months, introduces the new syntactic device of group effects. No matter what the sequence of words at this stage, it is obvious that what H. Paul has judiciously set apart and enumerated as the first device—I mean the plain contact effect—taks full sway here. One has to guard oneself rigorously and severely against imputing syntactic refinements to early child language without justification. For example, substantives and verbs, nouns and adjectives are by no means separated yet at the stage of the several-word sentence without inflection. Up to now we simply do not know how these differentiations develop. One thing however is tangible: *papa brav* ('Papa good') or *papa mö* (*mö* = *Schnee*, 'Papa stomps around in the snow') or *haim mimi* ('home, drink milk') or *mama etze* ('Mama sit down') or whatever may be the form of these first two-word sentences or the later accumulations of words in several-word sentences—contain two or more statements which operate in contact and somehow form a unit. The unity of the speaking situation, of the motivation for speaking, masters, unifies, joins the multiplicity of word meanings, aided of course by the old musical devices and the gestures.

Concerning the interesting new acquisition of word modifications and of inflected syntax, I have written in detail in another place and do not intend to repeat it here. We have scarcely taken the first steps into this wonderful field of research and are waiting for the linguistic specialist, the comparatist, and linguistic theorist, who combines the biological-psychological instinct of the child-research worker with the comprehensive grasp of the historian, and competently leads the investigations to new results. The crucial question of linguistic theory is, of course, whether the basic rules of ontogenesis have such profound general psychological foundations that they are valid for phylogenesis as well.

OTTO JESPERSEN〜〜〜〜〜〜〜〜〜〜〜〜

17 The distinguished Danish linguist Otto Jespersen devoted his life to the study of the English language and was the author of one of the few large English grammars of the historical-comparative school, *A Modern English Grammar on Historical Principles* (7 volumes; Heidelberg, London, and Copenhagen, 1928–1949). Jespersen was one of very few early linguists who paid more than passing attention to child language. He published a book on child language in 1916, *Børnesprog*, second ed. under a changed title (Copenhagen, 1923). The results were incorporated in his introduction to linguistics, *Language: Its Nature, Development and Origin* (London and New York, 1922). The work is divided into four "books," the second being called "The Child" (pp. 101–88). This is the only introduction to linguistics in which child language plays a major part. Jespersen coordinates the results of many previous studies of child language, arranged by general linguistic principles. His style is lucid and readable. A few passages are given here as samples of his presentation.

W. F. L.

From LANGUAGE: ITS NATURE, DEVELOPMENT AND ORIGIN

SENTENCES

In the first period the child knows nothing of grammar: it does not connect words together, far less form sentences, but each word stands by itself. 'Up' means what we should express by a whole sentence, 'I want to get up,' or 'Lift me up'; 'Hat' means 'Put on my hat,' or 'I want to put my hat on,' or 'I have my hat on,' or 'Mamma has a new hat on'; 'Father' can be either 'Here comes Father,' or 'This is Father,' or 'He is called Father,' or 'I want Father to come to me,' or 'I want this or that from Father.' This particular group of sounds is vaguely associated with the mental picture of the person in question, and is uttered at the sight of him or at the mere wish to see him

Reprinted from Otto Jespersen, Language: Its Nature, Development and Origin *(London: George Allen and Unwin Ltd.; New York: The Macmillan Company; 1959), 133–39, by permission of the publishers; first published in the United States in 1922.*

or something else in connection with him.

When we say that such a word means what we should express by a whole sentence, this does not amount to saying that the child's 'Up' *is* a sentence, or a sentence-word, as many of those who have written about these questions have said. We might just as well assert that clapping our hands is a sentence, because it expresses the same idea (or the same frame of mind) that is otherwise expressed by the whole sentence 'This is splendid.' The word 'sentence' presupposes a certain grammatical structure, which is wanting in the child's utterance.

Many investigators have asserted that the child's first utterances are not means of imparting information, but always an expression of the child's wishes and requirements. This is certainly somewhat of an exaggeration, since the child quite clearly can make known its joy at seeing a hat or a plaything, or at merely being able to recognize it and remember the word for it; but the statement still contains a great deal of truth, for without strong feelings a child would not say much, and it is a great stimulus to talk that he very soon discovers that he gets his wishes fulfilled more easily when he makes them known by means of certain sounds.

Frans (1;7) was accustomed to express his longings in general by help of a long *m* with rising tone, while at the same time stretching out his hand towards the particular thing that he longed for. This he did, for example, at dinner, when he wanted water. One day his mother said, "Now see if you can say *vand* (water)," and at once he said what was an approach to the word, and was delighted at getting something to drink by that means. A moment later he repeated what he had said, and was inexpressibly delighted to have found the password which at once brought him something to drink. This was repeated several times. Next day, when his father was pouring out water for himself, the boy again said *van, van,* and was duly rewarded. He had not heard the word during the intervening twenty-four hours, and nothing had been done to remind him of it. After some repetitions (for he only got a few drops at a time) he pronounced the word for the first time quite correctly. The day after, the same thing occurred; the word was never heard but at dinner. When he became rather a nuisance with his constant cries for water, his mother said: "Say please"—and immediately came his "Bebe vand" ("Water, please")—his first attempt to put two words together.

Later—in this formless period—the child puts more and more words together, often in quite haphazard order: 'My go snow' ('I want to go out into the snow'), etc. A Danish child of 2;1 said the Danish words (imperfectly pronounced, of course) corresponding to "Oh papa lamp mother boom," when his mother had struck his father's lamp with a bang. Another child said "Paa hen corn cap" when he saw his father give corn to the hens out of his cap.

When Frans was 1;10, passing a post office (which Danes call 'posthouse'), he said of his own accord the Danish words for 'post, house, bring, letter' (a pause between the successive words)—I suppose that the day before he had heard a sentence in which these words occurred. In the same month, when he had thrown a ball a long way, he said what would be in English 'dat was good.' This was not a sentence which he had put together for himself, but a mere repetition of what had been said to him, clearly conceived as a whole, and equivalent to 'bravo.' Sentences of this kind, however, though taken as units, prepare the way for the understanding of the words 'that' and 'was' when they turn up in other connections.

One thing which plays a great role in children's acquisition of language, and especially in their early attempts to form sentences, is Echoism: the fact that children echo what is said to them. When one is learning a foreign language, it is an excellent method to try to imitate to oneself in silence every sentence which one hears spoken by a native. By that means the turns of phrases, the order of words, the intonation of the sentence are firmly fixed in the memory—so that they can be recalled when required, or rather recur to one quite spontaneously without an effort. What the grown man does of conscious purpose our children to a large extent do without a thought—that is, they repeat aloud what they have just heard, either the whole, if it is a very short sentence, or more commonly the conclusion, as much of it as they can retain in their short memories. The result is a matter of chance—it need not always have a meaning or consist of entire words. Much, clearly, is repeated without being understood, much, again, without being more than half understood. Take, for example (translated):

Shall I carry you?—Frans (1; 9): Carry you.
Shall Mother carry Frans?—Carry Frans.
The sky is so blue.—So boo.
I shall take an umbrella.—Take 'rella.

Though this feature in a child's mental history has been often noticed, no one seems to have seen its full significance. One of the acutest observers (Meumann [E., *Die Sprache des Kindes*, Zürich, Zurcher and Furrer, 1903], p. 28) even says that it has no importance in the development of the child's speech. On the contrary, I think that Echoism explains very much indeed. First let us bear in mind the mutilated forms of words which a child uses: *'chine* for machine, *'gar* for cigar, *Trix* for Beatrix, etc. Then a child's frequent use of an indirect form of question rather than direct, 'Why you smoke, Father?' which can hardly be explained except as an echo of sentences like 'Tell me why you smoke.' This plays a greater role in Danish than in English, and the corresponding form of the sentence has been frequently remarked by Danish parents. Another feature which is nearly constant with Danish children at the age when echoing is habitual is the inverted word order: this is used after an initial adverb (*nu kommer hun*, etc.), but the child will use it in all cases (*kommer hun*, etc.). Further, the extremely frequent use of the infinitive, because the child hears it towards the end of a sentence, where it is dependent on a preceding *can*, or *may*, or *must*. *Not eat that* is a child's echo of 'You mustn't eat that.' In German this has become the ordinary form of official order: "Nicht hinauslehnen" ("Do not lean out of the window").

NEGATION AND QUESTION

Most children learn to say 'no' before they can say 'yes'—simply because negation is a stronger expression of feeling than affirmation. Many little children use *nenenene*

(short ĕ) as a natural expression of fretfulness and discomfort. It is perhaps so natural that it need not be learned: there is good reason for the fact that in so many languages words of negation begin with *n* (or *m*). Sometimes the *n* is heard without a vowel: it is only the gesture of 'turning up one's nose' made audible.

At first the child does not express what it is that it does not want—it merely puts it away with its hand, pushes away, for example, what is too hot for it. But when it begins to express in words what it is that it will not have, it does so often in the form 'Bread no,' often with a pause between the words, as two separate utterances, as when we might say, in our fuller forms of expression: 'Do you offer me bread? I won't hear of it.' So with verbs: 'I sleep no.' Thus with many Danish children, and I find the same phenomenon mentioned with regard to children of different nations. Tracy says ([Tracy, Frederick, *The Psychology of Childhood*, Boston, D. C. Heath & Company, 1893] p. 136): "Negation was expressed by an affirmative sentence, with an emphatic *no* tacked on at the end, exactly as the deaf-mutes do." The blind-deaf Helen Keller, when she felt her little sister's mouth and her mother spelt 'teeth' to her, answered: "Baby teeth—no, baby eat—no," i.e., baby cannot eat because she has no teeth. In the same way, in German, 'Stul nei nei—schossel,' i.e., I won't sit on the chair, but in your lap, and in French, 'Papa abeié ato non, iaian abeié non,' i.e., Papa n'est pas encore habillé, Suzanne n'est pas habillée (Stern [Clara and William Stern, *Die Kindersprache*, Leipzig: Barth, 1907], pp. 189, 203). It seems thus that this mode of expression will crop up every where as an emphatic negation.

Interrogative sentences come generally rather early—it would be better to say questions, because at first they do not take the form of interrogative sentences, the interrogation being expressed by bearing, look, or gesture: when it begins to be expressed by intonation we are on the way to question expressed in speech. Some of the earliest questions have to do with place: *Where is . . .?* The child very often hears such sentences as 'Where is its little nose?' which are not really meant as questions; we may also remark that questions of this type are of great practical importance for the little thing, who soon uses them to beg for something which has been taken away from him or is out of his reach. Other early questions are 'What's that?' and 'Who?'

Later—generally, it would seem, at the close of the third year—questions with 'why' crop up: these are of the utmost importance for the child's understanding of the whole world and its manifold occurrences, and, however tiresome they may be when they come in long strings, no one who wishes well to his child will venture to discourage them. Questions about time, such as 'When? How long?' appear much later, owing to the child's difficulty in acquiring exact ideas about time.

Children often find a difficulty in double questions, and when asked 'Will you have brown bread or white?' merely answer the last word with 'Yes.' So in reply to 'Is that red or yellow?' 'Yes' means 'yellow' (taken from a child of 4;11). I think this is an instance of the short memories of children, who have already at the end of the question forgotten the beginning, but Professor Mawer thinks that the real difficulty here is in making a choice: they cannot decide between alternatives: usually they are silent, and if they say 'Yes' it only means that they do not want to go without both or feel that they must say something.

PREPOSITIONS AND IDIOMS

Prepositions are of very late growth in a child's language. Much attention has been given to the point, and Stern has collected statistics of the ages at which various children first used prepositions: the earliest age is 1;10, the average age is 2; 3. It does not, however, seem to me to be a matter of much interest how early an individual word of some particular grammatical class is first used; it is much more interesting to follow up the gradual growth of the child's command of this class and to see how the first inevitable mistakes and confusions arise in the little brain. Stern makes the interesting remark that when the tendency to use prepositions first appears, it grows far more rapidly than the power to discriminate one preposition from another; with his own

children there came a time when they employed the same word as a sort of universal preposition in all relations. Hilda used *von*, Eva *auf*. I have never observed anything corresponding to this among Danish children.

All children start by putting the words for the most important concepts together without connective words, so 'Leave go bedroom' ('May I have leave to go into the bedroom?'), 'Out road' ('I am going out on the road'). The first use of prepositions is always in set phrases learned as wholes, like 'go to school,' 'go to pieces,' lie in bed,' 'at dinner.' Not till later comes the power of using prepositions in free combinations, and it is then that mistakes appear. Nor is this surprising, since in all languages prepositional usage contains much that is peculiar and arbitrary, chiefly because when we once pass beyond a few quite clear applications of time and place, the relations to be expressed become so vague and indefinite, that logically one preposition might often seem just as right as another, although usage has laid down a fast law that this preposition must be used in this case and that in another. I noted down a great number of mistakes my own boy made in these words, but in all cases I was able to find some synonymous or antonymous expression in which the preposition used would have been the correct one, and which may have been vaguely before his mind.

The multiple meanings of prepositions sometimes have strange results. A little girl was in her bath, and hearing her mother say: "I will wash you in a moment," answered: "No, you must wash me in the bath"! She was led astray by the two uses of *in*. We know of the child at school who was asked "What is an average?" and said: "What the hen lays eggs on." Even men of science are similarly led astray by prepositions. It is perfectly natural to say that something has passed over the threshold of consciousness: the metaphor is from the way in which you enter a house by stepping over the threshold. If the metaphor were kept, the opposite situation would be expressed by the statement that such and such a thing is outside the threshold of consciousness. But psychologists, in the thoughtless way of little children, take *under* to be always the opposite of *over*, and so speak of things 'lying under (or below) the threshold of our consciousness,' and have even invented a Latin word for the unconscious, viz. *subliminal*.[1]

Children may use verbs with an object which require a preposition ('Will you *wait* me?'), or which are only used intransitively ('Will you *jump* me?'), or they may mix up an infinitival with a direct construction ('Could you hear me sneezed?'). But it is surely needless to multiply examples.

When many years ago, in my *Progress in Language*, I spoke of the advantages, even to natives, of simplicity in liguistic structure, Professor Herman Möller, in a learned review, objected to me that to the adult learning a foreign tongue the chief difficulty consists in "the countless chicaneries due to the tyrannical and capricious usage, whose tricks there is no calculating; but these offer to the

native child no such difficulty as morphology may," and again, in speaking of the choice of various prepositions, which is far from easy to the foreigner, he says: "But any considerable mental exertion on the part of the native child learning its mother tongue is here, of course, out of the question." Such assertions as these cannot be founded on actual observation; at any rate, it is my experience in listening to children's talk that long after they have reached the point where they make hardly any mistake in pronunciation and verbal forms, etc., they are still capable of using many turns of speech which are utterly opposed to the spirit of the language, and which are in the main of the same kind as those which foreigners are apt to fall into. Many of the child's mistakes are due to mixtures or blendings of two turns of expression, and not a few of them may be logically justified. But learning a language implies among other things learning what you may *not* say in the language, even though no reasonable ground can be given for the prohibition.

---

[1] H. G. Wells writes (*Soul of a Bishop*, 94): "He was lugging things now into speech that so far had been *scarcely above the threshold* of his conscious thought." Here we see the wrong interpretation of the preposition *over* dragging with it the synonym *above*.

JEAN PIAGET

18 The Swiss psychologist Piaget made a mark in child-language research with his emphasis on the egocentric component of children's speech. He was sharply attacked by many, but since he is an influential psychologist whose postulates have played a pivotal role in the discussion, he occupies an important position, as Fritz Schultze did forty years earlier for similar reasons. His method will appeal to many at the present time because he operates with statistics. His attention is centered on ages 4–8 with emphasis on age 6.

The French original of the following excerpt is in Piaget's *Le Langage et la pensée chez l'enfant* (1923, second edition 1930). The passage is taken by permission from pp. 33–40 of the English translation, *The Language and Thought of the Child*, London-New York, third edition, 1959.

An interesting critic of Piaget's theories about the language and thought of the child and the development of the child's reasoning was the Russian, Lev Semenovich Vygotsky. An English translation of his 1934 book was published in 1962: *Thought and Language*, M.I.T. Press, now available in paperback. See especially Chapter 2, "Piaget's Theory of Child Language and Thought," pp. 9–24, and portions of Chapters 6 and 7. Piaget's *Comments on* these critical remarks are attached to the English edition of Vygotsky's book as a separate 14-page pamphlet. In a foreword to John H. Flavell's *The Developmental Psy-*

chology of Jean Piaget (Princeton, 1963) he defended his convictions against Flavell's critique.

Piaget is a scholar of awe-inspiring productivity. Since 1923 he has written many studies of links between language acquisition and the development of cognitive processes. A summary is contained in his book, *Le Structuralisme* (Paris, 1968) in a collection of popularizations, "Que sais-je"? The following short excerpt is from his early and controversial study.

W. F. L. & A. B. A.

From THE LANGUAGE AND THOUGHT OF THE CHILD

CONCLUSIONS

Having defined, so far as was possible, the various categories of the language used by our two children, it now remains for us to see whether it is not possible to establish certain numerical constants from the material before us. We wish to emphasize at the very outset the artificial character of such abstractions. The number of unclassifiable remarks, indeed, weighs heavily in the statistics. In any case, a perusal of the list of Lev's first 50 remarks, which we shall give as an example for those who wish to make use of our method, should give a fair idea of the degree of objectivity belonging to our classification. But these difficulties are immaterial. If among our results some are definitely more constant than others, then we shall feel justified in attributing to these a certain objective value.

The measure of egocentrism
Among the data we have obtained there is one, incidentally of the greatest interest for the study of child logic, which seems to supply the necessary guarantee of objectivity: we mean the proportion of egocentric language to the sum of the child's spontaneous conversation. Egocentric language is, as we have seen, the group made up by the first three of the categories we have enumerated—*repetition*, *monologue*, and *collective monologue*. All three have this in common that they consist of remarks that are not addressed to anyone,

or not to anyone in particular, and that they evoke no reaction adapted to them on the part of anyone to whom they may chance to be addressed. Spontaneous language is therefore made up of the first seven categories, *i.e.*, of all except *answers*. It is therefore the sum total of all remarks, *minus* those which are made as an answer to a question asked by an adult or a child. We have eliminated this heading as being subject to chance circumstances; it is sufficient for a child to have come in contact with many adults or with some talkative companion, to undergo a marked change in the percentage of his answers. Answers given, not to definite questions (with interrogation mark) or commands, but in the course of the dialogue, *i.e.*, propositions answering to other propositions, have naturally been classed under the heading *information and dialogue*, so that there is nothing artificial about the omission of questions from the statistics which we shall give. The child's language *minus* his answers constitutes a complete whole in which intelligence is represented at every stage of its development.

The proportion of egocentric to other spontaneous forms of language is represented by the following fractions:

$$\frac{Eg.\,L}{Sp.\,L} = 0.47 \text{ for Lev,} \quad \frac{Eg.\,L}{Sp.\,L} = 0.43 \text{ for Pie.}$$

(The proportion of egocentric language to the sum total of the subject's speech, including answers, is 39 percent for Lev and 37 per cent for Pie.) The similarity of result for Lev and Pie is a propitious sign, especially as what difference there is corresponds to a marked difference of temperament. (Lev is certainly more egocentric than Pie.) But the value of the result is vouched for in yet another way.

If we divide the 1400 remarks made by Lev during the month in which his talk was being

Reprinted from Jean Piaget, The Language and Thought of the Child (*London: Routledge & Kegan Paul Ltd., 3rd ed., 1959; New York: Humanities Press, Inc., 1962*), 34–40, *by permission of the publishers.*

studied into sections of 100 sentences, and seek to establish for each section the ratio $\frac{Eg.\,L.}{Sp.\,L.}$, the fraction will be found to vary only from 0·40 to 0·57, which indicates only a small maximum devation. On the contrary, the *mean variation*, *i.e.*, the average of the deviations between each value and the arithmetical average of these values, is only 0·04, which is really very little.

If Pie's 1500 remarks are submitted to the same treatment, the proportions will be found to vary between 0·31 and 0·59, with an average variation of 0·66. This greater variability is just what we should expect from what we know of Pie's character, which at first sight seems more practical, better adapted than Lev's, more inclined to collaboration (particularly with his bosom friend Ez). But Pie every now and then indulges in fantasies which isolate him for several hours, and during which he solioquizes without ceasing.

We shall see in the next chapter, moreover, that these two coefficients do actually represent the average for children between the ages of 7 and 8. The same calculation based on some 1500 remarks in quite another classroom yielded the result of 0·45 (a. v. = 0·05).

This constancy in the proportion of egocentric language is the more remarkable in view of the fact that we have found nothing of the kind in connection with the other coefficients which we have sought to establish. We have, it is true, determined the proportion of socialized factual language (*information* and *questions*) to socialized nonfactual language (*criticism, commands,* and *requests*). But this proportion flutuates from 0·72 to 2·23 with a mean variation 0·71 for Lev (as compared with 0·04 and 0·06 as the coefficients of egocentrism), and between 0·43 and 2·33 with a mean variation of 0·42 for Pie. Similarly, the relation of egocentric to socialized factual language yields no coefficient of any constancy.

Of all this calculation let us bear only this in mind, that our two subjects of 6½ have each an egocentric language which amounts to nearly half of their total spontaneous speech.

The following table summarizes the functions of the language used by both these children:

	Pie	Lev
1. Repetition	2	1
2. Monologue	5	15
3. Collective Monologue	30	23
4. Adapted Information	14	13
5. Criticism	7	3
6. Commands	15	10
7. Requests	13	17
8. Answers	14	18
Egocentric Language	37	39
Spontaneous Socialized language	49	43
Sum of Socialized language	63	61
Coefficient of Egocentrism	0·43	0·47
	∓0·06	∓0·04

We must once more emphasize the fact that in all these calculations the number of remarks made by children to adults is negligible. By omitting them we raise the coefficient of egocentrism to about 0·02, which is within the allowed limits of deviation. In future, however, we shall have completely to eliminate such remarks from our calculations, even if it means making a separate class for them. We shall, moreover, observe this rule in the next chapter where the coefficient of egocentrism has been calculated solely on the basis of remarks made between children.

Conclusion

What are the conclusions we can draw from these facts? It would seem that up to a certain age we may safely admit that children think and act more egocentrically than adults, that they share each other's intellectual life less than we do. True, when they are together they seem to talk to each other a great deal more than we do about what they are doing, but for the most part they are only talking to themselves. We, on the contrary, keep silent far longer about our action, but our talk is almost always socialized.

Such assertions may seem paradoxical. In observing children between the ages of 4 and 7 at work together in the classes of the *Maison des Petits*, one is certainly struck by silences, which are, we repeat, in no way imposed nor even suggested by the adults. One would expect, not indeed the formation of working groups, since children are slow to awake to social life, but a hubbub caused by all the children talking at once. This is not what happens. All the same, it is obvious that a child between the ages of 4 and 7, placed in the conditions of spontaneous work provided by the educational games of the *Maison des Petits*, breaks silence far oftener than does the adult at work, and seems at first sight to be continuously communicating his thoughts to those around him.

Egocentrism must not be confused with secrecy. Reflection in the child does not admit of privacy. Apart from thinking by images or autistic symbols which cannot be directly communicated, the child up to an age, as yet undetermined but probably somewhere about seven, is incapable of keeping to himself the thoughts which enter his mind. He says everything. He has no verbal continence. Does this mean that he socializes his thought more than we do? That is the whole question, and it is for us to see to whom the child really speaks. It may be to others. We think on the contrary that, as the preceding study shows, it is first and foremost to himself, and that speech, before it can be used to socialize thought, serves to accompany and reinforce individual activity. Let us try to examine more closely the difference between thought which is socialized but capable of secrecy, and infantile thought which is egocentric but incapable of secrecy.

The adult, even in his most personal and private occupation, even when he is engaged in an inquiry which is incomprehensible to his fellow beings, thinks socially, has continually in his mind's eye his collaborators or opponents, actual or eventual, at any rate members of his own profession to whom sooner or later he will announce the result of his labors. This mental picture pursues him throughout his task. The task itself is henceforth socialized at almost every stage of its development. Invention eludes this process, but the need for checking and demonstrating calls into being an inner speech addressed throughout to a hypothetical opponent, whom the imagination often pictures as one of flesh and blood. When, therefore, the adult is brought face to face with his fellow beings, what he announces to them is something already socially elaborated and therefore roughly adapted to his audience, *i.e.*,

it is comprehensible. Indeed, the further a man has advanced in his own line of thought, the better able is he to see things from the point of view of others and to make himself understood by them.

The child, on the other hand, placed in the conditions which we have described, seems to talk far more than the adult. Almost everything he does is to the tune of remarks such as "I'm drawing a hat," "I'm doing it better than you," etc. Child thought, therefore, seems more social, less capable of sustained and solitary research. This is so only in appearance. The child has less verbal continence simply because he does not know what it is to keep a thing to himself. Although he talks almost incessantly to his neighbors, he rarely places himself at their point of view. He speaks to them for the most part as if he were alone, and as if he were thinking aloud. He speaks, therefore, in a language which disregards the precise shade of meaning in things and ignores the particular angle from which they are viewed, and which above all is always making assertions, even in argument, instead of justifying them. Nothing could be harder to understand than the notebooks which we have filled with the conversation of Pie and Lev. Without full commentaries, taken down at the same time as the children's remarks, they would be incomprehensible. Everything is indicated by allusion, by pronouns and demonstrative articles—"he, she, the, mine, him, etc."—which can mean anything in turn, regardless of the demands of clarity or even of intelligibility. (The examination of this style must not detain us now; it will appear again in Chapter III in connection with verbal explanation between one child and another.) In a word, the child hardly ever even asks himself whether he has been understood. For him, that goes without saying, for he does not think about others when he talks. He utters a "collective monologue." His language only begins to resemble that of adults when he is directly interested in making himself understood; when he gives orders or asks questions. To put it quite simply, we may say that the adult thinks socially, even when he is alone, and that the child under 7 thinks egocentrically, even in the society of others.

19

One of the very best general psychological (not strictly linguistic) studies of child language is M. M. Lewis's book *Infant Speech: A Study of the Beginnings of Language* (London: Routledge & Kegan Paul Ltd.: New York: Harcourt, Brace & World, Inc.; 1936). The second edition (1951) added, as chapter 13, an article on the learning of tenses which had previously (1937) appeared in the *British Journal of Educational Psychology*, VII (1937), 39–56. This article is here presented as a sample of Lewis's sensible, nontechnical method of presentation and analysis. His own observations of the boy K, who is not identified, form the basis of the treatment.

THE BEGINNING OF REFERENCE TO PAST AND FUTURE IN A CHILD'S SPEECH

1. INTRODUCTION

In this paper I propose to deal with the way in which reference to the past and to the future come to be differentiated in the early stages of a child's adoption of conventional language.

It is a surprising fact that this is a topic on which hitherto very little work has been done. There has been much discussion of the manner in which the child acquires grammatical forms—the parts of speech, for instance, or past and future tenses. But only very recently, with the growth of general interest in the functions of language, has any attention been paid to the occurrence of these functions in the life of the child. We can observe this change of emphasis if we compare earlier work like that of Stern with the more recent work of Charlotte Bühler. Where Stern deals almost exclusively with the appearance of grammatical forms such as the parts of speech, the sentence and the subordinate clause, Bühler is concerned rather with the occurrence of such functions as narration and explanation. But even Bühler, I think, omits to consider the origin and

growth of these functions, in relation to the child's earlier linguistic development. This is a question, I suggest, well worthy of study; and in this paper I am making an attempt to indicate how two of these functions—reference to the past and to the future—may begin to arise.

2. THE FREEING OF LANGUAGE FROM DOMINANCE BY THE IMMEDIATE SITUATION

Reference to the past and to the future are two aspects of one very great advance in the life of the child. At first his language is exclusively concerned with the immediate situation in which it is spoken; then gradually it begins to be freed from the dominance of this present situation—he begins to deal with things that are absent. Perhaps the most striking instance of this greater freedom occurs when he spontaneously begins to speak of the past, to narrate. Karl Bühler and Charlotte Bühler have both emphasized the importance of this step. The latter tells us (p. 148) of their daughter Inge that when she was just eighteen months old she said, on being brought back one day from a walk, *daten lalala;* she had seen some soldiers singing in the street (soldaten lalala).

I do not think there can be any doubt about the importance of this new development in a child's life. What I am very doubtful about, however, is whether it is, as Charlotte Bühler seems to suggest, a sudden step. I shall try to show that this advance must be studied in the light of other aspects of the child's linguistic development: that reference

Reprinted from The British Journal of Educational Psychology 7.39–56 *(1937) by permission of the author*.
A paper summarized at the meeting of the British Association, Section J. Blackpool, 1936.

to the past and reference to the future emerge side by side, and are due very largely to social influence, particularly as this is exerted when he takes part in linguistic intercourse with those around him.

To study this—or in fact any aspect of linguistic development—we need detailed observations of a child, showing not only what he said on successive occasions, but what was happening when he spoke. But since earlier observers, as I have said, have been more concerned with form than with function, published observations of this kind are lacking. I shall, therefore, confine myself to showing what occurred in the case of a boy, K, whom I had the opportunity of observing constantly throughout his first three years. Examples of my observations are given in the series at the end of this paper.

In his case the first clear instance of spontaneous narration occurred some six months later than that of Inge Bühler. At 2; 0, 20 (Series III), on being brought back from a walk, he was evidently trying to recount what he had seen: *mɔukα*[1], he said, several times. His father asked, *motor-car*? He said *nɔu*, and repeated *mɔukα*. Then his father thought of *moo-cow*, and said this; the child replied, with evident satisfaction, *mukα*.

Now my observations of this child show that, so far from this being a sudden advance, it takes its due place in an ordered series of gradual steps in which we may trace his progress from his earliest attempts at conventional speech. This progress I shall attempt briefly to describe.

3. FUNCTIONS OF THE CHILD'S EARLIER UNDIFFERENTIATED SPEECH

If we observe children before they acquire conventional language, and while they are beginning to acquire it, we find that they use speech in three different ways: (*a*) in accompaniment to an act; (*b*) declaratively; (*c*) manipulatively. By accompaniment I mean this: while performing some movement the child utters a word which does not appear to refer to the situation in any way, but has become through training linked up with the

---

[1] The records of K are given in the script of the International Phonetic Association.

situation, and is indeed an intrinsic part of the performance of the movement.

Thus K, in his fourteenth month (1; 1,8), having learned to cover his head when his mother said *Peep-bo*, repeated the action spontaneously six times, saying *ɛbɔ* each time. Next day when his mother playfully held a cloth in front of his father's face, the child pulled it away, saying *ɛbɔ*; and again later he seized a shawl, put it on his head, and said *ɛbɔ*.

By declarative speech I mean the child's use of a word merely to draw the attention of others to some object, as for instance when K in his nineteenth month (1; 6, 11), said *tita* pointing to a picture of a watch. And by manipulative speech I mean the child's use of a word not only to draw our attention to an object, but by way of demanding that we shall satisfy his needs in relation to that object; for instance, K in his nineteenth month (1; 6, 9) reached up towards a drawer in which chocolate was kept and said *gɔga*.

Now it is reasonable to call the declarative and the manipulative uses of language *instrumental;* language in these cases is a social instrument by means of which the child draws others into his circle of activity. And it is very important to recognize this instrumental function of speech; for we find that the clue to the growth of reference to the past and future lies in this, that it grows directly out of the child's instrumental use of language. In his efforts to satisfy his needs, he refers at first only to the situation actually present, then he begins to refer to situations which are absent. Finally, under the stress of adult influence in linguistic intercourse, this reference to absent situations begins to be differentiated into reference to the past and to the future.

Thus we have to consider four phases of his development: first, the beginning of reference to absent situations: second, the growth of linguistic intercourse; third, the growth of reference to the past; fourth, the growth of reference to the future.

4. REFERENCE TO ABSENT SITUATIONS

In considering first the beginning of reference to absent situations, we have to notice that this occurs in the child's response to what others say to him as well as in his own speech.

(a) *Response to adult reference.*

When adults speak to the child, they constantly make reference to absent objects, a process which, of course, inevitably has its effect upon the child's own use of speech. In the case of K, the first instance of this kind which I observed occurred at 1; 1, 5 (Series I). The child had, since his tenth month, regularly responded to the phrase *Where's ballie?* by touching or grasping a ball lying before him. On the occasion in question, at 1; 1, 5, when the ball was out of sight, the adult's remark had still the same effect of inciting the child to act; and this activity involved an absent object. An exactly similar instance occurred at 1; 3, 5 (Series I). Now, as I have tried to show elsewhere (pp. 150, 304), reference of this kind to an absent object named by others does not suddenly appear fully fledged in the course of the child's development. It is a slow process, arising at first from the child's concern with the situation present before him, and constantly determined by this interest, the need to act in the present situation. The child's response to *ballie* or *apple* is far from being a simple link between an object and a name. For even when the ball or apple is present, we find that the child's response to *Where's ballie?* or *Where's apple?* is at first not so much a direction of attention towards the particular object as the initiation of an act which involves this object. The adult's remark incites the child to perform a particular act. Now when the adult says *ballie* or *apple* in the absence of the object, the child is again put into a state of readiness to perform the act, and looks round for the object which is essential to its performance.

But while the child's early response in such cases is not simply reference to an absent object but largely a concern with the situation actually before him, there is no doubt that it is out of such a response that reference to absent objects ultimately develops. For this to occur, two factors are necessary; the intervention of another speaker, and the pressure of the child's needs with regard to the situation actually present.

(b) *Rudimentary reference to absent objects in the child's own speech.*

We find these two factors also essential in the growth of the child's own spoken reference to absent objects: the child's need to deal with a situation and the cooperation of another speaker in helping him to do so. In the speech of K, the first instance of any reference to an absent object occurred at 1; 4, 17 (Series I): at breakfast the child turned towards the cupboard where honey was usually kept and said *ha*—a demand to be given the honey which was not yet before him. At 1; 5, 22 again, he caught at his father's coat and tried to get at his watch pocket, saying urgently *tik, tik*; at 1; 6, 9, he crawled towards the bureau where chocolate was usually kept, and reached up to the drawer, saying *gcga, gcga*. All these are cases in which the child is using words manipulatively, in the effort to draw attention to an object which he wishes to be brought into the present situation. And in all these cases it is clear that the child's utterance is much more an expression of his needs within the present situation than any reference to an absent object.

But all the time, reference to absent objects is undoubtedly growing, being continually fostered by what the adult does in response to the child's remarks. If when he says *tik tik* we show him the watch, or give him chocolate when he says *gɔga*, we are clearly aiding the process of reference to the absent object. An instance of the kind of advance that may be made is seen in my example from K's record at 1; 6, 13—four days after the last one given above (Series I). Here when the child was given a banana, he waved this aside and demanded *gɔga, gɔga*, although neither the time nor the place was normally associated with the eating of chocolate.

These then are the elements out of which reference by the child to absent objects, either in the speech of others or in his own speech, will grow. He responds by acts to the speech of others, and they respond by their acts to his speech. But now a much more potent factor enters, which greatly hastens the whole process: the adult engages in conversation with the child.

5. THE GROWTH OF LINGUISTIC INTERCOURSE

In the case of K, this very important development took place at about the age of 1; 6—the child began to respond to speech by speech. How did this occur? Throughout the child's experience, the adult comes before him as a being who both acts and speaks; at first the child responds only by acting and making his own primitive sounds, and gradually these sounds develop into speech, so that at last the child responds to the adult's acts and speech by speaking as well as acting. When this occurs, so that the child is responding by speech to speech, language has begun to be freed for him from the dominance of the present situation.

In the case of K we can trace three stages in this development:

(1) (Earliest months): the child responds to the adult's *acts* by *acts* and some utterance of sounds.

(2) (Towards the end of the first year): the child responds to the adult's *speech* by *acts*; and to his *acts* by *speech*.

(3) (About 1; 6): the child responds to the adult's *speech* by *speech*.

In this third stage, with which we are here concerned, we can notice two successive phases: the child responds by speech to speech, at first in the *presence* of the situation referred to; later, in the *absence* of that situation.

6. LINGUISTIC INTERCOURSE

(*a*) *With reference to the present situation.* Early examples of the former of these two phases, in the case of K, are given in Series II. At 1; 5, 10—the first case noted by me—it is the child who speaks first, and the adult then incites him to further speech. At 1; 6, 3, we have an interesting case: the child's remark *bɑ*—of the kind that he frequently made in accompaniment to an act—is given by the adult's question something of a more definite direction towards a coming situation. At 1; 6, 9, we have a case in which the child

is incited to manipulative speech: his mother says *I've got something nice for you*, to which he replies, *gɔga*—an expression of his desire to secure the object; and at 1; 6, 16, we have an example of declarative speech when the child is asked *What can you see?* and replies *fafa*, by which he draws attention to the flowers and perhaps expresses his delight in them. In all these cases a striking thing has happened: the child has at last shown that he understands the speech of others, not merely by performing some act, but actually by answering in words. He has entered upon what is perhaps the most distinctive feature of his human heritage—conversation.

Yet striking as this conquest undoubtedly is, we must recognize that it is in no sense a sudden change in the child's behavior. Until this moment the child has frequently used these kinds of speech either spontaneously or in response to another's acts: now he begins to use them in response to another's words. But there is no sudden change from one stage to the next. For when linguistic intercourse begins, it is not that the child replies simply by speech to speech; it is rather that he responds by speech and acts to speech and acts. Thus in the case at 1; 6, 3, it was the circumstances of the situation, as well as the remarks and gestures of the adult, which incited the child to say *ba* while he was walking to the bathroom. So also in the two subsequent instances.

In none of these cases is it true to say that the adult's remark evoked speech which otherwise would not have occurred; it is rather that the child would very likely have spoken in any case, because of the circumstances of the situation, and that the adult's remark made this more certain. But in saying this we must be careful not to minimize the decisive part played by the adult in inciting the child to speak. We must remember that all through the child's history the speech of those around him is peculiarly directed towards evoking from him not merely a response, but a *spoken* response. The importance of this in securing imitation by the child is already well recognized; but I do not think sufficient attention has hitherto been given to its function in arousing the child to a spoken response to the meaning of what he hears. The adult, by gestures and intonation, continually incites the child to speak, and encourages him with signs of approval when he has spoken. The resulting linguistic intercourse is without doubt the most powerful of all the means by which the society around the child fosters his advance in the mastery of language. For through conversation, more than any other factor, the child is helped to free his speech from the dominance of the present situation.

(b) Intercourse with reference to an absent situation.

We see how this may come about if we look at the two instances at 1; 9, 2 and at 1; 10, 15 (Series IV). In the former instance the child begins by rattling at the door and clamoring *ti: ti:* and *ai-i: ai-i:*—this we may regard as speech with a manipulative intention, called forth by the facts of the situation: it is the time of day when Eileen customarily appears with tea for the child's mother and a biscuit for him, and he is demanding that she shall now appear. But now when the adult asks: *What will Eileen bring us?* and the child replies *ti:*, this word takes on something of a forward-looking reference—it refers to the coming of Eileen; and clearly it is the adult's question which has suggested this forward direction to the child.

A similar development occurs in the second case. The child is clamoring *hɔum, hɔum,* but one need not suppose that there is in this much, if any, forward-looking reference to the child's home—it is rather that he wishes his carriage to be turned and wheeled homewards, very much as has occurred on previous occasions when an adult with him has said: *Now it's time to go home.* But now when the adult asks: *Whom do you want to see?* and the child replies *gæni,* there cannot, I think, be any doubt that there must be some forward-looking reference to the absent person, a reference that we may call manipulative because it is a demand that something shall be done for the child with regard to this person. And again it is reasonable to say that this forward-looking attitude has been suggested by the incentive of the adult's speech.

In both these cases, it is clear, there were already the rudiments of reference to an absent situation before this occurred in response to the adult's remark: the child said *ai-i:* and *hɔum* spontaneously. Rudimentary spontaneous reference to absent situations was, in fact, characteristic of K throughout the first three-quarters of his second year, as we have already seen illustrated in Series I. Nevertheless, it is evident that adult speech plays a leading part in the further development of this reference. Adult speech makes reference to absent situations incomparably more definite: for the adult's question is a means of drawing the child's attention to the absent situation, while at the same time it incites him—by intonation and gesture—to speak. Thus, much more certainly than ever before, the child's attention to absent situations will tend to be accompanied by his utterance of appropriate words, and the more that absent situations become linked up with words, the easier does it become to attend to them. In this way, it also becomes possible for the child to attend to remoter and remoter objects; for while his own rudimentary reference to absent objects arises almost inevitably from his needs with regard to a present situation, the adult in conversation may lead him further and further away from what is actually present. Further, the adult's remarks give a *direction* to the child's reference to what is absent; the child comes to learn that under certain conditions, a particular manner, gesture, intonation of the adult means recall of the past or anticipation of the future. And finally, something will be due to imitation. As the child realizes that the adult does refer to the past or the future, he too will come to do so more frequently, and linguistic intercourse of this kind will make him more aware of what may have been dawning upon him (but if so, dawning very dimly) that just as words enable him to deal with a present situation by calling in social aid, so they may help him to deal with absent situations.

Before we consider the details of this development, we must notice the relations between the stage already reached and the child's earlier behavior.

7. GRADUAL NATURE OF THIS ADVANCE

For striking as this advance may be—the beginning of linguistic intercourse in which both adult and child refer to an absent situation—here again we have to deny any sudden step. From the time when the adult's remark first causes the child to speak with reference to the present situation, up to the advance which we are now discussing, a series of changes may be observed showing progressively a greater freeing of the child's speech from the dominance of the actual situation. Let us look at our examples. In our earlier instances in Series III, at 1; 6, 3 and 1; 6, 9 the child's reply *ba* or *gɔga* is still very much determined by the facts of the present situation; this situation including, let us observe, not only the child's physical environment and the adult's acts, but also the features of the adult's speech—its intonation, rhythm, and stress. At the same time, in saying *gɔga* the child is in a rudimentary fashion certainly referring to the absent chocolate. And as we pass to subsequent observations, we find that the child's response is determined to a smaller and smaller extent by the characteristics of the actual situation, and that more and more the effect of the adult's remark is to direct the child's attention and speech to what is absent. Thus in our case at 1; 9, 2 (Series IV), there is still no doubt that the child's reply *ti:* is determined in some measure by the customary features of the present situation, and even by the word *Eileen*, which under these conditions has frequently been linked for him with the word *ti:*. In our next case, at 1; 9, 9, the dominance of the present situation is clearly less, though still powerful; the child's reply *ba: ti* still being determined in some measure by the customary features of the situation. At the same time the forward reference is correspondingly clearer, as may be seen by the child's behavior in tugging at the dressing-gown—he is looking forward to seeing his father shave.

Two cases in Series III show this process advanced a stage further. At 1; 10, 13, we see that the *physical* features of the present situation have ceased to be dominant although its *verbal* features may still influence the child's reply. Thus, while the child's reply almost pure reference to an absent situation, yet the word he uses, *gæni*, may perhaps be partly evoked by the word *cakes* with which it has probably been linked in the past.

And when we come to the case at 1; 11, 2, there seems nothing at all in the adult's remark to evoke any particular word from the child; there is not even the incentive of a question addressed to him. When, therefore, the child says *bʌti* and *gɔgi* he is really joining in conversation intelligently, with clear reference to the past.

We see then how, by a series of small steps, the child's reference to absent situations is progressively freed from the dominance of the present situation, and that a decisive factor in this progress is provided by the incentive of linguistic intercourse with others. We have still to see how this reference becomes specifically directed to the past and to the future.

8. THE DEVELOPMENT OF REFERENCE TO THE PAST

The primary effects of linguistic intercourse in fostering the child's reference to the past is, I think, this: it directs his attention to a past event and at the same time evokes from him words which were uttered at the time of that past event. Take, for instance, our first case, at 1; 8, 22 (Series III). A conversation is going on between adult and child; when the former asks, *Where's Da gone?* the child replies, more or less meaningfully, *gɔ:*. The adult pursues the topic and asks, *Where?* to which the child replies, with rather less meaning, *dɑ*. The adult's third question, *Yes, but where?* does at last evoke an answer, *ku:l* (school), which can be regarded as meaningful; but it is clear that no hard-and-fast line can be drawn between this and the two earlier replies. In all three cases, the intonation and gestures of the adult suggest to the child the utterance of a vocal response, and what the child then says is called forth partly by the form of the adult's words at this moment and partly by recall of what had on the past occasion been spoken by adult or child. It is reasonable to suppose that in this instance the adult had previously said *Da has gone to school*, and it is not unlikely that the child had imitated this immediately. When, therefore, the adult subsequently says *Where's Da gone?* he is to a very large extent evoking from the child the word *school* which he had previously heard, and perhaps even said.

I have analyzed this case at some length because it brings out a point which, I think, may sometimes be neglected: that linguistic intercourse between adult and child, even though it is meaningful, does at the same time evoke from the child responses which are at the verbal level and to that extent meaningless. When, for instance, K at 1; 8, 25, said *dæda* in reply to *Who gave you that box?* or at 1; 10, 13, *gæni* in reply to *Who made the cakes for you?*, it is clear that the connection between *box* and *dæda* and between *cakes* and *gæni* had more likely than not been established on the past occasion, so that the adult's words now were evoking something of that verbal connection. We must not, in fact, make too sharp a distinction in the child's linguistic development between meaningful and meaningless utterance.

At the same time it would be false to minimize the fact that, in the instances we have just considered, the child makes a true reference to the past. The adult, in the very act of reinstating a verbal connection made in the past, is thereby also recalling for the child the circumstances of that past event. So that when the child says *ku: l* or *dæda* or *gæni* he may reasonably be regarded as referring to the event which the adult has mentioned. As I have pointed out above, the child's speech is first freed from the dominance of the physical features of the present situation, then from the dominance of its verbal features, so that in our case at 1; 11, 2, we seem at last to have true reference to a past event.

With the next cases in our series, 2; 0, 20, and 2; 0, 22, we come to a further stage in the process: spontaneous reference to the past— on his return from a walk the child, for instance, spontaneously says *mɔukɑ*. Without much doubt, he is recalling the exciting experience just past, and with it the word uttered *then*, either by him or the maid, or both. This utterance is spontaneous, but the part that may be played by the adult in fostering such utterance is seen in the conversation that immediately follows. The adult questions the child, with two effects: on the one hand, he helps to make the child's utterance more precise and bring it nearer to conventional adult speech; on the other hand, he shows an interest in the child's reference to the past and so incites the child to further behavior of this kind. It is hardly necessary to emphasize how much difference it would make to the child's speech about the past events if his remarks continually failed to arouse any interested response from those about him.

9. THE DEVELOPMENT OF REFERENCE TO THE FUTURE

Just as in the growth of reference to the past, the child's reference to the future is determined by the behavior of adults in linguistic intercourse with him. It is, of course, true the rudiments of reference to the future exist in the child's speech long before he engages in any linguistic intercourse, but I do not think there can be any doubt that it is this latter activity which gives his rudimentary future reference the definiteness which it comes to have in conventional speech. In the case of K, the first glimmer of future reference in response to an adult occurs at 1; 6, 3, but his first clear spontaneous future reference not until 2; 1, 23 (see Series IV).

The general development of reference to the future seems to be as follows. Much of the child's speech, precisely because it is manipulative, and directed towards securing the satisfaction of needs, has from an early period something of a forward-looking direction. The adult, by questions and remarks, frequently incites the child to refer to his needs, and thus to make a manipulative reference to the future; and sometimes also incites him, by speaking of future events which resemble past experiences, to make a purely descriptive or declarative reference to these events. Ultimately, the child comes to refer to the future quite spontaneously.

Let us take a few landmarks in the progress of K. At 1; 6, 3 we saw, he says the word *ba* while marching towards the bathroom, when he is asked, *Where are you going?* Here the adult's question gives the child's reply a glimmer of forward direction; a function which, in our next case at 1; 8, 24, has become rather more definite. When the child says *gɔga*, he certainly expresses his need within the present situation, and possibly refers to something beyond it. It is the adult who makes this reference more specific by replying *When we go out*, for the child's immediate response *tata* unquestionably refers to the future.

It is important to notice that this reference to the future is made possible because the future resembles the past, and that the child's replies at this stage are determined by past occasions. Thus the remark *When we go out* recalls to the child occasions of going out, and it is this recall, as well as the need for chocolate, which evokes from him the reply *tata*. For some time in the child's development this effect of the past remains an important factor, as may be seen from our examples at 1; 11, 9, and 2; 0, 10. In the former case, when the child is asked *What is Baby going to have for breakfast?* and replies *agu*, the adult has helped the child to recall breakfast; so too in the second case when the adult says *I must take you to have your hair cut* and the child replies *ʃiʒiʒ*. Observations such as these make it reasonable to suppose that at this early stage the direction of the child's reference—whether to past or to future—is indefinite, and that at first he refers, and is helped to refer, to an absent situation, rather than to a definitely past or future one. We find two things helping to give this reference a forward-looking direction: first, the pressure of the child's own needs, secondly the influence of others in linguistic intercourse with him.

The observations before us give us a glimpse of the manner in which these factors work. The child's reply becomes progressively less dependent upon the actual physical conditions of the present situation or upon the verbal form of the adult's remarks. Thus at 1; 8, 24, the phrase *when we go out* almost inevitably suggests the reply *tata*, but at 1; 11, 9, *breakfast* rather less necessarily suggests *agu*, and at 2; 0, 10 *hair cut* even less necessarily *ʃiʒiʒ*. In all these cases we see that the child's speech is freeing itself from the dominance of the present and is being given a future direction by the pressure of his needs: *tata*, *agu*, and *ʃiʒiʒ* all express, with varying degrees of urgency, his desire to secure satisfactions to come, or at least to communicate his feelings about them.

This is the personal factor, proceeding from the child himself; but no less important,

I think, is the social factor, the pressure that is exercised upon the child from without. Each of these acts of linguistic intercourse is *followed* by the event to which it refers; and this the child must come to realize. He must realize also that a certain intonation and manner when the adult speaks signify the future. In this way, the adult does much to give the linguistic act a twist in the future direction.

Gradually, with the concurrence of these two factors, the personal and the social, there comes a time when the child refers to the future, in almost complete independence of present circumstances. Thus at 2; 0, 16, when K's father says *I must get up*, his response *pu dædi, bæŋkets of* is almost a spontaneous expression of his intention; five weeks later, at 2; 1, 23, the final stage is reached: on hearing a story the child remarks, without any incentive from an adult, [K] *tell it nau*—a completely spontaneous reference to the future.

Thus from the stage when a child first begins to make some slight reference to an absent situation because this is bound up with his present needs, we find the adult progressively intensifying and clarifying the child's reference to the future, so that at last this is made spontaneously and with increasing awareness that it is the future that is referred to.

10. CONCLUSION

In this brief survey I have tried to show by considering the facts of one child's development, how unlikely it is that the occurrence of reference to the past or to the future is a sudden event in a child's life. I suggest instead that it arises as the result of a number of factors, of which the most important are the child's own manipulative and declarative needs in speaking, and the influence of adult reference to past and future in linguistic intercourse. It is this last factor above all which I should like to stress, not because I consider it the most important—this is difficult to estimate—but because it has hitherto been so much neglected. In a recent very interesting paper, Sauvageot has suggested that the notion of tense—past, present, and future—may differ according to the linguistic community, being closely bound up with the means of linguistic expression: and may therefore be less fully developed in speakers of Slavonic languages than among Western Europeans. The account I have here given of the one child observed by me suggests that in the development of children's speech the factor of social intercourse may similarly play a decisive part, helping to make reference to the past and to the future the very definite functions with which we are familiar in our everyday language.

11. SUMMARIES OF OBSERVATIONS

SERIES 1:   Rudimentary reference to absent objects.

Age	Circumstances	Adult's speech	Child's speech	Conventional equivalent
1; 1, 5	C playing with toy.; has not played with ball all day; at this moment it is lying in corner of room, in shadow. M says:	Baby, where's ballie?		
	C turns round and crawls towards ball. On the way he halts at the coal-box, a favorite plaything. When M repeats phrase C returns journey, seizes ball, and looks at M.			
1; 3, 5	C has been nibbling an apple while crawling about on the floor, and has thrown it into a corner. M does not know this, and asks the question: Whereupon C crawls straight towards the apple and brings it to her.	Where's apple?		
1; 4, 17	At breakfast time turning towards the cupboard where the honey, which he generally has at breakfast, is kept, says:		ha.	Honey.
1; 5, 22	F sitting down. C spontaneously comes over to him, seizes lapels of coat and tries to push them apart, saying:		tik, tik.	Tick, tick.
1; 6, 9	C crawls over to bureau, reaches up to drawer where chocolate is kept, and says:		gɔga, gɔga.	Chocolate.
1; 6, 13	At dinner C is offered a banana. He waves this away and says:		gɔga, gɔga.	Chocolate.

Note: A = adult; C = child; F = father; M = mother.

SERIES 2: Beginning of linguistic intercourse.

Age	Circumstances	Adult's speech	Child's speech	Conventional equivalent
1; 5, 10	M dressing C in front of gas fire. C points to fire and says in a delighted tone: M asks, pointing to fire: C replies:	 What's that?	aha; fa. fa.	Aha; fire. Fire.
1; 6, 3	About bath time C climbs upstairs, M following him. At the landing she asks: C makes straight for bathroom, saying:	Where are you going? 	 ba.	 Bath.
1; 6, 9	Standing by bureau in which chocolate is kept, M says: C replies:	I've got something nice for you. 	 Gɔga, gɔga.	 Chocolate.
1; 6, 16	M wheels C's carriage towards bed of tulips and asks:	What can you see?	fa, fa.	Flower.

SERIES 3: Growth of reference to the past.

Age	Circumstances	Adult's speech	Child's speech	Conventional equivalent
1; 8, 22	Conversation between A and C:	Where's Da gone? Where? Yes, but where?	gɔ. dɑ. ku:l.	Gone. Da. School.
1; 8. 25	M. finding C with box which F had given him, asks;	Who gave you that box?	dæda.	Dadda.
1; 10, 13	F, referring to cake in C's hand:	Who made the cakes for you?	gæni.	Granny.
1; 11, 2	M, speaking to A, trying to recall name of people met nearly a month before, when C had been present: C, who is listening, says:	What was the name of those people? 	 bʌti, gɔgi,	 Bertie, doggie.
2; 0, 20	On his return from a walk with the maid, says: F asks: F asks again:	 Motor-car? Moo-cow?	mɔukɑ. nɔu. mukɑ.	 No! Moo-cow!
2; 0, 22	Picking up a book which he had lost the previous day, and which Da had found, says:		dɑ faind it.	Da find it.

SERIES 4:   Growth of reference to the future.

Age.	Circumstances.	Adult's speech.	Child's speech.	Conventional equivalent.
1; 6, 3	About bath-time C climbs upstairs, M following him. At the landing she asks: C makes straight for the bathroom, saying:	Where are you going?	bɑ.	Bath.
1; 8, 24	C speaking to M, says appealingly M replies: C says:	When we go out.	gɔga. tata.	Chocolate. Tata.
1; 9, 2	Early in the morning in M's room. C goes to door, rattles the handle and says: Then adds: M asks: M continues:	What will E bring us? What else will E bring us?	ti: ti: ai-i: ai-i: ti: biki.	Tea. Eileen. Tea. Biscuits.
1; 9, 9	In the morning C sees F getting out of bed; F asks: C goes to where F's dressing-gown is and pulls it over to F.	Where's Daddy going?	bɑ:ti.	Bathroom.
1; 10, 15	M wheeling C in carriage. C says: M asks:	Whom do you want to see?	hɔum. gæni.	Home. Granny.
1; 11, 9	Before breakfast M asks:	What is baby going to have for breakfast?	agu.	Egg.
2; 0, 10	M addressing child:	I must take you to have your hair cut.	ʃiʒiʒ.	Scissors.
2; 0, 16	F, in bed, says: C (immediately):	I must get up.	pu daedi, bæŋkets ɔf.	Pull Daddy (out of bed, and) blankets off.
2; 1, 23	M has told him a story. After hearing it three times he says:		(K) tel it nau	(K) tell it now.

REFERENCES

C. und W. Stern. *Die Kindersprache*, 4te Aufl, 1928.

C. Bühler. *Kindheit und Jugend*, 1931.

M. M. Lewis. *Infant Speech*, 1936.

A. Sauvageot. *La Notion de Temps et son Expression dans le langage*, in *J. de Psych.*, 1936.

20 Probably the most important theoretical work of recent times is Jakobson's *Kindersprache, Aphasie und allgemeine Lautgesetze* (Upsala, 1941), reprinted in his *Selected Writings*, vol. I (Hague, 1962). A shorter version, "Les Lois phoniques du langage enfantin et leur place dans la phonologie générale," was written a little earlier but published later (1949), as an appendix to the French translation of Trubetzkoy's *Grundzüge der Phonologie* (reprinted in *Selected* Writings, vol. I). A translation of this version is included here by permission.

Jakobson does not report any observations of his own, but uses those available in the literature, particularly in the first minute study of child language on a phonetic basis, by Antoine Grégoire. Jakobson, one of the founders of the Prague school of linguists (to which Prince Trubetzkoy, another Russian, also belonged), the first group of structural linguists, discusses the principles of phonemic opposition (contrast) as they develop in child language, break down in aphasia, and dominate the languages of the world. He was the first to grant child language a central position in the theory of language.

Jakobson's theory of child language can be said to have brought order into the bewildering array of facts accumulated by observation, which seemed to lack a common denominator until his broad principles were applied to them.

W. F. L.

Cf. Leopold's evaluation incorporated in his "Patterning in Children's Language Learning" in this volume, and his paper "Roman Jakobson and the Study of Child Language," in *For Roman Jakobson*, ed. Morris Halle et al. (The Hague: Mouton, 1956), pp. 285–88. An English translation of Jakobson's *Kindersprache, Aphasie und allgemeine Lautgesetze* is now available: *Child Language, Aphasia and Phonological Universals* (New York: the Humanities Press, 1969).

A. B. A.

THE SOUND LAWS OF CHILD LANGUAGE AND THEIR PLACE IN GENERAL PHONOLOGY

A brilliant work of Grégoire which has recently appeared with the title, *L'apprentissage du langage* (Liège, 1937), marks an epoch in the study of the beginnings of child language. According to the eminent Belgian linguist, the investigator must have lived day by day, hour by hour in the company of the

Reprinted from Roman Jakobson, Selected Writings (*The Hague: Mouton & Co., 1939; reprinted 1962*), *1.317–327, by permission of the author.*

Communication prepared at Charlottenlund, Denmark, in the summer of 1939 for the Fifth International Congress of Linguists at Brussels, September, 1939, and published as a supplement to *Principes de phonologie* by N. S. Trubetzkoy (Paris, 1949).

infants and must have watched, moment by moment, the external manifestations of their activity; on the other hand he must be extremely exact in the difficult recording of the linguistic phenomena and in reporting their conditions and functions. Grégoire's microscopic analysis combines these two qualities and makes it possible to evaluate and utilize correctly the numerous data of earlier publications. Some of these presented keen and judicious observations of competent linguists, but too compactly and fragmentarily. Others were patient monographs of psychologists and educators who unfortunately often lacked linguistic methods.

The abundance of our experiences permits a structural analysis of the incipient language and an investigation of its general laws, or laws which tend to be general, if one prefers a more cautious formulation. Besides, Grammont stated this principle at the beginning of our century with impressive precision. "There is," he says, "in the language of the child neither incoherence nor the effect of chance ... He misses the aim, to be sure, but he always deviates from it in the same way... The constancy of this deviation gives his speech its interest. At the same time it makes it possible to understand the nature of the modification." What then is the law of this deviation in the successive acquisition of phonemes?

Since Buffon the "principle of least effort" is often cited; articulations which are easy to produce are said to be learned first. But an essential fact of the small child's linguistic development clearly refutes this hypothesis. During the babbling stage (*période du babil*) the child produces the most varied sounds with ease (for example clicks and palatalized, rounded, affricated, hissing, uvular consonants, etc.), nearly all of which he eliminates when he proceeds to the stage "of a few words" (to use Oscar Bloch's term), that is to say, when he adopts the first semantic values. It is true that some of the sounds which tend to disappear are unsupported by the example of the speech of the environment, where they do not exist. But there are others which share the same fate although they are present in the speech of the adults, and the child reacquires them only after long efforts. This is often the case with velars, sibilants, and liquids. The child used these articulations frequently in babbling. The motor image was therefore familiar to him and the acoustic image must also have been present. The son of the observant Serbian scholar Pavlovič said *tata* for *kaka* although he distinguished the two words *kaka* and *tata* by ear. And Passy reports the case of a small child who substituted the form *tosson* for the words *garçon* ('boy') and *cochon* ('pig'), but became annoyed when his mother imitated him and made no difference between these two words. Facts of this kind are well known. The attempt has been made to attribute this loss of articulation (*phonation*) to the absence of a link between the acoustic and motor images; but as the observers report, the child sometimes begins to pronounce the *K* in the first words he imitates and then

suddenly gives up the velars, obstinately replacing them by dentals.

The sorting (*tri*) of sounds in passing from babbling (*babil*) to speech, in the full sense of the word, can thus be explained only by the act of transition itself, that is, by the phonemic function which the sound acquires. The child passes little by little from spontaneous, aimless soliloquy to a sort of conversation. Trying to conform to the environment, he learns to recognize the identity of the phonic phenomenon which he hears and utters, which he keeps in his memory, and which he reproduces at will. The child distinguishes it from the other phonic phenomena which he hears, remembers, and imitates, and this distinction, conceived as an intersubjective and constant value, strives for a meaning. To the wish to communicate with others is added the ability to communicate something to them. These first distinctions, which tend to become significant, require phonic oppositions which are simple, clear, stable, suitable to be imprinted on the memory and to be realized at will. The phonetic abundance of babbling (*gazouillis*) gives way to phonemic restriction.

The intimate link between the sorting of phonemes on the one hand and the unmotivated, plainly conventional character of the linguistic sign on the other is confirmed by the fact that exclamations and onomatopoeias do not obey this restriction. These vocal gestures which, in the speech of adults as well, tend to form a separate layer, seem actually to favor sounds not permitted otherwise. The expressive value of what is unusual rather than what conforms to a model is just what makes children use in their onomatopoeias rounded palatal vowels, while otherwise they continue to replace them by unrounded or even velar vowels. Thus a boy of eleven months mentioned in the well-known book of C. and W. Stern reproduces the motion of horses and wagons by *öö*; the little Grégoire uses these sounds at 19 months to render the striking of clocks; and the daughter of Marcel Cohen imitates the barking of the dog by means of the same vowels in her fifteenth month. Changing this onomatopoeia into a simple designation of the dog *oo*, she adapts the vocalism to the phonemic system which she has at her disposal at the time.

Eliminating these special cases and following the formation of the phonemic system in child language step by step, we notice rigid regularity in the sequence of these acquisitions, most of which form strict and stable series in chronological order. This regularity has struck observers for almost a century. No matter if the children are French or English, Scandinavian or Slavic, German or Japanese, Estonian or New Mexico Indian, every careful linguistic description uniformly confirms that the relative chronology of certain innovations is always and everywhere the same. On the other hand the pace of their succession is very variable; two successive elements which follow each other immediately in some cases can be separated by several years in the development of others. Being something like a slow motion film, these cases of deferred phonemic development are especially instructive.

Ordinarily the vowel system begins with a wide vowel and the consonant system at the same time with a front stop; generally they are *A* and a labial stop. The first consonantal opposition is between nasal and buccal, the second between labials and dentals (*P–T, M–N*).

These two oppositions form the minimum consonantism of the living languages of the world and cannot be absent except in cases of extrinsic and mechanical changes. An example is the absence of labials in Tlingit (and in some forms of women's speech in central Africa) which is due to artificial mutilation of the lips, and even in these cases the class of the labials tends to be represented in the phonemic system by specific substitutes.

Subsequent to the two consonantal oppositions mentioned, a narrow vowel comes to be opposed to the wide vowel in child language, and the next phase of the vocalism brings either a third degree of openness or a split of the narrow phoneme into palatal and velar vowels. Either one of these two processes leads to a system of three vowels, which is the minimum vowel system of the living languages of the world. This minimum vowel system as well as the minimum consonant system evidently requires the presence of phonemes which combine two "differential

elements" to use Saussure's terminology (thus in the "triangular" system of the vowels *U, A, I*, the phoneme *U* is velar by opposition to *I* and narrow by opposition to the phoneme *A*, and in the "linear" system the middle vowel is compex: wide by opposition to the narrow one and at the same time narrow by opposition to the wide one).

When we turn to the acquisition of the child's consonantism or of vocalism going beyond the demonstrated minimum, we notice that the sequence corresponds exactly to the general laws of irreversible solidarity which govern the languages of the world synchronically.

Thus in the phonemic system of the child, the acquisition of the velar and palatal consonants presupposes the acquisition of labials and dentals, and in the languages of the world the presence of palatovelars implies the simultaneous existence of labials and dentals. This solidarity is irreversible: the presence of labials and dentals does not imply the presence of palatovelars, as is proved, for example, by their complete absence in the language of Tahiti and in the Tataric of Kasimov as well as by the absence of velar and palatal nasals in many languages.

The acquisition of fricatives presupposes the acquisition of stops and in the same way the existence of the former implies that of the latter in the phonemic systems of the world. There is no language without stops, but on the other hand there are some languages, in Oceania, Africa, and South America, which lack fricatives completely; examples in the Old World are Kara-Kalpak and Tamil, both of which lack independent fricative phonemes.

The acquisition of affricates in child language in opposition to the corresponding stops presupposes the acquisition of the fricatives of the same series; likewise in the languages of the world the opposition of the dental, labial, and palatovelar affricate to the corresponding stop implies the presence of a dental, labial, or palatovelar fricative.

No horizontal opposition of vowels of greater openness can be acquired by the child unless his vowels of lesser openness acquire the same opposition. This evolutionary order corresponds exactly to the general synchronic law formulated by Trubetzkoy.

The child's acquisition of rounded front vowels, which are secondary in Rousselot's terminology, presupposes the acquisition of primary vowels, that is to say, rounded back vowels and the corresponding unrounded front vowels. The secondary series implies the presence of the primary vowels of the same degree of openness in the languages of the world.

The relatively uncommon oppositions in the languages of the world are among the last acquisitions of the child. Thus the second liquid is among the last accretions of the child's phonemic system, and the sibilant R (ř), an extremely rare phoneme in the languages of the world, is usually the last phoneme to be learned by Czech children. In the various Indian tribes which use glottalized consonants the children learn them late, and nasal vowels appear in the speech of French and Polish children later than all other vowel phonemes.

It would be easy to add to the number of coincidences between the developmental sequence of child language and the general laws which the synchrony of the languages of the world reveals, and more analogous correspondences will surely be found as exact linguistic information about the children of varied ethnic groups is accumulated. But it is possible now to draw conclusions from the very fact of the parallelism which I have pointed out.

Every phonemic system is a stratified structure, that is, it consists of superimposed layers. The hierarchy of these layers is nearly universal and constant. It appears in the synchrony as well as in the diachrony of language; we are therefore dealing with a panchronic order. When there is a relation of irreversible solidarity between two phonemic units, the secondary unit cannot appear without the primary unit, and the primary unit cannot be eliminated without the secondary unit. This order prevails in the existing phonemic system and governs all its changes. The same order determines language-learning, as we have just seen, a nascent system, and—let us add—it continues to prevail in language disorders, a system in dissolution.

For example, as the observations of psychiatrists show, nasal vowels tend to disappear first in language disorders; the opposition of liquids is likewise apt to vanish; secondary vowels succumb sooner than primary; fricatives and affricates change into stops; velar consonants are lost sooner than front consonants; and labial consonants as well as the vowel A are the last phonemes to resist destruction, exactly as in the beginning stage of child language. The higher layers are removed before the lower ones. Aphasic losses reproduce in inverse order the sequence of acquisitions in child language. A thorough phonemic analysis of aphasia (that is, language disorders of an internal nature, without damage to the speech organs) is apt to shed light on the correspondences under consideration, which are equally fruitful for the psychiatrist and the linguist.

Some isolated points of contact between child language on the one hand and the phonemic inventory of certain so-called primitive languages on the other have been pointed out before; but these languages were viewed as survivals which, so to speak, reflected the childhood of mankind, and reference was made to the biogenetic law of Haeckel, according to which the individual recapitulates in his development the phylogenesis, the development of the species. However, the scarcity of phonemes in a given language is not necessarily a primordial poverty. On the contrary, historical study frequently discloses that the impoverishment is of recent date. What remains conclusive in the agreement between child language and the languages of the world is solely the identity of structural laws which regulate any change in individual and social speech. In other words, the same stable hierarchy of units governs all increases and decreases in the phonemic system.

But it does not suffice to point out the regularity of this hierarchy; it needs to be explained by a demonstration of its necessity. It is obvious that isolated explanations are not sufficient. The laws of child language cannot be separated from the corresponding facts in the languages of the world. For instance the early appearance of labial and dental consonants in child language as compared with velars has been noticed, and the attempt has been made to explain it by the habitual motion of sucking. But it would be difficult to find even a fervent Freudian who would be willing to invoke infantile memories to explain another manifestation of the same law, namely the dropping of velars in certain Tataric or Polynesian languages. Instead of facing the totality of phonemic oppositions successively acquired by the child, people fragmented this organized structure. Thus in attributing the priority of the labials to the protrusion of the lips one overlooked that the primary opposition, the best defined and most stable, that between buccal and nasal labials, remains in that case completely incomprehensible.

However, the phonemic hierarchy is rigidly consistent. It follows the principle of maximum contrast and in the sequence of oppositions it proceeds from the simple and homogeneous to the complex and differentiated. Let us confine ourselves for the moment to a rapid citation of a few examples.

The stage of babbling (*babil enfantin*) begins with undetermined sounds which observers say are neither consonants nor vowels or, what amounts to the same, are both at once. The babbling stage ends with the well-defined separation of consonants and vowels. From the motor aspect the two categories stand in the opposition of restriction (*resserrement*) and dilation (*dilatation*). The wide vowel *A* offers maximum dilation; on the other hand the stop consonants show zero openness, and among the stops the labials are the ones which close the buccal cavity completely. It was to be expected *a priori* that exactly this maximum contrast would be chosen to initiate the distinction between vocalism and consonantism at the threshold of child language, and experience confirms this expectation.

The opposition between the two categories arises in the beginning on the axis of successiveness. The labial stop combined with the vowel forms the germ of the syllable. The opposition of phonemes on the other axis, that of simultaneousness, according to Saussure's good terminology, does not yet exist. And yet it is this opposition which is the necessary premise for the distinctive function of phonemes. The syllable, a phonemic frame, requires a phonemic content, frame and content being two solitary concepts, as Viggo Brøndal has pointed out.

Open tract and closed tract—or in other words vowel and consonants—this is where a new development enters. The first opposition on the axis of simultaneousness arises in this way—the opposition of buccal and nasal stops. While the vowel is characterized by the absence of closed tract, the consonant splits itself into two parts, one provided with a single closed tract and the other one which adds an open collateral tract to the first one and thus synthesizes the specific features of the buccal stop and the vowel. This synthesis is the natural consequence of the opposition consonant-vowel, whereas the nasal vowels, opposed to the buccal as a double open tract to a single open tract, represent a much more specialized and less contrasting fact in the language. That is why nasal vowels, just like consonants with double closure, appear rarely in the languages of the world and very late in the speech of children destined to speak these languages. On the other hand the universal opposition of the nasal and the buccal consonants is the first opposition which tends to assume a significative function in child language.

To clarify the second consonantal split let us recall briefly the ingenious discoveries of Koehler and of Stumpf, from which linguistics has not yet drawn all the conclusions it could. It is to these masters of modern acoustics that credit is due for having recognized and stated two irreducible types among speech sounds. Comparable to the colors, the speech sounds are chromatic in different degrees or achromatic on the one hand, clear (acute) or dark (grave) on the other. This latter opposition gains in importance as the chromatism decreases. Among the vowels, *A* is the most chromatic sound and is least suitable for the opposition of clear and dark; on the other hand the narrow vowels are most inclined toward this opposition and least chromatic. These two dimensions of the vowel triangle, of which the horizontal *U–I* is the base line and the vertical *A* the altitude, correspond, according to the brilliant analysis of Stumpf, to two psycho-physiological processes: the "*U–I* Process" which concerns the opposition between clear and dark, and the "*A*-Process" which determines the degree of chromatism. The first process is basic (heavy line in our graph) whereas the second is accessory (light line in our graph):

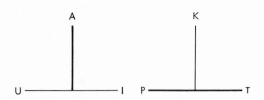

This scholar realizes that there are no languages whose vowel system is founded solely on the basic process. Did it perhaps exist by itself only in a prelinguistic period?, Stumpf asks himself hesitantly. But this assumption does not solve the problem in any way. Linear vocalism does exist in the languages of the world which we know, but it suppresses precisely the base line of the triangle. Thus the vowel system is reduced to the vertical (1) in several languages of the West Caucasus which Trubetzkoy has analyzed, and (2) in child language (as well as that of aphasics) at the stage when they make no distinction between the various vowels of the same degree of openness (for example, between *U* and *I*) utilizing them as combinatory or stylistic variants or using only one of them. These facts would seem to prove an indefensible paradox: one would have to say that the basic process is inseparably tied to the accessory process, whereas the latter can exist alone!

Nevertheless this apparent contradiction disappears when one views vocalism and consonantism as two parts of a whole and draws (as Stumpf did not) the consequences from his enlightened definition, according to which it is the presence of definite chromatism (*ausgeprägte Färbung*) which primarily distinguishes vowels from consonants. It being established that vowels are chromatic phonemes *par excellence*, then it is *A*, the summit of the chromatism, which appears as the optimum vowel, *princeps vocalium*, according to Hellwag's phrase. The vertical *A*, which differentiates the degrees of

chromatism, is naturally the principal pivot, sometimes the only one, of the vocalism. Consonants are phonemes without definite chromatism; the opposition of clear and dark, a contrast which increases as the chromatism diminishes, represents therefore the principal pivot of the consonantism. Acoustic analysis shows that the labials oppose a dark tone quality to the clear tone quality of the dentals. Since, according to Stumpf, the dark tone quality represents the quantitative maximum of the process under discussion, it follows that the labials offer the consonantal optimum.

Several laws obtain their internal explanation at the same time; namely, the priority of the labial consonants and of the vowel *A*; the precedence of the base line in buccal and nasal consonantism, i.e. of the split into labials and dentals; the precedence of the altitude in the vocalism, i.e. of its differentiation according to the degree of openness; and finally the sequence of the split of the vowels into velars and palatals proceeding from the narrow to the wide.

In the acquisition of language the first vocalic opposition is later than the first consonantal oppositions. There is accordingly a stage during which the consonants already fulfill a distinctive function, whereas the single vowel so far only serves as a support for the consonant and as a vehicle for expressive variations. Thus we see that consonants take on the function of phonemes before the vowels. Otherwise expressed, the first to appear are the achromatic phonemes which split along the horizontal, the line of black and white. After that the chromatic phonemes arise and become differentiated along the vertical, the lines of the degrees of chromatism. The precedence of the basic process with reference to the accessory process is thus completely confirmed.

The achromatic sounds, or more exactly, the sounds without definite chromatism, display, as Stumpf has already pointed out, various degrees of chromatism. Thus the two dimensions which correspond to those of the vocalism reoccur in the consonantism, but in inverse hierarchical order. The linear vocalism is vertical whereas the linear consonantism is reduced to the base line. The palatovelar consonants show the minimum of achromatism. Being remote, just like the wide vowels, *von der Linie der blossen Hellig-keiten*, as Stumpf expresses it, they are relatively unlikely to split according to their clear and dark character into two distinct classes, palatals and velars. They form therefore the peak of the consonantal triangle. The phonemes of the peak denote a higher degree of specific intensity than those of the corresponding base line. Keep in mind that, all other things being equal, the wide vowels are above the narrow ones in perceptibility, and the palatovelar consonants above the corresponding front consonants. Hence what is merely an epiphenomenon for the vocalic oppositions is the very essence of the palatovelar consonants. Stumpf subjected *K*, *T*, and *P* to acoustic filtration. When *T* and *P* are well on the way to disappearance, there still remains of the velar the rattling of a quick tap (*bruissement d'un coup sec*). The velars are reduced to the glottal stop (an indeterminate stop phoneme) in languages with linear consonantism and often in child language (or aphasic speech) of the corresponding stage.

It is clear that the opposition of vowels and stops, or in other words, that of openness and closure, precedes the opposition of complete closure and partial closure, that is, the opposition of stops and fricatives. The opposition of *U* and *I* involves two parallel distinctions, namely that of velars and palatals and that of rounded and unrounded. The separation of these two distinctions, which makes it possible to combine two inverse peculiarities in a rounded palatal and an unrounded velar phoneme is of course a secondary acquisition. The complex nature of affricates is of exactly the same order.

If one continues comparing the linguistic acquisitions of the child with the typology of the languages of the world, one glimpses the fact that the grouping of phonemes and the system of the grammatical meanings are equally subject to the rule of the superposition of functions.

The universality and the inner logic of the stated hierarchical order appear to make it possible to postulate it also for the evolution of speech (glottogony). This immutability justifies for example the verification and acceptance of the ingenious hypothesis recently put forth by P. van Ginneken (and earlier by Noiré) concerning the rudiments of human language: consonantal oppositions precede vocalic oppositions. To be sure, this scholar assumes a still older stage, that of clicks; but he points out himself that these are by their function not yet phonemes, but simply vocal gestures which are, properly speaking, a prelinguistic, extra-linguistic layer and, I should like to add, a postlinguistic one, as the study of aphasia shows. Trombetti's hypothesis about the priority of the stops is also confirmed, contrary to the priority of the affricates which Marr postulates.

I have tried to bring out the rigorous stratification of some phonemic oppositions and to show how this order appears. The principle is so simple that it seems trite: it is impossible to put on the roof without having built the frame of the house, just as one cannot take away the frame without carrying away the roof. But this is the principle which the dynamics and statics of language follow. It coordinates facts which have been considered disparate; it eliminates some supposedly "insoluble puzzles;" and it gives a unified direction to apparently incompatible and blind laws. The phonemic development of the child as well as the development of aphasia is, in its great outline, merely the corollary of this principle.

All this goes to prove that the choice of differential elements within a language is by no means arbitrary and fortuitous, but is, on the contrary, ruled by laws (or tendencies) of universal and constant validity. We have rapidly surveyed some laws of implication: the existence of a unit *Y* implies the existence of a unit *X* in the same phonemic system. It would be possible to examine another series of laws which are no less important for the typology of languages. They are the laws of incompatibility: the existence of a unit *Y* excludes the existence of a unit *X* in the same phonemic system.

Under the spell of the antiteleological (*antifinaliste*) spirit of the end of the century, F. de Saussure—in spite of his pioneering courage—expresses the following conviction: "In contrast to the false idea which we often have of it, language is not a mechanism created and arranged for the sake of the concepts to be expressed." Now however we are in a position to make this rejoinder: in contrast to the destructive, hypercritical attitude of that period, it is common sense, it is precisely the idea which we, the speaking subjects, often have of language which is perfectly valid: language is actually an instrument governed and arranged for the sake of the concepts to be expressed. It takes the sounds effectively and transforms this natural material into contrasting qualities suitable for carrying the meaning. The laws of phonemic structure just broached prove it.

H. V. VELTEN

21 Velten is one of the first students of child language who has applied Jakobson's new insights (with special reference to his famous *Kindersprache, Aphasie, und allgemeine Lautgesetze* [Uppsala, 1941]) into the study of phonology in general, and the phonemic development in child language in particular. Velten studied the slow process of language-learning by his daughter Joan, by applying Jakobson's basic phonemic patterns, with certain modifications. He tried to cover the lexical area as well, although on a rather limited corpus.

A. B. A.

THE GROWTH OF PHONEMIC AND LEXICAL PATTERNS IN INFANT LANGUAGE

This study is based on a record of my daughter Joan's speech from her eleventh to her thirty-sixth month.[1] It will deal chiefly with phonemic and lexical matters. For, apart from other reasons which will be discussed below, the morphological and syntactical development in the language of English-speaking children has been well described in numerous works, while only two authors have hitherto been concerned, implicitly or explicitly, with problems of phonemics in infant language,[2]

and as regards vocabulary patterns, it is impossible to glean any information from the customary alphabetical word lists.[3]

In a multitude of books on infant language it has been established that the acquisition of language properly speaking is preceded by a period, called 'babillage' (by H. Delacroix), 'Lallperiode' (by K. Bühler), or babbling stage, during which the speech organs are developed and incessantly exercised. Even the most outlandish sounds, i.e. speech sounds which the child has certainly never heard, may be produced and perfectly articulated during this time. An American child may pronounce velar spirants, voiceless nasals, retroflex sibilants, etc. During the early stages a uvular *r* is quite common.[4] Joan was particularly addicted (3d to 8th) to velar *g*-sounds and to voiceless palatal spirants.[5]

Reprinted from Language *19.281–292 (1943) by permission of the author and the Linguistic Society of America.*

[1] The month during which a given linguistic form was acquired will be referred to by an ordinal number in parentheses.

[2] Cf. A. Grégoire, Bibliothèque de la Fac. de Philos. et Letters de l'Univ. de Liège (1937) and R. Jakobson, *Språkvetenskapliga Sällskapets i Uppsala Förhandlingar* (1940–42), pp. 1–83. Jakobson has gathered all the evidence that can be gleaned indirectly from other works and gives an exhaustive general bibliography (pp. 78–83).

[3] Cf. W. v. Wartburg, *Mél Charles Bally*, 11 (Geneva, 1939): 'Es wird nie möglich sein, das Wesen des Sprachschatzes . . . zu erfassen, solange nicht die alphabetische Reihenfolge ersetzt wird durch ein der Sprache in ihrem jeweiligen Zustand selbst abgelauschtes Darstellunggssystem.'

[4] Cf. A. Grégoire, *Journal de Psychologie*, XXX (1933), 376–78.

[5] During this period, sound may of course be used in a purely expressive function, e.g. to indicate pleasure or displeasure. The following two utterances

At the end of this stage, i.e., with the first appearance of phonemes, the ability to produce a multitude of speech sounds seems to vanish overnight.[6] However, it is of course not a physical ability that has disappeared. The use of distinctive sounds is at first severely restricted because a child does not acquire a phoneme system by random selection or by taking it over ready-made from the language of the adults, but by proceeding, step by step, from the greatest possible phonemic distinction to smaller and smaller differentiations. This process is identical for children of all linguistic communities.[7] That is to say, the relative chronology is the same, although the absolute time scale varies considerably. For some children have acquired the standard phonological system of their parents' speech at the age of eighteen months,[8] while others of equal mental and physical ability do not pronounce certain phonemes until they are six years old or even older.[9] As regards Joan's speech, the growth of the phoneme pattern appears to have been comparatively slow, whereas the expansion of her vocabulary has been relatively rapid[10] (a combination

which accounts for the occurrence of an unusually large number of homonyms; see below).

The order in which the first six phonemes (comprising 15 phonemic oppositions) appear in infant language is the following.[11] (1) The basic pair of phonemes consists of a vowel (usually of the widest opening) and a consonant which is produced by a complete closure of the oral and nasal cavities. (2) The subsequent, and ever narrowing, phonemic distinctions arise through the addition of (a) a continuant, i.e., a sound halfway betwen a vowel and a stop, (b) a second stop sound, (c) a second continuant, and (d) a second vowel. The two continuants are either the nasals m and n or, more rarely, a sibilant and a labial spirant. The first pair of stops is, of course, p–t. The second vowel, which is either i or u, does not appear until this quadrangular system of consonant oppositions has been established, namely (1) $\frac{p\,m}{t\,n}$ or (2) $\frac{p\,f}{t\,s}$.[12]

Joan's speech has the initial pattern (2). Her first words, in chronological sequence, are (end of 11th), *ap* 'up,' *ba* 'bottle, bang'; (12th) *bas* '(omni) bus, box,' *ba·'za*, later *baza'* 'put on,' *za* 'that' (demonstrative or deictic particle); (13th) *da* 'down,' *at* 'out,' *ba·'ba* 'away, outside,' *bat* 'pocket'; (14th) *af*, which after assiduous practice changes to *faf* 'Fuff' (the name of the family cat), *bada'* (replaces *baza'*); (15th) *bus* 'push,' *uf* 'dog' ('woof'), *ba·* 'pie'; (16th) *dat* 'duck,' *bap*[13] 'lamb'; (17th) *am* 'cereal' (i.e. the capital letter M, which the child first discovered on a box of cereal), *an* 'N,' *n̥* (later *un̥*) 'in'; (18th– 20th) *da·* 'doll,' *as* 'S,' *u̥* 'O' (or anything ring shaped, e.g. a tire), *a* 'R,' *nas* 'nice,' *na·'na* 'banana'; (21st) *wa·* 'Y,' *ats* 'X,' *du'du* 'Doudou' (character in a French children's tale; used later as the name of a doll), *hwut*

---

carried over from the babbling stage survived in Joan's speech: (1) *ñañaña* expresses annoyance; it disappears as soon as *nu* 'no' is acquired (22d); (2) *ẽ* (pronounced like French *hein* or the similar interrogative sound often heard in English) is used in response to question to show delight at being the center of interest; it turns into *a·* 'yes' (19th), which is later used as an emphatic or contradictory affirmative particle (like French *si*), after the variants *ha·*, *u·*, *hu·* 'yes' (22d) have been developed.

[6] A period of complete silence sometimes intervenes between the babbling stage and the acquisition of language; cf. E. Meumann, *Die Sprache des Kindes* (Zurich, 1903), p. 23; Jakobson, *op cit.*, p. 16.

[7] There is ample evidence concerning European children (in the territory of Germanic, Romance, Slavic, and Finno-Ugrian languages), as well as American Indian and Japanese children; cf. Jakobson *op. cit.*, p. 32.

[8] Cf. Grammont's remark about his children in a letter quoted by L. Ronjat in *Le développement du langage observé chez un enfant bilingue* (Paris, 1913), p. 57.

[9] See Ronjat, *op. cit.*, p. 58; Jakobson, *op. cit.*, p. 33.

[10] The average number of words a normal child knows at a given age is often quoted in popular works on child psychology. But such figures are all but meaningless because of the enormous individual variation.

[11] Cf. Jakosbon, *op. cit.*, p. 37, and the same author's a paper in V° Congr. Intern. des Linguistes, *Résumés des communications* (Bruges, 1939), p. 28.

[12] In this paragraph I have restated Jakobson's observations in terms which do not alter his basic principle, but take into account a larger measure of initial variation than he allowed for.

[13] A word invented by the child when looking at a picture of a lamb. Since it was adopted by the adults of the household it persisted for many months until it was replaced by *za·b* (27th).

'foot.' Note that—like *p* and *b*, *s* and *z*, *t* and *d*—*hw* (a strongly aspirated *w*-sound) and *f* are allophones of one phoneme, the voiceless form being used in final position only.[14] Initial *f* appears at first only in words which also end in *f*: *faf* 'cat' and (22d) *fuf* 'fish' (with *-f* for *-s* by assimilation). During the latter part of the 22d month, however, *hw*-changes to *f*, and henceforth *f* occurs in all positions.

The small number of morphemes employed so far is entirely out of proportion with the enormous linguistic effort actually expended by the child. The acquisition of the initial vocabulary can be divided into the following (partly overlapping) stages.[15]

(1) The first words are used to accompany action or to call for action. Thus *ap* 'up' (used before the child could walk) signifies 'I am standing up' or 'I want to change my position,' 'I want to be taken out of here'; *ba* 'bottle, cup' means e.g. 'I want my milk' or 'I am having my orange juice'; *baza'* 'put on' is a peremptory command to put the lid on the sugar bowl; *bas* calls attention to a passing bus or expresses a desire to see cars go by;[16] etc.

(2) The *ba*—*bada'* stage, as it may be called, accompanies the unceasing practice of coordinating hand and eye. Everything that can be handled is divided into (a) movable parts that may be joined together, such as boxes with hinged covers, doors and books to be slammed shut, napkins and papers that can be folded over, coats that are to be buttoned, and all kinds of fasteners like buckles, snaps, safety pins, or zippers; and (b) detached parts to be experimented with, which may turn out to have a natural affinity (such as saucepans and lids, cups and saucers, etc.) or not (e.g. shoes and pencils, lamps and ash-

trays). Process (a) is called *ba*, process (b) *bada'* (if successful). This habit does not come to an end until most of the functions of *ba* are taken over (22d) by *zat* 'shut,' *bat* 'button, buckle,' and *nap* 'snap.' *ba* is last heard (30th) in reference to the closing of a safety pin. *buda'* (< *bada'*) disappears when *an* 'on' has become firmly established (23d).

(3) The deictic or *za* stage is a period of incessant linguistic effort (14th–22d). The child will point to an object, saying *za*; then, upon being told that it is, e.g., a clock, she will take me by the hand and insist on inspecting every time piece in the house and on having the name repeated before each one. She does not use the name herself, but her response to questions or requests shows that she remembers them very well—until, toward to end of this stage she suddenly blossoms out with a large active vocabulary. For a considerable time thereafter, she responds to new words elicited by *za* with an insistent *mu·* 'more,' i.e., a demand for more specimens of the same object or being. This process of linguistic identification has been described in many works on infant language. It means simply that the visual world of lights, shadows, colors, surfaces, angles, and outlines is being sorted out into objects by means of language. At first, the child is not at all interested in finding out what the objects with which she is becoming familiar are used for.[17] Nor is there the slightest difference in her reaction to inanimate objects as compared to living beings. (For many months, by the way, *za* refers to persons as well as things, and *fat* [22d] represents 'what' and 'who'—although the child understands *who* and would have no difficulty in pronouncing it.)

(4) The stage of classification (22d ff.), (a) by identifying objects with the persons who use them, (b) by size, (c) by color, and (d) by opposites, involves intricate and overlapping vocabulary patterns (to be described in a separate paper). Stage 4 is characterized by the great frequency of paratactic duplicate

---

[14] Although many children use at first only voiceless oral consonats, this initial phonetic variation of voiced and voiceles sounds is by no means uncommon. Cf. W. F. Leopold's record of his daughter's vocabulary in "Speech Development of a Bilingual Child," *Northwestern University Studies in the Humanities*, VI (1939), which lists voiceless finals, but almost no voiceless initials, except for some interjections.

[15] I wish to emphasize that these stages are based on observations of linguistic behavior. They are not intended to present any psychological or logistic theories whatsoever.

[16] *bas* does not occur in reference to a stationary car until a later stage.

[17] In her play (22d–28th), she uses anything for any purpose. She will, for example, rock a toothbrush to sleep, put a shoe in the oven to bake, and offer food to anything under the sun—a process which reaches its logical limit with the gesture of offering bacon to the eggs. This is not to be confused with a later stage of play when an avowed pretense is made that certain things *represent* other objects or beings.

statements, such as (23d) *za nu· but wut du·—
za zua dud du·'bu* 'that (is) big red chair, that
(is a) little green table' (a remark made upon
seeing a green table, no red chair being present
or having been mentioned). When this habit is
well established, the child sometimes produces
the most far-fetched contrasts. This stage is
mentioned here merely by way of anticipation; for it takes us beyond the period under
discussion.

To return to phonemic matters, from the
very beginning of the slow initial development
(11th–21st), words which introduce a new
sound have at first the character of loan
words. Thus a period of seven months follows upon the appearance of the vowel *u*
before a two-vowel system is established (22d;
see below). Up to then *u* remains a rare and
'foreign' sound (comparable, e.g., to the nasal
vowels of French loan wores in English);
and it occurs at first only in words that have
/u/ or /uw/ in English, whereas later it represents all mid and high vowels. Similarly, the
first morpheme of the structure CVC, *bas*,
does not automatically transform the initial
prosodic system, which renders English CVC
as consonant + short vowel, and English CV
as consonant + long vowel.[18] It is only after
a large number of new words of the type CVC
have been adopted that an old form like *ba*
'bottle' changes to *baz* (22d). Even then, *ba*
'bang, shut' remains unaltered for no less than
18 months, and the demonstrative *za* continues to be used side by side with *zat* 'that';
for from almost every stage of the development some of the most frequently used morphemes are retained without change—just
like the archaic forms[19] that can be traced

in most languages whose history is known
over a certain length of time.

After the 21st month Joan's preference for
closed syllables asserts itself, and the type
CVC outnumbers all others for almost a year.
The structure CVCV is at first often reduced
to CVC, as in *daba* 'grandpa' (22d), which
after a day or two assumes the permanent
form *dap*. English clusters are represented by
a single phoneme, except in the case of final
ts for Engl. [ts, dz, č, j, ks, gz]. Nursery words
of the conventional reduplicated type are rare
in the child's speech since she has never been
taught any such terms, except for *ba·'ba* (which
takes over some of the functions of the earlier
at 'out') and *ma'mma* (24th), which first
occurs (22d) in the compounds *ma'mma-bu·'*
'mother bear' and *ma'mma-da't* 'm. duck'
(appearing in picture books).

Since French and Norwegian are frequently
spoken in the household and used to address
the child (though less often than English),
she acquires at an early date a large passive
vocabulary, and is able to follow fairly complicated directions, in these languages. But
when her general active vocabulary begins to
increase (22d ff.), almost only English words
are adopted; and during the subsequent year
no more than two dozen French and Norwegian words appear in everyday usage
(although a good many more are employed
occasionally), as compared to thousands of
English terms. Normally Joan responds in
English when addressed in French or Norwegian. Morphologically and syntactically
her language is entirely modelled on English,
and phonologically (as regards the development beyond the initial universal stage of
infant language) it is based on her mother's
General American speech.[20] Of the morphemes

---

[18] In the initial stage of many children's speech,
the universal rule that morphemes are composed of
no more than two different phonemes persists even
when 5 or 6 phonemes have been acquired, so that
this prosodic system is retained much longer than in
Joan's speech. The form *da·* 'doll,' by the way, is no
exception, since English final *l* appears as a vocalic
element in the child's language; cf. the section on the
liquids below.

[19] They are, however, not often recognized as such.
To give an example at random, French forms like
époux, jaloux, etc. (which have not undergone the
general change from OFr. [u], i.e. orthographic *ou*,
to Mod. Fr. [ö], orthogr. *eu*) may simply be regarded
as survivals. Thus there would be no need for most
of the elaborate explanations offered in historical
grammars to account for these and similar exceptions
from a given diachronic development.

---

[20] It is well to be wary of attributing individual
particularities in an infant's pronunciation to dialectal
or other special influences. In Joan's language, e.g.,
the high vowel *u* resembled at first a narrow Scandinavian *o*-sound, as in Norw., Swed. *sol* [sω·l] 'sun,'
Swed. *blomma* [blω·ma] 'flower.' I should have been
inclined to ascribe this to Norwegian influence (even
though short [ω] does not occur in in Norweigian) if
I had not heard the identical sound in the speech of
small children who have certainly never heard a word
of Scandinavian. Since this sound changes, by almost
imperceptible stages, to [u], the transcription *u* has
been used from the beginning. It is to be noted that
Joan's *u* and *u·* differ solely in quantity throughout
period described in this paper.

listed above only a few were used to represent French words, such as *ba* 'balle,' *bas* 'poche,' *bat* 'boîte'. Her first Norwegian words appear somewhat later (22d): *mat* for Norw. *mat* [maˑt] 'food,' *dus* for *gris* 'pig,' and *zuwa* for *sove* 'sleep.' Incidentally, *zuwa* is the only word of her language in which *w* follows upon *u;* it later changes to *suwa* (24th), then to *suva* (36th).

During a five-week period beginning early in the 22d month the child's vocabulary increases from 30 morphemes to 150, i.e., if allowance is made for homonyms, from 40 words to over 200. Only 28 of these morphemes contain one or several newly adopted sounds, namely 13 terms with initial *h* given in the comprehensive list below; 6 with final *z* (for Engl. intervocalic liquid and intervocalic *t*), cf. *maz* '(to)morrow' (which soon changes to *maza*), *haz* > *haza* 'Harry,' *baz* 'bottle, butter,' *buz* 'a picture of Napoleon,' *daz* (> *taz* [24th]) 'color,' *waz* 'water'; and 9 with final *b* or *d* (which appear as allophones of -*m* and -*n* in words beginning with consonants or *hu*-), i.e., *bub* 'broom,' *bud* 'spoon,' *dab* 'jam,'

dud 'train,' *fub* 'swim,' *wub* 'room,' *wud* 'rain,' *hun* 'home,' *hub* for Norw. [hun] 'dog.'[21] All other morphemes that appear during this period are composed of the previously acquired 9 phonemes, namely (1) *p/b* for Engl. [p, b, v-], (2) *t/d* for E[t, d, k, g, č-, j-], (3) *f* for E[f, hw-, sw-], [-θ] and [-ð] after labials, and [-v], (4) *s/z* for E[s, š, z, ž], [θ] and [ð] initially and after dentals [l-, j-], (5) *m* for E[m], (6) *n* for E[n, ŋ], (7) *w* for E[w, r-, -v-], and (8–9) the two vowel phonemes. Thus the utilization of all theoretically possible combinations of these 9 phonemes rises, for monosyllables, from 26 per cent to about 86 per cent.[22] Cf. the following list.

ba 'shut'   *da* 'down' (later *daw*)
na   '(French) non'   *za* 'that'

(These are the only four forms with stressed short vowels in open syllables. Such vowels are long in all other words in this list, while closed syllables invariably have short vowels. It will therefore not be necessary to indicate the quantity by means of symbols.)

bu 'bear'	*ba* 'pie'	*fu* 'fall' *fa* 'fly'	*mu* 'more'	*wu* 'wall'	*wa* 'Y'
du 'toe'	*da* 'star'	*zu* 'sole'	*nu* 'no'	*hu* 'hole'	*ha* 'yes'
up 'open'	*ap* 'up'	*uf* (> *wuf*) 'dog'	*af* 'off'	*am* 'arm'	*aw* 'hurt'[23]
ut 'egg'	*at* 'out'	*us* (< *hus*) 'horse'	*as* 'ice'	*un* 'in'[24]	*an* 'on'
uts 'oats'	*ats* 'ants'				
bup 'book'	*bap* 'lamb'	*buf* 'beef'	*baf* 'bath'	*buts* 'peach'	
but 'bread'	*bat* 'bad'	*bus* 'push'	*bas* 'brush'	*bats* 'box'	
dup 'drip'	*dap* 'cup'	*duf* 'stove'[25]	*daf* 'coffee'	*daw* 'towel'	
dut 'coat'	*dat* 'cut'	*dus* 'dress'	*das* 'glass'	*dats* 'touch'	
fup 'sweep'	*fap* 'flop'	*fuf* 'fish'	*faf* 'cat'	*fats* 'fast'	
fut 'foot'	*fat* 'white'	*fus* 'face'	*fas* 'faucet'	*futs* 'fix'	
zup 'soup'	*zap* 'shop'	*zuf* 'leaf'	*zaf* 'laugh'	*zuts* 'seeds'	
zut 'suit'	*zat* 'light'	*zus* 'shoes'	*zas* 'sauce'	*zats* 'socks'	
	map 'mop'	*maf* 'mouth'	*mun* 'moon'	*man* 'man'	
mut 'milk'	*mat* 'mud'	*mas* 'mouse'	*muts* 'mix'	*mats* 'match'	
	nap 'snap'	*nuf* 'sniff'	*naf* 'knife'	*nam* 'thumb'	

---

[21] *h* and -*z* represent additions to the phoneme system, -*b* and -*d* do not—as would appear clearly in a phonemic transcription employing one symbol for each of the allophone pairs, *p/b*, *t/d*, *m/b*, *n/d*, e.g. P, T, M, N. The phonetic directions would merely have to state that P and T are voiced in nonfinal position, and that noninitial M and N are denasalized after oral consonants and *hu*-.

[22] This percentage would be even higher if allowance were made for theoretical combinations which could not possibly represent any English words. As a matter of fact, even some of these are utilized later;

cf. *muf*, which is used as the name of a dress in *muf-dus* (23d).

[23] This is of course an interjection. Its pronunciation indicates that it has the structure VC; later it changes to *awa*, which, like the forms *dawa*, *fawa*, etc., listed below, quite clearly has an open juncture between the first *a* and the *w*.

[24] Final -*ṇ* in *uṇ* and -*ṃ* in *aṃ* 'M' are retained until the 25th month, when they change to -*n* and -*m*.

[25] *f* for Engl. final *v* occurs only during this period; it is later replaced by *w* (zero after *u*), as in *zaw* 'love,' *du* 'stove' (23d).

nut 'neat'	*nat* 'night'	*nus* 'nurse'	*nas* 'nice'	*nan* 'lion'
nats[26] 'lunch'	*wap* 'wipe'	*wuf* 'roof'	*waf* 'rough'	*wuts* 'weeds'
wut 'wet'	*wat* 'rock'	*wus* 'rose'	*was* 'wash'	*wats* 'watch'
hup 'help'[27]	*hap* 'frog'	*hus* 'hose'	*ham* 'ham'	*han* 'hand'
hut 'head'	('hop')		*has* 'house'	*hats* 'high chair'
	hat 'hot'			

There are two forms consisting of a single phoneme, *u* 'ear' and *a* 'eye'; two of the structure VCC,[28] namely *aps* 'apple sauce' (which a few weeks later changes to *abus*) and *daws* 'trousers' (later *dawzas*);[29] but not a single word of the type VCV.

Of the 20 dissyllabic morphemes used in this period, one has the structure CVV, i.e. *zua* 'liver,' later also 'little' (see the section on the liquids below); all others are of the type CVCV or CVCVC, cf.[30] *dawa* 'tower, cover,' *fawa* 'flower,' *bawa*[31] 'bottom,' *hama* 'hammer,' *bubu* 'baby,' *budu* (for earlier *but*) 'pudding,' *dubu* 'table,' *zudu* 'sugar,' *nudu* 'noodle(-soup), naked,' the names *dudu* and *mamma* quoted above, *dabu* 'W' (early 22d; the first morpheme composed of more than three different phonemes), *badu* (replacing *nana*) 'banana,' *buda'* 'put on,' *wabut* (with five different phonemes) 'rabbit,' *babus* '(a picture of) puppies,' *nabud* 'napkin,' *nadaw* 'night gown,' *hamaz* > *hamuz* 'cat food' ('hamburger'). Finally, there must be added the curious name *bub-bu* (taken from the refrain [bum bum] of a Norwegian nursery rhyme) which Joan chooses for herself; the compound *han-bu* 'hand bag'; and the first compound the child forms of her own accord: *faf-daw* 'Fuff towel' (a towel with the picture of a cat). From now on unstressed syllables are, as a rule, no longer completely disregarded, but English posttonic syllabics, including syllabic liquids and nasals, are rendered as *u* (*a* after *w*, *u*, or *z*).

Only one meaning has generally been given for each of the morphemes listed. The following examples will indicate the large number of homonyms represented by some of them.

bat 'black, pat, bark, spot, block, pocket, bought, button, bent, bite'

but 'brick, pig, bead, bed, break, board, boat, bird, put, boot'

bu 'boy, pea, beer, bare, pear, ball, blow, bowl, blue'

nu 'new, knee, near, nail, no'

These examples illustrate, furthermore, the regular correspondence between the child's two vowels and the accented syllabics of English, i.e. *a* = Engl. [æ, a, ɔ, ʌ], [ɛ] before Engl. nasal or liquid [aɪ], *u* = Engl. [ɪ, iˑ], [ɛ] before stop or spirant, [eˑ, ɔr], [ɔl] after Engl. initial oabials, [oˑ, ə·, v, uˑ, ɔɪ, ɪu].

The child's phoneme system and the phonemic structure of English are obviously noncongruent. That is to say, not only does almost every unit of the child's system render several English phonemes, as might be expected, but, conversely, the phonetic variants of a given English unit may appear as different phonemes in the child's language. In the consonant system this fact appears most clearly in the representation of the English liquids. For apart from the 6 examples with *z* for Engl. intervocalic liquid, which survive for 20 months, Engl. *l* and *r* are from now on (23d–42d) consistently represented as follows.

---

[26] Of the forms with initial *n* by assimilation or by transference, only *nam* 'thumb' survives for a considerable time; *nats* and *nan* are soon replaced by *zats* and *zad*.

[27] This word survives for twenty months, although after the end of this period Engl. [ɛl] is rendered as *aw*, as in *bawt* 'belt'.

[28] Except for the morphemes with final *ts* listed so far. Plural forms in *-ts*, such as *wuts* 'weeds', *zuts* 'seeds' (i.e. inedible parts of one's food), have been quoted only if the singular is rare or does not occur in the child's speech. *-ts* for *Eng. -st*, by the way, appears only in the two forms *fats* 'fast' and *wuts* 'waste(-basket)'.

[29] This is the first appearance of *aw* before consonant. *has* 'house', *maf* 'mouth', *mas* 'mouse' are retained for two months before they become *haws*, etc.

[30] The word accent will henceforth be marked only if it is not on the initial syllable.

[31] With *-w-* in place of *-z-*. Assimilation of this type is considered an important characteristic of infant speech by Wundt, Grammont, and Ronjat (18–20; cf. the literature quoted there). The only other instances in Joan's language are the words *bup* and *fuf* quoted above, and the regular use (for over two years) of *f* for Engl. *th* after labials, cf. *baf* 'bath,' *maf* 'mouth,' as over against *dus* 'tooth,' *das* 'cloth'.

z = Engl. pretonic (clear) *l*, as in *zuf* 'leaf,' *zudu* 'lady,' *zat* 'like, lock,' *zap* 'lap,' *buza'd* 'belong.'

z, by the way, also renders French (uvular) *r*, as in *zaw* 'Raoul'; *mazua'* 'Montréal,' i.e. [mõreα'] in French—not French Canadian— pronunciation; *za dad* (24th) 'prends garde' (Engl. *pr-* would be represented as a simple labial stop).

w = (1) Engl. posttonic (dark) *l* after [ɛ, æ, ʌ]; cf. *waw* 'well,' *maw* 'smell,' *baw* 'bell,' *bawt* 'belt,' *dawa* 'jelly,' *zawa* 'yellow,' *saw* (27th) 'shell, shall,' *dawat* 'gallant,' *daw* 'gull'; and after Engl. [wa], as in *wawas* 'Wallace.'

w = (2) Engl. initial *r*, or intervocalic *r* after [a, æ, ɛ], as in *wat* 'right,' *wabu* 'rubber,' *wud* 'ring,' *wuts* 'reach'; *sawa* (24th) 'sorry,' *mawa* 'Mary, marry,' *dawa* 'carry, cherry.'

zero = (1) Engl. final *r* and *r* in clusters; cf. *fa* 'far,' *du* 'door,' *but* 'bread,' *munu* 'morning,' *dat* 'dark.'

zero = (2) Engl. *l* after [ɔ], as in *a* 'all,' *da* 'doll,' *ta* (24th) 'call,' *ta'd* (27th) 'called' (after Engl. initial labials: *bu* 'ball,' *fu* 'fall,' *wu* 'wall'); after [aɪ] as in *fa* 'while'; after [aʋ], as in *aw* 'owl'; and after consonants, cf. *fa* 'fly.'

Both English liquids appear of course as zero after all the vowels which are represented by *u* in the child's speech; cf. *pu* (24th) 'spill, peel, pail, pole, pearl, pull, pool, spoil'; *pua* (26th) 'paring, pouring, purring, pillow, peeler, pulling,' *mua* 'mirror,' *wua* 'worry,' *ua* 'early.' (In all these forms final *a*—for *u* by dissimilation—represents the unstressed syllable.)

The consonant correspondences given so far remain unchanged for 10 months, except for the appearance of a phonemic distinction between voiced and voiceless stops. This process is inseparably connected with a simultaneous vocalic development. It passes through the following 5 stages.

(1) *a'* appears (23d) in stressed closed syllables for Engl. [a], i.e., the General American syllabic of *part, pot, pod;* cf. *da'p* 'top' (as over against *dap* 'cup, cap') *da't* 'dark,' *na'p* 'knob.'[32]

(2) *a'* and *u'* are used (24th) to render all Engl. accented syllabics, except [ɪ] and [ʋ], before Engl. voiced stops and spirants; cf. *ba't* 'bad' (but *bat* 'back'), *ma't* 'mud' (*nat* 'nut'), *wu't* 'red, wade' (*wut* 'wet,' *wuts* 'waste'), *bu't* 'bead' (but *but* 'beat') *nu's* 'nose' (*dut* 'goat'), *fu't* 'food' (*dup* 'coop'). The child's language thus turns the English nondistinctive variation of vowel quantity into a phonemic difference, while still disregarding the distinction between Engl./p, t, k, s/ and /b, d, g, z/—a type of phenomenon that can often be observed in the speech of foreigners. This vowel lengthening process quickly affects the whole vocabulary, but after barely three weeks it is partly reversed in stage (3b).

(3) Three changes occur simultaneously. (3a) Final *b* and *d* are employed (instead of -*p*, -*t*, as heretofore) to represent Engl. voiced stops. This introduces two new phonemes: whereas previously only two of the three labials [p, b, m] or of the three dentals [t, d, n] could be distinguisheed in any given position, it is now possible to differentiate all three, though only when they occur as finals in words with initial nasal or vowel or *ha-*; cf. *mu't* 'meat', *mu'd* 'maid', *mu'n* 'moon,' *u't* 'eat, eight,' *u'd* 'old,' *u'n* 'own,' *hat* 'hat,' *had* 'hug,' *han* 'hen.' The phonemic oppositions concerned are neutralized in all other positions, i.e., /p—b/ and /t—d/ in nonfinal position (cf. *du* 'do, tea, toe,' *bu'du* 'bacon, broken, birdie'), /b—m/ and /d—n/ in words with initial oral consonant or *hu-* (as in *wub* 'rib, rim,' *bud* 'big, bin,' *za'd* 'yard, long,' *babu* 'puppy, bubble, plumber,' *hud* for 'hood' and for Norw. *hun* 'she').

Concomitantly, -*z* (replacing -*s*) is now used for Engl. final [z, ž], as in *nu'z* 'nose,' *hu'z* 'hose,' *wu'z* 'rouge,' a change which does not involve any addition to the phoneme inventory since -*z* had appeared previously (cf. note 21). Final or medial *z* for Engl. intervocalic *t* is retained; and -*z*- is now employed also for Engl. intervocalic /j/, as in *faza* 'fire.'

(3b) *a'* for Engl. [ʌ] and *u'* for Engl. [ɛ], which had become long during stage (2), are shortened again as in *wud* (< *wu't*) 'red,' *mad* (< *ma't*) 'mud.'

(3c) *u* for Engl. [iˑ, eˑ, oˑ, əˑ, uˑ], which had up to now remained short before finals representing Engl. voiceless consonants, becomes *u'* in all stressed syllables; cf. *du's* 'grease, goose,' *zu't* 'lake,' *du't* 'coat,' *hu't* 'hurt.'

---

[32] That is to say, *a'* represents Engl. [a] in all newly acquired words. It has not yet spread to all old morphemes when stage (2) sets in. In stressed open syllables *a* has of course been long from the beginning, except for the four forms, *ba, da, na, za*, quoted above.

To sum up, the changes 1, 2, and 3b–c constitute an extension of phonemic vowel quantity (which had previously applied only to stressed final open syllables, cf. *ba* 'shut,' *ba·* 'pie') and result in the following correspondences.

a = Engl. [æ, ɔ, aɪ] before voiceless consonants; [ɛ] before Engl. liquids or nasals or intervocalic *t*;[33] [ʌ] in any position.

a· = Engl. [æ, ɔ, aɪ] before voiced consonants; [a] in any stressed syllable.

u = Engl. [ɛ] before stop or spirant; [ɪ, ʋ] in any position.

u· = Engl. [ɔl] after Engl. initial labial; [i·, e·, ɔr, o·, ə·, u·, ɔɪ, ɪu] in any stressed syllable.

This system of 4 distinctive syllabics remains unaltered for 9 months; and only one phonetic change is to be recorded for this period (24th–33d). Beginning with the word *sɪt* 'sit,' *ɪ* appears as an allpohone of short *u* before dentals in accented syllables (25th). Accordingly, *fut* 'foot,' *dud* 'good,' *bus* 'bush,' *futs* 'fix,' *udz* 'edge,' *duza* 'dizzy' change to *fɪt*, *dɪd*, etc., while *fup* 'whip,' *fub* 'swim,' *wuf* 'wolf,' etc., retain *u*. A phonemic opposition /u—ɪ/ is not established until the 36th month.

(4) The oppositions /p—b/, /t—d/, and /s—z/ cease to be neutralized in initial position (25th), so that it is now possible to distinguish *pats* 'pencil, pants, plants' from *bats* 'bench, box, blocks,' *tu·d* 'cold, cord, toad, stone, turn, clean, queen, train, chain' from *du·d* 'green, Joan,' *sa·d* 'side, sign, slide, sand, song' from *za·d* 'yard, lawn, lion, line, (a)long,' *pu·bu* 'people, paper, purple' from *bu·bu* 'baby,' *ta·budz* 'cabbage' from *da·budz* 'garbage,' *sa·du* 'shadow' from *za·du* 'ladder,' and many other forms which previously were homonyms.

The changes described under (3a) and (4) are exceedingly rapid and differ from all previous and most later ones in that they leave no residue whatsoever.

(5) The oppositions listed under (4) cease to be neutralized in medial position also (27th); cf. *papu* 'puppy' (*pabu* 'probably'), *nu·tu* 'naked' (*nu·du* 'needle'), *du·sa* 'grocer' (*du·zu* 'daisy'). Note that -*t*- represents Engl. /k/ or /č/ since *z* continues to render Engl.

intervocalic *t*, as in *zazu* 'letter' (27th), *zu·zu* 'later' (28th). This final stage in the process of introducing the phonemic distinction between voiced and voiceless consonants, which is separated from the previous stages by a lengthy interval, takes no less than three months to spread to a major portion of the previously acquired vocabulary.

Simultaneously with the change recorded under (5) there appears the third consonant cluster (after -*ts* and -*dz*) of the child's language, namely final -*st*. For a period of two or three weeks this produces a considerable number of hypernormalisms. For when *pu·s* 'post' changes to *pu·st* (27th), a number of forms with -*s* for Engl. -*s* also change temporarily to -*st*. This phenomenon has frequently been observed in infant language, but in general it does not play an important part in Joan's linguistic development.

The increased use of plurals and the gradual appearance of possessive and third person forms bring into use the further final clusters -*ps*, -*fs*, -*bz*, -*mz*, -*nz*. For this (27th–30th) is a period of rapid morphological and syntactical development. In swift succcession there appear prepositions, demonstratives, auxiliaries, articles, preterite forms, conjunctions, and possessive and personal pronouns. It would seem normal that the first grammatical forms to occur in the language of an English-speaking child should be those with an -*s*/-*z* morpheme. But it is of course impossible to make any general statement about morphological development in infant speech since it is entirely dependent on the morphophonemic structure of the particular language that is being learned. And as regards syntax, only one observation can be made that holds good universally, namely that it begins with complete anarchy. Even when Joan's utterances are as yet restricted to two morphemes (early 22d), there occur such contradictory formations as *hat dap* 'Grandfather's hat,' *pat zu* 'Pat's shoe,' *mut-daf* 'milk (for) coffee,' i.e., 'coffee cream,' *fut-zas* 'food saucer,' i.e., 'a small plate for food'; and shortly thereafter longer statements of an erratic order can be recorded, cf. *as haza waz* 'Harry's ice water,' *buf mamma faf* 'beef mother (gives to the) cat,' *baba nabud wut* 'gone (are the) red napkins'. By the end of the 33d month, however, the syntax of Joan's speech, in which long compound sentences have now become

---

[33] Cf. *baza* 'better,' *faza* sweater,' *zazu* 'letter' (with *u* after *z*, which appears during the 27th month).

quite frequent, is generally in conformity with standard English, and so, on the whole, is the morphology (except for some analogical weak preterite forms).

As to the number of phonemes and words, the child's language has now (30th) 524

tap 'cup, type'	ta·p 'top, stop'	tup 'step'	tu·p 'tape, stoop'
tab 'tub, come'	ta·b 'time, climb'	tub 'Tim'	tu·b 'cream, comb'
taf 'tough'	ta·f 'calf, scarf'	tuf 'stiff'	tu·f·[34] 'tooth'
tat 'cat, cut'	ta·t 'tart, clock'	tɪt 'cook'	tu·t 'take, cake'
tad 'tug'	ta·d 'can, child'	tɪd 'skin'	tu·d 'turn, cold'
tas 'crush'	ta·s 'cloth, cross'	tɪs 'kiss'	tu·s 'case, chase'
taz 'color'	ta·z 'stars, cars'		tu·z 'cheese'
taw 'tell, towel'			

morphemes (= well over 100 words), namely 366 monosyllabic (excluding inflected forms ending in consonant + s) and 158 polysyllabic ones. The following list of morphemes with initial t + VC may serve as a sample.

This represents a utilization of 96 per cent of all possible phoneme combinations. The corresponding figures for the whole vocabulary are: morphemes of the type CVC, 65 per cent; all monosyllables, 62 per cent; type CVCV, 19 per cent. There are only 32 examples of the structure CVCVC(C), and (barring compounds) only 15 forms of more than two syllables, such as tawafud 'telephone,' dawaput 'davenport,' satupud 'centipede,' u·putats 'apricots,' maduzu·'d magazine', subuwɪ't 'cigarette,' tasatu·'t 'street crossing' (literary 'cross the street'). Note that this last word is not, phonologically speaking, a compound in the child's language; cf. on the other hand ta·'fa-tu·'t 'coffee cake,' u·'-pu·'d 'airplane,' ta·'p-tu' 'cocktail' (with p by dissimilation; the cluster pt does not occur within a single morpheme).

The phonological changes which occur during the remainder of the third year may be briefly summarized as follows.

(1) The neutralization of the oppositions /b—m/ and /d—n/ after oral consonants disappears (30th–33d), first in final, then in medial position; and, simultaneously, ɪ appears in unstressed closed syllables (before dentals only, as heretofore); cf. u·pin 'apron,' fa·ma 'farmer,' sa·min 'salmon' (for earlier u·pud, fa·ba, sa·bud).

Nasals appear in clusters, as in antu (< atu) 'uncle,' zasɪns pu·t 'licence plate.'

(2) Three phonemes and one new phoneme combination enter the language (33d–36th), namely (a) ɪ·[35] for Engl. [i·, e·], as in dɪ· 'day,' wɪ·d 'read' (< du·, wu·d); (b) -v, as in zav (< zaw) 'love,' then -v-, as in bɪ·vin (< bu·in < bu·a) 'bathing,' and finally v-, as in vɪndu (< bidu) 'vinegar'; (c) the phonemic opposition /u—ɪ/ appears in unstressed open syllables (but is neutralized in all other positions); cf. du·mɪ 'gloomy,' wɪ·dɪ 'weedy' (compare wɪ·du 'reader'); (d) ɪ appears after a, as in faɪ 'fly, why,' baɪt 'bite,' taɪt 'kite.'

The further development during the fourth year need not be described here since it proceeds according to the same principles as heretofore. But it may be mentioned that during a period of seven weeks (42d–44th) there appear no less than five new vowel sounds (all of which occur as allophones before they become additions to the phoneme system), i.e., in chronological order, e, ɛ, o, ɔ. æ. Shortly afterwards all the child's vowels begin to acquire for the first time the exact phonetic characteristics of the corresponding English sounds. Thus ɪ is raised until it is identical with the syllabic of English meet, while e and o are lengthened and sometimes pronounced with a gilde toward [ɪ] and [v].

To sum up, the analysis appears to show that the development of a child's language may, to some extent, serve as a miniature working model (on a greatly compressed time scale) of diachronic linguistics. Needless to say, this does not mean that infant speech recapitualtes the history of the parents' language or of human speech in general. But the chronological sequence of its structural patterns enables us to observe, within the

---

[34] Occurs only in tu·f-bas 'tooth brush' (with f for s by assimilation).

[35] Pronounced exactly as the vowel in Swed., Norw. le 'laugh'; cf. note 20.

space of a few days or weeks, such phenomena as the transformation of phonetic
variants into phonemes, the treatment of
loan words, the appearance of hypernormalisms, and the survival of forms which have
remained exempt from change.

ANTOINE GRÉGOIRE

22 Grégoire, Professor of Classical Languages at the University of Liège, Belgium,
was the first linguist to publish an exhaustive study of child language. He reported
about the speech development of his two sons during the first two years in
minute detail: "L'apprentissage du langage," (Liège and Paris, 1937). Ten
years later (1947) a second volume followed which continued the study into the
later years, with emphasis on the third year. Whereas the first volume had concentrated on the learning of sounds, the second takes the whole grammar into
account.

The value of the study lies in its completeness and its inventory of linguistic
facts. Taking out a small section as a sample would not do justice to it. The
following article is one that appeared under the title, "L'apprentissage du langage" in the Netherlands, in *Lingua*, I (1948), 162–74. It is a summary of some
of the results of volume II, intended as advance information, but actually delayed until after the publication of the volume. It does not show Grégoire at
his best, but must suffice for an anthology. The article is shortened; omissions
are indicated. Study of Grégoire's whole work is rewarding.

W. F. L.

L'APPRENTISSAGE DU LANGAGE

In 1941 R. Jakobson definitively demonstrated
the importance of child language for linguistics. In his pioneering book he made use of
the data I had collected for the first two years
of each of my two sons.[1] Therefrom he derived
the laws of general phonetics and stated that
they also operate in the primitive stage of
languages as well as in the speech of aphasias,
that is, of patients who have to relearn the
use of sounds and their semantic function.
Winding up his investigation of universal
phonetic principles, the author added that
one would find just as much in the areas of
morphology and syntax. I promised him I
would continue my study of the learning of
my two sons during the third and the following years. . . .

My attention has been devoted especially
to the third year. This year generally[2] stands
out as the stage at which one puts in the hands
of a young virtuoso the instrument which he
will learn to play in order to use it for the rest
of his life. Such a rapid success was hardly
foreseeable after the first two years. Of course,
as early as the first year, perhaps sooner than
one thinks, the child listens to the speech of
the environment with ever increasing atten-
tiveness. After one year his personal chatter
has less interest for him. He is fascinated,
without realizing it himself, by the colloquial
language. He succeeds in acquiring some
words which designate one thing or another
or are suitable for recalling, for requesting
an action, a gesture, a game. As far as conversation is concerned, he uses at the end of

---

Reprinted in translation by the editors from Lingua
*1.162–164, 168–169, 170–172 (1948) by permission of
the North-Holland Publishing Company.*

[1] R. Jakobson, *Kindersprache, Aphasie und allgemeine Lautgesetze* (Upsala, 1941). I have summarized
and appraised this work in an article in the *Revue
belge de philologie et d'histoire*, V, no. 21 (1942),
388–94.

[2] As far as can be determined in view of the scarcity
of other studies of the same kind.

the second year one-element sentences consisting of a single word or a few words which include only one major word. Here is a sample, from the 21st month, of three such communications which my younger son put together: *coco; ti-ng, ti-ng; tu tu.* He says this in the morning, in bed, to express the idea: "I, Coco, hear the sparrows chirp; soon I'll have breakfast with confitures (jam)." During the first six months of the third year puzzles of this kind remain common, but in the meantime several colloquial French sentences are learned. From then on the child commands regular sentences: subject, verb, attribute; pleonastic sentences with double subject: "papa, il travaille" ('Papa, he is working') and especially the other type: "il travaille, papa," and he adds imperative sentences, questions, and exclamations. Subordinate clauses headed by conjunctions (for example "when") do not appear until the last months and then rarely. . . .

At the same stage these children give a more surprising demonstration of their preferences. The phrase which they favor is the following: "les vaches qui courent!" ('the cows which run'). This elliptic expression is not registered in any grammar. The first linguist who called attention to it is the late Albert Séchehaye. He quotes the example which he has heard: "Madame, votre broche qui tombe" ('Madam, your brooch which is falling'), said by a streetcar conductor. This linguist thought the phrase came from child language or from popular speech. That does not mean that it was invented by children or for their benefit. It seems to be so far-spread that it must have appeared in the spoken language long ago.[3]

To summarize: in little more than one year

---

[3] I have not investigated its development. The relative pronoun *qui* ('who') demands a principal clause which exists in the forms "il y a . . . qui . . ." ('there is . . . which . . .'), "c'est . . ." or "ce sont . . . qui" ('it is . . . which'), two emphatic formulas, or as a statement like "vois, voyez" ('see') which is also found in expressions like "voici . . . qui . . ." and especially "voilà . . . qui . . ." ('here is, there is . . . which . . .'). Just the same, it is quite possible that a single exclamation of surprise, of fear, of astonishment like "les vaches!" ('the cows!') is immediately followed by its explanation, "qui courent . . ." ('which run').

the young children have attained a very rich achievement. After the babbling of their first year, unformed, unorganized, often without meaning, they have now mastered varied speech, rich in shading and forcefulness, because they have acquired several of the most expressive modes of speech.

Child phonology. . . .[3a] We examine first two phonetic phenomena which would have led, if the environment had not objected, to two serious omissions in the speech of the two brothers. One of these omissions could have been expected all the more because it has taken place for centuries in a world language like English and in a Romanic dialect, Walloon. Terminal *r* in unstressed position disappears in popular French, in Walloon, and in French influenced by Walloon: *quat'*, in Walloon *qwat'; maît'*, in Walloon *maîs';* in English in words of the type *fa:, fo:* or *foə, fiə* (*far, four, fear*), etc. The same happens in a word-final consonant cluster; cf. Walloon *pwèt'* ("porte"), *cwèt'* ("corde") and even medially, for example *pwètrè* ("porterait"), cf. *pwèrté* ("porter"); in English, *niəli* for *nearly*, pronounced exactly like *really*.

These instances show that the masses, in a distant period, paid little attention to the articulation of a faintly audible consonant which occupied a weak position. Its absence did not obscure the word or its meaning. This is proved by the fact that these words have passed into the normal language.

How did the two children I studied treat that *r* at the time when they endeavored to imitate the pronunciation of their family more accurately? They did not show much interest in the handling of the *r*. The older boy succeeded in paying more and more attention to the consonant before the end of the third year, in general after the seventh month. He owed this relative successfulness to the solicitude with which his parents surrounded him and also to his constant wish to do better. The younger, less supervised, neglected the consonant longer. But at various times he

---

[3a] [In Grégoire's usage, "phonology" includes "phonetic," "morphological," and "syntactic phonology." The omitted paragraph defends this usage. Translator's note.]

profited from the influence of his brother who was his chief teacher in this regard.[4]

Before leaving the above-mentioned consonant, a discrepancy concerning it should be mentioned which is surprising at first glance, but becomes revealing later on. The readers of my first volume remember that at the age of $2\frac{1}{2}$ months the two children produced the groups *ere, re, erere*,[5] repeated to the point of boredom, in an exercise of babbling which lasted several minutes in the case of the older. The *r* survived in such groups until the 14th month with the younger and a little longer with the older, along with the synonymous groups *ram ram*. Now the *r* heard in the beginning stage was precisely the untrilled pharyngeal *r* used in the French of the environment which the children, two years later, had such trouble to reproduce correctly. Why were the groups *ere*, etc., given up and then forgotten completely? Obviously because the hearers did not take up these groups, vague signs of good humor. The children themselves allowed them to disappear.[6]

At the same stage as the *r*, the development of the so-called hissing consonants, *s* and *z*, and of those sometimes called hushing sounds, *sh* and *j* ([š, ž]) also present surprises of a very subtle nature. It takes the children considerable time until these four consonants correspond in their speech exactly enough to the sounds they represent [!] in French.

---

[4] The acquisition of *r* amounts to a long, patient conquest. The progress is described in detail in my forthcoming book. I mention here one fact, selected from the more interesting ones. A phonological need guaranteed the presence of the *r* in the forms of the future. No form with hiatus, as would be *fea* for "fera" ('will make') has ever been heard. The end of the third year is also the time when the future gains ground.

[5] Later on trilled uvular *r* was added and even trilled labial *r* (in the cluster *br*).

[6] What is the explanation for the unexpected skill of the children in producing the *r* spontaneously shortly after their birth? In the first volume I have claimed a physiological reason. The normal position of the baby at this stage is to lie on his back. The breath strikes the walls of the pharynx. They are slightly contracted or simply narrowed. Under the influence of the friction of the air they produce the fricative of *ərə*. As for the *ə*, it is the neutral vowel, approximately the same in French, German, and English.

Let me first emphasize the following fact: if a language contains these four consonants and if the two groups have approximately the same frequency, as is the case in French, one notices very early the astonishing number of confusions which occur in the use of the two groups. One also finds that these exchanges tend to favor the hissing sounds: they are preferred to *ch* and *j*. If the educator did not resist these tendencies their fate would be decided. The hushing sounds would be in danger of giving way to the hissing sounds. The latter have the advantage over the former of being a perfectly clear hiss. The articulation is not complicated on either side, but the speaker tends to exchange them, with unfortunate results. His hearing is not always sufficiently acute to make him watch his step. It is well known that many people lisp. Many *s* and *z* sounds resemble poorly articulated *ch* or *j* sounds. Actually, most of the time the tongue tip, which is normally lowered behind the alveoles of the lower teeth, is placed behind the upper alveoles or at least between the two rows of teeth.

The number of lispers is thus thought to be considerable. Just the same, if exact counts were made, ... persons with speech defects who mispronounce *ch* and *j* are [!] at least as numerous as those who lisp, but ordinarily people criticize their defect less than they condemn the one which affects *s* and *z*.

Actually observers notice that current words like "déjà," "jamais," "le chat" are pronounced as if they were spelled *déjyà, *jyamais, *chya; that is to say, *ch* and *j* are more and more palatalized...

The preceding examples deal with phonetics. It is obvious that there is much similarity between child language and primitive or popular speech. The same relationship exists for morphology and syntax. I shall present some examples selected from the most original ones.

The goal toward which the child strives, especially from the third year on, is to acquire the language of the environment. But he does not accomplish the task in the manner of a parrot who succeeds phonetically without understanding anything. The child knows what he is saying (except for error, which is of course always possible). But he is an individual; he is himself, endowed with faculties which he applies. He is not afraid of displaying them unless his educators instill fear in him. Besides, numerous occasions, when his desire for action can operate, exist in all languages of the world, at least in the Indo-European languages and their descendants. None of them is without obscurities, complications, lack of uniformity, exceptions, annoying difficulties, even inconsistencies. Such irregularities, most commonly remnants of earlier layers, confuse the child. He resorts to a simplification of the divergences as much as he can, yielding without being told, to powerful analogies, true or false. Whole nations have done the same and continue to do so, but on a much more limited scale, because of the written language, of more and more wide-spread education, and the spirit of teaching, which is generally conservative and sometimes timorous. Because of his youth the child hardly feels fear. He operates with the bold freedom of a novice apprentice. It does not enter his mind that he might be making mistakes; he is guided by logic—elementary, to be sure, because of the absence of factual knowledge.

(1)   In my first book I discussed the feeble role which the articles play, especially the definite article, with which the two children still have difficulty, even the older one.[7] This lack of interest in expressing it causes the special confusions called agglutination and apheresis. Phenomena of this kind extend throughout the third year and, accidentally, even beyond. In the beginning the most common words like "oeuf" ('egg') "âne" ('donkey'), "arbre" ('tree'), "oiseau" ('bird'), "église" ('church') show how vague the impression was which the articles made on their minds by the fact that they became attached to the nouns. These words become disguised in their initial by an n or a z (the s of the plurals les, des) or by an added t (after "grand," "méchant," etc.). Here is a little scene observed accidentally, without coaching. The older boy is corrected not with reference to the article, but to improve the termination

-rbr(e). The child says at first "(re)gardez le grant arpe" ('look at the big tree'), employing the usual linking. He repeats: "gardez le z-abe," then again "le beau z-abe" ('the pretty tree'), which he changes into "le beau t-arbe." Upon being questioned further concerning the word he returns to an initial z: "c'est un z-arbre" ('this is a tree') and then resumes the t. At the beginning of the fourth year he still said "un petit n-arpe" ('a little tree') (because of un-n-arbre), "le grand n-arpe" and even "au l'arpe" ('to the tree').

(2)   La and là are phonetically identical, but they are separated by many features. The article is weak as has been seen; it is reduced to l' in l'alaisse and is even incorporated in "une l-alaise." The adverb là remains stable at all times in child language, being protected by its meaning ('there') and by its relative independence.

But children indulge in bold constructions of which we disapprove by habit and which we call mistakes. The following ones nevertheless demonstrate coincidence of functions or meaning which the little ones notice. It induces them to treat the two words là and ça too much alike. They even make them synonyms, as in the expression "accroché à là" ('hooked on to there') which would normally be "accroché à cela" or "à ça" ('to that'). In this last example, ça plays the part of a noun. The child draws a conclusion from that: he uses it as such, with the article, saying: "moi, je vais (re)ga(r)der le ça" ('I am going to look at the that') (namely, the pretty thing here).[8] The adverb là which we just saw as an equivalent of ça, also gets its turn, in the expression "su(r) là" ('on there,' namely, on the water), said in the second month of the third year. It reappeared four months later: "pas su(r) là" ('not on there').

(3)   The pronominal part of French grammar, in spite of the simplifications which have improved it, compared to Latin, still contains so many peculiarities that children two years old do not easily acquire a complete knowledge of it. The older of the two children, who always tries to do well, is guilty of excessive logical exactness with regard to the forms

---

[7] The more conscientious of the two and the only one at this stage, thus he is more supervised and guided.

[8] The object in question is a pretty paper knife. The handle is a very small imitation doe leg made of horn, with real fur.

of the relative pronoun.[9] The sentence in question is "toute la chaudière *qui* tombe!" ('the whole kettle which is falling!'). The child who knows this type of expression, as we have seen, creates this example himself, but modifies the *qui* as follows: "toute la chaudière *qu'elle* tombe" ('. . . that it falls'). Gender has never been discussed with him, neither for the feminine nor for the masculine, but he knows when a kettle is involved one says "*elle* tombe" ('she falls')[10] like "*une grande* chaudière" ('a big kettle,' fem.).

(4) The system of conjugations is quite a problem in spite of the numerous and important simplifications which the spoken language has introduced into it, in the forms as well as the tenses, moods, and voices. During the third year the trend is well established so that the children follow the easy model of the first conjugation for the irregular forms or types of forms which burden the others. To mention just one example, the infinitive *buver* [instead of boire 'drink'], already recorded by R. de Gourmont as existing, is found again, reinvented by the younger boy.

The older, who is quicker in acquiring the forms which are considered correct, errs in a different way. He submits less easily to the conjugation of verbs which combine several roots of disparate appearance. The best example of it is "je vais—nous allones—j'irai" ('I go—we go—I shall go'). . . The child naturally favors "aller." He derives from it a regular future "nous *allerons*,"[11] eliminating the isolated root of which "irai," etc., are the sole remnants.

---

[9] The most dangerous pronoun of all for beginners, no matter what their language.

[10] H. Frei, in *La grammaire des fautes*, p. 189, cites cases of *qu' elle* for *qui* gathered from the letters of prisoners of war, e.g. "ce n'est pas ma soeur *qu'elle* écrit" ('it is not my sister that she writes'). [In the colloquial language "qu'il" can be pronounced like "qui." Thus the change to "qu'elle" (fem.) from "qu'il" (masc.) can be considered an instance of hypercorrectness. Translator's note.]

[11] H. Frei does not mention this neologism with regard to the verb "aller" in the popular correspondence which he has examined.

(5) Reflexive verbs seem very convenient to us; we could not do without them. But they carry with them the great difficulty of the reflexive pronouns, and the child does not find his way through them. The simple verb can sometimes play the part of the reflexive verb: *i sauffe, papa* (= "papa se chauffe," 'Papa warms himself'), says the child of two and a half years as well as *le chat chauffe* ('the cat warms'—behind the glass, in the sun) and *la boisson* "chauffe" ('the beverage warms, becomes warm'). In French there are verbs with transitive and intransitive meaning (be the shade of meaning passive or reflexive) such as: "on peut *varier* la couleur; la couleur *varie*" ('onê can change the color; the color changes'); "son humeur *varie* tout le temps" and even "il *varie* tout le temps" ('his mood always changes; he always changes'). . . The older boy creates for himself without trouble a convenient concept of certain verbs by making their semantic and grammatical function flexible without impairing their clarity. For example, for months he uses the everyday verb *lever* ('to rise') by giving it the meaning of "se lever," "levez-vous" ('get up') or of "levez-moi" ('lift me' out of my chair), not counting the meaning "faire (se) lever" ('make get up'). It took him a long time before he adopted the reflexive construction. At the beginning of the fourth year he even invented a reflexive verb by widening the meaning of the verb: "tu vas *te mourir!*" ('you will die yourself,' i.e., "te tuer," 'kill yourself').

(6) During the third year the children usually accomplish the important task of assimilating part of the common vocabulary. What they had learned during the preceding years was minimal, for words noted when heard: the older boy 132 words, the younger 113. The following year yielded more. The older boy attained a total of 1293 words. This figure is a little higher than the average which Stern and his wife have established by combining a certain number of other counts published earlier. Their average lies between 1000 and 1100 words. . . .

23 About the author and his work see above in the introductions to the selections on "The Study of Child Language and Infant Bilingualism" and to "Patterning in Child Language".

The present selection on "Semantic Learning in Infant Language" is a more detailed treatment of a topic that was included in the third volume of his *Speech Development of a Bilingual Child*, which was published in the same year.

A. B. A.

SEMANTIC LEARNING
IN INFANT LANGUAGE

The literature of child language is full of discussions concerning the growth of 'concepts.' Preyer made it the center of his careful factual record,[1] and many writers since his time have debated the problem, arguing for or against him, or attacking it independently. Stern[2] is one of those who have tried to come closer to a solution by establishing a hierarchy of concepts of different scope: individual concepts, plural concepts, general generic concepts.

Essentially this whole discussion is a fight about terms and their definitions. There are several different levels of concepts, with varying degrees of abstractness and precision, in the language of adults. We must obviously expect the small child's concepts to be less abstract and less precise than the maturest concepts of adults. But it must also be emphasized that many of the working concepts of adults on an everyday level are imperfectly circumscribed and differ from a child's concepts only in degree of vagueness. Also, the belief that any words have sharp, logical, unified, unvarying meanings in the developed language is a superstition which has been exposed for a long time, but which is slow to die. Erdmann showed nearly fifty years ago[3] that the meaning of words, regarded descriptively, varies from situation to situation, and that there is hardly any word, even in the reaches of scholarly language, for which one definition is invariably correct.[4]

Lewis[5] stresses the fact that the semantic categories of adults as of children are practical, functional rather than scientific. Otherwise, the fact that not only children's words, but the words of adults as well, have a wavering and ill-defined reference, is not

---

Reprinted from Word 4.173–80 *(1948) by permission of the Linguistic Circle of New York, Inc. Volumes 3 and 4 of Leopold,* Bilingual Child, *mentioned in the notes as forthcoming, appeared in 1949.*

[1] W. Preyer, *Die Seele des Kindes* (Leipzig, 1882; seventh ed., 1908); *The Mind of the Child* (New York, 1888–89). I cite the second volume of the English edition. Preyer's work is a classic in the field of child-language study.

[2] Clara und William Stern, *Die Kindersprache* (Leipzig, 1907; fourth ed., thoroughly revised, 1928). This comprehensive monograph aims at combining the linguistic with the psychological approach. It is still the most important book on most aspects of child language.

[3] Karl Otto Erdmann, *Die Bedeutung des Wortes* (Leipzig, 1900; fourth ed. 1927). I used the third edition, 1922.

[4] The school of descriptive ('general') semantics, which has recently succeeded in capturing the attention of educated laymen in this country, has resumed the work of dispelling the fog of linguistic superstition by pointing out the haze of meaning in which words are enveloped. This part of its endeavor is a valuable contribution to a better appreciation of the language tool. The public is beginning to see that abstract words like *democracy, individualism, reactionary* have a diffused semantic content and appeal less definitely to the intellect than they seem to do at first glance. Erdmann makes it clear that this consideration applies as well to simpler words which are within the child's range of experience. Cf. Leo Weisgerber, *Muttersprache und Geistesbildung* (Göttingen, 1929), pp. 62–66.

[5] N. M. Lewis, *Infant Speech* (London, 1936), p. 220. This is one of the best books on child language by nonlinguists.

often faced in the discussion of children's concepts.[6]

The views concerning children's concepts range all the way from acceptance of a 'great of generalizaion'[7] to denial of the existence of concepts until after several years; the application of one word to a variety of situations is then explained by the poverty of the vocabulary and the operation of vague associations.[8] Many authors distinguish between child 'representations' and adult 'notions'[9] or recognize variations in the precision and scope of concepts.[10] The growth of concepts beyond the range of active vocabulary is emphasized by Cohen, Preyer, and Müller.[11] The best summary of studies of children's concepts up to 1929 is that of Köhler [see footnote 6].

I abstain from adding to the abstract discussion of 'concepts,' which is rather

fruitless as long as this vague word is not clearly defined. I turn instead to a consideration of meanings behind the words used by my daughter Hildegard, whose language-learning I have studied in detail.[12] My experience confirms that caution is necessary in the interpretation of the fact that words are used in a wide range of applicability. Hildegard and her younger sister Karla both made excessive use of the word *pretty*, not because a strong power of abstraction allowed them to subsume a great number of impressions under one abstract concept, but because they lacked specific terms for many things and had to be satisfied with a vague emotional reaction. Karla dropped, Hildegard reduced the use of *pretty* as soon as a more adequate vocabulary had been acquired.[13]

Hildegard was from birth exposed to two languages, English and German, simultaneously, and built her own early speech from selected vocabulary items from both languages. This situation enables us to see that in her case meanings and their phonetic means of expression did not form an indissoluble unit. There were numerous instances in which she used words from both languages, simultaneously or successively, for the same purpose.[14] In view of the crudeness of the linguistic system which she built up in the first two years, it would be quibbling to claim that such pairs of words did not cover exactly the same ground. She used English *hot* and German *heiss* exchangeably at 1.8.[15] She answered the challenge, "Say 'no more'," instantly with 'no mehr' 1.9, keeping the familiar English *no*, but substituting her active German word for the merely understood

---

[6] A good passage from E. Winkler, *Grundlegung der Stilistik* (Bielefeld and Leipzig, 1929) is cited by Elsa Köhler, *Kindersprache und Begriffsbildung* (Jena, 1929), p. 202 f. Cf. Wilhelm Ament, *Die Entwicklung von Sprechen und Denken beim Kinde* (Leipzig, 1899; reprint, 1912), pp. 32 f., 149–51, 155.

[7] H. Taine, "Note sur l'acquisition du langage chez les enfants et les peuples primitifs," *Revue philosophique*, I (1876), 3–23, according to Preyer p. 226. Cf. Köhler, p. 178.

[8] Wilhelm Wundt, *Völkerpsychologie*, vol. I, part 1 (Leipzig, 1900; fourth ed., 1921; I quote from the third edition, 1911), 301f. Leopold Treitel, "Haben kleine Kinder Begriffe?" *Archiv für die gesamte Psychologie*, III (1904), 345; Edward Conradi, "Psychology and Pathology of Speech Development in the Child," *Pedagogical Seminary*, XI (1904), 341–44.

[9] R. Cousinet, "Le rôle de l'analogie dans les représentations du monde extérieur chez les enfants," *Revue philosophique*, LXVII (1907), 162.

[10] K. Reumuth, *Die logische Beschaffenheit der kindlichen Sprachanfänge* (Leipzig, 1919), according to Köhler, p. 194. D. Usnadze, "Die Begriffsbildung im vorschulpflichtigen Alter," *Zeitschrift für angewandte Psychologie*, XXXIV (1919), 138–212, according to *Zeitschift für Psychologie* no. 122 (1931), 152. Henri Delacroix, *Le langage et la pensée* (Paris, 1924; second ed., 1930), p. 299. W. Nausester, "Die grammatische Form der Kindersprache," *Zeitschrift für pädago gische Psychologie*, VIII (1906), p. 228. E. Meumann in a book review, *Archiv für die gesamte Psychologie*, XI (1908), 158 f.

[11] Marcel Cohen in a discussion of a paper by Oscar Bloch, *Journal de Psychologie*, XX (1923), 637. Preyer, p. 92. Paul Müller, "Die Begriffe der Sechsjährigen," *Archiv für die gesamte Psychologie*, no. 72 (1929), 117.

[12] Werner F. Leopold, *Speech Development of a Bilingual Child; "A Linguist's Record* (henceforth cited as *Bilingual Child*): vol. I, "Vocabulary Growth in the First Two Years" (Evanston, 1939); vol. II, "Sound-Learning in the First Two Years" (Evanston, 1947; *Northwestern University Studies in the Humanities*, nos. 6, 11). This article consists of selected sections from vol. III, "Grammar and General Problems in the First Two Years," which is forthcoming in the same series.

[13] Erdmann, pp. 196–98 makes a valuable distinction between abstracts of a lower order which result from intellectual vagueness, and abstracts of a higher order which result from intellectual discipline.

[14] *Bilingual Child*, I, 176–79.

[15] 1.8 means at the age of 1 year and 8 months.

English *more*. She heard the remark, 'Look at the cars,' and reacted with the word 'Auto,' German by the test of her pronunciation, 1.10, to show us that she had understood. She used German *nass* and English *all wet* as synonyms 1.10 and once uttered the hybrid *all nass*. Although such amalgamations proved that her bilingualism had not reached the stage in which she disposed of two separate language instruments, they showed that something had developed behind her words which was not simply identical with their phonetic complex or indissolubly tied to it. In fact, it is one of the advantages of bilingualism that the child was at no time the slave of words; she always focused her attention on the sense behind the phonetic configurations. A strict behaviorist would have to assume that the use of two different linguistic signs discloses a difference in the purpose or functional value of the utterances. Such a conclusion would be manifestly absurd when applied to the bilingual synonyms in Hildegard's language. English *come on* meant exactly the same thing, or served the same purpose, as German (*komm*) *mit*!, even though the German version seemed to consist only of a preposition or adverb.

Thus Hildegard disposed of meanings which could be detached from the phonetic words used to express them in one language and attached to different words of the other language. Meanings which existed apart from fixed phonetic representations may well be called concepts, provided that the definition of a concept for this purpose is held down to a level corresponding to the child's development.

I shall leave aside the semantic aspects implicated in the formation of grammatical categories. The latter represent forms of thinking and as such overlap with one of the domains of semantics. A sharp line of demarcation cannot be drawn. The term 'plural concepts,' which has been used for the definition of one kind of noun concepts, throws a light on the contact which exists between semantic and grammatical categories. A concept which includes several individuals of the same kind in the semantic domain of a word is not far removed from a grammatical pattern which serves to designate several individuals of the same kind. For method-

ological reasons, however, a separation of these overlapping areas is necessary.[16]

In examining Hildegard's vocabulary under the aspect of meaning, it is necessary to keep in mind that meanings are necessarily hazy and vague at first; that the dearth of vocabulary compels the child to use words for purposes to which they are not adapted from the adult point of view; and that meanings become progressively sharper and closer to the standard. This process is parallel to the gradual refinement of the phonetic and syntactic systems, although the progress is in most areas less easily definable than the evolution of contrasting phonemic series.[17]

The names of colors are interesting because Hildegard distinguished colors without really learning to name them during the first two years. At 1.8 I called the last empty pages of her picture book 'weiss.' Her reaction was: 'Schnee? No!' She associated the word for 'white' with snow, and apparently only with snow; she was puzzled that the word was used for something that was obviously not snow. During 1.9 I often presented the names of colors to her, usually when we looked at pictures together. Sometimes she assorted her building blocks by shape and color. Once when she had assembled green blocks, I told her to add the remaining green ones. She did so and stated correctly, with the German word 'alle!' that there were no more of this color. Then she showed me a white one, and I named the color for her. At once she brought another one of the same color and echoed excitely, 'weisser!' This word, premature also in the reproduction of the adjective ending, was the only name of a color which she said to the end of the second year, and it remained a nonce word.[18] She did use *light* and *dark* 1.10, and *dunkel*, the German equivalent of *dark*, two months earlier; but they would hardly be called color names, and were not used as such.

Thus a conception of colors had begun to develop, but they were not expressed linguistically. She used the classifying prin-

---

[16] The learning of plurals will be treated in *Bilingual Child*, III, §567.

[17] For the phonemic development, see *Bilingual Child*, II.

[18] Her sister Karla learned to name several colors 1.10; cf. *Bilingual Child*, I, p. 129, note 273.

ciple of colors in acts, but not in words. She had grasped it by means of words which she heard, but it existed in her detached from any active phonetic forms. Her behavior proved the existence of a set of concepts which were not indissolubly linked with movements of the organs of articulation.[19]

In other areas of the infant vocabulary, every observer notices that the meanings which the child attaches to words taken over from the standard do not at once agree with the standard. Meanings are learned gradually, just as phonetic forms are.

Complete failures are rare (and therefore striking), particularly in the case of a child like Hildegard, who was cautious in the use of new words and did not attempt to incorporate them into her vocabulary until she felt some confidence that she could cope with them phonetically and semantically. There is nearly always some agreement between the standard meaning and the child's meaning; but the outlines of the latter are often less sharp than those of the former, even considering the fact that standard meanings themselves are less stable than the naive observer is inclined to think.

Chambers[20] has a neat metaphor to illustrate the haziness of meaning and the growth in clarity. The child's intellectual landscape is like a meadow in a dense fog. Near-by objects are clear. Those next removed in distance are dim. Remote ones are in a light of mystery. Beyond that lies the great unknown. 'The child unquestionably perceives the world through a mental fog. But as the sun of experience rises higher and higher these boundaries are beaten back.' 'The inexperienced user of a new word chops now on one side, now on the other side of the line.'[21]

Several authors attempt to break down the growth of semantic precision into categories.

One aspect of this process is the progress from predominantly emotional and volitional tinge to clearer and clearer objective reference, which has perhaps been analyzed best by Lewis.[22]

Considering the types of words used rather than the purpose of the whole utterance, Bloch[23] makes the point that proper names are the first to have exact meaning.[24] That is to be expected, because the variability of reference of standard words applies least to names. Still, even in this domain, children's usage is not without vacillation. Bloch himself excepts *Papa* and *Mama*, which are rather late in having exact meaning, not because the child recognizes the shifting reference of the words in standard usage, but because he extends their application for a while to all men and women regardless of their relationship to any other person; Hildegard did this with 'Papa' for one month 1.2–3. For four months, 1.5–9, she called an older girl, who visisted her occasionally, by her name, Rita, but used the same name for Rita's friend Helen. The latter never came without Rita, and since the two girls' position in her life was of merely incidental importance, she felt no need for separately identifying names until a later time, when the progressing refinement of linguistic thinking granted Helen her own distinctive name, although her importance remained peripheral.

The association between separate semantic units and corresponding separate phonetic complexes is much less close in child language than it is in standard languages. The linguistic accident of homonymy is a restricted phenomenon in the latter, whereas it plays a considerable part in child language.[25] Unless the history of each child form is established carefully, observers are likely to be misled by homonyms into assuming many more instances of unorthodox handling of

[19] The section on colors (596) is followed in *Bilingual Child*, I, by an examination of numerals, abstracts, original word formation, paraphrases, child etymology, original creation (597–603).

[20] W. G. Chambers, "How Words Get Meanings," *Pedagogical Seminary*, XI (1904), 30 ff.

[21] The same article presents an interesting demonstration of the haziness and the growing clarity of the meaning of selected words at a later age. Cf. Robert Macdougall, "The child's speech," *Journal of Educational Psychology*, IV (1913), 34.

[22] Lewis, pp. 143 ff., 212, 221. Much about this aspect is incorporated in the discussion of syntactic growth, *Bilingual Child*, III, §§507–41.

[23] Oscar Bloch, "Les premiers stades du langage de l'enfant," *Journal de Psychologie*, XVIII (1921), 706. This linguist's articles are among the best studies of child langauge.

[24] Cf. Ov. Decroly, *Comment l'enfant arrive a parler* (Liège, 1933), p. 121.

[25] *Bilingual Child*, II, §§458 f. gives an extensive, list of Hildegard's homonyms; cf. also I, p. 172 f.

meaning than necessary.[26] Many solutions remain problematic at best. Much that happens in children's language learning can only be surmised. The processes of the acquisition of the speaking faculty, interesting as their study is for general linguistics, are anything but simple and obvious. Casual references to child language, often delivered with naive confidence even by linguistic scholars, cannot be trusted.

The learning of meanings is both similar to, and different from, phonetic, morphological, and syntactic learning. As the child gropes for the exact phonetic form and learns to imitate it with growing exactness, he keeps on widening and restricting meanings, until they coincide with the standard model, with many failures along the way. Semantic learning is much more difficult, because the standard language itself is arbitrary in the range of applications which it allows for different words, and shifts meanings with the context, whereas the phonetic material of word stems is relatively fixed and tangible. It is more difficult, too, than the learning of morphological devices and of means to express syntactic relationships, because these devices are limited in number. Yet, the learning of meanings begins much earlier, because words without meanings are useless for the purposes of communication. A primitive communication can be achieved without morphological elements, but not without meanings somewhat related to the standard ones.

The child learns a word as applied to a certain situation, but not, as a rule, from a single application. The word occurs again and again in situations which are similar, but not completely identical. When the child is able to grasp the similarity of a situation with one previously experienced, the word connected with it will eventually emerge from memory, first passively, later actively.[27] In learning to group different situations under the same phonetic complex, the child tries to follow the same procedure as the standard speakers, but does not always succeed at once. 'A child is often faced by some linguistic usage which obliges him again and again to change his notions, widen them, narrow them, till he succeeds in giving words the same range of meaning that his elders give them.'[28] This process must be grouping and the way beset with failures, caused not only by the lack of experience on the part of the child, but also, it cannot be said too often, by the arbitrary and accidental practices of the standard language.

Let us present a few examples. If a child hears the word *brush* applied to a hair brush, many repeated occurrences in the same connection will bring about a firm association between the word and the object. The word is however also used for a clothes brush, for a shoe brush, and even for a toothbrush; the distinguishing prefix is omitted at least in the corresponding verb, which, in English, has the same form. The child must at first be puzzled by the use of the same word for so many objects or uses, when these objects differ greatly in shape, size, even material: shoe brushes are often made of lamb's wool. Since each of these uses occurs many times, always linked with the same word, the child will learn to associate the word with all of them and will perhaps eventually understand subconsciously that the similarity lies in the function. Let us assume then that the child sees a painter's brush for the first time, knows no word for it and calls it *brush*, because the function is again similar and the shape immaterial. He has performed an extension of meaning, which will evoke no comment from the English-speaking observer, because his language does the same. Let a German-speaking child perform the same extension of meaning, and the adults will laugh, or think the utterance odd, because standard German calls the first-named objects *Bürste*, but the painter's brush *Pinsel*.[29] As a further

---

[26] Change of meaning and overlapping of homonyms must be kept apart in semantic analyses of standard words as well; cf. Hans Sperber, *Einführung in die Bedeutungslehre* (Bonn and Leipzig, 1923), p. 87.

[27] The priority of comprehension over speaking will be dealt with in *Bilingual Child*, III §§643–37.

[28] Otto Jespersen, *Language* (London and New York, 1922), p. 117.

[29] At 5.3, while in Germany, Hildegard actually used *Bürste* instead of *Pinsel;* cf. *Bilingual Child*, IV, "Diary from Age Two" (forthcoming), §869; but by that time it was probably not an original extension, but English influence. A good example of similar import, based on an observation of Stern's, is given by Lewis, pp. 191, 212.

step, the disapproval of the adults will of course induce eventual correction of the misapplication; but the fault of the intermediate mistake is not the child's.

On the other hand, when the child uses one and the same word for a handkerchief, a towel, and a napkin, as Hildegard did, the adults do not approve, although the function of wiping parts of the body links these objects more closely than brushes are linked by their functions. In fact, in this case German can use one word, *Tuch* 'cloth', for all three of them: *Taschentuch*, *Handtuch*, sometimes *Mundtuch*. Shape and material offer no sufficient inducement for distinction. How is the child to know at once that in this case the slight differences in function call for entirely different words?

The standard languages use the word *glass* both for the material and for objects made of it: drinking glasses within the small child's range of experience; other objects like eye glasses, spy glasses, magnifying glasses, etc., on higher levels. In Hildegard's early language, the word *bottle* covered at one time a similar semantic range. She used it for several kinds of objects made of glass. Of course, the adults did not approve of this extension of meaning. The child was right in taking a clue from the material for the definition of a bottle; but she had to learn that shape and function also enter into it. The shape of bottles varies greatly. When Hildegard called a vaseline jar a bottle, she had the criteria of material and shape on her side and was not far from the truth with regard to function. The separate word *jar* for this purpose is a linguistic luxury for which the young child could not have the appropriate appreciation.

If the child learning to speak used for each object exactly the word which the standard speakers use for it, in close imitation, no semantic mistakes would occur; but the ability to speak would be greatly hampered. To simplify the learning process and to extend the range of expressible experiences, the child must form his own semantic clusters. Mistakes attest the independent linguistic operations of the child, which lead more rapidly to real speech than pure imitation, in spite of the lost motion of mistakes. As in the domains of morphology and of word formation, independent applications of standard principles with nonstandard results are doomed to eventual extinction, as the relentless corrective force of the standard language ideal imposes itself on the child's speech.[30]

As the vocabulary grows, each item needs to embrace less and less semantic territory; or, expressed in reverse, as meanings become more sharply defined, more and more words are needed to express the meanings now excluded from the semantic sway of words in the earlier, limited vocabulary. Addition to the vocabulary and reduction of individual semantic complexes are two facets of one process. Both are features of the progressive mastery of the standard model. It is best not to assign priority to either of them. At early stages, rough classifications suffice. With advancing maturity, finer subdivisions are needed, and new words are learned to satisfy the urge for expressing them.

The process is parallel, in its general outlines, to the learning of sounds, grammatical forms, and syntactic constructions. The material to be learned is taken over in an organization which reproduces at first only the crudest outlines of the standard organization. Little by little, finer classifications of the standard are recognized and reproduced. This requires the addition of more and more items of vocabulary, which cover less and less semantic territory. The outlines of the areas to which each word is applicable become more and more distinct, and coincide progressively with standard practice.

The tangible progress from a single series to two contrasting series and later to finer subdivisions applies less clearly to semantics than it does to sounds and syntax. The only semantic area in which it can be followed

---

[30] Semantic learning is of course not limited to infant language. For uncommon words it continues through life. Ernst Tappolet, "Die Sprache des Kindes," *Deutsche Rundschau* no. 131 (1907), p. 405, shows that the meaning of the relatively common verb *sell* was still too restricted in the language of a six-year-old child, who protested that houses cannot be sold because they cannot be carried away. The following sections of *Bilingual Child*, III (608–32) explore in detail the changes of meaning (extensions and restrictions) operating in the child's language.

definitely is that of opposites,[31] in which the standard languages themselves show the

[31] *Bilingual Child*, III §§625–27. H. V. Velten, "The Growth of Phonemic and Lexical Patterns in Infant Language," *Language*, XVIX (1943), 281–92, sees the problem; but his child was so slow in learning to speak that the article is much more enlightening with regard to the growth of phonemic patterns than with regard to the problem at hand.

sharpest logical cleavage by contrast. Hildegard's appreciation of the principle of semantic contrast came relatively late, in step with the increasing intellectualization of her language. It went hand in hand with a liking for antithetical statements in the field of syntax.

EVELYN G. PIKE

24 Evelyn Pike's report on "Controlled Infant Intonation" is one of the first of its kind on child intonation. Naturally, the study of child intonation has important theoretical implications, some of which were pointed out in subsequent research on child language.

In this study, Evelyn Pike describes an experiment in which she, and later also her husband, Kenneth L. Pike, by design exposed their younger daughter, Barbara, in her initial stage of language acquisition, to intonation contours of certain words which were deliberately changed from the normal pattern of English. This experiment was carried out during the Pikes' stay with the Aztecs, so that there was no interference of normal English speech.

A. B. A.

CONTROLLED INFANT INTONATION

With the first words which she spoke, our daughter, Judith, used a rising intonation. Such an intonation is so common among small children that I have associated it with "baby talk."[1] The possibility of controlling our intonation in speaking with her didn't occur to me until Judith's intonation habits had become already well established; and this, much sooner than most of her other speech habits. I assume this to be because for some time small children tend to use a very limited

Reprinted from Language Learning 2.21–24 (*1949*) *by permission of the author and* Language Learning.

[1] "Baby talk" in this sense is used as applying to the phonetically modified forms the child says in his effort to repeat the normal speech that he hears from his elders. Among other varieties of baby talk is that which children use because they hear forms spoken by their elders deliberately modified to mimic the children.

number of intonation contours which are repeated on many different combinations of segmental items. My husband and I had already tried a similar approach, for Judith, as regards the segmental phonemes—the consonants and the vowels. We had deliberately avoided the use of words specially modified in their consonants and vowels so that the period during which she used "baby talk" seemed to us and a number of others to be considerably shorter than we have observed it to be in other children whose parents used special word forms in speaking to the children. Therefore, with our second daughter, Barbara, I determined to try a type of controlled intonation designed to eliminate from her speech the intonation of "baby talk."

The rising intonation that Judith used seemed to correspond to the 2–1, or 3–1? contour of adults. Thus she would say with that rise: *Dog? Dog?* or *Horse? Horse?* or *Flower? Flower?* (With strong phonetic modifications, such as [ho^{i}š] for *horse*, and [ša^u] for *flower*.[2]

Judith was not the only person who used this intonation for these isolated words. Both her father and I and all the neighbors, in trying to get Judith to talk would point to objects, name them, and pronounce the name with a rising 2–1 or 3–1 intonation. The reason for this seemed to be that the speakers' attitudes in saying *Baby*, while pointing to a doll for example, included the meanings: *Do you want the baby?* or *Can you say the word baby?* or *Do you understand the word baby?* These attitudes tended to force the speakers to use a rising intonation. Now in adult conversation, the question might be asked this same way, but the response *Yes*, or *No*, would usually be given with a falling pitch. Judith, however, instead of using the intonation normal for the response, merely mimicked the intonation which she heard.[3]

Our living situation at the time Barbara was ready to learn to speak made the intonation experiment possible. We had no near English-speaking neighbors, but mostly Aztecs and Mixtecos. Judith was in school during most of Barbara's waking hours, and my husband was away, so I could control all direct English which she heard; later, upon my husband's return, he joined in controlling the speech which Barbara heard.

---

[2] For an analysis of American intonation, see Kenneth L. Pike, *Intonation of American English*, *University of Michigan Publications in Linguistics I* (Ann Arbor: University of Michigan Press, 1945). As indicated there, American English intonation contours are best described in terms of four relative heights at which the intonations begin and end. These may be symbolized by the numbers 1, 2, 3, and 4, with 1 as the highest pitch and 4 as the lowest.

[3] I was interested to observe children's speech in Mixteco village of San Miguel el Grande, Oaxaca, Mexico. They also repeat the pitch of the voice used in speaking directly to them. One of the first two words spoken by a child who visited our home frequently were [táà] 'father' and [čóʔò] 'let's go.' In each word there was a falling pitch comprised of a high tone followed by a low tone. This was the correct pitch sequence as used by the parents and is not altered by the attitude of the speaker nor is it changed in questions; the pitch is lexical. Thus, from the beginning, the pitch of the child's voice for these words was normal Mixteco. Little children learn lexical tone as they learn segmental items of their language.

First, I wished to obtain the intonation falling from pitch 2 to 4, a contour normal to English as a response to the question *Do you understand that this is a baby?* Assuming that the child would mimic my own pitch contours, I controlled my speech by using a 2–4 falling intonation. That is instead of pointing to a doll and saying, *Baby?* with a rising intonation, I would say it with a falling one. Rather than implying *Do you understand that this is a baby?* I said, *Baby!* and implied, *This is a baby*, or *Here is baby*. In repeating the same word several times in succession with the first syllable on pitch 2 and the second on pitch 4, I used the falling intonation on the word each time it was uttered even though in normal spoken English such a sequence might induce a rise on all pronunciations of the word but the last.

Baby was, therefore, the first word Barbara spoke. Much of the time she pronounced the vowel of the second syllable differently from the vowel of the first syllable, so that this word deliberately given by Barbara could be distinguished readily from nonsense chatter in which the vowels of all the syllables tended to be identical for any one specific sequence but might vary from sequence to sequence. During the first week that she began to use this word, Barbara used only a falling intonation, or occasionally a level one; she did not use rising intonation at all. She would point to her dolls, or pat herself, and say *Baby* with a falling intonation roughly equivalent to the one I had used in speaking to her.

About the same time I was trying to teach her a new word and a different intonation. The word chosen was *Daddy!* and the intonation was that of a call; the first syllable was long and extra high, on pitch one, and the second was somewhat long and on pitch 2 or 3. In one room with Barbara I would call and point toward the other room, where my husband was staying out of sight. He would then answer. After some days, Barbara one day called out, in the same intonation, when my husband was in the next room and I was not with her; she seemed very gratified when she heard him respond. However, this intonation she did not use much after that, nor did we use it much in speaking to her.

With the same word but a different intonation—a contour falling from 3 to 4 or from 2 to 4—I then started teaching her to associate her father, mother, sister, and herself with their names and point to them when they were mentioned. She soon learned to say *Daddy* in this lower (and quieter) general pitch of the voice. She also learned to pat herself and say *Baby* in that intonation. Instead of learning to say *Judy* and *Mommy*, however, she extended the term *Daddy* to all three or to anyone else who seemed to give her pleasure. In each case she would use the falling intonation.

After she was using both words well, I had to leave Barbara with another American family. These people had not been told of the experiment which I was conducting, so naturally enough they made no attempt to control their intonation, but used the rising intonation on the word *Baby*. When we returned after about four days' absence, Barbara had largely stopped using the falling intonation and had substituted a rising one on *Baby*. With the word *Daddy*, which the neighbors had not had occasion to use, Barbara continued to use the falling intonation. As we again began to use the falling intonation on the word *Baby*, Barbara began to use that intonation also, but never stopped using the rising one frequently.

This little experiment indicated to me that children mimic pitch very early; that those used by their elders spoken directly to them are the ones they learn first; that if the child's speech is to have the normal English intonation, those who work with him must modify their intonation to conform to that which is normal for the kind of responses that the child is learning to make.

DOROTHEA McCARTHY

25 Dorothea McCarthy may be considered among the pioneers of the study of child language. Her first study appeared in 1929 and her first monograph, *The Language Development of the Preschool Child*, appeared in 1930 (University of Minnesota Press, 1930, 174 pp.). This chapter on "Language Development" appeared in the 1950 edition of the *Encyclopedia of Educational Research*.[1] Her comprehensive monograph-length review of the literature on child language, "Language Development in Children," appeared first in L. Carmichael, ed., *A Manual of Child Psychology* (New York: John Wiley & Sons, Inc., 1946), pp. 476–581, and constituted a significant contribution to the study of child language at that time. The revised, and even more comprehensive review, including some clinical material, was published in the second edition of Carmichael's *Manual* (1954), pp. 492–630, and has served as a very useful reference work. A recent work of hers is the chapter on "Affective Aspects of Language Learning" in *Perceptual Development in Children*, eds. A. H. Kidd and J. L. Rivoire (New York, 1966), pp. 305–43.

A. B. A.

LANGUAGE DEVELOPMENT

Language is a major key to the child's mental life; many thought processes involve subvocal words, some form of oral expression is neces-

sary for the communication of ideas to others, and a certain basic mastery of linguistic skills is an essential prerequisite for academic achievement.

The many biographical studies of the child study movement around the turn of the cen-

Reprinted from W. S. Monroe, ed., Encyclopedia of Educational Research (*1950*), *165–72, by permission of the author and the American Educational Research Association.*

[1] In the 1960 edition of this *Encyclopedia*, the chapter on "Language Development" was written by J. R. Carroll (included in this volume).

tury were replete whith isolated observations of the language of single children who were for the most part precocious and observed by biased relatives under varying conditions. These studies were of little scientific value, but they were suggestive and helpful in laying the groundwork of casual observation which necessarily preceded scientific observation and control. Since the appearance of the pioneer studies of Madorah Smith in 1926 and McCarthy in 1930, there have been a number of important investigations of the language of children of preschool age which have yielded considerable uniformity of results, and a fairly accurate description can now be given of linguistic development in the age range of two to five years. Davis carried on similar work up to the nine-year level. The most significant and promising work on the prelinguistic babblings of infancy has been done by Irwin and his associates since 1941. Young compared contrasting socioeconomic groups in various situations. Shire studied the predictive value of measures of linguistic development for first-grade reading, and Yedinack dealt with their interrelationships in normal second-grade children and in similar groups having functional articulatory and reading difficulties. The most intensive and complete review of the literature in this area is by McCarthy.

INFANT VOCALIZATIONS

All normal children begin to use the organs of speech shortly after birth in vocalization which takes on a playful character as the child exercises his vocal mechanisms in the so-called babbling stage. Chen and Irwin, who studied 95 infants, found that the average child uses about seven different sounds in the first two months and that this number increases to about twenty-seven by 2.5 years. At first, the sounds are predominantly vowels in a ratio of roughly 2 : 1. This ratio reverses at the end of the first year when consonant types exceed the vowels, and by 2.5 years about one-and-one-half times as many consonants as vowel types are uttered. At this age the child uses practically all the vowels needed for adult speech but only about two thirds of the consonants. In terms of frequency of occurrence, vowels are five times more frequent than consonants in the first two months, and these two kinds of phonemes appear with about equal frequency by the middle of the third year of life. No sex differences were noted in the first year, but after that age girls exceed the boys slightly in the number of phoneme types uttered. Irwin and curry report that only four vowels occur with appreciable frequency in newborns. the most frequent being æ which occurred in all subjects. Vowels made with the front part of the oral cavity are more frequent than those made with the back part, and the course of vowel development during the first year appears to be characterized by the increasing use of back vowels. Irwin found the opposite trend in the use of consonants, the utterances of six-month-old babies being characterized by the predominance of the aspirate sound h and glottal and velar sounds, with absence of labial and dental sounds. When considering the place of phonation the development for consonant sounds, therefore, if one accepts the inclusion of the aspirate h as a speech sound, appears to be from back to front, while that for vowels is from front to back. Ombredane and Lewis both agree with this finding, the former describing speech sounds as progressing from those involving strong muscular tension (glottic) to those involving weak muscle tension of the more mobile organs of speech. This later use of the lips in consonant formation, he considers, marks the beginning of cortical functioning. Lewis points out that the sounds made with the back part of the oral cavity are those which are associated with states of comfort (such as feeding), whereas those made with the lips occur more often in states of discomfort, and are associated with the anticipatory mouthing movements of the hungry infant.

It is particularly interesting to note that feeble-minded four-year-olds approximate the utterances of normal children less than one year of age. In the first six months of life children in an orphanage group have been found markedly retarded when compared with children living in a normal family environment. Children from upper socioeconomic groups begin to excel those from lower socioeconomic groups by about one year of age. Girls begin to excel boys at the age of the appearance of the first word.

An analysis by McCarthy of the linguistic items reported in eight major infant studies that employed observational techniques showed that a few vowel sounds characterize the utterances heard in the first two months and that cooing and responses to the human voice are reported between the second and the fourth months. Vocalizations expressive of pleasure are reported between the third and seventh months and those expressive of recognition between the seventh and eighth months. Greater variety in syllabification is found from the fourth to the sixth month and rudimentary imitation of sounds from the sixth to the tenth month. Interjectional sounds and listening to familiar words are reported at about eight months; responses to gestures and to "bye-bye" between nine and twelve months. Differential responses to different words are reported in the ninth and tenth months. The appearance of two or more sequential words is reported quite consistently at one year of age, and the naming of single objects and pictures occurs normally in the latter half of the second year. There is a steady increase in the number of items children can name and point to on request from the twenty-first to the thirty-sixth month. The first phrases, sentences, pronouns, and prepositions all emerge and round out the most advanced linguistic accomplishments of the second year.

IMITATION AND COMPREHENSION

Since the child learns whatever language he hears spoken, it is evident that imitation of a sort plays an important role in his acquisition of oral speech. From among utterances in the vocal repertoire of the babbling stage, adults in the environment select for approval and repetition those combinations of sounds which most closely resemble real words in the mother tongue. An interesting controversy on the exact role of imitation in language acquisition has been carried on in the literature. One of the best presentations in this area is to be found in Lewis's *Infant Speech*. Most writers are agreed, however, that the child does not learn to make new sounds by imitation, but that his attention is called to those sounds in his own vocal repertoire which are close approximations to real words and

thus they are repeated more often. He may also learn through imitation new groupings of sounds he already uses spontaneously. It is entirely possible for some sounds which seem like words to be used in mere sound play and without real meaning. Most writers seem agreed, however, that comprehension of the language of others precedes the actual use of language by the child.

THE FIRST WORD

Just when the child uses his first word is difficult to determine. It is usually thought of as the first use of sound *with meaning*, but it is necessary to make several observations on the consistency of a sound in identical or similar situations on different occasions, and also to note behavior in other situations, in order to make sure that the sound is not being used on other occasions or to designate other objects or persons than that for which it was originally employed. Most of the data available on the first word come from biographical studies of rather accelerated children of the upper socioeconomic levels. Bateman, the Sterns, Bühler, and Decroly, summarizing material of this sort, find the average age for appearance of the first word about 11 months. This corresponds to reports of parents on the age of talking of gifted children. Mentally defective children, on the other hand, are always much later in the use of the first word. Mead reported 38.5 months for a group of feeble-minded children in contrast to 15.3 months which she found to be the average age for normals.

In form, the first word is usually a monosyllable or a reduplicated monosyllable like *mama*, *bye-bye*, and the like. It usually functions as a name or has a strong emotional tone such as in an interjection. Single words are often used in isolation with accompanying gestures and inflections which give them the force of whole sentences and hence they are often spoken of as one-word sentences or rhemes.

GROWTH OF VOCABULARY

The study of vocabulary is fraught with so many serious methodological problems that few studies yield comparable results or any consistent picture which is readily describable. The first difficulty is that of deciding on the proper criterion for *knowledge* of a word; a word may be in one's speaking vocabulary or only in one's understood vocabulary. Furthermore, one may know a single meaning for a word and later come to know it in an entirely different connotation. The second problem, discussed at length by Seashore and Eckerson and by M. K. Smith, involves failure to define *the word* as the unit of measurement, i.e., failure to distinguish between roots and derivatives, between commonest and multiple usages, and the like. A third issue basic to vocabulary measurement, discussed by Williams, centers about the problems of methods of sampling dictionaries of various sizes in choosing words for vocabulary tests. Some tests use abridged dictionaries, others unabridged ones. Some choose a sample by taking the bottom word on every *n*th page, whereas others count ordinal positions of the words. In the former method more common words are more likely to be chosen because of greater space allotments.

The most widely quoted study on preschool vocabulary estimates is that of M. E. Smith, who measured understood vocabularies of 273 children ranging in age from 8 months to 6 years by means of a sampling of the Thorndike 10,000-word list. Her results may be summarized in terms of the following estimates for the several age levels: 1 year, 3 words; 2 years, 272 words; 3 years, 896 words; 4 years, 1540 words; 5 years, 2072 words; 6 years, 2562 words.

The only procedure which overcomes the major sampling difficulties stressed by Williams and by Seashore is the Seashore and Eckerson Test for which special methods for the early grades were devised by M. K. Smith. This method, which is claimed to be highly reliable (+.90 for grades 5–9), yields extraordinarily high estimates of total vocabulary, estimates which are of an entirely different order of magnitude than those reported in earlier work. For grade 1 she reports the average number of words in the total vocabulary as 23,700 with a range from 6000 to 48,800, and for grade 12 it had risen to 80,300 with a range from 36,700 to 136,500.

With the present confusion in the literature, accurate estimates of average vocabulary for any age level are practically impossible. It is probably safe to say, however, that the average child on entering school has a vocabulary of at least several thousand words instead of the popular estimates by teachers and laymen of three to four hundred words. In general, vocabulary estimates are much higher in recent investigations which employ more refined techniques than in the earlier ones.

Analyses of children's oral language according to parts of speech fall into three types of studies. The first type, suitable only for the small vocabularies of the second and third years of life when some record of total vocabulary is feasible, always yields a high percentage of nouns (about 60 per cent) and about 20 per cent verbs. This is roughly the proportion of nouns to verbs in the language. An entirely different picture of the proportions of the various parts of speech is obtained in the second type of study, in which no attempt is made to determine total vocabulary but a fairly long sample of running conversation or of compositions or letters is analyzed. In this method, nouns are only about 20 per cent of the words used, due largely to the necessities of sentence structure; and naturally, other percentages are shifted accordingly.

A third type of analysis for parts of speech, based on number of *different* words rather than total number of words in a running sample, reveals that language is made up largely of a small number of frequently occurring words (articles and prepositions being relatively frequent) and that there is relatively infrequent use of the great majority of words in the total vocabulary. This approach gives a still different picture of the proportions of the various parts of speech. For example, a study by Zyve of the conversations of kindergarten children yielded 51 per cent nouns using the number of different words as the base, but only 15 per cent nouns when computed according to the total words used.

Johnson and his cowrkers at Iowa have developed the "type-token ratio" (TTR). This is the ratio of the number of different words (types) to the total words (tokens) in a sample of oral or written language. It is considered indicative of variability or flexibility of language usage. Chotlos, who applied this technique and several others to 3000-word samples of written language from 108 children, concludes that the more highly developed the individual in terms of age and intelligence, the more highly differentiated his language structure.

COMPREHENSIBILITY

There are very marked individual differences in the comprehensibility of children's speech. Some children speak very clearly almost from the onset of speech; others suffer from prolonged infantile forms well into the early school years. Most writers find that the greatest improvement in clarity of articulation normally occurs between 2 and 3 years of age and that practically all speech is comprehensible after 3.5 years. Wellman and others report a correlation of +.80 between age and ability to give speech sounds. The child whose speech is developing normally usually drops all serious letter substitutions by 4 or 5 years of age. Only a few children account for the occurrence of speech errors beyond age 6, and these apparently are the speech defectives who need some form of therapy. There are no really satisfactory measures of articulation for preschool children which have been adequately standardized. Most available tests require too difficult vocabulary and are too time consuming because they test for relatively rare sounds.

QUANTITATIVE MEASURES

The most objective and reliable measures of children's language are those which measure amount of language per unit of time, and thus yield a measure of talkativeness, and those involving the average number of words per response. The measures of rate show wide individual differences, and while in general the amount of speech per unit of time does show an increase with age, especially in the preschool years, it appears to be symptomatic of personality traits and indicative of situations. Amount of speech in a given time is therefore less satisfactory as a developmental index than the average length of response. The latter measure has been used quite satis-

factorily in all the major investigations. It is a highly sensitive index that reveals developmental trends from infancy to maturity and also reflects sex, occupational, and intellectual group differences with remarkable consistency.

In general, it appears that the child of 18 months is essentially in the one-word sentence stage, only occasionally combining 2 words. One year later the most typical sentences are 2 and 3 words in length. By 3.5 years the average child uses complete sentences averaging about 4 words in length, although he is capable of an occasional sentence which is much longer (25 or 30 words). By school entrance the average sentence length is about 5 words and by 9.5 years it is about 6 or 7 words.

Studies involving the average length of sentence in written language have been reported by Heider and Heider and by Stormzand and O'Shea. Their data indicate that the average length of sentence in written language is about 11 words per sentence at 9 years, about 13 at 12 years, about 17 at 15 years, and about 20 words at the adult level.

SENTENCE STRUCTURE AND GRAMMATICAL FORM

Students of child language have been concerned not only with the quantitative approach regarding the number of words known and the length of the sentences into which they are grouped but also with the qualitative aspects of sentence formation. Among the early writers, Nice gave the best description of four stages of sentence development in the oral language of young children, although the age levels she designates are for precocious rather than average children. She recognizes (a) the single-word stage below 12 months; (b) the early-sentence stage about the middle of the second year, which is characterized by a preponderance of nouns, lack of articles, auxiliaries and copulative verbs, prepositions, and conjunctions; (c) the short sentence stage of from 3.5 to 4.5 words, which is lacking in inflections and in which only one or two sentences in 50 are compound or complex; (d) the complete sentence stage attained at about 4 to 5 years of age, consisting of 6 to 8 words and characterized by greater definiteness and complexity and by the use of inflections and relational words.

In the studies by McCarthy, Day, and Davis the functionally complete although structurally incomplete sentences have been recognized. The percentage of such responses decreases with age throughout the preschool period, but even by 9 years they still constitute about one third of the responses given in oral speech. Much intelligible conversation therefore goes on in fragmentary sentences which are not necessarily an indication of immaturity in individuals who can and do use complete sentences when the occasion demands. Simple sentences without phrases show a steady increase until 4 years of age, when their proportion begins to decline due to the appearance of more advanced forms of sentence structure.

The beginnings of the use of prepositions herald the use of phrases, and the use of connective words is symptomatic of the use of the compound and complex sentence forms. All of these forms first appear among the most precocious children in the third year of life but never consitute a large proportion of child speech.

The category of elaborated sentences, first described by McCarthy and consisting of sentences involving two phrases, or two clauses, or a phrase and a clause, proved interesting as a developmental index. Such sentences are rare in the speech of preschool children, constituting only 6 per cent of the sentences at 4.5 years and about 10 per cent by 9.5 years. Shire found the percentage of elaborated sentences in oral language to be the best single predictor other than intelligence of success in first-grade reading. She also found that the oral language of children who were in the lowest decile of a group of 300 in first-grade reading was characterized by an absence of elaborated sentences, shorter average length of response, little use of connectives, and a lack of variety in word usage.

The best data on sentence structure in written compositions have been reported by Stormzand and O'Shea and by Heider and Heider. The first uses of prepositions, modifiers, and connectives seem to be important milestones, but once achieved they seem to lose developmental significance at higher ages.

Goodenough, McConnon, and Young have emphasized the importance of the situation in which language samples are obtained. More recent studies have given detailed consideration to qualitative aspects of certain parts of speech. For example, Goodenough conducted an intensive study of pronouns, Grigsby of prepositions, and Carroll of adjectives. Lewis, Adams, and M. E. Smith have studied various verb forms, especially past and future tenses, and LaBrant concentrated on the clause as a unit of measurement in linguistic study.

Many minor studies have been reported by educators on the incidence of various types of grammatical errors in the oral and written language of school children. Most of them are quite pessimistic, indicating lack of success on the part of the school in eradicating errors which seem to be more a function of family and cultural example and usage and to be little influenced by traditional classroom techniques. Davis points out, however, in a more optimistic article that many of these reports have been based on mere enumeration of errors and have not considered the number of times there was opportunity for error. In general she found that the ratio of correct to incorrect usages increased with advancing age. The measures she employed were related to socioeconomic status. The influence of the school in eliminating errors was most marked in the less privileged groups, where there was the greatest need for improvement.

FUNCTIONS OF LANGUAGE

Psychologists have long concerned themselves not only with the problem of how the child talks but also with why he talks. The functions that language serves in the child's life are of primary concern in the study of the motivations of language. Traditionally grammarians have approached this problem from an analysis of written language into declarative, interrogative, imperative, and exclamatory sentences. But, as has been pointed out, so much of children's oral language is fragmentary and structurally incomplete that this method is not suitable.

Piagét in his *Language and Thought of the Child* suggested a new approach to this aspect of language. After noting that young children often talk about themselves and the activities they are engaged in at the moment without addressing anyone or expecting a hearer to understand or answer, he classified approximately 40 per cent of child language as *egocentric*, the remainder being some form of *socialized* speech which is addressed to a hearer and which requires a reply.

Studies of children's language which have been concerened with this aspect of the problem fall into two main groups, and there has developed what appears superficially to be a controversy over the degree of egocentrism as reflected in children's language. Studies by McCarthy, Day, Davis, and Johnson and Josey which employed a literal interpretation of the definitions of Piagét's categories failed to substantiate his claims and found only very small percentages (3 to 10 per cent) of children's speech to be egocentric. Other writers, particularly Fisher and Rugg, Krueger, and Sondergaard, agree with Piagét in finding a high percentage (approximately 40 per cent) of egocentrism. However, rather than adhering to his definitions of the categories included in this heading they have looked to the content and form of the sentences and have classed them as egocentric if they employed the first personal pronoun, referred to the self, or were self-assertive, even though they were addressed to a hearer who was expected to reply. Interestingly enough a study by Henle and Hubbell reveals that conversations of college girls are just as egocentric as are those of preschool children according to this type of criterion, so perhaps degree of egocentrism is not as significant an indicator of maturational trends as it was once though to be. The apparent controversy is undoubtedly due to differences in interpretation of terms, to the differences in the situations in which samples are recorded, and to individual differences in the personality traits of the children studied.

The actual percentage of socialized speech obtained in any study depends on the policy adopted in regard to classification discussed under egocentrism. The percentages of questions and of anwers depend on the degree of participation of the adult in the situation. However, several trends in regard to categories of socialized speech appear to be valid.

There is a strong affective element in the early speech of children, for they seem to speak first about the things they feel strongly about such as wishes, commands, treats, and other emotionally toned responses. Among children 1.5 to 2.5 years of age responses which are mere naming of objects, pictures, and the like are prominent while they are asking "what" questions and building up a basic vocabulary of nouns. Only somewhat later, 3 to 4 years of age, do remarks associated with the situation emerge. Such responses are indicative of the child's increasing ability to recall information and to bring his past experiences to bear on the present situation, to talk about the future and related items, and to integrate his experiences and talk about them.

The category of children's questions has received special attention, not only in the major developmental studies but also in separate studies by Piagét, E. A. Davis, M. E. Smith, and Lewis. This area was reviewed by Fahey in 1942. In general the percentage of questions obtained in any one study is highly dependent upon the situation in which the language is sampled, more questions being asked of adults than of children. The number of questions seems to be a function also of intellectual level, and children from upper socioeconomic levels have been found to ask more questions than those from lower socioeconomic levels. There is little agreement among the various studies in regard to the types of questions asked. Piagét stresses the affective rather than the intellectual aspects of the early "why" questions, and Lewis emphasizes the playful and attention getting character of much of the child's question-and-answer activity. He also brings out that children in building up their knowledge in various areas often ask questions to which they already know the answer. This is in effect making tentative statements and seeking social sanctions for their formulations by way of corroboration or rejection by others.

INTERRELATIONSHIPS OF VARIOUS MEASURES OF LANGUAGE DEVELOPMENT

In spite of the wide variety of measures of linguistic development which have been employed, there has been little work directed to the question of the relative importance of the various measures or to any form of integration of them into a single linguistic index. Most of the analyses have yielded sets of mutually interdependent measures which are difficult or impossible to manipulate statistically.

Williams working at the preschool level studied articulation, vocabulary, correctness of word usage, and length, completeness, and complexity of sentence. All were scored with satisfactory reliability in terms of arbitrarily quantified measures. Complete data were avaliable on only thirty-eight three- and four-year-olds. A rather strong positive relationship was found among the various language measures with the exception of the two vocabulary indices, which appeared to be relatively independent of other aspects of language.

Yedinack studied the interrelationships of language measures in second-grade children chosen from 89 classes of 2147 pupils. Functional articulatory disabilities were found in 3.31 per cent, serious reading disabilities in 3.12 per cent, and both handicaps in 1.26 per cent. Marked overlapping of linguistic defects was found. Forty per cent of the reading disability cases also had functional articulatory defects, and 38 per cent of the cases identified as having articulatory difficulties were also seriously retarded in reading.

She selected a control group of 74 normal readers and speakers who matched the disability groups in age, sex, and school grade. In general, rather substantial correlations ranging from .54 to .93 were found among the variables of length, completeness, and complexity of sentence structure. Vocabulary and articulation were relatively independent of other measures of language and also of oral and silent reading ability in these comparatively homogeneous groups. Yedinack concludes that the interrelationships of her various language measures were not markedly different in the groups having articulatory and reading difficulties from those in the control group of second-graders who were normal in speech and reading.

RELATION OF LANGUAGE DEVELOPMENT TO
OTHER ASPECTS OF DEVELOPMENT

Since there is no general index of linguistic development available, there is little direct evidence of its relationship to other aspects of the child's development. In regard to motor behavior, language is usually thought of as a substitute for gestures and other overt responses. Shirley and Brigance report a cyclical relationship between language and motor development in the first two years: there seem to be plateaus in language development when the child is learning to walk or acquiring some other motor skill which requires his undivided attention. Bilto reports that 90 speech defective children between 9 and 18 years of age were markedly inferior on three sets of motor tasks. The literature on the relationship between lateral dominance and language development is confused; much further work from the genetic, dynamic, and neurological points of view is needed in this area before conclusions can be stated.

In relation to intellectual development the evidence is more clearcut. Feeble-minded children are always late in learning to talk, and a child who talks early is quite likely to be above average in intelligence. Although delayed speech is often symptomatic of general mental retardation, there are many other reasons why a child may be late in talking. Sirkin and Lyons report that only one third of a group of feebleminded individuals speak normally, and speech correction work was ineffective below a mental age of 5.5 years. Intellectually gifted children are always accelerated in language development, and vocabulary tests are quite generally recognized to be the best single indicators of general intelligence.

All the developmental trends reported with chronological age in the normative studies of language development also appear when the data are analyzed according to mental age groups, and all the group differences in linguistic development which have been reported are parallelled by differences in IQ. It is also interesting to note that all measures of infant intelligence have proved unsuccessful before the age when language appears. The approach of Irwin analyzing the prelinguistic babblings of infants appears to be most promising in this regard.

As pointed out above, children first use language to express content which has a strong emotional tone. Further evidence of the relationship between emotional and linguistic development comes chiefly in a negative way from the study of clinical deviants. Many speech defects, particularly stuttering and infantile speech, are symptoms of emotional maladjustment. Many clinical cases of delayed speech have been traced to emotional trauma, and mutism is a frequent symptom of childhood schizophrenia. There is also growing body of clinical evidence that severe reading disabilities are due to deep-rooted problems of maladjustment often associated with the dynamics of the family relationships. It thus appears that experimental work on the relationship between emotional and linguistic development is indicated.

Further evidence is also needed on the relationships between linguistic and social development. From studies and casual observation of young children it is evident that the child is decidedly an individualist in his play until the onset of language. Mallay reports that as the child learns to make verbal rather than motor approaches to other children his socialization is facilitated. Schmidt has shown that speech therapy given to a group of mental defectives facilitated their social development. I. P. Davis reports a positive correlation between maturity of articulation and acceptable social behavior. She states that this may indicate either that the factors which retard a child's speech also retard his social development or that a speech difficulty may contribute to social retardation.

EFFECT OF ENVIRONMENTAL FACTORS

There is abundant evidence in the literature (Davis, Day, McCarthy, Young) to show that children from the upper socioeconomic groups are more advanced in all aspects of language development. Since intelligence is usually measured by means of verbal tests, it is difficult or impossible from available data to say whether these differences are due to differences in intellectual capacity or whether the differences in intelligence test scores merely reflect more basic differences in language development.

Drever, Bean, and others report that increases in children's vocabulary are almost always associated with travel and other broadening environmental experiences. The age of the child's associates also appears to make a difference in his linguistic development; children who associate chiefly with adults are usually precocious in language development. Only children are especially advanced, even more so than would be expected on the basis of age, intelligence, and socioeconomic status. Institution and orphanage environments seem to produce children with a paucity of linguistic skill, their retardation in this respect being much more serious than their intellectual retardation.

Multiple births also seem to produce an environmental situation which is not conductive to optimum linguistic growth. Day found a two-year retardation in the language of twins at 5 years of age. Davis found that the handicap tended to be overcome to some extent after school entrance. Triplets and the famous Dionne quintuplets have also been found to be even more seriously retarded than twins. Apparently such children have a very intimate and satisfying social experience in which they do not need language as much for communication as the children who grow up as singletons.

Several studies, particularly those by Young McConnon, M. E. Smith, and Williams and Mattson, indicate that language samples vary greatly with the situation in which the sample is recorded. Smith found, for example, that children use longer sentences and ask more questions when alone with an adult than when in a group of children.

INDIVIDUAL DIFFERENCES

The extremes of individual differences in language development are indeed striking. They range all the way from the mutism of the adult idiot, the deaf-mute, or the child schizophrenic to the gifted child who begins to use words at 8 months and sentences by one year of age. Individual differences in linguistic development closely parallel differences which have been found in intellectual development, and differences in language development contribute greatly to differences in intellectual development that have thus far been measured. It is interesting to note that all intelligence tests which have proved to have a satisfactory degree of validity are heavily weighted with verbal items.

Sex differences in language development are small but consistently favor the girls. Whenever groups of boys and girls are well matched in age, intelligence, and socioeconomic status, and when the situation in which responses are recorded does not favor the interests of either sex, language differences in favor of girls appear in a wide variety of measures which reveal developmental trends. When they do not appear, their absence can nearly always be accounted for on the basis of selection on one of the above-mentioned factors. The evidence in articulation, comprehensibility of speech, and incidence of speech defects and reading disabilities also tends to favor the girls; boys much more often develop some form of language disorder.

The few studies which have been conducted on the language development of handicapped children indicate that there are important differences in language depending on the nature of the handicap. For example, Maxfield found that blind children tend to ask more questions, give fewer commands, and have an unusually high percentage of emotionally toned responses when compared with seeing children. The interesting studies by the Heiders on deaf children indicate that the sentences of the deaf are shorter than those of hearing children, include relatively more simple and fewer compound and complex sentences, fewer verbs, and relatively more infinitives and prepositional phrases than the sentences of normal children.

CONCLUSION

In general it appears that recent years have seen a marked increase in interest in language as a psychological phenomenon. This interest has been primarily in language as a form of social behavior rather than as a form of thought. The research in the field has been characterized by a relentless search for new and better tools and by the application of these technqies to larger numbers of normals in more carefully controlled situations as well as to deviant groups. The age ranges studied have spread from the preschool level downward into infancy and upward into the school ages. There is need for much better integration of clincial observa-

tions and developmental normative studies on both normal and abnormal groups.

BIBLIOGRAPHY

Adams, Sidney. "Analysis of Verb Forms in the Speech of Young Children, and Their Relation to the Language Learning Process." *Journal of Experimental Education*, VII (1938), 141–44.

Bateman, W. G. "Papers on Language Development: I. The First Word." *Pedigogical Seminary*, XXIV (1917), 391–98.

Bean, C. H. "An Unusual Opportunity to Investigate the Psychology of Language." *Journal of Genetic Psychology*, XL (1932), 181–202.

Bilto, E. W. "A Comparative Study of Certain Physical Abilities of Children with Speech Defects and Children with Normal Speech." *Journal of Speech Disorders*, VI (1941), 187–203.

Brigance, W. N. "The Language Learning of a Child." *Journal of Applied Psychology*, XVIII (1934), 143–54.

Brodbeck, A. J., and Irwin, O. C. "The Speech Behavior of Infants Without Families." *Child Development*, XVII (1946), 145–56.

Bühler, Charlotte. *Kindheit und Jugend*. Third ed. Leipzig: Hirzel, 1931.

Carroll, J. B. "Determining and Numerating Adjectives in Children's Speech." *Child Development*, X (1939), 215–19.

Chen, H. P., and Irwin, O. C. "Infant Speech, Vowel and Consonant Types." *Journal of Speech Disorders*, XI (1946), 27–29.

Chotlos, J. W. *A Statistical and Comparative Analysis of Individual Written Language Samples*. Psychological Monographs, Vol. 56, No. 4 (1944). pp. 77–111.

Davis, Edith A. "The Form and Function of Children's Questions." *Child Development*, III (1932), 57–74.

——. *The Development of Liguistic Skill in Twins, Singletons with Siblings, and Only Children from Age Five to Ten Years*. Institute of Child Welfare Monographs Series, No. 14. University of Minnesota Press, 1937. 165 pp.

——. "Accuracy versus Error as a Criterion in Children's Speech." *Journal of Educational Psychology*, XXX (1939), 365–71.

Davis, Irene P. "The Speech Aspects of Reading Readiness." *Newer Practices in Reading in the Elementary School*. Seventeenth Yearbook, N.E.A., Department of Elementary School Principals, 1938. 704 pp.

Day, Ella J. "The Development of Language in Twins: I. A Comparison of Twins and Single Children." *Child Development*, III (1932), 179–99.

Decroly, O. *Comment l'enfant arrive à parler.* Vols. I and II. Cahiers de la Centrale. (Revu et complété par J. Decroly et J. E. Segers.) Cent. du P.E.S. de Belgique, Vol. 8, 1934.

Drever, J. "A Study of Children's Vocabularies: I, II, and III." *Journal of Experimental Pedagogy*, III (1915–16), 34–43, 96–103, 182–88.

Fahey, G. L. "The Questioning Activity of Children." *Journal of Genetic Psychology*, LX (1942), 337–57.

Fisher, Mary S. *Language Patterns of Preschool Children.* Child Development Monographs, No. 15 (1934). 88 pp.

Goodenough, Florence L. "The Use of Pronouns by Young Children: A Note on the Development of Self-Awareness." *Journal of Genetic Psychology*, LII (1938), 333–46.

Grigsby, O. J. "An Experimental Study of the Development of Concepts of Relationship in Preschool Children as Evidenced by their Expressive Ability." *Journal of Experimental Education*, I (1932), 144–62.

Heider, F. K., and Heider, Grace M. *A Comparison of Sentence Structure of Deaf and Hearing Children.* Psychological Monographs, Vol. 52, No. 1 (1940). pp. 42–103.

Henle, Mary, and Hubbell, Marian B. " 'Egocentricity' in Adult Conversation." *Journal of Social Psychology*, IX (1938), 227–34.

Irwin, O. C. "The Profile as a Visual Device for Indicating Central Tendencies in Speech Data." *Child Development*, XII (1941), 111–20.

———, and Curry, T. "Vowel Elements in the Crying Vocalization of Infants Under Ten Days of Age." *Child Development*, XII (1941), 99–109.

Johnson, E. C., and Josey, C. C. "A Note on the Development of the Thought Forms of Children as Described by Piagét." *Journal of Abnormal and Social Psychology*, XXVI (1931), 338–39.

Johnson, W., et al. *Studies in Language Behavior.* Psychological Monographs, Vol. 56, No. 2 (1944). 111 pp.

LaBrant, Lou L. *A Study of Certain Language Developments of Children in Grades Four to Twelve Inclusive.* Genetic Psychology Monographs, Vol. 14 (1933). pp. 387–491.

Lewis, M. M. *Infant Speech: A Study of the Beginnings of Language.* Harcourt, Brace & World, Inc., 1936. 335 pp.

———. "The Beginning of Reference to Past and Future in a Child's Speech." *British Journal of Educational Psychology*, VII (1937), 39–56.

———. "The Beginning and Early Functions of Questions in a Child's Speech." *British Journal of Educational Psychology*, VIII (1938), 150–71.

Mallay, Helena. "A Study of Some of the Techniques Underlying the Establishment of Successful Social Contacts at the Preschool Level." *Journal of Genetic Psychology*, XLVII (1935), 431–57.

Maxfield, Kathryn E. *The Spoken Language of the Blind Preschool Child: A Study of Method.* Archives of Psychology, No. 201 (1936). 100 pp.

McCarthy, Dorothea. *The Language Development of the Preschool Child.* Institute of Child Welfare Monographs Series, No. 4. University of Minnesota Press, 1930. 174 pp.

———. "Language Development in Children." In Carmichael, Leonard, ed., *A Manual of Child Psychology.* John Wiley & Sons, Inc., 1946. pp. 476–581.

———. *The Psychologist Looks at the Teaching of English.* Independent School Bulletin, No. 5, 1947. pp. 3–11.

McConnon, Kathleen. *The Situation Factor in the Language Responses of Nursery School Children.* Doctor's thesis. University of Minnesota, 1935.

Mead, C. D. "The Age of Walking and Talking in Relation to General Intelligence." *Pedagogical Seminary*, XX (1913), 460–84.

Nice, Margaret M. "Length of Sentences as a Criterion of a Child's Progress in Speech." *Journal of Educational Psychology*, XVI (1925), 370–79.

Ombredane, André. "Études sur le langage. Sur les premières manifestations du langage enfantine et sur la prétendue loi de Fritz Schultze." *Hygiene Mentale*, XXX (1935), 69–89.

Piaget, Jean. *Le langage et la pensée chez l'enfant.* Neuchâtel et Paris: Delachaux et Niestlé. *The Language and Thought of the Child.*

M. Warden, trans. Harcourt, Brace & World, Inc., 1926. 246 pp.

Rugg, Harold; Krueger, Louise; Sondergaard, Arenso. "Studies in Child Personality: I. A Study of the Language of Kindergarten Children. *Journal of Educational Psychology*, XX (1929), 1–18.

Schmidt, Bernardine G. "Language Development as an Aid to the Social Adjustment of Mental Defectives." *Mental Hygiene*, XXV (1941), 402–13.

Seashore, R. H. "The Measurement and Analysis of Extent of Vocabulary." *Psychological Bulletin*, XXX (1933), 709–10.

———, and Eckerson, L. D. "The Measurement of Individual Differences in General English Vocabularies." *Journal of Educational Psychology*, XXXI (1940), 14–38.

Shire, Sister Mary Louise, O.S.U. *The Relation of Certain Linguistic Factors to Reading Achievement of First Grade Children.* Doctor's thesis. Fordham University, 1945.

Shirley, Mary M. *The First Two Years: A Study of Twenty-five Babies: II. Intellectual Development.* Institute of Child Welfare Monograph Series, No. 7. University of Minnesota Press, 1933. 513 pp.

Sirkin, J., and Lyons, W. F. "A Study of Speech Defects in Mental Deficiency." *American Journal of Mental Deficiency*, XLVI (1941), 74–80.

Smith, Madorah E. *An Investigation of the Development of the Sentence and the Extent of Vocabulary in Young Children.* University of Iowa, Studies in Child Welfare, Vol. 3, No. 5 (1926). 92 pp.

———. "The Influence of Age, Sex, and Situation on the Frequency, Form, and Function of Questions Asked by Preschool Children." *Child Development*, IV (1933), 201–13.

———. *Some Light on the Problem of Bilingualism as Found from a Study of the Progress in Mastery of English among Preschool Children of Non-American Ancestry in Hawaii.* Genetic Psychology Monographs, Vol. 21 (1939). pp. 121–204.

Smith, Mark K. *Measurement of the Size of General English Vocabulary Through the Elementary Grades and High School.* Genetic Psychology Monographs, Vol. 24 (1941). pp. 311–45.

Stern, Clara, and Stern, William. *Monographien über die Seelische Entwicklung des Kindes. I. Die Kindersprache.* Third ed. rev. Leipzig: J. A. Barth, 1922. 434 pp.

Stormzand, M. J., and O'Shea, M. V. *How Much English Grammar?* Warwick and York, 1924. 224 pp.

Wellman, Beth L., et al. *Speech Sounds of Young Children.* University of Iowa, Studies in Child Welfare, Vol. 5, No. 2 (1931). 82 pp.

Williams, H. M. "Some Problems of Sampling in Vocabulary Tests." *Journal of Expermental Education*, I (1932), 131–33.

———. "An Analytical Study of Language Achievement in Preschool Children. Part I." In *Development of Language and Vocabulary in Young Children.* University of Iowa, Studies in Child Welfare, Vol. 13, No. 2 (1937). pp. 9–18.

Williams, R. M., and Mattson, Marion L. "The Effect of Social Groupings upon the Language of Preschool Children." *Child Development*, XIII (1942), 233–45.

Yedinack, Jeanette G. "A Study of Linguistic Functioning of Children with Articulation and Reading Disabilities." *Journal of Genetic Psychology* (In press).

Young, Florene M. *An Analysis of Certain Variables in a Developmental Study of Language.* Genetic Psychology Monographs, Vol. 23 (1941). pp. 3–141.

Zyve, Claire I., "Conversation Among Children." *Teachers College Record*, XXIX (1927), 46–61.

26 Yuen Ren Chao is one of the first few linguists who devoted special attention to the study of child language before the middle of this century. In 1935 he published a study in Chinese with an English summary on "Three Examples of the Dialectal Nature of Abnormal Pronunciations" (*Bulletin, National Research Institute of History and Philology, Academia Sinica*, V [1935] 241–53). In this study Chao has recorded the phonologies of three now standard dialects, two of which were children's speech. As mentioned by Chao in the following selection, the next worthwhile work on Chinese child language was *Studies in Child Psychology* (in Chinese, Shanghai, 1947) by the Shanghai psychologist H. C. Chen, whose point of view was psychological more than linguistic.

The present study, published in 1951, is a description of the speech of his granddaughter "Canta" at the age of 28 months (in 1949). Canta, although born and reared in the United States, was surrounded at that age mainly by speakers of Standard Mandarin. Canta's speech is, therefore, considered by Chao as "a form of Mandarin—or Mandarin in the making." There were a few English words in her speech, but "she adapts them into her own phonological system much more than do the bilingual speakers around her."

As stated by Chao, this is a synchronic rather than developmental study, over a "specious present" of about one month in which he attempts to treat aspects of phonology and grammar, as well as vocabulary.

A. B. A.

THE CANTIAN IDIOLECT: AN ANALYSIS OF THE CHINESE SPOKEN BY A TWENTY-EIGHT-MONTHS-OLD CHILD

With all the increase of interest and of the amount of work done in the descriptive treatment of the Chinese language and languages in China, little attention has yet been given to the language of the Chinese-speaking child. Dr. H. C. Chen (Ch'ên Ho-ch'in), the well-known child psychologist of Shanghai, has made some study of children's speech,[1] and the present writer has recorded the phonologies of three non-standard dialects, of which two were children's speech.[2] In the present study an attempt will be made to give a fairly all-round description of the speech of a Mandarin-speaking child, to include the phonology, grammar, and vocabulary, as well as to give indications, where it is relevant, of the situations in which the words or sentences were actually used.

The subject of this study is one of the writer's grandchildren, whose name, for present purposes, shall be "Cantian 49," or "Cantian" for short.

Although born and reared in America, Canta has had an almost entirely Chinese language environment. More than half the people around her are speakers of Standard Mandarin, and the others are also speakers of Mandarin of sorts. Canta's speech is is therefore also a form of Mandarin—or Mandarin in the making. Some contact with English, as well as borrowings from

Reprinted from University of California Publications in Semitic Philology *11.27–44 (1951) by permission of the author and the University of California Press.*

[1] *Êrh-t'ung hsin-li chih yen-chiu* [*Studies in Child Psychology*] (Shanghai, 1947), Vol. II, 203–81. The point of view here is, however, more psychological than linguistic.

[2] "Three Examples of the Dialectal Nature of Abnormal Pronunciation" (in Chinese, with English summary), *Bulletin, National Research Institute of History and Philology, Academia Sinica*, V (1935), 241–53.

English in the Chinese she hears, has resulted in a few English words in her speech, but she adapts them into her own phonological system much more than do the bilingual speakers around her.

Since a child's language changes more rapidly than that of an adult, it might seem possible here to make a diachronic study in the history of one person's language. For example, an early record of about one year ago shows that there was only one general fricative, no semivowel in any position, and one instead of two rising tones, so that [hɛ] high-rising was either *shye* 'shoe' or *shoei* 'water,' which are now distinguished in speech. Unfortunately the early records were rather incomplete. Pressure of work and a period of absence, during a time when there were rapid changes in Canta's speech, resulted in a very unsatisfactory state of the early records. The present study is therefore only a synchronic one over a "specious present" of about one month, and earlier materials are mentioned only for incidental comparison.

1. PHONOLOGY

For typographical convenience and for easy reference to the grammatical and lexical sections, National Romanization[3] will be used for citing forms in the environmental language, and an adapted form of the system will be used for the subject's language. Only a minimum of phonetic symbols (in square brackets) will be used, and for finer phonetic details more use will be made of descriptions than of the "narrow" forms of symbols.

A familiar feature of children's language

is underarticulation and consequent reduction of many distinctions. In interpreting the values of the sounds described below, it should be borne in mind that sounds represented by the same symbol, say *t*, are considerably less clearly and less strongly articulated in the subject's speech than in the environmental adult language.

In our citations of Cantian forms, a semiphonemic notation will be used, which will give some idea of the actual allophones under one phoneme if they differ considerably in value or, as with respect to the mid vowels, if the phonemic instability is too great to permit a synchronic snapshot to be in sharp focus.

The initial consonants of Cantian are as shown in the accompanying tabulation.

	Unaspirated voiceless plosives	Aspirated voiceless plosives	Nasals	Fricatives
Labials	b	p	m	f
Dentals or palatals	d	t	n	s
Velars or glottals	g	k		h

The initial *b* is practically the same in value and distribution (i.e., occurrence in words learned from adult language) as in Standard Mandarin ("S.M."), with the usual voicing in unstressed intervocalic position, as *bah.ba* [ˈpàba]:[4] *bah.ba* 'papa.' Initials *p* and *m* have also the same values and similar distribution as in S.M., as *pah: pah* 'afraid'; *mae: mae* 'buy.'

The phoneme /f/ varies between a labiodental value [f] and a bilabial value [φ], a difference which will be recorded in our citations. The variation is partly conditioned in that the bilabial value is more likely to go with *u* and the other value with other sounds, but there is a slight amount of free variation. In distribution this phoneme occurs in words derived from S.M. *sh* (i.e., [ʂ]), *h*, as well as from *f*, as *φu: shu*

---

[3] An easily accessible exposition of the system can be found in the author's *Mandarin Primer* (Cambridge Mass: 1948), esp. chap. ii. The system of tonal spelling, from a reader's point of view, can be summarized as follows: (4) Syllables ending in *-h*, *-ay*, *-ey*, *-w*, *-nn*, *-ng* (pronounced with *-ng*), *-ll* (pron. with vocalic *r*) are in 4th Tone (falling), (3) Syllables with doubled vowels or with the combinations *ae*, *ao*, *oe*, *ea*, *oa*, *co* are in 3d Tone (low-dipping). (2) Syllables not in 3d or 4th Tone are in 2d Tone (high-rising) (a) if they have initial or medial *y* or *w*, or (b) if they have *-r* after a vowel, or (c) if they have *m-*, *n-*, *l-*, *r-* but not *mh-*, *nh-*, *lh-*, *rh-*. (1) Syllables not in 4th, 3d, 2d Tones are in 1st Tone (high-level). Atonic or neutral tone syllables are marked by a dot placed *before* the syllable.

[4] When there is a colon between cited forms, the form or forms before the colon are in Cantian and those after it are in S.M.

	/d/	Dental, *d* [t]	Palatal, *dj* [t′]	[tś]
			CANTIAN	
S.M. dental plosive	*d*[t]	*dah* [ta] : *dah* 'big'	*djiaw* [t′iau] : *diaw* 'dropped'	*djih* [tśi] or [ti] : *dih* 'floor'
S.M. dental affricate	*tz*[ts]	*doh* [tɔ] : *tzuoh* 'sit'		*djih* [tśi] or [t′i] : *tzuh* 'writing'
S.M. retroflex affricate	*j*ᵣ[tʂ]	*da* [ta] : *ja* 'prick'		
S.M. palatal affricate	*j*ᵢ[tś]		*djiaw* [t′iau] : *jiaw* 'shout'	*dji* [t′śi] or [t′i] : *ji* 'chicken'

'book'; *ɸua: hual* 'flower'; *faandji: farng.tzy* 'house.'

The unaspirated voiceless initial /d/ (apart from becoming voiced under the same conditions as *b*) has three values, a dental value *d* [t], a palatal plosive [t′] (not simply dental palatalized),[5] and a palatal affricate [tś], the last two to be romanized as *dj* in our citations. These three values are either phonetically conditioned or in free variation and are allophones of the same phoneme /d/. The dental value occurs after back vowels, the two palatal values (plosive and affricate) in free variation with each other occurring after other vowels, with more use of the affricate when the entire final is *i*. As several S.M. initials are rendered by this one phoneme, its allophones cut across the S.M. initials in a somewhat complicated fashion. The following examples will exhibit the type of relations referred to.

The pure dentals were attained only re-

cently. Before that, all front stops had been palatal, so that [hiᶦt′ău] served both for S.M. *shii-jeau* 'wash the feet' and *shii-tzao* 'take a bath.'

The initial /t/ behaves quite similarly to /d/. Examples are, dentals in *tan* (t'an]: *tang* 'soup'; *ta.ta: tsa.tsa* 'wipe a little'; *tar: char* 'tea'; palatal plosives in *tjyɛn: tyan* 'sweet' or *chyan* 'money'; *daatjih.iė: datih.lė* 'sneeze'; *tjihte: chihche* 'automobile.' A noticeable difference in the treatment of the aspirated palatal initial is the greater use of the affricative value, due no doubt to the greater likelihood of friction when there is aspiration. Thus, not only words with *i* as complete final have affricative initials, as when *dj* occurs, but also words with *i* as medial. In other words, not only the syllable *tjih*, but also words like *tjyɛn* cited above, often begin with (tś'] as well as with (t′'].

The nasal initial /n/ has a palatal value and will be written *ń* in the citations as a reminder orthography. It has not yet acquired a completely dental articulation before non-palatal sounds, as *d* and *t* have done. Thus, *ńa: na* 'take'; *ńaw: naw* 'to be fussy' or *niaw* 'urine.'

At the end of a syllable /n/ has also a palatal value, *ń*, before a pause but assimilates to the articulation of the following sound, *m* before *p*, *ng* before *k*, etc. We shall write final *n* without modification in our orthography except that a few occurrences of final *m* are so written when it is part of the point under discussion. Final *n* is usually quite weak, even weaker than in S.M.; in fact, it sometimes amounts to no more than a final nasalization of the preceding vowel.

The phoneme /s/, orthographically *ś*, is very

---

[5] Front palatal plosives are so rare in languages that there are no symbols for them in IPA. I only know of their existence in Tibetan (Lhasa dialect), in some of the dialects of Shantung, such as of Lintzu, and in Karlgren's reconstruction of Ancient Chinese. On the other hand, they are fairly common in children's speech. Why? There is perhaps a physiological reason for this. As soon as the tongue takes a *front* palatal position, the area of contact is so large that it would be very difficult to release the closure cleanly enough to avoid friction, and any friction there would result in an affricative sound, as when French palatalized dental *Tiens, tiens!* [tjɛ̃ tjɛ̃] becomes palatal affricative [tśɛ̃ tśɛ̃]. On the other hand, since a child's tongue is smaller than an adult's (even though its jawbones, as Jespersen showed, are not much smaller), there is less chance that friction will develop, and during the period when dentals are not clearly formed, palatal plosives are then likely to result.

weakly articulated, with wide passage and little friction. Consequently the point of articulation is less sharply defined, but distributed over a palato-alveolar region similar to the *esh* sounds in languages, like English, in which palatal and retroflex fricatives are not distinguished. Examples are: *śaa.iė: saa.le* 'spilt.'

Words with S.M. *shu* or *shu-* are normally rendered by *φu*, as *φu: shu* 'book'; *φuai: shuai* 'stumble'; *φuo: shuo* 'say.'[6] But the word for water is so frequent that it begins to break the general pattern and forms a vanguard syllable *śoci*, which is quite out of step with the other forms. (Originally it had been *hε* and later *φoei*, now discarded.)

The velar plosives *g* [k] and *k* [k'] became normalized to standard values very early. There was no noticeable tendency to substitute *dau* ('knife') for *gau* 'cake,' so common among Chinese children, though not so nearly universal as generally supposed. There was some substitution of *k* for *h* for a brief period, but it passed long before this recording.

The fricative initial /h/ before open vowels is a glottal [h], as *hao: hao* 'good,' as against the velar or pharyngeal fricative [χ] in S.M. Before medial *u*, there is stronger articulation in the lips than at the back of the tongue or at the glottis, so that S.M. *hual* 'flower' becomes *φua* and S.M. *huay* 'bad' becomes *φuay* in Cantian. Consequently, words with *hu-* in S.M. are transferred to Cantian *φ*, which is an allophone of /f/. When, however, *u* is the whole final and not a medial, S.M. *h* is kept as [h] and therefore also Cantian /h/, as *huudji: hwu.tzy* 'mustache.'

The medials have developed in a way typical of children's speech, namely, omitted at first (*baw* for *biaw*), added as part of the consonant (*ńaw* for *niaw*), and finally fully admitted. At the stage recorded, the status of the medials is as follows.

For *i* after labials it tends to be present when stressed, but absent in proclitic position. There is, however, some free variation in stressed positions. Thus, *beau: beau* 'watch';

baw or *biaw: bu yaw* 'don't want'; but, *be donn: bye dong* 'don't move.'

For the medial *u* the final *uo* usually loses the medial and has the value *o* [ɔ], as *doh: tzuoh* 'sit,' though in *φuo* it is kept. The initials *g*, *k*, *h* generally retain the medial *u*, as *huoo: huoo* 'fire.' In proclitic position, however, the *u* is usually lost, as *.hotjoei: huootoci* 'ham.' With other finals the medial *u* after dentals takes a somewhat palatal value, as *tjoei* [t'‥üĕi]*: toei* 'leg'; after other initials its value is [u], as *guai:* [*kuāi*]*: guai* 'good.'

The medial *iu* or *ü* occurs only in the word *yueh.iȧn: yueh.liang* 'moon,' where it has the same (front) value as in nuclear position, as in *yu: yu* 'fish.'

Of semivowels occurring initially, *i* is more underarticulated and less clearly palatal or dental, just as *ś* is underarticulated and not clearly dental or retroflex or palatal. In distribution Cantian initial *i* includes S.M. *l-* and *r-* as well as original *i-*, as *yai: lai* 'come'; *yėh: reh* 'hot'; *yaw: yaw* 'want.' A nasal ending sometimes results in a substitution of a nasal initial in place of S.M. *l-*, as *ńeen: leeng* 'cold'; *ńiindah: liingdall* 'necktie.'

There are fewer endings in Cantian than in S.M. The endings *-i* and *-u* are extremely open, so that the resulting diphthongs are very close to monophthongs. In proclitic position, they are quite lost, as *haakann* or *.hakann: haokann* 'pretty.' There is only one nasal ending, which is usually palatal in articulation, as *tjwan:* either *chwan* 'ship' or *chwang* 'bed';[7] *don: jong* 'clock.'

The retroflex ending *-l* in S.M. (i.e., [-r]) is simply dropped and only the vowel is retained, as *wa: wal* 'to play.' A middle central vowel in S.M. is given the low vowel value, as *.daydah: tzayjell* 'it's here'; *ahyi: ellyi* 'second aunt.' Note also that, in dropping the ending, it is from the form heard that the ending is dropped and not from the morpheme alternant that would be used in S.M. if there were no suffix. For example, S.M. *yihdeal* 'a little' is Cantian *.idjea* and

---

[6] In this connection it may be noted that along a region from about central Anhwei to central Shensi there are many dialects in which S.M. *shu or shu-* is rendered by *φu* or *fu*, for example, Sian *fu* 'book,' *fei* 'water.'

[7] The mid-lower Yangtze Mandarin in Grandma's speech equates *chwan* 'ship' with *chwan* 'bed,' but, this being part of the Cantian system, Grandma's equating was probably not the main cause of this coalescence.

not *.idjean, such as occurs in djean.śin: dean.shin 'refreshment.'

The vowel system is less amenable than S.M. to reduction to three phonemes: high, mid, and low.

The apical high vowel y has in S.M. a dental value in tzy, tsy, sy (Wade-Giles ŭ) and a retroflex value in jy, chy, shy, ry (Wade-Giles ih). The first type is combined in Cantian with the high front vowel i, as wah.dji: wah.tzy 'stocking.'[8] The second type is kept distinct and has a value intermediate between a retroflex apical vowel and a palatal i, just as the Cantian consonant ś is intermediate between retroflex [ʂ] and palatal [ś]. Examples are tjy: chy 'eat'; śy: shy 'wet.'

For some reason this vowel did not for a long time combine with the unaspirated initial dj, thus tjyy (with aspirated initial) both for S.M. jyy 'paper' and for S.M. chyy 'ruler.' In proclitic position, tjy becomes tu or tji, as .tufann or .tjifann: chy-fann 'eat dinner,'

The other high vowels i, u, iu have the same values [i, u, ü] as in S.M. and approximately the same distribution, apart from changes into i and u from the apical vowel, as just noted.

As for the low vowel or low vowels, a usually has a central or slightly fronted value. In this connection, note that the palatal or semipalatal articulation of ń and ś has had serious effects on the vowel system. While the separation of pure dentals, retroflexes, and palatals in S.M. makes it possible to deal with vowels in an extremely simple fashion, the absorption of the medial in Cantian ń and ś, and to a less degree in dj and tj, has made it necessary to set up more vowels. Thus, S.M. shian and san can be phonemicized as /sian/ and /san/, where the medial will take care of the difference in vowel qualities [ɛ] and [a]. But in Cantian it will be necessary to recognize śɛn and san having different vowel phonemes. Again, in the contrast between tiyàn: chyang 'wall,' where the Cantian a remains a low vowel, and tjyɛn: chyan 'money,' where Cantian

ɛ and S.M. a are both the same half-low vowel, we find an additional situation where an extra vowel phoneme is needed.

The mid vowel or vowels are also more complicated in Cantian than in S.M. Simple stressed e has the same back unrounded value as in S.M., but with less tendency to become an ascending diphthong. For S.M. uo and ou, diphthongs of smaller range are used. After dentals, and in unstressed positions for all initials, uo becomes o, as already noted, and ou becomes e. After initial semivowel i- there are two vowels [ə] and [ɛ], according to the alophone in S.M. Thus, there is contrast between yëh [jə]: reh 'hot' and yee [jɛ]: yee 'also.' The problem of two kinds of mid vowels, one central and one back, has plagued phonemicists of the Peiping dialect,[9] who have used somewhat drastic solutions. There the problem has to do with such contrasts as are found in ge'l 'song' versus gel 'root,' where words with retroflex suffixes derived from stems ending in e and those ending in e plus -i or -n are involved. Here the same problem comes up even in root words.

When the mid vowel e is followed by endings -i and -n it has a rather more fronted value than S.M., as men: men 'door.' The change from S.M. mid vowel in -el to the low vowel a (with dropping of the retroflex ending) has already been noted in our discussion of endings.

Another special vowel quality in Cantian is in what in National Romanization is written ong, the actual S.M. vowel in it being an open u. But the Cantian forms for the ong words have a fairly open—medium—o sound. After velar initials it tends to be a nasalized vowel. After initials it is followed by the usual palatal nasal ending (unless assimilated). The treatment of S.M. ong is therefore another reason for using an "allograph" o, if not a phoneme,

The difficulty with the vowel system is that it is in a state of extreme flux, where the various changes from one stage to the next in the approach to adult language are not going on all in step, thus resulting in internal

---

[8] In this particular suffix, an earlier form, after the -.dji form was begun, was an ejected 't, with closed glottis and dental oral explosion, resulting in a high-pitched expiratory click. This was used for about two months and abandoned about four months ago.

[9] See Lawton M. Hartman 3d, "The Segmental Phonemes of the Peiping Dialect," Language, XX (1944), 35–36; Charles F. Hockett, "Peiping Phonology," Journal of the American Oriental Society, LXVII (1947), 259–67.

inconsistencies. Some of this is true of historical change in adult language, as seen in various phonemic anomalies, such as, for example, the lone word *d'i* 'earth' in Ancient Chinese, the only instance of a dental stop with that type of final. But in adult language there is usually time for some stabilization to set in, so as to allow the phonemician to catch his breath, whereas here the vowels float about and will not stay put until they attain adult S.M. status.

The tones of Cantian are much more regular and stable, though distinctly different from S.M. in several respects. Canta acquired tones very early, as most Chinese children do. Isolated tones of stressed syllables are practically the same as in S.M. In terms of the four-interval, five-point system of tonal notation,[10] starting from 1 up to 5, the tones of S.M. are: 1st Tone, high-level, "55:"; 2d Tone, high-rising, "35:"; 3d Tone, low-dipping, "214:"; and 4th Tone, high-falling-to-low, "51:."

Like that of most Mandarin-speaking children, Canta's modification of 3d Tone into "half 3d," that is, low-falling "21:," comes sooner than the modification of 3d Tone into 2d Tone before another 3d Tone. This is also true of other Cantian tones. Some of the half 3d-Tone words were of course learned as fixed combinations and never heard as full 3d Tones, as in *yiidji* ("21: 55:"): *yii.tzy* 'chair.' But even in made-up combinations in which the first syllable is known in full 3d-Tone form, the change into half 3d Tone seems already to have been acquired, as *yeou* ("214:") 'have' in end position, versus *yeou tarn* ("21: 35:") 'have candy.' There are occasional slips, as *Dah yeou* ("214:") *tjwan* 'There is a ship here,' followed immediately by *Dah yeou* ("21:") *yu* 'There is a fish here,' where the 3d-Tone word *yeou* before a 2d Tone was given the full 3d Tone the first time and then a half 3d Tone right afterward.

The raising of a 3d-Tone word before another 3d Tone is, however, only beginning to be learned. Thus, *Beau yeou* ("21: 214:") 'The watch is there,' instead lf normal S.M.

"35: 214:." On one occasion she said *Bii yeou* 'The pencil is there' first in the tones "21: 214:"; then, after a few seconds, she corrected herself and gave the S.M. form "35: 214:"

The shifting tones of *i* 'one' and *bu* 'not,' which in S.M. are in the 4th Tone before 1st, 2d, and 3d Tones, and 2d before the 4th Tone, are usually generalized into the 4th Tone by most Mandarin-speaking children before they learn the shift. There is not enough material on *i* to judge by. The tone of *bu* is still 4th before all tones, as *buh day djii.śa : bwu tzay dii.shia* 'is not below.'

A feature of Canta's stress system that is of great phonological importance is the existence of true proclitic syllables, that is, weak and atonic syllables before a tonic stress. In S.M., weak and atonic ("neutral tone") syllables occur mostly in enclitic positions. Cantian has such forms too, as *poh.de : poh.le* 'has broken.' But while S.M. has no true iambs[11] but only quasi-iambs with half stress in initial position and full stress in end position in a polysyllabic group, the same combination in Cantian is often a true iamb, with neutral tone and quite weak stress for the first syllable, as *.be|ńa : |bye|na* 'Don't take it!'

When this initial weakening does occur, there is great reduction in medial, ending, and even the vowel. Thus, *śoei : shoei* 'water,' but *.śi|djiaw : |shuey|jiaw* 'to sleep'; *śao : sheau* 'small,' but *.śa|yi : |sheau|yi* 'little aunt.'

The pitch of neutral tone in proclitic position is middle or half-high. The pitch for enclitic position is approximately as in S.M. After the 1st Tone, if it is not a sentence particle, it is half-low, as in S.M., as *φua.dji* ("55 : .2:") : *shua.tzy* 'brush.' If, however, it is a sentence particle, it stays up, as *Danńhe* ("55 : 55:") : *Tzang.le* 'It's got dirty.' This gives a peculiarly Cantian intonation.

After a 2d-Tone word, which ends at pitch "5:," a neutral tone in S.M. comes down to the middle "3:." But the Cantian syllable in such a position stays up at "5:" and is usually not weak, that is, it is actually a 1st Tone. Moreover, the original 2d Tone

---

[10] See Y. R. Chao, "A System of Tone-letters," *Le Maître phonétique* (1930), p. 24. A rough approximation to the tone values can be obtained by humming the numerals in quotes as *do, re, mi, fa, sol,* e.g., "35:" as *mi-sol* (on a sliding scale, of course).

[11] This view is not generally accepted. For present purposes it would be sufficient to say that for many of those forms in S.M. which are only quasi-iambs, Cantian has true iambs.

usually changes into a half 3d Tone,[12] as *biitji* ("21 : 55:") : *byi.ti* ("35 : .3:") 'mucus from the nose.'

In *aadotjeandji* ("21: 55: 21: 55:") : *eel* (*.dou*)*chyan.tzy* ("21: .2: 35: .3:") 'earring,' the last two syllables *tjeandji* have the same tonal pattern as in *djeandji : jean.tzy* 'scissors.' Moreover, *yiidji* serves both for *yi.tzy* 'soap' and *yii.tzy* 'chair,' a point tested by showing Canta alternately a piece of soap and a chair in quick succession and asking what they were. She made no effort to distinguish them and seemed mildly amused that they had the same name. That she had heard the 2d Tone plus neutral at least sometimes is shown in her self-correction when she echoed someone's mentioning *shyebar.tzy* 'shoehorn,' first as *śerbaadji* ("35: 21: 55:"), and then corrected herself by saying with S.M. tones *śerbar.dji* ("35: 35: .3"). The tonal pattern of the last two syllables is, however, still rare with her.

After the 3d Tone, as seen in the example just given, a neutral in S.M. is given a high pitch "55:" (instead of the usual "4:"). It is not weak and should also be considered as being in the 1st Tone. After the 4th Tone, the pitch of a neutral tone is low, as in S.M.

The initial of a neutral-tone syllable in enclitic position undergoes certain changes. Some of these changes are as in S.M., such as the voicing of *b, d, g*, etc., as already noted. If the preceding syllable ends in a nasal, a following unstressed plosive (occasionally stressed ones, too), whether aspirated or unaspirated, becomes a nasal. Thus, the names of the colors with the subordinative particle *.de* attached take the following forms:

horn.ńe : *horng.de* 'red'; *hoanńhe* : *hwang.de* 'yellow'; *ńaanńhe* : *lan.de* 'blue'; but *yuh.de* : *liuh.de* 'green.' For *pyngguoo* 'apple,' which she spoonerizes into what would be **kwenpoo*, she actually says *.kemmoo* (".4 : 214:").

This assimilatory feature has resulted in a peculiar difficulty in her terms of address. People in the family have the publicly used terms: *bah.ba* 'papa' and adapted English forms *mha.mhi* 'mommy,' *guam.pa* 'grandpa,' *guam.ma* 'grandma.' She had difficulty in saying the last two and started to use spoonerized forms *pan.ngua* and *mam.ma*. She was laughed into correcting herself, but because of this law of nasal assimilation the only phonologically possible form in the Cantian system is *guam.ma* for both *guam.pa* and *guam.ma* Under correction by people in the house, with displaced contrasting stress on |*pa* and |*ma*, she could force herself to say *.gem|pa*, *.gem|ma* (with English intonation on the contrasting syllables). But the term she naturally uses for either grandparent at latest recording is still *gam.ma* and *gem|pa* in free variation, with a slight preponderance of the former for 'grandpa' and the latter for 'grandma.' She also fails to respond distinctively if told by a third person to give something to *guam.pa* (or *guam.ma*), and she would act according as one or the other grandparent is likely to be the person concerned, irrespective of the form spoken.

Canta's speech, like that of many other children, includes spoonerisms, sometimes resulting in permanent forms which replace the originals entirely. The following instances have been recorded:

Cantian actual	Cantian prototype	S.M.	Meaning
.kemmoo	**.penguoo*	*pyngguoo*	'apple'
.kem.modjy	**.penguoodjy*	*pyngguoojy*	'apple cider'
djinn.hite	*djih.hinte*	*tzyhshyngsche*	'bicycle'
pan.ngua	**guam.pa*	*"guam.pa"*	'grandpa'
śayii	*iaśyy*	*lhashyy*	'go to stool'
śentja	*tjennśa*	*chennshal*	'shirt'
Tarn biau,	*Tarn dan,*	*Tarng tzang,*	'The candy is dirty, I don't want it any more'
dann.ńe.	*biaw.de.*	*bu yaw.le.*	
twen.huen	*hwen.tuen*	*hwen.tuen*	'One Ton' (stuffed dumplings)
tjy.śe	*śy.de*	*shy.de*	'wet'

[12] This is an instance of the lack of synchronism between tone and segmental elements, where an intrasyllabic rise (for the 2d Tone) is delayed and becomes an intersyllabic rise. The same phenomenon has been observed in the early speech of Canta's third aunt (who was one of the subjects of the study referred to in note 2 above), though she could not, of course, have influenced her.

Once, when a recording machine was used to record her speech and she heard the sentence *Yi.geh kuohren tzoou.de puh.tzy.lii chiu .le* 'A rich man has gone into a store,' she repeated it as *Pohyèn doou kuh.dji .iè* 'Broken man gone into the pants.' Since then she has called phonographs or disk records "pohkuh.dji."

2. GRAMMAR

Just as the sounds are underarticulated in Cantian, so are the sentences undercon-structed. It is true that the topic-comment relation in standard Chinese subject-predicate relation is already a looser relation than that of actor-action, and that the direction of action of verbs can be outward or inward according to (linguistic or situational) con-text; hence there is nothing specially Cantian in construction in sentences like: *Bey bii .bu nonndu* : *Woo bii bwu nonq-diou* 'I, pencil don't cause to lose,—I won't lose my pencil.' But since the verb-object order is not used in Cantian except in fixed combinations, the preceding construction bears a larger share of syntactical burden than it does in S.M. For example, *Yi jidaa wey* 'Aunt egg feed' : *Yi wey (woo) jitzeel* 'Aunt feed (me) eggs.' *Bey hairyaw dey.geh day* 'Baby still want this wear.' Since *hairyaw* is used for *yaw* 'want' in general, and *dey.geh* is used for both S.M. *jey.geh* and *ney.geh*, and the thing referred to was a brooch at some distance, it should be translated as *Woo yaw day ney.geh* 'I want to wear that.' But it would be misleading to leave the analysis there and regard 'wear that' as simply verb-object transposed. The real construction, in view of other parallel forms, is that of a subject-predicate clause serving as object of *hairyaw*. The constructional translation, with idiomatic equating of syntactic words, is, therefore, 'I wish that that be worn.'

There is a predominance of a few typical beginnings and endings (other than particles) of sentences over all other forms. Typical beginnings are:

Bey . . . 'I, the Baby . . .'

Śennday . . . : *Shianntzay* . . . 'Now . . .'

Ah, . . ., *ah*! for example, *Ah, deh φu, ah!* 'Look, this is a book, look!' This form was later abandoned in favor of the next.

Tjin! : *Ting!* 'Listen,' but actually used

for either looking at something or listening to something. This was also abandoned and replaced by the currently used form below.

Ńeekann or *.ńekann* or *.ńekan* : *Nii kann* '(You) look!' or, less frequently,

Ń-ńau! : *Nii chyau*! '(You) look!'

Deh or *Deh.hy* or *Deh.śy* : *Jeh.shy* 'This is.'

Hairyaw : *hairyaw* 'still want,' 'want more,' but actually used as *yaw* in asking for things even for the first time. It is often used before a sentence in the sense of 'I wish that...' as: *Hairyaw Bey tarntjyn wan.ńe* '(I) wish (that) I (be helped down from the piano stool because my) playing the piano is finished.'

Buh 'not' is also often used to negate whole sentences, as *Buh śoei ge dah* : *Shoei buh* (or *bye*) *ge .de jell* 'Don't put the water here.'

Common predicates are:

. . . *baw* or *biaw* : . . . *bu yaw* 'don't want,' 'not wanted' (name of thing not wanted in subject position and less frequently in object position).

. . . *ńaa.tji.de?* : . . . *naal.chiu.le?* 'Where is . . . gone to?'

. . . .*daydah* or . . . .*daydah.ńe* : *tzay*[13] *jell* (.*ne*) '. . . is here.'

. . . *fanndah* : . . . *fanq .de jell* 'Put the . . . here.' (*Fanq*, used by half the people in the house, is not the usual S.M. word for 'put,' as the next is.)

. . . *gedah* : . . . *ge .de jell* 'Put the . . . here.'

. . . *wan.ńe* : . . . *wan.le* 'finished . . .' is used as a complete predicate rather than as a complement as in S.M. Thus, *tjyfann wan.ńe* in normal S.M. construction would be *chy-wan.le fann .le* or *chy-fann chy-wan.le* 'have finished eating.' Once in a while the S.M. repetitive construction is used, as *Bey tjifann tjibaa.ue* : *Bey chy-fann chy-bao.le* 'I have finished eating dinner.'

Subordination is mostly in the same word order as in S.M., but the subordinative particle .*de* is not used except in fixed com-binations. Examples are *Bey wah.dji* : *Bey* (.*de*) *wah.tzy* 'My stocking'; *Mhamhi geei śer djiaw .de* (i.e., ...*le*) 'The shoe Mommy gave me has come off'; *Deh. hy gam.ma mae* ("21:") *bii* ("214:") : *Jeh.shy guam.pa mae .de bii* 'This is the pencil grandpa bought.' But at least once, clearly enough from the

---

[13] S.M. does have a form *day* 'to be at,' but it is not frequently heard around the house.

situation, a restrictive modifier followed: *Deh.hy Bey śer baw* : *Nah.shy Bey bu yaw .de shye* 'Those are my discarded shoes.'

It is not common for Chinese children to make up compounds other than transient compounds such as numerals plus classifiers. This is also true of Cantian, with two or three interesting exceptions. One is *djihśoei* : *dihshoei* 'ground-water,' which she applies to 'sea, river, lake, pond, inlet.' The first time she made this up was when she saw a pond. The other is *huooden* : *huoodeng* 'fire-light' a term she invented when she saw lit candles at a house she was visiting. On most previous occasions, when the word *deng* was heard, it referred to electric lights. Rice soup is called *fannhetan*, where *hetan* : *hetang* 'drink soup' is used as a noun for 'soup.'

Parts of speech and form classes in general are greatly underdifferentiated, and one instance of use in agreement with S.M. syntax should not be taken as conclusive evidence that certain words are being used in the same function as in S.M. We have just noted that, in the compound *fannhetan*, *hetan* is not verb-object, but a noun. The sentence *Bey hairyaw gaybey.uo* seems to mean 'I want to cover myself with the quilt,' an interpretation apparently confirmed when she is satisfied when so covered. But on another occasion she said *Bry taandji, deh gaybey.uo— bry gaybey.uo, gaybey.uo śannyou.ue* : *Bwu.shy taan.tzy, jeh (shyh) (gay)bey.uo—bwu.shy (gay)bey.uo, (gay)bey.uo shang-lou .le* 'It's not a blanket, it's a quit—it's not a quilt, the quilt is gone upstairs.' The obvious conclusion is that *gaybey.uo* 'to cover with a quilt' in S.M. is in Cantian a noun 'quilt.' But the obvious is not necessarily true. To attribute a noun or a verb category to the Cantian syntax is to read too much adult grammar into it. Actually, both verbal expressions in S.M. like *gay-bey.uo*, and substantive expressions like *shoei* when occurring in Cantian, are still undifferentiated in her language. *Śoei* : *shoei* in *Deh.hy śoei* 'This is water' seems to be a substantive, but most of the time it means 'I want to have a drink of water.' *Śoou* : *shoou* 'hand,' but in *Bey śoou deng* it means '(I) touch the (the lamp).' *Kannbaw* 'to read a newspaper' in S.M. is either 'to read a newspaper' or 'newspaper.' *Biitji* : *byi.ti* 'mucus from the

nose' in S.M. also means in Cantian 'wipe my nose' and 'tissue paper.' When *tayyeh .ue* : *tay reh .le* was spoken for taking off a bib in order to put a pin on the dress below, it was not a wrong statement about her sensation of warmth, but a real request.

Like most other children, Canta finds personal pronouns, or "shifters," difficult to acquire. The only personal pronoun that Canta uses is *ńii*, and mostly in special combinations. *Ńeekann* : *Nii kann* 'Look' has already been noted. The form *gĩ*, from *geei nii* 'for you' (i.e., for Canta herself), is often used. The active independent use of *ńii* is established by a sentence *Gam.ma day ńii* (stressed) *tu.tjiu* : *Guam.ma day nii chu.chiu* 'Grandma will take you (i.e., me) to go out.' Previous to this utterance the word *nii* had not been heard for at least half an hour. The pronouns *woo* and *ta* and their compounds are not in the Cantian vocabulary.

Numerals do not form a significant part of the vocabulary. She recites the numerals for fun in random order, but not to use them as numbers. The form *i.geh* is used, but more frequently for several things than for one thing, the reason being that when there are several things other people often count *yi.geh*, *leang.geh*, *san.geh*, etc., and the first word gets better remembered. Plurality of things is expressed by repeating the name of the thing, as *tjihte, tjihte, tjihte* 'many automobiles.' At one stage, when Little Aunt had been correcting her *geng* for *deng* 'light' by making her say "*de-de-deng*," she began to call a light *dededen*. Then, passing the Bay Bridge one night, with its many lights along the way, she said, "De-de-de-de-de-de- . . . -den!"

The perfective particle *.le*, often with the 'new-situation' meaning, had been acquired for some time, with the phonetic substitution *.ię*, but recently she was dissatisfied with the palatal articulation and so changed it to *.de*, which is dental enough, like *.le*, though not so good with respect to manner of articulation. But it continues to be *.ię* after words ending in *-i*, *.ue* after words ending in *-u*, and *.ńe* after nasal endings. Thus, *yai.ię* : *lai.le* 'has come'; *hao .ue* : *hao .le* 'all right now'; *ńeen.ńe* : *leeng .le* '(I'm) getting cold.' That this particle has been learned as an active and independent lexical unit is shown by the following examples. .Ńekann Bey doh.śa (1-second pause) .de : Nii kann Bey tzuoh .shia .le 'Look, I've sat down'; daatjih.iė .de : daa-tih .le '(I have) sneezed,' where the .iė in daatjih.iė is from the fixed form daa-tih .le, while the .de was added as the particle meaning 'here is something happening.'

Questions understood and asked are mostly limited to the form . . . shyh sheir 'Who is . . .?' . . . tzay naal.ne? 'Where is . . .?' and Jeh.shy sherm.me? 'What is this?' The form Nah.shy sherm.me? 'What's that?' is understood but not used. There is an abbreviated Cantian form .De.me? often used in asking the names of things (near or distant). When not so abbreviated, a rising-tone interrogative interjection (not a particle) is often added after a comma-length pause: Deh. hy śe. me, ə̃?

The active use of śe.me sherm.me 'what' in attributive position was a very recent acquisition. The first recorded use was Deh śe.me te? : Nah.shy sherm.me che? 'What (sort of) vehicle is that?' Deh śe.me ha?: Nah.shy sherm.me hual? 'What (sort of) flower is that?'

Other forms of questions, such as questions involving yaw.bu.yaw, yeou.mei-.yeou, etc., questions ending in .ma and involving interrogative words other than those mentioned above, are not in active use. The sentence Deh.hy bu.hy yaφa : Jeh.shy bwu.shy yashua was apparently a question of the A-not-A form. But the actual stress and intonation and the situation showed that it was not a question, but a statement: 'This is a not-toothbrush.' Real questions in the A-not-A form or .ma form are not even understood unless helped out by the situation, in which case an apparent answer is not really an answer to the question, but rather an utterance made in response to the situation. Thus, no answer could be elicited from the question Shianqpyi tzay naal jao.jaur .de? 'Where did you find the eraser?' In her active use of the form . . . .daynaa .de? apparently meaning 'where is . . .?' it is as much a command to look for something as a question about the location. Now that the eraser is found, there is no point in asking where it was found. As usual, I think it is more accurate to regard this as evidence, not for the primacy of the pragmatic function of language, but for the lack of differentiation of the early functions of language. In fact, for months after Canta began to say hɛ at the sight of water or while drinking water, it never occurred to her that the same sound could be used a a means of obtaining water to drink.

There is a larger proportion of foreign loans in interjections than in other words. There is Ouch! for minor hurts, Oh-oh! ("5: 22:") for minor mishaps, Hi! for greeting other children, 'bye! (with Chinese voiceless initial but English intonation "423:") for parting. These are used along with the usual Chinese interjections Oio! Aio! Aiio! Ah! etc. A voiced h with a prolonged neutral vowel ə is used for expressing impatience or exasperation, which can shade into actual crying in extreme cases. A very constant stylistic feature of Canta's speech is the changing of speaking to singing at the moment when there is evidence that a repeated request is acceded to, even though no overt action is taken. Thus, if Bey yaw he śoei 'I want a drink of water' is repeated several times and the tone becomes more and more impatient, the moment someone acknowledges the request and says, say, 'I'll get you some water as soon as I am through with this,' then the same words Bey yaw he śoei will be sung to various improvised tunes (not in adult scales). If the initial request is repeated four or five times, a promise to grant it will invariably be followed by singing of the words.

In more complicated organization of words into sentences there is some experimentation in putting building blocks together, whether they form any building she has seen before or not. Some of these turn out to be quite normal S.M. constructions, as:

Bey śannpyi daynah .ńe : Bey shianqpyi tzaynall .ne 'I, eraser is there.'

Gam.ma i.śan dah yeou .ue, ńiindah dah yeou .ue : Guam.pa i.shang jell yeou.le, liingdall jell yeou .le 'Grandpa clothes here are, necktie here is.'

But some sentences are difficult to understand without the help of the situational context. Examples are:

Kaiden nah : kai-deng nall,—kai nall .de deng 'Turn on the light over there.'

Hetan śoou : he tang shoou, —na shoou he tang 'drink soup with the hand.'

Ńeekann Bey yee tjy djidaa wan.ńe : *Nii kann Bey yee chy-wan.le jitzeel .le* 'Look, I've also finished eating my eggs.'

Bey hairyaw tjoei danńha : *Bey hairyaw toei tzang .le, —Woo yaw tsa.tsa toei, woo toei tzang .le* 'I want to have my leg wiped, my leg is dirty.'

Gam.ma yeou ("214:") *bii* ("21":") *śannpyi* : *Guam.pa yeou bii shianqpyi* 'Grandpa has pencil eraser.' In view of the full 3d Tone on *yeou*, the true analysis should probably be 'Grandpa (does) have (when it is a question of) pencil eraser.'

Bey hairyaw kannbow day naa.tji .de? : *Bey hairyaw kannbaw daw naal chiu .le, —Woo yaw kann* (*.de*) *baw naal .chiu .le?* 'Where is the newspaper I want to read?'

Bey yeandjin me'oou.ue djinn.dji Canta : *Bey yean.jing meiyeou.le jing.tzy Canta* 'My eyes have no glasses (to) mirror Canta.' The translation of *djinn.dji* by the verb 'to mirror' is not so far-fetched as it might seem, since Cantian nouns and verbs are not such distinct things as in S.M.

(At top of her voice, *ff*:) *Dahdjinn!* : *dahjinq,tzy* 'big mirror.'

(Someone says: *Bye jiaw!* 'Don't shout!')

(Then, after 2 min., *p*:) *Bey śennday .budjiaw* (*mf*:) *Dahdjinn* (*pp*:) *wan.ńe*. Here, the specially greater loudness on repeating the word *dahdjinn* was obviously to quote her own previous shouting, but the construction is quite a mixed one, consisting of *Bey shianntzay bwu "Dahjinq" .le* 'I am no longer shouting "Big mirror"' and *Jiaw "Dahjinq" jiaw-woan.le* 'I am through shouting "Big mirror."'

Cantian 49 has just emerged from the prattling stage. But under emotion, especially of exciting interest, such as trying to narrate a scene of a recent past, there are still long and rapid strings of unphonemicizable sounds, mixed here and there with real words. Such passages are difficult to transcribe, even from the phonograph recordings.

There is occasional intentional playing with language. Words and phrases are often sung to improvised tunes, as has been noted above. Sometimes a syllable would be put through the four tones, although Canta has not heard the order of the tones more than ten times. In playing with the tones on more than one syllable, there is often substitution of intersyllabic change for intrasyllabic change, as has already been noted in her speech pattern. Thus, the four tones played on her own name "Canta" take the form "5: 55:," "5: 35:," "21: 5," "55: 1:."

In playing with tones, the resulting syllables are usually not expected to make sense. Once, when she said the word *.śidjao* : *shii-tzao* 'take bath' in four tones ".5: 55:," ".5: 35," ".5: 214:," ".5: 51:," she was surprised and amused that the last one made sense, since in proclitic position *śuey* normally becomes *śi* and the result is *.śidjiaw* : *shuey-jiaw* 'go to sleep,' which is what she does after taking her bath.

There is often intentional misnaming of things. Thus, after having learned that a cushion is called *djɛnn.dji* : *diann.tzy* and not *taandji* : *taan.tzy*, the word for 'blanket,' she often answers uniformly "taandji" when asked what various other things are. Since the word *taandji* was once used as the wrong name for something, a more subtle interpretation for it, when it continues to be used for everything, might be 'wrong name for that thing.'

3. VOCABULARY

Only active vocabulary spoken on her own initiative and not by immediate echoing is included here. Items which are obsolete at this stage are so marked. Needless to say, bound forms are not taken out of context and given what would be the S.M. meaning. Thus, while both *ńaw* : *naw* 'fussy, make noise' and *.beńaw* : *bye naw* 'don't make such a noise' are included, only *.bedonn* : *bye donq* 'don't move' is entered, since **donn* : *donq* 'move' is not known to have occurred in any other context. As in S.M., the main stress in a group is always on the last syllable not preceded by a dot, which is a sign for weak stress, or "neutral tone."

On the orthography used here see page 117, esp. footnote 3.

A!: *A!* (with initial glottal stop, in both Cantian and S.M. after a proposal, with an 'all is well' intonation) 'shall we?' 'let's'

aadoutjɛɛndji: *eelchyan.tzy* 'carring'

aadou: *eel.dou* 'ear'

ah.dji: *wah.tzy* 'stocking,' obsolete, superseded by *wah.dji*

Ahyi: *Ellyi* 'Second Aunt,' term of address

Ahyiah.ɸu: *Ellyi.fu* 'Second Uncle,' term of address

Aio! or *Aiio!*: (*same*) 'Goodness!'

au.djin: *iodine* '(tincture) of iodine'

audjyn: *iodine* 'soy bean sauce'; 'dark gravy' (second syllable given a 2d Tone, apparently to distinguish it from real iodine)

baw: *baw* 'newspaper'

baw, *biaw*: *bu yaw* 'don't want'; 'I don't want it'

baede: *bair.de* 'white'

beau: *beau* 'a watch'

.beda: *byejel* '(safety) pin'

.bedonn: *bye donq* 'don't move'

.bena: *bye na* 'don't take it'; 'something not to be taken,' as *Deh.hy.bena* 'this is . . .'

.benaw: *bye naw* 'don't make such a noise'

.benga: *biinggal* 'crackers'

.benonn: *bye nonq* 'don't play with that'; 'something not to play with'

.betuu: *bye tuu* 'don't spit it'; 'to eat down,' as *Bey.betuu wan.ne* 'I have finished not-spitting it (i.e., swallowing it)'

bey: *baby* 'doll'; also applied to children of the same age as herself or older

Bey or *Bey.bei*: *Baby* 'I, the Baby'

biaw, *baw*: *buyaw* 'don't want'; 'I don't want it'

bi.bi: *pipi* (Fr.) = *śańaw*

biidji: *byi.tzy* 'nose'

biitji: *byi.ti* 'mucus from nose'; 'wipe my nose'; 'tissue paper'

bindjyn: *bingchiling* 'ice cream'

bo.bo: *bor.bo* 'Uncle,' addressing men of father's generation

bu, *bu.hy*, *bry*: *bwu.shy* 'is not'

.budjiaw: *buhjydaw* 'I wonder' (not used as direct reply 'I don't know,' which is expressed by mere silence)

.budjuey: *bwuduey* 'that's wrong'

buhśaa: *buh saa* 'will not spill'

buhtern.ńe: *buh terng.le* 'doesn't hurt any more'

'bye [*ḅai*]: 'Goodbye!'; 'leave, go away'

da: *ja* 'prick'

daa: *daa* 'beat, strike'

daambann.ńe: *tzeem bann.ne?* 'what shall we do?' (spoken in fun, apparently without knowing what this expression is used for)

daatjih.ie: *daa-tih.le* 'sneeze'

dah: *dah* 'big'

dahdjinn: *dah-jinq.tzy* 'big mirror'

dahkoou: *dahkoou* 'with wide-open mouth'

dahtaan: *dahchaang* 'overcoat'

dan: *tzang* 'dirty'

danńhe: *tzang .le* 'dirty, soiled'

.danaa.tji.de: *daw naal .chiu .le* 'where is . . . gone to?'

dannge: *dah.muge* 'thumb'

dao: *jao* 'look for'

daśann: *jawshiangjing.tzy* 'camera'

dau: *dau* 'knife'

day: *day* 'take along'

day: *day* 'put on'; 'wear'

daydah, *.daidah*: *tzayjell* 'it's here'

.day ńaa.ńe: *tzay naal.ne* 'where is . . . ?'

daynah, *.dainah*: *tzaynall* 'is there'

dededen: *deng* 'lamp, light' (obsolete)

.de.me: *Jeh sherm.me* 'what is this?'

deh, *deh.hy*: *jeh.sh* 'this is'

den: *deng* 'lamp, light'

denn.dji: *deng.tzy* 'a stool'

dey.geh: *jay.geh* 'this, that'

djeandji: *jean.tzy* 'scissors'

dijean.śin: *dean.shin* 'refreshment'

djeau: *jeau* 'foot'

djeou, *djeou-pas-bon*: *jeou* 'wine'; 'wine, which is no good (for children)'

djeudji: *jyu.tzy* 'orange.' (This is the family usage. In S.M., *jyu.tzy* is 'tangerine' and *chern.tzy* is 'orange.')

dji: *ji* 'chicken'

−.dji (or *dji* after 3d Tone): *.tzy* noun suffix

djiandjeou: *deanjeou* 'tincture of iodine'

djiannh(u)ah: *diannhuah* 'telephone'

djiannte: *diannche* 'streetcar'

djiaw: *jiaw* 'shout'

djiaw.iė: *diaw.le* 'come off'; 'dropped'

djidaa: *jitzeel* 'egg'

djieedji: *dye.tzy* 'plate, saucer'

.djigaa: *tzyhgeel* 'myself'

djih: *dih* 'floor, ground'

djih.hinte, *djinn.hite*: *tzyhshyngche* 'bicycle'

djih.śa: *dih.shia* 'floor, ground'

djihśɛrdah: *jih shyedall* 'tie the shoestring'; 'shoestring'

djihśoei: *dihshoei* 'ground-water,' applied to pond, sea, etc.

djii.śa: *dii.shia* 'below'

djin: *ding* 'nail, screw'

djinn.dji: *jinq.tzy* 'mirror'

djiuśoei: *jyu.tzyshoei* 'orange juice'; 'organge'

djoadji: *joa.tzy* 'paw'

djoei: *tzoei* 'mouth'

djudju: *dudu* 'train' (obsolete, too childish for her)

djyy = (second) *tjyy*

doh.śa: *tzuoh.shia.lai* 'sit down'

don: *jong* 'clock'

doou: *tzoou* 'walk'; 'go, leave'

do.śan: *juo.shanq* 'is on the desk'

duh.dji: *duh.tzy* 'belly'

"*ẽ*"— : "*ẽ*"— 'uh—'; '—er—'

"*ẽ*"? (long rising tone): *ar?* 'huh?'

ein (sic!): *ian* 'cigarette'

faandji, *hoandji*: *farng.tzy* 'house'

fann: *fanq* 'put'

fanndah djinn.dji: *fanqdah-jinq* 'magnifying glass'

fannhetan : *fanntang* 'rice soup'

feidji : *feiji* 'airplane'

φoei : *shoei* 'water' (obsolete, replaced by *śoei*)

φu.dji : *shu.tzy* 'comb'

φuh : *shuh* 'tree'

φu : *shu* 'book'

φua.dji : *shua.tzy* 'brush'

φuai : *shuai* 'fall, stumble'

φuaya, yaφua : used for both *shuaya* 'brush the teeth' and *yashua* 'toothbrush'

φuo : *shuo* 'say'

φu-tour : *shu-tour* 'comb the hair'

ga : *gal* 'liver'

ga.ga : *caca* (Fr.) = *iaśyy*

gan ńhe : *gan.le* 'dry'

gau : *gau* 'cake'

gaybey.ue : (*gay*)*bey.uo* 'quilt'

ge : *ge* 'put'

ge.bey : *ge.bey* 'arm'

geei : *geei* 'give'

.gī : *geei.nii* 'for you' (i.e., me)

gon, gon.gon : *gong.gong* term of address for men who are of grandfather's generation, or who look so

gon.bo : *gongbor* 'greatuncle–uncle,' Cantian term of address for an intermediate generation

gongonntjihte : *gonggonqchihche* 'bus'

goou : *goou* 'dog'

guai : *guai* 'good' (of children)

guanmen : *guanmen* 'shut the door'

gunae : *goodnight* 'good night'; 'to kiss'

gwu.tu : *gwu.tou* 'bone'

haakann, .hakann : *hakann* 'pretty'

haatji, haatjy : *haochy* 'good to eat'; 'to eat'

.ha.duduh : — 'How do you do?'

hairyaw, hairyaw yaw : *yaw* 'want'; 'want some more'

hao : *hao* 'good'; 'not dirty'; 'not wet'

hao .ue : *hao .le* 'all right now'

.hayou : *hwangyou* 'butter'

he : *he* 'drink'

.hei.djidjia, hweidjia : *hwei-jia* 'home'

hetan : *he tang* 'soup'

Hi ! [*hai*] :— 'Hi!'

hoanńhe : *hwang.de* 'yellow'

horn.ńe : *horng.de* 'red,' any bright color

.hotjoei : *huootoei* 'ham'

h(u)a : *hual* 'flower'

h(u)ah : *huah* 'draw'; 'write'

huoo : *huoo* 'fire'

huooden :— 'candle'

h(u)oote : *huooche* 'train'

huudji : *hwu.tzy* 'mustache'

hwen.tuen, twen.tuen, twen.huen : hwen.tuen 'one ton' (stuffed dumplings)

.hy, .śy, śyh : *.shy, shyh* 'is'

ia.dji : *ia.tzy* 'duck'

iaia, ia.ia :— 'to rock' (as rocking chair); 'to sway' (as tree) (a made-up word)

iaśyy, śayii : *iha-shyy* 'go to stool'

i.djea : *yihdeal* 'a little'

i.ge : *yi.ge* 'several' (sic!)

i.śan : *i.shang* 'dress'

kafei, kafei-pas-bon : *kafei* 'coffee'; 'coffee, which is no good (for children)'

kaiden : *kai-deng* 'turn on the light'; 'the light'

kaimen : *kai-men* 'open the door'

kannbaw : *kann-baw* 'read the newspaper'; 'newspaper'

kei.śi :— 'kiss'

.kemmoo : *pyngguoo* 'apple'

.kenmoodjy : *pyngguoojy* 'apple cider'

koh.dji, obsolete form for both *kow.dji* and *kuh.dji*, q.v.

kow.dji : *kow.tzy* 'button'

ku : *ku* 'cry'

kuay.dji : *kuay.tzy* 'chopstick'

kuhdah : *kuhdall* 'belt' (not necessarily for *kuh.dji* 'pants')

kuh.dji : *kuh.tzy* 'pants'

maa : *maa* 'horse,' also applied to 'seahorse' when seen in a picture for the first time

maedon.śi : *mae dong.shi* 'buy things'

mam.ma : *guan.ma* 'grandma' (obsolete)

maw.dji : *maw.tzy* 'hat'

meeimhau : *mei:mau* 'eyebrows'

meiyeou.ue : *meiyeou.le* 'have not'; 'there is not'; 'not there'

men, mhein : *men* 'door' (second form made up for fun)

me'oou.ue : *meiyeou.le* 'have not'; 'there is not'; 'not there'

mey.mei : *mey.mei* 'younger sister,' applied to girls (sometimes boys) of the same age as herself or younger

mha.mhi ("55 : 22 :") :— 'mommy,' term applied to her own mother only

mhamhi ("5 : 5 :") :— 'Look!' term used for introducing a remark to anyone

mhau (with very fronted and long a) : *mhau* 'cat'

.mεnbau : *miannbau* 'bread'

mεnn : *miann* 'noodles'

mhein, see *men*

ńaanńhe : *lan.de* 'blue'

naa.tji.de : *naal .chiuh .le* 'where is . . . gone to?'

ńaeńhai : *nae.nai* term of address for women of grandparents' generation, usually prefixed by surname

ńao : *neaul* 'bird'

ńaw : *naw* 'be fussy'; 'make noise'

ńaw : *niaw* 'urine'

ńean = *yean*

ńeen : *leeng* 'cold'; 'to be stripped to the waist'

ńeekann, .ńekann, .ńekan : *nii kann* 'look' (directing attention)

ńii : *nii* 'you' (Canta herself only)

ńiindah : *liingdall* 'necktie'

ńiou : *niou* 'ox, cow'

ńiounae : niounae '(cow's) milk'

ń-ńau : nii chyau '(you) look!'

ńoan.ɸu : noan.huo 'warm'

nonndu : nonq-diou 'cause to be lost'

nonnɸuay : nonq-huay 'to spoil by playing with'

oh-oh ("5 : 22 :") :— 'oh-oh' used as in English

oiv! ("5 : 5 :") : *oio!* interjection for a sudden (but not too important) turn of events. Cf. preceding item

ouch ! :— 'ouch!'

pah : pah 'afraid,' used principally when in danger of falling

pair : pair '(playing) card'

pam.ma, pam.pa, pan.ngua : guam.pa 'grandpa' (obsolete)

par : par 'crawl'

parn.hɛ : parng.shie 'crab'

pas bon :— (with voiceless initial in both words) 'tastes bad'; also used as suffixes to *kafei, djeou,* and *tar,* q.v.

penntour .ue : penq.le tour .le 'I bumped my head'

pih.bu, pih.u : pih.gu 'buttocks'

poh kuh.dji : poh kuh.tzy 'broken trousers,' term applied to phonographs or records

śaabiah : sheaubiall 'small pigtail'

śaa.iė : saa.le 'spilt'

saańhuńhu : sheaunhiounhiou 'little finger'

saańhe : saan.le 'come loose'

Śaayi = .Śayi

.śabɛnn.dji = śaabiah

.śag(u)ah.dji : sheauguah.tzy 'undershirt'

śahyeu : shiah-yeu 'rain'

śahyou : shiah-lou 'go downstairs'; 'downstairs'

śan : suan 'sour'

śańaw : sa-niaw 'urinate'

śandjiau : shiangjiau 'banana'

śanntjwan : shanq-chwang 'go up the bed' 'on the bed'; 'bed'

śannyou : shanq-lou 'go upstairs'; 'upstairs'

.śanpyi, śannpyi : shianqpyi 'rubber (band)'; 'eraser'

śao : sheau 'small'

śaur : shaurl 'spoon'

śạw : shiạw 'laugh'

.Śayi, Śaayi : Sheauyi 'Little Aunt,' term of address

Sayi : Śanyi 'Third Aunt,' term of address (for a different person from above)

.śɛbaadji, śɛrbar.dji : shyebar.tzy 'shoehorn'

sɛbon (with voiceless *b*) :—'c'est bon,' i.e., 'tastes good'

.śɛdah : shyedall 'shoestring'

.śɛdjih : shiee-tzyh 'to write'

śɛɛ : shiee 'to write'

śɛh.śɛ, hɛh.hɛ : shieh.shie 'Thank you' (in response to something given)

śɛnnday : shianntzay 'now'

śerm.me, .śe.me : sherm.me 'what'; 'what kind of'

śɛr, śeir : shye 'shoe'

.śibuh : sueibuh 'diaper'

.śidao, .śidjeau : shii-tzao 'take bath'

.śidjeau : shii-jeau 'wash the feet'

.śi.djia-i : shueyjiaw-i 'nightshirt'; 'bathrobe'

.sidjiaw : shuey-jiaw 'go to bed'; 'sleep'

Śihyi 'Fourth Aunt' = *.Śayi*

śinn : shinn 'letter'

śinn.śin : meaning unknown, occurring in *Gam.ma buhyeou śinn.śin.*

śiou.śi :— 'Susie' (formerly *hiou.hi*)

śiow.dji : shiow.tzy 'sleeve'; term also applied to undershirt the sleeve of which is sucked

soei : shoei 'water'

śoo.iė : suoo.le 'locked'

śoou : shoou 'hand'; 'touch with hand'

śooudjiah : shooujiuall 'handkerchief'

śooudjin : shoou.jin 'towel'

śy.de : shy.de 'wet'

śyh = .hy

śy.iė : shy.le 'it's (got) wet'

śyi.śí : shii.shi 'just wash'; 'give it a washing'

śyy : shyy 'excrement'

't (glottalized *t* with oral explosion) : *.tzy,* noun suffix, now replaced by *.dji,* q.v.

ta : cha 'fork'

taandji : taan.tzy 'blanket'

ta.mi :— 'Tommy'

tan : chuan 'put on'; 'wear'

tann : tanq 'hot'

Tan.ta : Kan.ta 'Canta'

tao.ue : chaur.le 'it's (got) wet'

tar, tar-pas-bon : char 'tea'; 'tea, which is no good (for children)'

tarn : tarng 'eandy'; 'sugar'

tarntjyun : tarn-chyn 'play the piano'

ta.ta : tsa.tsa 'wipe a little'

tay : tsay 'vegetable'

.tayėh.ue : tay reh.le 'too hot'; 'take off' (a sweater, a bib, etc.)

tay djonn.ńe : tay jonq.le 'it's too heavy'

tay.iang : tay.iang 'sun,' sometimes also applied to the moon

tayśɛrn : tay shyan 'too salty'

tern : terng 'it hurts'

tjɛnbii : chianbii 'pencil'

tjibaa.ue : chy-bao.le 'have eaten enough'; 'I want to leave the table'

tjeai.de : chii.lai.le 'have got up'

tjennśa : chennshal 'shirt'

tjih : tsyh '(small) fishbone'

tjihte : chihche 'automobile'

tjihtjyou : chihchyou 'balloon'

tjin : ting 'listen!' previously also used for 'look!'

tjoei : toei 'leg'

tjuan.hu : chuang.hu 'window'

tjuei.tjuei : chuei.chuei 'blow' (hot food, etc.)

tjwan : chwan 'ship'; 'bed'

tjy, tji : chy 'eat'

tjyăn : chyang 'wall'
tjyɛn : chyan 'money, coin'
tjyɛn : tyan 'sweet'
tjyfann, tjifann : chy-fann 'eat dinner'
tjyy : chyy 'ruler'
tjyy, djyy : jyy 'paper' (can say *djyy* with effort)
to : tuo 'take off'
tośɛr : tuoshye 'slipper'
tośɛr : tuo shye 'take off shoes'
tooufa : tour.fa 'hair' (of the head)
tu.chiu : chu.chiu 'go out'
tufann = tjyfann
tuh.dji : tuh.tzy 'rabbit'
twen.tuen = huen.tuen
wa : wal 'play with'
wan.ńe, woanńhe 'finished,' applied to many things, as *Kaiden wan.ńe* 'Turn on the lights finished,' i.e., 'The lights are out'
wey : wey 'to feed'; also used for 'help' in general such as taking her by the hand in going downstairs
woan : woan 'bowl'
yaφua = φuaya
yah : lah 'hot' (of taste)

yai : lai 'come'
yai.e : lai.le 'has come'; 'here is . . .'
yăn : yang 'sheep'
yeaba : laa.ba '(toy) horn'
yean, ńean : lean 'face, cheek'
yeandah : yeanjienql 'eyeglasses'
yeandjin : yean.jing 'eye'
yee : yee 'also'
yėh : reh 'warm, hot'
yɛnn.dji : yuann.tzy 'garden'
yi : yi 'aunt'
yiidji : yi.tzy 'soap'
yiidji : yii.tzy 'chair'
.yobo (pause) *śibiin : luo.bosybiing* 'hot biscuits stuffed with radish shreds'
yoobo : luo.bo 'radish'; 'turnip'
you : you 'grease' (on fingers or clothes)
yow : row 'meat'
yu : yu 'fish'
yu : liu 'donkey' (pronounced *yœ* when trying to distinguish from above)
yueh.iȧn : yueh.liang 'moon'
yuh.de : liuh.de 'green'; 'blue'
yun.tai : yun.tsai 'cloud'

MARCEL COHEN〜〜〜〜〜〜〜〜〜〜〜〜〜〜〜〜〜〜

27 Cohen, very well-known as a specialist in Semitic languages and an authority on the languages of the world in general, is one of the relatively few linguists who paid serious attention to child language at an early date, since 1925. His major contribution to the study of children's language learning is "Sur l'étude du langage enfantin," *Enfance* V (1952), 181–249, in which he combines methodological postulates and theoretical considerations with selected observations made on his seven children and grandchildren (one more child, recently born, appears in a footnote). One chapter in translation is included here as a sample of his approach.

The names of the children (in this selection J. and J.–L.) are given only in abbreviated form. Age is indicated by months (18 = 1;6). The phonetic transcription is not explained, but should present no difficulties.

W. F. L.

ACQUISITION AND PRACTICE OF CHILD LANGUAGE

In regard to the spoken language, the period considered here extends from the first at-

Reprinted in translation by the editors from Enfance *5.205–209 (1952) by permission of the author and* Enfance.

tempts to reproduce the spoken language of adults until the moment when grammar begins to be used.

But this period must be subdivided, keeping in mind the different stages, the boundaries of which can hardly be drawn exactly. On the other hand, noticeably more so than in the complete speech of the adults, elements other than properly so-called words come into play and must be closely examined if one really wants to understand the exercise of the intellect and its instrument of communication at the age considered.

It is necessary to distinguish many elements and operations without forgetting that in practice they are intermingled at every moment. The account must therefore in its turn be subdivided into sections. But certain considerations apply to everything and must be stated first.

On the one hand the child responds by imitation, or rather by the effort to imitate, to training from adults, to acquire sounds and their combinations as well as to learn the meanings attached to these combinations.

On the other hand the child perceives more or less well, imitates in part mechanically, and remembers much more than what is deliberately taught.

From still another point of view, he is not simply an imitator. In response to urgent needs which he cannot satisfy by devices which he has not yet learned, he resorts often enough to inventions (*créations*) which in large part are comprehended and accepted by adults. (Some of them remain useless because they are not understood.)[1]

Invention does not stop with early childhood; it merely takes other forms after the approximate normalization of the inventory of sounds. In childhood and later, fanciful use of "mouth noises" must be taken into account. On the other hand more or less active invention is practiced by adults in the creation of words (particularly nicknames given to children and other persons), sometimes of grammatical elements (analogical forms of conjugation, extension of derivative suffixes, etc.), and especially in the coherent arrangement of the discourse (the different elements of personal style).

When we separate different components of the language material in the study and in the account, the parallelisms of development must not be forgotten: during the period when the child has acquired only a part of the phoneme inventory, he is also limited in his realization of the combinations of these phonemes into a child's equivalent of words; in his simultaneous command of many of these word equivalents; finally in their arrangement into wholes. At every stage there is a structure in which the different elements are interdependent. On the other hand the stages overlap because of the perseverance of elements previously acquired and by the premature emergence of some elements, often sporadically. One must also keep in mind the possibility of certain retrogressions. These phenomena are moreover normal in the development of adult speech forms and appear when they are considered historically.

Sounds (*examined in isolation*)
Through imitation the youngster must acquire, little by little, the total inventory of articulations which serve to form words (or "phonemes") in the language or languages he is learning.

It is a matter of the activities and the positions of small organs (vocal cords, tongue, velum, and their neighbors) moved by very small muscles with micromovements difficult to control and on the whole not easily accessible to visual observation. The task is very difficult, in spite of the preliminary exercise of babbling (*gazouillis*), in which moreover by no means all articulations appear. It is to be considered that on the whole the child always reaches the end of the period of pregrammatical acquisition without having command of all the phonemes or the ability to use them with accuracy.

A small number of phonemes is necessary to form terms which are not homonyms; without phonemes no comprehension would be possible. Thus, in spite of certain homonymies which are eventually tolerated, in spite of the abundance of related meanings (in the child's usage) which can be given to a single term, the child cannot be considered a beginner in speaking until a certain number of phonemes, contrasting with each other and forming so-called phonemic oppositions, have become established in his speech.

Let us remember that French, considered in its actual pronunciation (not its spelling), has 35 phonemes, 20 consonants and semi-

---

[1] About inventions of the child, see in addition to various passages of Werner F. Leopold's work, *Speech Development of a Bilingual Child* (Evanston: Northwestern University Press, Vols. I–IV, 1939–1949) the article by the same author, "Original Invention in Infant Language," *Symposium* (Syracuse University), III (May, 1949).

vowels, and 15 vowels. The phonemes prove to be more or less difficult to execute successfully. A considerable number of young Frenchmen who are quite capable of fluency in prattling (*bavardage*) reach school age without being able to pronounce the hushing sounds well (voiceless *š* spelled *ch;* voiced *ž* spelled *j* or *ge*) by opposition to the hissing sounds, voiceless *s*, voiced *z*. Consonants which are "difficult" at the moment can either be replaced by "easier" consonants, thus *t* for *k*, which threatens to multiply the homophonies, or be articulated imperfectly, thus palatalized *s* [*s'*] for *š*, or be omitted, leaving empty slots in the table of phonemes and "zero consonants" in the words. This is especially common for the liquids *r* and *l*.

The respective position of consonants and vowels and of consonants with reference to each other is not a matter of indifference. A consonant may be used only initially (at the beginning of the word) and not be spoken terminally, or it may not form clusters with all the others, or certain others. Thus a child may pronounce *rond* ('round') correctly, but omit the *r* in *grand-père* ('grandfather'), [gãpe].

It will be necessary to observe a large number of children in all countries to discover the principles of acquisition. It is important to realize that this is one of the areas in which individual differences loom large.

In order to appraise the sound inventory of a child and its acquisition, the environment must of course be taken into account. Originality or deficiency must not be attributed to the child when it is only a matter of imitation.

No study of sound acquisition by the subjects observed will be given here.[2] The readers can themselves extract certain information from the data given in the following sections. But by way of example I shall give some indications about J. and J.-L.

These two cousins, only a month apart in age, brought up in Paris in very similar circumstances, show a clear and instructive contrast in the time of acquisition of the phonemes.

J. (Some notes from the period 18–20.)

---

[2] Reference is made to the studies of Leopold (vol. I and especially vol. II) and of Grégoire, *L'apprentissage du langage*, Liège–Paris, 1937).

Distinguishes *p, t, k* very well from each other, *b, d, g* are generally merged (*confondus*) with them: thus three series of stops, but voiced and voiceless are merged.

Uses the nasals *m, n*, and a sort of *ñ* (*gn*).

Uses a good *l* in various positions; *r* is generally missing.

Dental fricatives (hissing sounds) and prepalatal fricatives (hushing sounds) as well as labiodentals are missing. Examples: *a* (*chat* 'cat'), *õ* (*on*) (*garçon* 'boy' and *bouchon* 'cork'), *iñ* (*cygne* 'swan'), *ö* (*eu*) and *lö* (*fleur* 'flower'), *wa* (*voir* 'see'), *yõ* (*avion* 'airplane').

[*f* and *v* are noted at 21, *s, š, z*, and *r* begin at 22.]

J.–L. (Record made by his father, at 19 and 7 days.) Distinguishes *p, t; k* is generally replaced by *t; k* is exceptional. Voiced *b* and *d* generally amalgamated with *p* and *t;* voiced articulation is exceptional; *g* is noted as missing, thus *asõ* (*garçon*).

The nasals *m* and *n* are used; *l* is completely missing (pronunciation zero) as well as *r*.

The voiceless sibilant *s* is well established, but pronounced with a little lisp (*zozotée*). *z* seems to be missing: *meõ* (*maison* 'house'); *š* is established, quite distinct from *s*, a little palatalized: *š'a* (*chat*); *ž* is missing: *Jean-Louis* is reduced to *a–i*.

The *f* is well established (but bilabial); *v* is missing.

[*l* appears sporadically at 22, but a summary made at 24 notes: absence of *k, š, l, r*; at 25 *r* begins to be established; at 26 *r* and *l* are noted as generally used; *k* and *g* seem to have begun to be used.]

Interesting observations for J. show that two or more stages of acquisition can be represented during the same over-all phase, that is, at the same time, in different words acquired at different times or under different circumstances or having special phonetic shapes.

At 19 1/2 −20 he showed three treatments of initial *m:*

m in *mãmã* (repetitive word, entirely nasal), which was acquired at 17;

zero in *ayi* (*merci* 'thank you,' *a-i* (*Marie*);

p in *pal o pye* (*mal au pied* 'foot hurts') (favored by the following *p*?).

At 21, *p* is introduced in *payi* (*Marie*).

At 23 the name is corrected (or relearned) in the form *mai*.

(Note of May 1952.) At the age of acquired speech and running conversation, differences continue between the articulations of the two subjects. At 2 years 9 months, J.'s articulation is normal, but voiceless sounds are still sometimes reminiscent of voiced ones (which is no longer observed at 2 years 10 months). At 2 years 9 months, J.–L. articulates some instances of *š* poorly and often pronounces *z* for *ž* (of which, however, he had produced examples early). He replaces the palatals *k* and *g* by the dentals *t* and *d*.

LEON KACZMAREK

28 Since the end of World War II several major studies of language acquisition have been published in eastern Europe. Among them is the Polish work of Kaczmarek, *Kształtowanie się mowy dziecka*, which reports in careful detail about the language-learning of a few children in one family, with generalizations about child language. Reference is made to much of the international literature; among the authorities cited is Stalin. Kaczmarek divides language-learning into four stages, making a neater distinction between cooing, babbling, and imitative speaking than many other students of child language. He pays much attention to intonation. Paragraphs dealing with these aspects are in the following selection translated from the German summary (pp. 69–71).

W. F. L.

A GENERAL VIEW OF THE FORMATION OF CHILD LANGUAGE

The gradual improvement of the means of communication makes it possible to distinguish four stages in the child's acquisition of language, as follows:

(1) the developmental stage of melody, at age 0–1, which comprises roughly the first year of life; the melody is usually accompanied by facial expression and gestures;

(2) the developmental stage of word structure, at age 1–1; 6 (2); the melody has, as far as expression is concerned, the function of an element modifying the meaning;

(3) the developmental stage of specific child language, at age 2 (3)–7; (analogical formations, neologisms, blends, etc.); a special intensity of this characteristic child language can be observed in the first phase;

Reprinted in translation by the editors from the author's German summary of his Kształtowanie Sie Mowy Dziecka *by permission of Poznańskie Towarzystwo Przyjaciół Nauk, Wydział Filologiczno-Filozoficzny, Prace Komisji Filologicznej, Tom XV, Zeszyt 2 (Vol. 15, No. 2), Poznań, 1953.*

in the further development its peculiarities decrease steadily until the speech becomes adapted to the general language.

Chronologically the acquisition and development of the child's language takes the following shape:

Developmental stage of melody; 0–1. The first sound of the child, i.e. the first cry, must also be viewed as the first expression of independent life, the activity of breathing being connected with it.

For a considerable time the crying or weeping caused by hunger, thirst, inner pains, wetting, etc., remains the only sound the child produces. In the beginning it is neither conscious nor does it serve a purpose. For the environment however it is the signal that the child needs help. In the course of time, i.e. in the second half of the first year of life, the child notices that upon his crying somebody comes who satisfies his needs. In general this is of course the mother. This very fact, the child's realization that by crying he can achieve his purpose, is of great importance for the development of speaking. It is actually the germ of the appreciation that articulated sound structures can be used in a similar way.

Approximately in the second month (sometimes sooner or later) the infant begins to coo when he feels comfortable. He usually engages in cooing after feeding, during the bath, after a change of diapers, while being rocked, and under similar circumstances. It occurs, like the movements of arms and legs, unconsciously, self-impelled; in other words it is in the nature of unconditioned reflexes. As numerous authors of specialized works affirm, deaf children also coo. Cooing stops with children of normal development toward the end of the third quarter of the first year; with deaf children it ends about the eighteenth month.

In the second half of the first year, toward the end of the third quarter, the child begins to babble, that is to say to emit sounds and to repeat them consciously. Thus we are confronted with with conditioned reflexes. He does not only repeat his own sounds but also imitates sounds from the environment. These sounds are already articulated. Their variety is great and the articulation is distinct. The latter fact is undoubtedly connected with the ability to stand, as was already pointed out by Baudouin de Courtenay, who said that the child cannot use the organs of speech in the same way as adults until he can walk or at least stand upright.

In contrast to adequate articulation in babbling, the pronunciation of whole words is extremely variable at this stage of development, that is to say it is still awkward. This points to the lack of relationship between babbling (cooing even more so) and speaking. Babbling is therefore to be regarded at best as practice for pronunciation. The definitely melodic character of babbling (caused by the use of sounds of varying pitch and different length and intensity), the rhythmic character of babbling and finally its continuance even after the mastering of language all lead to the conclusion that it represents a kind of singing.

For the development of real speaking we must look for other causes. I am thinking first of the emotionally tinged activity of the child's environment; second, of the understanding of the speech of the environment corresponding to the level of the child's mind and senses; and third, of the child's response to the initiative of the environment by the use of language which precedes articulated speech, namely by consciously produced cries. That means the child acquires speech only in a human environment. Acquisition of language outside of human society is impossible. That is proved by examples of complete isolation of children and the development of so-called wolf children. The speed of speech acquisition depends on the amount of attention the child gets. Here lies the reason for the uneven development of children from different social environments.

The emotionally based activity of the environment, which starts with the birth of the child, is usually very intensive. Whatever attention the child gets in connection with his attitudes and conditions serves as a stimulus for numerous and varied utterances. These continue later, and the child learns while playing.

WERNER F. LEOPOLD

29 This paper is based on Leopold's comprehensive study on *Speech Development of a Bilingual Child*, which appeared in four volumes between the years 1937 and 1949 (cf. the introduction to "The Study of Child Language and Infant Bilingualism" at the beginning of this volume). This voluminous work is a comprehensive and very detailed examination of the language-learning process, mainly in the first two years, analyzing it from the various linguistic aspects: lexical, phonological, syntactic, and semantic. This was probably the most detailed study attempted until that time. Since we have not included a chapter from the four volumes in this reader, the student is urged to acquaint himself with the work itself.

This article includes a summary of patterning development in the areas of phonology, morphology, syntax, and lexicon. Jakobson's distinctive features theory is advocated. The impact of bilingualism on language development is also discussed.

A. B. A.

PATTERNING IN CHILDREN'S LANGUAGE LEARNING

The problem of how children learn to speak has always engaged the marginal attention of linguists.[1] Too often their references to it have been casual and, on closer inspection, erroneous. The obvious requirement that reliable data must be collected before conclusions are drawn has too often been neglected. But well-known names of linguists appear among the contributors of special studies, for instance Jacob Grimm, Schleicher, Grammont, Marcel Cohen, Jespersen, Gutzmann, Meringer, Antoine Grégoire, Passy, Debrunner, as well as names of famous non-linguists like Taine, John Dewey, Wundt, Buffon, Darwin, Stanley Hall, Romanes.[2] But psychologists and educators have devoted more serious attention to child language than linguists have generally done.

The crushing bulk of data amassed in thousands of studies from many lands and many fields of scholarship[3] threatened to overwhelm the student who tried to discover great lines of development in child language. It looked as if every child went its own way in mastering the language of its environment.

One scholar after another tried to establish a generally valid sequence in the acquisition of sounds, for example. But no two lists agreed sufficiently to show a consistent line of development. There were those who were ready to give up and who declared that each child has its own language and its own sequence of learning, and that no principles of general validity can be found. Cross sections of group observations, often based on the speech of thousands of children of a certain age, did their share in reducing the weight of the less common features and in establishing averages.[4] But even in the results of such studies, the variations within each category remained large, and furthermore, the diachronic aspects of gradual growth were brought out less clearly than in individual biographic studies.

The scholar who cut the Gordian knot was Roman Jakobson, now of Harvard University, in his study of child language, aphasia, and general sound laws (1941). The study is written in German and was published in a place where it is not easily accessible.[5] It is not so well known as it should be. It has opened a new era in child-language research and at the same time fixed the position of child linguistics within the competence of general linguistics.

The decisive progress is due to the application of phonemic analysis. As one of the originators of the phonemic method in the Linguistic Circle of Prague, Jakobson was eminently qualified to apply its principles to child language. Even though his postulates need correction in details, the application of

Reprinted from Language Learning 5.1–14 (*1953*).

[1] This article is a revised and extended version of a paper presented at the meeting of the Linguistic Society of America in New York on December 30, 1951.

[2] For bibliographical data see my *Bibliography of Child Language* (Evanston, Ill.: Northwestern University Press, 1952). Otto Jespersen's book, *Language* (London and New York, 1922; reprint, 1949), is the only introduction to linguistics which accords major consideration to child language. Some of the best studies of child language have been published by students and teachers of languages, e.g., Egger, a classical philologist in France; Humphreys, a professor of Greek at Vanderbilt University; Deville in France; and Gheorgov in Bulgaria.

[3] Authors from many fields have written about child language: philosophers, anthropologists, biologists, students of medicine, law, astronomy, etc.; cf. the index in the *Bibliography of Child Language*.

[4] Best recent summary: Dorothea McCarthy, "Language development in children," in Leonard Carmichael, ed., *Manual of Child Psychology* (New York and London, 1946), pp. 476–581.

[5] Roman Jakobson, *Kindersprache, Aphasie und allgemeine Lautgesetze* (Uppsala, 1941; Språkvetenskapliga Sällskapets i Uppsala Förhandlingar, 1940–42). An earlier version in French is appended to the French edition of N. S. Troubetzkoy, *Principes de phonologie* (Paris, 1949).

structural views to child language was nothing less than revolutionary.[6]

As in many epochmaking inventions and innovations, the fundamental change in the approach was really quite simple. Instead of trying to find the sequence in which children learn sounds, which has proved futile, the attention must be focused on the sequence in the acquisition of sound categories. To establish the categories, a knowledge of phonetics was of course necessary, and many eager students of child language lacked it. Some based their accounts of sound learning on initial letters of words in standard spelling; the "c's" of English "cat," "cellar," and "church" made strange bedfellows. But even the majority withbetter phonetic sense, phoneticians included, did not detach their attention from individual sounds. Their lists for the sequence of sound acquisition showed a frustrating lack of agreement. Individual differences obstructed the search for a common denominator.

As soon as we think in terms of sound categories instead of individual sounds, the blurred outlines gain shape. We find that the speed and time of sound acquisition varies enormously between different children; but the sequence in categories and the relative chronology are always and everywhere the same, at least in great outlines. So Jakobson claims (p. 32 f.), and I believe he is right.

It is not difficult to see a priori that this must be so. It is safe to assume that the small child's perceptive faculties develop gradually. When the child's attention turns to language, it will first distinguish in what it hears only the coarser contrasts, and will need time to appreciate the finer subcontrasts between the sounds which reach its ear. The same applies to the efforts to reproduce the sounds in its own articulation. As the small child must learn control of the muscles in arms, hands, legs, and body, so it needs to learn the much more delicate control of the muscles in the tongue and the other organs needed for speech. Naturally this is a long drawn-out process, and the child learns the coarser, approximate movements sooner than the fine intermediate adjustments.

In the field of vowels this means that the child learns to distinguish, passively and actively, low vowels from high vowels first, then the mid vowels, and eventually the breakdown of these three major levels into still more refined subdivisions. It also means that a twofold distinction between front and back vowels is made sooner than a threefold distinction between front, back and central vowels. Complicated vowels like German and French [y] and [ϕ], which combine tongue and lip position for front and back vowels, come still later. That is the reason for many substitutions. If a child, for instance, replaces [ʌ] regularly by [a], the reason is that the central retracted vowel is not yet in its phonemic system, but [a] is. We know that some languages get along with but three vowels, [i], [u], and [a]. Those engaged in speech therapy or reeducation would do well to start with this coarsest vowel contrast.

This should however not be taken to mean that children's earliest vowel systems consist necessarily of the lowest vowel and the two highest vowels. In the case which I studied,[7] the vowels of the first few weeks (which I call the crying stage) were all low and favored front articulation. The brief cooing phase of the second month was characterized by a co-existence of low front and center vowels ([a, æ, ɛ : ʌ, ə]) and high back [u] and [ʊ];

---

[6] I give Jakobson full credit for the new approach, although, as always happens with new inventions and discoveries, he had predecessors. For instance, the Viennese medical speech therapist, Emil Froeschels, now also in the United States, established as early as 1925 the reverse parallelism between structural growth in child language and structural decay in aphasia, one of the leading ideas of Jakobson's study. Jakobson however went much more deeply into the building-up process of child language.

[7] Instead of making too many generalized statements, for which the time is not ripe, I base this paper largely on the data assembled in my study of two children's language-learning, *Speech Development of a Bilingual Child* (Northwestern University Studies) (4 vols.; Evanston, Ill. 1939–1949) henceforth referred to as *Bil. Ch.* The bilingualism involved is English and German. The volumes deal primarily with my older daughter, but give data about my second daughter as well. I spoke only German to the children. In this paper, as in *Bil. Ch.*, the emphasis is on the formative stage of the first two years. I apologize for the generalization implied in the title of this article. It takes a tentative step in the direction of generalization, but it is understood that future studies are likely to lead to modifications. Age indications like 1; 2 mean at the age of 1 year and 2 months.

higher front vowels were missing. The high back vowels together with all kinds of back consonants have given the cooing phase its name. The back consonants of this phase are what observers have in mind when they state that infants begin with all kinds of sounds not used by their environment.

This phase should be, but usually is not, sharply separated from the following long babbling stage, the stage of speech exercises consisting of more varied sounds without meaning. In this stage the high back vowels and the central vowels disappear. All sounds were more fronted and articulated much more distinctly. I found an opposition of low and high front vowels in the ninth month. Three front levels ([e] had been added) existed by the eleventh month. Thus, three levels of front vowels were used before the opposition front—back came into play. Of course we cannot speak of phonemic contrasts in babbling, which is, by definition, speech exercise without meaning. Jakobson and others exclude babbling from their analyses. I find striking oppositions however, which might perhaps be characterized as a sort of experimental prepatterning. The postulated phonemic contrast between fully open vowels and fully closed stops was also prepatterned in babbling combinations like [baba, dididi], and so was the early structural syllable pattern, consonant—vowel, both of which were carried over without break or relearning into imitative speaking with meaning.

In the case I studied the speaking stage began in the last three months of the first year, overlapping with babbling, which continued for many months. The low vowels were carried over from babbling. The [æ] of crying and babbling, however, was now dropped. Standard [æ] was replaced by [a]. Standard central [ʌ] was also replaced by [a]. As late as the last month of the second year, the child's [da] stood for Jack and *cover* as well as for *down*, John, and German *da* and *tragen*. Homophony did not bother the child at all; [maɪ maɪ] was not an exclamation, but meant *my money*.

Thus phonemic contrasts became more clearcut. The highest front vowel [i] was acquired in the tenth month in an imitated word, with the allophones [ɪ] and [y], the latter being used after the bilabial phoneme [b p]. In the first month of the second year, the high [i] was contrasted with low [a] and experimentally with high back [u], so that briefly the coarsest three-vowel system was realized. However, the [u] did not yet become established. Instead, two months later (1; 2) the mid front [e] was learned in the new word *baby*, which had long remained passive in spite of its great interest value for the child. In this word a clear contrast between mid front and high front vowels existed.

Thus three series of front vowels were learned before the contrast front—back was tackled in earnest. High back [u] and [ʋ] were added lastly to the vowel system in the middle of the second year, that is, four and five months later (1; 6–7). Both functioned as representatives of all standard high and mid back vowels. Mid back vowels were either raised to [u], or lowered to [a], and sometimes split into both contrasting vowels as [au]— eloquent testimony to the fact that the mid back vowels did not yet exist as phonemes in the child's vowel system.

Mid back [ɔ] was quite common in unstressed syllables in the later months, because they receive less attention, which favors a vowel of indifferent formation. In fact, it seems likely that the striving for phonemic contrast is not characteristic of unstressed syllables, an aspect which Jakobson neglects. Still, since [ɔ] was in stressed position an allophone of the high back vowel, the same might be claimed for the unstressed vowel. The mid back vowel in stressed position was learned in the 23rd month. Three back levels were then distinguished, but [o] and [ɔ] remained allophones of one phoneme.

Central vowels in stressed position were not learned at all during the first two years; [ʌ] was represented by [a] as late as 2; 4. Central [ə] (schwa) was learned in unstressed syllables during the second half of the second year, because its neutral character made it suitable in such a position; before that time unstressed syllables had been omitted. Even in unstressed position [ə] had to struggle for a place in the vowel system and did not become well rooted until the last month of the second year. The front—back range hardly achieved a three-unit distinction in the first two years.

I had recognized the contrast pattern in

vowel learning before I read Jakobson's study. I am indebted to him for the application of the same principle to consonant learning. It is well known that children generally favor front consonants in their early imitative speaking. This has been variously explained by their accessibility to visual observation, by the greater mobility of lips and tongue tip, by the preceding practice in sucking and tactile exploration, and by their different acoustic qualities. Usually children reproduce bilabial stops early and correctly, and dental stops next, whereas velar stops are later and are frequently replaced by dental stops. There are however enough contrary examples where velars take the place of dentals, to show that the child is phonetically able to pronounce both. The reason for their intermingling is that the child's phonemic system has only reached the stage of two series, one labial and one nonlabial. [t] and [k], [d] and [g] can, at an early stage, be allophones of one phoneme—actually all four can be one phoneme, because the contrast voiced—voiceless can also be late. In the case studied by me, [b] was used in the first word (0; 9); [d] was used in words at 0; 10, whereas [g] was not acquired until 1; 7 and [k] at 1; 8, after long experimentation. The separation of voiced and voiceless stops did not begin to be achieved until the very end of the second year.[8] A clear distinction between three series of stops—labials, dentals, and velars—came after the end of the second year.[9]

The nasals showed the sway of the two-series system even more clearly. The bilabial [m] was learned at 1; 2. It contrasted with the two buccal stops, [b] and [d], which up to that time had been the only consonants for four months. The second nasal to be imitated was the dental [n] of standard words. It was reproduced at 1; 7–8, but took, in the child's version, the phonetic form of velar [ŋ] for three months. The velar continued to occur as an allophone after alveolar [n] had been learned in correct articulation. Velar [ŋ] never represented the [ŋ] of standard words, but was used only as a substitute for standard [n], [g] and [k]; standard [ŋ] was omitted by

the child. Again the three-series stage came after the end of the second year.

Fricatives have an intermediate articulation comparable to the mid vowels. To produce a contrast with the open articulation of vowels, it is easier to make a complete closure with lips or tongue in stop position than to make the fine adjustment necessary for producing breath friction. That is why children often substitute stops for fricatives: [p] for [f], [t] for [s], etc. My older daughter did so only for the very late dental fricatives of English, in the fourth year; but the younger also used [t] for [s], "kisses" beoming [kɪtət]. The older daughter learned one fricative very early, at 1; 1, namely the bilabial glide [w], which functioned as a substitute for the labiodental fricative [v]. Thus, as far as degrees of openness are concerned, the three series, vowels—fricatives—stops, existed as early as 1;2. Two months after, [j] was added, with an allophone [ʒ] another three months later, so that we have then two contrasting series of fricatives in initial position (if indeed the classification of [w] as a fricative is allowed).

In terminal position the situation was different. The ends of words received less attention, and the child did not strive for contrast. Just as mid vowels and schwa ([ə]) were favored in terminal unstressed syllables, the half-open fricatives were satisfactory as terminal consonants when these were no longer omitted, from 1; 7. The single fricative [ʃ] was learned as a substitute for all apical fricatives at 1;7, three months earlier than [t] as a terminal stop. Thus, for example, [θ] and [ð] appeared initially as the stops [d] and [t] in "through" 1; 11 and "this" 1; 8–2; 1, but terminally as [ʃ] in "mouth" 1; 10. For four months, [ʃ] was the only terminal fricative. In the last month of the second year, the velar fricative [x] was used in agreement with the standard, in German words; as a phonetic unit (off-glide after back vowels) it had been used four months earlier. Thus we have then two series of fricatives initially and terminally, but not the same ones for the two positions. The third fricative, [f], developed very slowly from the middle of the third year, in either position.

Affricates occurred very early in cooing and

---

[8] Cf. *Bil. Ch.* vol. II, §414.
[9] Cf. *Bil. Ch.* vol. II, §417.

babbling. But in imitated words they occurred for a long time only for standard stops and standard fricatives, faultily articulated. As imitative sounds they were first replaced by one of the two components. Only in the last third of the second year was standard [tʃ] imitated, in voiceless or voiced form. Being compromise sounds, affricates represent a subcontrast which is naturally learned fairly late.

The so-called liquids are among the latest sounds of children. Not infrequently they are not yet mastered at school age. In the first two years of my older daughter, [r] and [l] were oftened rendered by the same substitutes; more commonly, initial [r] was [w], initial [l] was [j]. Terminally both became vowels, when they were not omitted altogether. The [l] was learned in the middle of the second year as a feeble phonemic unit; the [r] not until the fourth year. Both were used in approximately correct articulation very early in one or two isolated words. But linguists interested in children's language have learned to discount instances of premature phonetic perfection in isolated words, which are imitated by themselves without being fitted into the phonemic system of the stage. Such instances merely prove that the phonetic capacity of the child can be well ahead of the phonemic development. The child does not abstain from the use of certain sounds because it cannot hear or articulate them, but because they do not yet fit the phonemic stage.

I am convinced that Jakobson's phonemic analysis of sound learning is the way out of the difficulties presented by the puzzling individual differences between children. It is not yet in final shape. Velten, in a study of a slow sound learner,[10] has used it and modified the analysis, which proved to be too rigid. I have suggested other corrections in my books. But the linguistic study of children's language learning will have to build henceforth on Jakobson.

In the field of vocabulary, there is much discussion in the literature about action words versus naming words, about emotional and

volitional urges versus factual objectivity, and that sort of thing; but no agreement has been reached. The child names objects and actions and feelings, everything that is interesting for some reason. There is no doubt that wish components are stronger at first than later; but dispassionate statements also occur early. At any rate, every child makes a selection from the presented vocabulary with sovereign independence according to its needs and stage of maturity, and does not always agree with adults in judging the usefulness of lexical items.

In the learning of word meaning, however, it is possible to observe the coarseness of early semantic classifications and the gradual refinement of the semantic system in the direction prescribed by the environment. It is a tremendous task for the child to learn the adult ways of classifying the phenomena of the world, and it is fascinating to follow the development from dim unconventional clusters to categories sanctioned by the environment, by means of constant semantic extension and restriction. In some categories, like adjectives and adverbs, clear contrast patterns proceeding from simple to more complex can be observed. But these processes cannot be illustrated in a brief survey.[11]

In the field of grammar, syntax comes before morphology. The student of child language becomes very conscious of the fact that morphological devices are a luxury of fully developed languages. The small child gets along quite well without them, for a short or a long time.

Most children begin with sentences of one word.[12] Presumably their attention is captivated by a single word of the presentation, the semantic peak of a sentence, which in Germanic languages is also the phonetic peak through stress. The word may be a noun, an adjective, a verb of the adult sentence, but it serves for the child as the vehicle of a complete statement. This is where a great number of nonlinguists have

---

[10] H. V. Velten, "The Growth of Phonemic and Lexical Patterns in Infant Language," *Language*, XIX (1943), 281–92.

[11] The process of semantic learning is studied in detail in *Bil. Ch.* vol III, §592–634.

[12] The statement is based on an impression gained from the literature; it is not backed by statistics. We have too few linguistically expert studies of child language to generalize safely. Again I lean in the following on my own data for one child.

erred. They like to count the number and percentages of parts of speech in children's early vocabularies. But the child does not yet recognize the syntax of the standard language and makes its own statements in an unorganized, one-word form. The one-word period lasts a long time, in the case I observed, nearly a year, from the ninth to the twentieth month. Parts of speech mean nothing during this stage as far as the child's syntax is concerned. The only syntactic device used early in my case was the interrogative intonation; it was employed to ask for information or, much more commonly, to request a permission, rarely to ask for the name of a thing.

There is often a transition from the one-word phase to the two-word phase in the form of two one-word sentences following each other.[13] The approach to the syntactic pattern subject—verb, for instance, was made by my daughter in the form *Mama? sh!* 1; 6, which should be interpreted as "What is Mama doing? She is sleeping!" All that was needed to turn this question and answer into one complete sentence was to omit the interrogative intonation; this was done two months later. Thus the subject—verb pattern was learned at 1; 8. Other two-word sentences consisted of verb plus object, one month later. *Drinks milk* meant "the cat is drinking milk," the subject being understood from the situation. There were even sentences containing both subject and object, but then the two-word span did not allow a verb to be expressed.

The interval between two-word sentences and three-to-four-word sentences was only three months. Many of these longer sentences were still grammatically incomplete, the extra word or words being used up for other purposes: two-word verbs of the type "wake up," adjectives or possessives, or adverbs. During the last month of the second year, the complete, pattern, subject—verb—object, was learned. Some early examples still betrayed, by striking pauses, the effort needed to combine the two patterns, subject—verb and verb—object, into one; but almost immediately such statements were made fluently.

---

13 Marcel Cohen, "Sur l'étude du langage enfantin, *Enfance*, V (1952), 181–249, is dubious about this transition. It is unmistakable in the case studied by me.

Other utterances had been syntactically complete (complete in rough outlines, that is) before this time, because for the frequent imperative no subject is needed, and for intransitive verbs no object. I have disregarded early complete sentences like *I see you* 1; 5, because they were learned by mechanical phonetic imitation as units. The use of such stereotype phrases has nothing to do with the child's learning to put words together in an original sentence.

My child was syntactically well equipped by the end of the second year. The length of sentences increased soon. All that remained to be learned was the addition of minor items like articles, copulas, prepositions, and of course the syntactical patterns of subordination, which belong to a much later stage.

Morphology is different. Practically no morphological devices (formal indications of declension and conjugation) were learned by my daughter during the first two years. Her speech type was isolating. Syntactic relationships were made clear by word order, which generally followed the standard. But there were enough sentences with unorthodox arrangement to show that not even this principle was fully acquired. Occasionally the word on which the interest was centered was placed first. This left room for misunderstandings, as when she said, commenting on the barking of a dog: *Meow bites Wauwau*, 1; 11. She may have meant that a cat was biting a dog; but it is also possible that she used misleading word order. Imperfections of communication were an incentive to learn standard morphological features, which she did during the third year.

The neglect of endings, stem modifications, etc., is exactly in line with the postulated principle that the child learns in every area of language first a coarse pattern, which is later refined by the development of subcontrasts and formal distinctions. The intellectual task of recognizing and recreating the patterns and subpatterns of adult sentences with their formal means of expression must of necessity begin with a picture in hazy outlines, which become clearer and clearer as experience and maturity grow.

My child operated functionally, in the second year, with what we would call singulars and plurals of nouns, with present, past, and future of verbs, etc., but managed to make herself understood without the use of formal signs. There were indeed forms of nouns based on standard plurals, and forms of verbs based on past tenses; but they were used for singular and present tense as well, and not contrasted with other forms of the same word. A few real plural endings appeared at the end of the second year, but they were not yet added consistently. The possessive ending was attached only to the names *Mama* and *Papa*, and not regularly so. The verb appeared invariably in the unmodified pure stem form, for the third person signular as well as for past, future, etc.: the verb was in the single item phase. During the third year the more important morphological forms were learned, with many mistakes along the way. Such mistakes are more interesting than correct forms, because they show the grasping of a pattern more clearly. The only auxiliary verb during the second year was *don't*, which she heard all too frequently. It was a real auxiliary when another verb was added, as she did readily. She even used it with German verbs: *Don't spiel*, 1;11, for "Don't play." There was no passive voice until much later, the passive being a dispensible stylistic luxury.

I have said very little about the bilingualism involved in the case which I studied. The contrast between two languages, English and German, was an added complication for the learning of this child. On the basis of the evidence it is to be counted among the finer distinctions which were learned late. In the initial stages the bilingual presentation merely meant a larger vocabulary to choose from. The child chose either the German or the English item at her own discretion, leaning at first more on German, later more and more decidedly on English, and welded one language instrument out of the two presentations. She did not mind hybrid phrases, substituting for instance the German adjective *nass* in the English idiom *all wet* 1; 10, and similarly *right da* 1; 11. Very often the crude phonetic form of the child's words could equally well stand for the English or the German model, because the vocabulary of the two languages is closely related on the elementary level: English *book* and German *Buch* resulted in the same form as long as the terminal consonants remained unrepresented.

The single item phase with respect to bilingualism lasted for years. The split into two contrasting languages, distinguished by the person addressed, first showed rudimentarily and vacillatingly toward the end of the second year. Consciousness of dealing with two languages began early in the third year. The active separation of the two languages did not start in earnest until the very end of the third year. Increasingly, from then on, the learning of English and German proceeded separately. Eventually English was greatly predominant. The case I studied is not one of near-perfect bilingualism like that studied by Ronjat.[14]

The most striking effect of bilingualism was a noticeable looseness of the link between the phonetic word and its meaning. The child never insisted on stereotype wording of stories, as monolingual children often do, and even made vocabulary substitutions freely in memorized rhymes and songs. The unity of phonetic word and meaning, which is postulated by some scholars, was definitely not a fact for this child, who heard the same thing constantly designated by two different phonetic forms. This separation of word and meaning may be considered beneficial, because it favors content over form, thinking over verbiage. It may also be appraised as a handicap, because it results in a less unified, less forceful view of the world. That is a matter of conviction.

At any rate, bilingualism is such a widespread phenomenon in the world of language that it deserves to be studied exactly by linguists. In children's language-learning it can be observed in a nascent state, with the detail of a slow-motion picture and the speed of a fast-motion picture. The same advantage holds for all other linguistic phenomena, which show in child language as under a magnifying glass.

[14] Jules Ronjat, *Le développement du langage observé chez un enfant bilingue* (Paris, 1933) (French-German bilingualism). The only other booklength case study of child bilingualism previous to my own study is Milivoïe Pavlovitch, *Le langage enfantin: acquisition du serbe et du français par un enfant serbe* (Paris, 1920) (successive bilingualism).

ROBERT W. ALBRIGHT AND JOY BUCK ALBRIGHT~~~~~~~~~~~

30 The authors offer a transcription of speech samples of a 26-month-old child. The corpus of 237 utterances is presented in phonetic transciption. The prosodic features are accounted for through the accompanying marking of stress, intonation, and pitch, which is not so common in the literature. They were especially impressed by the seeming variability of speech forms used by this child, and they discuss it briefly, adding some interesting complex substitution rules.

Cf. their methodological article on "Application of Descriptive Linguistics to Child Language," *Journal of Speech and Hearing Research,* I (1958), 257–61, which is actually based on the present one.

A. B. A.

THE PHONOLOGY OF A
TWO-YEAR-OLD CHILD

Introductory. In studying a sample of the conversation of a young child, the authors were impressed by the seeming variability of speech forms used by their informant. For exam'le, the pointing formula *That's a—* occurred as [d'ætsə], [d'æsə], [dówsə], ['æsə], [ázə], [d'əts], [d'æzə], the pronominal form *I* as [áy], [á], ['ə], [ə], the interrogative form *what* as [hw'ə], [hw'ət]. [hwəš], and the nominal form *taxi* as [t'æksiy], [tá·siy], [táʷksiy], [táʷxtiy], [g'ət'æksiy].[1] There was a good deal of variability even when the speech forms occurred in similar environments. Thus, *microphone* occurred twice as a single utterance between, pauses; the first time as [màytuɸówn], the second time in the more

Reprinted from Word *12.382–390 (1956) by permission of the authors and the Linguistic Circle of New York, Inc.*

The authors would like to acknowledge a grant-in-aid that was provided by the Social Science Research Center and the Faculty Research Grants Committee of Cornell University to conduct research into child language. Also, they would like to express their appreciation of the helpful criticism they have received from the linguists in Cornell's Division of Modern Languages, and from Y. R. Chao of the University of California.

[1] See Tables 1 and 2 below for the values assigned to the symbols. Since not all vowel symbols could be set with each accent mark by the printer of this journal, the stress symbols sometimes precedes the vowel symbol in our transcription. Thus, ['a] = [à], [^e] = [ê], etc.

conventional form [màykrəfówn].

It is important to consider that the variability may have been exaggerated by listeners unaccustomed to the child's speech. Also, a child's phonemic system is in the process of development, and the sound patterning is probably less regular than that of adult speech.[2]

1. *The informant.* He was 26 months old and had grown up in an English-speaking household with his parents and a three-months-old sister. During his first ten months of life, he lived in Europe, after which he returned to this country where he has been living in New York City. The parents have spoken only English in the home; they grew up in Denver, Colorado, and use the dialect of that region.

The child and his parents have established the habit of repeating utterances, and this repetition of part or all of the utterance spoken by the adult occurred many times. It does not seem to have interfered with the child's speech development, however, and it was often helpful to the authors later when the sample was being transcribed phonetically.

2. *Procedure.* The informant's conversation was tape-recorded over a period of two hours. Interruptions by his baby sister, and periods of silence or vocal play left a remain-

[2] Y. R. Chao suggested this in personal correspondence, and described it as "lower phonemic consistency."

der of about an hour and a half of connected discourse containing 232 utterances. This discourse was transcribed phonetically. Next, the first 100 utterances of the sample were analyzed in terms of the phones, their frequency of occurrrence, and their environments. As mentioned in the introduction, the child's language was well developed, and the 100 utterances contained many phones in a great variety of environments. Following this analysis, the method of minimal pairs was applied to the entire body of 232 utterances. Because the linguist's method of "equivalence of repetition" is not applicable to such young children who either cannot or will not engage in repeating minimal pairs, the authors used what may be described as a method of "equivalence of recurrence." For most speech sounds, recurrences were frequent enough to provide contrasts in different environments, although for one or two sounds there was inadequate data.

3. *Corpus in phonetic transcription*.[3] 1. [²âpəèyaw³sáyt¹↓] *I play outside*. 2. [²àswîŋādærieʷ³háy¹↓] *I swing on that real high*. 3. [²nə³seʷiŋ¹↓] *In a swing, no swing*, or *a swing*. 4. [²hwˆəts¹datdá·y³↑] *What's that, daddy?* 5. [³kórdə²↓] *Recorder*. 6. [³hér²↓] *Here* (?). 7. [²d'æ³bábp²↓] *That's Bob*. 8. [²d'æs³jéy·²↓] *That's Joy*. 9. [²dæs³məʷmiy¹↓] *That's mommy*. 10. [³bənánùs¹↓] *Bananas*. 11. [²əhˆæəb³éʷtən'ænə¹↓] *I have a banana*. 12. [³t'æksiy¹↓] *Taxi*. 13 [¹hw'ətsíy³↑] *What's this?* 14. [²d'æsə³tâ·síy¹↓] *That's a taxi*. 15. [²dəmênərinərə³t'æksiy¹↓] *The men are in rrr a taxi*. 16. [²d'ætsə³m'æˆn¹↓] *That's a man*. 17. [²d'ætsəg'ə³t'æksiy¹↓] *That's a (ge) taxi*. 18. [³kídiy¹↓] *Kitty*. 19. [²hîsə³n'ə·b'əs¹↓] *Here's another bus*. 20 [²dˆæs'ə³lániy¹↓] *That's a laundry* (truck). 21. [²'əsə³méytow¹↓] *That's*

a tomato. 22. [²d'æsəs·³tápiŋ¹dây²↑] *That's a stopping, daddy*. 23. [²dˆæsə³stápiŋ¹↓] *That's uh stopping*. 24. [³stáplàyt¹↓] *Stop light*. 25. [²ən¹hw'əsd'æ³↑] *And what's that?* 26. [²ən¹ùwz'æ³↑] *And who's that?* 27. [²âzə¹b'əstúw³↑] *That's a bus, too?* 28. [²dˆæs¹bəstúw³↑] *That's bus, too?* 29. [²d'æ¹sənb'əs³↑] *That's an bus?* 30. [²dˆətsəgèʷt³kr'əʷk¹↓] *That's a truck* (regressive assimilation of final [k] probably produces the inserted get–). 31. [²d'ætsum³kówd¹↓] *That's umm coal* (?). 32. [³kú·tr'ək¹↓] *Coal truck*. 33. [²əbdˆæsə³kóˆtrəkhùw¹↓] *And that's a coal truck, too*. 34. [²dˆæsə³kúwlb'əs¹↓] *That's a school bus*. 35. [²dˆæsək'əb'əs¹↓] *That's a schoolbus*. 36. [²dˆæsə—ə—³číldrənìt¹↓] *That's a children it* (*in it?*). 37. [²čílrənìə³b'əs¹↓] *Children in a bus*. 38. [²d'æs³máy¹↓] *That's my*. 39. [²dêsdèz³míye¹↓] *There's, there's Mia*. 40. [²p'əkityzsèr³tûw¹↓] *Bucky's there, too*. 41 [²ənd'æsə³gás¹↓] *And that's a gas* (gas truck). 42. [²dəb'əkiyb'əkiyb'əkiyindədèr¹túwtûw³↑] *The Bucky, Bucky in the there too, too?* 43. [²b'əkiyinder³tûw¹↓] *Bucky in there, too*. 44. [²d'æzəbêʷ³tr'ək¹↓] *That's a good* (?) *truck or That's a truck*.[4] 45. [²dˆæs'əm·s·³mówk¹↓] *That's umm smoke, or possibly some smoke*. 46. [²ìnə³tréyən¹↓] *In a train*. 47. [²d'æsdə³tréyən¹↓] *That's the train*. 48. [²d'æsəw³ràyt¹↓] *That's all right*. 49. [³b'ɜnáwt¹↓] *Burn out*. 50. [²àylâyki—bə³n'ænə¹↓] *I like* (or *like it*) *banana*. 51. [²wìyhˆæφtuwìyh'æφtuwìy³h'æφtùw¹↓] *We have to, we have to, we have to* (receive treatment for a cut). 52. [³k'ət¹↓] *Cut*. 53. [³k'ɜdər¹↓] *Recorder*. 54. [²jêkəlíns·¹kráy³↑] *Jacqueline her* (or *err*) *cry?* 55. [²jêkəlinfiyə¹bétɜ³↑] *Jacqueline feel better?* 56. [²áybêysənf'ɜ³jékxein¹↓] *I* (*bring?*) *some for Jacqueline*. 57. [²jêkliàw³sáy¹↓] *Jacqueline outside*. 58. [²wəsdìs¹dáy³↑] *What's this* (?), *daddy?* 59. [²máytu³φòwn¹↓] *Microphone*. 60. [²f'ɜ̂ə³téyp¹↓] *For the tape*. 61. [²jêkuinplèyiŋ ³əsáy¹↓] *Jacqueline playing outside*. 62. [²jêklinz³slìypìˆŋ¹↓] *Jacqueline's sleeping*. 63. [²îəsəlìtə³t'æksiybùk¹↓] *It's a* (or *here's a*) *little taxi book*. 64. [²nùnùdâyplèyn¹dət'æksiy³bùk¹↓] *No, no daddy, playing* (*with?*) *the taxi book*. 65. [²nòwnòw¹dây²nòwtêykətə³wéydət^æsiybùk¹↓] *No, no, daddy, no take it*

---

[3] Corresponding English forms are provided as a rough translation to help the reader, and are not presumed to be equivalent speech forms of child and adult language. The diacritics have the following values: ´ˆˋ indicate heavy, medium, and light stress with the fourth degree of extremely light stress left unmarked; after a vocalic symol ʷ stands for rounding and ˆ stands for raising; clause terminals are shown by ↑, ↓, and → for rising, fading, and sustained; pitch levels are numbered in ascending order of 1, 2, 3, with 2 for mid or average pitch; · and : represent length and extra-length; ~ represents nasalization.

[4] Cf. inserted [get-] in utterance 30, and [gə-] in utterance 17.

away the taxi book. 66. [²rîystə¹b'ə^wkìy³↑] *Reads to Bucky?* 67. [²îyztə³súz'ən¹↓] *Reads to Susan.* 68. [³ríyt'ət¹↓] *Read it.* 69. [³b'əkìy¹↓] *Bucky.* 70. [²b'əkiy³b'ŏd¹↓] *Bucky gone (?).* 71. [²bˆəkiygòwtəòwshəhə³sáy¹↓] *Bucky go to out huh, huh side.* 72. [²bˆəkiyg'o·tə³'ɜk¹↓] *Bucky gone (?) to work.* 73. [²s'ə^wiywéntə³w'ərkmâmìy¹↓] *Susie went to work, mommy.* 74. [²míyəwêntə³y'ɜk¹↓] *Mia went to work.* 75. [³dˆæs¹w'əns²tày³d'ætw'ən¹↓] *That's one, daddy, that one.* 76. [²bˆəkíydu³w'ɜk¹↓] *Bucky do work.* 77. [²âygòwnəst'əməp³híe^wə¹↓] *I going to come (?) up here.* 78. [²bˆəkiymèks³háwsəz¹↓] *Bucky makes houses.* 79. [²bˆəkiymèy³háwsəs¹↓] *Bucky make houses.* 80. [²dèi¹b'ə^ws¹↓] *There bus.* 81. [²bˆəkiydràyvzðə³b'əs¹↓] *Bucky drives the bus.* 82. [²bˆəkiygòwðə³gúw¹↓] *Bucky go the school.* 83. [²³aháytiŋmâmiy¹↓] *I hiding, mommy.* 84. [²³aháydiŋmâmiy¹↓] *I hiding, mommy.* 85. [²hî—hîr—aygimdæbâaənə³fláydày¹↓] *H— here, I give that Bob another fly, daddy.* 86. [²aygìbdəbâbdə³fláydày¹↓] *I give the Bob the fly, daddy.* 87. [²bâbiyùwkêč³əfláy¹↓] *Bob, he you catch a fly.* 88. [³fláy¹↓] *Fly.* 89. [²'əsə³fláy¹↓] *That's a fly.* 90. [³yíŋet¹↓] *Swing it.* 91. [³šr^wátət¹↓] *Swat it.* 92. [²ay³búpdày¹↓] *I burp, daddy.* 93. [³kówdə¹↓] *Recorder.* 94. [²d'əz¹dêsφèyrékərz³↑] *Does this play records?* 95. [³máykrəfówn¹↓] *Microphone.* 96. [²nôwaydò³wátuw¹↓] *No, I don't want too.* 97. [²ày³pléyd¹↓] *I played.* 98. [²ə²p'ɔərt¹↓] *I pour it.* 99. [²ày³p'ɔt¹↓] *I pour it.* 100. [²ayp^ɔtitòws³fáwrz¹↓] *I pour it those flowers.* 101. [²ðəflâwràrə³drínkət¹↓] *The flower are a drink it.* 102. [²əflâwràwɔdríŋ³ket¹↓] *The flower are a (or want to) drink it.* 103. [²flâwə'ə³s'ɜsity¹↓] *Flower are thirsty.* 104. [²flâwə'ətə³tríŋk¹↓] *Flower are (or want) to drink.* 105. [²âytèykəwayd'ɔnðə³kár¹↓] *I take a ride on the car.* 106. [²dâyaynìydætsyâtə³níydæ¹↓] *Daddy, I need that swat, I need that.* 107. [²hwèzfláy¹dâ:iy³↓] *Where's fly, daddy?* 108. [³dézəflày¹↓] *There's a fly.* 109. [²dòws³báps¹↓] *Those Bob's.* 110. [²d'əs¹bát³↑] *Those Bob?* 111. [²àyhêytində³fláy¹↓] *I hitting the fly.* 112. [²yôwlət'ə³mámiy¹↓] *Roll it to mommy.* 113. [²d'æsə³tífe^wn¹↓] *That's a telephone.* 114. [²dèsə³b'ɔ¹↓] *There's a ball.* 115. [²dèsə³bòwisy¹↓] *There's a bouncy (?).* 116. [²èsə³b'ɔ¹↓] *There's a ball.* 117. [²wânəríyd'æ³↑] *Want to read that?* 118. [²h'əm³↑] *Humm?* 119. [²də³táksì¹↓] *The taxi.* 120.

[³táxtìy¹↓] 121. [²dàsə³táksiy¹↓] *That's a taxi.* 122. [²əyìyu³wíyd'ət¹↓] *I see (or need) you read it.* 123. [³nów²nów¹↓] *No, no.* 124. [²dˆæsə³b'ə^w¹↓] *That's a bus.* 125. [²àyr^wîydiŋ³b'ə^ws¹↓] *I riding bus.* 126. [²d'æˆt¹↓] *That.* 127. [²dˆætsə³b'ɔs¹↓] *That's a bus.* 128. [²hwì^ws¹d'æ³↑] *What's that?* 129. [²àys³níy:¹↓] *I sneeze.* 130. [²hw'ədá³↓] *What's that?* 131. [³klóws¹↓] *Clothes.* 132. [²âyəniŋčɔ³klów¹↓] *Ironing the clothes.* 133. [²də³šús¹↓] 134. [²ɔ³βúsnàwm^əmiy¹] *All bust now, mommy.* 135. [²nówp³↑] *Nope.* 136. [²əw'ə^wn³dìsm^əmiy¹↓] *I want this, mommy.* 137. [²bíɜ¹↓] *Beer.* 138. [²dêsə³mámìy¹↓] *This of mommy (possessive probably).* 139. [²d'æs³táys¹²d'æstàys³tûw¹↓] *That's daddy's, that's daddy's, too.* 140. [²ayw^ᶜadìs·³mâ¹↓] *I want this more.* 141. [²'æsəkíytə³môwtów¹↓] *That's a mosquito.* 142. [²dèsəkíyəbày³tûw¹↓] *That's a mosquito bite, too.* 143. [²dèsə³kíxebàytûw¹↓] *That's a mosquito bite, too.* 144. [²dèsə³kíykəbàyt¹↓] *That's a mosquito bite.* 145. [²hw'əsd'æ³↑] *Waht's that?* 146. [²hw'əsdə¹mâmìy³↑] *What's the (or that), mommy?* 147. [²dówsə³hówsəmâmìy¹↓] *Those are horsy, mommy.* 148. [²wùkətən³d'æsəhôwziymámiy¹↓] *Look it, and that's a horsy, mommy.* 149. [²tímìy¹↓] *Timmy.* 150. [²pûdiŋšuzə³á·n¹↓] *Putting shoes on.* 151. [²d'ædæ³š'əbù¹↓] *That, that shovel.* 152. [²dæsdə³peyo¹↓] *That's the pail.* 153. [²wùs³ás¹↓] *What's that (?)?* 154. [²îtsə—²hw'ə³d'æ¹↓] *It's a—what that?* 155. [²d'æsəm:³báy¹↓] *That's a boy* 156. [²d'æs³b'əti¹↓] *That's bunny.* 157. [²hw'əstə¹m'əmi²↑] *What's that, mommy?* 158. [²hw'əstə¹tá·y³↑] *What's that, daddy?* 159. [³k'əpìy¹↓] *Cuppy (for cup).* 160. [²h^ᶜuw^xashi¹s'əβər³↑] *He wants his supper?* 161. [²d'æsə³b'ədiy¹↓] *That's a birdy?* 162. [²dəwîtow³béybìy¹↓] *The little baby.* 163. [²dəbìgb^ərdiŋ'ɔiŋəgè³tíydiŋ¹↓] *The big bird going to get eating.* 164. [²jôygòwinyə³ká¹↓] *Joy go in the car.* 165. [²dôydètdow³t'əmàmiy¹↓] *Joy get those come (receives mail), mommy.* 166. [²hûwtə¹mámìy³↑] *Who come, mommy?* 167. [²ˀe^w¹tat³↑] *Who's that?* 168. [²àypubá:³d'æti¹↓] *I put back, daddy.* 169. [²ay³putæ¹tay²↑] *I put that, daddy.* 170. [²âypu³b'æ¹d'əyə¹↑] *I put back to you (returned something).* 171. [³dúwə^{w¹}↓] *Stool.* 172. [h^ᶜə↓] *Huh?* 173. [³háy¹↓] *High.* 174. [²dérdàtsə³lîtòw¹↓] *There, that's a little.* 175 [²dahìhih'əhə³há·¹↓] (Vocal play). 176. [²kəwàwkə³wáw¹↓] (Vocal play). 177. [³káw¹↓] (Vocal play).⁵ 178. [²hw'ətdúwən¹jôy³↑] *What doing, Joy?* 179. [²hwˆətdùwænjóy¹dây³↑] *What doing Joy, daddy?* 180. [²hw'ətjúwənjóy¹dâtiy²↑] *What doing Joy, daddy?* 181. [²hwˆəšdùwinjóy¹-dây²↑] *What's doing Joy, daddy?* 182. [²hwˆətsjùwiŋ³jóy¹jàdi²↑] *What's doing Joy, daddy?* 183. [³júwiŋ¹↓] *Doing* (in response to Father's question, "What's what!"). 184. [²ðˆæmìykəgûd³twéyˆn¹↓] *That make a good train.* 185. [²dà³gúin¹↓] *Doll going.* 186. [²čuwčuw³trey¹n²čuwčuwčuwkə³wæts¹↓] (Nursery language plus vocal play). 187. [³nyá:¹↓] *No* (in play with father). 188. [³nát¹↓] *Not.* 189. [²imâmìyz³nóy¹↓] *It's mommy's dolly* (*?*). 190. [²ay³h'æpsəmâmìy¹↓] *I have some, mommy.* 191. [²ayw¹asəm—³pí?òwz¹↓] *I want some picklés.* 192. [²àyniydìysəm³píkəm'əmiy¹↓] *I need eat some pickles, mommy.* 193. [²a³iýdìt¹↓] *I eat it.* 194. [²ìsmáyz³↑] *Is mine?* 195. [²əmbêybìywũzəbìyə³hí³¹↓] *The baby wants to be up* (or *a*) *here.* 196. [²hwêzə³gów¹dày²↑] *Where's you go, daddy?* 197. [²hwèstə³p'ə^w¹tây²↑] *Where's the boat, daddy?* 198. [³bówt¹↓] *Boat.* 199. [²p'ɔ¹k'ɔn³↑] *Boat gone?* 200. [²wˆɜgowiŋɔnə³báy:kbigbìgbôwt¹↓] *We're going on a great* (*?*) *big, big boat.* 201. [²hwə's'əstiŋ¹dây³↑] *What's this thing, daddy?* 202. [²hwèsə³tréyn¹↓] *Where's a train?* 203. [²əmhwìsəmhwêsənˆəðər³tréyn¹↓] *Umm, whisa-where's another train?* 204. [²wˆɜsànəı³bút¹↓] *We'res* (plural?) *on a, in boat.* 205. [²də³bút¹↓] *The boat.* 206. [²înðə³βáφ'ər¹↓] *In the water.* 207. [¹ríβ'ər³↑] *River?* 208. [³hwê¹zə²rívf'ər¹↑] *Where's a river?* 209. [²wˆərgòw³sítìn¹↓] *We're go sit in.* 210. [²w'ərgôwìŋnə³bówt¹↑] *We're going the* (or *in the*) *boat.* 211. [²w'egwˆəinìn³bówt¹↓] *We're going in boat.* 212. [²wˆɜgòˆiŋìnə³bówtm'əmiy¹↓] *We're going in a boat, mommy.* 213. [²nòwdêywɜgòwiy³íθt¹↓] *No, they were going with* (this is his usual form for negation—the *no* having the initial position in the utterance). 214. [²ày³k'ət¹ətdây²↑] *I cut it, daddy.* 215. [²àygônànəs³bówt¹↓] *I going on this* (*?*) *boat.* 216. [³jêkəin²gòwninə¹bówdày:²↑] *Jacqueline going in a boat, daddy.* 217. [³kágòwiŋ¹an:²dôwt¹↓] *Car going on*

boat. 218. [²ˆəpsðə³púsfədàwn¹↓] *Oops, the purse fall down.* 219. [²ənd'əndə³číyšfədàwn¹↓] *And then the cheese fall down.* 220. [²ay³níyd'æt¹↓] *I need that.* 221. [²nôw³-nówp'ədət¹↓] *No, no put it.* 222. [²pùtə³hí³¹↓] *Put a* (or *it*) *here.* 223. [²sétayesêyd'æsə³-séyd¹↓] *Seed, daddy, a seed that's a seed.* 224. [²asàwədâya³sá:ri¹↓] *I sorry, daddy, I sorry.* 225. [²hàtəklîynit³'əp¹↓] *Have to clean it up.* 226. [²lòwgu³téy¹↓] *Look it tape.* 227. [²hwêrðæ³téymámiy¹↓] *Where that tape, mommy?* 228. [²l^əkə³dærékərdmàmiy¹↓] *Look at that record, mommy.* 229. [²lùkədæ³rékər¹↓] *Look at that record.* 230. [³dá¹↓] *That.* 231. [²da³rék'ə^w rd¹↓] *That record.* 232. [²nôwag'ɔnan³súw¹↓] *No, I going on stool.*

4. Consonant sounds

TABLE 1: Consonant sounds.

	Labial and labio-dental	Dental and alveolar	Palatal	Velar	Glot-tal
Stops	p b	t d		k g	?
Fricatives	f v φ β	s z ð	š ž	x	h
Affricates			č ǰ		
Nasals	m	n		ŋ	
Glides	w	l r w	y ɥ		

Initial clusters in utterances: fl kl tr dr kr pl st.
Final clusters in utterances: ns nt ŋk ps rd rt rz ts θt.

5. Vowels and diphthongs⁶

TABLE 2: Vowels and diphthongs.

	Front	Central	Back
High	i		u
Mid	e	ə ɜ	o
Low	æ	a	ɔ
Diphthongs:	aw ay		
	ow ey		
	uw iy		
	oy		

---

⁶ The symbols i, e, æ, ə, u, o, ɔ, and a represent the sounds in b*i*t, b*e*t, b*a*t, *a*bove, l*oo*k, l*o*pe, l*a*w, and l*o*p; ə is the syllabic *r* heard in eastern New England. The diphthongs are those heard in b*ough*, b*eau*, b*oo*, b*uy*, b*ay*, b*ee*, and b*oy*.

6. *Alternations of sounds.* The following alternations are not presented as allomorphs of phonemes in the child's language, but rather as variants which did occur more than once in the discourse sample and, in some cases, frequently.

(1) *Alternation of stops.* Before back vowels, voiceless and voiced [p] alternated freely. [b] was frequently replaced by [m] in uttterance segments such as [gim] and [gib] corresponding to English *give*. Aspirated and unaspirated [t] alternated freely in the medial position, and [t] alternated freely with zero in consonant clusters when [t] preceded [s], [n], or [d].[7] Voiceless and voiced [k] alternated freely in the initial and medial positions in utterances. [t] replaced [k] occasionally when followed by [ə]. [k] alternated with zero after vowels plus length, and after diphthongs.

(2) *Alternation of fricatives.* [f] was replaced medially by [φ], or [p] before voiceless consonants, and by [β], [b], or [v] before voiced consonants. [s] was replaced occasionally by [z], [š], [ž], or zero.

(3) *Alternation of affricates.* It is interesting that the sounds [č] and [ǰ], which are difficult for most children, were seldom replaced by other sounds even though they occurred frequently in a few nouns. Their freedom from the variation so characteristic of most of the sounds may be accounted for by the fact that they were restricted in their occurrence, and were not subjected to the changing pressures of various sound environments the way other sounds were. Thus, their seeming stability was probably more of a passivity.

(4) *Alternation of Glides.* [w] alternated with [l] initially in utterance segments. [l] was replaced by zero following [u] and [ɔ], and by [o] following [e] and [t]. [ł] was an alternant of [l] before back vowels and after back consonants. [ɥ] occurred a few times in place of [r] and [w].

[w] alternated with [r] before [i], and in clusters of a stop plus [r] in segments such as

[tweyn] and [treyn] corresponding to English *train*. [w] replaced [r] in combinations of a vowel plus [r] before [ay]. In sequences of [aw] plus [i] followed by a vowel, [r] was replaced by [ə]. Zero [0] was an alternant of [r] in clusters of [r] plus a stop, and in clusters of a stop plus [r]: [ko0dɜ] ∽ [kordɜ], and [mayt0uφown] ∽ [maykrəfown] corresponding to *recorder* and *microphone*. Syllabic [r] was replaced by [u] before a stop: [bup] corresponding to *burp*.

[o] and [u] replaced [w] in clusters of a consonant plus [w]. [y] had no alternants.

(5) *Alternation of nasals.* The short and long forms of [m] and [n] alternated in the child's language similarly to the allomorphic patterning of these sounds in conventional English.[8] [n] alternated with [ŋ] after [i], and with [˜] when preceded by a vowel, similarly to the way these sounds alternate in adult English: [gowin] ∽ [gowiŋ] ∽ [gõ] for *going*.

(6) *Alternation of Vowels.* [i] was replaced by [ə] before [t], and often by [i·] medially and finally. [e] and [e·] alternated before stop consonants, and the lower front vowel [æ] alternated freely with raised [æ^] after [d] and [m]. [u] was replaced by [ə] in unstressed syllables, and by [o] before voiced, velar consonants. [u·] was occasionally replaced by ['ə]. [a] was replaced by·['ə] and [ɔ] in combination with nasal consonants, and by [ɔ] following a bilabial. [o] was replaced by [ɔ] and [u] occasionally. [ə] was replaced by [u] before the voiceless fricatives [f], and [s]; ['ə] was replaced occasionally by [ɔ] or [u] preceding [s], [k], or [m].

(7) *Alternation of diphthongs.* [aw] occurred medially only. [ɔ] and [o] replaced [aw] before [s], but preceding [t] the diphthong [aw] had no alternants.

[ay] occurred initially, medially, and finally in many different environments. [á], ['ə], and [ə] were alternants of [ay] in the utterance segment corresponding to English *I*.

[oy] occurred frequently in the utterance segment [ǰoy]. It was occasionally replaced by [ey]: [ǰey] ∽ [ǰoy].

---

[7] This may have been a mark of open juncture, but we were unable to establish it on the basis of this data.

[8] See Trager and Smith, *An Outline of English Structure* (Norman, Oklahoma, 1951), p. 34.

JOHN L. FISCHER

31

This study is concerned with sociolinguistic aspects of children's speech: the choice of the variants -in and -ing for the present participle ending in twenty-four children of a New England village. The author learned that the choice between these two variants is related to sex, class, personality, mood, —"socially conditioned variants" or "sociosymbolic variants." He also discusses the impact of social factors on linguistic change.

In the past decade, very important developments have taken place in the new field of socio-linguistics. Of special importance are studies by scholars like Einer Haugen, Uriel Weinreich, Dell Hymes, John Gumpertz, William Labov, Joshua A. Fishman, William Bright, and others. For a general idea about this newly developing field, the student is advised to consult the following anthologies, which are easily accessible and contain various helpful reference lists:

1. *Language in Culture and Society*, Dell Hymes, ed. (New York: Harper & Row, Publishers, 1964).

2. *Sociolinguistics*, William Bright, ed. (The Hague: Mouton & Co., 1966).

3. *Explorations in Sociolinguistics*, Stanley Lieberson, ed. (Bloomington: Indiana University Press; The Hague: Mouton & Co., 1966) (& *International Journal Of American Linguistics*, XXXIII, No. 4, October 1967).

4. *Readings in the Sociology of Language*, Joshua A. Fishman, ed. (The Hague: Mouton & Co., 1968).

A. B. A.

SOCIAL INFLUENCES ON THE CHOICE OF A LINGUISTIC VARIANT

During the year 1954–55 my wife and I were engaged in a study of child rearing in a semi-rural New England village.[1] In the course of the study I had occasion to record two or more interviews on Audograph discs or tapes, with each of the 24 children of our sample. Previously certain inconsistencies in the children's speech had attracted my attention, especially the variation between -*in* and -*ing*

for the present participle ending.[2] Accordingly, in transcribing the discs and tapes, I decided to note the choice of these two variants, and this paper is intended to summarize and discuss this information.

To begin with, all of the 24 children, except three, used both forms to some extent at least. The three exceptions used only the -*ing* form, and since they were less loquacious than most of the other children, it is possible that a larger sample of their speech would have revealed the use of the other variant as well. This may then be regarded as a case of so-called free variation of two linguistic forms within a local speech community, and within the

Reprinted from Word *14.47–56 (1958) by permission of the author and the Linguistic Circle of New York, Inc.*

[1] This study was part of a larger cross-cultural study of socialization financed by the Ford Foundation and under the general direction of John Whiting of the Harvard Graduate School of Education and others.

[2] The variation in this dialect between -*in* and -*ing* in the participle ending does not extend to words with a final -*in* in an unstressed syllable in standard speech. This variation is therefore probably best viewed as a case of free alternation of two allomorphs which happen to differ in respect to one phoneme, rather than as a case of phonological free variation.

speech of most individual members of our sample community. In general, the choice of one or the other of the variants would not affect the denotation of acts, states, or events by the word.

"Free variation" is of course a label, not an explanation. It does not tell us where the variants came from nor why the speakers use them in differing proportions, but is rather a way of excluding such questions from the scope of immediate inquiry. Historically, I presume that one could investigate the spread of one of these variants into the territory of another through contact and migration, and this would constitute one useful sort of explanation. However, another sort of explanation is possible in terms of current factors which lead a given child in given circumstances to produce one of the variants rather than another, and it is this which I wish to discuss here.

Before discussing the determinants of selection of the variants it will be helpful to understand a little of the general background of the data. The 24 children in our sample consisted of an equal number of boys and girls, both divided into two equal age groups, ages 3–6 and 7–10. By the time the recordings were made my wife and I had been observing the children periodically for eight to ten months and most of the children were fairly well acquainted with us. Most of the children were interviewed in an office in our house, which was located in the middle of the village. Most of the children had visited our house before, some a number of times. Four younger children who had not were interviewed in their own homes. Three general types of text were obtained:

(1) Protocols for all children for a verbal thematic apperception test (TAT) in which the children were asked to make up stories starting out from short sentences given by the investigator.

(2) For older children only, answers to a formal questionnaire.

(3) For a few of the older children, informal interviews asking them to recount their recent activities.

I shall present first some counts of variants in the TAT protocols, since this test was administered to all the children. As is shown in Table 1, a markedly greater number of

girls used *-ing* more frequently, while more boys used more *-in*.

TABLE 1.   Number of children favoring *-ing* and *-in* variant suffixes in TAT protocols according to sex.

	-ing > *-in*	*-ing* $\leqslant$ *-in*
Boys	5	7
Girls	10	2

Chi square: 2.84; 05 < P < .1 (by two-tailed test)

This suggests that in this community (and probably others where the choice exists) *-ing* is regarded as symbolizing female speakers and *-in* as symbolizing males.

Within each sex, differences in personality are associated with the proportion of frequency of *-ing* to *-in* as illustrated in Table 2.

TABLE 2.   Frequency of use of *-ing* and *-in* in TAT protocols of two boys.

	-ing	*-in*
"Model" boy	38	1
"Typical" boy	10	12

Chi square: 19.67; P < .001

The first boy was regarded by his teacher and others as a "model" boy. He did his school work well, was popular among his peers, reputed to be thoughtful and considerate. The second boy was generally regarded as a "typical" boy—physically strong, dominating, full of mischief, but disarmingly frank about his transgressions. The "model" boy used almost exclusively the *-ing* ending here, while the "typical" boy used the *-in* ending more than half the time, as shown above.

In Table 3 below, one may also note a slight tendency for the *-ing* variant to be associated with higher socioeconomic status, although this is not statistically significant with a sample of this size. The community studied is fairly small and does not have strong class lines, which is probably why more marked results did not appear.[3]

TABLE 3.   Number of children favoring -ing and -in endings according to family status.

Family status	-ing > -in	-ing ≤ -in
Above median	8	4
Below median	7	5

Chi square (corrected): 0; P > .9

Besides asking *who* uses which variant and how much, we may also ask whether there are situational differences in *when* a single speaker uses these variants. One variant in the situation may be described as degree of formality: in the children's terms I would think of this as degree of similarity to a formal classroom recitation. The best child to examine for this variable is the "model" boy of Table 2 since he was interviewed in all three situations mentioned above and was obligingly talkative in each. As Table 4 shows, the frequency of choice of variants changed from an almost exclusive use of -ing in the TAT situation to a predominance of -in in the informal interviews.

TABLE 4.   Frequency of -ing and -in in a ten-year old boy's speech in three situations in order of increasing informality.

	TAT	Formal interview	Informal interview
-ing	38	33	24
-in	1	35	41

Chi square: 37.07; P < .001

[3] Most previous studies of sociological factors connected with linguistic variants have been concerned with linguistic indices of class, caste, or occupational groups. Group boundaries have been regarded, implicitly or explicitly, as barriers to communication analogous to political boundaries, geographical distance, etc. The emphasis in this paper is rather on variations within a face-to-face community whose members are in frequent free communication: variations between social categories of speakers and between individual speakers, and situational variations in the speech of individual speakers, as noted below.

Of course, these three situations should not be regarded as exhaustive of the frequency range of these variants in this boy's speech. In the interviews I myself used the -ing variant consistently and this probably influenced the informant's speech somewhat. Probably in casual conversation with his peers the -in/-ing ratio is even higher than in the informal interview.

Another measure similar in implication to the frequency of variants by type of interview would be differences in frequency between the beginning and later parts of a single interview. Especially in the TAT protocols, which are the most formal texts, I noticed for a number of children that the -ing frequency was higher in the beginning of the interview and later dropped off, presumably as the child became more relaxed and accustomed to the situation. In only one child was the reverse trend noted, and there are reasons to believe that this particular child may have become more tense during the administration of the test.

A linguist might ask whether there is any association between the suffix variants and specific verbs. The corpus is not large enough to establish stable frequency indices for the suffixes of individual words, but there is certainly a trend for markedly "formal" verbs to have the -ing suffix and markedly "informal" verbs to have the -in suffix. The first boy in Table 2 above, for instance, used -ing in *criticizing, correcting, reading, visiting, interesting,* and used -in in *punchin, flubbin, swimmin, chewin, hittin.* For some common verbs, however, such as *play, go,* and *do* he used both alternatively. Probably only a few verbs are formal or informal enough in their connotations so that the same variant would always be used with them. Of course, the choice of verb vocabulary is itself related to personality and situational factors.

In brief, then, the choice between the -ing and the -in variants appear to be related to sex, class, personality (aggressive/cooperative), and mood (tense/relaxed) of the speaker,[4] to the formality of the conversation and to the specific verb spoken. While these are "free variants" in the standard type of description of languages in which only

[4] And doubtless of the person spoken to, although this was not investigated.

grammatical facts and differences in none but "denotative" meaning are taken into account, if we widen our scope of study to include the meaning of these variants to the conversants we might call them "socially conditioned variants," or "sociosymbolic variants," on the grounds that they serve to symbolize things about the relative status of the conversants and their attitudes toward each other, rather than denoting any difference in the universe of primary discourse (the "outer world").[5]

What are the wider implications for linguistics of such an analysis of social factors influencing choice of linguistic variants? For one thing, many linguists have recognized that "free" variation is a logically necessary stage in most or all linguistic change.[6] Less widely appreciated but also recognized by some is another fact: Although the mechanisms of psychic economy are becoming better understood in diachronic phonemics, they are not always sufficient to explain

fully the progressive adaption of variant forms, and that people adopt a variant primarily not because it is easier to pronounce (which it most frequently is, but not always), or because it facilitates some important distinction in denotational meaning, but because it expresses how they feel about their relative status versus other conversants.

The clearest and most comprehensive statement of social factors in linguistic change which I have encountered is found in an article by Martin Joos dealing with medieval sibilants.[7] He speaks of "the phonetic drift, which was kept going in the usual way: that is, the dialects and idiolects of higher prestige were more advanced in this direction, and their speakers carried the drift further along so as to maintain the prestige marking difference against their pursuers. The vanity factor is needed to explain why phonetic drifts tend to continue in the same direction; the 'inertia' sometimes invoked is a label and not an argument." This protracted pursuit of an elite by an envious mass and consequent "flight" of the elite is in my opinion the most important mechanism in linguistic drift, not only in the phonetic drift which Joos discusses, but in syntactic and lexical drift as well.[8]

The study of social factors in linguistic drift is in the field of the sociology of language rather than linguistics proper. However,

---

[5] Uriel Weinreich has suggested to me the term "symptomatic signs," after Karl Bühler, as an alternative for "sociosymbolic variant" which already has a basis in established usage. However, it seems to me that "symptomatic signs" might be in one sense too broad and in another too narrow: too broad in the sense that it might be interpreted to refer to "non-linguistic" features of speech such as general pitch, loudness, timbre, rate, etc., and too narrow in the sense that Bühler appears to regard the symptomatic function as, ideally, purely expressive of the speaker, while I am looking for a broader term which would cover this function but also include expression of the dyadic relationship between the conversants. This cannot simply be taken care of by adding in Bühler's "signal" function which deals with the "appeal" to the listener, since at least some aspects of the relationship do not exist primarily either in speaker or listener but rather *between* them, e.g. relative age, relative rank. See Karl Bühler, *Sprachtheorie* (Jena, 1934), esp. p. 28. Whether I should here introduce a term incorporating "symbol" is a further question which I acknowledge but do not discuss here, as it is complex and is not directly relevant to the main argument of the paper.

[6] I find in checking over the literature that this statement seems to be based more on my impressions of conversations with linguists than on published statements. One clear statement of this principle, however, is to be found on p. 367 of Hans Vogt's paper on "Language Contacts," *Word*, X (1954), 365–74. A more general statement applying to any type of cultural element, and by implication linguistic elements, can be found in Ralph Linton's *The Study of Man* (N. Y., 1936), p. 280.

[7] Martin Joos, "The Medieval Sibilants", *Language*, XXVIII (1952), 222–31; reprinted in M. Joos ed., *Readings in Linguistics* (Washington, 1957), pp. 377–380. Others have separately recognized the importance of fashion in linguistic change, especially in the spread of standard dialects, and to a lesser degree have recognized the complementary process of using distinctive linguistic features to emphasize social exclusiveness. J. O. Hertzler in "Toward a Sociology of Language," *Social Forces*, XXXII (1953), 109–19, gives a bibliography including studies of both sorts. Joos's statement however appears to me to be unique in his recognition that the two processes combine to constitute a self-perpetuating cycle. Since Joos is noted for his rigorous definition of the scope of linguistics proper it is perhaps all the more interesting that he should throw in this "sociological" aside.

[8] Incidentally, this flight-pursuit mechanism might be regarded as an explanation of the constant rate of decay of basic "noncultural" vocabulary postulated by Morris Swadesh's theory of glottochronology. To make it suffice one would also need to assume that all societies possess some form of elite group—if only the "ideal conformist" in some societies—and that mass envy of the elite and ambition to join them are

this study can not reach ultimate fruition without certain linguistic studies by competent linguists. I refer here to studies of individual variations in linguistic forms in small, face-to-face speech communities, and of variations in these forms in the speech of single individuals in a range of social situations. Studies of this sort constitute tasks of respectable magnitude which have, in the main, been neglected.[9]

A student of social factors in the choice of linguistic variants would wish to know for a fairly large stratified sample of a speech community how often members of a given subgroup used a sizable sample of series of socially significant variants, and for at least some of the subgroups one would want to know how these frequencies of choice of variants changed under different situations and in the presence of conversants of different social status and personal relationships. A linguist as such would not wish to analyze these social factors in great detail. But it would be well within the scope of linguistics to identify individual informants in a unitary speech community by name or code number and group them according to their similarity or dissimilarity in the use of variants in some standard situation, say, in conversation with the linguist. The psychologist and sociologist could then take these groups and see what sense they made in their terms. In practice, of course, such a rigorous separation between linguistics and the more general social sciences is not required since linguists and other laymen are presumably capable of making a number of distinctions of considerable sociological interest, such as male versus female, etc.

A word about the relation of the proposed study to dialectology is appropriate here. It has generally been the aim of dialectologists to describe linguistic variations between groups which are separated by some communications barrier, especially geography or social class. What I am advocating here is the study of linguistic variations within small groups where there is free and relatively intense communication, so that as far as possible the lack of contact between speakers is not a reason for failure to use the same forms. Of course in a large society such as ours, small closed groups are rare, and some of the variation among the individuals of any group picked for study will be due to the fact that they have different contacts outside the group. But this empirical fact does not reduce the importance of studying variation within the face-to-face community, although it suggests that the best place to study such variation would be on a remote Pacific atoll with a small, long-established population.

What I am proposing might be called comparative idiolectology rather than dialectology. Ideally, a thorough description of a single dialect would be based on the study of a sizable sample of the idiolects in a local speech community, in the same way that a thorough description of a language would be based on the study of a sizable sample of its dialects. In comparative idiolectology one might, as a device of fieldwork, still concentrate on a single informant, but one would want to follow him around with a portable recording machine and note changes in his speech in different settings and situations and with different conversants. Moreover, since phenomenologically language is as much listening as speaking one would be led to analyze what was said comprehensibly to him by others as well as what he said himself.

The untrained listener will not, of course, generally be able to reproduce or identify the differences in the speech of others whom he encounters, unless he is an accomplished mimic. But he does react to these differences by making interpretations about the social situation on the basis of them and will be able to tell when a speaker is talking like a woman, like an upper class person, like a

---

everywhere the same. These assumptions may seem radical and against common sense, but they are not as easy to refute as one might think. Needless to say, one would not assume that the elite is always a property or authority elite. In politically and economically undifferentiated societies, the most important criterion might be technical skill and productivity in consumer goods, admired personality traits, etc.

[9] The classic study in this field is Louis Gauchat's "L'Unité phonétique dans le patois d'une commune", *Aus romanischen Sprachen und Literatur* (Halle, 1905), p. 124. Other references are cited by W. von Wartburg, *Problemes et méthodes de la linguistique* (Paris, 1946), p. 33 (footnote). Modern techniques, of course, open entirely new perspectives for research.

relaxed person, etc., even though he cannot specify all the variant forms on which he bases his judgment.[10] (This is not to deny the presence or importance of other "non-linguistic" features of speech as well as things entirely unconnected with speech such as dress, physical appearance, gestures, etc., which also serve as cues for judgments of the conversational situation.)

In analyzing sociosymbolic variants there will obviously be a certain amount of association between variant series. In many of the series at least one variant could be distinguished as "formal," and another as "informal." But it is a question for empirical investigation whether this distinction applies to all variant series, and, if so, with how much force. I have suggested above a number of factors which influence the -in/-ing distinction. Conceivably they all bear on formality, that is, compliance, tenseness, femaleness, and high class all make for formal behavior. But even if this is true for these factors in American culture, are they a unitary complex in all cultures, and may there not be other social factors affecting sociosymbolic variants which are independent of the formality complex? Are variants associated with being female always associated as well with formality? In three languages with which I am acquainted, English, Japanese, and Ponapean, I can think of a number of instances where this link is found, but there also appear to be exceptions. In Ponapean, for instance, a minority of women have an unusual allophone for the r phoneme, but this seems to have no relation to the degree of formality. Lisping in English is regarded as feminine, but would indicate little about degree of formality.

Even where the same factor determines the choice of alternants in several series of variants, the breaking point for each series will probably be different. For instance, in the TAT texts discussed above, three of the

children used the pronunciation [ey] for the indefinite article a. This pronunciation can be regarded as formal to the point of being artificial and is much more restricted for speakers in this community than the -ing variant of the present participle ending, yet the direction of social symbolism is the same, though not the intensity. In other words, [ey] in itself is more a sign of formality than -ing though both are signs of formality. The "formality" index of a given text would be determined by the variant chosen in several series of sociosymbolic variants, each of which would have a different sociosymbolic level with respect to formality. Presumably these series could be ordered in terms of increasingly greater thresholds of formality required to bring about the shift from the informal to the formal form.

I have been stressing here the synchronic implications of sociosymbolic variants. The diachronic implications are at least equally interesting. Obviously the threshold for a given variant does not necessarily remain the same, generation after generation. If a particular variant has for whatever reason greater prestige, it will gradually be adopted in more situations by more people: its threshold will be lowered. But as its threshold is lowered and approaches universality in the speech community, its sociosymbolic load is reduced and eventually vanishes. One could hardly convey much of an air of informality, for example, by saying [ə] for the indefinite article, though saying [ey] would be quite stilted. But presumably new series of variants keep arising to replace those which achieve uniformity in this way.

Now what is meant by "variants of greater prestige"? One could determine which of a pair of variants had the greater prestige by noting which tended to "spread" when two conversants who in other situations differed in their choice came together. But the grounds of prestige clearly vary according to individuals and societies. A variant which one man uses because the wants to seem dignified another man would reject because he did not want to seem stiff. Societies likewise have characteristic average value preferences. Using the variable of formality, it is quite possible that one society would show a tendency, at least in some situations, to show

---

[10] The "tape experiment" described by Putnam and O'Hern investigates language and social status in this manner, although the speakers were not members of a single face-to-face community, so the complication of barriers to communication is introduced. See G. N. Putnam and E. M. O'Hern, "The Status Significance of an Isolated Urban Dialect," Language, XXXI, Supplement, Language Dissertation, No. 53 (1955).

a preference for adoption of formal forms of speech, and another in analogous situations show a preference for informal forms. These preferences could in turn be related by persons so inclined to social structure. One would end up with a statement not simply of the direction of linguistic drift, but what this drift meant psychologically and what social changes might check it. It would be very interesting, for instance, to find and examine cognate variants from some related

societies with differing descent practices, and see whether the current drift is in the direction of femininization or masculinization. Such data would not only illuminate the mechanism of linguistic drift, but would provide students of social structure with extremely valuable indices of the distribution of envy and cross-segmental identification in the communities speaking the language studied.

JEAN BERKO GLEASON

32 The aim of this study was to test children's productive knowledge of English morphology by eliciting various inflections and derivations. Preschool and first-grade children (ages 4–5, and 5–6–7, respectively) were shown pictures of objects, features, or actions, accompanied by brief statements of the experimenters. In order to discover the child's real productive mastery of English morphology, a number of "nonsense words" were introduced by the experimenters in those utterances. These nonsense words are forms that might be admissible phonologically, but happened not to be in use in English, e.g. *zib*, *wug*, *rick*, *gling*, *gutch*.

This study has become a "classic," by demonstrating new methods in psycholinguistic research, and was instrumental in producing related studies by others, including some on younger children. Cf. "The Development of Grammar in Child Language," by Miller and Ervin, in this volume. For comparison with studies on Russian, cf. Dan Slobin's paper "The Acquisition of Russian as a Native Language," in Smith, F., and G. A. Miller, eds., *The Genesis of Language* (Cambridge, Mass.: The M.I.T. Press, 1966), pp. 129–48.

A. B. A.

THE CHILD'S LEARNING
OF ENGLISH MORPHOLOGY

In this study[1] we set out to discover what is learned by children exposed to English morphology. To test for knowledge of morphological rules, we use nonsense materials.

Reprinted from Word *14.150–177 (1958) by permission of the author and the Linguistic Circle of New York, Inc.*

[1] This investigation was supported in part by a fellowship from the Social Science Research Council. During the academic year 1957–58 the writer completed the research while holding an AAUW National Fellowship. A dissertation on this subject was presented by the writer to Radcliffe College in April, 1958. I am indebted to Professor Roger W. Brown for his inspiration and his help in the conduct of this study.

We know that if the subject can supply the correct plural ending, for instance, to a noun we have made up, he has internalized a working system of the plural allomorphs in English, and is able to generalize to new cases and select the right form. If a child knows that the plural of *witch* is *witches*, he may simply have memorized the plural form. If, however, he tells us that the plural of *gutch* is *gutches*, we have evidence that he actually knows, albeit unconsciously, one of those rules which the descriptive linguist, too, would set forth in his grammar. And if children do have knowledge of morphological rules, how does this knowledge evolve? Is there a progression from simple, regular rules to the more irregular and qualified rules that are adequate fully to describe

English? In very general terms, we undertake to discover the psychological status of a certain kind of linguistic description. It is evident that the acquisition of language is more than the storing up of rehearsed utterances, since we are all able to say what we have not practiced and what we have never before heard. In bringing descriptive linguistics to the study of language acquisition, we hope to gain knowledge of the systems and patterns used by the speaker.

In order to test for children's knowledge of this sort, it was necessary to begin with an examination of their actual vocabulary. Accordingly, the 1000 most frequent words in the first-grader's vocabulary were selected from Rinsland's listing.[2] This listing contains the most common words in the elementary school child's vocabulary, as taken from actual conversations. compositions, letters, and similar documents. This list was then examined to see what features of English morphology seem to be most commonly represented in the vocabulary of the first-grade child. From this we could decide what kind of extensions we might expect the child to be able to make. All of the English inflexional morphemes were present.

The areas that seemed to be most promising from this examination were the plural and the two possessives of the noun, the third person singular of the verb, the progressive and the past tense, and the comparative and superlative of the adjective. The pronouns were avoided both because of the difficulty involved in making up a nonsense pronoun, and because the pronouns are so few in number and so irregular that we would hardly expect even adults to have any generalized rules for the handling of new pronouns. Moreover, we do not encounter new pronouns, whereas new verbs, adjectives, and nouns constantly appear in our vocabularies, so that the essential problem is not the same. The past participle of regular or weak verbs in English is identical with the past tense, and since the regular forms were our primary interest, no attempt was made to test for the past participle. A number of forms that might

suggest irregular plurals and past tenses were included among the nouns and verbs.

The productive allomorphs of the plural, the possessive, and the third person singular of the verb are phonologically conditioned and identical with one another. These forms are /-s ∽ -z ∽ -əz/, with the following distribution:

/-əz/ after stems that end in /s z š ž č ǰ/, e.g. *glasses, watches;*

/-s/ after stems that end in /p t k f θ/, e.g. *hops, hits;*

/-z/ after all other stems, viz. those ending in /b d g v ð m n ŋ r l/, vowels, and semivowels, e.g. *bids, goes.*

The productive allomorphs of the past are /-t ∽ -d ∽ -əd/, and they are also phonologically conditioned, with the following distribution:

/-əd/ after stems that end in /t d/, e.g. *melled;*

/-t/ after stems that end in /p k č f θ š/, e.g. *stopped;*

/-d/ after stems ending in voiced sounds except /-d/, e.g. *climbed, played.*

The progressive -*ing* and the adjective -*er* and -*est* do not have variants. It might also be noted that the possessive has an addittinal allomorph /-ø/; this occurs after an inflectional /-s/ or /-z/, so that if the form *boy* is made plural, *boys*, the possessive of that plural form is made by adding nothing, and indicatedin writing only by the addition of an apostrophe: *boys'.*

The children's vocabulary at the first-grade level also contains a number of words that are made of a free morpheme and a derivational suffix, e.g. *teacher,* or of two free morphemes, e.g. *birthday.* The difficulties encountered in this area are many. First, it might be noted that there are not many contrasts, i.e., not many cases of the same derivational suffix being added to different bases to produce forms of like function. Although *beautiful* and *thankful* both appear on the list, it does not seem that these examples are numerous enough for us to expect a young child to be able to append -*ful* to a new noun in order to produce an adjective. Word derivation and compounding are furthermore often accompanied by changes in stress and pronunciation, so that

---

[2] H. D. Rinsland, *A Basic Vocabulary of Elementary School Children* (New York: The Macmillan Company, 1945).

the picture is additionally complicated. There seemed to be enough examples of the pattern ′ ‵, as in *bláckboàrd* as against *blàck boárd*, and of the diminutive-affectionate *-y*, the adjectival *-y*, and the agentive *-er* to warrant testing for these forms.

So far as the general picture is concerned, all speakers of the language are constrained to use the inflectional endings and apply them appropriately to new forms when they are encountered. We are not so often called upon to derive or compound new words, although by the time we are adults we can all to some extent do this. From the children's actual vocabulary we were able to make an estimate of the kind of morphological rules they might be expected to possess, and from these items a test could be constructed. It was noted, moreover, that in the child's vocabulary there are a number of compound words, like *blackboard* and *birthday*. It is entirely possible to use a compound word correctly and never notice that it is made of two separate and meaningful elements. It is also possible to use it correctly and at the same time have a completely private meaning for one or both of its constituent elements. In order to see what kind of ideas children have about the compound words in their vocabularies, it was decided to ask them directly about a selected number of these words.

Within the framework of the child's vocabulary, a test was devised to explore the child's ability to apply morphological rules to new words. He was called upon to inflect, to derive, to compound, and, lastly, to analyse compound words.

MATERIALS AND PROCEDURE

In order to test for the child's use of morphological rules of different types and under varying phonological conditions, a number of nonsense words were made up, following the rules for possible sound combinations in English. Pictures to represent the nonsense words were then drawn on cards. There were 27 picture cards, and the pictures, which were brightly colored, depicted objects, cartoon-like animals, and men performing various actions. For reasons that will be discussed later, several actual words were

also included. A text, omitting the desired form, was typed on each card. An example of the card to test for the regular plural allomorph in /-z/ can be seen in Figure 1.

THIS IS A WUG.

NOW THERE IS ANOTHER ONE.
THERE ARE TWO OF THEM.
THERE ARE TWO _____.

FIGURE 1.   The plural allomorph in /-z/.

The subjects included 12 adults (seven women and five men), all of whom were college graduates. Many of these adults had also had some graduate training. All were native speakers of English.

The child subjects were obtained at the Harvard Preschool in Cambridge and the Michael Driscoll School, in Brookline, Massachusetts. At the Preschool, each child was brought to the experimenter, introduced, and told that now he was going to look at some pictures. The experimenter would point to the picture and read the text. The child would supply the missing word, and the item he employed was noted phonemically. After all of the pictures had been shown, the child was asked why he thought the things denoted by the compound words were so named. The general form of these questions was "Why do you think a blackboard is called a blackboard?" If the child responded with "Because it's a blackboard," he was asked, "But why do you think it's called that?" The children at the preschool ranged between four and five years in age. Twelve girls and seven boys were asked all items of the completed test, and two groups, one of three boys and three girls and one of five boys and three girls, were each asked half of the inflexional items in preliminary testing.

At the Driscoll School, the experimenter was introduced to the class and it was explained that each child was going to have a turn at looking at some pictures. The procedure from this point on was the same as for the Preschool. All children in the first grade were interviewed. There were 26 boys and 35 girls in this group. Ages ranged from five and one half to seven years.

The following is the order in which the cards were presented. Included is a statement of what was being tested, a description of the card, and the text that was read. Pronunciation is indicated by regular English orthography; a phonemic transcription is included for first occurrences of nonsense words.

1. Plural. One bird-like animal, then two. "This is a wug /wʌg/. Now there is another one. There are two of them. There are two ——."

2. Plural. One bird, then two. "This is a gutch /gʌč/. Now there is another one. There are two of them. There are two ——."

3. Past tense. Man with a steaming pitcher on his head. "This is a man who knows how to spow /spow/. He is spowing. He did the same thing yesterday. What did he do yesterday? Yesterday he ——."

4. Plural. One animal, then two. "This is a kazh /kæž/. Now there is another one. There are two of them. There are two ——."

5. Past tense. Man swinging an object. "This is a man who knows how to rick /rik/. He is ricking. He did the same thing yesterday. What did he do yesterday? Yesterday he ——."

6. Diminutive and compounded or derived word. One animal, then a miniscule animal. "This is a wug. This is a very tiny wug. What would you call a very tiny wug? This wug lives in a house. What would you call a house that a wug lives in?"

7. Plural. One animal, then two. "This is a tor /tɔr/. Now there is another one. There are two of them. There are two ——."

8. Derived adjective. Dog covered with irregular green spots. "This is a dog with quirks /kwərks/ on him. He is all covered with quirks. What kind of dog is he? He is a —— dog."

9. Plural. One flower, then two. "This is a lun /lʌn/. Now there is another one. There are two of them. There are two ——."

10. Plural. One animal, then two. "This is a niz /niz/. Now there is another one. There are two of them. There are two ——."

11. Past tense. Man doing calisthenics. "This is a man who knows how to mot /mat/. He is motting. He did the same thing yesterday. What did he do yesterday? Yesterday he ——."

12. Plural. One bird, then two. "This is a cra /kra/. Now there is another one. There are two of them. There are two ——."

13. Plural. One animal, then two. "This is a tass /tæs/. Now there is another one. There are two of them. There are two ——."

14. Past tense. Man dangling an object on a string. "This is a man who knows how to bod /bad/. He is bodding. He did the same thing yesterday. What did he do yesterday? Yesterday he ——."

15. Third person singular. Man shaking an object. "This is a man who knows how to naz /næz/. He is nazzing. He does it every day. Every day he ——."

16. Plural. One insect, then two. "This is a heaf /hiyf/. Now there is another one. There are two of them. There are two ——."

17. Plural. One glass, then two. "This is a glass. Now there is another one. There are two of them. There are two ——."

18. Past tense. Man exercising. "This is a man who knows how to gling /gliŋ/. He is glinging. He did the same thing yesterday. What did he do yesterday? Yesterday he ——."

19. Third person singular. Man holding an object. "This is a man who knows how to loodge /luwdž/. He is loodging. He does it every day. Every day he ——."

20. Past tense. Man standing on the ceiling. "This is a man who knows how to bing /biŋ/. He is binging. He did the same thing yesterday. What did he do yesterday? Yesterday he ——."

21. Singular and plural possessive. One animal wearing a hat, then two wearing hats. "This is a niz who owns a hat. Whose hat is it? It is the —— hat. Now there are two nizzes. They both own hats. Whose hats are they? They are the —— hats."

22. Past tense. A bell. "This is a bell that can ring. It is ringing. It did the same thing yesterday. What did it do yesterday? Yesterday it ——."

23. Singular and plural possessive. One animal wearing a hat, then two. "This is a wug who owns a hat. Whose hat is it? It is the —— hat. Now there are two wugs. They both own hats. Whose hats are they? They are the —— hats."

24. Comparative and superlative of the adjective. A dog with a few spots, one with several,

and one with a great number. "This dog has quirks on him. This dog has more quirks on him. And this dog has even more quirks on him. This dog is quirky. This dog is ——. And this dog is the ——."

25. Progressive and derived agentive or compound. Man balancing a ball on his nose. "This is a man who knows how to zib /zib/. What is he doing? He is ——. What would you call a man whose job is to zib?"

26. Past tense. An ice cube, then a puddle of water. "This is an ice cube. Ice melts. It is melting. Now it is all gone. What happened to it? It ——."

27. Singular and plural possessive. One animal wearing a hat, then two. "This is a bik /bik/ who owns a hat. Whose hat is it? It is the —— hat. Now there are two biks. They both own hats. Whose hats are they? They are the —— hats."

28. Compound words. The child was asked why he thought the following were so named. (No pictures were used for these items.)

    a. afternoon
    b. airplane
    c. birthday
    d. breakfast
    e. blackboard
    f. fireplace
    g. football
    h. handkerchief
    i. holiday
    j. merry-go-round
    k. newspaper
    l. sunshine
    m. Thanksgiving
    n. Friday

It took between ten and fifteen minutes to ask a child all of these questions. Even the youngest children have had experience with picture books, if not actual training in naming things through pictures, and no child failed to understand the nature of the task before him. It was, moreover, evident that a great number of these children thought they were being taught new English words. It was not uncommon for a child to repeat the nonsense word immediately upon hearing it and before being asked any questions. Often, for example, when the experimenter said "This is a *gutch*," the child repeated, "*Gutch*." Answers were willingly, and often insistently,

given. These responses will be discussed in the following section.

RESULTS

Adult answers to the inflectional items were considered correct answers, and it was therefore possible to rate the children's answers. In general, adult opinion was unanimous—everyone said the plural of *wug* was *wugs*, the plural of *gutch* was *gutches;* where the adults differed among themselves, except in the possessives, it was along the line of a common but irregular formation, e.g. *heaf* became *heaves* in the plural for many speakers, and in these cases both responses were considered correct. If a child said that the plural of *heaf* was *heafs* or *heaves* /-vz/, he was considered correct. If he said *heaf* (no ending), or *heafès* /-fəz/, he was considered incorrect, and a record was kept of each type of response.

Sex differences
The first question to be answered was whether there is a sex difference in the ability to handle English morphology at this age level. Since it seemed entirely possible that boys entering the first grade might be on the whole somewhat older than girls entering the first grade, it was necessary to equate the two groups for age.

TABLE 1. Distribution of children at each age level for comparison of the sexes.

Age	Boys	Girls	Total
4	2	2	4
4 : 6	1	1	2
5	2	2	4
5 : 6	2	2	4
6	10	10	20
6 : 6	6	6	12
7	5	5	10
Total:	28	28	56

The children were divided into seven age groups. Since at each of these levels there were more girls than boys, a random selection of the girls was made so that they would match the boys in number. The distribution of these ages and the number in each group can be seen in Table 1. This distribution was utilized only incomparing the performance of the boys with that of the girls; in all other instances, the responses of the entire sample were considered.

The groups of 28 boys and 28 girls thus selected were compared with one another on all inflectional items. The chi square criterion with Yates' correction for small frequencies was applied to each item, and on none was there a significant difference between the boys' and girls' performance; boys did as well as girls, or somewhat better, on over half the items, so that there was no evidence of the usual superiority of girls in language matters. From this it would appear that boys and girls in this age range are equal in their ability handle the English morphology represented by these items.

Age differences

Having ascertained that there was no difference between boys' and girls' answers, we combined the sexes and went on to compare the younger with the older children. The oldest children at the Preschool were five years old, and the youngest at the Driscoll School were five and one half years, so that the dividing line was made between the schools. Chi square corrected for small frequencies was again applied to all inflectional items. First graders did significantly better than

TABLE 2. Age differences on inflectional items.

Item	Percent-age of correct preschool answers	Percent-age of correct first grade answers	Signifi-cance level of difference
Plural			
glasses	75	99	.01
wugs	76	97	.02
luns	68	92	.05
tors	73	90	—
heafs	79	80	—
cras	58	86	.05
tasses	28	39	—
gutches	28	38	—
kazhes	25	36	—
nizzes	14	33	—

preschoolers on slightly less than half of these. The differences can be seen in Table 2.

Item	Percent-age of correct preschool answers	Percent-age of correct first grade answers	Signifi-cance level of difference
Progressive			
zibbing	72	97	.01
Past tense			
binged	60	85	.05
glinged	63	80	—
ricked	73	73	—
melted	72	74	—
spowed	36	59	—
motted	32	33	—
bodded	14	31	.05
rang	0	25	.01
Third singular			
loodges	57	56	—
nazzes	47	49	—
Possessive			
wug's	68	81	—
bik's	68	95	.02
niz's	58	46	—
wugs'	74	97	.02
biks'	74	99	.01
nizzes'	53	82	.05

Formation of the plural

The nature of the children's answers can best be seen through a separate examination of the noun plurals, the verbs, and the possessives. The percentage of all children supplying correct plural endings can be seen in Table 3. The general picture indicates that children at this age have in their vocabularies words containing the three plural allomorphs /-s ∾ -z ∾ -əz/, and can use these words. The real form *glasses* was included here because we knew from a pretest that children at this age generally did not make correct application of /-əz/ to new forms, and we wanted to know if they used this form with a common English word. Evidently they have at least one actual English model for this contingent plural. In uncomplicated cases children at this age can also extend the use of these forms to new words requiring

/-s/ or /-z/, as indicated by the high percentage of right answers for *wug and *bik, a form used in the pretest and answered correctly by a correspondingly high number of children. For the items *wugs and glasses there is, moreover, a significant difference between the younger and older groups. For glasses they progress from 75 per cent right to 99 per cent right in the older group, a change that is significant at the 1 per cent level. The few wrong answers in these cases were either a complete failure to respond, or a repetition of the word in its singular form.

TABLE 3. Percentages of children supplying correct plural forms.

Item	Allomorph	Per cent correct
glasses	/-əz/	91
wugs	/-z/	91
luns	/-z/	86
tors	/-z/	85
heafs, -ves	/-s/ /-z/	82
cras	/-z/	79
tasses	/-əz/	36
gutches	/-əz/	36
kazhes	/-əz/	31
nizzes	/-əz/	28

From this it is evident that however poorly children may do on extensions of the rule for forming the plural of glass, they do have this item in their vocabulary and can produce it appropriately. During the period from preschool to the first grade, those who do not have this item acquire it. They can also extend the rule for the addition of the /-s/ or /-z/ allomorph where the more general rules of English phonology dictate which of these forms must be used. During this period they perfect this knowledge.

The ability to add /-z/ to *wug and /-s/ to *bik does not alone prove that the child possesses the rule that tells which allomorph of the plural must be used: English phonology decrees that there cannot be a consonant cluster */-kz/ or */-gs/. The final consonant determines whether the sibilant must be voiced or unvoiced. The instances in English where there is a choice are after /l/ /n/ and /r/, and after a vowel or semivowel. Thus we have minimal pairs like: ells: else; purrs: purse; hens: hence; pews: puce. In forming the plural of *wug or *bik, the child has only to know that a dental sibilant must be added; which one it is is determined by the invariant rules of combination that govern English consonant clusters. If, however, he is faced with a new word ending in a vowel, semivowel, /-l/, /-n/, or /-r/, he himself must make the choice, because so far as English phonology is concerned he could add either a /-z/ or an /-s/ and still have a possible English word. We would expect him, therefore, to have more difficulty forming the plural of a new word ending in these sounds than in cases where phonology determines the form of the sibilant. These problems are represented by the forms *cra, *tor, and *lun. As Table 3 indicates, the percentages correct on these items were respectively 79, 85, and 86. The difference between performance on *wug and *cra is significant at the 5 per cent level.

During the period from preschool to the first grade, they improved markedly in their handling of *cra and *lun. The differences between the younger and older groups were significant at the 5 per cent level. The case of adding /-s/ to these forms did not, however, arise. The child here, as in so many other stages of language-learning, answered complexity with silence: the wrong answers were invariably the unaltered form of the singular.

The only other case to be answered correctly by the majority of the children was *heaf. Since adults responded with both *heafs and *heaves /-vz/, both of these answers were considered correct. It must be noted that although 42 per cent of the adults gave *heaves as the plural of this item, employing what would amount to a morphophonemic change along the lines of: knife: knives; hoof: hooves, only three children out of a total of 89 answering this item said *heaves; 9 or 10 per cent added nothing, and an additional four formed the plural with the wrong allomorph, i.e. they said /hiyfəz/, treating the /-f/ as if it belonged to the sibilant-affricate series. /f/ is, of course, phonetically very similar to /s/, and one of the questions suggested by this problem was whether children would generalize in the direction of phonetic similarity across functional boundaries—/f/ is distinguished phonetically from /s/ only in that it is grave and /s/ is acute. It is, so to speak, no more different from /s/ than /z/ is, and it is as similar to /s/ as /ž/ is to /z/. It does not, however, so far as English phonology is concerned, function like /s š z ž č ǰ/, none of which can be immediately followed by another sibilant within the same consonant cluster. The high percentage of correct items indicates that /f/ had already been categorized as belonging to the consonant class that can be followed by /-s/, and the phonetic similarity between /f/ and the sibilants did not lead the children to generalize the rule for the addition of the /-əz/ allomorph in that direction. Nor could any irregular formation be said to be productive for children in this case, although for adults it apparently is.

The proportion of children's right answers suddenly drop when we come to the form *lass. As Table 3 shows, 91 per cent of these children when given the form glass could produce the form glasses. When given the form *lass, a new word patterned after glass, only 36 per cent could supply the form *lasses. The picture becomes progressively worse with the other words ending in sibilants or affricates, and by the time we reach the form *niz, only 28 per cent answered correctly. *Niz, of these four, is the only one that ends in a sound that is also the commonest plural allomorph, /-z/, and the children did the worst on this item. What is of additional interest is that on these four items there was no significant improvement from the prechool to the first grade. The difference between performance on *cra, the worst of the other items, and *tass, the best of these, was significant at the .1 per cent level. Again, the wrong answers consisted in doing nothing to the word as given. It must be noted, however, that in these items, the children delivered the wrong from with a great deal of conviction: 62 per cent of them said "one *tass, two *tass" as if there were no question that the plural of *tass should and must be *tass. From this it is evident that the morphological rules these children have for the plural are not the same as those possessed by adults: the children can add /-s/ or /-z/ to new words with a great deal of success. They do not as yet have the ability to extend the /-əz/ allomorph to new words, even though it has been demonstrated that they

have words of this type in their vocabulary.

The form "kazh" /kæž/ wa added here once again to see in what direction the children would generalize. /ž/, although it is in the sibilant-affricate group, is very rare as a final consonant in English: it occurs only in some speakers' pronunciation of garage, barrage, and a few other words. As Table 3 indicates, the children treated this word like the others of this group. It might also be noted here that for the forms *gutch and *kazh, some few children formed the plural in /-s/, i.e., /gʌčs/ and /kæzs/. Ten per cent did this for *gutch, and 5 per cent for *kazh, errors that indicate that the phonological rules may not yet be perfectly learned. What is clearest from these answers dealing with the plural is that children can and do extend the /-s/ and /-z/ forms to new words, and that they cannot apply the more complicated /-əz/ allomorph of the plural to new words.

Verb inflections

The children's performance on the verb forms can be seen in Table 4. It will be observed that the best performance on these items was on the progressive, where they were shown a picture of a man who knew how to *zib and were required to say that he was *zibbing. The difference between *zibbing and the best of the past tense items, *binged,

TABLE 4. Percentages of children supplying correct verb forms.

Item	Allomorph	Percentage correct
Progressive		
zibbing	/-iŋ/	90
Past tense		
binged, bang	/-d ∞ æ ← (i)/	78
glinged, glang	/-d ∞ æ ← (i)/	77
ricked	/-t/	73
melted	/-əd/	73
spowed	/-d/	52
motted	/-əd/	33
bodded	/-əd/	31
rang	/æ ← (i)/	17
Third singular		
loodges	/-əz/	56
nazzes	/-əz/	48

was significant at the 5 per cent level. The improvement from the younger to the older group was significant at the 1 per cent level; fully 97 per cent of the first graders answered this question correctly. Here, there was no question of choice; there is only one allomorph of the progressive morpheme, and the child either knows this -ing form or does not. These results suggest that he does.

The results with the past tense forms indicate that these children can handle the /-t/ and /-d/ allomorphs of the past. On *binged and *glinged the percentages answering correctly were 78 and 77, and the older group did significantly better than the younger group on *binged.

Actually, the forms *gling and *bing were included to test for possible irregular formations. A check of English verbs revealed that virtually all in -ing form their past tense irregularly: sing: sang; ring: rang; cling: clung, and many others. The only -ing verbs that form a past tense in -ed are a few poetic forms like enringed, unkinged, and winged, and onomatopoeias like pinged and zinged. Adults clearly felt the pull of the irregular pattern, and 50 per cent of them said *bang or *bung for the past tense of *bing, while 75 per cent made *gling into *gland or *glung in the past. Only one child of the 86 interviewed on these items said *bang. One also said *glang, and two said *glanged— changing the vowel and also adding the regular /-d/ for the past.

The great majority on these forms, as well as on *ricked which requires /-t/, formed the past tense regularly. There was a certain amount of room for variation with the past tense, since there is more than one way of expressing what happened in the past. A number of children, for example said "Yesterday he was *ricking." If on these occasions the experimenter tried to force the issue by saying "He only did it once yesterday, so yesterday once he—?" The child usually responded with "once he was *ricking." Taking into account this possible variation, the percentages right on *rick, *gling and *bing represent a substantial grasp of the problem of adding a phonologically determined /-t/ or /-d/.

With *spow the child had to choose one or the other of the allomorphs, and the drop to 52 per cent correct represents this additional complexity. Several children here re-

tained the inflectional /-z/ and said /spowzd/, others repeated the progressive or refused to answer. No child supplied a /-t/.

On *motted, the percentage correct drops to 33, although the subjects were 73 per cent right on the real word melted, which is a similar form. On *bodded they were 31 per cent right, and on rang only 17 per cent right. The older group was significantly better than the younger on rang and *bodded. What this means is that the younger group could not do them at all—not one preschool child knew rang—and the older group could barely do them. What emerges here is that children at this age level are not able to extend the rule for forming the past tense of melted to new forms. They can handle the regular /-d/ and /-t/ allomorphs of the past in new instances, but not /-əd/. Nor do they have control of the irregular past form rang, and consequently do not form new pasts according to this pattern, although adults do. They have the /-ed/ form in actual words like melled, but do not generalize from it. With ring, they do not have the actual past rang, and, therefore no model for generalization. In the children's responses, the difference between *spowd, the worst of the items requiring /-t/ or /-d/, and *molted, the best requiring /əd/ is significant at the 2 per cent level. For *mot and *bod, the wrong answers, which were in the majority, were overwhelmingly a repetition of the present stem: "Today he *bods; yesterday he *bod." To the forms ending in /-t/ or /-d/ the children added nothing to form the past.

The third person singular forms require the same allomorphs as the noun plurals, /-s ∾ -z ∾ -əz/, and only two examples were included in the experiment. These were *loodge and *naz, and required the /-əz/ ending. Fifty-six per cent of the children supplied the correct form *loodges, and 48 per cent supplied *nazzes. The wrong answers were again a failure to add anything to the stem, and there was no improvement whatsoever from the younger to the older group on these two items.

Formation of the possessive
The only other inflectional items statistically treated were the regular forms of the possessive. The percentages of children supplying right answers can be seen in Table 5.

In the singular, the problem was the same as for the noun plurals, and the children's difficulty with the /-əz/ form of the allomorph is mirrored in the low percentage who were able to supply *niz's /-əz/ when told "This is a niz who owns a hat. Whose hat is it? It is the——?" For *bik's there was a significant improvement at the 2 per cent level between the younger and older groups. For *niz's the younger group did no worse than the older group.

In the plural possessives the problem is somewhat different: since these words are already regularly inflected, the possessive is formed by adding a morphological zero. The children did not add an additional /-əz/ to these forms, and in the case of *nizzes', they erred on the side of removing the plural -es, e.g. for the plural possessive they said simply *niz in those cases where they gave the wrong answers.

It was the adults who had difficulty with the plural possessives: 33 per cent of them said *wugses /-zez/ and *bikses /-sez/, although none said *nizeses /-əzəz/. This is undoubtedly by analogy with proper nouns in the adults' vocabulary, i.e., no adult would say that if two dogs own hats, they are the *dogses /-zəz/ hats. However an adult may know a family named Lyons, and also a family named Lyon. In the first instance, the family are the Lyonses /-zəz/ and if they own a house, it is the Lyonses' /-zəz/ house; in the second instance, the family are the Lyons and their house is the Lyons' /-nz/. The confusion resulting from competing forms like these is such that some speakers do not make this distinction, and simply add nothing to a

proper noun ending in /-s/ or /-z/ in order to form the possessive—they say "it is Charles' /-lz/ hat." Some speakers seem also to have been taught in school that they must use this latter form. It seems likely that the children interviewed had not enough grasp of the /-əz/ form for these niceties to affect them.

Adjectival Inflection

The last of the inflectional items involved attempting to elicit comparative and superlative endings for the adjective *quirky. The child was shown dogs that were increasingly *quirky and expected to say that the second sas *quirkier than the first, and that the third was the *quirkiest. No statistical count was necessary here since of the 80 children shown this picture, only one answered with these forms. Adults were unanimous in their answers. Children either said they did not know, or they repeated the experimenter's word, and said "*quirky, too." If the child failed to answer, the experimenter supplied the form *quirkier, and said "This dog is quirky. This dog is quirkier. And this dog is the——?" Under these conditions 35 per cent of the children could supply the -est form.

Derivation and compounding

The children were also asked several questions that called for compounding or deriving new words. They were asked what they would call a man who *zibbed for a living, what they would call a very tiny *wug, what they would call a house a *wug lives in, and what kind of dog a dog covered with *quirks is.

Adults unanimously said that a man who *zibs is a *zibber, using the common agentive pattern -er. Only 11 per cent of the children said *zibber. Thirty-five per cent gave no answer. 11 per cent said *zibbingmàn and 5 per cent said *zibmàn, compounds that adults did not utilize. The rest of the children's answers were real words like clown or acrobat.

For the diminutive of *wug, 50 per cent of the adults said *wuglet. Others offered little *wùg, *wuggie, *wugette, and *wugling. No child used a diminutive suffix. Fifty-two per cent of the children formed compounds like báby *wùg, teény *wùg, and little *wùg. Two children, moreover, said a little *wug is a *wig, employing sound symbolism—a narrower vowel to stand for a smaller animal.

TABLE 5. Percentages of children supplying correct possessive forms.

Item	Allomorph	Percentage correct
Singular		
wug's	/-z/	84
bik's	/-s/	87
niz's	/-əz/	49
Plural		
wugs'	/-∅/	88
biks'	/-∅/	93
nizzes'	/-∅/	76

For the house a *wug* lives in, 58 per cent of the adults formed the asyntactic compound *wúghoùse*. Others said *wuggery*, *wúgshoùse*, and *wúghùt*. Again, no child used a suffix. The younger children did not understand this question, and where the older children did, they formed compounds. Eighteen per cent of the first graders said *wughoùse*. Others suggested birdcage and similar forms. What emerges from this picture is the fact that whereas adults may derive new words, children at this stage use almost exclusively a compounding pattern, and have the stress pattern at their disposal: the adults unanimously said that a dog covered with *quirks* is a *quirky* dog. Sixty-four per cent of the children formed the compound *quirk dòg* for this item, and again, no child used a derivational suffix.

Analysis of compound words

After the child had been asked all of these questions calling for the manipulation of new forms, he was asked about some of the compound words in his own vocabulary; the object of this questioning was to see if children at this age are aware of the separate morphemes in compound words. The children's explanations fall roughly into four categories. The first is identity: "a blackboard is called a *blackboard* because it is a blackboard." The second is a statement of the object's salient function or feature: "a blackboard is called a *blackboard* because you write on it." In the thirdtype of explanation, the salient feature happens to coincide with part of the name: "a blackboard is called a *blackboard* because it is black;" "a merry-go-round is called a *merry-go-round* because it goes round and round." Finally, there is the etymological explanation given by adults —it takes into account both parts of the word, and is not necessarily connected with some salient or functional feature: "Thanksgiving is called *Thanksgiving* because the pilgrims gave thanks."

Of the children's answers, only 13 per cent could be considered etymological. Most of their answers fell into the salient feature category, while the number of identity responses dropped from the younger to the older group. Many younger children offered no answers at all; of the answers given, 23 per cent were identity. Of the older chil-

dren, only 9 per cent gave identity answers, a difference that was significant at the 1 per cent level.

As we might expect, the greatest number of etymological responses—23 per cent—was given for *Thanksgiving*, which is an item that children are explicitly taught. It must be noted, however, that despite this teaching, for 67 per cent of the children answering this item, Thanksgiving is called *Thanksgiving* because you eat lots of turkey.

The salient feature answers at first seem to have the nature of an etymological explanation, in those instances where the feature coincides with part of the name—72 per cent of the answers, for instance, said that a fireplace is called a fireplace because you put fire in it. When the salient feature does not coincide with part of the name, however, the etymological aspects also drop out. For *birthday*, where to the child neither the fact that it is a day nor that it is tied to one's birth is important, the number of functional answers rises: it is called *birthday* because you get presents or eat cake. Only 2 per cent said anything about its being a day.

The child approaches the etymological view of compound word through those words where the most important thing about the word so far as the child is concerned coincides with part of the name. The outstanding feature of a merry-go-round is that it does, indeed, go round and round, and it is the eminent appropriateness of such names that leads to the expectation of meaningfulness in other compound words.

Although the number of etymological explanations offered by the children was not great, it was clear that many children have what amounts to private meanings for many compound words. These meanings may be unrelated to the word's history, and unshared by other speakers. Examples of this can be seen in the following.

"An airplane is called an *airplane* because it is plain thing that goes in the air."

"Breakfast is called *breakfast* because you have to eat it fast when you rush to school."

"Thanksgiving is called that because people give things to one another." (Thingsgiving?)

"Friday is a day when you have fried fish."

"A handkerchief is a thing you hold in your hand, and you go 'kerchoo'."

These examples suffice to give the general

nature of the private meanings children may have about the words in their vocabulary. What is of additional interest, is that the last explanation about the handkerchief was also offered by one of the college graduate adult subjects.

We must all learn to handle English inflection and some of the patterns for derivation and compounding. So long as we use a compound word correctly, we can assign any meaning we like to its constituent elements.

CONCLUSION

In this experiment, preschool and first-grade children, ranging from four to seven years in age, were presented with a number of nonsense words and asked to supply English plurals, verb tenses, possessives, derivations and compounds of those words. Our first and most general question had been: do children possess morphological rules? A previous study of the actual vocabulary of first graders showed that they know real items representing basic English morphological processes. Asking questions about real words, however, might be tapping a process no more abstract than rate memory. We could be sure that our nonsense words were new words to the child, and that if he supplied the right morphological item he knew something more than the individual words in his vocabulary: he had rules of extension that enabled him to deal with new words. Every child interviewed understood what was being asked of him. If knowledge of English consisted of no more than the storing up of many memorized words, the child might be expected to refuse to answer our questions on the grounds that he had never before heard of a *wug, for instance, and could not possibly give us the plural form since no one had ever told him what it was. This was decidedly not the case. The children answered the questions; in some instances they pronounced the inflectional endings they had added with exaggerated care, so that it was obvious that they understood the problem and wanted no mistake made about their solution. Sometimes, they said "That's a hard one," and pondered a while before answering, or answered with one form and then corrected themselves. The answers were

not always right so far as English is concerned; but they were consistent and orderly answers, and they demonstrated that there can be no doubt that children in this age range operate with clearly delimited morphological rules.

Our second finding was that boys and girls did equally well on these items. Sometimes the girls had a higher percentage of right answers on an item, and more often the boys did somewhat better, but no pattern of differences could be distinguished and the differences were never statistically significant. These findings are at variance with the results of most other language tests. Usually, girls have been shown to have a slight advantage over boys. In our experiment, girls were no more advanced than boys in their acquisition of English morphology. Since other language tests have not investigated morphology *per se*, it is easy enough to say that this is simply one area in which there are no sex differences. A reason for this lack of difference does, however, suggest itself: and that is the very basic nature of morphology. Throughout childhood, girls are perhaps from a maturational point of view slightly ahead of the boys who are their chronological age mates. But the language differences that have been observed may be culturally induced, and they may be fairly superficial. Some social factor may lead girls to be more facile with words, to use longer sentences, and to talk more. This can be misleading. A girl in an intellectual adult environment may, for instance, acquire a rather sophisticated vocabulary at an early age. This should not be taken to mean that she will learn the minor rules for the formation of the plural before she learns the major ones, or that she will necessarily be precocious in her acquisition of those rules. What is suggested here is that every child is in contact with a sufficiently varied sample of spoken English in order for him to be exposed at an early age to the basic morphological processes. These processes occur in simple sentences as well as in complex ones. Practice with a limited vocabulary may be as effective as practice with an extensive vocabulary, and the factors that influence other aspects of language development may have no effect on morphological acquisition. Since, moreover, this type of inner patterning is clearly a cognitive process, we might expect it to be related to intelligence more than to any other feature. Unfortunately, there were no IQ's available for the subjects, so that a comparison could not be made, and this last must remain a speculation.

Our next observation was that there were some differences between the preschoolers and the first graders. These were predominantly on the items that the group as a whole did best and worst on: since no child in the preschool could supply the irregular past *rang*, and a few in the first grade could, this difference was significant. Otherwise, the improvement was in the direction of perfecting knowledge they already had—the simple plurals and possessives, and the progressive tense. The answers of the two groups were not qualitatively different: they both employed the same simplified morphological rules. Since this was true, the answers of both groups were combined for the purpose of further analysis.

Children were able to form the plurals requiring /-s/ or /-z/, and they did best on the items where general English phonology determined which of these allomorphs is required. Although they have in their vocabularies real words that form their plural in /-əz/. in the age range that was interviewed they did not generalize to form new words in /-əz/. Their rule seems to be to add /-s/ or /-z/, unless the word ends in /s z š ž č ǰ/. To words ending in these sounds they add nothing to make the plural—and when asked to form a plural, repeat the stem as if it were already in the plural. This simplification eliminates the least common of the productive allomorphs. We may now ask about the relative status of the remaining allomorphs /-s/ and /-z/. For the items like *lun* or *cra*, where both of these sounds could produce a phonologically possible English word, but not a plural, no child employed the voiceless alternant /-s/. This is the second least common of the three allomorphs. The only places where this variant occurred were where the speaker of English could not say otherwise. So far as general English phonology is concerned a /-z/ cannot in the same cluster follow a /-k-/ or other voiceless sound. Once the /-k-/ has been said, even if

the speaker intended to say /-z/, it would automatically devoice to /-s/. The only morphological rule the child is left with is the addition of the /-z/ allomorph, which is the most extensive: the /-əz/ form for him is not yet productive, and the /-s/ form can be subsumed under a more general phonological rule.

What we are saying here is that the child's rule for the formation of the plural seems to be: "a final sibilant makes a word plural." The question that arises is, should we not rather say that the child's rule is: "a voiceless sibilant after a voiceless consonant and a voiced sibilant after all other sounds makes a word plural." This latter describes what the child actually does. However, our rule will cover the facts if it is coupled with a prior phonological rule about possible final sound sequences. The choice of the voiceless or voiced variant can generally be subsumed under phonological rules about final sound sequences; the exceptions are after vowels, semivowels, and /l- n- r-/. In these places where phonology leaves a choice, /-z/ is used, and so the child's conscious rule might be to add /-z/. It would be interesting to find out what the child thinks he is saying—if we could in some way ask him the general question, "how do you make the plural?"

Another point of phonology was illustrated by the children's treatment of the forms *heaf* and *kazh*. It was demonstrated here that the children have phonological rules, and the direction of their generalizations was dictated by English phonology, and not simple phonetic similarity. /-ž/ is a comparatively rare phoneme, and yet they apparently recognized it as belonging to the sibilant series in English, and they rarely attempted to follow it with another sibilant. The similarity between /f/ and the sibilants did not, on the contrary cause them to treat it as a member of this class. The final thing to be noted about *heaf* if that several children and many adults said the plural was *heaves*. This may be by analogy with *leaf: leaves*. If our speculation that the /-z/ form is the real morphological plural is right, there may be cases where instead of becoming devoiced itself, it causes regressive assimilation of the final voiceless consonant.

The allomorphs of the third person singular

of the verb and the possessives of the noun are the same as for the noun plural, except that the plural possessives have an additional zero allomorph. These forms were treated in the same way by the children, with one notable exception: they were more successful in adding the /-əz/ to form possessives and verbs than they were in forming noun plurals. They were asked to produce three nearly identical lorms: a man who *nazzes; two *nizzes; and a *niz's hat. On the verb they were 48 per cent right; on the possessive they were 49 per cent right, and on the noun plural they were only 28 per cent right. The difference between their performance on the noun plural and on the other two items was significant at the 1 per cent level. And yet the phonological problem presented by these three forms was the same. For some reason the contingent rule for the formation of the third person singular of the verb and for the possessive is better learned or earlier learned than the same rule for the formation of noun plurals. The morphological rule implies meaning, and forms that are phonologically identical may be learned at different times if they serve different functions. These forms are not simply the same phonological rule. Since their different functions change the percentage of right answers. Perhaps the child does better because he knows more verbs than nouns ending in /s z š ž č ǰ/, and it is possible that he has heard more possessives than noun plurals. It is also possible that for English the noun plural is the least important or most redundant of these inflections. This is a somewhat surprising conclusion, since nouns must always appear in a singular or plural form and there are ways of avoiding the possessive inflection: it is generally possible to use an of construction in place of a possessive—we can say the leg of the chair or the chair's leg, or the chair leg although in cases involving actual ownership we do not say of. A sentence referring to the hat of John sounds like an awkward translation from the French. And no child said it was the hat of the *niz. The children's facility with these forms seems to indicate that the possessive inflection is by no means dying out in English.

Of the verb forms, the best performance was with the present progressive: 90 per cent of all the children said that a man who knew how to *zib was *zibbing. Undoubtedly, children's speech is mostly in the present tense, and this is a very commonly heard form. Explanations of what is happening in the the present all take this form. "The man is running" — or walking or eating or doing something. The additional point is that the -ing forms are not only very important; this inflection has only one allomorph. The rules for its application are completely regular, and it is the most general and regular rules that children prefer.

The children's handling of the past tense parallels their treatment of the plurals, except that they did better on the whole with the plurals. Again, they could not extend the contingent rule. Although they have forms like melted in their vocabulary, they were unable to extend the /-əd/ form to new verbs ending in /t d/. They treated these forms as if they were already in the past. They applied the allomorphs /-d/ and /-t/ appropriately where they were phonologically conditioned, and only /-d/ to a form like *spow, where either was possible. This suggests that their real morphological rule for the formation of the past is to add /-d/, and under certain conditions it will automatically become /-t/. Many adult speakers feel that they are adding a /-d/ in a word like stopped; this may be because of the orthography, and it may be because they are adding a psychological /-d/ that devoices without their noticing it.

Whereas the children all used regular patterns in forming the past tense, we found that for adults strong pasts of the form rang and clung are productive. Since virtually all English verbs that are in the present of an -ing form make their pasts irregularly, this seemed a likely supposition. Adults made *gling and *bing into *glang and *bang in the past. New words of this general shape may therefore be expected to have a very good chance of being treated according to this pattern—real words like the verb to string for instance, have been known to vacillate between the common productive past and this strong subgroup and finally come to be treated according to the less common pattern. The children, however, could not be expected to use this pattern since we could not demonstrate that they had the real form rang in their repertory. They said *ringed. At one point, the experimenter misread the card and told the child that the bell *rang*. When the child was asked what the bell did, he said, "It **ringed*." The experimenter then corrected him and said, "You mean it *rang*." The child said that was what he had said, and when asked again what that was, he repeated, "It *ringed*," as if he had not even heard the difference between these two allomorphs. Perhaps he did not.

The adults did not form irregular pasts with any other pattern, although a form was included that could have been treated according to a less common model. This was the verb **mot*, which was of the pattern *cut* or *bet*. There are some 19 verbs in English that form their past with a zero morpheme, but this group does not seem to be productive.

The cases of **gling*, which became **glang* in the past and **mot*, which became **motted* suggest some correlates of linguistic productivity. About nineteen verbs in English form their past tense with a zero allomorph. About 14 verbs form their past like *cling*, and seven follow the pattern of *ring*. Within these last two groups there are words like *win*, which becomes *won*, and *swim*, which becomes *swam*. We can also find words similar to *win* and *swim* that are quite regular in the past: *pin* and *trim*. But virtually all of the verbs that end in *-ing* form their past in *-ang* or *-ung*. There are approximately 10 of these *-ing* verbs.

The productivity of the *-ang* and *-ung* forms proves that new forms are not necessarily assimilated to the largest productive class. Where a small group of common words exist as a category by virtue of their great phonetic similarity and their morphological consistency, a new word having the same degree of phonetic similarity may be treated according to this special rule. *Ox* : *oxen* is not similarly productive, but probably would be if there were just one other form like *box* : *boxen*, and the competing *fox* : *foxes* did not exist. With **mot*, the zero allomorph is not productive because although it applies to more cases than are covered by the *-ing* verbs, it is not so good a rule in the sense that it is not so consistent. The final /-t/, which is the only common phonetic element, does not invariably lead to a zero allomorph, as

witness *pit* : *pitted*, *pat* : *patted*, and many others.

Although the adults were uniform in their application of *-er* and *-est* to form the comparative and superlative of the adjective, children did not seem to have these patterns under control unless they were given both the adjective and the comparative form. With this information, some of them could supply the superlative.

Derivation is likewise a process little used by children at this period when the derivational endings would compete with the inflectional suffixes they are in the process of acquiring. Instead, they compound words, using the primary and tertiary accent pattern commonly found in words like *bláckboàrd*.

The last part of the experiment was designed to see if the children were aware of the separate elements in the compound words in their vocabulary. Most of these children were at the stage where they explained an object's name by stating its major function or salient feature: a blackboard is called a *blackboard* because you write on it. In the older group, a few children had noticed the separate parts of the compound words and assigned to them meanings that were not necessarily connected with the word's etymology or with the meaning the morphemes may have in later life. Not many adults feel that Friday is the day for frying things, yet a number admit to having thought so as children.

These last considerations were, however, tangential to the main problem of investigating the child's grasp of English morphological rules and describing the evolution of those rules. The picture that emerged was one of consistency, regularity, and simplicity. The children did not treat new words according to idiosyncratic pattern. They did not model new words on patterns that appear infrequently. Where they provided inflectional endings, their best performance was with those forms that are the most regular and have the fewest variants. With the morphemes that have several allomorphs, they could handle forms calling for the most common of those allomorphs long before they could deal with allomorphs that appear in a limited distribution range.

33 Child syntax has been treated by Henry and Renée Kahane and Sol Saporta in their monograph, *Development of Verbal Categories in Child Language, International Journal of American Linguistics*, XXIV, number 4 (October, 1958) [Publication nine of the Indiana University Research Center in Anthropology, Folkore, and Linguistics]. A section of it is presented here as a sample of the method used to analyze categories in contrasting terms.

The abbreviations used in the selection refer to the publications which have furnished the source materials in three languages:

DialNo	E. C. Hills, "The Speech of a Child Two Years of Age," *Dialect Notes*, IV (1914), 84–100.
Leop	W. F. Leopold, *Speech Development of a Bilingual Child*, Vols. III and IV (Evanston, 1949).
MenGr	D. R. Major, *First Steps in Mental Growth* (New York, 1906).
PEC	C. W. Valentine, *The Psychology of Early Childhood*, 2nd ed. (London, 1943).
PedSem 11	A. F. and I. C. Chamberlain, "Studies of a Child," *Pedagogical Seminary*, XI (1904), 264–91, 452–83.
PedSem 36	K. Foulke and S. M. Stinchfield, "The Speech Development of Four Infants under Two Years of Age," *Pedagogical Seminary*, XXXVI (1929), 140–71

The Source for the German material is E. and G. Scupin, *Bubis erste Kindheit* (Leipzig, 1907); for French: A. Grégoire, *L'Apprentissage du langage*, Vol. II (Liège, 1947)—two boys, Ch(arles) and E(dmond).

W. F. L.

DEVELOPMENT OF VERBAL CATEGORIES IN CHILD LANGUAGE

1.2. *Tense.* Two contrasting patterns develop from the noncontrasting form: the contrast between NONPAST and PAST (1.21) and the contrast between NONFUTURE and FUTURE (1.22). The noncontrasting form (*do*) of the i-stage continues in both categories into the ii-stage as one member of the oppositions (*do: did* and *do: 'll do*).

1.21. *Non-past vs. past.* The examples are arranged as follows. In the i-stage the one

Reprinted from International Journal of American Linguistics *24.34–37* (*Oct. 1958*) *by permission of the authors.*

noncontrasting form (*do*) expresses the two categories of non past (i.α) and past (i.β). In the ii-stage, the same two categories are expressed by contrasting forms; nonpast (ii.α) is again expressed by the form *do*, and past (ii.β) is expressed by the form *did*. Adverbs found with the category nonpast (α) are: *now, today; maintenant* ['now']; *jetzt* ['now]', *immer* ['right now (sic)'], and, probably, *ei* ['hey']. Adverbs found with the category past (β) are: *yesterday, just, the other day, last morning* ['yesterday morning'], *a long time ago, sometime* ['a while ago (sic)'], *once a while* ['a while ago (sic)']; *hier* ['yesterday']; *gestern* ['a while ago (sic)']. In most sections there are two patterns: minus adverb (a) and plus adverb (b). In addition, English, in the ii-stage, has a third pattern: plus the auxiliary *do* (c). One set of examples will illustrate.

i.α   1; 9. 'i'ie boys no' *bi* ['little boys don't
      bite']~ PedSem 36.156.
ii.α 2; 5. wauwau *is coming* now ['the dog is
      com-: ing now'] Leop 4.25.
i.β   1; 9. good Beech *fall* down ['good Beecher
      feel down'] PedSem 36.157.
ii.β 2; 8 I *taw* a blue bird once a while ['I saw
      a blue bird a while ago'] PedSem 11.291.

1.*a*. The noncontrasting form means nonpast

English.   1; 9. 'i'ie boys no' *bi*' ['little boys
don't bite'] PedSem 36.156 | 1; 11. mama
wash hands ['mama is washing my hands']
Leop 3.39 | 1; 11. mama *hang* up stockings
['mama is hanging up the stockings'] Leop
3.44 | 1; 11. papa *read* book ['papa is reading
a book'] Leop 3.39 | 2; 3. Wut *want* tamp put
on ['Ruth wants a stamp to put on (this
letter)'] PedSem 11.290.

French.   1; 8.Ch. *è chonne* (elle, i.e. la
cloche, sonne) ['it's ringing'] 114, 373 | 1; 11.
Ch. *a* pu (il n'y en a plus) ['there is nothing
more'] 373 | 2; 0. Ch. n'*a* pas faim la lune
['the moon isn't hungry'] 191 | 2; 2.E. les
vasses (vaches) lè *cou* (elles courent) ['the
cows are running'] 195 | 2; 4. Ch. *est* mésante
(méchante) a closse (la cloche) ['the bell is
naughty'] 192.

German.   1; 6. wauwau *beiss* (beisst) ['a
dog bites'] 77 | 1; 8. Bubi *weint* ['Bubi is
crying'] 83 | 1; 11. Bubi snupfen (schnupfen)
habt (hat) ['Bubi has a cold'] 96 | 2; 0. da
hängt papa ['there is a picture of my daddy']
100 | 2; 0. *is* da vogel nein *is* keine vogel
['there's the bird; no, the bird's not there']
100.

1. *β*. The noncontrasting form means past

English.   (a) Minus adverb. 1; 9. good
Beech *fall* down ['good Beecher fell down']
PedSem 36.157 | 1; 10. nau'y fok *eat* dim boy
['the naughty fox ate the ginger bread boy']
PedSem 36.158 | 1; 11. mama *kiss* my ['mama
kissed me'] Leop 3.40 | 2; 0. Dane *step* on
my finger ['Clarence stepped on my finger']
DialNo 4.91 | 2; 3. no *ope* doah ['I did not
open the door'] MenGr 312 (b) Plus adverb.
2; 6. some time Oda *do* that ['Oda did that a
while ago (sic)'] Leop 4.30.

French.   2; 5.Ch. des petits garçons qui
vont dessus ['little boys who were riding on it,
i.e. the merry-go-round'] 261.

German.   (a) Minus adverb. 2; 5. mama *hat*
ein pickerle (pickelchen) Bubi hat's raus-
gemacht ['mama had a little pimple which
Bubi squeezed out'] 137 (b) Plus adverb.
2; 8. gestern *sind* die strimpfel (strümpfchen)
klatsenass (klatschnass) ['the socks were soak-
ing wet a while ago (sic)'] 156.

2. *α*. The contrasting form means non-past

English.   (a) Minus adverb. Examples in
1.21.i.*α*. (b) Plus adverb. 2; 5. wauwau *is
coming* now ['the dog is coming now'] Leop
4.25 | 3; 3. papa now *have* you enough money
to go to Germany? Leop 4.43 (c) Plus the
auxiliary *do*. 3; 5. what *do* we *do* today Leop
4.47.

French.   (a) Minus adverb. Examples in
1.21.i.*α*. (b) Plus adverb. 2;3. Ch. 1' (elle) *est*
chaude le (la) boite maintenant papa ['daddy,
the box is warm now'] 192.

German.   (a) Minus adverb. Examples in
1.21.i.*α*. (b) Plus adverb. 2; 3. *bin* ich immer
miede (müde) ['right now (sic) I'm tired']
122 | 2; 3. jetz *is* ristig (richtig) ['now it is
right'] 120 | 2; 9. was *bist* du denn jetz papa
bist du ein grosspapa ['what are you now,
daddy, are you a grandpa?'] 169 | 2; 9.
jetz *is* der Bubi nich mehr krank jetz *bin*
ich gesund ['now Bubi is not sick any more,
now I'm well'] 177 | 2; 10. jetz *hab* ich swarze
(schwarze) haare ['now I have black hair']
180 | 2; 1. ei kanne *tanzt* Bubi ['hey, Bubi is
dancing with the pitcher'] 108 | 2; 2. ei Bubi
geht passiern (spazieren) ['hey, Bubi will go
for a walk'] 116.

2. *β*. The contrasting form means past

English.   (a) Minus adverb. 2; 4. I *kissed* you
Leop 4.19 | 2; 0. Dane *ate* apple all up ['Cla-
rence ate the apple all up'] DialNo 4.91 |
2; 5. where you *was* ['where were you?']
Leop 4.26 | 2; 6. what you *did* mama ['what
did you do, mama?'] Leop 4.30 | 2; 10. I
throwed it away ['I threw it away'] Leop 4.37

(b) Plus adverb. 2; +. other day I *was* there mama ['I was there the other day, mama'] PedSem 11.463 | 2; 4. just *woke* up ['I just woke up'] Leop 4.20 | 2; 6. I *went* nini mummy last morning ['I went nini (?) with mummy yesterday morning'] PEC 442 | 2; 10. I *had* a drink once a while ['I had a drink a while ago (sic)'] PedSem 11.483 | 3; 1. I *saw* a man a long time ago yesterday PEC 443 (c) Plus the auxiliary *do*. 2; 3. what *did* you *buy* Leop 4.17 | 2; 4. *did* papa *like* my ice cream Leop 4.22 | 2; 8. *did* you *track* zis dis ['did you crack this dish?'] PedSem 11.290 | 2; 10. I *did* not *be* naughty ['I was not naughty'] Leop 4.36 | 2; 11. I *did* not *broke* it ['I did not break it'] Leop 4.38.

French. (a) Minus adverb. 2; 6.Ch. le carrousel ti (qui) *tournait* à l'envè (envers)

['the merry-go-round was turning around backward (sic)'] 130, 198 | 2; 6; Ch. i (il) *courait* is vite bébé ['Bébé was running so fast'] 130, 193 | 2; 7.E. i *kiyait* (il criait) fort ['he was shouting loudly'] 131, 189 | 2; 11.Ch. i *avait* pas (il n'y avait rien) dedans ['there was nothing in it'] 196 (b) Plus adverb. 3; 0.Ch. hier tu n'*étais* pas ici ['yesterday you were not here'] 121.

German. 2; 0. *war* das ['what was it?'] 101 | 2; 1. ach blume fort mama blume *war* drinne ['oh, mama, the flower which was inside (the vase) is gone'] 106 | 2; 9. was *war* d'nn (denn) das was hier milch gegossen hat ['who (sic) spilled milk here?'] 173 | 2; 9. *war* das ssön (schön) ['wasn't that swell?'] 1 69 | 2; 10. das kinderle (kindchen) *war* unatig (unartig) ['the child was naughty'] 189.

ROBBINS BURLING

34

This is one of the few studies on child language and infant bilingualism that involve a nonwestern language—in this case Garo, in India. It studies the development of speech and linguistic interference in a young American child, Stephen (the author's son), who was brought to the Garo environment at the age of one year and four months (in 1956). Burling raises several theoretical problems, especially while comparing his findings with those of Leopold, and contests some of Leopold's conclusions, such as the problem whether or not syntax precedes morphology in the grammatical development, or the connection between sound and meaning.

A. B. A.

LANGUAGE DEVELOPMENT OF A GARO AND ENGLISH SPEAKING CHILD

Toward the end of October, 1954, I arrived with my wife and small son Stephen in the Garo Hills district of Assam, India, where we were to spend most of the next two years making a social anthropological study of the

Reprinted from Word *15.45–68 (1959) by permission of the author and the Linguistic Circle of New York, Inc.*

Garo.[1] These people, one of India's tribal populations, number a quarter of a million and speak a language belonging to the Bodo group of Tibeto-Burman.[2] When we arrived, Stephen (who was born on the last day of May, 1953), was one year and four months old and was just beginning to attach meanings

[1] This paper is an expanded and revised version of one read at the 1958 summer meeting of the Linguistic Society of America. The opportunity to work in the Garo Hills was provided by a fellowship from the Board of Overseas Training and Research of the Ford Foundation.

[2] I have assembled a descriptive grammar of the Garo language which is to be published shortly.

consistently to some of the vocal activity that he had been emitting in profusion for many months. His first few words were English, but he immediately came into regular contact with Garo speakers and soon added Garo words to his vocabulary; in fact, for the greater part of the time we were there, his Garo was significantly more fluent than his English. Since there have been few studies of child language in non-Indo-European languages, I kept a record of my son's linguistic development and have assembled the results here.

The study of a child's speech is a delightful one, not the least satisfying aspect being the frequent enjoyment that one's informant shows in having so much attention paid to him by his father. Nevertheless, it is beset with difficulties that never arise in the study of adult language. Children won't repeat themselves the way good adult informants can be persuaded to do. It is next to impossible to try to compare minimal pairs directly, both because of the poverty of the children's vocabulary and because of the difficulty in getting them to repeat forms. Moreover children speak with less precision and much less consistency than adults. With wide variation within the limits of a phoneme and with the difficulty of comparing minimal pairs it is frequently impossible to specify precisely the time when the child first makes a new contrast within the range of speech sounds that had formerly been a single phoneme. Nevertheless the ideal for which I have striven is an analysis of the successive additions of the distinctive features rather than a detailed description of the ever changing phonetic minutiae of his speech.

Stephen began to use Garo words within a few weeks of our arrival, but his English vocabulary grew steadily and it was several months before Garo became clearly predominant. The eventual triumph of Garo was aided by a protracted hospitalization of his mother which, except for short visits, removed him from close contact with his most important single English model. She was hospitalized through most of March and April, 1955, when he was one year and nine and ten months old. At this time, I spoke to him frequently in Garo, which diluted the effectiveness of the second major English source.

Even after this the continued illness of his mother forced him into greater contact with Garos than might otherwise have been the case. The result was steady progress in the Garo language, which I believe he learned in much the same way as any Garo child.

PHONEMES AT ONE YEAR AND FOUR MONTHS

When we arrived in the Garo Hills, Stephen was one year and four months old and had a total vocabulary of a mere dozen words, but even those required a considerable phonemic inventory. He seemed to distinguish three vowel positions; a low unrounded vowel, generally central, though sometimes varying toward the front, as in *papa* 'papa'; a high front unrounded vowel as in *kiki* 'kitty'; and a mid or high mid back and strongly rounded vowel, as in *tu* 'door.'

As these examples also show, he clearly distinguished three stops in roughly the positions of *p, t* and *k*. Usually the stops were unaspirated and somewhat varyingly or mildly voiced, and in this case they were used with voiced vowels. Occasionally, however, the stops were strongly aspirated and without voicing, and in such cases they were invariably accompanied by unvoiced vowels, resulting in an explosive whisper: [k'aₐk'aₐ] 'custard,' [p'aₐ] 'up.' He interpreted all English voiced stops as unaspirated, but voiceless stops were sometimes interpreted in one way and sometimes in another, although he was generally consistent for any one word. For instance, 'papa' and 'kitty' never had aspiration, while 'custard' and 'up' always did. He also confidently used two nasals, *m* and *n*, as in *ma* 'more' and *nana* 'banana.' I never heard the nasals used except with fully voiced vowels. He had then three vowels, five consonants, and a distinction of voice and aspiration that cut across both the vowels and stops.

At this time all of his words were of the form CV or CVCV; if the latter, the two syllables were always identical. The first progress after our arrival came at one year and five months when he learned suddenly and decisively to use two different syllables in the same word, including either different vowels or different consonants. "Kitty' was then pronounced as *kiti* rather than as the earlier *kiki* and one of his first Garo words was *babi* (standard Garo *ba-bir-si*) 'cook,' his name for our cook.

If this appears to be an extensive phonemic repertory, it should be emphasized that it was available to Stephen at the very threshold of his use of meaningful speech. Though I did not keep careful records of the preceding period, my impression is strong that most if not all of the distinctions which I have described were present in the babbling which preceded his real speech.

Though these phonemes were first used for English words, he soon began using them in Garo words as well. For a considerable time he formed words from both languages with what amounted to a single phonemic system, and so for the first part of the record it is largely possible to ignore the existence of two languages. For the remainder of the paper, rather than adhering to strictly chronological account, I will discuss in turn the development of various aspects of his speech, and in the final section I will make a few general observations and some comparisons with other children whose speech development has been described.

CONSONANTS

About a month after our arrival, at one year and five months, he began to use a lateral in *lala* 'Emula,' the name of his Garo "ayah" (nurse). Soon afterward he began experimenting with affricates and spirants. The affricate was established first in *ci* 'cheese,' but by the age of one year and seven months, he had both this affricate and a spirant in *sosa* (Garo *so-si-a*) 'wet.' Both *š* and *č* were pronounced intermediate to the position of the nearest English sounds (*s* and *š*; *ts* and *č*) and from the beginning were very similar to the Garo phonemes.

At about the same time he began to use a labiodental approximating English *f*, and with refinement in the voiced/voiceless opposition that was achieved just shortly afterwards, he briefly used *v* as well. Garo does not have phonemes near to this position, and presumably as a result, *f* and *v* failed to become established. In fact they disappeared completely for a period and were replaced in English words by the bilabial stops.

The disappearance of *f* and *v* can be taken as marking his real transition to the Garo language. Everything earlier might be considered to be just as much English as Garo, but only Garo influence can explain the loss of these phonemes. He began to use *f* and *v* once more at two years and four months, but even at 2 ; 7 (years and months), a full year after they first appeared, these consonants were inconsistently articulated.

By 1 ; 7, the rather ephemeral distinction between voiced and unvoiced vowels, and the associated distinction between unaspirated and aspirated consonants, had disappeared, being replaced by a consistent distinction between voiced and unvoiced stops. At that time *p t k* and *b d g* became consistently distinct in the prevocalic position, and the associated vowels were invariably voiced. Stephen's pattern then came considerably closer to both that of Garo and of English, since the languages share the voiced/voiceless contrast. In Garo the contrast is made only for syllable initials, and this is the only position in which Stephen made it for most of our stay.

At just about the same age (1 ; 7), he began to use *w* and *h* both for the English phonemes, and for the Garo phonemes, which are phonetically similar to those in English, as in *hai* which in Garo means 'let's go' and the English word *wet*.

At 1 ; 9, he added *n* to his roster of phonemes. This does not occur initially in either Garo or English and so its appearance had to await the development of more complex syllables than he had had when the other nasals were first used. An example is *do ʔoŋ* (Garo *jo ʔ-oŋ*) 'bug.' This example also shows that at this same age the inervocalic glottal stop appeared. It was several months before he could use the glottal stop in the other positions in which it occurs in Garo.

With the addition of these phonemes, there was only one other Garo consonant outstanding: *j*, a voiced affricate which is intermediate as to position between English *dz* and *ǰ* and is thus the voiced counterpart of the Garo *c*. A *j* first appeared at one year and ten months, but for several months thereafter, Stephen used it only irregularly, frequently substituting *d* both for the *j* phoneme of Garo and for its nearest equivalents in English.

As soon as *j* was well established (by two years and three months), Stephen had all of the basic phonemic distinctions of the Garo consonants.

Correct pronunciation involves more than simply keeping the phonemes distinct from each other, however, and further refinement in his consonants consisted of increased precision and vigor in articulation, wider distribution of some consonants, growing sensitivity to allophonic distinctions, and better mastery of clusters.

An example of the way in which he gradually gained precision in his articulation is provided by his velar stops. He had had these since we arrived in the Garo Hills, but at first it was impossible to describe them more precisely than simply velar stops. Possibly because of the sheer small size of the mouth, but also because of imprecision and variation, one could not hope to specify the exact point of articulation. By one year and three months, however, his *k* and *g* had settled into the far back postvelar position which is characteristic of Garo, and he interpreted English *k* and *g* the same way, giving a distinctively foreign quality to English words with these phonemes.

At 1; 6 his syllable pattern was expanded to include the CVC pattern when he was able to use a final *t* in *dut* 'milk.'[3] Final *n* followed at 1; 7 in *mun* 'moon,' ŋ appeared finally (its only position) only at 1; 9 and final *m* and *l* appear in my records at 1; 10. The *k* sound was used finally by 2; 0 but *p* was not regularly used in that position until 2; 4. Until then, he substituted either *k* or *t* in place of final *p*, as in *jit* 'jeep,' and *cik-a* (Garo *cip-a*) 'shut.' The *s* sound was used finally as early as it was used in any other position and in this Stephen surpassed the Garo pattern, which has final *s* only in a small number of imperfectly assimilated loanwords.

From the beginning his word-final stops were unreleased and therefore corresponded to the Garo allophonic pattern. This was

carried over into English so that the final consonants of such words as *bed* were consistently unreleased. Medially he was at first inconsistent. Stops might be aspirated once and unaspirated the next time, so that at 1; 10 he pronounced 'papa' either as [p'ap'a] or as [p'apa]. At 2; 0 he learned to make the consistent distinction between syllable initial and syllable final allophones of the stops which contrast with each other medially, syllable initials being aspirated like word initials, and syllable finals being unaspirated. Garo has no true medial consonants since every one must be associated with either the preceding or following vowel, and the difference can be summarized by specifying the position of syllable juncture. At two years, then, with the establishment of some of the consonantal allophones, syllable juncture was also becoming established.

There is a single phoneme in Garo which if syllable initial is a flap, but if syllable final varies from a lateral much like the English *l* to a sound intermediate between a lateral and a flap, with considerable free variation. At first, Stephen pronounced every instance of this phoneme as [l], which amounted in some cases to the use of the wrong allophone of the correct phoneme. Thus in place of Garo *ra-ma* 'road,' he would say [lama]. This is a substitution which I heard small Garo children make, and in fact Garos recognize it as typical childish speech. At two years and three months, Stephen began to shift his initial examples of this phoneme in the direction of a flap and by 2; 5 he could execute an expert flap. However, even at 2; 7 he occasionally continued to replace the flap with [l] in words that he had known for a long time. New words were pronounced correctly, but some that had become firmly fixed before he was able to articulate correctly were slow to shift.

At two years and five months, also, he was suddenly able to use the glottal stop in clusters (phonetically these are glottalized consonants, though I find it easier to analyze them as clusters), and also in the phonetically distinct situation of preceding a consonant in the following syllable. He was then able to produce beautifully such Garo words as *na ʔŋ -ni* 'your'; *ma ʔn-a* 'to be able'; and *a ʔ-kor* 'hole,' and also said /jʌ ʔm-bo/ with a glot-

---

[3] Those acquainted with the Indic languages may recognize some familiar items in my examples. Garo has borrowed heavily from Bengali, including the word for "cow's milk" as opposed to "mother's milk." Stephen learned these as Garo words, which indeed they are, and I do not distinguish between them and older Garo words.

talized *m* substituting for the *mp* cluster of the English 'jump,' together with the Garo imperative suffix -*bo*, so this word expressed the command 'jump!', an example of the phonetic and morphological assimilation of English words into Garo that was typical of his speech.

Garo is not rich in consonant clusters, but my data are not complete even for those which it has. An isolated initial *st* cluster appeared as early as 1; 10 in *stas* (English 'stars') but these were not regularly used for many months. Initial combinations of a stop with *r*, which are the commonest Garo clusters, apparently first began about 2; 5. At 2; 8 he could make the initial *hw* in English, and could consistently add English plural *s* after other consonants, but other English clusters were still regularly simplified.

The result of this progressive development was a steady approach to the Garo consonantal pattern. He used more consonants prevocalically than postvocalically, which is in accordance with the Garo pattern, and his allophones were settling down to the Garo pattern.

At 2; 8 Stephen's English consonantal system still had several lacunae. The single Garo *s* was used in place of the four English phonemes /z, ž, s, š/. Though he eventually learned to make a voiced spirant in imitation, he never did so spontaneously. English *r* was replaced by *w;* post-vocalically it was sometimes omitted all together. He never substituted the phonetically very different Garo *r*. The spirants *θ* and *ð* were replaced by various other phones: *den* 'then,' *ti* 'three,' *ala* 'other,' *samsiŋ* 'something,' *bæfwum* 'bathroom.' The labiodentals *f* and *v* were fairly distinct by 2; 8. Occasionally they were pronounced as good labiodental fricatives, but more often were bilabial fricatives. Even this latter position kept them distinct from any other phoneme. He did not keep voiced and voiceless consonants distinct in the final position.

VOWELS

I have pointed out that at the time of our arrival Stephen had three distinct vowels. At 1; 6 several new vowels appeared with great rapidity, and for some time his vowels were in such a state of flux that it was difficult to analyze them systematically. His vowels were always much less well defined than the consonants, and more variable in successive utterances. He sometimes experimented with various vowels, used one briefly and then abandoned it. I once heard him pronounce the word 'moon' with high front rounded and unrounded vowels, a mid central vowel, and a high back rounded vowel in rapid succession, giving every appearance of groping for a sound that suited him. At 1; 6 vowel clusters first appeared with *ai* in *kai* 'Karen.' The two vowels were quite distinct and most easily considered as separate syllables. Other vowel sequences soon appeared: *i* following a front rounded vowel toward the end of the month, and *oi, au, ui,* and *ia* occurred occasionally at 1; 7, all of them being bisyllabic. Most of these were relatively rare at this time, but by then *ai* was well established and frequently used. It is the commonest vowel sequence in Garo. By the end of 1; 7 I felt that mid front and back vowels were fairly well established, as in *we* 'wet' and *po* 'Paul,' though 'teddy' was still pronounced occasionally as *tidi* rather than as *tedi*.

Various other vowels were heard occasionally. He used a mid central unrounded vowel in [vʌvʌvʌ] for a noise that a dog makes, with the vowel more emphasized than most examples of the mid central English vowel. A mid front rounded vowel was recorded first in conjunction with a following *i*, but later also alone in [tö] 'toy,' which was also sometimes [töi]. This even appeared briefly in an unvoiced from in [k'öʌk'iʌ] 'cookie.' This and a higher front rounded vowel occurred occasionally through 1; 7, but by the end of that month, I was inclined to feel that they were nondistinctive variants of the back rounded vowels. The use of [ʌ] was occasional, but not consistent until later. By the end of 1; 7, then, he seemed to be settling into a five-vowel system much like the Garo one.

For some time after this, however, *e* gave him trouble and it was only six months later, when he was just two years old, that it was unambiguously distinct from both *a* and *i*. In fact, for a while the *e* disappeared, and once when he was one year and ten months old, I was unable even to get him to imitate it successfully, though he would imitate many other vowels easily. When trying to imitate *e* he would substitute either [i] or [ai]. The failure of the *e* to become well established until later seems surprising both since *o*, which first appeared at about the same time, was by 1 ; 10 thoroughly established, and because both Garo and English have unrounded vowels in the mid front position, so there would seem to have been ample chance for him to hear these vowels, and model his own speech upon them.

At 1 ; 10 the mid central [ʌ] was reasonably well established in English words, and by his second brithday, the mid front *e* was again secure. At two years and one month, he seemed to be differentiating a separate and lower vowel from *e* toward the *æ* position of English, although Garo has no comparable vowel. The addition of [ʌ] and *æ* represented his first enduring progress beyond Garo.

By 2 ; 1 Stephen's vowel system was well enough defined and his articulation precise enough to make possible a more conventional synchronic description:

/e/ was a front mid, unrounded vowel. It was close to the correct position of Garo but was used also for the English /e/ of 'bed,' which is similar.

/æ/ had become distinct from /e/ and was used in English words only, even though these were generally incorporated into Garo sentences.

/a/ remained a low central vowel, used for both the Garo and the English vowels which are similar to each other.

/o/ was a back rounded vowel, intermediate to the cardinal positions of [o] and [ɔ], and therefore close to the proper position for the Garo vowel. It was also used for English words with similar vowels.

/u/ was settling down to the position of conventional Garo: high, usually central and not quite so sharply rounded as the early high back vowel from which it has been derived. This vowel appeared also in such English words as 'turn.'

/ʌ/ remained rarer than the other vowels. It was phonetically not too different from the nonfinal allophone of the Garo /i/ (for a discussion of which see just below), but as his speech developed /ʌ/, which was used only in English words, seemed clearly to become

separated from /a/ while the nonfinal allophone of Garo /i/ was derived from the more extreme high front [i]. That is, if there was uncertainty about an English word containing /ʌ/, the uncertainty always was whether or not it was distinct from /a/.

/i/ was a high front and unrounded vowel, something like the English vowel in 'beat' but with no glide. The Garo /i/ has several striking allophones, but for the most part at this time, Stephen used a high front unrounded vowel in all positions.

He used vowel sequences of all sorts easily. He did not tend to diphthongize them, but maintained the syllabic division between them which is appropriate to Garo.

The most serious imperfection in his Garo vowel system at 2 ; 1 was the absence of some of the allophones of /i/. Improvement came at 2 ; 3 when he began to make a consistent allophonic distinction between the /i/ of open and closed syllables. Nonfinal Garo /i/ was then pronounced somewhat lower than final /i/ in just about the position of English vowel [ɪ] in 'hit.' This was not yet exactly the proper position of the Garo allophone, which in adult speech is pronounced considerably to the rear of the English [ɪ], but at least some allophonic distinction was being made. The same phone [ɪ] was used in English words such as 'hit' while [i] was used for the English nucleus [iy]. In his speech the contrast between the high [i] and the slightly lower [ɪ] was actually phonemic, since the higher one could be used in English words where it appeared nonfinally (such as 'feet'), though this is an impossible position for the similar allophone of the Garo vowel. What in Garo were allophones were actually separate phonemes in Stephen's speech of the time, since he used them in English words, in positions not found in Garo. The next step in the development of his high front vowels was not clearly established until 2 ; 8, when the nonfinal allophone of the Garo vowel shifted securely to the rear to its proper position [i]. This meant that [ɪ] was used only in English words and [i] only in Garo words. But by this time, as is described below, several other developments had brought about a systematic separation of the vowel systems of English and Garo.

At 2 ; 7 Stephen had still not acquired any

further distinctively English vowels. For the complex vowel nuclei of English he either used nonfused sequences of Garo-like vowels, or simple Garo vowels. Thus for /ey/ of 'make' he generally substituted the Garo sequence /e-i/ without the fusing of the English nucleus. Similarly for /ay/ of 'pie' and /aw/ of 'out' he substituted /a-i/ and /a-u/ respectively. For /iy/ of 'heat' he substituted the simple high Garo /i/, for /ow/ of 'boat' the Garo /o/, and for /uw/ of 'food' the Garo /u/.

I have described Stephen as having phonemes that are distinctively Garo ([ʔ]) and others that are distinctively English ([ʌ, æ]), as well as many that were used in words of both languages. At least until early in his third year, however, his speech was most efficiently described as a single phonemic system. It was an approximation to Garo, with the addition of a few phonemic distinctions which are not found in that language. Even at the age of 2;7 his Garo was clearly better than his English, and he could still be described as speaking a variety of Garo that happened to have a great many English loan words. Some of the phonemes of his speech were found only in these loan words, but there was no indication that he recognized these words, or these phonemes, as having any special status. Other English phonemes were interpreted by him according to Garo speech patterns.

By 2;8 and 2;9 I felt that Garo and English were becoming differentiated as phonemic systems. Many English vowels now seemed to be becoming fixed in positions slightly different from the nearest Garo vowels, although since the differences were often small and since there was so much free variation in his speech, it was not easy to specify exactly the moment of separation.

At this time [ɪ] was used exclusively for the English phoneme and the nonfinal allophone of the Garo high front vowel had moved away to the rear. English /e/ also seemed to be consistently pronounced slightly lower than the Garo /e/ and English /ɔ/ of 'dog' was now lower than Garo /o/. The high back vowels seemed less stable but again English /u/ of 'put' was at least sometimes pronounced further to the rear than the high mid Garo /u/. I could detect no distinction between Garo and English /a/, which are virtually identical in adult speech.

Most of the complex nuclei were becoming more thoroughly untied as diphthongs in the manner appropriate to English rather than to Garo. This was true of /ey, aw, ay, ɔy, ɔw/ and /uw/. For /iy/ he continued to use the high front Garo /i/ which lacked any glide.

In other words, in the two months from 2;7 to 2;9 a systematic separation of the two vowel systems took place, and it was impossible to continue to describe them as one system. This is in contrast to the consonants, where—except for the addition of f and v—Stephen never went beyond the Garo system, and for as long as we were in India, he simply used the closest available Garo phones as replacements for the English phonemes.

SUPRASEGMENTALS

Garo, although a Tibeto-Burman language, does not have phonemic tone, and so the history of Stephen's speech cannot include the development of recognized tones. However, he fleetingly used a distinction which, even if idiosyncratic, was based partly upon tone. At the age of 1;6, I noticed that he made a fairly clear and consistent distinction between the words 'papa' and 'bye-bye' on the basis of length and tone. Both had unaspirated consonants and voiced vowels, but the word 'papa' was pronounced with a higher tone and very rapidly, while the word 'bye-bye' was pronounced with a lower tone and more slowly. Some other words seemed to have similar characteristics, though none were as clear as this pair, and the distinction did not last for long.

A month later at 1;7, length was clearly used as a distinctive feature of certain words which represented noises, such as [di:di::] to represent the noise of an automobile horn, and [ʔoʔoʔo::] for the sound of a crowing rooster. (This rather marginal use of the glottal stop actually preceded its use in non-onomatopoetic words by at least a month.)

At 1;7 he used the exaggeratedly high and then falling intonation which is used by Garos to emphasize great distance. Even by two years, however, his speech was not connected enough to do more than begin to catch incipient intonational patterns. At two years he sometimes used the slightly rising intonation which terminates Garo words, and I heard the typical low and falling English intonation with the word 'there' to convey the sense of 'there, that's done.' Stress does not have an important role in Garo, and I heard no significant stress variations, except for the emphasis of shouting.

MORPHOLOGY AND SYNTAX

At one year and seven months, I began to notice a few utterances which, from an adult point of view consisted of more than one morpheme. He would say *cabo* (< Garo, *ca?*–'eat' and *-bo*, the imperative suffix);

galaha (< Garo *gar-* 'fall' and *-a-ha* 'past'); *kukigisa* (Garo *cookie ge-sa*) 'one cookie'; *giboi* 'good boy.' At 1; 10 he was occasionally attaching the form *-gipa* to strings of speech or to nonsense, but only occasionally in positions where this suffix (which makes modifiers out of verbs) could have made any sense. I also recorded different inflectional forms of the Garo first person singular pronoun, *aŋa aŋasa*, and *aŋnisa*, which have somewhat diverse meanings, though presumably he learned these individually and did not construct them himself. His closest approach to

DEVELOPMENT OF LANGUAGE SKILLS BY STEPHEN BURLING

Age (years and months)	Consonants	Vowels	Other linguistic progress	Important nonlinguistic events
1; 4	p t k m n	i u a		Arrival in Garo Hills
1; 5	l			
1; 6	c	Vowels rapidly shifting		
1; 7	s w h (f) (v) voiced/voiceless contrast	i u (e) o a		
1; 9	ŋ			Mother in hospital
	intervocalic?			
1; 10	(j)	ʌ		„ „ „
1; 11			First unambiguous morpheme substitution	
2; 0		e	Syllable and word juncture in Garo	
2; 1		æ		
2; 2			Recognizes the existence of two languages	Living away from Garo, but contact with Garo continues
2; 3	j [r] allophone of l	ɪ		Return to Garo Hills
2; 5	Clusters with glottal stops			
2; 6			English developing rapidly	
2; 8		Systematic differentiation of Garo and English vowel systems		

substitutability was in phrases with the word *ba-o* 'where' as in *po bao* 'where's Paul?' I heard this word used once or twice with nouns other than 'Paul,' but was still doubtful that these were formed by him. It seemed more likely that all were learned as entire phrases. His speech could thus not be described as having utterances of more than one morpheme, since the constitutents were not substitutable. Gradually he acquired more such forms, particularly combinations of verb bases with one or another of the principal verb suffixes which indicate such things as tense. He regularly used the suffix which he heard most often with the verb, as the imperative forms of 'eat' and 'get dressed' and the past of 'fall,' since 'falling' was most often discussed after it happened.

Then on the first day of May, at one year and 11 months, I was sure for the first time that he could use suffixes freely and add any one of several suffixes to any verb. This was a decisive step and after that, he constantly produced new forms. On virtually the same day, he also was able to form syntactical constructions with a noun subject and a verb. Both morphological and syntactical constructions came at the same time and once the initial ability to make substitutions was gained, he went foward rapidly with more and more complex constructions.

From his first use of the constructions of verb with a principal suffix, he used the suffixes *-gen* 'future,' *-bo* 'imperative,' *-a-ha* 'past,' and *-a* 'present or habitual,' which are probably the ones most commonly used by adults. Shortly there followed *-gi-nok* 'immediate' or 'intentional future' and *-jok* 'recent past,' but even a month later at two years these were not used so readily as the others.

Soon after his second birthday he was beginning to use some of the adverbial affixes, which form a characteristic feature of Garo. These affixes are placed directly after the verb base but before the principal verb suffix, and modify the meaning of the verb base in various ways. Early in his third year it was difficult to know how freely he was using these, but the ability to form new constructions with them seemed to be beginning. By then I had recorded the following: *-ja-* 'negative,' *-eŋ-* 'continuous,' *-at-* 'causative,'

-ba- 'progression toward the speaker,' *-aŋ-* 'progression away from the speaker,' and *-be-* 'very.'

Shortly after his second birthday I had also recorded a few constructions with another class of verb suffixes, a class which follows the principal verb suffixes, and which can be called terminators. He did not use these frequently but I recorded *-ma* 'neutral interrogative,' *-mo* 'interrogative anticipating agreement,' and *-de* 'emphatic.'

He also used a few noun suffixes, though none of them as freely as the principal verb suffixes. The most frequently used was *-ci* 'in the direction of,' while its more emphatic and precise near synonym *-ci-na* was somewhat less frequent. At various times *-ba* 'also,' *-ni* 'possessive,' and *-na* 'dative' were used, most commonly with the pronoun for 'I.'

The third and last inflected class of Garo is that of numerals, which are formed from numeral classifiers and the quantifiers. Just before his second birthday Stephen began to experiment with combinations of classifiers and quantifiers, putting them together in the correct way, but with no apparent understanding of their meaning. A few days after his birthday, however, he saw a small bug, and said *jo ʔoŋmaŋsa* 'one bug,' including quite correctly the classifier used for all animals, *maŋ-*. A few days later I recorded him saying *gegini* in referring to two pieces of a cookie, correctly joining the classifier *ge-* to the word for 'two,' *-gin-i*.

The only English morphological construction which he had even incipiently used was the plural, which I recorded in isolated instances such as *ais* 'eyes' and *stas* 'stars.' But the plural marker was not used freely and could not be substituted. Although this English plural marker appeared substitutable or elaborated the way the Garo affixes had. At the same time he gradually acquired a few English phrases such as 'get down,' 'come in,' and 'good night,' all of which were of course learned as units, and their parts were not substitutable in any way.

Stephen's first freely formed constructions involving more than one word were those which combined a noun as a subject and a verb as a predicate. The construction in Garo is much like that in English, but his first sentences were clearly Garo. For one thing, they almost at once included a Garo principal suffix on the verb, so the sentences included three morphemes. Examples are: *ba-bi on-a-ha* 'Babi (the cook) gave (it to me)' and *do ʔo bilaŋaha* 'bird flew away.' He continued often to use verbs alone without a subject, but since this conforms to adult Garo, where the subject need not be expressed if no ambiguity arises, this was not a babyish trait on his part.

Soon after his use of subject-verb sentences, he started to use verbs with nouns in other cases. My first recorded example is on May 17, two and one half weeks after his first construction: *papaci reaŋna* 'go to Papa.' On June 4 I recorded two three-word sentences (four and five morphemes respectively): *aŋa tolet naŋa,* 'I need toilet,' and *lala bi taleŋa* 'Emula is preparing the bed.' In both these examples one word was derived from English, though the word order, morphology and phonology were all completely Garo. This assimilation of English words into Garo was characteristic of his speech for as long as we were in the Garo Hills.

By 2; 0 he was also using possessives correctly, attaching the possessive suffix to one noun, most frequntly *aŋa* 'I,' and then following it by a name of the thing possessed. At that time also there were the first constructions of a noun with a numeral, examples of which have alrady been given. By early June, then, just after his second birthday and a bit over a month after he first clearly used morpheme substitution, he had used the following constructions (those marked with* were used most freely and frequently, while those in parentheses were only incipient, and those left unmarked were well established, though not among the commonest):

   Morphological constructions
      verb base plus adverbial affix
   * verb base (with or without an adverbial affix) plus principal verb suffix
      complete verb plus terminator
      noun plus principal noun (case) suffix
      (numeral classifier plus quantifier to form a numeral)
   Syntactical constructions
   * noun (in various cases) plus verb to form sentence
   * possessive noun plus noun
      (noun plus numeral)

Even at this early stage I had never noticed him using obviously incorrect morpheme order. He spoke in a simplified way, of course, and sometimes left things out, but he did not reverse the proper position of morphemes or words. This is perhaps not remarkable since given the freedom of word order (not morpheme order within the words), incorrect word order is not easy to achieve in Garo. In learning these constructions, he apparently always used the construction first in certain specific examples which he learned as a whole and by rote. After using several of these for a while, he would learn to generalize on the construction, and to substitute different morphemes or words in the same construction.

For the next few months, until 2; 3, his grammatical development was largely a matter of consolidating and improving the steps that had already been begun in May at 1; 11. By September he was freely and correctly using many adverbial affixes and principal verb suffixes. Both these classes had been considerably expanded. At 2; 1 I recorded his use of the general suffix *-kon* 'probably,' and by 2; 2 he was using it in such a way as to show that he understood its meaning. At 2; 2, I recorded the suffix *-ode* 'if,' but could not tell whether he understood its meaning or could use it freely. These innovations are significant in that they involve members of still another class of suffixes that had not been represented earlier and which are inserted after the principal suffix but before the terminator if there is one. He also used several of the principal noun suffixes (case markers) correctly and readily. Of the noun suffixes, the possessive marker continued to be used most regularly. His syntax included the simple form of the Garo sentence with nouns in various cases, followed by the verb. However, he sometimes put one noun, often a pronoun, after the verb, which is a correct Garo way of giving emphasis to the noun. More elaborate constructions, with phrases, clauses, conjunctions, and the like, were still absent from his speech.

The only English construction which he could freely use at 2; 3 was that with 'more,' such as *mo ci* 'more water.' Here *ci* is the Garo for water, but the construction is quite foreign to Garo, and is clearly English. The few other

English phrases which he used, including even such complex ones as 'what are you doing,' had been memorized as units and the parts were not separable.

By the age of two and a half, he had the system of verb inflection essentially complete, including the use of at least some of the members of every class of verb suffix, and all of the common ones. He used many adverbial affixes easily. I heard examples of as many as three adverbial affixes in one word, which is as many as adults commonly use, though it is not a formal limit. He had also begun to use members of a group of verb suffixes which can convert verbs to a substantive function. At 2;6 he was able to use the important verb suffix *-gi-pa*, by which Garo verbs are put into a form which can be used to modify nouns. He had used *-gi-pa* much earlier, appending it to strings of nonsense, but such "babbling" had stopped by 2;1, and now the suffix was used correctly and with understanding, A few weeks after this appeared, he added the somewhat similar suffix *-a-ni*, which is used to make abstracts from verbs, such as 'heat' from 'hot' or 'walking' from 'walk.'

He also used members of every class of noun suffix, though he did not use every single suffix. He used most of the principal noun suffixes and a good many of the secondary noun suffixes which follow the principal suffixes, and he frequently and easily used the terminating noun suffixes *-san* 'only', *-dake* 'like, in the manner of,' *-ba* 'also,' and *-de* 'indeed.' Personal pronouns, which in Garo act grammatically like nouns, were added slowly. He had used *aŋa* 'I' since 1;11, but *na ʔa* 'you sg.' was recorded only at 2;4, *ciŋ-a* 'we exclusive' at 2;5, and *bi-a* 'he, she' at 2;6. Others were even later.

At 2;6 he could use numbers incompletely and tried to count, but frequently got the order reversed. Two months later he was able to count to ten with occasional mistakes in Garo, and more consistently correctly in English, and he understood the numbers at least to three. He used several numeral classifiers in Garo quite readily, though except for *-sak* (for people) and *-maŋ* (for animals) it was doubtful whether he really understood their meaning.

He was weaker in the use of particles. He used few adverbial particles except *bak-bak* 'quickly,' and only a few of the conjunctions. Lacking most of the conjunctions, he was able to form few complex sentences, though by 2;6 he was making the balanced type of Garo sentence in which two similar verbs, one generally positive and the other negative, are paired together with their associated nouns, without an intervening conjunction.

Reduplication is used grammatically in a number of ways in Garo, but by this time I had not yet detected Stephen using any reduplicated forms. The slow acquisition would seem to indicate that the grammatical reduplication of adult speech has little to do with the reduplicated forms of infantile speech which occur so ubiquitously and which Stephen had used from the beginning of his speech.

SEMANTICS

Besides making steady progress in phonology and grammar, Stephen spoke about a continually widening range of subjects. In some cases he learned a new word in either Garo or English, and for some time used that word in all circumstances, without ever using an equivalent in the other language. In other cases, however, he simultaneously learned English and Garo words with approximately the same meanings, as though once his understanding reached the point of being able to grasp a concept he was able to use the appropriate words in both languages. I first recorded the English word *swallow* and the Garo *min-ok-a* 'swallow' on the same day. He learned to count in the two languages in parallel fashion, and could recite numbers in either one and keep the two sets generally distinct even before he became confident and consistent in reciting them in the right order. It was clear that in both languages he could recite numbers before he had any real ability to count or to understand the meaning.

By one year and ten months he was beginning to use color terms in both English and Garo, with great interest, but with little understanding. He would point to something and mention a color term in either language that had no relationship to the color of the object. When later at 2;9 he suddenly grasped the meaning of color terms, and was able to consistently call a red thing red, he was able to do so in both English and in Garo simultaneously. At about the same time he started to use various indicators of time, such as *last night*, *yesterday morning*, and corresponding Garo terms, again with little understanding except that he kept terms for past time separated from those for the future. This imprecise use of time markers was in striking contrast to his correct use of spatial terms such as *here*, *there*, and various Garo equivalents, which he had started to use correctly much earlier.

At 2; 9 Stephen began for the first time to ask explicitly about words. He would occasionally start to speak, pause, point to something, and ask *wats dis;* receiving an answer, he would proceed to use the word in his sentence. He asked such questions equally well in both English and Garo. He also talked about words, though it was difficult to know how well he grasped the sense of the sentences he used. For instance, he would point to his nose and say *in English it is nose*, or *in Gawo it is giŋ-tiŋ*, but he would sometimes get these reversed and call a Garo word English or vice versa. When he was two years and ten months old, I was able to interest him in playing a game with me. I would ask him a question such as "What does hand mean," and he would promptly supply the Garo equivalent; or, if I supplied him with a Garo word, he would return the English. He gave no indication that he noticed which language I presented him with, but consistently gave the opposite one. When I asked for the meaning of the word "table" however, for which the Garos use a word borrowed from English which is phonetically similar to the original, Stephen paused only briefly and then supplied the translation "dining room table." At 2; 9 also, he started using the word *said* and its Garo equivalent *a-gan-a* correctly and with understanding in dicrect speech— another indication of his growing awareness of speech as a phenomenon that can be talked about. In either Garo or English he was able to say such things as *I said "sit down!"*

BILINGUALISM

As early as the age of 1; 6, not quite two months after our arrival, I recorded what then seemed to me like translation. If we asked him if he wanted milk, he would unhesitatingly indicate the affirmative with the Garo equivalent *dut* 'milk.' However, six months later I could still find no evidence that he was really aware of the existence of two different languages in his environment. As in the case of *milk* and *dut* he did recognize that there were two words for certain things and sometimes he would say them together, one after the other, clearly recognizing that they were equivalents. But all his constructions at that time were completely Garo, the only significant English influence being lexical.

We spent about two months from the middle of July to the middle of September (2; 1 to 2; 3) in Gauhati, Assam, away from the Garo Hills, where Stephen came into contact with several English speakers, as well as numerous Assamese speakers. He continued to be cared for to a great extent by his Garo "ayah." who even sought out the companionship of other Garos, so his contact with that language was never broken. But while we were in Gauhati, I began to feel that he really recognized the existence of the separate languages. He quickly learned who did not speak Garo and rarely attempted to speak to them. He was always more shy with them than with Garo speakers. By 2; 3 he could understand a considerable amount of English, but spoke little. He then showed a facility for translating exactly what was said in English into idiomatic Garo. If I asked him a question in English, he was likely to give an immediate and unhesitating reply in Garo.

After returning to the Garo Hills, life was somewhat more normal. He had more continuous and intimate contact with his mother than he had had for some months. This finally resulted at the end of 1955, when he was two and one half years old, in an explosive expansion of his ability in English. Though his English never caught up with his Garo as long as we stayed in the Garo Hills, he developed a taste for speaking English with native English speakers and to my chagrin he came to prefer to speak English with me. Occasionally, when I failed to understand his still very foreign English, he would with obvious condescension translate into Garo, which, being said more correctly, was easier to understand. He translated without hesitation and with no apparent difficulty in switching from one language to the other. He frequently spoke to me in idiomatic English and immediately repeated it in just as idiomatic Garo for someone else's benefit.

We remained in the Garo Hills until October, 1956, but the pressure of other work prevented me from keeping detailed records of Stephen's speech after April (2; 10), while his increasing tendency to speak English with me and the increasing skill with which he spoke in both languages made it both more difficult and less rewarding to do so. When we left the district, there was still no doubt that Garo was his first language (when he spoke in his sleep, it was in Garo) but English had become a flexible means of expression as well. We spent about a month traveling across India. At first he attempted to speak Garo with every Indian he met, but by the end of the month was learning that this was futile. I tried to speak Garo with him from time to time, but he rarely used full Garo sentences even then.

The last time he ever used an extensive amount of Garo was on the plane leaving Bombay. He sat next to a Malayan youth who was racially of a generalized southern mongoloid type, so similar to many Garos that he could easily have passed for one. Stephen apparently took him for a Garo, recognizing the difference between him and and the Indians that had failed to understand his language in the past weeks. A torrent of Garo tumbled forth as if all the pent-up speech of those weeks had been suddenly let loose. I was never again able to persuade him to use more than a sentence or two at a time. For a couple of months he would respond to Garo when I spoke to him, but he refused to use more than an occasional word. After this, he began failing even to understand my speech, though it was frequently difficult to know just how much was really lack of understanding and how much was deliberate refusal to cooperate. Certainly at times he would inadevertently give some sign that he understood more than he meant to, but increasingly he seemed genuinely not to understand, and within six months of our departure, he was even having trouble with the simplest Garo words, such as those for the body parts, which he had known so intimately.

CONCLUSIONS

In the preceding sections I have described the manner in which one child acquired speech. A few general observations about his linguistic development and a comparison of it with that of some of the other children whose language-learning has been previously described remain to be made.

The earliest stage recorded here, with three stop positions, three widely spaced vowels, and two nasals, corresponds closely to the pattern which Jakobson suggests to be characteristic of an early stage of speech, except that to these Stephen added temporarily the cross-cutting distinction of aspiration in the consonants and unvoicing of the vowels.[4] Stephen was not slower to articulate velar stops than the others, unlike some children that have been studied.[5] Some advances, notably the acquisition of the voiced/voiceless contrast, were systematic and added several new phonemes together, though even this was not carried so far as to add a voiced spirant, which Garo lacks, or (until later) a voiced affricate, which Garo does have. Other phonemes seemed to be added individually and it is difficult to see any consistent pattern in their order of appearance.

Viewing his speech as developing by the successive addition of distinctions, or minimal contrasts, provides for the most part an efficient means for analyzing his progress. However, progress was not without its interruptions. Some new steps, such as the acquisition of the contrast between voiced and unvoiced stops or the ability to make glottalized consonants, appeared so rapidly as to be almost datable to the day. In most other cases, however, months elapsed between his first tentative efforts to use a new sound, and its final unambiguous incorporation into his phonemic system. This meant that his language was progressing on several fronts simultaneously and later developments were

---

[4] Roman Jakobson and Morris Halle, *Fundamentals of Language* (The Hague, 1956), pp. 37–42.

[5] Werner F. Leopold, *Speech Development of a Bilingual Child* (Evanston, Illinois, 1939–1949), vol. II, 417.

often beginning before earlier ones were completed.

Apparently Stephen developed phonemic contrasts more rapidly than some children in comparison with the speed of expansion of his vocabulary. Velten, for instance, notes the large number of homonyms in his daughter's speech which appeared as her vocabulary outstripped her ability to produce phonemic contrasts adequate to keep all the items distinct from one another.[6] This was never the case with Stephen, and from a linguist's point of view the problem was more often finding minimal pairs for comparison. Homonyms arising from failure to make the proper contrasts were not common.

It was notable that in the earliest stages of his speech, he briefly used several distinctions (voiceless vs. voiced vowels, tone, length) that are found in neither of the languages that he was learning. One presumes that if these features had been present in his environment he would have started learning them from that time. It might be suggested then that learning a language is not only a matter of learning not to make certain phones, but also of learning not to make certain contrasts which arise apparently spontaneously as a child first tries to speak.

Two and a half years seems remarkably early to have acquired all of the phonemes and all of the important allophones of the language. However, the fact that at the age of four years and four months, almost a year after returning to the United States, he had not yet completed his English phonemic inventory ($/\theta/$ and $/ð/$ were inconsistently articulated) would seem to deny any extraordinary precociousness, although in general he did seem to be an early talker. Perhaps this provides some objective measure of one's intuitive feeling that Garo does have a simpler phonemic system than English.

Most studies of child language have put heavy stress on the number of words used in a sentence. This is true of much of the psychological literature, but it is also true of Leopold's work. My feeling as I observed Stephen's language, and my conclusion now, is that the number of words or morphemes is perhaps the least important criterion of grammatical progress. What from an adult point of view are multimorphemic words, or multiword sentences, were used before their complex nature was recognized by Stephen. The most significant single advance in his ability came when he learned to make substitutions, and once this was achieved, he was soon able to make sentences with not just two morphemes but with three and more. One simply cannot reasonably speak of a two-morpheme stage of his speech development. (Since Garo has such complex word formation, it is more significant to consider the number of morphemes in a sentence than the number of words.)

It has generally been assumed that syntactical constructions precede morphological ones. Leopold states baldly, "In the field of grammar, syntax comes before morphology. The student of child language becomes very conscious of the fact that the morphological devices are a luxury of fully developed languages. The small child gets along quite well without them, for a short or long time."[7] It is difficult and perhaps arbitrary in many languages to draw the line between morphology and syntax, but it is extremely convenient to make such a distinction for Garo, since there are stretches of several syllables set off by characteristic junctures which can be called words, and the grammatical devices used to form these words are very different from those used to join words together. If the distinction is made, Stephen defied the generalization that syntax comes first by learning to make both types of constructions simultaneously. Some reasons for this are obvious: What I am calling morphology in Garo is much more essential than the morphological processes of English, or even of the other European languages. Morphology is not a "luxury" of the fully developed language. Moreover, it is far more regular, and therefore no doubt easier to learn than the morphology of European languages. What I am calling Garo morphology, then, has somewhat the character of syntax in the European languages, but Stephen's method of learning this morphology was not com-

---

[6] H. V. Velten, "The Growth of Phonemic and Lexical Patterns in Infant Speech," *Language*, XIX (1943), 287.

[7] Werner F. Leopold, "Patterning in Children's Language Learning," *Language Learning*, V (1953–1954), 10.

parable to that by which other children have been observed to learn English syntax. Most histories of child speech have reported a period in which many words are used together with minimal regard for the standard order. Children have been described as using ill-connected sequences of words, and only gradually learning to join them closely together with proper order, juncture and intonational pattern.

One of the striking features of Stephen's speech was the rarity with which he reversed the order of morphemes or words. This was true of his earliest Garo sentences and also was true of his English when it finally began. This was in marked contrast to my own daughter who learned English as her first language two years later, and to other children such as Velten's daughter.[8] My daughter regularly produced such garbled masterpieces as *reading a mommy a book Nono* 'Mommy is reading a book to Nono (her nickname)' or *Nono falling Nono jammies pant* 'Nono's pajama pants are falling down.' Stephen never distorted normal order in this way. I do not know whether this is due to peculiarities of the Garo language or to Stephen. It is true that word order is freer in Garo than in English, but he was consistent in phrases where word order is not optional (such as that formed from a possessor and possessed noun) and he was entirely consistent from the very beginning in the order of morphemes within words, which is as rigid in Garo as word order in English, even though these morphological constructions were as early as syntactical constructions. I could readily observe the gradual acquisition of new grammatical constructions and repeatedly the same pattern was followed. He would first learn a number of examples of the construction by rote and at this stage it was generally difficult to tell whether he understood the meaning of the construction or not, though for the most part this seemed unlikely. He would then generalize the construction and learn to substitute other appropriate forms in the same construction. Even after this, one could not always be sure whether the meaning was grasped or whether he was simply generating sentences mechanically and for the pleasure of it.

---

[8] Velten, 290.

Whatever the case, however, these constructions were rarely grammatically incorrect, and sooner or later it would become clear that he was using them under semantically appropriate conditions. Considering the progressive acquisition of new constructions brought the same clarification to his grammatical development as considering the successive acquisition of phonemes brought to the analysis of the phonetic record.

As soon as Stephen began to form constructions of his own, he incorporated English morphemes and words into Garo sentences. He appended Garo suffixes to English words without the least hesitation, but there was never any doubt that his early sentences were Garo, since the morphology and syntax were Garo even if the lexical items came from English. I once heard the sentence *mami laitko tunonaha* 'mommy turned on the light' where the roots of every word were English, but the suffixes (*-ko* 'direct object marker' and *-aha* 'past tense'), word order, and phonology were Garo and there was no doubt that the sentence should be considered a Garo one. When he finally began to form English sentences, he just as readily adopted Garo words into English. This mutual borrowing was made easy partly because his models did the same. All the English speaking adults around him constantly used Garo words in their speech, and Garos borrow readily from English. However many morphemes might be borrowed, there was seldom any question as to which language he was using since affix morphology and syntax were either all Garo or all English. After his vowel systems became differentiated at 2 ; 8, the phonology was also appropriate to the choice of grammatical system. It was only shortly before the systematic separation of the vowels that he used many English sentences. Before that, he spoke with a single linguistic instrument, forged largely from Garo, but with the addition of English vocabulary and a few extra English phones. Later, when he did have two linguistic systems, the two never appeared to interfere with each other. He spoke one language or the other, never a mixture of the two.

One final comparison with Leopold's daughter is worth making. Leopold insists that a striking effect of bilingualism was the looseness of the link between the phonetic word and its meaning.[9] His daughter never insisted on stereotyped wording of stories. Leopold believed that this was due to the fact that she heard the same thing constantly designated by two different phonetic forms, so that form and meaning were not rigidly identified with each other. There can never have been a child more obsessional in this respect than Stephen. When we read to him, he instantly protested the slightest alteration in any familiar text. This was true even though we read to him in his second language, English, where one would suppose the form and meaning to be least rigidly identi-

fied. It must have been an idiosyncratic trait rather than bilingualism that freed Leopold's daughter from insistence upon stereotyped wording.

In the fall of 1958, at the age of five and a half, Stephen is attending kindergarten in the United States. He speaks English perhaps a bit more fluently and certainly more continuously than most of his contemporaries. The only Garo words he now uses are the few that have become family property, but I hope that some day it will be possible to take him back to the Garo Hills and to discover whether hidden deep in his unconscious he may not still retain a remnant of his former fluency in Garo that might be reawakened if he again came in contact with the language.

---

[9] Leopold, *Language Learning*, V, 13.

A. R. LURIA

35 Here is a sample of the work on children's speech by the well-known Russian psychologist, A. R. Luria, of the University of Moscow. This study was published in *Word* (1959), in 2 parts: Part 1 deals with the development of the directive function of speech in early childhood, and Part II deals with the dissolution of the directive function of speech in connection with pathological conditions of the brain.

For some of his other studies, as well as those by other Russians, see his lists of references following each part. Another work by this prominent Russian psychologist, in collaboration with F. I. Yudovich, is available in English: *Speech and the Development of Mental Processes in the Child*, London, 1959. Cf. also footnote 6, in part 2 of this selection.

A. B. A.

THE DIRECTIVE FUNCTION OF SPEECH IN DEVELOPMENT AND DISSOLUTION

PART I: DEVELOPMENT OF THE DIRECTIVE FUNCTION OF SPEECH IN EARLY CHILDHOOD

Along with the semantic and syntactic functions of speech, it is necessary to distinguish also its pragmatic or directive function. In the development of behavior this function

Reprinted from Word *15.341–352, 453–464 (1959) by permission of the author and the Linguistic Circle of New York, Inc.*

manifests itself in the fact that a word gives rise to new temporary connections in the brain and directs the system of activity of the child that has mastered it.

It was a full quarter of a century ago that the eminent Soviet psychologist L. S. Vygotskij pointed out the role played by the words of adults in the development of the child's mental processes and formulated his well-known thesis that what the child at first does with the help, and on the instructions, of the adult, he later begins to do by himself, supporting himself with his own speech; that speech as a form of communication with adults later becomes a means of organizing the child's own behavior, and that the function which was previously divided between two people later becomes an internal function of human behavior (Vygotskij, 1934, 1956). In the twenty-five years that have elapsed since Vygotskij's death the problem of the role of the word in the organization of mental life has been the subject of numerous Soviet investigations (Rozengardt, 1948; Ljublinskaja, 1955; Luria, 1955, 1956a, 1958; Kol'cova, 1958; and many others).

There arises, however, the question of how this pragmatic, directive function of the word is formed, and how its formation relates to the formation of the significative or generalizing functions of the word. A brief review of the pertinent experiments forms the topic of the present communication.

1

A child at the beginning of its second year of life is already in command of a considerable number of words. He understands such expressions as *cup, cat, fish, horse*, and can without difficulty hand someone the object if it is mentioned. But is the pragmatic, directive function of speech at this stage as effective as its significative, nominative function? Can the cited word always direct the child's activity with full effectiveness?

An answer to this question is suggested by the experiments which we have carried out in collaboration with A. G. Polijakova.

Before a child aged 1; 2 to 1; 4, we placed some object, e.g. a toy *fish*, and asked him to hand it to us; the child did this without particular difficulty. We then asked him, in the same situation, to hand us the *cat*. The child at first looked at us in disbelief, then began to look around until he found the object which had been named. It would seem that the adult word fully determined the child's action.

Let us, however, repeat this experiment in a somewhat more complicated situation. Let us place before the child two objects: a toy *fish* at some distance from it, and half way toward the fish a brightly colored toy *cat*. If in this situation we ask a child of 1; 0 to 1; 2 to hand us the *fish*, his behavior will be different. The uttered word will evoke

in him an orientational reaction, and his glance will be fixed on the fish; but his hand, stretched out toward the fish, will stop half way, turn toward the cat, and instead of giving us the fish that was requested, the child will grasp the *cat* and offer it to the experimenter. The directive function of the word will be maintained only up to the moment when it comes into conflict with the conditions of the external situation. While the word easily directs behavior in a situation that lacks conflict, it loses its directive role if the immediate orientational reaction is evoked by a more closely located, or brighter, or more interesting object.

It is only at the age of 1; 4 to 1; 6 that this phenomenon disappears and the selective effect of words is maintained even in conditions in which the components of the situation conflict with it.

We can easily disturb the directive function of the word in still another way. It is known that the word physiologically excites a certain system of connections in the cortex. In the normal, mature nervous system these connections possess considerable mobility and easily replace each other. As has been shown in many investigations (cf. Luria, 1956b, 1958; Homskaja, 1958), the mobility of the connections evoked by the word (or, as I. P. Pavlov called it, by the second signal system of reality), is even greater than the mobility of connections evoked by immediate signals.

However, the mobility of nervous processes in a very small child is still quite inadequate, and connections evoked by the word possess a considerable inertia at the early stages of development. Taking this inadequacy of the mobility of connections in the early stages of development as a premise, we can measure the effectiveness of the directive function of the word.

We place before a child of 1; 0 to 1; 2 two toys: a fish and a horse, this time placing them at the same distance and giving them dimensions and colors that are equally attractive. We ask the child to give us the *fish*: he does this easily. We repeat this experiment three or four times, and the effect remains the same. In exactly the same tone of voice, we now utter a different instruction and ask the child to hand us the *horse*.

Despite the fact that the meaning of this word is well known to the child, the inertia of the connections evoked by the first word is so great that in many cases the child again offers the experimenter the fish. The directive function of the changed verbal instructions is here vitiated by the inertia of the connection that has been established.[1]

The loss of the directive function of a word whose meaning is well known can also be observed in an experiment involving actions designated by verbs. If we give a child of 1; 2 to 1; 4 a stick on which rings are placed and we instruct him, "Put on the ring," he does this easily. With equal ease he will, in another situation, execute the instruction, "Take off the ring." However, if the child has several times *put on* a ring and is holding the next ring in his hands, the instruction "*Take off* the ring" loses its directive meaning and begins to function nonspecifically, merely accelerating the activity of *putting on* the ring onto the stick (Poljakova's and Ljamina's experiment).

The directive role of the word at an early age is maintained only if the word does not conflict with the inert connections which arose at an earlier instruction or which began with the child's own activity.

2

Experimental research can do more than ascertain the bare fact that the directive role of words is not fully effective at an early age. Such research can also *measure* the relative effectiveness of verbal signals as compared to the directive role of immediate, visual signals. In order to make this comparison as vivid as possible, we pass on to some experiments with somewhat older children—aged from 1; 4 to 1; 6 on the one hand, and from 1; 8 to 2; 0, on the other hand.

Let us first establish how effective the orienting (attention directing) and directive

role of a visual signal and its trace can be at this stage. We place before a child two inverted objects, a cup and a tumbler of nontransparent plastic. As the child watches, we hide a coin under the cup, which is placed to the left, and we ask the child to "find" it. For a child of 1; 4 to 1; 6, this constitutes an interesting and meaningful task, which he solves without difficulty. We repeat this experiment three or four times, each time holding the coin under the cup within sight of the child. The solution will invariably be successful. Now, without interrupting the experiment, we change its conditions and hide the coin not under the cup on the left, but under the tumbler on the right. A certain proportion of children of the younger group will follow not the changed visual signal (more precisely, its trace), but the *influence of the inert motor stereotype*, and will put out their hands toward the cup on the left, carrying out the habitual movement reinforced in the previous experiment; only then will they turn to the tumbler under which the coin is hidden.

Let us now weaken the influence of the visual signal. We repeat the first experiment, but impose a short, 10-second delay between the hiding of the coin under the cup and the execution of the movement. This forces the child to act according to the *traces* of the visual signal whose effectiveness we are considering. The majority of children in the younger group successfully execute this task; only a few, the very youngest, cease to subordinate their actions to the visual instruction and begin to grasp both objects, losing track of the task of finding the coin that is hidden under one of them.

However, we again modify the conditions and after repeating the experiment three or four times with the cup and the 10-second delay we hide the coin under the tumbler located on the right, all within sight of the child. The picture now changes substantially. The ten-second delay turns out to be sufficient for the visual signal to yield its place to the decisive influence of the reinforced motor habit. The overwhelming majority of children now repeat the movement directed toward the cup on the left, ceasing to be directed by the image of the coin hidden under the tumbler on the right.

---

[1] In a number of cases such an experiment may not give the desired results. This happens when the dominant role in the child's behavior continues to be played by the *immediate orientational response to objects*. In such cases the child will alternately hand the experimenter now this object, now the other, and the directive function of speech will fail to be exercised from the start.

This orienting, directive influence of the visual signal is maintained better among children of the older group (1; 8 to 2; 0). Even when the execution of the movement is delayed, they solve the task well, directing their search to the object under which they saw the coin being hidden. This means that the orienting, directive role of the visual image becomes so effective at the end of the second year of life that the child submits to it completely, and successfully overcomes the inertia of the motor connections which have arisen.

A completely different picture appears in those cases where we replace the immediate, visual signals by verbal ones. For this purpose we again place before the child the two abovementioned objects, a cup and a tumbler, but this time unseen by the child, we slip the coin under the left-hand cup. In order to orient, i.e. to direct the actions of the child, we now draw upon a word rather than a visual image. We tell the child: "The coin is under the cup . . . Find the coin!" This instruction attunes the child completely and the game continues, but its results turn out to be profoundly different. While the trace of an immediate visual impression caused all children of the younger group to reach with assurance for the cup under which they saw the coin being hidden, the verbal instruction turns out to be wholly insufficient for this directive role: a considerable proportion of the children of this age lose track of the task and begin to grasp *both* objects before them. When we repeated the experiment with a ten-second delay in the execution of the action, this loss of directed activity among the children of the younger group was almost universal.

We then returned to the experiments with the immediate (nondelayed) execution of the action. When we reinforced the required reaction by repeating the instructions several times, "The coin is under the cup . . . Find the coin!", the children of the younger group turned out to be capable of executing it in an organized way: the word achieved the required directive function, and the children reached for the object named. However, if we altered the verbal instruction and, without changing the intonation, said, "Now the coin is under the tumbler . . . Find it!", only an insignificant proportion of the children changed their movements, while the great majority repeated their previous movement. When a ten-second delay was imposed on the execution of the task, all the children of the younger group failed to let their action follow the changed verbal instruction; they continued to execute the stereotyped movement that had been reinforced in the previous experiment and, as before, turned to the cup on the left.

The children of the older group (1; 8 to 2 years), who solved these tasks with uniform success when the directive role was played by a visual signal (in experiments with delayed as well as with immediate execution), turned out to lag behind when they had to execute the task according to verbal instructions. They did carry out both tasks well if they were allowed to make the necessary movement immediately; then they would turn to the cup after the instruction "The coin is under the cup . . . Find the coin!" and to the tumbler if the instruction was "The coin is under the tumbler . . . Find the coin!" However, it was enough to delay the execution of the instructions by ten seconds for this orienting, directive role of the verbal instruction to be insufficiently effective. After three repetitions of the experiment with the instruction "The coin is under the cup . . . Find the coin!" the transition to another command—"The coin is under the tumbler . . . Find the coin!"—deprived the verbal instruction of its directive role, and the child continued inertly to execute the former habitual movement. In these cases the kinesthetic stereotype which had been worked out earlier overcame the insufficiently established effect of the word.

A comparative analysis of the orienting or directive functions of visual and verbal signals allows us to see how late the directive role of the word is formed in early childhood.

3

While the directive function of straightforward, "deictic" speech is already formed around the age of 2, the kind of speech that involves more complicated preliminary connections—connections which precede the action and organize it in advance—acquires a regulative function considerably later, and its development occupies the entire third and partly the fourth year of life.

This time let us turn to a child with a more complicated, involved instruction. "When the light flashes, you will press the ball (rubber bulb)" or ". . . you will raise your hand." Such a verbal instruction, formulated this time in a syntactically complex, "conditional" *sentence*, does not require any immediate realization of an action. It must close a preliminary verbal connection, giving to the appearance of a stimulus ("light") a conditional meaning of the signal for action ("you will press the ball"). The directive role is played here not by a separate word, but by a relation, a synthesis of words entering into a sentence; instead of an immediate, "triggering" role it acquires a preliminary, conditional, "pretriggering" function.

It has been shown experimentally (Jakovleva, 1958; Tikhomirov, 1958) that the possibility of establishing such a pretriggering system of connections on the basis of speech —not to speak of the possibility of subordinating further conditional reactions to it—is something unattainable for a child of 2 to $2\frac{1}{2}$ years, and sometimes even for a 3-year-old child.

The younger children of this group (1; 10 to 2 years) appear unable to realize that synthesis of separate elements which is required by the instruction formulated in the sentence. Each individual word contained in the sentence evokes in the child an immediate orienting reaction, and as soon as he hears the beginning of the sentence, "When the light flashes . . .," the child begins to look for the light with its eyes; when he hears the end of the sentence—". . . you will press the ball"—he immediately presses the device in his hand. At this stage the separate words have already acquired an effective triggering function, but the creation, by means of words, of a preliminary pretriggering system of connections, which requires the inhibition of immediate reactions and their separation into individual fragments, turns out to be unattainable. This is why the actual presentation of a light signal—the flash of light— does not at this stage lead to a conditioned movement, and evokes only an immediate orienting reaction: the child begins simply to inspect the light, which has not yet become

for him a conditional signal for the pressing of the ball.

It would, however, be incorrect to believe that the formation of this more complex form of directive speech—the closing of conditional, pretriggering connections— depends entirely on the ability to relate words which comprise a sentence, i.e. to do the work of synthesizing the elements of a sentence into a single system. Even when a child, some time later, is able to do this synthesizing work and begins to "understand" the meaning of the whole sentence well, the effective directive role of the sentence can still remain absent for a long time.

Let us adduce the experiments which demonstrate this interesting fact.

We present a child at the end of the third year of his life (2; 8 to 2; 10) with an instruction of this kind, and we see a picture which differs basically from the one that we have just described. A child at this age will as a rule make the required connection without particular difficulty, and when the light flashes he will press the ball; however, he will be unable to stop the movements which have been triggered by speech and he will very soon begin to press the ball regardless of the signal, continuing involuntarily to repeat the previous movements. Even the repetition of the instruction or the reinforcement of the inhibitory link which is hidden in it—even the request to "Press *only* when the light flashes" and "*Not to press* when there is no light"—all this turns out to be powerless to stop the motor excitation that has begun; on the contrary, this excitation is sometimes even *reinforced* by the inhibitory instruction, which in the given case turns out still to lack its inhibitory meaning and continues to act *nonspecifically*, only strengthening the dominant motor response.

While speech at this time has already acquired an effective connection closing triggering function, it has thus not yet acquired an effective inhibitory role.

This weakness of the inhibitory function of speech, as was shown by the observations of Tikhomirov (1958), can be seen most vividly by means of special experiments. Let us complicate the instruction described above and present it to a child of 3 to $3\frac{1}{2}$ years. We will ask it to *press* the ball every time a *red* light goes on, and *not to press it* when a *blue* light goes on; in other words, we will place the child in circumstances in which speech requires a complex *selective* reaction— positive with respect to one signal (red) and inhibitory with respect to another (blue). We let the child repeat the instruction and we are persuaded that all the information included in the sentence has reached him and is retained. Does this mean that it also possesses an effective directive role?

The experiment shows that this practical correspondence between the semantic meaning of the sentence and its directive role does not appear for a long time. Having understood the meaning of the instruction and repeating it correctly, the child is practically unable to execute it: the excitation provoked by the signal turns out to be so considerable and diffuse that after only a few attempts the blue signal, too, begins to evoke in the child impulsive motor responses. At first he attempts to control them but later, as his excitement grows while the directive function of the inhibitory verbal instruction weakens, he begins to perform the movements without any restraint.

In clashing with the inert excitation evoked by a positive signal, the inhibitory link in the verbal instruction is crushed. At first the child retains the entire instruction, but though he repeats it correctly, he is nevertheless unable to subordinate his actions to it. It is not uncommon for the inert excitation evoked by the positive part of the instruction to become so overwhelming that, under the influence of his own impulsive reaction, the child loses the inhibitory link contained in the verbal signal and begins to assure the experimenter that the instruction required him to press the ball in response to both signals presented to him.

Thus the insufficient mobility of the child's neurodynamics at first destroys the directive role of the verbal instruction, and later distorts the entire system of links contained in it.

4

The question now arises: Can we reinforce the regulating function of verbal connections, and if so, how can this be done most effec-

tively? The solution of this question may bring us closer to the description of certain mechanisms of the directive function of speech.

The experiments carried out by Paramonova (1956) showed that there are very simple means for heightening the directive influence of speech when the effect of the traces of a verbal instruction turn out to be insufficient.

Let us carry out an experiment of the kind already described with a 3-year-old child. We ask him to press a ball in response to every *red* signal and to refrain from pressing it in response to every *blue* one. We introduce only one change into this experiment: we accompany each flash of the red light with the direct command "Press!" and every flash of the blue lamp with a similar command, "Don't press!" If such plainly directed speech is introduced, it allows the child quickly to work out a fairly effective system of selective reactions. What could not be attained through *preliminary* connections evoked by a verbal instruction turns out to be easily attainable if we draw upon the *immediate* influence of verbal commands. In direct speech, the directive function has been fairly effectively established; its influence is therefore capable of concentrating the course of nervous processes and of producing a differentiated habit.

In the experiments just described we drew upon the directive function of verbal commands in order to make more precise the influence of verbal instructions and to secure the organized course of the child's motor responses. Could we not, however, for this purpose draw upon the *child's own speech* and have it support the traces of the verbal instruction, which weaken relatively fast? After all, as L. S. Vygotskij has already shown, the function which at first is distributed between two people can easily turn into an internal psychological system, and what a child today does with help, he will tomorrow be able to do on his own. The investigation of the *directive possibilities of the child's own speech* can uncover a new and essential side of his linguistic development.

We repeat the experiment described, but introduce some substantial changes. In order to make it easier for the child to carry out his task correctly, we ask him *to give himself supplementary verbal commands*, accompanying each appearance of a red signal with the word "Press!", and the appearance of each blue signal with the words "Don't press!" Will this utilization of the child's own commands reinforce the action of the verbal instruction and strengthen its directive role?

The experiment shows that it is not so simple to obtain a directive influence from the child's own speech, and that over the first years of life the directive role of the child's own speech undergoes a complex course of development.

Let us begin with children of 2 to 2½ years and simplify our experiment for this purpose. We ask the child to respond to each flash of the red light by pressing the ball; but in order to remove those excessive movements which, as we have indicated above, are not subject to the control of an inhibitory instruction, we ask the child to accompany each motor reaction with the word "Press!" (or even with something easier to pronounce, such as "Now!", to which we assign the meaning of a self-command). The experiments of S. V. Jakovleva (1958) have shown that the active speech of a child at this age is so insufficiently developed, and the underlying neurodynamics so inert, that the child of 2 to 2½ years of age still finds difficulty in coordinating his verbal commands with the signal and frequently begins to utter excessive, stereotyped commands. It is significant that even if the child succeeds and begins to say "Press!" (or "Now!") only when the signal appears, his entire energy is diverted to the utterance of this word, and the motor reaction which is supposed to be associated with it becomes extinct. The child at this age cannot yet create a *system* of neural processes that includes both verbal and motor links, and the word does not play any directive role.

As O. K. Tikhomirov's experiments (1958) showed, it is only at 3 years of age that the neurodynamics which underlie the speech processes are sufficiently mobile for the child to time his own verbal command with the signal and for the command to exert a directive influence on the motor response as it becomes a mobile link in a unified system with it. While the child is unable to

control his excessive, diffuse pressings of the ball according to the preliminary instruction, he easily achieves this control when he begins to give himself the commands "Press!" and "Don't press!" In concentrating the diffuse excitation, the child's own verbal responses, functioning on a feedback principle, here acquire their directive function.

However, is this directive function of the child's own speech fullfledged? Control experiments have answered this question in the negative and have permitted us to see more deeply into the mechanisms of the early forms of the directive function of speech.

Let us return again to the more complicated experiment described above. We present a child of 3 to 3½ years with the instruction to press a ball every time a red light flashes and to refrain from pressing it when there is a blue flash, but we give him the possibility of accompanying each red signal with his affirmative command "Press!" and every blue signal with his own inhibitory command, "Don't press!" Does the directive role of the child's *inhibitory* verbal response have the same, full value as his *positive* verbal response?

The experiments which have been conducted for this purpose have disclosed some very substantial peculiarities of the regulating effect of the child's own speech. The verbal responses "Press" and "Don't Press" turn out to have a complex structure. Physiologically they are, first of all, motor responses of the speech apparatus and are thus always connected with the positive phase of an innervation. But in virtue of their *meanings* they are systems of connections which, in the former case, have a positive, and in the latter case, an inhibitory signal value. Which side of the child's own speech—the motor ("impulsive") or semantic ("selective") side— here influences the motor processes and acquires the directive role?

The experiments of O. K. Tikhomirov yield an answer to this question. A child of 3 to 3½ years easily responds to each light signal with the required word, but in uttering the command "Don't press" in response to the blue signal, he not only fails to restrain his motor responses, but *presses the ball even harder*. Consequently, the child's own verbal reaction "Don't press" exerts its influence not in its semantic aspect, i.e. not by the selective connections which are behind it, but by its immediate "impulsive" impact. This is why the directive influence of a child's own speech at this stage still has a nonselective, nonspecific character.

At least one more year must pass before the directive role goes over to the selective system of semantic connections which are behind the word, and—as Tikhomirov has observed—it is only at the age of 4 to $4\frac{1}{2}$ years that the verbal response "Don't press" actually acquires the inhibitory effect specific to speech.

However, for this stage of development one circumstance is typical: as soon as the directive role passes to the semantic aspect of speech and that aspect becomes dominant, external speech becomes superfluous. The directive role is taken over by those inner connections which lie behind the word, and they now begin to display their selective effect in directing the further motor responses of the child.

The development of the pragmatic, directive aspect of speech constitutes a new chapter in psychology and psycholinguistics. It still has almost no facts to operate with that are derived from systematic investigation. However, by establishing the fact that by no means all the information carried by speech ipso facto acquires a directive value in determining human behavior, and by investigating the formation patterns of this directive role of speech, this chapter has already opened important new vistas for the scientific investigation of the organization of human behavior.

REFERENCES

Homskaja, E. D. (1958). "An Investigation of the Influence of Speech Responses on Motor Responses in Children with Cerebroasthenia" (in Russian), *ibid.*, pp. 131–259.

Jakovleva, S. V. (1958). "Conditions of Formation of the Simplest Types of Voluntary Movement in Children of Pre-School Age" (in Russian), in Luria (1958), pp. 47–71.

Kol'cova, M. M. *O formirovanii vysšej nervnoj dejatel'nosti rebënka* [On the Formation of the Child's Higher Neural Activity.] Leningrad, 1958.

Ljublinskaja, A. A. *Rol' jazyka v umstvennom razvitii rebënka* [The Role of Language in the Mental Development of the Child] (= Leningradskij Pedagogičeskij Institutim. Gercena, *Učenye zapiski*, vol. 112 [1955]).

Luria, A. R. "The Role of the Word in the Formation of Temporary Connections in Man," (in Russian) *Voprosy psikhologii*, I (1955), 73–86.

———. "On the Directive Role of Speech in the Formation of Voluntary Movements," (in Russian) *Žurnal vysšej nervnoj dejatel'nosti*, VI (1956), 645–62.

———. ed. *Problemy vysšej nervnoj dejatel'nosti rebënka.* [Problems of the Higher Neural Activity of the Child.] Vols. I and II. Moscow, 1956, 1958.

———, and F. Ia. Yudovich *Reč' i razvitie psikhičeskikh processov rebënka.* Moscow, 1958. English version: *Speech and the Development of Mental Process in the Child.* London, 1959.

Paramonova, N. P. (1956). "On the Formation of Interactions Between the Two Signal Systems in the Normal Child" (in Russian) in Luria, ed. [Problems of the Higher Neural Activity of the Child.] Vol. I. Moscow, 1956. Pp. 18–83.

Rozengardt-Pupko, T. L. *Reč' i razvitie vosprijatija v rannem detstve* [Speech and the Development of Perception in Early Childhood.] Moscow, 1948.

Tikhomirov, O. K. (1958). "On the Formation of Voluntary Movements in Children of Pre-School Age" (in Russian) in Luria, ed. [Problems of the Higher Neural Activity of the Child.] Vol. II. Moscow, 1958. Pp. 72–130.

Vygotskij, L. S. *Myšlenie i reč'* [Thought and Language.] Moscow, 1934.

———. *Izbrannye psikhologičeskie issledovanija* [Selected Psychological Studies.] Moscow, 1956.

PART II: DISSOLUTION OF THE REGULATIVE
FUNCTION OF SPEECH IN PATHOLOGICAL
STATES OF THE BRAIN

1

Since Hughlings Jackson, almost one hundred years ago, first called attention to the problem of the "dissolution" of speech, the pathology of speech processes has occupied an important place in clinical and psycho-linguistic research. However, while the study of disturbances of the phonetic, morpho-logical, syntactic, and semantic aspects of speech is reflected in many hundreds of publications dealing with the problems of aphasia,[1] the disturbance of the pragmatic or directive function of speech in patho-logical states of the brain has hardly been the object of investigation. Nevertheless, the study of such disturbances deserves to occupy a leading place in the effort to understand the "dissolution" of mental activity in pathological conditions.

In order that the system of connections that arises on the basis of speech efficiently determine further activity, it is not enough that the information carried by speech reach the subject. A number of further conditions must be fulfilled; important among them is the maintenance of the strength, the equilib-rium, and the mobility of the neural pro-cesses which determine the flow of higher neural activity.

If one of these conditions is disturbed, the directive function of speech connections may suffer substantially. The system of connections which has arisen on the basis of speech may either become pathologically weakened, so that its directive influence is rapidly extinguished; or it may become pathologically inert, so that the switch to a new system of connections, replacing the previous ones, is impossible; or, finally, a change in the equilibrium of stimulating and inhibiting processes, which so commonly arises in pathological states of the brain, can actually cause the directive influence of speech connections to become sharply handicapped. Can we forget those patients with a distinctly expressed neurosis in whom the conservation of information received through speech does not guarantee the con-servation of that organized, "voluntary" character of behavior which is typical of normals? Consequently we have every reason to expect that pathological states of the brain which are accompanied by a disturbance

in the strength of neural processes, their equilibrium, and their mobility, will produce conditions which will be patently reflected not only in the significance and communica-tive aspects of speech, but also in the realiza-tion of its directive function.

But there is a still more significant reason for investigating speech disturbances caused by brain pathology. Everything we know about the complex structure of the human cerebrum warrants the belief that the rela-tion between all the aforementioned aspects of speech activity—semantic, syntactic, and pragmatic (directive)—is preserved in unequal measure in different forms of brain pathology, and we expect that the distur-bances of the process of analysis of informa-tion carried by speech and of the realization of its directive influence will not always proceed in parallel. In other words, we may expect that pathological states of the brain may bring about a disturbance of *different links of that chain of processes* which enable man to obtain an adequate picture of his environment and correctly to regulate his mental activity. Hence an analysis of the changes in speech connections under pathological conditions of the brain will reveal to us new possibilities for investigating the structure and the dynamics of the direc-tive function of speech, with which we are now concerned.

Let us pass on to the relevant facts.

2

We begin our analysis with those cases in which the directive influence of speech appears to be blocked in its executive link so that the information, which reaches the patient fully, seems to be completely incapa-ble of determining his subsequent activity, but in which certain circumstances may completely eliminate this defect.

Over thirty years ago we had occasion to carry out a series of experiments on patients affected by Parkinson's disease.[2] In these cases, lesions in the subcortical motor centers soon make it impossible to evoke voluntary movement by verbal instructions.

---

[1] We have dwelled on these problems in detail elsewhere; cf. Luria [Traumatic Aphasia], 1947; "Brain Disorders and Language Analysis," 1958. References are fully identified at the end of this article.

[2] The data of these experiments were first published in our book, *The Nature of Human Conflicts* (Luria, 1932).

The injured subcortical apparatus excites repeated tonic responses, and the pathologically perseverating tension of all muscles is an obstacle to the execution of the instruction. It is easy to imagine such a difficulty in carrying out a voluntary movement if one briefly tenses all the muscles of one hand and then tries to move it without relaxing the tension.

However, the difference in the cases of Parkinsonism lies in the fact that the cortical motor apparatus remains fully intact. Consequently, if the center of gravity of the motor act is shifted to *cortical mechanisms* and the influence of subcortical components is thus removed, or at least diminished, it is again possible for the patient to execute the movement. And it is for this reason that a patient with Parkinson's syndrome who is unable to execute extended automatic movement dependent on subcortical mechanisms, easily carries out movements in response to external conventional signals which are effected at the cortical level.

This can be demonstrated by means of a simple experiment. A patient is asked to beat a simple rhythm with his finger. After 20 to 30 seconds his movements will begin to be extinguished, the general tension of the muscles will rise sharply, and the movement will stop. The patient is then asked to beat his finger in response to the verbal signals, "Now! Now!" This task, which is dependent on the cortical level of regulation, is completely accessible to him, and the movement can be continued for some time. Next, the patient's movement is tied even more closely to his speech system by attaching a symbolic function to his movements. He is asked to reply to the experimenter's questions by beating out the necessary numbers with his finger. If we then ask him, "How many wheels on a car?" or "How many points on a compass?" we see that the same patient who had failed in the previous experiment and could not automatically strike the table with his fingers even two or three times, easily begins to do so, switching his movements into his speech system and subordinating them to the complex dynamic constellation of cortical connections.

It is hardly necessary to emphasize how distinctively the preserved directive function of speech connections is thus brought out. This function overcomes the inertia of neural processes which arose as a result of injury to the subcortical motor apparatus.

The discovery of this phenomenon served as the beginning of a whole series of investigations concerning the functional compensation for defects arising from brain injuries.[3] But the experiment may not seem convincing enough. After all, it may be objected, the lesion is here restricted to *subcortical* connections, while the cortex is completely intact. Can the directive function of speech be maintained in cases where the *cortex itself* is in a pathological state?

This question is answered by a series of experiments conducted by E. D. Homskaja (1956, 1958), nearly thirty years after the abovementioned observations had been made.

The cerebro-asthenic syndrome is clinically well known. After an infectious illness or a trauma to the brain, the cortex frequently passes into a pathological state characterized by stimulational weakness. The strength of neural processes appears to be weakened, and the equilibrium of the basic neural processes is affected. Particularly severe is the impairment of the most complex processes of active inhibition; every frustration, no matter how small, is manifested in the diffusion of an excited, irritated state. Educators in children's clinics and in special schools are familiar with children who react with excitement to every difficulty and are unable to refrain from excessive agitated movements even when the teacher asks them to control themselves.

What has been said is enough to warrant the assumption that in these children the directive function of speech traces is impaired; the information of the prohibitory command of the teacher is fully perceived by them, but it does not achieve the required effect.

Let us follow this weakening of the directive function of speech traces in special experiments. A cerebro-asthenic child, seated before a signal device, is given a rubber bulb and is asked to press the bulb at every flash of a *red* light and to refrain from pressing

---

[3] Luria (1948). An English translation is in preparation.

it at every flash of a *blue* light.[4] If these signals are presented slowly, with relatively substantial intervals between them, the child of 9 to 12 years can carry out the task without difficulty and without error. However, if the signals are made shorter and the intervals between them are reduced so that the flashes come at a rapid pace, the situation changes radically. Then the child, though he remembers well what he is supposed to do, turns out to be incapable of carrying out his task, and in response to the rapidly presented blue (inhibitory) signal he impulsively presses the bulb, often accompanying these excessive pressings with a delayed reaction, "Oops!" or with the exclamation, "Wrong again!..." The inhibitory processes in the cortex of such a child are so weak, and the excitatory ones so easily diffused, that the traces of the verbal instruction cannot overcome the pathological state of the child's neurodynamics and adequately direct his behavior. Consequently, the directive function of the verbal traces is substantially impaired in such children.

But can we not strengthen this directive function in some way and thus compensate for the defects of the child's neurodynamics?

Let us return to the experiments which we have already described,[5] tracing the evolution of the directive function of speech. We replace the motor response to the red signal by a verbal response, "(Press) now!" and we ask the child to reply to every blue (inhibitory) signal with the words "Don't (press)!"

The verbal responses of a child with the cerebro-asthenic syndrome suffer from the impairment of his neurodynamics considerably less than do his motor processes. Therefore a child who responds with many impulsive movements is able to avoid giving incorrect, impulsive, *verbal* responses completely. Could we not utilize this fact in order to compensate the defects of his motor processes by means of his own speech?

For this purpose, the motor and verbal responses of the child may be united. The child is asked, at the appearance of every *red* flash, to say "Press!" and to press the

bulb, but at the appearance of every *blue* flash to say "Don't!" and to refrain from pressing it. These experiments, conducted by E. D. Homskaja, showed to what degree the *immediate* directive influence of loud speech is intact in these children. When the verbal and motor responses were unified, it became evident that *the child's own verbal commands were directing his motor responses,* and in these "unified" experiments the impulsive motor reactions to inhibitory signals disappeared almost completely. The directive function was here characteristically played not by the innervation of the verbal reaction itself, but by that system of selective connections which stand behind the word. When Homskaja replaced the child's own selective commands, "Press!" and "Don't press!", by monotonous repetition of "I see! I see!" at the appearance of every signal, no directive influence of speech on the flow of motor reaction was obtained. The external speech activity of the child, intact in its neurodynamic peculiarities and in its complex semantic structure, retained its directive function as well, and it was this circumstance that made it possible to draw upon the child's own speech as a means of compensating for the defects in its behavior.

3

But there are also cases of pathological brain states in which a massive impairment of neurodynamic processes affects the speech system as well, and the directive role of speech then becomes deeply impaired. The strength, equilibrium, and particularly the mobility of neural processes in these cases turn out to be pathologically altered to such an extent that the normal flow of the speech processes themselves, and the normal organization of the connections which are based on them, are profoundly disturbed.

One set of instances can be found in connection with oligophrenia. The form of deep mental retardation bearing this label develops as a rule after inflammation, intoxication, or trauma affecting the child's brain even at the fetal stage, at the time of birth, or in very early childhood.

The profound retardation of such children

---

[4] The procedure of such an experiment was described in detail in Part I of this article; see above, p. 190.

[5] See above, p. 191.

is manifested in the entire organization of their complex neural activity, but as was shown in special investigations (Lubovskij, 1956; Meščerjakov, 1956, 1958; Pevzner, 1956; and others), the damage is greatest in those forms of neural organization which are the basis of speech activity or which are achieved by means of speech.

These children form complex temporary connections with difficulty, and find it especially hard to carry out those operaions of abstraction and generalization which are accomplished by means of speech. Consequently the information which reaches them is greatly reduced, and its organization is simplified. A newly established connection is easily destroyed under the influence of external agents (or "noise"). However, if a system of connections does become consolidated, it becomes pathologically inert and almost incapable of being restructured (Luria, 1956, 1958a; Pevzner, 1956). It is particularly characteristic of these children that the dynamics of neural processes underlying speech activity are in their case impaired not less, but more than the dynamics of neural processes which are materialized in simpler sensory-motor reactions.

Can speech, under these circumstances, retain that directive function on which we drew when we wanted to compensate for the functional defects of children with cerebro-asthenic syndromes? Experiments have answered this question in the negative.

A child with oligophrenia is subjected to the experiment previously carried out to demonstrate the intactness of the directive function of speech in cerebro-asthenic children, but under somewhat modified circumstances. An oligophrenic child aged ten to twelve with a profound form of mental retardation is asked to press a bulb in response to a *red* flash and to refrain from pressing it in response to a *blue* flash. After the habit, following a certain amount of drill (of course, with the signals being slowly presented), is sufficiently well established, we try to restructure it. This time the child is asked to change the previous condition and to respond to every *blue* signal by a motor reaction, but to refrain from any movement at a *red* signal.

Experiments have shown (Lubovskij, 1956,

et al.) that this task, so simple for a normal child (or even for the cerebro-asthenic children described above), is often beyond the powers of a child with severe oligophrenia. At first he correctly follows the new verbal instruction, but he retains it only for a short time, and if the experiment is interrupted by a brief pause or if some sharp extraneous signal is introduced, the directive influence of the new instruction is destroyed and the child begins inertly to carry out the old system of connections, pressing at *red* flashes and refraining from pressing at *blue* flashes.

Can we draw on the child's own speech in order to overcome this pathological inertia in the way we utilized it with the cerebro-asthenics? All attempts to resort to the oligophrenic child's own speech reactions have resulted in failure.

In the experiments of Lubovskij (1956), Homskaja (1956), and Marcinovskaja (1958), a child was asked to replace his motor reactions by verbal ones, replying, according to the changed verbal instructions, "Don't press!" to every *red* signal and "Press!" to every *blue* one. While the child with the cerebro-asthenic syndrome had found no difficulty in such a restructuring of verbal responses, a child with profound oligophrenia often stumbled over this task. Having learned, in the first experiment, correctly to answer "Press!" to a *red* signal, and "Don't press!" to a *blue* one, these children were unable to restructure their verbal responses afresh and obstinately retained the old pattern even under the new conditions.

The inertia of neural processes which is typical of the speech activity of these children, also produces additional difficulties. Having begun to say "Press!" and "Don't press!", our subjects would continue inertly to repeat the alternation of these two verbal responses, regardless of the signals presented to them. Here meaningful speech was replaced by a mechanical stereotype, and its complex functions had decayed.

To the question whether such inert speech, which easily turns into a mechanical stereotype, can play a directive role, experiments have also given a negative answer. A child with profound oligophrenia is handed a bulb and is asked, in unifying his motor and verbal reactions, to respond to every *blue* signal by "Press!" and at the same time to press a bulb, but at a *red* flash to say "Don't press!" and to refrain from pressing the bulb.

Marcinovskaja's observations (1958) have shown that many severe oligophrenes find this task completely unattainable. While they respond to the signal verbally, they completely cease to press the bulb; or else, reacting by a movement, they cease to respond verbally. Even if the coordination of speech and movement is possible for such a child, his stunted, inert speech is still unable to play a directive role. Accompanying his movements by inert verbal reactions which easily get stuck and lose their meaning, the child, instead of improving, worsens his motor reactions.

It is evident that the directive function of speech is deeply impaired in these cases.

It is interesting that in the experiments with oligophrenia, speech turns out to be dynamically affected even in its contentive, meaningful function. When, for example, in Meščerjakov's experiments (1958) an oligophrene was asked to define the meaning of words presented to him by the labels "living" and "nonliving" he did this only for a relatively short time, and as soon as the experimenter twice repeated the alternation of these terms ("living—not living, living—not living"), the child's further effort at classifying the named objects decayed into an inertly alternating repetition of these two responses. The profound impairment of the dynamics of neural processes—and particularly of their mobility—deprives the word of its significative as well as of its directive role.

It is apparent how different this form of brain pathology is from that described above and how profoundly the speech processes may suffer when their neurodynamic basis is affected.

4

The two illustrations just adduced have shown that pathological states of the brain may bring about an impairment of the verbal system of connections in various of its links, and that while in some cases the directive function of speech may remain relatively intact, in others it is grossly affected.

In both illustrations presented so far we were dealing with the general disturbance of cortical function—though unequal, to be sure, in type and extent.

But might we not take one further step and attempt to discover whether the several divisions and zones of the cortex have a differential connection with the directive role of speech process? May we not expect that injury to some parts of the cortex might produce a substantial impairment in the reception of information carried by speech, while the injury to other sectors will affect the speech process in other links, leaving the reception of speech messages relatively intact, but causing a disturbance of its directive function? Every discovery in this domain would be significant for the further analysis of the structure of speech processes and for the investigation of their underlying cerebral mechanisms.

Elsewhere (Luria, 1947, *et al.*) we have already discussed the fact that a lesion of limited areas of the cortex may cause the subject to be incapable of controlling the phonetic, lexical, and logical-grammatical code of his language. The role played in this process by the temporal regions of the cortex, with their function of auditory analysis, and the parieto-occipital region of the cortex, which makes it possible to realize simultaneous syntheses (basically spatial ones), is well known.

Do all these lesions at the same time produce an impairment of the directive function of speech, or can we find cases in which the phonetic, lexical, and logical-grammatical structure of speech is preserved while its directive role is impaired?

We are still at the very beginning of this investigation, but the facts obtained so far already suggest a basis for an answer to this question.

Lesions in those sections of the cortex which reflect and elaborate exteroceptive information or, to use a label of I. P. Pavlov's, the cortical sections of the analyzers of the external world, inevitably produce an impairment in the perception of whole visual-spatial or auditory structures and make far more difficult the deciphering of those complex phonetic, lexical, and sometimes even logical-grammatical codes on which human speech is based. However, while they affect the phasic or semantic aspects of speech, they do not necessarily disturb its directive role.

We have had the opportunity to observe many scores of patients whose analysis and synthesis of visual images was disturbed, who recognized visually presented complex objects with difficulty, and for whom visual information was so reduced that they could simultaneously perceive only one visual unit. However, they carried out a process of organized search, pursuing individual fragments, directing their activity to the task which had been verbally formulated for them —and, collecting the pieces of visual information thus obtained into a system of meaningful connections secured by speech, they compensated for the defects of their receptor apparatus.

We have had the opportunity, too, to observe numerous cases in which the impairment of the analysis and synthesis of the phonemic structure of language resulting from lesions in the temporal regions of the cortex, deprives the patient of his ability to perceive speech addressed to him, but by shifting to an analysis of speech sounds with the support of a visually perceived oral image, the patients were able to perform this task and to compensate for their defects to a certain extent.

We have observed a great number of cases in which, as a result of lesions in the parieto-temporal cortex the patient was unable to synthesize the signals into one structural whole and to grasp complex logical-grammatical constructions; but such patients successfully replaced their impaired simultaneous synthesis by consistent consecutive syntheses of separate elements of information being put in. With the support of auxiliary means, such patients effected the reception of this information by other, roundabout ways.

In all these cases[6] the impairment connected with the input of information was successfully compensated for by the intact state of more complex and higher levels. It is enough to see the perseverance with which patients of this type carry out their tasks and work on

themselves, to realize that the directive function of those neural connections which have arisen on the basis of speech is preserved in them.

Analogous facts could be observed in those patients who had lesions in the regions of the cortex related to effector processes, i.e. to the output of speech.

We have had numerous occasions to observe patients in whom lesions in the premotor zone of the cortex produced complete inability to form a well automatized motor habit, and who, for example, were unable to beat out a rhythm such as – –·· ·– –· · · However, if we added speech to the implementation of this task and asked the patient to dictate to himself, "One, two—one, two, three" or to say to himself, "Strong, strong, weak, weak, weak," or even to give himself auxiliary symbolic support by means of speech (one such patient imagined a row consisting of two large cannon and three small machine guns), the task, based on the system of directive connections arising on the basis of speech, was successfully achieved.[7]

In all these cases, lesions in specific areas of the brain bring about a noticeable impairment in the analysis and synthesis of visual, auditory, or proprioceptive signals, and sometimes cause severe defects in the decoding of speech, but they do not affect the directive function of speech.

There arises the question as to whether there are also opposite cases, in which the external organization of speech codes remains intact while the directive function of speech is affected. This problem was thoroughly analyzed in our laboratory. Despite the fact that these investigations are still in their infancy, there are already enough facts at our disposal to suggest that this type of dissociation is indeed possible.

According to the investigations of N. A. Filippyčeva (1952), B. G. Spirin (1951), A. I. Meščerjakov (1953), M. P. Ivanova (1953), and others, this type of impairment in the directive function of speech may occur when there are extensive lesions in the frontal zone of the cortex.

In experiments resembling those to which we have repeatedly referred, a patient with

---

[6] Analyzed in detail in Luria (1947, 1948).

[7] See also Luria (1948).

massive injuries to the frontal lobe is asked to press a rubber bulb in response to every *red* flash and to refrain from pressing it in response to every *green* flash. (In a variant experiment by E. D. Homskaja, still unpublished, the instruction called for *strong* pressure on red signals and *weak* pressure on blue signals.) It was apparent that this is a task of great difficulty. The inertia of excitations in the motor analyzer is so severe that movements, as soon as they are established, turn into stereotypes, and the patient begins alternately to press and to refrain from pressing—or to press the bulb with equal force—although he remains perfectly aware of the verbal instruction. The influence of connections set up by this verbal instruction turns out in their case to be too weak to counterbalance the stagnant processes in the cerebral apparatus that produces movements; the directive role of the connections is easily extinguished.

It is important to note that, as Homskaja showed, the inclusion of the patient's own active speech, so effective in the case of cerebral asthenia, is not only futile for the frontal patients, but occasionally even aggravates their performance. The speech of such a patient, falling under the influence of a pathological inertia and linked to his motor behavior with inadequate effectiveness, easily loses its directive function and is unable to compensate for the behavioral gap.

It is for these reasons that the recovery of function is so difficult for patients with massive frontal lobe injuries, and it is for this reason, too, that frontal lobe lesions cause damage to the structure of human behavior which is so profound and so hard to reverse.

This concludes our survey of the facts at our disposal that bear on that "dissolution" of speech of which Hughlings Jackson spoke and on the disturbance of its directive function, which interested us in particular. The analysis of the manner in which this important aspect of speech processes is formed and disturbed is still at its very beginning. However, there is already no doubt that the study of the directive function of speech in its development and dissolution represents an important chapter in psychology and psy-

cholinguistics, and that further work in this field will contribute many new facts concerning the laws governing the workings of human speech.

REFERENCES

Filippyčeva, N. A. *Inertnost' vysšykh korkovykh processov pri lokal'nykh poraženijakh bol'šykh polušarij mozga.* [The Inertia of Higher Cortical Processes in Local Lesions of the Major Hemispheres of the Brain.] Dissertation, USSR Academy of Medical Sciences. Moscow, 1952.

Homskaja, E. D. "On the Problem of the Role of Speech in the Compensation of Motor Reactions," (in Russian) in Luria, ed. [Problems of the Higher Neural Activity of the Normal and Abnormal Child.] Vol. I. Moscow, 1956. Pp. 284–309.

———. "On the Pathology of the Interaction of Signal Systems in Mentally Retarded Children," (in Russian) *ibid.,* pp. 310–16.

———. "An Investigation of Verbal Reactions to Motor Ones in Children With Cerebro-Asthenia," (in Russian) in Luria, ed., *ibid.* Vol. II. Moscow, 1958. Pp. 131–249.

Ivanova, M. P. *Narušenie vzaimodejstvija dvukh signal'nykh sistem v formirovanii sloznykh dvigatel'nykh reakcij pri poraženijakh mozga.* [Disturbances of the Interaction of the Two Signal Systems in the Formation of Complex Motor Reactions in Cases of Brain Lesions.] Dissertation, Department of Psychology, Moscow University. Moscow, 1953.

Lubovskij, V. I. "Some Peculiarities of Higher Neural Activity of Normal and Abnormal Children," (in Russian) in Luria, ed. [Problems of the Higher Neural Activity of the Normal and Abnormal Child.] Vol. I. Moscow, 1956. Pp. 129–96.

Luria, A. R. *The Nature of Human Conflicts.* New York, 1932.

———. *Travmatičeskaja afazija* [Traumatic Aphasia]. Moscow, 1947.

———. *Vosstanovlenie funkcij mozga posle voennoj travmy* [Recovery of Brain Functions After War Trauma]. Moscow, 1948.

———., ed. *Problemy vysšej nervnoj dejatel'nosti normal'nogo i anomal'nogo rebĕnka.* [Problems of the Higher Neural Activity of the Normal and Abnormal Child.] Vols. I and II. Moscow, 1956, 1958a.

————. (1958b). "Brain Disorders and Language Analysis," *Language and Speech*, I (1958), 14–34.

Marcinovskaja, E. N. "Disturbance of the Directive Role of Speech in Severely Retarded Children," (in Russian) in Luria, ed. [Problems of the Higher Neural Activity of the Normal and Abnormal Child.] Vol. II. Moscow, 1958. Pp. 267–95.

Meščerjakov, A. I. *Narušenie vzaimodejstvija dvukh signal'nykh sistem v formirovanii prostykh dvigatel'nykh reakcij pri lokal'nykh poraženijakh mozga.* [Disturbance of the Interaction of the Two Signal Systems in the Formation of Simple Motor Reactions in Cases of Brain Lesions.] Dissertation, Department of Psychology, Moscow University. Moscow, 1953.

————. "The Mechanisms of Abstraction and Generalization Processes in Mentally Retarded Children," (in Russian) in Luria, ed. [Problems of the Higher Neural Activity of the Normal and Abnormal Child.] Vol. II. Moscow, 1958. Pp. 295–389.

Pevzner, M. S. (1956). "Clinical Characterization of the Basic Variants of Defects in Oligophrenia," (in Russian) in Luria, ed. [Problems of the Higher Neural Activity of the Normal and Abnormal Child.] Vol. I. Moscow, 1956. Pp. 354–400.

Spirin, B. G. *Narušenie podvižnosti nervnykh processov posle operacij na golovnom mozgu.* [Disturbance of the Mobility of Neural Processes Following Brain Surgery.] Dissertation, USSR Academy of Medical Sciences. Moscow, 1951.

JOHN B. CARROLL

36 This is primarily a review of research in the field of language development in children, although the author has his own opinions about various problems, e.g. he doubts whether there is any relation between babbling and phonological development in the child's speech. Cf. Velten's article in this volume; and Jakobson's negative opinion on this matter, as stated in his *Kindersprache*, is of special interest. (See: Jakobson, Roman. *Child Language: Aphasia and Phonological Universals.* Translated by A. R. Keiler. The Hague: Mouton Publishers, 1968.)

As mentioned in the introduction to Dorothea McCarthy's reading above, this article by Carroll in the 1960 edition of the *Encyclopedia for Educational Research* replaces that of McCarthy of the 1950 edition, and thus reflects the linguistically oriented shift (the structural approach) in the study of child language through the 1950's. Carroll himself has been active in the area of psycholinguistics. Among his more recent works are *Language and Thought* (1964) and "Words, Meanings and Concepts," *Harvard Educational Review* (1964).

A. B. A.

LANGUAGE DEVELOPMENT

Of all the phases of child development, the learning of language has traditionally attracted most attention because of the complexity of language and the case and swiftness of learning. Granted, language is complex; but the case and swiftness of the child's

Reprinted from Harris Chester, ed., Encyclopedia of Educational Research, *3rd ed.* (1960), *744–752, by permission of the author and the American Educational Research Association.*

learning of his native language may be more apparent than real. Interest in studying child language learning stems from three sources: First, students of the science of language, such as Hockett and Jespersen, have wondered whether the gradual changes in languages over generations are to any extent caused by the variations observed in children's speech as compared with that of their elders; thus far, there is no positive answer to this question. Second, many psychologists feel that the study of the process whereby children learn to speak and understand language holds the key to many fundamental problems of behavior. Third, educators, parents, and others concerned with the welfare of children need information to help them decide whether the language development of a child is proceeding in a normal fashion, as well as information to guide the development of the curriculum in schools or to form the basis for special education programs for handicapped children.

Studies and observations of child language development were made even in ancient times, and by now the literature of the subject is enormous. A monograph-length summary has been provided by McCarthy (1954a), but Leopold's (1952) bibliography is also valuable, particularly for its coverage of non-English material. A useful manual for parents and teachers concerned with cases of delayed speech development was prepared by Beasley. . . .

THE NATURE OF LANGUAGE

One of the most important preludes to the study of child language development is the scientific description of the adult form of the language the child is learning. It is also possible, however, to describe the utterances of the child in scientific terms as constituting the child's *idiolect* or his own linguistic system.

Modern linguistics teaches that a language is a structured system of arbitrary vocal sounds and sequences of sounds which is used in interpersonal communication and which rather exhaustively catalogs the things, events, and processes of human experience (Carroll, 1953). The science of phonetics concerns the varieties of vocal sounds which are found to occur in the languages of the world; it is to be distinguished from *phonemics*, a branch of linguistics which deals with the phonemes, the minimal sound units which occur in a particular language and make differences in meaning. The difference between phonetics and phonemics is important for students of child language, because the child must learn, eventually, the precise variations of a phoneme in different circumstances. For example, in learning English the child learns to aspirate the phoneme *p* in *pin* but to pronounce it without aspiration in the word *spin*.

A further refinement of the theory of the phoneme has been provided by Jakobson, who considers the phoneme to be a bundle of "distinctive features." For example, a phoneme may be either consonantal or vocalic, nasal or oral, voiced or voiceless, and so forth. Jakobson proposes that the child learns the various distinctive features in a definite developmental sequence, the consonant-vowel distinction being learned first. He also observes that the distinctive features which occur most rarely in the languages of the world are generally also learned latest by children who speak the languages in which they occur. This would be true, for example, of the English distinction between *f* and voiceless *th*, for English is one or relatively few languages possessing this distinction. Leopold (1939–47), Velten, and others have started to apply Jakobson's theory to observational data and find it substantiated at least in broad outlines.

All the meaningful sound patterns of a language, including intonation patterns, vocal modifiers, and ways of making emphasis, can be precisely described as distinctive linguistic units having characteristic distributions and interrelationships in a language. Fries has presented a treatment of the major sentence types and syntactical features of English. The standard gestures and facial expressions of a culture can also be described.

A language also contains a system of socially shared meanings which must of course be learned by the child. There is some evidence that the particular set of meanings and categories provided by a language conditions the cognitive processes of the child. For example, the color terminology of a particular language may affect the child's ability to recognize and remember color differences. Brown (1956) has discussed the way in which a language provides categories for classifying experience. It should not be concluded, however, that language is *necessary* for cognition; Heider and Heider point to evidence that the deaf child without language organizes the world of his experience in much the same way as the hearing child does.

Within a speech community there are many types and varieties of languages and dialects, varying principally with geographical location and also with socioeconomic status and occupation. The kind of language the child learns—in all its detailed aspects of sound and meaning—is most likely to be that of his parents, which will seldom be precisely the dialect of the investigator. This rather obvious fact has been ignored in many studies of child language and has been the basis of serious methodological shortcomings. For example, some studies of the child's learning of speech sounds have erroneously assumed that there is one "standard" set of phonemes which all children are gradually approximating.

THE LANGUAGE LEARNING PROCESS

The child's learning of his mother tongue provides an admirable test case for any theory of learning that one might consider. Gestalt or field theories have had little to say about language learning except in the area of concept development, where the emphasis is on the development of the child's pre-linguistic perceptions. Werner and Kaplan have applied field theory to experimental analysis of how word meanings develop. Holt's associationistic reflex-circle theory of babbling has now been abandoned, for reasons summarized by Miller and Dollard. A purely Pavlovian or Watsonian view of language learning has been supplanted generally by some variety of reinforcement theory, in which it is held that the child tends to learn whatever responses are reinforced either by some immediate, drive-reducing reward or by some indirect secondary cue of an eventual reward; responses which are not so reinforced tend to drop out of the child's repertoire. The responses which are involved in these events may be direct responses to external stimuli, or they may be "operant" responses (such as "babbling") which are somehow internally initiated. The most ambitious effort to work out the details of such a theory as applied to language learning is Skinner's. This and other positions are summarized by Miller and by Osgood and Sebeok. Miller and Dollard hold that the child has no native instinct to imitate or copy behavior but can learn to do so even in rather early stages of language development when imitative behavior is rewarded. They also point out that imitation helps the child only in providing new *combinations* of responses which have already been learned by other means.

Mowrer theorizes that in the "cooing" and "babbling" stages of development the child's hearing of his own voice acquires secondary reward value because it is similar to his mother's voice. He has also proposed to explain predication by appealing to the theory of conditioning ("The Psychologist Looks at Language"). That is, when we say "John is a theif," we make "John" the conditioned simulus for whatever responses we have to "thieves." According to this theory, in learning to make sentences the child learns to manipulate verbal symbols as conditioned stimuli and responses.

The process of language learning can be described in general terms in this way: throughout his language development, the child learns what verbal or gestural responses will get what he wants or fend off what he dislikes, and what responses on the part of others are the cues for what he wants or does not want. In effect, he is learning the "semantics" of the language. At first the responses involved are very gross or global, but gradually they become differentiated and structured. Somewhat as a linguistic scientist learns what distinctions are crtical in a previously unanalyzed language, the child discovers the critical distinctions in his language by an unconscious trial-and-error process. He learns to imitate the responses of others, but he also learns to try new responses and combinations of responses and to generalize. His errors and sometimes his "bright sayings" are the result of a failure to recognize a critical distinction in sound form, or meaning, or the result of a false analogy into which he is trapped by the inconsistencies of the language. There are probably clear and relatively uniform developmental sequences in the distinctions learned, but investigators have failed to trace these in sufficient detail and have almost completely overlooked such features of language as intonation patterns, which are very likely among the first items distinguished (Lewis). If such developmental scales could be established, they would probably be more meaningful than such indices of language development as mean sentence length. It would probably be found, too, that the over-all frequency with which items occur in the speech heard by the child has an important relation to the developmental sequences in which the items are learned. At the same time, it is probable that the frequencies heard by the child may not correspond to those in general adult speech. Recent psycholinguistic investigations reviewed by Miller and by Osgood and Sebeok suggest that linguistic frequencies go far in explaining a variety of phenomena in language behavior, such as word association, tachistoscopic word reading, and so forth.

METHODOLOGY OF RESEARCH

The foregoing remarks will serve to emphasize that one of the most important methodological considerations is a scientific conception of the nature of language in general and of the characteristics of the particular language or languages involved in any investigation. Psychologists and educators investigating child language have generally failed to take account of advances in linguistic studies; by the same token, linguists who have studied child language have missed many opportunities for interpreting their observations in psychological terms. Psychologists should give more consideration to the linguists' units of analysis such as the phoneme and morpheme.

Methodology must be guided by the investigator's purposes. If these are simply to provide an accurate description of the *idiolect* of a particular child at a particular stage of development, or over several stages of development, the investigator must pretend that he is a linguistic scientist studying a new language or dialect, and he must use the tools, procedures, and units of analysis of the linguistic scientist. The most extensive and careful studies are those of the linguists Cohen, Grégoire, Leopold, ("Bibliography of Child Language") and Velten. Only from such studies can come the kind of data needed to establish precise scales of language development in terms of the linguistic items distinguished by the child at various stages. Unfortunately, most of the available studies report only *items*, and it is difficult to derive from such data information concerning the *distinctions* which the child makes between items.

If the purposes are to provide normative observational data on grosser aspects of language development, the usual considerations concerning cross-sectional and longitudinal sampling studies apply. Among the classic studies of this type are those of Davis (1937), Fisher, McCarthy (1930), and Shirley, to which must be added that of Templin.

In either case, careful attention must be given to the conditions under which the verbal responses are elicited, for it has been repeatedly demonstrated (Hahn, Jakobson) that different kinds and frequencies of responses depend on the situation: free play, supervised play, play inside or outdoors, conversation with adults, or the like. Careful time sampling and situation sampling designs seem to be in order if one wants purely normative or "typical" data; even the "classic" studies have shortcomings in this respect. Information on typical behavior needs to be supplemented, however, with some sort of testing to determine the limits or ranges of behavior; for example, to determine the range of vocabulary, accuracy of sound production and discrimination, or knowledge of concepts. It should be remembered, too, that particularly in the detailed observational studies it is as important to determine what the child understands as to record what the child says. It would also be useful to describe the linguistic environment of the child, that is, to specify utterances the child hears.

One of the basic drawbacks in the available research literature is that it is based mainly on observations in naturalistic settings. Theories of language-learning cannot ultimately be tested unless an experimental approach is adopted. Oddly enough, one never seems to think of "teaching" a child his language in the early phases or of investigating the effects of specific practices in such teaching. Miller and Dollard propose several experiments dealing with the babbling stage. Dawe found that language training given to children in an orphanage was very effective. Brown (1957) used an experimental approach to demonstrate that preschool children have already acquired the distinctions between particular and mass nouns in English. More studies of this kind are needed.

ASPECTS OF LANGUAGE DEVELOPMENT

Intensive studies of infant vocalization, from radically different points of view, have been made by Irwin and Lewis. Despite the fact that the phonetic diversity noted during the period of babbling increases considerably, these phenomena have little specific relevance for the development of true language. It is as if the child starts learning afresh when he begins to learn to utter meaningful speech. The course of development of the child in learning the phonemic structure of a language has been studied best by such linguists as Cohen, Grégoire, Jakobson, Velten, and Voegelin and Adams, but never on the basis of a sufficient number of cases. The critical age range of 24 to 36 months is particularly in need of study with adequate samplings. Templin conducted tests of sound discrimination ability and articulation ability with carefully constructed samples of sixty children at each of eight age levels from three to eight years. Unfortunately, her results on sound discrimination are not presented in terms of separate phonemes. Rearranging her data on articulation, however, we find that at age three, 90 percent or more of the children could articulate the phonemes *n, t, g, m, b, d, w, h, p,* and *k;* from 70 to 80 percent articulated correctly *f, ng, l, s, y;* from 50 to 69 percent articulated *v, r, sh, j, ch;* while only 10 to 49 percent articulated correctly *z, zh, th* (voiced), *th* (voiceless), and *hw.* By age six the only sounds which were not correctly articulated by 90 percent or more of the subjects were *s, sh, th* (voiced), *z, zh, hw,* and *ch.* Templin's tests of sound discrimination and articulation ability are suitable for providing measures of language development for comparison with her normative data. Schneiderman and Williams found substantial relationships between articulation ability and other indices of language development.

Potter and Peterson found the formants of vowels uttered by children systematically different from those of adults, presumably because of the different shpae and size of the vocal cavity.

Morphology

In linguistics, morphology deals with the forms and grammatical inflections of words as they undergo modification for tense, number, case, person, and so forth. There is abundant evidence to support the notion that the child learns these forms first by imitating the various inflected forms as they occur in sentences or phrases heard from other, more mature speakers. For example, the child usually learns *am, are, was, is, sing, sang, sung,* and so forth as separate items in their own contexts. It is impossible for him to learn *all* possible forms in this way, and usually sometime during the third year the child may be heard experimenting with false analogical forms like *bringed.* The period from three to eight is marked by considerable difficulty in learning irregular forms, but the fact that analogical formations occur at all attests to the ability of the child to respond to patterning in language at an early age. Templin found that grammatical errors decrease from age three to eight. Noel found that children's language usage is closely related to that of their parents.

Syntax

Brown, as we have seen, has shown that preschool children have already learned the distinction between mass and particular nouns. Presumably they learn the form-class allegiances of words very early—for example, whether a word can be used as a noun or as a verb. The semantic context undoubtedly furnishes a cue for this learning, but more detailed studies are needed to investigate the dynamics and sequence of learning. The essentially normative studies by Davis (1938) and Templin of the distribution of parts of speech are of little use, for they simply reflect adult language characteristics; these distributions change little with age.

Carroll (1939) and Guillaume theorize that the child learns syntax by first imitating whole sentences or phrases and then differentiating the component parts as the function of these parts is learned. Further research should inquire into the developmental sequence with which various sentence types, as described by Fries, are learned. Data from the investigations of Grégoire, Leopold (1939–47), and others offer possibilities for further comparison and analysis. Important studies of syntax in the written work of older children and of deaf children have been made by Heider and Heider, LaBrant, and Walter.

Vocabulary

There exist numerous investigations, admirably summarized by McCarthy (1954a), as to the sheer number of different words in the active or passive vocabulary of the average child at various ages. These investigations are plagued by several methodological difficulties, but it may suffice to state that children's, and adults' vocabularies are generally much larger than they are popularly believed to be. For example, Mary K. Smith, estimated the vocabulary of the average child in Grade I as 23,700, and in Grade XII, 80,300. The most recent normative data available are contained in Templin's study of ages three to eight, using different measurement procedures and yielding estimates of vocabulary somewhat more conservative than Smith's.

Estimates of vocabulary do not take multiple meanings or homonyms into account. Even so, there is no such thing as an exact referential meaning of a verbal symbol, although the referential meanings may achieve a fair degree of standardization in the adult speech community. The meanings of a word for a particular individual, as Carroll (1953) has pointed out, depend upon his experiences with it. This being so, the meanings of a word for a child vary much more than adults are likely to imagine. For example, a three-year-old may not recognize the rather subtle distinction observed by adults between *needing to do something* and *wanting to do something* and may use the former in the sense of the latter. The mere acquisition of a word is often only the first step in a long series of trials and explorations which the child must make with it. Feifel and Lorge, Leopold (1939–47), Velten, and Werner and Kaplan have investigated the dynamics by which multiple meanings are acquired and by which the child's concept of a word may change.

Martin's study of how children develop meanings of quantitative words such as *some*, *any*, and *several* is a good example of the kind of detailed study needed in this area. Strauss and Schuessler's study of children's concepts of money is of methodological interest because it shows that the developmental sequence can be described as a highly reproducible cumulative scale. Doubtless word meanings could be scaled in this manner. Dale and Reichert have provided an exhaustive bibliography of vocabulary studies.

STAGES OF DEVELOPMENT

As in other phases of child development, it is difficult to delineate clearcut stages of devel-

opment in language learning; the criteria commonly used are somewhat arbitrary and exist from the adult's point of view. For example, the appearance of the "first word," usually thought to mark the start of true language development, may simply represent a point where the child's voco-motor control catches up with a previously developed ability for "voluntary" symbolic communication. A more important point in development, usually allowed to go unnoticed by parents, may be that at which the child first begins to discriminate words or intonation patterns in adults' utterances. The most complete discussion of stages of development in the first two years is provided by Lewis.

The first few months
Vocalizations, crying, cooing, and miscellaneous nondescript sounds of the first three or four months are probably most significant in that, in addition to exercising the maturing speech apparatus, they make it possible for the infant to learn, through appropriate reinforcement, the instrumental, communicative character of vocal sounds, as when crying brings relief from hunger or pain. Some investigators believe that cries are differentiated for discomfort, pain, and hunger, although this differentiation may have a purely organic basis. Certain it is that the infant early develops the capacity of reacting differentially to adult voices.

The "babbling" stage
The cooing of the first several months gradually develops into a much more phonetically diversified type of random vocalization usually called babbling, employing both vowels and consonants. Irwin has traced age trends in the degree of phonetic diversity displayed. Irwin is wrong in speaking of phonemes at this stage, because the sounds have not acquired any semantic distinctiveness. Babbling is probably mainly unlearned, but in the period from six to ten months of age it may provide a context for rudimentary imitative behavior if there is appropriate reinforcement. We have already mentioned the need for experimental research at this stage. The particular sound types uttered by the babbling child have little relevance for later learning, for the types appear in more or less random sequences which bear little relation to the

sequence observed after true language learning starts. In fact, after babbling stops (usually before the end of the first year) the child may appear to have temporarily lost the ability to produce certain sounds. Jakobson's theory of the sequential acquisition of phonemic distinctive features explicitly applies *only* to the period after true language acquisition has started, and not to the babbling period.

The beginnings of language comprehension
In the latter part of the babbling period, usually from eight to ten months, but sometimes earlier, there are the first evidences of understanding and recognition of certain symbolic gestures, intonations, words, and phrase structures on the part of the child. This is an extremely important period of language development; research should investigate the extent to which individual differences in language development depend upon the amount and variety of the child's linguistic experience at this stage. The child gradually becomes capable of distinguishing the more frequently occurring phonemes of the language but does not attain full mastery in this respect until the age of four to six years or even later. At first, only the larger linguistic units are distinguished (phrases or single words); later (at two or three years of age) closely similar words can be distinguished on the basis of minimal phonemic differences (for example, *heard* and *hurt*). Understanding of commands usually starts at about 10 to 12 months.

The beginnings of symbolic communication
The first active, meaningful, "voluntary" use of vocal language approximating words in adult language is usually found at about the end of the first year, although it is difficult to distinguish such an event from mere babbling or imitation. Even before this time, the infant has probably already learned to use verbal behavior instrumentally; his chief problem is mobilizing his speech apparatus to action in an appropriate situation. The beginnings of active speech are usually somewhat gradual; for about six months after the "first word" the child's vocabulary may not extend beyond a handful of words (Smith, Madorah E., 1926), but thereafter a rapid increase

ensues. Lewis has shown that the first words reported by various investigators have a definite phonetic structure and tend to feature labial and dental consonants. The utterances learned in the period between 12 and 18 months are particularly likely to be learned as whole units even when from the adult point of view they are composed of several words, and their pronunciation is extremely imprecise. This is also the period of the "one-word sentence," when a single word or word-like utterance can stand for a multiplicity of meanings and can be used in many different situations.

The beginnings of differentiated speech communication
Toward the end of the second year of life, when there is also a rapid growth of vocabulary, the child starts indulging in what might be called "linguistic experimentation." Perceiving that segments of utterances can be similar while other segments differ, he starts experimenting with endless variations such as "Give me the ball," "Give me the blocks," and so forth. This behavior lays the foundation for the development of truly articulated sentence structure (Carroll, 1939; Guillaume). Lewis provides an analysis of the process by which the child approximates accurate pronunciation of words and socially approved grammatical expression.

Later stages
After the beginning of differentiated speech communication, when the child first starts to manipulate the syntactical structures of language freely, it is less useful to distinguish stages in development. Language development is rapid in all respects. By the age of about six, the average child has mastered nearly all its common grammatical forms and constructions—at least those used by the adults and older children in his environment. After the age of six there is relatively little in the grammar or syntax of the language that the average child needs to learn, except to achieve a school imposed standard of speech or writing to which he may not be accustomed in his home environment. Vocabulary learning, however, continues until late in adult life. Linguists like Hockett believe, in the light of their experiences with

teaching foreign languages, that at the age of puberty linguistic habits somehow solidify in such a way that new phonemic systems become much more difficult to acquire. Ruesch has delineated a number of stages in the whole life of the individual with respect to the kinds of communicative problems he faces. In early childhood (two to five years) communication is with one person at a time; in later childhood (6 to 12 years), the child learns to communicate with groups; the adolescent (12 to 18 years) resumes communication with age mates of the opposite sex; in young adulthood communication is mostly with age superiors; in middle and later adulthood there is a gradual change-over from intake to output of information.

GROSS INDICES OF LANGUAGE DEVELOPMENT

To meet the need for a simple way of gauging a child's general stage of language development, several American investigators have provided normative data on such indices as amount and rate of talking, mean sentence length, and percentage of compound and complex sentences. These studies have been well summarized by McCarthy (1954a), who concludes that mean sentence length is the most "reliable, easily determined, objective, quantitative, and easily understood measure of linguistic maturity." Rules have been formulated by Davis (1937) for dividing utterances into sentences or "expression units"; it is possible that these rules could be made more objective by the application of purely linguistic criteria (intonation patterns, pausal phenomena, sentence structure types). The method has been applied to written as well as to spoken language. In Templin's careful study of spoken language (Templin), the mean length of fifty sentences obtained in a specified child-adult situation for ages three, four, five, six, seven, and eight are 4.1, 5.4, 5.7, 6.6, 7.3, and 7.6 words, respectively. These lengths are significantly greater than those reported twenty or more years earlier by Davis (1937) and McCarthy (1930) for a closely comparable testing situation; possibly this means that contemporary children are learning language better because of increased verbal stimulation and greater permissiveness in child-adult relations.

One can still have reservations concerning the reliability and objectivity of this index, in view of its sensitivity to the type of situation, examiner-child rapport, the subjectivity of sentence division, and other factors. There may be more promise along lines suggested by Métraux, who presents "profiles" of the speech behavior of children 18 to 54 months of age. Sievers has constructed a general language development examination based on psycholinguistic theory. She tested decoding, associational, and encoding functions with respect to semantic, grammatical, and integrational responses.

INTERRELATIONSHIPS AMONG ASPECTS OF LANGUAGE DEVELOPMENT

Several aspects of language development can be distinguished on logical, linguistic, or psycholinguistic grounds, and it is conceivable that under certain constellations of training or reinforcement conditions these aspects might develop rather independently. Nevertheless, under typical conditions most aspects are rather highly related. In summarizing such studies as those of Williams and Yedinack, McCarthy (1954a) concludes that most of the usual indices of maturity (vocabulary, articulation ability, sentence length, speech errors) are strongly related, with the exception of vocabulary. This is the conclusion one can draw from Templin's results, which also show that the correlations tend to decrease toward the older ages. In Sievers' study of 228 children aged two to six years, however, most of the functions tested were reported to have low intercorrelations. These abilities were more diverse than those studied by Williams and by Yedinack, and the results were not unexpected.

There has been much interest in the relation between language maturity and measures of intellectual functioning such as MA or IQ. The results depend so much on the respective measures used that it is impossible to state any generalization other than to the effect that whenever the measures employed cover obviously overlapping functions or content the relation will be high; otherwise the relationships tend to be considerably lower, although still positive. Spiker and Irwin, who studied 117 infants aged one month to 28 months, report generally low but significant correlations between certain indices of phonetic frequency or diversity and the 1939 Kuhlman Test of Mental Development. Madorah E. Smith (1957) found the number of different words in speech samples from children aged two to five to be correlated with MA to the extent of .48. Templin found substantial correlations between her vocabulary measures and IQ at ages six to eight, but much lower correlations for articulation ability, sound discrimination, length of remarks, and number of different words in speech samples; these results are generally consistent with those reported by Schneiderman.

CONDITIONS AFFECTING LANGUAGE DEVELOPMENT

All the available evidence, as summarized by McCarthy (1954a, b), supports the general prediction that the quality of a child's early linguistic environment is the most important external factor affecting the rate of language development. Bossard has documented the very wide variations which exist in the role of language in family life, and Milner has demonstrated that this variation is associated with children's language performance in the first grade. Since family patterns of behavior vary to a considerable extent with socioeconomic status, we can easily account for the findings of Templin and others that language development is faster in the upper socioeconomic levels. Nevertheless, Noel found no significant correlation between children's grammatical errors and occupational level of parents, although quality of language usage was related to the extent to which parents participated in outside activities involving language. The important study by Wood showed not only that presence of articulatory defect in children tended to be associated with parent neuroticism, but that psychotherapy given to mothers yielded improvement in their children's articulation. There are many practices in child rearing that might account for these relations; for example, oversolicitousness, failure to provide situations stimulating talking, excessive use of baby talk, and unconscious attitudes of rejection.

Additional confirmation of the general

prediction regarding rate of speech development comes from studies of special groups. Davis (1937) found that only children (who would have more dealings with adults) develop language facility faster than children with siblings, and these in turn faster than twins. Orphaned or institutionalized children develop more slowly (Moore) but can be trained (Dawe). Degree of association with adults is a factor (McCarthy, 1930). Siblings, particularly when they are twins, will occasionally develop "secret languages." Linguistic investigations reported by Forchhammer and Jespersen indicate that such languages are probably always variants of the adult language being learned.

On the matter of sex differences in language development, the research literature as summarized by McCarthy (1954a) provides general confirmation of the popularly held notion that girls develop language competence faster. Nevertheless, the differences are not pronounced, and Sievers and Templin have shown a substantial number of differences favoring boys. Perhaps changes in child-rearing practices in American culture in the past generation have tended to minimize sex differences in language development. McCarthy (1953) has attempted to explain the small trends favoring girls, and particularly the much higher incidence of language disorders in older boys, by theorizing that for various reasons identification and warm exchange of affection with the mother can be more complete in the case of female infants. Olson and Koetzle observed that although boys may talk less, they talk faster.

Speech development in handicapped children
Blindness *per se* does not have a retarding effect and may actually stimulate the development of language in special directions whenever the child discovers language to be a means of getting additional support from the environment, as Maxfield's results suggest. Deafness, on the other hand, necessitates special measures to aid the child's language development. Keys and Boulware found that there is little permanent advantage in language-learning gained by children who hear but lose hearing before school age as compared with children who never hear at all. The most thorough treatment of language

learning in the deaf is presented by Heider and Heider. The phenomenon of deafness could permit a test of the hypothesis that without an auditory channel an individual could never learn to talk correctly and naturally.

THE FUNCTIONS OF LANGUAGE IN THE LIFE OF THE CHILD

In the early phases, language behavior is very closely related to the satisfaction of the immediate physiological needs and wants of the child, but as he matures this relation may become increasingly indirect, in pace with his growing curiosity about the nature of his complex environment and its meaning for him, and also in pace with the widening of his circle of relationships with other people. Toward the end of the second year of life the normal child starts an intense use of language to explore his relations with people and things. He learns to ask questions and thus to seek help from other children or adults in learning the names of things, learning the categories in which his language orders the world, and learning the freedoms and sanctions of his relations with others. Thus, the trend is from an affective-motivational role of language to a cognitive one. Fahey has reviewed research on the questioning activity of children. Pyles showed that verbalization (in this case, the learning of names for novel shapes) aided learning in a concept formation experiment. Kuenne found that transposition behavior, for example, the ability of a child to make a consistent choice of the larger (or smaller) of two squares regardless of the absolute sizes of the squares, was a function of mental age and hence presumably of the progress the child had made in the use of language. Language development is normally a very good index of the general level of cognitive functioning of the child.

The role of language in play and self-stimulation should not be overlooked, as Lewis has stressed. Babbling is a form of play, and after the child has acquired some mastery of true language he continues to talk to himself partly for pleasure.

Much controversy and research was provoked by Piaget's declaration that the speech of the young child tends to be "egocentric"

and that "socialized" speech attains importance only at a later stage of development, perhaps at age seven or eight. Piaget was one of the first to employ what are now called techniques of content analysis to attempt to demonstrate the importance of egocentricity. Though he found 38 percent of the remarks of two children aged six and a half to be egocentric, other investigators have not been able to obtain values as high as this when they have tried to follow Piaget's rules of analysis literally (McCarthy, 1930). With changed rules of analysis, which, for example, identify remarks containing first-person subjects as "egocentric"—a dubious procedure—several investigators, as summarized by McCarthy (1954a), have obtained high percentage of "egocentric" speech. But with such a criterion even adult speech proves to be highly egocentric, as Henle and Hubbell showed. Fortunately, interest in this rather fruitless controversy has waned in recent years. Its essential fallacy was the assumption that the analysis of the verbal response alone—without reference to the situational context in which responses were made—could be made the basis of an inference concerning the intention of the child. The varying results obtained by different investigators were due to different ways of defining egocentricity, differing situations in which verbal behavior was observed, and differences in the personalities of the children observed.

Instead of studies of "egocentricity," more studies are needed of the manner in which children learn to control social situations by language. Métraux's "profiles" of speech development include descriptions of the tendency of the child to verbalize with regard to his own and others' behavior. Hahn found that there was a high correlation between the child's leadership abilities and his willingness to give class speeches of the "show-and-tell" variety; it would appear that language ability is a key to social success even at the first-grade level.

IMPLICATIONS FOR LANGUAGE-ARTS TEACHING

By the time he arrives at school age, the normal child, according to Noel, has already learned to speak with whatever sound system, grammar, and vocabulary are characteristic of the kind of language he has heard most frequently at home or in his neighborhood. His teachers must ponder the extent to which they can simply build upon his previously acquired capabilities and the extent to which they can attempt to alter a system of habits which not only are highly practiced, but also probably serve a supportive role in the child's adjustment to his nonschool environment. Educational research concerning language-arts teaching in the primary and elementary grades has not been sufficiently cognizant of these considerations and provides few guides to good practice. Language-arts teaching in these grades is not merely a process of teaching new habits and skills, but often a process of changing habits. Experience indicates that spoken language development should run ahead of the development of competence with reading and writing. That is, at least in the primary grades the child should generally learn language patterns (new words, grammatical constructions, and so forth) in the spoken language before they are introduced in printed form. The child needs many opportunities for practice in speaking and understanding language in different types of situations.

The school can foster the cognitive development of the child best when it is realized that the child brings to his school years a rather large variety of concepts, as represented by a large vocabulary, but that the many gaps which still exist in his verbal response system must be filled in as natural a way as possible. This can be done by providing many pertinent experiences and establishing learning conditions which will allow the child to see relevant distinctions in meaning and differential classification of concepts.

REFERENCES

Beasley, Jane. *Slow to Talk: A Guide for Teachers and Parents of Children with Delayed Language Development*. Bureau of Publications, Teachers College, Columbia University, 1956. 109 pp.

Bossard, James H. S. *The Sociology of Child Development*. Harper & Row, Publishers, 1954. 788 pp.

Brown, Roger W. "Language and Categories." In Bruner, J. S., *et al. A Study of Thinking*. John Wiley & Sons, Inc., 1956. pp. 247–312.

———. "Linguistic Determinism and the Parts of Speech." *Journal of Abnormal and Social Psychology*, LV (1957), 1–5.

Carroll, John B. "Determining and Numerating Adjectives in Children's Speech." *Child Development*, X (1939), 215–29.

———. *The Study of Language: A Survey of Linguistics and Related Disciplines in America*. Harvard University Press, 1953. 289 pp.

Cohen, Marcel. "Sur l'étude du language enfantin." *Enfance*, V (1952), 181–249.

Dale, Edgar, and Reichert, Donald. *Bibliography of Vocabulary Studies*. Rev. ed. Ohio State University Press, 1957. 174 pp.

Davis. Edith A. *The Development of Linguistic Skill in Twins, Singletons with Siblings, and Only Children from Ages Five to Ten Years*. University Minnestoa Press, 1937. 165 pp.

———. "Developmental Changes in the Distribution of Parts of Speech." *Child Development*, IX (1938), 309–17.

Dawe, Helen C. "A Study of the Effect of an Educational Program upon Language Development and Related Mental Functions in Young Children." *Journal of Experimental Education*, XI (1942), 200–209.

Fahey, George L. "The Questioning Activity of Children." *Pedigogical Seminary*, LX (1942), 337–57.

Feifel, Herman, and Lorge, Irving. "Qualitative Differences in the Vocabulary Responses of Children." *Journal of Educational Psychology*, XLI (1950), 1–18.

Fisher, Mary S. *Language Patterns of Preschool Children*. Child Development Monographs, No. 15, 1934. 88 pp.

Forchhammer, Egil. "Über einige Fälle von eigentümlichen Sprachbildungen bei Kindern." *Archiv für die Gesamte Psychologie*, CIV (1939), 395–438.

Fries, Charles C. *The Structure of English: An Introduction to the Construction of English Sentences*. Harcourt, Brace & World, Inc., 1952. 304 pp.

Grégoire, Antoine. *L'apprentissage du langage*. Droz. Vol. 1, 1937. 288 pp. Vol. 2, 1947. 491 pp.

Guillaume, P. "Les débuts de la phrase dans le langage de l'enfant." *J. de Psychologic Normale el Pathologique*, XXIV (1927), 1–25.

Hahn, Elise. "Analyses of the Content and

Form of the Speech of First Grade Children." *Quarterly Journal of Speech*, XXXIV (1948), 361–66.

Heider, Fritz K., and Heider, Grace M. *A Comparison of Sentence Structure of Deaf and Hearing Children*. Psychology Monographs, Vol. 52, No. 1, 1940. pp. 42–103.

Henle, Mary, and Hubbell, Marian B. " 'Egocentricity' in Adult Conversation." *Journal of Social Psychology*, IX (1938), 227–34.

Hockett, Charles F. "Age-Grading and Linguistic Continuity." *Language*, XXVI (1950), 449–57.

Irwin, Orvis C. "Development of Speech During Infancy: Curve of Phonemic Frequencies." *Journal of Experimental Psychology*, XXXVII (1947), 187–93.

Jakobson, Roman. *Kindersprache, Aphasie, und allgemeine Lautgesetze*. Almquist and Wiksell, 1941. 83 pp.

Janus, Sidney Q. "An Investigation of the Relationship Between Children's Language and Their Play." *Pedagogical Seminary*, LXII (1943), 3–61.

Jespersen, Otto. *Language: Its Nature, Development and Origin*. Holt, Rinehart & Winston, Inc., 1922. 448 pp.

Keys, Noel, and Boulware, Louise, "Language Acquisition by Deaf Children as Related to Hearing Loss and Age of Onset." *Journal of Educational Psychology*, XXIX (1938), 401–12.

Kuenne, Margaret R. "Experimental Investigation of the Relation of Language to Transposition Behavior in Young Children." *Journal of Experimental Psychology*, XXXVI (1946), 471–90.

LaBrant, Lou L. "A Study of Certain Language Developments of Children in Grades Four to Twelve Inclusive." *Genetic Psychology Monographs*, XIV (1933), 387–491.

Leopold, Werner F. *Speech Development of a Bilingual Child: A Linguist's Record*. Northwestern University Press, 1939–47. 4 Vols. 188; 295; 200; 176 pp.

———. *Bibliography of Child Language*. Northwestern University Press, 1952. 115 pp.

Lewis, M. M. *Infant Speech: A Study of the Beginnings of Language*. See. rev. ed. Humanities Press, Inc., 1951. 383 pp.

Martin, William E. "Quantitative Expression in Young Children." *Genetic Psychology Monographs*, XLIV (1951), 147–219.

Maxfield, Kathryn E. *The Spoken Language of the Blind Preschool Child: A Study of Method*. Archives of Psychology, No. 201. Columbia University Press, 1936. 100 pp.

McCarthy, Dorothea. *The Language Development of the Preschool Child*. University Minnesota Press, 1930. 174 pp.

———. "Some Possible Explanations of Sex Differences in Language Development and Disorders." *Journal of Psychology*, XXXV (1953), 155–60.

———. "Language Development in Children." In Carmichael, Leonard, ed., *A Manual of Child Psychology*. Sec. ed., John Wiley & Sons, 1954a. pp. 492–630.

———. "Language Disorders and Parent-Child Relationships." *Journal of Speech and Hearing Disorders*, XIX (1954), 514–23.

Métraux, Ruth W. "Speech Profiles of the Preschool Child 18 to 54 Months." *Journal of Speech and Hearing Disorders*, XV (1950), 37–53.

Miller, George A. *Language and Communication*. McGraw-Hill Book Company, 1951, 298 pp.

Miller, Neal E., and Dollard, John. *Social Learning and Imitation*. Yale University Press, 1941. 341 pp.

Milner, Esther. "A Study of the Relationship Between Reading Readiness in Grade One School Children and Patterns of Parent-Child Interaction." *Child Development*, XXII (1951), 95–112.

Moore, Jean K. "Speech Content of Selected Groups of Orphanage and Non-Orphanage Preschool Children." *Journal of Experimental Education*, XVI (1947), 122–33.

Mowrer, O. Hobart. *Learning Theory and Personality Dynamics*. The Ronald Press Company, 1950. 776 pp.

———. "The Psychologist Looks at Language." *American Psychologist*, IX (1954), 660–94.

Noel, Doris I. "A Comparative Study of the Relationship Between the Quality of the Child's Language Usage and the Quality and Types of Language Used in the Home." *Journal of Educational Research*, XLVII (1953), 161–67.

Olson, Willard C., and Koetzle, V. S. "Amount and Rate of Talking of Young Children." *Journal of Experimental Education*, V (1936), 175–79.

Osgood, Charles E., and Sebeok, Thomas E., eds. *Psycholinguistics: A Survey of Theory* and Research Problems. Waverly, 1954. 203 pp.

Piaget, Jean. The Language and Thought of the Child. Trans. M. Warden. Harcourt, Brace & World, Inc., 1926. 246 pp.

Potter, Ralph K., and Peterson, Gordon E. "The Representation of Vowels and Their Movements." Journal of the Acoustical Society of America, XX (1948), 528–35.

Pyles, Marjorie K. "Verbalization as a Factor in Learning." Child Development, III (1932), 108–13.

Ruesch, Jurgen. Disturbed Communication; the Clinical Assessment of Normal and Pathological Communicative Behavior. W. W. Norton & Company, Inc., 1957. 337 pp.

Schneiderman, Norma. "A Study of the Relationship Between Articulatory Ability and Language Ability." Journal of Speech and Hearing Disorders, XX (1955), 359–64.

Shirley, Mary M. The First Two Years: A Study of Twenty-Five Babies: II. Intellectual Development. University of Minnesota Press, 1933. 513 pp.

Sievers, Dorothy Jean. Development and Standardization of a Test of Psycholinguistic Growth in Preschool Children. Doctor's thesis. University of Illinois, 1955.

Skinner, B. Frederick. Verbal Behavior. Appleton-Century-Crofts, Inc., 1957. 478 pp.

Smith, Madorah E. "An Investigation of the Development of the Sentence and the Extent of Vocabulary in Young Children." University of Iowa Studies in Child Welfare, III (1926), 1–92.

———. "Relation Between Word Variety and Mean Letter Length of Words with Chronological and Mental Ages." Journal of Genetic Psychology, LVI (1957), 27–43.

Smith, Mary K. "Measurement of the Size of General English Vocabulary Through the Elementary Grades and High School."

Genetic Psychology Monographs, XXIV (1941), 311–45.

Spiker, Charles C., and Irwin, Orvis C. "The Relationship between IQ and Indices of Infant Speech Sound Development." Journal of Speech and Hearing Disorders, XIV (1949), 335–43.

Strauss, Anselm, and Schuessler, Karl. "Socialization, Logical Reasoning, and Concept Development in the Child." Americal Sociology Review, XVI (1951), 514–23.

Templin, Mildred C. Certain Language Skills in Children: Their Development and Interrelationships. University of Minnesota Press, 1957. 183 pp.

Velten, H. V. "The Growth of Phonemic and Lexical Patterns in Infant Language." Language, XIX (1943), 281–92.

Voegelin, Charles F., and Adams, Sidney. "A Phonetic Study of Young Children's Speech." Journal of Experimental Education, III (1934), 107–16.

Walter, Jean. "A Study of the Written Sentence Construction of a Group of Profoundly Deaf Children." American Annals of the Deaf, C (1955), 235–52.

Werner, Heinz, and Kaplan, Edith. "Development of Word Meaning Through Verbal Context: An Experimental Study." Journal of Psychology, XXIX (1950), 251–57.

Williams, Harold M. "An Analytical Study of Language Achievement in Preschool Children. Part I." University of Iowa Studies in Child Welfare, XIII (1937), 9–18.

Wood, Kenneth S. "Parental Maladjustment and Functional Articulatory Defects in Children." Journal of Speech and Hearing Disorders, XI (1946), 255–75.

Yedinack, Jeanette G. "A Study of the Linguistic Functioning of Children with Articulation and Reading Disabilities." Pedagogical Seminary, LXXIV (1949), 23–59.

ROMAN JAKOBSON ‿‿‿‿‿‿‿‿‿‿‿‿‿‿‿‿‿

37 Here is another sample from Roman Jakobson's work on child language. This great scholar, whose impact on the linguistic treatment of child language can hardly be overestimated, certainly needs no further introduction here. Cf. the introduction to his "Les Lois Phoniques . . .", and see his next reading on "Phonemic Patterning," with Morris Halle.

The anthropologist George Peter Murdock, published in 1957 his "World Ethnographic Sample," including among the tables of kinship 1,072 parental terms (531 for mother, and 541 for father). In a linguistic seminar in 1959 he tried to verify, on the basis of these data, the alleged tendency of historically unrelated languages "to develop similar words for father and mother on the basis of nursery forms," and challenged linguists to "clarify the theoretical principles that account for those established facts" of convergence. The present paper by Jakobson is a linguist's response to this challenge.

A. B. A.

WHY "MAMA" AND "PAPA"?

In Spring 1959, during a linguistic seminar at the Center for Advanced Study in the Behavioral Sciences, George Peter Murdock endeavored to verify the alleged tendency of unrelated languages "to develop similar words for father and mother on the basis of nursery forms." Murdock's (1957) tables of kinship terms assembled for his "World Ethnographic Sample" supplied the investigation with 1,072 terms (531 for mother and 541 for father). The valuable seminar report has recently been published by Murdock (1959). As the author concludes, "the purpose of this paper is merely to present the data, which clearly confirm the hypothesis under test"—a striking convergence in the structure of these parental kin terms throughout historically unrelated languages. He asks whether linguists—"now that the facts are established"—could not "clarify the theoretical principles that account for them." On May 26, 1959, at the same seminar, I ventured to answer Murdock's call, and now I am happy to contribute those remarks to the book dedicated to Heinz Werner.

"The child," H. Werner (1940) stressed, "grows out of his child's world into an alien world of adults. His behavior is the result of an interaction between these two worlds." One could add that likewise the behavior of adults with regard to the child they nurse and educate is a result of an interaction between both worlds. In particular, the so-called

Reprinted from Roman Jakobson, Selected Writings (*The Hague: Mouton & Co., 1939; reprinted 1962*), *538–545, by permission of the author.*

Written in Stanford, California, 1959, for *Perspectives in Psychological Theory*, dedicated to Heinz Werner (New York, 1960).

"baby talk" used by the grownups when speaking with infants is a kind of pidgin, a typical mixed language, where the addressers try to adjust themselves to the verbal habits of their addressees and to establish a common code suitable for both interlocutors in a child-adult dialogue. The socialized and conventionalized lexical coinages of this baby talk, known under the name of nursery forms, are deliberately adapted to the infant's phonemic pattern and to the usual make-up of his early words; and, on the other hand, they tend to superimpose upon the child a sharper delimitation and higher stability of word meaning.

Some of such nursery forms overstep the limits of the nurseries, enter into the general usage of the adult society, and build a specific infantile layer in standard vocabulary. In particular, adult language usually adopts the nursery forms designating each of the two mature members of the nuclear family. Very frequently these intimate, emotional, childishly tinged words coexist with more general and abstract, exclusively adult parental terms. Thus, for instance, in English, *mama* (*mama, mammy, ma, mom, mommy*) and *papa* (*pap, pappy, pa, pop* or *dada, dad, daddy*) differ in use from the higher terms *mother* and *father*; in a similar way, Russian distinguishes *mama* and *papa* or *t'at'a* from *mat'* (Common Slavic *mati*) and *otec* (Common Slavic *otĭcĭ*). In Indo-European the intellectualized parental designations **mātēr* and **pətēr* were built from the nursery forms with the help of the suffix *-ter*, used for various kin terms. I am inclined to trace to these prototypes not only the cited English nouns and the Slavic *mati* but also the root of the Slavic paternal term *ot-* and similar forms in some other Indo-European languages: cf. Vasmer's (1954) data on Rus. *otec*. The root in question could have lost its initial *p-* through an infantlike elimination of consonantal diversity in **pətēr* when this adult term went down into the nursery.

As an instructive example of the difference in formal and functional properties between the two levels of parental appellations, the use of Bulgarian words *mama* and *majka* "mother" may be cited. The nursery forms like *mama*, adequately characterized by E. Georgieva (1959) as intermediate between common and proper nouns (*polunaricatelni, naricatelno-sobstveni imena*), can be used in standard Bulgarian neither with articles nor with possessive pronouns. The bare *mama* means either "my, addresser's mother" or "I, addressee's mother." As to the term *majka*, it may appear with any "short possessive pronominal form" (*ti, mu, i, vi, im*) except the first person pronoun *mi*. One's own mother is spoken of in Bulgarian as *mama* or occasionally as *majka* "mother," as far as it is clear from context or situation whose *majka* is meant. Finally, in a distancing fashion, the expression *mojata majka* "the mother of mine" may be used, while the turn *majka mi* "my mother" is ordinarily avoided. If the parental terms assembled by Murdock could be divided into these two— *mama-papa* and *mother-father*—classes, his statistical test would yield even more overwhelming results.

Nursery coinages are accepted for a wider circulation in the child-adult verbal intercourse only if they meet the infant's linguistic requirements and thus follow the general line of any interlanguage, as formulated in the indigenous name for Russenorsk, the hybrid tongue of Russian and Norweign fishermen: *moja på tvoja* "mine in your way" (Broch, 1927). Those settled nursery forms adopted by speech communities ostensibly reflect the salient features and tendencies of children's speech development and their universal homogeneity. In particular the phonemic range of the intimate parental terms proves to be "severely limited." The principles underlying the successive stages in the child's acquisition of language enable us to interpret and clarify the "cross-language parallels" in the structure of such terms throughout the world. Consonantal clusters appear in no more

than 1.1 per cent of the 1,072 parental terms counted by Murdock, and child's speech at its early stages uses no consonantal groups but only combinations of consonants with vowels. Such combinations are nearly constant in the *mama-papa* words, and purely vocalic roots are exceptional: only three among the tabulated instances.

Stops and nasals—briefly, consonants formed by a complete oral closure—predominate in parental terms. According to Murdock's tabulation, stops and nasals approach 85 per cent of nonsyllabics. The exact ratio cannot be stated, because all nonsibilant fricatives are lumped together with corresponding stops.

Labial and dental—briefly, backward flanged, or, in acoustical terminology, diffuse consonants—prevail over velars and palatals—briefly, forward flanged (hornlike), acoustically compact consonants. More than 76 per cent of all the terms counted include a labial or dental as opposed to more than 10 per cent with velars and palatals. A more exact computation would ask for a split of Murdock's class of sibilant fricatives into hissing (diffuse) and hushing (compact) consonants.

Wide vowels, especially /a/, are obviously preponderant, but it is impossible to extract numerical data from Murdock's table, because the narrower and wider vowels within each of the three classes—front, unrounded back, and rounded back—are lumped together, and the relation—/e/:/i/ = /a/:/ə/ = /o/:/u/—which underlies many vocalic patterns is disregarded.

The contrast between the consonantal presence and rocalic absence of an obstruction in the vocal tract finds its optimal expression when a consonant with a complete oral closure, and especially a backward flanged consonant with a closure in the front of the oral cavity, is opposed to a forward flanged vowel with a wide frontal opening. On the acoustical level, vowels differ from consonants by a sharply defined formant structure and a high total energy. The compact vowel displays the maximal energy output, while the diffuse consonant with an oral occlusion represents the maximal reduction in the energy output. Thus nursery names for mother and father, like the earliest meaningful units emerging in infant speech, are based on the polarity between the optimal consonant and the optimal vowel (Jakobson and Halle, 1957).

The principle of maximal contrast accounts for the constituents common to the majority of the *mama-papa* terms. As to the order of these constituents, the sequence "consonant plus vowel" appears to be almost compulsory; yet this question has been omitted in Murdock's test. During the babbling period in the infant's development, many of the uttered syllables consist of a vocalic sound succeeded by a consonantal articulation. The most natural order of sound production is an opening of the mouth followed by its closure. Among Russian interjections, one observes such infantile sound gestures as ['ap] and ['am]; when changed into verbal roots, they are adapted to the Russian phonemic pattern by subsituting a fricative velar for the initial aspiration: *xapat'*, *xamat'*, *xamkat'*. As soon as the child moves from his babbling activities to the first acquisition of conventional speech, he at once clings to the model "consonant plus vowel." The sounds assume a phonemic value and thus need to be correctly identified by the listener, and since the best graspable clue in discerning consonants is their transition to the following vowels, the sequence "consonant plus vowel" proves to be the optimal sequence, and therefore it is the only universal variety of the syllable pattern.

Among 436 dentals and palatals, briefly, medial, acoustically acute consonants (the T, N, C, and S classes in Murdock's table), there are 159, or 39 per cent, which are followed by a palatal, i.e., acute vowel, while among 507 labials and velars, briefly peripheral, acoustically grave consonants (Murdock's P, M, K, and ŋ classes) only 88, or 17 per cent, are accompanied by acute vowels. The considerably higher percentage of acute vowels after acute rather than grave consonants reflects an assimilative influence of consonantal tonality upon the tonality of the subsequent vowel, and the same tendency is manifest in the early stage of children's speech. At this stage, vocalic differences do not possess their own phonemic value, and the consonant functions as the only carrier of significative distinctions, the only genuine phoneme. The *mama-papa* terms, like the

primary word units in infant language, do not comprise different consonants, and a dissyllabic form usually reiterates one and the same consonant. At first child's language is devoid of any hierarchy of linguistic units and obeys the equation: one utterance–one sentence–one word–one morpheme–one phoneme–one distinctive feature. The *mama-papa* pair is a vestige of that stage of one-consonant utterances.

The reduplication of syllables, while passed over in Murdock's test, appears, however, as a favorite device in nursery forms, particularly in parental terms, and in the early word units of infant language. At the transition from babbling to verbal behavior, the reduplication may even serve as a compulsory process, signaling that the uttered sounds do not represent a babble, but a senseful, semantic entity. The patently linguistic essence of such a duplication is quite explicable. In contradistinction to the "wild sounds" of babbling exercises, the phonemes are to be recognizable, distinguishable, identifiable; and in accordance with these requirements, they must be deliberately repeatable. This repetitiveness finds its most concise and succinct expression in, e.g., *papa*. The successive presentations of the same consonantal phonemes, repeatedly supported by the same vowel, improve their intelligibility and contribute to the correctness of message reception (cf. Pollack, 1959).

The most spectacular results of Murdock's test concern the distribution of nasal and oral consonants between maternal and paternal terms: 55 per cent of the words denoting mother and only 15 per cent of those dentoing father belong to M, N, and ŋ consonant classes. Thus the traditional assertions that "the mother is usually named with an *m*-form, the father with a *p*, *b*, *t*, or *d*-form" (Lewis, 1951) obtain an instructive statistical corroboration. The origin and the evolution of the *m*-form can easily be traced, if one rejects any, as Lewis says, "mystical" beliefs in the weak *m* "suited to name a woman" or in the "centripetal" connotation of the nasals as opposed to the "centrifugal" meaning of the oral stops, as well as the equally superstitious speculations about the child's "meaningless" syllables, "arbitrarily" interpreted and taught by the grownups to the children "in the nurseries of all countries" (Jespersen, 1922).

Often the sucking activities of a child are accompanied by a slight nasal murmur, the only phonation which can be produced when the lips are pressed to mother's breast or to the feeding bottle and the mouth is full. Later, this phonatory reaction to nursing is reproduced as an anticipatory signal at the mere sight of food and finally as a manifestation of a desire to eat, or more generally, as an expression of discontent and impatient longing for missing food or absent nurser, and any ungranted wish. When the mouth is free from nutrition, the nasal murmur may be supplied with an oral, particularly labial release; it may also obtain an optional vocalic support. Eloquent material on the shape and function of those nasal interjections has been collected by such sagacious observers of infant speech as Grégoire (1937), Leopold (1939), Smoczyński (1955), and others. It should be noted in this connection that of the two Russian catching interjections ['ap], ['am] the latter and the corresponding verbal root xam- are associated with nutrition.

Since the mother is, in Grégoire's parlance, *la grande dispensatrice*, most of the infant's longings are addressed to her, and children, being prompted and instigated by the extant nursery words, gradually turn the nasal interjection into a parental term, and adapt its expressive make up to their regular phonemic pattern. Some investigators, however, for example, Leopold (1947), insist that not seldom this transition from the *m*-interjection to the maternal term proved to be delayed, and one of the two parental terms, *papa*, appeared as the first thoroughly designative verbal unit, whereas, for instance, the form *mama* existed in the language of Leopold's daughter as an interjection only: "it had no intellectual meaning and cannot be considered to be a semantic alternative of *papa*, which was learned with real meaning at 1; 0. *Mama* with the standard meaning was not learned until 1; 3."

The transitional period when *papa* points to the parent present, while *mama* signals a request for the fulfillment of some need or for the absent fulfiller of childish needs, first and foremost but not necessarily for the mother, is attentively described by Grégoire: "Edm. a paru réclamer sa maman, absente

ce jour-là, en disant [mam: am: am:]; or, c'est [papa] qu'il émet, lorsqu'il la voit rentrer. . . . Edm. me voit lui préparer une tartine; il énonce [mamã], et non [papa]." Likewise Smoczyński's children in the middle of their second year, when begging for something from their father, addressed him: [mama ma-ma ma:-ma:-ma:].

The priority of paternal terms with their oral stop, in relation to the maternal terms with nasal, is well founded both on the semantic and on the phonological level. Parsons' (1955) observations on the preoedipal mother-child identity in its plain contradistinction to the father's role give an answer to the question why the first distant, merely deictic, rudimentarily cognitive attitude in child's verbal behavior is embodied in the paternal term, which "heralds just the transition from affective expression to designative language" (Jakobson, 1941), whereas in the maternal term, the purely referential value arises in a later (Parsons would probably suggest—oedipal) stage. It would be interesting to examine whether there is a difference in the settlement of *mama* "with the standard meaning" in the speech development of boys on the one hand and girls on the other. On the phonological level, it may be observed that the optimal consonant-vowel contrast is achieved by the backward flanged vowel. The addition of a new, open resonator brings the nasal consonants closer to vowels and thus attenuates the maximal contrast. The phonemic formation of nasal consonants implies the existence of the consonant-vowel contrast and is a superstructure upon this contrast.

Although the *mama-papa* terms are nursery words, they conform to the developmental character of infant language, and neither their penetration into the national language nor their international diffusion invalidates this basic conformity. Therefore the complete exclusion of "forms resembling *mama* and *papa*" from Murdock's text, "unless comparative data on related languages clearly demonstrated their indigenous origin," seems to be superfluously rigorous.

The captivating test of the eminent anthropologist deserves to be continued and developed. The phonemic relation between the maternal and paternal term should be examined and tabulated. How frequently do both terms belong to the nasal or to the oral class? How often do both of these terms contain a labial or both of them a dental? What are the types of combination between the opposition labial-dental and nasal-oral within the pairs of parental terms? Reinforced, multiform polarizations seem to play here a noticeable role. Cf. such pairs as Russian *mama-t'at'a*, where the feature nasal-oral is combined with the two tonality features—grave-actue and sharp (palatalized)–plain (nonpalatalized). The coincidence of the latter two features creates the optimal contrast of high and low tonality.

Among familial terms the nursery forms are not confined to parental designations, and it would be a tempting task to trace how the different degrees of relationship designated correspond to the development of the child's language. Thus Russian *baba* "grandma" and *d'ad'a* "uncle" (cf. *papa* and *t'at'a*) introduce the voicing of consonants, a later feature in the phonemic patterning of Russian (and all Slavic) children. The terms *d'ed* "grandpa" and *t'ot'a* shift from /a/ to other vowels, which belong to the later phonemic acquistions of children. Nurse is called either *mamka*, a diminutive from *mama*, or *n'an'a* "nanny," opposed by its nasals of high tonality (sharp and acute), briefly by a typically diminutive sound symbolism, to *mama* with its nasals of low tonality (plain and grave).

We observe that only seniors in age and function are supplied here with nursery names, and we face the relevant question: for what kinsmen are there such names in a given language or stock of languages? A wide field is open for productive joint work of linguists, anthropologists, and experts in psychology of mental and behavioral development.

BIBLIOGRAPHY

Broch, O. "Russenorsk." *Archiv für slavische Philologie*, XLI (1927), 209–62.

Georgieva, E. "Mama i majka." *Bŭlgarski ezik*, IX (1959), 287–89.

Grégoire, A. (1937), *L'apprentissage du langage*. Bibliothèque de la Faculté de Philosophie et Lettres de l'Université de Liège, 73.

Jakobson, R. "Kindersprache, Aphasie und allgemeine Lautgesetze." *Uppsala Universitets årsskrift* (1942), 1–83.

———, and Halle, M. "Phonology in Relation to Phonetics." *Manual of Phonetics*, ed. L. Kaiser. Amsterdam: North-Holland Publishing Company, 1957. pp. 215–51.

Jespersen, O. *Language, Its Nature, Development and Origin*. London and New York: The Macmillan Company, 1922.

Leopold, W. F. *Speech Development of a Bilingual Child*, I: *Vocabulary Growth in the First Two Years*. Evanston and Chicago: Northwestern University Press, 1939.

———. *Speech Development of a Bilingual Child*, II: *Sound Learning in the First Two Years*. Evanston: Northwestern University Press, 1947.

Lewis, M. M. *Infant Speech*. New York: The Humanities Press; London: Routledge & Kegan Paul, Ltd., 1951.

Murdock, G. P. "World Ethnographic Sample." *American Anthropologist*, LIX (1957), 664–87.

———. "Cross-Language Parallels in Parental Kin Terms." *Anthropological Linguistics*, I (1959), 1–5.

Parsons, T. "Family Structure and the Socialization of the Child." *Family Socialization and Interaction Process*, by T. Parsons and R. F. Bales. New York: The Free Press, 1955.

Pollack, I. "Message Repetition and Message Reception." *Journal of the Acoustical Society of America*, XXXI (1959), 1509–15.

Smoczyński, P. "Przyswajanie przez dziecko podstaw systemu językowego." *Societas Scientiarum Lodziensis, Section 1, no. 19* (1955).

Vasmer, M. "otéc," *Russisches etymologisches Wörterbuch*, II (1954), 290. Heidelberg: Carl Winter, 1953–1955.

Werner, H. (1940), *Comparative Psychology of Mental Development*, 2nd rev. ed. New York: International Universities Press, 1957.

ROMAN JAKOBSON AND MORRIS HALLE

38

This selection is a chapter from Roman Jakobson and Morris Halle's work on *Phonology and Phonetics*. The student will find it interesting to compare this chapter with Jakobson's earlier work on "Les Lois Phoniques . . . ," which is included in this volume.

Roman Jakobson needs no further introduction here. See the introduction to "Les Lois Phoniques . . ." and the preceding reading "Why Mama and Papa ?"

Morris Halle, Professor of Linguistics at M.I.T., is certainly known to all readers with a linguistic or psycholinguistic background through his extensive contributions to generative grammar, especially generative phonology. He is the author of *The Sound Pattern of Russian* (1959), *Preliminaries to Speech Analysis* (with Roman Jakobson and C. G. M. Faut) (1963), *Fundamentals of Language* (with Roman Jakobson) (1956), *The Sound Pattern of English* (with Noam Chomsky) (1968), and "Phonology in a Generative Grammar," *Word, XVIII* (1962), 54–72.

A. B. A.

PHONEMIC PATTERNING

4.1 STRATIFICATION: NUCLEAR SYLLABLE

Ordinarily child language begins, and the aphasic dissolution of language preceding its complete loss ends, with what psychopathologists have termed the "labial stage." In this phase speakers are capable only of one type of utterance, which is usually transcribed as /pa/. From the articulatory point of view the two constituents of this utterance represent polar configurations of the vocal tract: in /p/ the tract is closed at its very end while in /a/ it is opened as widely as possible at the front and narrowed toward the back, thus assuming the horn shape of a megaphone. The combination of two extremes is also apparent on the acoustic level: the labial stop presents a momentary burst of sound without any great concentration of energy in a particular frequency band, whereas in the

Reprinted from Roman Jakobson and Morris Halle, Fundamentals of Language (*The Hague: Mouton & Co., 1956*), *37–51, and from Roman Jakobson, Selected Writings,* Vol. 1 (The Hague: Mouton & Co., 1962), pp. 491–504, *by permission of the authors.*

Written in Orleans and Cambridge, Mass., 1955, and published first in *Fundamentals of Language* (The Hague, 1956), then in a slightly revised and shortened version in the *Manual of Phonetics*, ed. by L. Kaiser (Amsterdam, 1957), and in German translation by G. F. Meier (Berlin, 1960).

vowel /a/ there is no strict time limitation, and the energy is concentrated in a relatively narrow region of maximum aural sensitivity. In the first constituent there is an extreme limitation in the time domain but no ostensible limitation in the frequency domain, whereas the second constituent shows no ostensible limitation in the time domain but a maximum limitation in the frequency domain. Consequently, the diffuse stop with its maximal reduction in the energy output offers the closest approach to silence, while the open vowel represents the highest energy output of which the human vocal apparatus is capable.

This polarity between the minimum and the maximum of energy appears primarily as a *contrast* between two successive units—the optimal consonant and the optimal vowel. Thus the elementary phonemic frame, the syllable, is established. Since many languages lack syllables without a prevocalic consonant and/or with a postvocalic consonant, CV (Consonant + Vowel) is the only universal model of the syllable.

4.12 THE ROLE OF THE NASAL CONSONANT

The choice between /pa/ and /a/ and/or /pa/ and /ap/ may become the first carrier of meaning in the very early stages of child language. Usually, however, the infant preserves for a time a constant syllable scheme and splits both constituents of this syllable, first the consonant and later the vowel, into distinctive alternatives.

Most frequently, the oral stop, utilizing a single closed tract, obtains a counterpart in the nasal consonant, which combines a closed main tract with an open subsidiary tract and thereby supplements the specific traits of a stop with a secondary vocalic characteristic. Before there appeared the consonantal opposition nasal/oral, consonant was distinguished from vowel as closed tract from open tract. Once the nasal consonant is opposed to the oral as presence to absence of the open tract, the contrast consonant/vowel is revalued as presence vs. absence of a closed tract.

Various further oppositions, modifying and attenuating the primary optimal contrast of consonant and vowel, follow. All these later formations reshape the mouth resonator in some way, while nasalization merely adds a secondary resonating cavity to the mouth resonator without changing its volume and shape.

The consonantal opposition nasal/oral, which belongs to the earliest acquisitions of the child, is ordinarily the most resistant consonantal opposition in aphasia and it occurs in all the languages of the world except for some American Indian languages.

4.13 THE PRIMARY TRIANGLE

The opposition nasal vs. oral stop, however, may be preceded by the split of the stop into two opposites, labial and dental. After the appearance of the contrast CV, founded upon one attribute of sound, loudness, the utilization of the other basic attribute, pitch, is psychologically inferable. Thus, the first tonality opposition is instituted: grave/acute, in other words, the concentration of energy in the lower vs. upper frequencies of the spectrum. In /p/ the lower end predominates, while in /t/ the upper end is the stronger one. It is quite natural that the first tonality feature should affect not the vowel /a/, with its maximal concentration of energy in a narrow central region of the spectrum, but the consonant /p/, with its maximal diffusion

of energy over a wide frequency band.

At this stage the pole of high and concentrated energy /a/ contrasts with the low energy stops /p/ and /t/. Both stops are opposed to each other by a predominance of one or the other end·of the frequency spectrum, as the gravity and acuteness poles. These two dimensions underlie a *triangular* pattern of phonemes (or, at least, of oral phonemes, if the nasality feature has already emerged) (Figure 1).

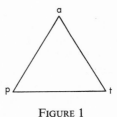

FIGURE 1

4.14 THE SPLIT OF THE PRIMARY TRIANGLE INTO TWO TRIANGLES, CONSONANTAL AND VOCALIC.

The rise of the consonantal tonality feature is followed by the first vocalic split. The polarity of two successive units, CV, based on the contrast of reduced and full energy, is supplemented by a polarity of two alternative vowels, founded on the opposition of lower and higher concentration of energy. The single compact /a/ finds its opposite in a diffuse vowel. Henceforth, both the consonantal and the vocalic section of the primary triangle contruct each its own linear pattern—the grave/acute consonantal axis and the compact/diffuse vocalic axis.

The consonants duplicate this originally vocalic opposition, and the consonantal baseline of the over-all triangle proves to be complemented by a consonantal apex—the velar stop that Grimm justly defined as the "fullest of all producible consonants." The tonality opposition, originally consonantal, may in turn be extended to the vocalic pattern: it is naturally the diffuse vowel that splits into grave and acute, complementing the vocalic apex of the over-all triangle with a /u/–/i/ base-line. In this way the originally single primary triangle is split into two autonomous two-dimensional patterns—the consonantal and the vocalic triangle (Figure 2).

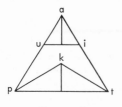

4.15 PATTERNING OF ORAL RESONANCE FEATURES

Both the vocalic and the consonantal pattern may subsequently pass from the triangular to the quadrangular pattern by superimposing the distinction between velar and palatal upon the wide vowels and/or upon the consonants. In this way the grave/acute feature spreads to the compact vowels and/or consonants. In the languages of the world, however, the triangular pattern prevails over the quadrangular for vowels and even more so for consonants—it is the minimum model, both for the vocalic and for the consonantal patterns, with the very rare exceptions in which either the vocalic or the consonantal pattern—but never both—is linear. In the rare cases of a linear patterning, the vowels are confined to the feature compact/diffuse and the consonants, almost unfailingly, to the tonality feature. Thus no language lacks the oppositions grave/acute and compact/diffuse, whereas any other opposition may be absent both from vowels and from consonants.

The alternation in the volume and shape of the mouth resonator is used for the grave/acute opposition. In the early stages of child language, in the advanced stages of aphasia, and in numerous languages of the world this alternation is reinforced by a variation in the size of one or both orifices of the mouth cavity. The restriction of the back and front orifices, together with an expanded and unified oral cavity, serve to lower the resonance frequencies, whereas the combined action of the dilated orifices and of a restricted and compartmented cavity raises the resonance frequencies. But the change in the size of each of these orifices may achieve an autonomous status and set in operation secondary tonality features (flatting and/or sharping).

The development of the oral resonance

features in child language presents a whole chain of successive acquisitions interlinked by laws of implication. We tentatively tabulate this temporal series in the following chart, using for the distinctions acquired the traditional articulatory terms and designating each of these acquisitions by a sequence of numbers preceded by 0., i.e. writing each sequence as a decimal fraction. The sequences were composed in such a way that if sequence S_1 is assigned to distinction A and sequence S_2 to distinction B, and S_1 is an initial subsequence of S_2 (i.e. S_1 is an initial subsequence of S_2 if the first digits of S_2 are identical with S_1; e.g. $S_1 = 0.19$ and $S_2 = 0.195$), then the acquisition of distinction B implies that of A. The number and numerical values of the digits have no other significance. It is obvious that only those distinctions are acquired by the child which are present in the language being learned.

Consonants: dental vs. labial	0.1
Vowels: narrow vs. wide	0.11
Narrow vowels: palatal vs. velar	0.111
Wide vowels: palatal vs. velar	0.1111
Narrow palatal vowels: rounded vs. unrounded	0.1112
Wide palatal vowels: rounded vs. unrounded	0.11121
Velar vowels: unrounded vs. rounded	0.1113
Consonants: velopalatal vs. labial and dental	0.112
Consonants: palatal vs. velar	0.1121
Consonants: rounded vs. unrounded or pharyngealized vs. non-pharyngealized	0.1122
Consonants: palatalized vs. non-palatalized	0.1123

4.16 SONORITY FEATURES IN RELATION TO THE OPTIMAL CONSONANT AND VOWEL

The reduced concentration of energy in the diffuse vowel moves it away from the optimal, compact vowel in the direction of the consonants and, conversely, the reduced spread of energy in the compact consonant diverts it from the optimal, diffuse consonant in the direction of the vowel.

In the nasal consonants the addition of the new, open resonator superimposes sharply defined nasal formants upon the spectrum of the oral stop. Nasal resonance brings consonants closer to vowels and, on the other hand, when superimposed upon a vocalic spectrum, damps the other formants and deflects the vowel from its optimal pattern.

The optimal, stop consonant finds its opposite in the constrictive, which attenuates the consonantal reduction of energy. Stops are an earlier acquisition of children and a later loss of aphasics than constrictive phonemes. There are in the world several languages without constrictives but no languages without stops.

The appearance of liquids, which combine the clearcut formant structure of a vowel with the consonantal reduction of energy, changes the contrast consonant/vowel into two autonomous oppositions, consonantal/nonconsonantal and vocalic/nonvocalic. While the consonantal feature, reduction of energy, is optimally represented by the stop, which tends toward a single pulse, the nonvocalic feature, absence of sharply defined formant structure, is optimally manifested by the strident consonant, which tends toward white noise. Therefore, the mutual emancipation of the two features, discontinuous/continuant on the one hand and strident/mellow on the other, implies the acquisition of a liquid that combines two autonomous features, the vocalic and the consonantal. Actually, mellow constrictives, as opposed to strident constrictives, or strident plosives (affricates), as opposed to mellow plosives (stops proper), do not appear in child language before the emergence of the first liquid, and, in aphasia, vanish when the liquids are lost.

Strident plosives, in contradistinction to mellow plosives, attenuate the consonantal reduction of energy. The mellow constrictives deviate from the nonvocalic optimum embodied in the strident constrictives, namely from their markedly noisy pattern. One and the same split of the consonantal feature, on the one hand, and of the nonvocalic feature, on the other, is manifested both in the appearance of the liquids and of the strident stops. This explains the "strange but widespread" interchangeability of strident stops and liquids, especially laterals, that have been noted in some Manchu-Tungus and Paleosiberian languages.[1]

Since nasality, by superimposing a clearcut

formant structure upon the consonantal pattern, brings consonants closer to vowels, and since liquids combine the consonantal with the vocalic feature, it is advantageous to range these two related classes of phonemes under a common heading: *sonorants*. On the other hand, the consonantal character of these two classes is strengthened in such relatively rare phonemes as the discontinous nasals (the so-called prenasalized stops) and the strident liquids (the sibilant laterals or vibrants).

The oral phonemes with an obstructed vocal tract have a noise source at the obstruction and may use voice—if at all—only as a supplementary source, whereas for the phonemes with an open tract, voice is the main source. While the optimal consonant is voiceless and the optimal vowel voiced, the voicing of consonants or, in very rare instances, the unvoicing of vowels, may be utilized as one of the various attenuations of the maximum contrast CV.

Sicce the consonant is primarily characterized by reduction of energy, the optimal consonant is lax, but may be subsequently opposed by a tense consonant, which attenuates the contrast between consonant and vowel. Normally, however, the voiced consonant is of lower energy than the voiceless one, and therefore, in the opposition of tense and lax consonants, the laxness is frequently accompanied by voicing and the tenseness by voicelessness, so that the consonant, optimal in one respect—the reduction of energy— deviates from the consonantal optimum in another—the presence of voice. If both oppositions act autonomously in a language, the doubly optimal consonant, lax and voiceless, is opposed by two phonemes, one, a voiceless tense and the other, a voiced lax, both of which, in different ways, shift the structure of the consonant toward that of the vowel. A further move in this direction is a consonant endowed with the distinctive features of tenseness and voicing, such as /dᶜ/ in some languages of India.

Normally, the toal energy of a vowel increases along with the concentration of energy (compactness), but in a tense vowel, as compared with the corresponding lax vowel, the total energy increases, whereas the concentration of energy decreases. This reversal separates the tense vowels from the vocalic optimum.

---

[1] K. Bouda, "Lateral und Sibilant," *Zeitshrift für Phonetik*, I (1947).

While reducing their time, the checked consonants increase their energy and thus attenuate the consonantal optimum. If a language possesses the two oppositions, checked/unchecked and tense/lax, then the optimal consonant, lax and unchecked, is opposed by two phonemes, the one checked (glottalized), the other tense. Furthermore, a double attenuation of the consonantal optimum may be presented by the rare combination of two distinctive features, tense and checked, within one and the same phoneme, such as the Avar /K'/.

Thus, all the inherent distinctive features actually rest upon two axes. On the one hand, the oppositions bearing upon the *sonority axis* display various fissions and attenuations of the primary contrast between the optimal consonant and the optimal vowel and thus give rise to more minute and specific distinctions. On the other hand, those oppositions that involve the *tonality axis*, perpendicular to the sonority axis, emerge originally as the counterpart and corollary of the contrast, "optimal vowel vs. optimal consonant" and, subsequently, as the corollary of the opposition, "optimal, compact vowel vs. attenuated, diffuse vowel" or "optimal, diffuse consonant vs. attenuated, compact consonant."

4.2   THE DICHOTOMOUS SCALE

In their recent, quite autonomous development, phonemic analysis and the mathematical theory of communication have arrived at fundamentally similar and mutually complementary conclusions, making possible a most productive cooperation.[2] Any spoken

---

[2] For procedures of the communication theory utilizable in phonemic analysis, see especially C. E. Shannon and W. Weaver, *The Mathematical Theory of Communication* (Urbana, 1949); C. E. Shannon, "The Redundancy of English," *Cybernetics*, Transactions of the Seventh Conference (New York, 1951); D. M. Mackay, "In Search of Basic Symbols," *Cybernetics*, Transactions of the Eighth Conference (New York, 1952); D. Gabor, "Lectures on Communication Theory," M.I.T., Research Laboratory of Electronics, *Report*, No. 238 (1953); E. C. Cherry, *Human Communication* (New York and London, 1957). Cf. I. Pollack, "Assimilation of Sequentially Encoded Information," *American Journal of Psychology*, LXVI (1953).

message presents the listener with two complementary alignments of information: on the one hand, the chain of phonemes yields sequentially encoded information; on the other hand, every phoneme is composed of several distinctive features. The totality of these features is the minimum number of binary selections necessary for the specification of the phoneme. In reducing the phonemic information contained in the sequence to the smallest number of alternatives, we find the most economical and consequently the optimal solution: the minimum number of the simplest operations that would suffice to encode and decode the whole message. When analyzing a given language into its ultimate constituents, we seek the smallest set of distinctive oppositions which allows the identification of each phoneme in the messages framed in this language. This task requires the isolation of distinctive features from concurrent or adjoining redundant features.

If, in a language, one and the same phoneme is implemented as a palatal stop before /i/, as a postalveolar affricate before /e/, and as a velar stop in all other positions, the invariant must be determined as a compact (forward flanged) consonant, distinct from the diffuse (backward flanged) consonants /p/ and /t/ of the same language. While, in such a case, the redundant features are condtitioned by the diverse distinctive features of the following phoneme, a striking example of redundant features linked to concurrent distinctive features may be found in the French consonantal pattern. Here, the compactness of the consonant is implemented by a velar articulation when lumped with plosiveness in /k/ and /g/, by a palatal articulation when lumped with nasality in /ɲ/, and by a postalveolar articulation when lumped with constrictiveness in /ʃ/ and /ʒ/.

Such a delimitation of distinctive and redundant features not only permits an identification of all the phonemes involved but is the unique solution, since any different analysis of these five phonemes deviates from the optimal solution. The fifteen French consonant phonemes under consideration require only five binary decisions: nasal/oral, and if oral then continuant/discontinuous, and tense/lax; compact/diffuse, and if diffuse then grave/acute. Each French consonant contains from two (compact nasal) to five distinctive features. If one deems the point of articulation distinctive, and the difference between constrictive and stop redundant, then the six French voiceless consonants— velar /k/, postalveolar /ʃ/, alveolar /s/, dental /t/, labiodental /f/, and bilabial /p/[3]—would require for their identification fifteen distinctions instead of three, according to the elementary mathematical formula cited by Twaddell (1935): "If x is the maximum number of significant phonological differentiations within a given articulatory range in a language, then $2x = n(n-1)$, where n is the maximum number of phonemes in that range." Some of the minute differences in the point of articulation have, moreover, the disadvantage of being acoustically hardly recognizable by themselves. Finally, such distinctions as /s/ vs. /f/ and /t/ vs. /p/ present an identical differential criterion, namely the opposition of an acute and grave consonant, based on the same difference in the size and shape of the mouth resonator. Again /k/ vs. /t/ and /ʃ/ vs. /s/ display (acoustically as well as genetically) one and the same opposition, based on a parallel relation of the front and back resonators, so that an attempt to operate with the two pairs of phonemes as if they were distinguished by two separate features introduces superfluous redundancies.

The reduction of language into distinctive features must be consistent. If, for instance, the Czech /l/, which can occur in identical positions with each of the 32 other phonemes of the language, is declared "an unanalyzable distinctive unit," its distinction from the other 32 phonemes would require 32 unanalyzable relations, whereas through the dissolution of the /l/ bundle into three features—vocalic, consonantal and continuous—its relation to all the other phonemes of the pattern is reduced to three binary selections.

The maximum elimination of redundancies and the minimum number of distinctive alternatives is a principle that permits an affirmative answer to the focal question raised by Chao in 1934 as to whether the task

of breaking down a given language into its ultimate components yields a unique solution.[4] Not less crucial is his later question (1954), whether the dichotomous scale is a pivotal principle which the analyzer can profitably impose upon the linguistic code, or whether this scale is inherent in the structure of language.[5] There are several weighty arguments in favor of the latter solution.

First, a system of distinctive features based on a mutually implicating relation between the terms of each binary opposition is the optimal code, and it is unwarranted to assume that the speech participants use a more complicated and less economic set of differential criteria in their encoding and decoding operations. Recent experiments have disclosed that multidimensional auditory displays are most easily learned and perceived when "binary coded."[6]

Second, the phonemic code is acquired in the earliest years of childhood and, as psychology reveals, in a child's mind the pair is anterior to isolated objects.[7] The binary opposition is a child's first logical operation. Both opposites arise simultaneously and force the infant to choose one and to suppress the other of the two alternatives.

Third, almost all of the distinctive features show an unquestionably dichotomous structure on their acoustical and, correspondingly, on their motor level. Among the inherent features, only the vocalic distinction compact/diffuse often presents a higher number of terms, mostly three. For instance, /æ/ is to /e/ as /e/ is to /i/: the geometric mean /e/ is noncompact in relation to /æ/ and nondiffuse in relation to /i/. Psychological experiments that obtained /e/ through the

---

[3] See L. E. Armstrong, *The Phonetics of French* (London, 1932).

[4] Y. R. Chao, "The Nonuniqueness of Phonemic Solution of Phonetic Systems," Academia Sinica, Institute of History and Philology, *Bulletin*, IV (Shanghai, 1934).

[5] Y. R. Chao, review of Jakobson, Fant, Halle, *Preliminaries ...*, in *Romance Philology*, VIII (1954).

[6] I. Pollack and L. Ficks, "Information of Elementary Multidimensional Auditory Displays," *Journal of the Acoustical Society of America*, XXVI (1954).

[7] See H. Wallon, *Les origines de la pensée chez l'enfant*, I (Paris, 1945). For the pivotal role of gradual binary fissions in child development, cf. T. Parsons and R. F. Bales, *Family, Socialization, and Interaction Process* (Glencoe, 1955).

mixture of /æ/ and /i/ confirm the peculiar structure of this vocalic feature.[8] Parallel experiments in mixing vowels situated on the tonality axis showed that grave and acute vowels, when sounded simultaneously, are not perceived as a single vowel: /u/ and /i/ do not merge into /y/. The feature grave/acute is a patently binary opposition. Since the second formant in /y/ is higher than in /u/ and lower than in /i/, and since in cavity length /y/ occupies a middle position in relation to /u/, with the longest, and /i/, with the shortest resonator, attempts were made to get along with one dimension for all three vowels.[9] But the chief genetic distinction is cardinally different: the disparity in the size of the lip orifice is primarily responsible for the opposition /y/ vs. /i/, and the disparity in the size and shape of the resonator itself for the opposition /y/ vs. /u/. On the acoustical level, the distinction of grave from acute in vowels is manifested in the relative proximity of the first and second formants, which has as its consequence a very striking weakening of the upper formants, whereas the distinction of flat from nonflat is mainly due to a lowering in the second formant.[10]

Similarly, the effort to project the vocalic oppositions tense/lax and compact/diffuse upon one and the same line is hampered by the salient difference between their physical essences,[11] by the dissimilar parts they play in linguistic structure, and by the considerable

disadvantages which their unidimensional treatment imposes upon the analysis.

Finally, the application of the dichotomous scale makes the stratified structure of phonemic patterns, their governing laws of implication, and the conclusive typology of languages so transparent that the inherence of this scale in the linguistic system is quite manifest.

4.3 THE SPATIO-TEMPORAL PATTERN OF PHONEMIC OPERATIONS

If there is a difference between the linguistic patterns of two speech communities, interlocution between members of the two communities demands an adjustment of the listener to the speaker and/or of the speaker to the listener. This adjustment may involve all the aspects of language or only a few of them. Sometimes the phonemic code is the only one affected. Both on the listener's and on the speaker's side there are different degrees of this adjustment process, neatly called *code switching* by the communication engineers. The receiver, trying to understand the sender, and/or the sender, in trying to make himself understood, concentrate their attention on the common core of their codes. A higher degree of adjustment apears in the effort to overcome the phonemic differences by switching rules, which increase the intelligibility of the message for its addressee. Having found these clues, the interlocutor may try to use them not only as a listener, but also in a more active manner, by adapting his own utterances to the pattern of his addressee.

The phonemic adjustment may cover the whole lexical stock, or the imitation of the neighbor's phonemic code may be confined to a certain set of words directly borrowed from the neighbor or at least particularly stamped by his use of them. Whatever the adjustments are, they help the speaker to increase the radius of communication, and if often practiced, they are likely to enter into his everyday language. Under favorable circumstances they may subsequently infiltrate into the general use of the speech community, either as a particular speech fashion or as a new pattern fully substituted for the former norm. Interdialectal communication and its influence on intradialectal communication

---

[8] See K. Huber, "Die Vokalmischung und das Qualitätensystem der Vokale," *Archiv für Psychologie*, XCI (1934).

[9] See, e.g., P. Delattre, "The Physiological Interpretation of Sound Spectrograms." *PMLA*, LXVI (1951).

[10] Cf. Jakobson, Fant, Halle, *Preliminaries . . .*, p. 48; H. K. Dunn, "The Calculation of Vowel Resonances, and an Electrical Vocal Tract," *Journal of the Acoustical Society of America*, XXII (1950), 650; K. N. Stevens and A. S. House, "Development of a Quantitative Description of Vowel Articulation," *ibidem*, XXVII (1955); detailed data are presented by Halle and Fant in the first two volumes of the series *Description and Analysis of Contemporary Standard Russian* (The Hague: Mouton & Co., 1959, 1960).

[11] See especially L. Barczinski and E. Thienhaus, "Klangspektren und Lautstärke deutscher Sprachlaute," *Archives néerlandaises de phonétique expérimentale*, XI (1935).

must be analyzed from a linguistic and, particularly, from a phonemic point of view.[12]

The problem of bridging space stops neither at the borders of distant and highly differentiated dialects, nor at the boundaries of cognate or even unrelated languages. Mediators, more or less bilingual, adapt themselves to the foreign phonemic code. Their prestige grows with the widening radius of their audience and may further a diffusion of their innovations among their monolingual tribesmen.

Not only the interdialectal, but also the interlingual adjustment may affect the phonemic code without limitation to borrowed words or even without any lexical borrowing. In all parts of the world, linguists have been surprised, as Sapir confesses, to observe "the remarkable fact that distinctive phonetic features tend to be distributed over wide areas regardless of the vocabularies and structures of the languages involved."[13] This far-reaching phenomenon still awaits systematic mapping and study in connection with the equally urgent inquiry into the typology of phonemic patterns.

The other possibility of phonemic adjustments to a different dialect or foreign language is a partial or total preservation of its phonemic structure in borrowed words. As noted repeatedly in the phonemic literature and closely examined by Fries and Pike, "the speech of monolingual natives of some languages is comprised of more than one phonemic system."[14] Such a coexistence of two systems within one language is due either to a phonemic difference between the original vocabulary and unassimilated loanwords, or to the use of two patterns, one native and the other imitative, as different styles of speech. Thus, spatial phenomena, namely interdialectual or interlingual isoglosses, especially isophones, may be projected into the framework of a single dialect, individual or social.

The same statement, *mutatis mutandis*, can be made about the time factor in language, particularly in the phonemic field. Any sound change, at its proceeding, is a synchronic fact. Both the start and the finish of a change coexist for a certain length of time. If the change differentiates the younger generation from the older, there is always some intercourse between the two generations, and the receiver belonging to one is accustomed to recode messages from a sender of the other. Furthermore, the initial and the final stage may co-occur in the use of one and the same generation as two stylistic levels: on the one hand, a more conservative and solemn, on the other, a more fashionable way of talking. Thus, synchronic analysis most encompass linguistic changes, and vice versa, linguistic changes may be comprehended only in the light of synchronic analysis.

The decisive factor in phonemic changes and in the diffusion of phonemic phenomena is the shift in the code. The interpretation of events in time and space is primarily concerned with the question: in what respect is the structure of the code affected by such shifts? The motor and physical aspects of these innovations cannot be treated as self-sufficient agents, but must be subordinated to the strictly linguistic analysis of their role in the coding system.

SELECTED BIBLIOGRAPHY

A.   Studies

Alarcos-Llorach, E. *Fonología Española*, I: Fonología general. Madrid, 1954.

Andrade, M. J. "Some Questions of Fact and Policy Concerning Phonemes." *Language*, XII (1936).

Avanesov, R. I. *Fonetika sovremennogo russkogo literaturnogo jazyka*. Moscow, 1956.

Axmanova, O. *Fonologija*. Moscow, 1954.

Bazell, C. E. "The Choice of Criteria in Structural Linguistics." *Word*, X (1954).

Bloch, B. "A Set of Postulates for Phonemic Analysis." *Language*, XXV (1948).

Bloomfield, L. *Language*. Chapters V–VIII. New York, 1933.

Buyssens, E. "Mise au point de quelques notions

---

[12] See "Results of the Conference of Anthropologists and Linguists," *Indiana Unversity Publications in Anthropology and Linguistics*, VIII (1953), 16 f., 36 ff.

[13] E. Sapir, "Language," *Selected Writings* (Berkeley and Los Angels, 1949), p. 25.

[14] C. C. Fries and K. L. Pike, "Coexistent Phonemic Systems," *Language*, XXV (1949).

fondamentales de la phonologie." *Cahiers Ferdinand de Saussure*, VIII (1949).

Chao, Y. R. "The Nonuniqueness of Phonemic Solutions of Phonetic Systems." Academia Sinica, Institute of History and Philology, *Bulletin*, IV. Shanghai, 1934.

Cherry, E. C., Halle, M., and Jakobson, R. "Toward the Logical Description of Languages in their Phonemic Aspect." *Language*, XXIX (1953).

Coseriu, E. and Vasques, W. *Para la unificacion de las sciencias fonicas*. Montevideo, 1953.

Dieth, E. *Vademecum der Phonetik*. Chapter III C. Bern, 1950.

Faddegon, B. "Phonetics and Phonology." *Meded. Kon. Nederl. Akad. Wetensch.*, Afd. Letterkunde, II (1938).

Fischer-Jørgensen, E. "Phonologie." *Archiv für vergleichende Phonetik*, V (1941); "On the Definition of Phoneme Categories on a Distributional Basis." *Acta Linguistica*, VII (1952).

Frei, H. "Langue, parole et différenciation." *Journal de Psychologie* (1952).

Fries, C. C. and Pike, K. L. "Coexistent Phonemic Systems." *Language*, XXV (1949).

de Groot, A. W. "Neutralisation d'oppositions." *Neophilologus*, XXV (1940).

Halle, M. "The Strategy of Phonemics." *Word*, X (1954).

Harris, Z. S. *Methods in Structural Linguistics*. Chicago, 1951; "From Phoneme to Morpheme." *Language*, XXXI (1955).

Hjelmslev, L. "Über die Beziehungen der Phonetik zur Sprachwissenschaft." *Archiv für vergleichende Phonetik*, II (1938).

Hockett, C. F. "A Manual of Phonology." *Indiana University Publications in Anthropology and Linguistics*, XI (1955).

Jakobson, R. "The Phonemic and Grammatical Aspects of Language in their Interrelations." *Actes du Sixième Congrés International des Linguistes*. (Paris, 1949).

———, Fant, C. G. M., and Halle, M. *Preliminaries to Speech Analysis*, third printing. Massachusetts Institute of Technology, Acoustics Laboratory, 1955.

Jones, D. *The Phoneme: Its Nature and Use*. Cambridge, 1950.

Juilland, A. G. "A Bibliography of Diachronic Phonemics." *Word*, IX (1953), 198–208.

Kořinek, J. M. *Úvod do jazykospytu*. Chapter II. Bratislava, 1948.

Kruisinga, E. "Fonetiek en fonologie." *Taal en Leven*, VI (1943).

v. Laziczius, J. "Probleme der Phonologie." *Ungarische Jahrbücher*, XV (1935).

Martinet, A. *Phonology as Functional Phonetics*. London, 1949; "Où en est la phonologie?" *Lingua*, I (1949).

Mattoso-Câmara, J. *Principios de Linguistica Geral*. Chapters I-II. Rio de Janeiro, 1944.

Pike, K. L. *Phonemics: A Technique for Reducing Languages to Writing*. Ann Arbor, 1947; *Tone Languages*. Ann Arbor, 1948; "Grammatical Prerequisites to Phonemic Analysis." *Word*, III (1947); "More on Grammatical Prerequisites." *Word*, VIII (1952); *Language in Relation to a Unified Theory of the Structure of Human Behavior*, II. Glendale, Calif., 1955.

Polak, M. "Fonetiek en fonologie." *Levende Talen* (1940).

Pos, H. J. "Phonologie en betekenisleer" *Mededelingen der Koninklijke Nederlandsche Akademie van Wetenschappen*, Afd. Letterkunde. NR, No. 13 (1938).

Sapir, E. *Selected Writings*. Berkeley and Los Angeles, 1949. Pp. 7–60.

Seidel, E. *Das Wesen der Phonologie*. Bucharest and Copenhagen, 1943.

Sotavalta, A. "Die Phonetik und ihre Beziehungen zu den Grenzwissenschaften." *Annales Academiae Scientiarum Fennicae*, XXXI, No. 3 (1936).

Stetson, R. H. *Motor Phonetics*. Amsterdam, 1951.

Swadesh, M. "The Phonemic Principle." *Language*, X (1934).

Trnka, B. "Určování fonému." *Acta Universitatis Carolinae*. Prague, 1954.

Trubetzkoy, N. *Principes de phonologie*. Paris, 1949. German text: "Grundzüge der Phonologie." *Travaux du Cercle Linguistique de Praque*, VII (1939).

Twaddell, W. F. "On Defining the Phoneme." Supplement to *Language*, XVI (1935); "Stetson's Model and the 'Supra-Segmental Phonemes'." *Language*, XXXI (1935).

van Wijk, N. *Phonologie: een hoofdstuk uit de structurele taalwetenschap*. The Hague, 1939.

Zwirner, E. "L'opposition phonologique et la variation des phonèmes." *Archiv für vergleichende Phonetik*, II (1938); "Phonologie und Phonetik." *Acta Linguistica*, I (1939).

B. Discussions

Akademija Nauk SSSR, Otdelenie literatury i jazyka, *Izvestija*, XI (1952) and XII (1953)—Diskussija po voprosam fonologii.

International Congresses of Phonetic Sciences, *Proceedings*, I–III (1933, 1935, 1938).

Journal of the Acoustical Society of America, XXII (1950)—Proceedings of the Speech Communication Conference at MIT; XXIV

(1952)—Conference on Speech Analysis.

Travaux du Cercle Linguistique de Copenhague, V (1949)—Recherches structurales.

Travaux du Cercle Linguistique de Prague, IV (1931)—Réunion phonologique internationale tenue à Prague; VIII (1939)—Etudes phonologiques, dédiées a la mémoire de N. S. Trubetzkoy.

ERIC H. LENNEBERG

39 Lenneberg has been working in the general area of psycholinguistics with special emphasis on the biological aspects and pathological cases of language acquisition and language development. He makes use of current work on generative grammar. This paper is a case report on an eight-year-old boy with a "congenital disability for the acquisition of motor speech skills (anarthria) which, however, has not impaired his ability to learn to understand language." The boy's crying and laughter sounded normal. He did not produce spontaneous words, but learned to imitate (repeat) a few words which were barely intelligible. But he could obviously understand and follow tape-recorded instructions which were transmitted to him through earphones without being able to see the examiner. Some of the questions and instructions were quite complex. An organic defect prevented this patient, like many others, from the acquisition of the motor skill necessary for *speaking* the language, but "evidence was presented for the acquisition of grammatical skills as required for a complete understanding of language." Lenneberg concludes that babbling and imitation are not essential in language acquisition and that speaking a language is not crucial for the development of *understanding*. Following Chomsky and Miller, he emphasizes the generative aspect. "Knowing a natural language is dependent upon the *acquisition of a single set of organizing principles*."

Lenneberg also edited the volume, *New Directions in the Study of Language* (Massachusetts Institute of Technology Press, 1964), and his recent most interesting book is *Biological Foundations of Language*, with appendices by Noam Chomsky and Otto Marx (John Wiley & Sons, Inc., 1967).

A. B. A.

UNDERSTANDING LANGUAGE WITHOUT ABILITY TO SPEAK: A CASE REPORT

Infants' random babbling is generally con-

Reprinted from Journal of Abnormal and Social Psychology 65.419–425 (1962) by permission of the author and the American Psychological Association.

This paper was written while the author was a National Institute of Mental Health Career Investigator (Grant M-2921).

sidered to play a major—by some, an essential—role in the acquisition and development of language. In fact, many psychologists believe that the main reason for the failure of mammals other than man to learn to speak or even to bring their vocalizations under new and varied stimulus control is due to their scanty random vocalizations. Recently it was discovered that dolphins make a great variety of vocal tract produced noises and, to be sure, the hope was soon expressed that these animals may with proper training learn to converse with their trainers in English. Incidentally, this hope was shared by Dr. Doolittle, Hugh Lofting's charming literary creation.

Our understanding of human behavior is often greatly enlightened by careful investigations of clinical aberrations and in many instances disease or congenital abnormalities provide conditions that may replace the crucial experiments on children that our superego forbids us to plan and perform. No psychological theory on verbal behavior can be successful unless it takes into consideration and accounts for the pathological variations that may be observed clinically. In the present paper I will present the case of a child who is typical of a large group of children with deficits in their motor execution of language skills but who can learn to understand language even in the total absence of articulation. This and similar clinical material forces us to review our theoretical formulations concerning the role of babbling and echoic responses in the acquisition of language and to review once more the relationship between understanding and speaking a language.

CASE REPORT

This is an 8-year-old boy who has a congenital disability for the acquisition of motor speech skills (anarthria) which, however, has not impaired his ability to learn to understand language.

Medical history
The mother, at the time of subject's birth, was a para I, gravida II white housewife who had enjoyed good health. Throughout her second pregancy she suffered from a mild chronic bronchitis but gestation was otherwise unremarkable. The baby was born 2 weeks prematurely by dates. Delivery was spontaneous, preceded by 6 hours of labor though the birth was precipitous. No other complications were recorded. The birth weight was 4 pounds 10 ounces. Good respiration was established within half a minute at which time the baby cried vigorously. He had good color and was at no time cyanotic or jaundiced. The following abnormalities were noted at birth: he had bilateral club feet (talipes

equino varus on left and metatarsus varus on right) and a fine white line in a sagittal direction on the upper lip. Otherwise the physical examination was reported to be within normal limits. The mother was told that the placenta had been too small to nourish the fetus adequately but no pathological report is available. The baby was placed in an incubator for 2 weeks and remained in the newborn nursery at the hospital for 2 months. He sat at 9 months and walked only at 2 years of age, earlier development having been handicapped by casts and corrective shoes. He has never been heard to use any words. He has had the usual complement of inoculations and there have been no severe diseases. At age 2 he fell on his head and required two stitches; the incident had no sequelae. The first pediatric examination recorded in the hospital chart (age 2 years) revealed anomalies of the eyes in addition to the anomalies of feet and lip. There was a right ptosis and a convergent strabismus.

Family history
The family history is noncontributory. The subject is the second of three children: both siblings are intelligent and well. The mother is now divorced and lives with the subject's grandmother. A home visit revealed a warm and socially adequate climate.

Physical and laboratory examinations
When first seen by the author the child had been brought to a neurological service with a chief complaint of failure to develop speech. He was then 3 years and 9 months, of markedly small stature but with a head circumference normal for his chronological age (49.6 centimeters). Anomalies of the eyes had been corrected surgically. He had single palmar creases in both hands but no other mongoloid stigmata. The only other abnormal finding on examination was an enlarged heart; no murmurs were heard. His oral cavity was of normal configuration and he had no difficulties in chewing, swallowing, sucking, blowing, or licking. Laryngoscopy was negative. On radiological evidence his bone age was 2:8 according to Todd's standards. A skull series was normal. All laboratory tests were negative, and there were no signs of

hypothyroidism or inborn errors of metabolism. An electroencephalogram was read as nondiagnostic though it was noted that activity in the right temporal area was less rhythmic than in the left.

Psychological tests

Tests were performed at 4, 5, and 8 years. Merrill-Palmer, WISC, Bender Visual Motor Gestalt, and Leiter International Performance tests were used, the examinations being administered by three different psychologists and at two different clinics. The subject always related easily to the examiner and gave no signs of emotional disturbance or psychiatric disease. IQ's were consistently in the 72–83 range but might have been consistently biased by the subject's inability to express himself verbally. He always gives an alert impression, reacts quickly to verbal instructions, and has always shown an adequate concentration span with little signs of distractibility or hyperactivity. At his most recent test no evidence of "organic" deficits was obtained although some "immaturity in his drawings" was noted. He is slightly retarded in his mental development but the deficit is definitely in the educable range and cannot explain his inability to speak.

Voice and speech

The child's crying and laughter have always sounded normal. He is also able to make other noises, for instance short cough-like grunts accompanying his pantomimed communications. While playing alone he will readily make noises that sound somewhat like Swiss yodeling (though he has never had any experience with these sounds!) and which do not resemble any kind of vocalization heard among normal American children. (Samples of these sounds are reproduced in a documentary film.) When the author first saw him he appeared to have some difficulty in bringing his voicing mechanism under voluntary control. For instance, he was unable to make the pointer of the VU meter in an Ampex tape recorder jump by emitting grunts into a microphone even though he was fully aware of the logical connection between sound and deflection of the pointer and was fascinated by it. He would hold on to the microphone and move his head and lips

toward it as if to prompt himself for the action; after a few futile attempts and with signs of rising frustration he would in desperation end up gesturing to the examiner's mouth inviting him to make the needle jump, or else simply resort to clapping his hands and accomplish his end this way. In recent years he seems to have learned to control his vocal apparatus to a greater extent. He has had speech training for a considerable length of time and can now repeat a few words after the speech therapist or his mother but the words are still barely intelligible and are never produced without the support from the speech correctionist or the mother (samples are reproduced in the film).

Some of the spontaneous sounds emitted by the patient at 4 years were analyzed spectrographically.[1] The spectrograms are grossly abnormal for a child of this age and resemble those of a neonate in a number of respects, such as the unsteadiness in the formant pattern, the intermittent bursts of nonharmonic overtones, and the almost random change in resonance distribution over the spectrum (Lenneberg, 1961). The spectrograms may be interpreted either as grossly immature or as evidence of a fixed central nervous system abnormality implicating the basic mechanisms for speech synergism.

From the patient's first visit to the clinic it has been obvious that he had a normal and adequate understanding of spoken language. He has been seen more than 20 times since then and the finding of full comprehension has been confirmed by neurologists, psychologists, speech therapists, medical residents, and other hospital personnel. A number of tape recordings have been made of interviews including a visit to the patient's home. Most of the examinations were done without the presence of his mother. At one time a short series of instructions were tape recorded and

---

[1] A 5-page table giving a transcript of commands, questions, and statements with classification of subject's response and a figure showing frequency cycles per second have been deposited with the American Documentation Institute. Order Document No. 7317 from ADI Auxiliary Publications Project, Photoduplication Service, Library of Congress; Washington 25, D. C., remitting in advance $2.50 for microfilm or $6.25 for photocopies. Make checks payable to: Chief, Photoduplication Service, Library of Congress.

TABLE 1.   Number of subject's correct, indecisive, and incorrect responses.

| Type of response required | Correct | | Indecisive | | Incorrect | | |
	No cue possible	Cue possible or certain	No cue possible	Cue possible or certain	No cue possible	Cue possible or certain	Total
Action	19	5	0	0	2	2	28
Yes-No nodding	2	11	0	3	0	1	17
Total	21	16	0	3	2	3	45

transmitted to the patient through earphones. He followed the instructions without being able to see the examiner.

Demonstration film
At age 8 years his capacity to comprehend was fully documented in a 16-millimeter sound film which is publicly available.[2] The film was not rehearsed and the examiner had been known to the patient by sight only. The demonstration includes the following items: ability to chew, swallow, and suck; sounds emitted while playing at age 4; tape recordings of mother's "conversation" with subject, recorded during a home visit; following commands and answering questions by nodding; a short story is told followed by questions on it which are couched in complex grammatical constructions such as the passive voice.

Interpretation
It is tempting to explain the patient's responses to verbal instructions by extralinguistic means. Perhaps he is merely responding to visual cues given by the examiner and has, in fact, not learned to understand English! Could children with his type of abnormality develop perceptual skills such as were observed in von Osten's famous horse, der kluge Hans, who supposedly could stamp his hoof in response to questions posed to him in German, but who, upon close examination by the psychologist Pfungst, had merely learned to observe the questioner, picking up minute motor cues related to posture and respiratory patterns which signaled to him whether to stop or to continue to stamp his

hoof? There is direct evidence against this hypothesis. The child described can react to tape-recorded instructions in the absence of any observer. Further, his responses do not merely consist of nodding but also of doing things which could under no circumstance be conveyed by inadvertent motor cues. In the film which documents the case, it is clear that the child frequently follows commands without looking at the examiner. Out of the 45 responses only 3 times was there vacillation between correct and incorrect answers and the last answer in each case is correct. On the other hand, there was no hesitation in the 3 instances when incorrect answers were given. There is no reason to assume that this child has superhuman ability to respond to visual cues instead of assuming that he has learned what every other child of his age has learned, namely, to understand English. Table 1 summarizes the child's performance. It is the result of a panel of three judges who scrutinized the film, viewing each command and its execution individually and with as many repetitions as was necessary in order to determine by unanimous agreement whether there was any likelihood of extralinguistic cuing.

Finally, we must consider the possibility that this patient had no understanding of syntactic connections but merely responded to key words in the commands and questions. This possibility is extremely unlikely in the face of his understanding of such sentences as "Take the block and put it on the bottle." "Is it time to eat breakfast now?" "Was the black cat fed by the nice lady?"

Diagnosis
The hospital's clinical diagnosis is multiple congenital anomalies, which, however, is a

---

[2] *The Acquisition of Language in a Speechless Child*, 16-millimeter sound film. Running time 18 minutes, distributed by Psychological Cinema Register, Pennsylvania State University.

wastebasket classification and of no heuristic value. Certainly it does not explain the absence of motor speech. The two most common causes for this deficit, peripheral deafness and severe emotional disturbance, may be readily ruled out on clinical evidence. Nor may we assume that the patient's mental retardation is a sufficient cause since the degree of deficiency revealed in his psychological tests is not ordinarily accompanied by any marked speech deficit. Patients with an IQ as low as 25 to 35 have a wide repertoire of sounds and frequently use a vocabulary of 50 or more words. Some authorities would classify this patient as having congenital or developmental motor aphasia. I am not in favor of such a classification on terminological grounds. Aphasia has come to designate loss of speech in persons who had been fluent before the onset of disease or trauma. The condition occurs in children (Guttmann, 1942) as well as in adults and presents a symptomatology that is distinct from any developmental condition. However, the most important reason for rejecting the term aphasia for cases such as described here is that aphasia has traditionally been applied to cortical and subcortical lesions. The present case, on the other hand, gives every indication of an abnormality on a lower level, probably mesencephalic, because of the association with the ocular abnormalities and the discoordination as seen in the spectrograms. The term congenital anarthria better characterizes the condition. Psychological tests make cortical or subcortical damage also unlikely and his excellent understanding of language supports this view.

DISCUSSION

Failure to learn to understand despite babbling and imitative facility

The case reported makes it clear that hearing oneself babble is not a necessary factor in the acquisition of understanding; apparently, hearing oneself babble is also not a sufficient factor. In a language acquisition study on home-raised mongoloid children (research in progress) I have gathered empirical evidence that these children are excellent imitators who babble abundantly and freely. In all cases they have a speaking command of at least single word utterances; yet their understanding of complex commands and questions (such as used in the demonstration film) is frequently defective (usually if their IQ is about 50 or below). Here the vocal play is present and motivation is provided through interaction with parents, but it does not enable these children to overcome their inborn cerebral deficit.

Relationship between speaking and understanding

We must now pose the problem: if the secondary reinforcement provided by hearing oneself babble is neither necessary nor sufficient for an acquisition of understanding of language, could learning to speak be an entirely independent task, justifying a theory that applies to it alone, but not to the learning of understanding? We will see that the answer to this question is a qualified *no*.

The case presented here—by no means unique—is particularly dramatic because of the vast discrepancy between understanding and speaking; a similar phenomenon in more attenuated form is extremely common. Understanding normally precedes speaking by several weeks or even months. The discrepancy is regularly increased in literally all types of developmental speech disorders and is best illustrated in a condition known in the profession as Delayed Speech. Pertinent are also those children who have structural deformities in the oral cavity or pharynx and who produce unintelligible speech for years— sometimes throughout life—without the slightest impairment of understanding. Congenitally deaf children also learn to comprehend language in the absence of vocal skills. Understanding in all of these circumstances is definitely prior to and in that sense independent from speaking.

However, there is no clear evidence that speaking is ever present in the absence of understanding. Speaking is to be understood here as the production of utterances that are bona fide examples of a natural language (such as English) with presumptive evidence of autonomous composition of grammatically acceptable sentences. An empirical test of speaking without understanding might be as follows: a child acquires nothing but words that have no meaning to him (by blind imitation) and learns the formal principles governing the generation of sentences. He will now utter sentences out of context and irrelevant to situations by established common sense standards; he would also have to be demonstrably incapable ever to respond appropriately to commands formulated in natural language. My assertion is that such a condition has never been described as a congenital, developmental problem (Mark, 1962). (Adventitious conditions such as sensory aphasia in the adult are problems in *partial loss*, not *partial acquisition* of language and are therefore not relevant to this discussion. Nor could case reports of psychotic children be adduced reliably because even if their utterances are primarily echolalic, there are usually indications that the child does understand, at least at times, what is said to him. In fact, this is usually the basis of the therapy given them.) It is thus likely that the vocal production of language is dependent upon the understanding of language but not vice versa. Though there is no conclusive proof of this hypothesis, there are theoretical considerations that make this likely. In order to make this latter point clear, a few general remarks on the nature of grammar are indispensable. My discussion will lean heavily on Chomsky's (1957) and Chomsky and Miller's (1962) work.

Wherever the word *imitation* is used in connection with language-learning it is assumed that subjects learn more than passive mirroring of sentences heard. The novel creation of sentences is a universally accepted fact. At first it was thought that this phenomenon could be accounted for by postulating that grammar simply reflected transitional probabilities between words. In this model the learning of grammar was thought to be like the learning of probabilities. Such learning has been demonstrated to occur for a great many mammals. If this model were acceptable, a child's exposure to certain contingencies should enable him to learn grammar in the absence of "understanding" the relationship between words. Chomsky has offered formal proof against left-to-right probabilistic models, and has shown how a different model can overcome some of the basic difficulties encountered by Markovian grammars. We shall not concern ourselves here with the

mathematical detail but shall merely demonstrate by a few examples (most of them suggested by Chomsky) that grammar simply cannot be explained in terms of learned sequential contingencies, and that therefore the understanding and producing of sentences cannot be equated with probability learning.

Consider the following two strings of words, (*a*) colorless green ideas sleep furiously, (*b*) furiously sleep ideas green colorless. In terms of transitional probabilities they are indistinguishable. Both sentences can only occur in a zero order of approximation to English. However, we can discriminate between them from the point of view of grammaticality. Sentence *a* strikes us as a possible sentence, whereas *b* does not. The difference between *a* and *b* could not possibly be due to association by contiguity for obvious reasons (Miller, Galanter, and Pribram, 1960). Nor is the sequence of form class markers -*less*, -*s*, -*ly* the hallmark of grammaticalness as shown by the sentence, (*c*) friendly young dogs seem harmless, which is grammatical though it reverses the order of the markers.

In order to account for the difference in our perception of *a* and *b* we might try to see whether sequential contingencies do exist, but instead of on the level of words, on the level of parts of speech (actually proposed by Jenkins and Palermo, 1961). If this were so the essence of the transitional probability model would be saved and the principal underlying the formation of sentences would still be simple enough to allow of the possibility of speaking without understanding. Unfortunately this model is no more successful in accounting for "sentencehood" than any other Markovian device. If we compare the strings, (*d*) occasionally call warfare useless, (*e*) useless warfare call occasionally, we find that now *d* is perceived as more grammatical than *e* though the order of parts of speech in *d* is that of *b* above which we rejected as less grammatical. This example shows that the traditional categorization in terms of parts of speech is certainly not successful in reinstating a Markovian model.[3]

---

[3] Nor is there any hope that eventually more efficient categories might be discovered since Chomsky's (1957) criticism is leveled against all finite state sentence generating devices. Compare his argument concerning mirror-image languages, and Miller's (1960) argument.

Mowrer (1960) has proposed that simple contiguity of words is sufficient explanation for the complex meaning that is conveyed by a sentence. Osgood (1957) on the other hand believes that grammatical order can be set aside by motivational factors and that with an increase of motivation word order would correlate with order of importance of words. Doubt is cast on both views, however, by comparison of sentences such as, (f) the fox chases the dog, (g) the dog chases the fox, which clearly make either position untenable. A child whose task it is to learn to produce sentences such as f and g in the appropriate physical environment must necessarily learn some principal of concatenation which goes *beyond* recognition of contiguity. It would be tempting to maintain that the principle to be learned is something like "First noun phrase is the actor or subject in a sentence." Yet, the patterning involved must be more complex and in a sense more abstract still, for even a preschool child would understand the sentence, (h) the fox is chased by the dog, as belonging to g and not to f. To explain this phenomenon we would now have to postulate that in addition to the principle above, the child would also have to learn that the presence of the morphemes *is, -ed, by* signals a reversal of the original principle. But sentence (i) the fox is interested by virtue of his nature in chasing the dog, eliminates this possibility because this sentence is understood as similar in meaning to f instead of g despite the presence of morphemes *is, -ed, by* occurring in essentially the same sequential order as in h. In other words, if we must learn to compose sentences that conform to English grammar, we can only learn to apply the structural principles of sentence formation by first learning to understand and to group sentences in accordance with similarity or differences in meaning. It is not possible to explain the grammatical phenomena demonstrated in the test sentences above by assuming that the entire sentence is in one way or another associated with the complex natural situation to which it refers. Sentences without any referential meaning such as, (i) A v's C, (k) C v's A, (l) C is v'ed by A, (m) A is v'ed by C, can easily be grouped in terms of similarity and dissimilarity of meaning. Therefore, the word *meaning* in this context refers to

grammatical understanding and not to an association between a symbol and a physical stimulus.

Obviously, we do not yet have a satisfactory model that might explain how grammar is learned. All we can say is that a child learns to produce novel sentences after hearing a number of utterances which were produced by formal laws of generation in addition to a number of other determining factors: he must be able to abstract the formal laws through observation (or be equipped to accept sentences as an input and recognize invariant patterns of complex relationship) before he can apply them to the production of new sentences. It is particularly important to realize that what the child learns during acquisition of grammar is the peculiar formal relationship that obtains between a number of different grammatical patterns, i.e., the relationship between active-passive, declarative-interrogative-negative, and many other similar relationships called *rules of transformation* (Chomsky, 1957; Harris, 1957). It is this latter ability—and only this—that enables any speaker of English to group the sentences f through i according to similarity in meaning. The psychological process involved here is more similar to the operation by which we know that:

$$w \left(\sqrt{w} \times \sqrt{w} \right)$$

and

$$\frac{w^6}{w^4}$$

can both be represented by w^2 than to an operation by which we know that the symbol S_4 is next in line to be generated after a train of symbols S_1, S_2, S_3, has been produced. This point is illustrated by Chomsky's examples of structural ambiguity. There are rules of transformations which convert sentences of the form (n) one visits relatives, (o) relatives are visiting, into a phrase, (p) visiting relatives. Because of the two different transformational origins this phrase is ambiguous and, when used in a sentence, may render that entire sentence ambiguous: (q) visiting relatives can be a nuisance.

The conclusion of this discussion is that *knowing a language* may be, and ordinarily is, manifested by two distinct behavioral manifestations: understanding and speaking. Upon careful analysis, however, both of these manifestations depend upon the application and use of a single set of grammatical rules; in the case of understanding, the rules are applied to the analysis, i.e., processing and organizing of input data; in the case of speaking, the same rules are applied to the organization of output data or responses. In the process of language-learning, the acquisition of grammatical rules must occur first in connection with analysing incoming sentences; then with producing outgoing sentences. The most important point here is, however, that *knowing* a natural language is dependent upon the *acquisition of a single set of organizing principles* and that this set of principles is merely reflected in understanding and speaking but is not identical with these skills.

SUMMARY

A case was presented, typical of a larger category of patients, where an organic defect prevented the acquisition of the motor skill necessary for *speaking a language*, but evidence was presented for the acquisition of grammatical skills as required for a complete *understanding of language*. Theories on the acquisition of speech and language must account for both motor and grammatical skills. Present theories assert that babbling, hearing oneself vocalize, and imitation are the cornerstones of speech development. These phenomena primarily relate to the development of the motor skills involved which, however, never develop in isolation, i.e., without simultaneous acquisition of grammatical skills. The case presented together with the language deficit in certain Mongoloids clearly shows that babbling, hearing oneself talk, and imitation are neither sufficient nor necessary factors in the acquisition of grammar, and since the motor skills alone are never shaped into "speaking without grammar," i.e., parroting without understanding, it is concluded that the present theories are inadequate.

REFERENCES

Chomsky, N. *Syntactic Structures*. The Hague: Mouton, 1957.

———, and Miller, G. A. "Introduction to the Formal Analysis of Natural Languages." In D. Luce, E. Galanter, and R. Bush, eds., *Mathematical Psychology*. In R. D. Luce, R. R. Bush, and E. Galanter, eds. *Handbook of Mathematical Psychology*, Volume II. New York and London, John Wiley & Sons, 1963, 269–321.

Guttmann, E. "Aphasia in Children." *Brain*, LXV, (1942), 205–19.

Harris, Z. S. "Co-occurrence and Transformation in Linguistic Structure." *Language*, XXXIII (1957), 283–340.

Jenkins, J. J., and Palermo, D. S. "Mediation Processes and the Acquisition of Linguistic Structure." Paper read at SSRC conference in Cambridge, Massachusetts, October 1961.

Lenneberg, E. H. "Speech as a Motor Skill with Special Reference to Nonaphasic Disorders." Paper read at SSRC conference in Cambridge, Massachusetts, October 1961.

Mark, H. J. "Elementary Thinking and the Classification of Behavior." *Science*, CXXXV 1962, 75–87.

Miller, G. A. "Plans for Speaking." In G. A. Miller, E. Galanter, and K. H. Pribram, eds., *Plans and the Structure of Behavior*. New York: Holt, Rinehart & Winston, Inc., 1960. pp. 139–58.

———, Galanter, E., and Pribram, K. H. *Plans and the Structure of Behavior*. New York: Holt, Rinehart & Winston, Inc., 1960.

Mowrer, O. H. *Learning Theory and the Symbolic Processes*. New York: John Wiley & Sons, Inc., 1960.

Osgood, C. E. "Motivational Dynamics of Language Behavior." In M. R. Jones, ed., *Nebraska Symposium on Motivation: 1957*. Lincoln: University of Nebraska Press, 1957. pp. 348–424.

40

This selection is taken from Ruth Weir's book *Language in the Crib* (Mouton, 1962). The book deals with "certain aspects of the language" (English) of her two-and-one-half year old son, Anthony, and attempts to study the child's language or his "idiolect" as a "self-contained system under special circumstances," i.e., his presleep monologues. These were also compared with his daytime language and the language of the surroundings. She recorded on tape those "half-dream soliloquies," as Roman Jakobson called them in his introductory chapter to this book, "Anthony's Contribution to Linguistic Theory," pp. 18–20, and she analyzed this material from the phonological, (pp. 28–68) morphological, (pp. 69–80) and syntactic (80–93) and lexical (93–100) points of view. She then added an interesting chapter on "Discourse Analysis" or the analysis of the paragraph (pp. 101–41), from which we drew our two selections (pp. 114–17, 121–23).

Weir recorded quite a few sets of utterances which she calls sequences. She finds three basic types of sequences which she calls *build-ups*, *break-downs*, and *completions*, all of which consist "of more than one unit of speech delimited by pauses."

An example for a build-up paragraph appears at the beginning of our first selection: *Daddy*# *Daddy bucket please*, etc. Break-down: *Anthony jump out again*# *Anthony jump*#, or: *Clock off* # *Clock* # *off* #. Completions: *Anthony take the*# *Take the book*#. Some aspects of "replacement sequences" are discussed in a recent study by Martin Braine "The Acquisition of Language in Infant and Child," in Carroll Reed, ed., *The Learning of Language* (forthcoming).

For a detailed review of *Language in the Crib*, see W. F. Leopold, *Language*, XL (April-June, 1964), 269–73; and Ursula Bellugi, *Harvard Educational Review*, XXXIV (1964), 332–34.

A. B. A.

PARAGRAPHS

Having tried to present each one of the language functions in separate examples, we now want to continue with longer and more complex paragraphs where there is usually an interplay of the various functions.

We can come back to our original example of a paragraph and try to analyze it:

(A)(1) *Daddy*
(2) *Daddy bucket please*
(3) *Another other book please*
(4) *Donkey*
(5) *Fix the donkey*
(6) *And the blue box and the big box*

Line (1) is a vocative, although the addressee

Reprinted from Ruth Weir, Language in the Crib (*The Hague: Mouton & Co., 1962*), 115–117, 121–123, *by permission of the publisher.*

is really not expected to respond. *Daddy* is repeated in line (2), still retaining its conative function but now the imperative is expanded by *bucket please*. This is a time in the child's life when he does use *please* fairly automatically in requests, unfortunately, a passing fancy. *Please* is repeated, but the vocative is omitted in line (3), the substitution item in the slot for *bucket* is now *book*, both containing the phonemes /b–k/, probably not accidentally. The noun phrase is now expanded by modifiers, *another other*, together referentially meaningless, but related to each other by one being included in the other. The "th" is the phoneme /d/, possibly part of the reason for the particular selection of these modifiers, as also reflected in line (5) where *donkey* again starts in /d/, the two consonants of the original *Daddy*. The choice of *donkey* is not accidental in other respects either: the first vowel is /A/, and not the also possible and elsewhere occurring /O/, followed by a nasal, the reverse of /A/ plus nasal of *another*. The second vowel is /I/, just like in *Daddy*. A new imperative, this time with the verb *fix* is in line (5) showing the primarily conative function of this paragraph, although the addressee, probably *Daddy*, is omitted. One more /d/, one of the favored consonants here, is added in *the*, making the line a non-elliptic sentence. Both /d/ and /n/ reappear in line (6) in *and the* twice, also serving as a conjunction exercise. The noun *box* now returns to the initial /b/ of *bucket* and *book*, repeated also in the modifiers *blue* and *big*. The final /ks/ of *fix* is mirrored twice in the same final cluster of *box*.

Let us now take a long sequence from the corpus which occurred in the middle of a tape, that is half-way after the child was put to bed and before he fell asleep. It presents a more complex picture and at the same time shows the various functions of language in different hierarchical arrangements:

(B)(1)   *That's office* (2×)
   (2)   *Look Sophie*
   (3)   *That Sophie*
   (4)   *Come last night*
   (5)   *Good boy*
   (6)   *Go for glasses*
   (7)   *Go for them*
   (8)   *Go to the top*
   (9)   *Go throw*
  (10)   *Go for blouse*
  (11)   *Pants*
  (12)   *Go for shoes*
  (13)   *Powder*
  (14)   *S'not dry*
  (15)   *Get powder on*
  (16)   *Shoe fixed* (2×)
  (17)   *And the shoe*
  (18)   *Some powder*
  (19)   *On the leg*
  (20)   *Anthony's leg*
  (21)   *Put in Daddy's legs*
  (22)   *Put some Mommy's legs*
  (23)   *Mommy's legs* (2×)
  (24)   *Mommy get some* (2×)
  (25)   *Soap*
  (26)   *Mommy took a shower*
  (27)   *Take some soap*
  (28)   *Down*

There seems to be little question that the first three lines of the sequence are related by sound play. The phonemic sequence /sÓfI/, phonetically [sófì], is repeated in every one of the first three lines. Except for the final /s/ in line (1), it is identical phonemically with line (3); syntactically they can be considered identical as well since the syntactic difference of *That Sophie* and *That's Sophie* is phonemically obliterated. Line (1) is said twice so that there is balance between the forms /sÓfIs/ and /sÓfI/. Both the first and the last lines begin with *that*. Moreover, if we take only the different sentences in the first three lines, the pattern of thesis, antithesis, and synthesis also emerges.

The emotive function is the predominant one in the next three lines which, however, are also tied to the preceding lines. *Sophie*, a family friend living out of town, had come for a visit which apparently had made an impression on the child. *Last night* is not factually correct, it was an afternoon visit, and not on the previous day. The time expression *last night* was a favorite one of the child's, perhaps because of its rhythm with the two vowels /A/ and the final /t/. The reason *Sophie* had made an impression on Anthony was because he was a *good boy* and in turn he was a *good boy* because of *go for glasses*. In addition to the primary emotive function of these lines there is again some sound play present. Lines (4), (5), and (6) begin in a velar, once voiceless, twice voiced; the voiced velar is repeated once more in line (6). Three [ɔ]'s follow each other in lines (5) and (6), the second word final, the first and third followed by another single phoneme.

The following lines are tied by substitution patterns, the child's practice of selection and substitution, or we can say that the function of metalanguage is the predominant one. Line (7) is a simple pronominal substitution for the noun in line (6). In lines (8) and (9) only the frame *go* remains, different form classes are substituted, but the vocabulary is related in terms of sound: every word in the substitution items begins with an alveolar phoneme, once the voiced /d/, three times the voiceless /t/. Basically, though, this is a transformation exercise. Lines (10) and (12) return to the original longer frame *go for*, also using unmodified nouns as substitutes in the pattern, keeping the grammatical structure the same with paradigmatic substitutions. The particular selection of *blouse* and *shoes* is determined by their final /s/ which is also the last consonant of the original *glasses*. *Blouse*, in addition, has an initial cluster of voiced stop plus /l/, as does *glasses*. *Pants* of line (11) is probably also meant as a substitution item for the pattern, but occurs without the frame. It too ends in /s/ as all other previous substitution items did.

The substitution pattern ceases to be the primary function of the next two lines where in line (13) *powder* alliterates with *pants* of line (11), and the /nts/ sequence of phonemes is repeated as /snt/ in line (14), as is the /dr/ sequence of line (13). The sentence in line (14) is probably one which the child has heard frequently.

The original substitution pattern is now changed in line (15) to *get*, still alliterating with *go*, however, using the last substitute of the previous pattern, *powder*, as the noun, and repeating the phonetic sequence [nɔ] in reverse as [ɔn]. *Shoe fixed* of line (16) is another substitute for the frame *get*, repeating one of the nouns of the first substitution pattern, without the final /s/.

Line (17) is a conjunction exercise, a very frequent practice with *and*. Line (18) has the third repetition of *powder*, and *some* can be related to *shoe* in the line above by the child's frequent confusion of /s/ and /š/ as was pointed out earlier. Lines (18) and (19) are a referential statement, part of the daily bathing routine of the child, and the completion sequence of the two lines is probably a quotation of a single adult sentence.

The next lines again present a substitution pattern, the frame being *leg* or *legs*, and the possessive case of nouns the selected grammatical relationship to be practiced since it also presents a final /s/ as did the nouns substituted in the former pattern. The first noun substituted, *Anthony's*, echoes the consonantal environment of *leg* of the previous line: /n/ and an alveolar stop. *Daddy's* and *Mommy's* follow since these three people are of greatest importance to the child, an emotive selection. The /t/ and /n/ of *Anthony's* in line (20) are repeated in the frame of line (21), with the addition of /p/ which

reappears in line (22), reminiscent of *powder* of lines (13), (15), and (18). Line (22) repeats *some*, containing the same phoneme sequence /Am/ as does the following *Mommy's*. *Mommy's legs* of line (23) is a type of phrase reduplication, a play with a whole phrase, here repeated twice, once with rising, once with falling intonation. Also repeated twice, both with sustained intonation, is line (24), using the pattern frame *get* from line (15) and repeating *Mommy* and *some* from line (22), the last line containing more than one phrase. Together with line (25), a vocative request is formulated, utilizing still a different function of language, the conative. The selection of the object of the sentence is again phonologically determined, alliterating with the immediately preceding *some*, and ending in /p/, the initial consonant of the first word of the preceding pattern. Line (26) is an imaginary statement of fact, evoked by the preceding and following word *soap*. However, relationships of sound are not irrelevant either. *Mommy* is repeated from line (24), and we have already commented on the relationship of /s/ and /š/ in the child's phonemic pattern. Lines (27) and (28) show the exercise of changing the past form of the word *took* to the nonpast *take*, a transformation practice, repeating the sequence *some soap*, and ending with *down*, containing the alveolar stop and nasal sequence of phonemes which had been played with in lines (19), (20), and (21).

Now another example which occurred at about the same relative time as the paragraph just discussed:

(C)(1) *Lock the door*
    (2) *Mail all the letter*
    (3) *Mailman*
    (4) *Doggie can bite the mailman*
    (5) *Bite all the letters*
    (6) *Mailman have a bite*
    (7) *Bite the letters*

An explanatory note for a better understanding of the paragraph may be in order. The dog in the household did not care for the mailman and had shown strong evidence of this dislike. If he possibly could, he would bite letters delivered through a slot in the front door—which delivery Anthony called mailing the letters—and he would have liked to accord the mailman the same treatment. The front door was always kept closed around the time the mailman was expected, and in addition secured by a chain so that Anthony would not inadvertently open it. Now back to the paragraph.

The first two lines are imperative, hence, their function is primarily conative, but also metalingual, since they have the same grammatical pattern. The consonants are interesting, however. All except /k/ are voiced, and they are only /l/, occurring four times, /d/, occurring also four times (here the pronunciation of "letter" is [lǽdə̀r]), /r/ twice, and /m/ only once. Line (3) repeats the /m/ and adds another nasal, /n/. Line (4) repeats all the preceding consonants except /r/, adds /t/ which then reappears in every succeeding line also, and reinforces the alveolar point of articulation by a voiced alveolar stop as well. Line (4) which is in the middle of the paragraph, is also the longest line, and could also be a quotation of adult speech, although the child has learned the construction of verb phrases with *can*. Line (5) repeats the original imperative pattern by substituting the verb *bite*, or more precisely it is the pattern of line (2), but this substitution exercise results in a misuse of syntactic liberty as a command is given ordering something which is not semantically acceptable. The nasals are reintroduced in line (6), *mailman*, and since the child knows that mailmen do not usually *bite*, the pattern is changed to a vocative imperative, performing also another transformation, that of the same phonemic shape assigned to another form class, here the original verb *bite* now appears as a noun, *a bite*. The end of the sequence, line (7), repeats the originally introduced pattern in line (1), repeating the substitution items of line (5), thus giving the sequence added symmetry.

A sequence using the functions of language somewhat differently, and occurring closer to the onset of sleep, is the following one:

(D)(1) *Hi big Bob*
   (2) *That's Bob* (2×)
   (3) *Big Bob* (3×)
   (4) *Little Bob*
   (5) *Big and little*
   (6) *Little Bobby*

   (7) *Little Nancy*
   (8) *Big Nancy*
   (9) *Big Bob and Nancy and Bobby*
(10) *And Bob*
(11) *And two, three Bobbys*
(12) *Three Bobbys*
(13) *Four Bobbys*
(14) *Six*
(15) *Tell the night, Bobby*
(16) *Big Bob*
(17) *Big Bob not home*
(18) *Nancy and Wendy*
(19) *Wendy gave Anthony's*
(20) *On Nancy*
(21) *Only Nancy could with the Kitty*
(22) *Mommy go sweep*
(23) *Aw, Nancy again*

It would perhaps be better to first comment on the cast of characters. The names are those of close family friends, the father's name is *Bob*, sometimes called "big Bob" by Anthony, an added redundancy to distinguish him even more clearly from his son *Bobby*; the mother's name is *Nancy*, and the children are named *Bobby* or *little Bobby* and *Wendy*.

The first line is simply a greeting intended for a real person who is not present, but whom the child sees rather frequently. *Big Bob* preferred by Anthony to *Bob* alone, probably because of alliteration. Line (2), repeated twice, identifies the person, and two of the repetitions of line (3) serve to clarify who it is, returning to the alliteration. In the third repetition the intonation is changed to a rising contour, showing the adjectives in still another function as they contrast with *little* in line (4). There is no such person as *little Bob*, the origin of this phrase could be the child's wish to make *Bob* little, but he has now engaged in a practice session of adjectival substitution, using the antonyms *big* and *little*, as they appear in line (5) as the synthesis from the previous thesis *big* and antithesis *little*. In line (6) *little Bobby* could just be mention of the child's name, but line (7), *little Nancy*, when no such person exists, shows clearly that the substitution game continues, as line (8) also shows. Line (9) introduces a new pattern. While retaining the modifier in *big Bob*, it is not used with the other names, and the purpose of this line is primarily an enumeration and practice in the use of the conjunction *and*. A chain is formed, the climax of the preceding lines, where each line contains only a single name. *And* is used before every name except the first. This is corrected in line (10) where even the adjective *big* is dropped before *Bob*. *And* also appears in line (11), and now the enumeration has become refined to the point of actual counting, forming a new chain with ascending numerals. Even the plural morpheme is used with the noun to confirm this. Lines (12) and (13) go on counting, using only one numeral per noun, and echoing in line (12) the end of line (11). Counting has now become all-absorbing, and only the numeral remains, without the noun, ending the chain of grading. Since the concept of numbers was only in the early stages of acquisition by the child, *six* was probably the highest numeral he could think of at the moment. Hence, to terminate this particular activity, the child's version of "Say good night to Bobby" or "Say good night, Bobby," an imperative, appears in line (15), keeping the name *Bobby*, with which he has practiced, still there. (It should be borne in mind that the initial consonant of "the" is /d/.) The two /b/'s in the last word of line (15), however, bring Anthony back again to his favorite *Big Bob* with three /b/'s, also typically returning to the beginning of the paragraph using a closed construction. In line (17) the /O/ phoneme is added two more times, also becoming the grand total of three. The /n/ in this line is probably a cue to the first word in line (18), *Nancy*, containing two /n/'s, followed by the echo of /En/ in *and* and *Wendy* which even alliterate further by the following /d/. The last word, *Wendy*, of line (18) is repeated as the first word of line (19) where the sequence /En/ reappears in *Anthony's*. The phoneme /g/ is also reintroduced and will again appear in line (22) and line (23) together with the sequence /En/ in *again* and *Nancy*. The possessive /s/ in *Anthony*'s in line (19) can only be explained if we look at its consonant pattern /n-n-s/ which is identical with that of *Nancy*. Line (20) begins with [ɔn], contained in the last word of the previous line, and alliterating with the other word in the same line. *On Nancy* in turn is reminiscent of *only Nancy* because of its rhythm in line (21). *Only* plus a name plus *could* is a favorite saying of the child and it appears here. The /w/, which thus far has been confined to *Wendy*, now reappears in line (21)

in *with* and in line (22) in *sweep*. *Kitty* is a repetition of the consonants /k-d/ of *could*.

An example of a combination of a grammatical exercise with sound play is the following paragraph occurring shortly after the child had been put to bed. We have indicated the first phonetic consonant of "throw" in brackets.

(E)	(1)	*Bobo's not throwing*	[t]
	(2)	*Bobo can throw*	[θ]
	(3)	*Bobo can throw it*	[θ]
	(4)	*Bobo can throw*	[θ]
	(5)	*Oh* (2×)	
	(6)	*Go* (3×)	

Line (1) is a negative statement true to fact, a description of a state, with the phoneme /O/ occurring in four out of the five syllables. The first consonant of *throwing* is [t], a usual substitution for the standard English phoneme /θ/. Here perhaps [t] rather than [f], another substitute for /θ/, is chosen because of the final released [t] of *not*. In line (2) the first statement is amended to an imaginary statement of fact, the pronunciation of *throw* is corrected to conform to standard English with [θ], also avoiding the troublesome sequence *not throwing*. Here, as in line (1), a correct standard grammatical pattern is used, as they are also in the following two lines, line (4) being a complete echo of line (2). In line (3), however, the grammatical pattern has been expanded to include an additional slot in the pattern, making it more complex, but still grammatically correct. In terms of sound, this addition, *it*, ends in [tʳ], the same consonant as the original *not* which led the child astray in the first appearance of *throw*. Now the troublemaker is safely at the end of the sentence. The paradigmatic exercise of the first four lines is clear: *throwing, can throw, can throw it, can throw*. The significance of the repetition of /O/ in line (1) is borne out by line (5), phonetically [oʊ], showing the practice of a complex vowel nucleus, a feature imperfectly learned in the child's system. [oʊ] is repeated twice in line (5) and three times in line (6) where it is combined with /g/ making a pseudo-word of it. That the primary function of *go* is sound play rather than a referential or conative one is confirmed by the child's squealing pronunciation of this line, an indication of play, and not of intended denotative meaning. The selection of the velar /g/ is perhaps also not accidental in view of the previously repeated /k/ in *can*.

Following is a paragraph immediately preceding the child's dropping off to sleep, characterized also by his rocking back and forth in the crib, an activity often accompanying his speech, immediately preceding sleep:

(F)(1) *Don't touch Mommy Daddy's desk*
  (2) *I should*
  (3) *He say so* (2×)
  (4) *Daddy's desk and Mommy's desk*
  (5) *Don't go on the desk*
  (6) *Don't take Daddy's glasses*
  (7) *Don't take it off*
  (8) *Don't take the glasses off*
  (9) *Daddy's wearing glasses*
 (10) *Daddy always*
 (11) *Dadada*
 (12) *Leave it*
 (13) *Daddy's glasses* (some whispering, banging, squealing)
 (14) *Doggie, Mommy, cookie* (2×) (unintelligible low volume with much banging, hitting of microphone, squealing)
 (15) *Mike* (15×) (Hitting of microphone, squealing) SLEEP

Interestingly enough, the things he is forbidden to do during the day preoccupy him at the moment of sleep. There are two very strict rules in the household: nothing on the parents' desks is to be touched, nor taken for play. No climbing on desks is permitted under any circumstances, although imitation of the cat who often walks on the desk is very tempting for the child. The other absolute, never to be tampered with, are eyeglasses which both parents wear, the father occasionally, the mother always. Line (1), then, is a repetition or reminder of a command the child has heard many times with great definiteness. The construction of the sentence is elliptic, the possessive does not appear with *Mommy*, and the conjunction *and* which we would expect between *Mommy* and *Daddy* is lacking too, probably in order to get more quickly to the alliterating *Daddy's desk*, the sound of which appeals to the child,

and is also evocative of *don't*, the underlying idea of this paragraph. The indication of two possessors, *Mommy* and *Daddy*, is also typical of the child's thought pattern in pairs. Line (2) offers at first glance linguistically a contradiction to line (1) on the basis of standard English, but we believe this to be an erroneous interpretation. The rules for answers to negative statements or commands in English are rather complex, and the child has not yet learned them. *I should*, therefore, is to be interpreted as "I should not touch." The use of the pronoun *I* instead of the much more frequent "Anthony" when the child talks about himself and the occurrence of the modal *should*, which is rare in his speech, make this a very important sentence for Anthony in that he is trying to show that he is grown-up and understands what the adult has forbidden him, by using the adult's language which he understands very well, but usually does not use. In line (3) another infrequent personal pronoun appears, *he*, the distinction in substitutions of *he* or *she* not being well learned by the child, again an attempt at adult speech with pronouns. The attempt here, however, is not as successful as in line (2), the third person singular marker is missing, more consonant with the child's usual speech pattern. The selection of *say so*, both beginning with /s/ which is frequently confused with /š/ by the child, is probably also conditioned by the *should* of the previous line.

Line (4) completes the elliptic line (1), now expanding the paired idea, but the order of *Daddy's* and *Mommy's* is reversed for two reasons: the child prefers the alliterating *Daddy's desk* to *Mommy's desk* on the one hand, and the line conforms to the next seven lines by beginning with /d/. The following four lines (lines [5] through [8]) are not only tied by the initial /d/, but all have as their first word the negative command *don't*. In listing what he is not supposed to do, the child then continues with *don't go on* in line (5), a phonemically related sequence by repeating /O/ three times and the longer /On/ twice, continuing with *the desk* which again alliterates since the consonant of the definite article is /d/. The linguistic structure of negative imperatives has been learned quite well, since the child has no doubt heard them very frequently. The next negative command in line (6) substitutes a new verb, *take* replacing *touch* and *go* of the previous pattern sentences, repeating the alveolar /t/ of *touch* and echoing the velar of *go* by a voiceless /k/. The favorite *Daddy's* reappears, but *glasses* has been substituted for *desk* in the same slot in the pattern. The reason is twofold: the child has never been forbidden to *take* the *desk*, a physical impossibility for him; *glasses* repeats the vowel [æ] and consonant /s/ of *Daddy's* which ends in a voiceless sibilant. Lines (7) and (8) are a substitution pattern exercise, showing again weakness in the correct pronominal choice, and the adding of *off* to the pattern of line (6), that is echoing the phoneme /O/ played with previously, and also using *take off* in connection with glasses, a frequent activity which the child has observed and mentioned. Line (9) shows a change of the pattern, using the *-ing* verb construction correctly, the best learned marked verb form. Since the mother, however, is the person who is the constant wearer of glasses, the following line (10) is not true to fact, and the occurrence of *Daddy* both in lines (9) and (10) is due to sound play as line (11) confirms. *Daddy always* of line (10) is a partial repetition of the consonants occurring in line (9), and since the child knows that Daddy does not always wear glasses, he drops the whole idea and goes on with just sound play in line (11). Line (12) now uses an affirmative command which parallels the meaning of the previous negative ones, and has as its object the pronoun *it*, the vowel phoneme of which is identical with that of *leave*, /l/. In line (13), *Daddy's glasses*, played with in line (6), is a substitution item for *it* of the previous line.

Following line (13), the recording becomes unintelligible. We can detect some whispering by the child which, however, is drowned out by his banging the side of the crib, and squeals follow. The next intelligible speech event is line (14), still having /d/ as its first consonant, but with a primarily phatic function. Three nouns are mentioned in sequence twice, all of which are of emotive content to the child, all also ending in /l/. In terms of sound pattern, the identical consonants /d/ of *Daddy* now have been dissimilated to /d-g/ of *doggie*, but identical consonants occur in the other two words, /m/ in *Mommy* and /k/ in *cookie*. Once again, some unintelligible speech follows, also accompanied by banging, squealing, and additional attention is focused on the microphone standing next to the crib, it being assaulted by various objects, judging by the recording. The last linguistic speech event, sounding like a phonograph record stuck in one place, is a repetition of the first syllable of the object which the child is hitting; the form *mike*, although frequent in standard English, is not a common expression in the household, and therefore not familiar to the child. Finally, after about fifteen repetitions of this syllable, Anthony has given up keeping the channel of communication open by linguistic means, he again resorts to throwing and squealing, and finally there is silence, sleep has overtaken him.

A type of paragraph which is infrequent, in that its primary function is narrative, is the following:

(G)(1) *See that*
  (2) *Walk with feet* (3 ×)
  (3) *Two feet*
  (4) *See*
  (5) *Twofeet and the horse*
  (6) *Like all other Indians*
  (7) *Twofeet had a horse* (2 ×)
  (8) *See cactus*
  (9) *And the grass*
 (10) *And flowers*

See that of line (1) could be interpreted as an imperative, or as an elliptic question which is more likely in view of the rising intonation contour which accompanies it and the context which follows it. Line (2) confirms that the child is pointing to or looking at something, namely his *feet*. Their observation evokes a statement of what they are used for, rather than a command which the form of line (2) would suggest.

MARTIN D. S. BRAINE

41

The two articles that follow, "On Learning the Grammatical Order of Words," by Martin D. S. Braine, and "Theoretical Notes on the Acquisition of Syntax: A Critique of 'Contextual Generalization,'" by Thomas G. Bever, Jerry A. Fodor, and William Weksel, constitute the first part of an interesting series of arguments and counter-arguments representing both psychological and linguistic points of view about language acquisition. See the summaries at the beginning of these selections.

It started with Braine's paper "On Learning the Grammatical Order of Words" (*Psychological Review*, LXX (1963), 323–48), in which he examined, on the basis of certain experiments, the possibility that grammatical structure is acquired by what he calls 'contextual generalization' (cf. summary below).

Braine's theory of the learning of grammatical structure is criticized in the following paper by Bever, Fodor, and Weksel "On the Acquisition of Syntax: A Critique of 'Contextual Generalization.'" (*Psychological Review*, LXXII [1965], 467–82.) They argue that the processes suggested by Braine cannot account for what children learn about the structure of relations between the sentences of their language.

In a way, this discussion echoes the clash between a behavior theory, with a basically empirical approach to learning, and the generative school of thought, with a rationalist approach concerning language acquisition, innate ideas, and abstract underlying structures (with transformations) for all sentences, etc.

A. B. A.

ON LEARNING THE GRAMMATICAL ORDER OF WORDS

The possibility is examined that grammatical structure is acquired by "contextual generalization"—a type of generalization which results from a S's learning the position of a unit in a sequence. Several experiments, in which S's learn miniature artificial languages, demonstrate and explore certain aspects of this type of generalization in verbal learning. From the experiments a theory of the learning of grammatical structure is developed. Confrontation of the theory with facts about the structure of natural languages, especially English, suggests that it may be tenable, provided its scope is narrowed in ways discussed, and provided that an additional assumption is made—that as well as learning the locations of units, S's form paired associates whose foci are closed-class morphemes, i.e., articles, auxiliaries, affixes, etc.

Reprinted from Psychological Review 70.323–348 (1963) *by permission of the author and the American Psychological Association.*

The writer is indebted to the Superintendent of Schools, and to the Principals of Woodlin and Rosemary Hills elementary schools, of Montgomery County, Maryland, for their cooperation in making available subjects and school facilities for Experiments I–IV. For Experiment V a similar debt is owed to James Hymes of the University of Maryland nursery school.

Just how virtually every human child contrives to learn his native language probably constitutes the most arresting mystery in psychology. A salient feature of the development is the relative rapidity with which the complexity of sentence structure increases during the initial period of acquisition. The purpose of the present paper is to explore the potentialities of the concept, "contextual generalization," for explaining the acquisition of grammatical structure, especially those aspects of grammatical structure which have to do with word order (which constitute much of the grammar in English).

For verbal learning, contextual generalization may be defined informally as follows: when a subject, who has experienced sentences in which a segment (morpheme, word, or phrase) occurs in a certain position and

242

context, later tends to place this segment in the same position in other contexts, the context of the segment will be said to have generalized, and the subject to have shown contextural generalization.

Thus defined, contextual generalization falls within the general rubric of stimulus and response generalization. One speaks of "stimulus generalization" when a subject, who has learned to make a certain response to a stimulus S_1, later makes the same response to a new stimulus S_2 which is like S_1. In stimulus generalization, the mediating property (the way in which S_2 is like S_1) is usually conceived to be some intrinsic property of S_1 and S_2, e.g., color, shape, etc. Similarly, in response generalization, the mediating property of R_1 and R_2 is usually thought of as some intrinsic property of the responses. Although the properties mediating generalization are usually intrinsic ones, there seems to be no particular reason why this should be so, and contextual generalization appears to be a special case where the mediating property is an extrinsic one, namely, temporal location in an utterance.

There are various suggestions in the literature that learning word order is similar to learning the associative connections manifest in word association tests. According to an early view of Miller (1951), "controlled associations are quite similar to the choice of successive words in speech [p. 186]." Consistently with this idea, Miller leaned heavily on the concepts of "contextual constraint" and "transitional probability"—"By grammatical habits we mean the operations of contextual constraints upon the sequence of symbols [p. 185]." While these concepts have been hown to be relevant to some verbal learning and memory experiments, no one has tried to develop these ideas to the point at which they can be taken seriously as a theory of the learning of grammatical structure. Perhaps this failure reflects the difficulties of such an enterprise.

A central difficulty of a theory based on learned associations between words is its clumsiness in handling generalization phenomena that obviously occur in verbal behavior. Thus, if we are told, for example, that *People kivil every day*, we are likely to deduce the existence of a verb *to kivil*, and to accept

sentences like *George kivils* as grammatical. Similarly, sentences like *Iron floats*, or *Colorless Green ideas sleep furlously* (Chomsky's 1957 example), would probably be recognized as having the structure of English even though it is doubtful that any of the words have ever previously been associated with each other in the experience of most English speakers; certainly such sentences would be considered more grammatical than *We are going to see him is not correct to chuckle loudly and depart for home*, in which the associational bonds between the words are quite strong (Miller, 1951, p. 81). It seems obvious therefore that there must exist generalization mechanisms in language learning whereby a word learned in one context generalizes to another context, even though no associations may have previously formed between the word and its new context.

In any explanation of the learning of grammatical structure it seems to the writer that some such generalization mechanism will have to occupy a central position. The present paper explores whether contextual generalization is a serious candidate for this role.

The paper is divided into two parts. The first part reports a series of experiments in which children learn some miniature artificial languages with nonsense syllables as words. Contextual generalization is first demonstrated as a phenomenon, and then various problems associated with the concept are explored. From the experiments, the general lines are sketched of a theory of the learning of grammatical structure based on contextual generalization—based, that is, on the notion that "What is learned" are primarily the proper locations of words in sentences.

Although experiments with artificial languages provide a vehicle for studying learning and generalization processes hypothetically involved in learning the natural language, they cannot, of course, yield any direct information about how the natural language is actually learned. The adequacy of a theory which rests on findings in work with artificial languages will therefore be judged by its consistency with data on the structure and development of the natural language. In the second part of the paper an attempt is made to confront the theory developed with known facts about the grammatical structure of natural languages, especially English, so as to discover the limitations of the theory, the stumbling blocks it faces, and the resources it can draw upon to meet the stumbling blocks.

EXPERIMENT 1: THE A + P LANGUAGE WITH WORD CONSTITUENTS

This experiment demonstrates, for a very simple language, that the position of a word in a verbal array can be the "functional stimulus" mediating generalization.

Method

Description of the language. There were two classes of words, A words and P words, and sentences were always two words long and consisted of an A word followed by a P word. The words were low association value nonsense syllables. *Kiv, juf,* and *foj* were the A words, and *bew, mub,* and *yag* the P words. Two words of each class were used during the initial learning, and the third was introduced in generalization trials.

Procedure. The subject was told that he was going to play a sort of word game in which he would learn a bit of a new language which might seem strange because he would not know what any of the words meant. The words (written on 1.5×3 inch cards) were shown to him and a consensus about their pronunciation was reached.

The "language" was taught through a series of sentence completion problems. A word was presented on the ledge of a board, either preceded or followed by a vacant position; A words were always presented on the left, and P words on the right of the vacant position. In each problem, the subject was given two words, one of each class, to choose from to complete the sentence by placing his selection in the vacant position. Before each problem the subject was asked "Do you remember how this one goes?" or "How do you think this one should go?" If he chose the correct word he won a poker chip (eight poker chips were worth a chocolate); if he chose wrongly he was shown the correct answer. After each problem, the correct

sentence was read aloud by him, and repeated by the experimenter.

In the initial learning two A words (*kiv* and *juf*) and two P words (*bew* and *mub*) were used. Four sentences can be formed from these, and eight sentence completion problems can be constructed since each sentence can be formed either by filling in the first word or by filling in the last word. The initial learning had two stages. Four of the eight problems were first selected and were presented in random order until learned to a criterion of seven successive correct responses (not including the first presentation of the first problem, which was used to demonstrate the procedure to the subject). Then the remaining four problems were presented once each, followed by all eight problems in random order until correct responses to seven successive presentations were made.

After the initial learning four generalization problems were each presented once to discover whether the subjects had registered the positions of the words used in the initial learning. A new A or P word was presented, with the alternatives always being words used in the initial learning. The generalization problems were (with the alternatives in parenthesis): *foj—(kiv, bew);—yag (mub, kiv);— yag (juf, bew); foj—(mub, juf)*.

Subjects. The subjects were 16 children, aged 9–6 to 10–5, 8 boys and 8 girls. Nonreaders were excluded.

Results

The initial learning was accomplished quite rapidly, two subjects making no errors whatever following the initial demonstration problem. As a demonstration of contextual generalization, the main interest of the experiment lies in the performance on the generalization problems. In 78 per cent of these problems the subjects filled the vacant position with the word that had occupied this position in the initial learning. Using the binomial expansion, one would expect by chance that, among 16 subjects, 5 subjects would respond correctly on either all four or three of the four generalization problems, 6 subjects on two problems, and 5 subjects on one problem or none. The obtained figures were 12, 4, and 0 subjects, respectively. The tendency to respond correctly is highly significant ($x^2 = 15.5$, $df = 2$, $p < .001$).

A vacant second position was filled in correctly in 91 per cent of the problems (13 subjects correct on both problems, and 3 subjects on one or none), as compared with 66 per cent for a vacant first position (8 subjects on both problems, and 8 subjects on one or none). Tested by chi square for correlated proportions, the difference between the positions is not statistically significant.

After the generalization problems, the subjects who had correctly completed at least three of the four sentences were asked why they picked the one they did. The two most frequent explanations were "It sounded right," and "I remembered" (when asked *what* they remembered these subjects said they did not know—further questioning usually elicited that they had not realized that all the sentences in the generalization problems were new). Only one subject said anything to indicate that he had noticed the constant positions of the words. These explanations suggest that the subjects responded unwittingly to the positional cue and that this cue was temporal rather than spatial in nature, and auditory rather than visual (i.e., the temporal position of the word in the sentence when read aloud or rehearsed subvocally, rather than its left or right position in the visual display). Further evidence for this is provided in a later experiment.

Conclusion

The results indicate that subjects who have experienced sentences in which words occur in a certain position and context tend to place these words in the same positions in new contexts. Such behavior indicates the learning of an association of words with their positions, the context generalizing. A suggestion as to the mechanism of contextual generalization is contained in the subjects' explanations of their responses: perhaps the repeated experience of a certain word in a certain position makes it sound familiar, and therefore sound "right" in this position, even though the original context be changed.

Discussion

Extrapolating from the above conclusion, it is possible to hazard a guess about the infant's learning of grammatical word order. Perhaps he constantly hears the same expressions recurring in the same positions in his verbal environment; these therefore come to sound familiar and therefore "right" to him in these positions, and consequently in his own language he reproduces the same positional relationships. Such a theory would make the learning of gramatical word order a special case of "Gibsonian" perceptual learning (Gibson and Gibson, 1955), i.e., a process of auditory differentiation, or of becoming familiar with, the temporal positions of expressions in utterances. Perceptual learning is usually assumed to be a rather primitive process and there is therefore no reason to suppose that it demands much in the way of intellectual capacity in the learner. Learning of this sort would therefore satisfy at least one requirement of any process postulated to be involved in first language learning, namely, that it not require intellectual capacities obviously beyond the reach of the 2-year-old.

The most immediate problem in the above line of thought concerns the definition of position. In the learning of a language more complex than the one used in this experiment, two closely related questions arise. One question concerns whether it is the absolute positions of expressions (e.g., first, second, etc.) that are learned, or the positions of expressions relative to other expressions. A less obvious but probably more important question concerns the nature of the elements that fill positions. It is perhaps most natural to assume that the word is the principal element whose position is learned. If the word is the only element whose position is learned, then for English, position must be defined relatively and not absolutely, since almost any English word can occur in any absolute position in a sentence. However, some exploratory work suggested that the relative positions of words were rather difficult to learn. It seemed, therefore, that it might be fruitful to question the assumption that there is anything inevitable about the word as the sole or principal element whose position is learned.

An alternative assumption is that the elements are hierarchically organized: a sentence would be assumed to contain a hierarchy of elements in which longer elements (e.g., phrases) contain shorter elements (e.g., words) as parts, with the positions that are learned always being positions within the next larger element in the hierarchy. A hierarchy of elements would require that expressions of any length can be elements whose position is learned; words (or morphemes) would be merely the smallest elements in the hierarchy. At each level in a hierarchical scheme position could be defined either absolutely or relatively. A simple example of a hierarchical scheme in which position is defined absolutely is provided by binary fractionation. In this scheme a sentence contains just two positions, a first and a last, and each expression in these positions can itself contain two positions, a first and a last, and each resulting expression is potentially divisible in turn in like manner, etc. It may be noted that this method of defining position seems relevant to English structure, e.g., the verb in English generally constitutes the first part of the last section of a sentence. A hierarchical organization of elements is assumed in immediate constituent analysis in structural linguistics (cf. Chomsky, 1957).

EXPERIMENT 2: THE A + P LANGUAGE WITH PHRASE CONSTITUENTS

This experiment was designed to investigate whether the ease and effectiveness of learning is related to the way in which position is defined for the subject. The learning of the same language was compared under conditions (a) when words were the units and the positional cues were relative, and (b) when phrases (either one or two words long) were the units and the positional cues were absolute—first and last. It was expected that Condition b would prove simpler. The initial learning procedure was designed to match that of Experiment 1, so that the learning scores could be compared with those for the apparently simpler language of Experiment 1.

Method

Description of the language. The language was that of Experiment 1 except that an additional word (*ged*) always preceded two of the three A words (*juf* and *foj*), and another additional word (*pow*) always followed one of

the P words (*bew*). Sentences could thus vary from two to four words in length, and the A and P words were sometimes first and second, and sometimes second and third; the relative ordinal positions were, however, the same as in Experiment 1, i.e., A words (*kiv*, *juf*, and *foj*) always immediately preceded P words (*bew*, *mub*, and *yag*).

An alternative way of specifying this language is to say that any of three A phrases (*kiv*, *ged juf*, *ged foj*) could be followed by any of three P phrases (*bew pow*, *mub*, *yag*). When described in this way the grammar is an exact replica of the grammar taught in Experiment 1, but with phrases instead of words as the immediate constituents.

Procedure. The procedure had four parts: initial learning, second learning, learning test, and recall test. To match Experiment 1, the initial learning used only two A terms (*kiv*, and *juf* preceded by *ged*) and two P terms (*bew* followed by *pow*, and *mub*). Using a sentence completion procedure as before, the language was taught in two ways. For one group of subjects (Group 1) only the position of the A or P word was left vacant in a problem, and the choices available for sentence completion were always an A and a P word. (For this group the two new words *ged* and *pow* never had to be filled in.) For another group of subjects (Group 2), the sentences were presented in each problem lacking the whole A or P phrase (ie., either one or two words as the case might be), and the choices available for completing the sentence were always a whole A and P phrase. (When the choices were of unequal length, these subjects of course were not given any cues as to the length of the sentence to be constructed.) The initial learning was exactly parallel to the initial learning in Experiment 1: to every sentence completion problem used then there corresponded a problem for each group in this experiment, and the order of administration of problems and the learning criteria were the same. Subjects who failed to complete the initial learning in 60 trials were not included in the remaining parts of the experiment.

The purpose of the second learning was to introduce and provide practice with the A term (*foj* preceded by *ged*) and the P term (*yag*) not used in the initial learning. Nine problems combined these new items with previously used words or phrases, and with each other; in a further six problems, each A and P word (or phrase) occurred twice, once as the correct alternative and once presented in the sentence for completion. In the second learning, as in the initial learning, Group 1 filled in A and P words only, and Group 2 the full A or P phrase.

In the learning test, each of the eight sentence completion problems of the initial learning were administered in turn to both groups with only the A and P words to be filled in. For Group 1 the learning test was simply a repetition of the same eight problems they had already learned to criterion.

In the recall test, the eight words of the language were handed to the subjects and they were asked to try to make a complete sentence of the language that they remembered. The request was repeated until they had offered four sentences.

Subjects. In each group there were 12 children, aged 9–7 to 10–7, 6 boys and 6 girls. Nonreaders were excluded.

Results

The first three lines of Table 1 show the learning scores for the two groups and for the subjects of the previous experiment. Since some subjects failed to reach the learning criterion, the scores are expressed in terms of the median and range. It can be seen that there is no difference between Group 2 and the subjects of Experiment 1 in either trials-to-learn, or errors.

Using the nonparametric Mann-Whitney sum-of-ranks test, it was found that Group 2 learned in fewer trials ($z = 2.7$, $p < .01$), and made fewer errors ($z = 1.7$, $p < .05$ for the one-tailed hypothesis), than Group 1.

In the eight problems of the learning test, there was only one error among the 12 subjects of Group 2, whereas 6 of the 10 subjects in Group 1 who took the test made one error apiece ($x^2 = 4.5$, $p < .05$). Subjects who had learned by filling in the whole A or P phrase therefore knew the relative positions of the individual words of the phrase even better than the subjects who had been trained to fill in the individual words.

In the recall test the subjects of Group 1 constructed an average of 2.6 sentences, as against 3.1 for Group 2. The results favor Group 2, as predicted, but the difference is not significant ($t = 1.2$). The difference between the groups might well have been greater if the experimenter had not foolishly limited the subjects to four sentences, thus imposing a ceiling on the recall scores to the probable detriment of the group with the higher mean score! It should also be remembered that the two worst subjects in Group 1 were excluded from the recall test because they failed to complete the initial learning.

Discussion

The similarity between the learning scores for Group 2 and for the language of Experiment 1 indicates that it matters little whether the elements in first and last position are words or variable length phrases (one or two words).

The results also indicate that the same language is learned more easily and effectively when the response units are phrases of variable length and the positional cues are first

TABLE 1. Learning and error scores in the various experiments.

Experiment	N	Percent subjects learning	Trials to learn Mdn. and range	Number errors Mdn. and range
I	16	100	10.5 (0−28)	4 (0−7)
II: 1	12	83	24 (5−60+)	5 (2−20+)
II: 2	12	100	9.5 (2−20)	3.5 (1−9)
III	24	100	11 (0−40)	3 (0−14)
IV: 1	6	33	50+ (29−50+)	20+ (10−20+)
IV: 2	14	64	32 (4−50+)	9 (3−20+)
V	12	100	13 (0−55)	4.5 (0−18)

and last, than when the response units are words and the positional cues are provided by the relative positions of the words to each other. This result is probably due to the greater informational economy of a first-last dichotomy; that is, to learn the absolute positions of the phrases fewer items of information would have to be registered than to learn the positional relationships between the words taken individually. Consider, for example, the complexity of a relative definition of the position of *bew*: *bew* precedes *pow*; it follows either *kiv*, *juf*, or *foj*, whichever of these appear; and it occurs next but one after *ged*, when *ged* is present. Obviously it is much simpler to take *bew pow* as a unit and state only that this occurs last. (Within a hierarchical scheme the position of *bew* could then be specified as the first member of a *bew-pow* unit.)[1]

The results of this experiment therefore suggest that learning is easier with a simple definition of position, and that a variable length element does not impair learning. Such a result would be expected under the assumption that position can be defined through a hierarchical scheme, since a hierarchical scheme permits a simple definition of position, but does so at the cost of a complex element.

EXPERIMENT 3: THE A + PQ AND AB + P LANGUAGES

The experiment was designed to explore the learning of locations in a language with a hierarchy of elements. Suppose a grammar in which a double binary fractionation of sentences is possible (i.e., not only a division of the sentence into an A and a P phrase, but also a further subdivision of at least one of the phrases into two parts). Such a gram-

mar would be exemplified in a language with four A phrases, a_1, a_2, a_3, a_4 (not necessarily of equal length), any of which may precede any of four P phrases, p_1q_1, p_2q_2, p_1q_2, p_2q_1. The P phrase has internal structure, consisting of a P word (p_1 or p_2) followed by a Q word (q_1 or q_2). With such a language, it was predicted that the subjects would not only associate phrases with their position within the sentence, but also associate words with their position within the phrase—contextual generalization should occur both between and within phrases.

For the above language, between-phrase generalization would be demonstrated in essentially the same way as in Experiment 1. At a certain point in the learning, an A and a P phrase (e.g., perhaps a_4 and p_2q_1), not yet experienced by the subject, would be introduced and presented in problems of the form $a_4(\ \ )$ and $(\ \ )p_2q_1$. If the subject has registered the positions of the A and P phrases in the previous learning, he should complete these sentences correctly, to form, e.g., $a_4p_1q_1$, $a_1p_2q_1$.

However, the more complex grammar brings a new factor up for consideration, not present in Experiment 1. In a language in which some of the phrases have internal structure, the component phrases of most new sentences will be formed by joining words not previously combined, and not represent new additions to the vocabulary. When new phrases are recombinations of familiar elements, any associations of a paired-associate type, which may have formed during the previous learning, will have an opportunity to facilitate generalization. In the case of the language outlined, where only one phrase has internal structure, such associations could facilitate solution only of generalization problems in which the unstructured phrase is to be filled in. Thus in problems of the form $a_4(\ \ )$, in which the structured phrase has to be filled in, a_4 is a new addition to the vocabulary so that no associations can have formed to it; whereas in problems of the form $(\ \ )p_2q_1$, associations could have formed between the familiar unstructured A phrases to be filled in and the words p_2 and q_1 of the phrase presented. Analysis of performance on such generalization problems may therefore give some indication of the extent of asso-

---

[1] One way (which would apply only to a language more complex than the one taught here) in which the complexity of a relative definition of position could be reduced, would be to arrange that a few elements recur in a very large number of sentences of the language. The subject might quickly learn to recognize these elements and they might then serve him as reference points in the sentence; the positions immediately preceding or following such elements would then be defined in a fairly simple manner. The familiar element would, so to speak, serve as a "tag" (cf. the discussion of "closed-class" morphemes, below).

ciative effects in this kind of generalization.

Within-phrase generalization would be demonstrated in problems of the form $a_n p_3(\ \ )$ and $a_n(\ \ )q_3$, where a_n is any A phrase (familar), and p_3 and q_3 are new words. If, in the previous learning, the subject has registered the positions of the P and Q words in the P phrase, he should complete the sentences correctly, to form, e.g., $a_n p_3 q_1$, $a_n q_1 p_3$. Since a_n can be any of the four A phrases, a generalization problem of the above form, e.g., $a_n p_3(\ \ )$, can be replicated four times, with a_1, a_2, a_3, a_4 serving in turn as the A phrase; in each replicaton a correct response will construct the same P phrase (e.g., $p_3 q_1$) in the context of a different A phrase. One can therefore ask whether the association of words with their within-phrase positions is demonstrated on the first problems, and also whether there is an increase in generalization with successive A phrase contexts. An increase might be due either to an increase in the strength of association of the word with its within-phrase position or to between-phrase contextual generalization of the new P phrase from one A phrase to another.

Method

Description of the languages. The two languages are defined in Table 2. In the AB + P language the structured phrase was in first position, in the A + PQ language in second position.

TABLE 2.   A + PQ language.

A phrase	P phrase	
Kivil (a_1)	mervo (p_1)	som (q_1)
Ob ordem (a_2)	yag (p_2)	eena (q_2)
Remin gice (a_3)	leck (p_3)	wimp (q_3)
Noot (a_4)		

Note: A $p_h q_h$ sequence constitutes a P phrase, and an A phrase followed by a P phrase is a sentence. The AB + P language is obtained by interchanging A and P phrases of the A + PQ language.

Procedure. The procedure had five parts: initial learning, second learning, between-phrase generalization test, third learning, and within-phrase generalization tests. Since the languages are mirror images, the procedure will be described only for the A + PQ language; the procedure for the AB + P language was an exact analogue—read A in place of P, B in place of Q, and P in place of A in the following description.

The initial learning was an exact problem-by-problem analogue of that used in the two previous experiments. *Kivil* and *Ob ordem* were the A phrases, and *mervo som* ($p_1 q_1$) and *yag eena* ($p_2 q_2$) the P phrases. The subjects always filled in the whole phrase, in the same way as Group 2 in the previous experiment. The initial learning, then, was comparable to the first experiments, two A phrases and two P phrases with, as yet, no elaboration of internal structure.

The second learning introduced a new A phrase (a_3: *Remin gice*) and a new P phrase ($p_1 q_2$: *mervo eena*). The first nine problems combined these new phrases with the previously used ones and with each other; then a random assortment of problems constructible from the six phrases were learned to a criterion of seven successive correct responses. The second learning thus introduced a new A term, unrelated to the previous A terms; the P term, however, was systematically generated by the combination of elements from the previously learned P terms.

The between-phrase generalization test consisted of six problems presented once each. The problems introduced a new A phrase unrelated to previous A phrases (a_4: *noot*) and a new P phrase generated by recombination of elements ($p_2 q_1$: *yag som*). These were presented three times each in the positions appropriate to their class, and in each problem a different one of the previously used phrases had to be filled in. In the three problems in which *yag som* was the phrase presented, the incorrect choice was always *mervo eena* (because otherwise the subjects might well solve these problems by adopting the hypothesis that the same word could not occur twice in a sentence).

In the third learning 15 problems constructible from the eight phrases were presented, most of which contained the two phrases just introduced in the generalization test. The purpose of the third learning was to familiarize the subjects with these new phrases.

The within-phrase generalization problems differed from all previous parts of the procedure in that sentences were presented lacking one word only, and in that subjects had to choose from three instead of two alternatives (because there were three parts of speech). Preceding the first generalization problem there were three "buffer" problems with these characteristics which contained no new words. There were 16 within-phrase generalization problems; these were arranged in four sets, each set comprising four problems. In two problems of each set, the P phrase presented was p_3 (*leck*) followed by the space to be filled in; in the other two problems it consisted of q_3 (*wimp*) preceded by the blank; the choices were always a P word, a Q word, and a word selected from one of the A phrases; each of p_1, p_2, q_1, q_2 were correct once. In the first set of problems the A phrase used was always a_1, in the second set a_2, in the third a_3, and in the fourth a_4. Thus, in the first set the problems were: *Kivil leck——(ordem, som, mervo); Kivil—— wimp (yag, eena, remin); Kivil——wimp (som, gice, mervo); Kivil leck——(ordem, yag, eena)*. In the second, third, and foruth sets of problems, in addition to replacement of the A phrase, the order of presentation of problems containing particular P phrases was varied, as also were the wrong alternatives. To give the subjects additional experience of the sentences used in each set of generalization problems before going on to the next set, between sets the subjects were given eight problems made up from the four sentences introduced in the set just completed. In these practice problems, the whole A or P phrase had to be filled in, as in the earlier learning.

If two sessions were required to complete the prcedure, the break between sessions always occurred during the second learning.

Subjects. Twenty-four children, aged 9–11 to 11–1, served as subjects. Each language was learned by 6 boys and 6 girls. Nonreaders were excluded.

Results

Table 1 shows the initial learning scores for the 24 subjects, who were treated as a single group since the scores were very similar for the two languages. It can be seen that the scores are almost exactly the same as those found in Experiment 1 and for Group 2 in Experiment 2.

In 74 per cent of the between-phrase generalization problems, the subjects filled the vacant position with the phrase which had occupied this position in the previous learning. Using the binomial expansion, one would expect that among 24 subjects, 8.25 subjects would be correct on either zero, one, or two of the six problems, 7.5 subjects correct on three problems, and 8.25 subjects correct on four, five, or six problems. The obtained figures were 2, 3, and 19 subjects ($x^2 = 21.8$, $p < .0001$). Since, as described in the procedure, three of the problems had the same wrong alternative (*mervo eena*), there was the possibility that subjects might have solved some of these by avoiding this couplet. This possibility is ruled out by the fact that the subjects made slightly fewer errors on the first of the three problems than on the other two, and also that they did not make more than the average number of errors on the one problem on which this couplet was correct.

It will be remembered that in the AB + P language the structured phrase was in first position, and in the A + PQ language in final position. The 12 subjects who learned the AB + P language correctly placed the structured phrase in first position in 83 per cent of the 36 relevant problems (3 problems per subject); they correctly placed the unstructured phrase in final position in 69 per cent of the problems. The corresponding figures for the subjedts who learned the A + PQ language were 75 per cent for the unstructured phrase in first position, and 69 per cent for the structured phrase in final position. These four percentages do not seem to differ from each other.

On the first set of within-phrase generalization problems the subjects filled 68 per cent of the vacant positions with the words that had previously occupied these positions (as against the 33 per cent expected by chance). Among 24 subjects one would expect from the binomial expansion that 14.2 subjects would make errors on all or all but one of the four problems, and that 9.8 subjects would make two or more correct responses. The obtained figures were 4 and 20, and the difference is highly significant ($x^2 = 18.0$,

$p < .0001$). Despite the small number of subjects for each language, the tendency to respond according to word position on the first set of within-phrase generalization problems is significant for each language individually (by a similar chi square test using Yates' correction).

In Figure 1 the results on all four sets of within-phrase generalization problems are presented, showing for each set the proportion of times that a given within-phrase position was correctly filled. It can be seen that correct responses occurred somewhat more frequently on the later sets than on the first, suggesting that some generalization from one sentence context to another occurred over and above the within-phrase generalization manifested by the better-than-chance success on the first set. Comparing the within-phrase positions with each other, Figure 1 suggests that the tendency to associate a word with its position may be greatest for the Q position in the A + PQ language (i.e., for the last word in the sentence), and about the same for the remaining three positions.

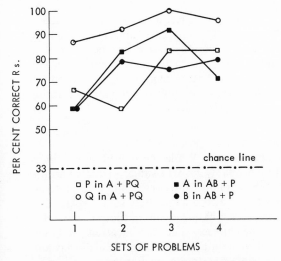

FIGURE 1. Proportion of sentences in each set of four within-phrase generalization problems in which a given position was correctly filled (e.g., the open squares indicate how often the P position in the A + PQ language was filled with a P word).

When asked how they knew what to pick, three subjects said something about position (e.g., "I don't know exactly; this one usually starts it"); the remaining subjects showed no insight. The most frequent answer made some reference to the sound of the sentence (e.g., "I don't know; I just put it because it sounds right"); a number of subjects said that they "remembered," and it was obvious that most subjects were quite unaware that many of the new sentences were new. One subject said she "tried them all out and picked the one that made the most sense"!

Discussion

The similarity of the initial learning scores to those in Experiment 1, and for Group 2 in Experiment 2, indicates that ease of learning is not related to such factors as number of words per phrase, number of syllables per word, exact phonetic or lexical constitution of the words, etc., at least within the limits that these factors were varied. Similarly, the results on the between-phrase generalization problems confirm and extend the observations of Experiment 1, in that they provide evidence that phrases as well as words tend to become associated with the sentence positions in which they recur, and thus to generalize to fresh contexts. Both these findings indicate that, within fairly wide limits, the constitution of the elements in first and last position is not an important variable for either learning or generalization.

It was noted in the introduction to the experiment that paired-associate links, formed between phrases and parts of phrases during learning, might act to facilitate solution of the between-phrase generalization problems in which the unstructured phrase was to be filled in. However, no evidence was found for such a facilitative effect, since the unstructured phrase was not filled in correctly more often than the structured phrase.

The results on the within-phrase generalization problems indicate that during learning the component words of the structured phrase become associated with their positions within the phrase. This finding confirms the assumption that elements can be hierarchically structured for the subject, that is, that locations with which expressions become associated can be locations within longer expressions whose location in the sentence is also learned.

This experiment completes the experiments which explore ways in which the structure of the verbal array may define positions for the subject. In Experiment 4 the question of the role of the oral-auditory cycle in this kind of learning is given further consideration.

EXPERIMENT 4: POSITIVE AND NEGATIVE INSTANCES

It was suggested earlier that the relevant positional cue was the temporal position of the word in the sentence as spoken, and not the left-right position in the visual display. It was also suggested that, since only the correct sentences were read aloud, the subjects had much more opportunity to become familiar with the sound of the correct sentences, their experience of ungrammatical sentences being confined entirely to subvocal rehearsal of the wrong answers to problems. In choosing between the alternatives on a given problem, the subjects would therefore be able to rehearse each alternative and select the one that sounded "right," i.e., familiar. Even in the subvocal rehearsal it is likely that the correct alternative would be rehearsed more often than the incorrect one, since if the subject happened to try the correct alternative first it would sound right, and the incorrect alternative might not then be rehearsed.

In ordinary discrimination-learning experiments, matters are usually arranged so that the subject has equal experience with both the positive and negative stimuli. In the previous three experiments, if the subjects' method of solution has been correctly interpreted, there was very unequal experience with correct and incorrect sentences, exposure to positive instances greatly predominating. First language learning by infants, it may be noted, occurs through exposure to positive instances almost exclusively.

The following modifications of the procedure used in Experiment 1 were made both to test the above interpretation of the subjects' method of solution, and also to explore the possible importance for language learning of the distinction between learning to discriminate positive from negative instances, and learning primarily through exposure to positive instances. It was predicted that

learning would be seriously impaired if the training procedure were altered so that the subjects had nearly equal familiarity with correct and incorrect sentences. Two procedures were designed, each modifying Experiment 1 in a slightly different way. The language in each case was the A + P language with word constituents, described for Experiment 1.

First modification

Procedure. The preliminary instructions, the rewards, the learning criteria, the sequence of presentation of problems, and the actual words used in each problem were exactly the same as in Experiment 1. The difference lay in the fact that each problem was not presented as a sentence completion problem; instead the correct and incorrect sentences involved in a problem were each written on separate cards, and were presented to the subject, one on his left and one on his right. He was instructed to read each one aloud and then to point to the one which "could be said in this language." He was told whether he was right, but neither sentence was read aloud following his response.

Six children, aged 9–6 to 10–7, served as subjects.

Results. The results are shown in Table 1 (Row IV: 1). Only two subjects reached the learning criterion, and both these required more trials and made more errors than any subject in Experiment 1. This procedural modification obviously impairs learning very severely indeed.

Second modification

Procedure. While the preceding modification probably gave the subjects equal exposure to the sound of the correct and incorrect sentences, it also altered the visual display, and the precise nature of the response demanded of the subject. The modification now described maintained the same visual display and the same response as in Experiment 1

The procedure was an exact duplicate of that in Experiment 1, except that in each problem before completing the sentence, the subject read aloud the sentences which would be produced by substituting each alternative in turn in the vacant position. After completing the sentence he was told whether he was correct, and if incorrect was shown the correct sentence, but he did not then read it aloud. If he read it aloud spontaneously he was told not to; the experimenter did not read the sentence aloud either. After a 2-second pause the next problem was set up.

Since each problem terminated with the correct sentence exposed visually to the subject, and since literate subjects have a tendency to read to themselves written words they see, there was probably somewhat more exposure (subvocal) to the correct than to the incorrect sentences. However, there was certainly far less differential exposure than in Experiment 1.

The subjects were 14 children, aged 10–1 to 10–10.

Results. The results are again shown in Table 1 (Row IV: 2). While the impairment of learning appears to be a trifle less serious with this procedure than with the preceding one, learning is obviously greatly impaired relative to the procedure used in Experiment 1 For both trials-to-learn and errors, the difference is highly significant ($p < .001$, and .0001, respectively, by the Mann-Whitney sum-of-ranks test).

Discussion

Since the difference between the second modification and the procedure used in Experiment 1 involved only the reading of the sentences, the results strongly support the previous interpretation of the basis of the subjects' responses. That is, the relevant cue was the temporal position in the spoken sentence and as learning progressed words or phrases came to sound familiar in the positions in which they recurred. The subjects were then able to respond correctly in generalization problems by picking the alternative which made the sentence "sound right."

It may be added that the deleterious effect on grammatical judgments of self-exposure to negative instances is a phenomenon within ordinary experience. For example, if a foreigner asks whether *different to, different than,* or *different from* is correct in English, or whether a sentence like *The child seems sleeping* is any less correct than *The book seems interesting,* one is usually much more confident of the answer if one responds at once than if one repeats each alternative 20 times before responding. The very act of repeating the

ungrammatical (or less grammatical) sequence a number of times seems to make it momentarily "sound right," and thus removes the usual basis for the judgment.

EXPERIMENT 5: THE A $+$ P LANGUAGE WITH 4-YEAR-OLDS

Experiments 1–4 were all performed with children about 10 years old. Since the theory developed claims to have relevance to first language learning, it assumes that the phenomena under study also occur readily in much younger children. Experiment 5 was designed to examine this assumption. An attempt was made to repeat Experiment 1 with preschool subjects making only such procedural changes as were necessitated by their illiteracy.

Method

Procedure. The following modifications were made to the procedure used in Experiment 1 with the older children. (*a*) Instead of nonsense syllables, animal noises served as the "words" of the languages; "sentences" were thus sequences like *moo meow, oink quack,* etc. (*b*) Instead of being written, each word was graphically represented by a picture of the animal or of its head, with the mouth open as if to talk. (*c*) The sentences were "read" from top to bottom rather than from left to right, i.e., a sentence was completed by placing a word (picture) in the vacant position above or below the presented word; this modification was introduced because it was thought that preschool children would more easily adopt a consistent top-to-bottom than left-to-right direction of reading. (*d*) A correct response was rewarded with a raisin, and if the subject wished he could exchange four raisins for an M & M candy. (*e*) There were several sessions rather than one; these were kept short, and second and subsequent sessions always began with one presentation of each of the first four problems; responses to these problems were not tallied if the subject had met the learning criterion on these problems in prior sessions.

Before the training began, a consensus, determined by the experimenter, was reached for each picture as to "what the animal said." Then the first problem was presented several times over and used as a vehicle for teaching the children to read the pictures smoothly in the top-bottom sequence; on subsequent prob-lems if the child had difficulty reading the sequence after his response, he was helped until he had read it at least once smoothly.

In addition to the above, a further modi-fication had to be introduced. On probelms in which the word presented (e.g., *moo*) was in top position, the child was instructed before his response: "Does it go *Moo* . . . , or *Moo* . . . ?"; during the first brief pause the experi-menter indicated one alternative with the end of his pencil, and during the second the other alternative. When the word presented (e.g., *quack*) was in bottom position, the instruc-tion was "Does it go . . . *quack*, or . . . *quack*?" with similar indication of the alternatives. The purpose of the instruction was to encour-age some sort of rehearsal of the alternative sentences. It was necessary because a picture appears to elicit vocal or subvocal rehearsal of a particular word less readily than does the written word. The experimenter was careful not to give voice or gestural cues which could guide the subject to the correct response.

Subjects. The subjects were 12 nursery-school children, aged 4–2 to 5–0.

Results

The learning scores are shown in Table 1. All subjects learned[2] and it can be seen that the median scores for both errors and trials to learn are very similar to those of the older subjects of Experiment 1. Although the upper end of the range is higher, two subjects com-pleted the initial learning without any errors whatever, just as in Experiment 1. On 75 per cent of the generalization problems the subjects filled the vacant position with the word that had occupied this position in the previous learning. This figure is close to the figure of 78 per cent found in Experiment 1. Vacant first and second positions were filled

in about equally often. One subject gave a crude but accurate statement of the prin-ciple involved.

While the procedure necessarily differs in too many ways from that of Experiment 1 to permit firm conclusions to be drawn from the comparison, it can nevertheless be stated that the preschool subjects did not find this task substantially more difficult than the older subjects found the analogous task in Experi-ment 1. Moreover, contextual generaliza-tion occurred in both age groups. While a comparison of age groups on a relevant task which involved neither reading nor simula-tion of reading in either group would be more satisfactory, the results nevertheless provide prima facie evidence of age group similari-ties in the learning processes involved.

GENERAL DISCUSSION

The remainder of the paper will consider how far a theory based on contextual gener-alization may provide a plausible account of the learning of the grammatical structure of natural languages, particularly English. As developed in the preceding experiments the theory consists of three proposals. (*a*) "What is learned" are the locations of expressions in utterances. (*b*) Units (i.e., expressions whose position is learned) can form a hierarchy in which longer units contain shorter units as parts, the location that is learned being the location of a unit within the next-larger containing unit, up to the sentence. (*c*) The learning is a case of perceptual learning—a process of becoming familiar with the sounds of expressions in the positions in which they recur.[3]

---

[2] The procedure proved not to be well adapted to some 4-year-olds. The initial teaching, the prelimi-nary instruction to each problem, and the require-ment of reading the picture sequences involved con-trols on the subjects' behavior which tended to arouse their opposition. This was generally handled by keep-ing the sessions brief, but nevertheless four subjects refused to cooperate after experiencing only one or two sessions. These subjects are omitted from the results (they were not learning more slowly than the others when they stopped).

[3] Certain cues not involved in the experiments could facilitate the learning of position in natural languages. In English, for example, various suffixes are associated with many nouns and verbs (e.g., *-ment*, *-ation*, *-ness*, etc., and *-ate*, *-ize*, etc.). Also, many of the more frequent nouns (especially those without suffices) are correlated with "object-like" features in the external world, and many verbs with "process-like" features. That quite young children know these correlates has been demonstrated by Brown (1957). Where they covary with position, all such cues, although only probabilistic, should facili-tate the learning of the locations of expressions. (In the experiments it is likely that learning and generali-zation would have been markedly assisted if the words belonging in a given position had been "tagged" in some way, e.g., by giving them all the same ending.)

With respect to Proposal (*b*), probably the simplest hierarchical scheme is provided by the binary-fractionation model. This model, in which position is defined through successive first-last dichotomies, is the one used in the design of Experiments 2 and 3, and can serve as a basis for discussion where a specific model is required.

One direct way in which the theory might be examined is by collecting data on the development of grammatical structure. The first word combinations of three children 18–24 months old studied by the writer have been shown to have a characteristic structure which was interpreted as indicating that what had been learned was that each of a small number of words belonged in a particular position in a word combination (Braine, 1963). Occasional reference to the subsequent development of these children will be made in the discussion.

The discussion will be concerned with some obvious facts about the structure of natural languages, English especially, which raise difficulties for the theory proposed. Each difficulty will be discussed in turn. Since it is hardly to be expected that the learning of all of the many kinds of grammatical regularities that exist will prove amenable to interpretation in terms of the above proposals, a purpose of the discussion will be to determine the range of phenomena to which the theory can hope to apply, and suggest ways of extending its scope.

Contrasting word order
Of the conceivable arrangements of any given set of morphemes, usually only a few are grammatically possible (e.g., *The man*, is possible in English whereas *Man the*, is not); the word order is said by linguists to be "restricted" to those that can occur (e.g., Harris, 1951, p. 184). When two (or more) arrangements are grammatically possible, sometimes the two orders are equivalent (e.g., *boys and girls, girls and boys*), in which case the order is said to be "free"; more often the two orders are nonequivalent (e.g., *Georege hit John, John hit George*, or *The child is inside the car, The car is inside the child*), in which case the orders are said to "contrast."

In mastering distinctions associated with contrasts between word orders, the child probably learns to respond to relationships quite different from any suggested so far in this paper. For example, in English both the sequences Noun + *inside*, and *Inside* + noun can occur; to use them appropriately the child must presumably learn to place *inside* before the word for the container and after the word for the contained object. One of the children the writer has studied uttered both verb-noun and noun-verb sequences at about 24 months of age, but he had apparently not learned that the agent of an action goes before the verb, and the object of the action typically after it, so that where English word order contrasts, his word order was free. Thus, among Gregory's utterances one finds *carry Mommy* (where Mommy is to do the carrying), *comes elevator, truck fix, fall down rabbit*, as well as the normal English word order, e.g., *Daddy fix, Mommy comes*, etc. Apparently the agent—action sequence is not necessarily primitive in the English sentence but can develop, at least in some children, as a polarization of a sequence which is initially more or less random. In a similar way one finds Gregory saying *inside* Doctor Z——(meaning that Dr. Z——is inside his office), *pocket inside*, as well as the normal order, e.g., *candy inside, inside pocket*.

It seems clear that the theory developed is not relevant to the learning of contrasts between word orders, and that its scope must be confined to the learning of restrictions on word order. This exclusion from the theory may be quite far-reaching: it seems probable that features of English word order which have to do with the difference between transitive and intransitive verbs, and with the distinction between the prepositional and adverbial use of words like *inside, on, off, down*, etc. (e.g., *the car outside, outside the car*, or *the light* [is] *on, on the table*) may not develop until the appropriate contrasts have been learned.

Cues to the "middle" of utterances
If, as claimed, children learn the sentence positions of words and phrases, they must have some way of identifying where in the sentence the initial phrase ends and the next phrase begins. In the experiments described, the boundary was clearly defined by the procedure: the subjects filled in the entire first

or last phrase. (In the one experiment where this was not true learning was impaired.) But what cues define borders between consituents for the 2-year-old learning the natural language?

One can only speculate about possible answers to this question. Two major types of cue offer themselves for consideration. The first have to do with intonation. By "intonation" is meant the variety of phenomena referred to by such terms as "stress," "pitch," "juncture," "off-glide," "on-glide," "contour," "superfix," "intonation pattern," etc. Just how much information about utterance structure is given by intonation is currently a matter of controversy in the linguistic literature. According to Trager and Smith (1951, pp. 67–77), the segmentation of an utterance into parts, and of the parts into parts, is almost completely specified by features of intonation. If this is true, most of the necessary information about the location of the boundaries between positions is contained within an utterance as spoken. However, the extent of the correlation between intonation phenomena and grammatical structure has been seriously questioned (e.g., Bolinger, 1957). Moreover, Trager and Smith's analysis assumes the existence of 12 phonemes which have to do with stress, pitch, and juncture. Recent work indicating that pitch and not intensity is the main cue to stress (Bolinger, 1958) would appear to put this phonemic analysis in jeopardy. It is doubtful, however, that anyone would claim that intonational phenomena provide no information about the partition of utternaces.

That intonation does provide information about segmentation is shown by the following demonstration. A five-word nonsense sentence, *Ob ordem kivil mervo eena* was recorded several times over, spoken in two ways. In one case the sentence was spoken with definite primary stress on the first syllables of the second and last words; in the other case stresses were placed on the third and last words; care was taken that there should be no special pause between any pair of words. Five people on the institute staff listened to each form of the sentence and wrote down a five-word English sentence which seemed to them grammatically similar to the model. It was predicted that the sentence would be

heard as composed of two parts, with the point of division located immediately following the word carrying the first main stress. Despite the crudity of the stimuli, the prediction was consistently borne out. In half the sentences a subject-predicate division was placed at the predicted mid-point (e.g., *The lády/goes into tówn, The algebra cláss-room/seated twénty*); in four sentences an initial prepositional phrase was separated off (e.g., *For swéetening/she preferred súgar, In this órder/words flý*); in the remaining sentence the midpoint divided the predicate-phrase (*They are góing/right awáy*—with a pronoun subject in English the first main stress tends to shift forward). If the length of the juncture between words, as well as the location of the first main stress, were manipulated, it may well be that the subjects could be led to be more consistent in the type of division they hear.

In addition to intonational phenomena, a role in defining the immediate constituents may well be played by the closed-class morphemes (i.e., articles, prepositions, auxiliary verbs, etc.—these classes are called "closed" because they contain only a small number of morphemes which change relatively slowly in the history of a language, whereas the "open" classes, i.e., nouns, verbs, and adjectives, contain enormous numbers of members and show a relatively fast turnover historically). Computer programs which analyze grammatical structure rely completely on the closed-class morphemes (Klein and Simmons, 1961). How much use the child makes of them probably depends on his level of development, since some of the closed-class morphemes tend to develop relatively late. However, even in the early stages of development when the child may not differentiate them clearly, they may nevertheless provide boundary markers for the utterance constituents. In ordinary conversation these morphemes are typically unstressed and poorly differentiated phonetically (cf./wənəgow/for *want to go*, / əpiysəkukiy/for *a piece of cookie*, /ələ/ for *all the*, etc.); conceivably they may serve in the early stages to provide a noise-filled physical separation between the stressed (and therefore phonetically clearer) meaning-bearing open-class words in the utterances the child is exposed to. Some support for this speculation is provided by one of the children studied by the writer at 24–27 months of age. Steven used two elements like these morphemes: one, which will be written *uh*, usually took the phonetic form /ə/; the other, which will be written *di* consisted of /d/ followed by a front or central vowel. Although they were devoid of meaning, definite rules seemed to govern Steven's use of these elements. Both could occur at the beginning or middle of almost any utterance; when one of them occurred at the middle of the utterance, it seemed to mark the boundary between immediate constitutents. Thus, in the corpus of Steven's utterances at this time there is a sequence *up uh top* (i.e., "up on top"), and another *up top uh Betty* (ie., "up on top of Betty"), where *uh* appears to have shifted forward to the phrase division. Similarly, there is *Bethy di sleepy bed* (i.e., "Bethy's asleep in bed"), and *no uh Daddy sleepy* (i.e., "Daddy's not asleep," or, "I don't want Daddy to sleep"), where there is again a shift to the phrase division. While Steven was the only one of the three children studied to develop elements of this kind, his apparent use of them as boundary markers may indicate how very young children tend to hear some closed-class morphemes, even if they do not incorporate them in their own speech in this way.

Positional regularities in English?

Since colloquial English constitutes both the terminal point of the child's own development and the verbal environment in which he develops, a theory which proposes that what is learned are the locations of words must suppose that rigid rules define what parts of speech can occur in what phrase and sentence positions in ordinary English grammar.

In discussing the extent to which such a correlation exists, it is convenient to follow recent work in linguistics which divides English grammar into two parts. According to Harris (1957) and Chomsky (1957), the grammar of a language can be hierarchized into an elementary part, called the "kernel" of the language, and a second part which consists of a set of transformational rules for deriving complex sentences from simple ones. The kernel grammar contains the definitions of the main parts of speech and describes rules for constructing simple declarative statements without complex noun or verb phrases. The transformational rules then carry these kernel sentences into other sentences, or into phrase or clause segments of sentences, which could not be derived in the kernel grammar. Thus from the kernel of English one could generate *The man is biting the dog*. The transformational rules would then show how to turn this into the passive, or into the negative, or into any of several questions (e.g., *Why is the man biting the dog?*), or into a relative clause (e.g., . . . *who is biting the dog* . . .), or into a noun phrase (e.g., *The man's biting the dog*, as subject perhaps of *is cause for surprise*), etc.

Obviously no set of rules defining the positions of words and phrases in simple declarative sentences like *The light is on* or *George walked across the street*, will also fit the part-of-speech positions in complex sentences of transformational origin like *She found them helping the man make it go* with its successive noun-verb sequences, or *The boy's pushing the lawnmower woke the baby* where the arrangement of words in the initial noun phrase is more like that of a normal sentence than of an ordinary noun phrase. Correlations of parts of speech and sentence positions must therefore be discussed separately for kernel sentences and for the derived transforms. Within the simple declarative kernel sentence there appears to be a standard arrangement of words and phrases which is normal for this type of sentence. (Whether this arrangmenet actually shows the detailed correlations of words and phrases with positions which is required by the theory proposed will be considered in the next section.) Similarly, in each type of transform there seem to be definite rules governing the positional arrangements of parts of speech which is standard for that type of transform. For example, all interrogatives are constructed according to a plan which is standard for interrogatives; similarly questions beginning with *what*, *where*, *why*, *when*, *how*, *who* have a common arrangment; relative clauses follow one of two main arrangements according to whether the pronoun is object or subject of its verb; transforms which occupy noun positions in other sentences follow one of several standard arrangements (e.g., *The boy's pushing the lawnmower, The light's being on, His braking the car at that moment,* etc., or *The reading of books, The acting of plays,* etc., or *For the light to the on, For him to brake the car at that moment,* etc., and several other forms); the same is true for the several other types of transform. In general, therefore, within the kernel and within each of the various types of transform there is a standard arrangement of parts of speech; the various standard arrangements are, however, all different from each other.

One way to formulate this state of affairs would be to regard English not as a unitary language, but as a family of sublanguages. The sentences in some of the sublanguages are complete English sentences; in others they do not occur alone, being merely clauses or phrases of English. The sublanguages differ in that the sequential arrangement of morphemes in each sublanguage is peculiar to that sublanguage. The languages have in common the fact that they all share the same vocabulary, and that any class of words which constitutes a part of speech in one sublanguage constitutes a part of speech in all the others. Moreover there are sentence-by-sentence correspondences between the sublanguages: to every sentence in each of the transformations there corresponds a sentence in the kernel (e.g., to *John was hit by George* in the passive transformation, there corresponds *George hit John* in the kernel). However, the converse, that to every sentence in the kernel there corresponds a sentence in each transformation, is not true since many of the transformations are defective vis-à-vis the kernel (e.g., there are no passive transforms of kernel sentences containing the verb *to be* or intransitive verbs). The kernel therefore has a privileged status since the sentences in each sublanguage apparently constitute a mapping of some large group of sentences of the kernel (cf. Harris, 1957, Footnote 61). It is worth noting that the changes in arrangement made in the various transformations are usually rather minor ones, and much of the normal word order of the kernel grammar tends to be retained (e.g., in the interrogative there is merely an inversion of subject and auxiliary verb; noun transforms like *The boy's pushing the lawnmower*

differ little in arrangment from the kernel sentences to which they correspond, i.e., *The boy was pushing the lawnmower,* etc.).

In attempting to account for the child's learning of this intricate set of structures, it seems to the writer that it would be sound strategy to aim first at finding an explanation for the learning of the kernel of the language, i.e., for the learning of the structure of the simple declarative English sentence. This constitutes enough of a problem already. Moreover, any proposed theory which fails to account for the learning of the kernel will, a fortiori, fail to account for the learning of the structure of the language as a whole. If a viable account of the learning of the kernel can be found, then the fact that all the sublanguages have so very much in common (the same vocabulary and parts of speech, and many of the same word arrangements) suggests that there may be some hope of treating the learning of the other sublanguages as a problem in transfer of training. In any case the remainder of this discussion will consider only whether the proposals advanced earlier can be worked into a defensible account of the learning of the kernel grammar.

Even with scope of the proposals narrowed in this way, there still remains the problem that the verbal environment in which the child learns contains both kernel and transforms, and therefore does not consistently present to him the same parts of speech in the same positions. It is difficult to evaluate this problem. On the one hand, it is noticeable that adults tend to simplify their language when speaking to very young children; also, since transforms usually change the normal word order in minor ways, it is probably true that most stretches of speech exemplify the normal positional arrangements more than they distort them. On the other hand, in the early stages of development the positional relationships in the child's own language obviously do not simply mirror the relationships in the adult English around him, but must be related to them in a much more complex manner. Almost nothing is known about the sequence in which various structures of English develop, so there is no point in discussing this question further.

Contingencies between positions

Even as a theory of the learning of the kernel grammar, the proposals advanced are insufficient. The fundamental stumbling block is that the parts of speech which can occur in one position are frequently contingent on what part of speech occurs in some other position. Another way of expressing this difficulty is to say that the proposals advanced predict more generalization than actually occurs in natural languages. Thus, if four parts of speech, A, B, C, and D, occur in sequences AB and CD, the theory predicts that sequences AD and CB should also occur, by generalization. Yet such unlimited generalization of context often fails to occur in natural languages.

The concept of a primary phrase. The above difficulty arises in part because the proposals advanced make no provision that sentences be segmented so that generalization only occurs between comparable units. Consider the predicate phrases in such sentences as *George is throwing, George is reading, George is throwing accurately, George is reading the book.* According to the binary fractionation model, in the first two sentences, the first predicate position is occupied by *is* and the second position by *throwing* or *reading;* in the other two sentences the first predicate position has *is throwing* or *is reading,* and the second position *accurately* or *the book.* If the content of the first position in one case is recombined with that of the second position in the other case one obtains such predicate phrases as *is accurately, is reading throwing.* As they stand, the proposals can be interpreted to predict that such recombinations would occur by generalization. To avoid such absurdities the theory clearly has to regard the predicate division of *George is throwing* into *is +* *throwing* as somehow less important than the predicate division of *George is reading the book* into *is reading + the book.* The simplest way to accomplish this is to set up a distinction between "primary phrases" and "components of phrases" (i.e., morphemes): *is throwing, the book, accurately* are "primary phrases," each having component morphemes (e.g., *is, throw, -ing; accurate, -ly*).

The proposals advanced must contain two levels, and must state specifically that it is the locations of expressions which are primary phrases, or whose parts are primary phrases, that are learned, and that within each type of primary phrase the locations of the component morphemes are also learned. With the proposals thus modified, one could say that the first part of a sentence is a noun phrase, and that the second part is either a verb phrase, or has as its first component a verb phrase. A statement of this kind is not possible unless a primary phrase such as a verb can be treated as a single unit, regardless of whether it is *throws, throw, is throwing, has thrown, has been throwing.*

Primary phrases typically consist of an open-class morpheme (e.g., noun, verb) together with one or more closed-class morphemes (e.g., article, auxiliary verb). Since the closed-class morphemes tend to be specific to the primary phrases to which they belong (e.g., articles to noun units, *-ly* to adverbial units), and tend to recur much more frequently than the open-class morphemes, they could serve as cues to "mark" or "tag" primary phrases. They would then facilitate the learning of the locations of primary phrases.

Some support for the concept of a primary phrase unit is provided by Glanzer (1962), who has shown that in paired-associate learning, although associates are learned more readily to open- than closed-class words in isolation, the opposite is true when the words are embedded in a nonsense syllable context. For example, although *of* is a more difficult associate than *food, tah of zum* is easier than *yig food seb.* Glanzer interprets the results to indicate that closed-class words are incomplete units when isolated from context.

The notion of a primary phrase also receives some confirmation in the stress sequences in English, since the normal English intonation seems generally to mark with some degree of strong stress the principal word of each primary unit in simple sentences (e.g., *Our néighbor is réading the ríot-act quite vocíferously to his chíldren in the gárden*).

One new problem is created by the concept of a primary phrase: one now has to enquire what makes the phrase a unit. What, if the metaphor will be forgiven, provides the psychological cement which binds the morphemes of a primary phrase more closely to each other than to other components of an utterance? Discussion of this question is temporarily deferred.

Contingencies still incompatible with the proposals. Even when utterances are treated as segmented into primary phrases in the above manner, there are still very many cases where the occupancy of one position is contingent on the occupancy of other positions. Thus, in many English dialects, a small class of verbs (e.g., *is, become, seem*) yield predicate phrases consisting of verb + adjective, whereas following other verbs one usually finds adverbs (e.g., *The wind became violent,* but *The wind blew violently; The opposition seemed skillful,* but *The opposition objected skillfully*). The widespread phenomenon of grammatical agreement constitutes another kind of contingency between positions. Consider, for example, the case of the arbitrary gender distinction in French. Masculine and feminine articles, and endings elsewhere in the sentence, occur in the same positions as each other; according to the theory as it now stands, their contexts should generalize feminine articles and endings occurring in association with masculine nouns and vice versa. A French child constructed according to the theory should get thoroughly confused. Since French children apparently contrive not to be, there is clearly something lacking in the proposals advanced. Within primary phrases a contingency of one morpheme on the presence of another in the same unit is particularly frequent. There is, for instance, the contingency between certain prepositions and verbs (e.g., *tear up, think over*), or between certain words and noun-making particles (e.g., *involve-ment,* but *depend-ence*). Such contingencies become very elaborate in the varied declensions and conjugations of highly inflected languages. Thus, to write a computer program which would produce Latin verb forms, one would have to proceed more or less by setting up paired lists A and a, B and b, C and c, . . . etc.; on List A would be the first conjugation stems, and on List a the first conjugation endings; Lists B and b,

C and c, D and d would cover the second, third, and fourth conjuagtions, and Lists E and e, F and f, . . . Z and z would take care of the irregular forms. A long disjunctive instruction would be required stating that a verb consists of a pair of items either from A and a, or from B and b, or C and c, . . . or Z and z. According to the theory proposed, such an intricate system should be very difficult to learn: the stems and endings should both generalize in the course of learning with the result that the whole complex system should collapse into simple structure—one set of stems and one set of endings; it would, according to the theory, be simpler that way. Yet apparently it was not. It is, of course, possible that the Roman child did overgeneralize in this way at some point in his development, much as English speaking children occasionally form participles like *singed* and *broked;* but such generalizations must clearly have been relatively transitory and easily corrected, otherwise the language itself would presumably have been less stable.

There are therefore two central problems which cannot be handled by the theory as it now stands: the contingencies between the contents of different positions, and the question as to what causes the morphemes of a primary phrase to "go together" as a unit.

Learning contingencies. Let us add to the theory the assumption that the subjects learning a language tend to form associations—similar to those studied in paired-associate experiments—between morphemes of the language, and let us see if the addition of this assumption can provide a solution to the above problems. The assumption itself is not an extravagant one. That English-speaking subjects do indeed form such associations is amply demonstrated by the work of Miller and Selfridge (1950) and others.

The notion that learned paired associations between morphemes play a role in learning grammatical strcuture can only be plausible under certain circumstances. If one is forced to assume that every member of one of the large open classes of morphemes becomes associated with every member of another such class, the sheer number of associations posited becomes astronomical, and the assumption therefore implausible. If, however, one can assume that the foci of associative bonds are typically members of the closed morpheme classes (i.e., articles, prepositions, plural -s, pronouns, auxiliary verbs, verb endings -*ing*, -*ed*, etc., adverbial -*ly*, noun and verb suffixes -*ment*, -*ence*, -*ize*, etc.), the assumed number of paired associates learned, though still large, is very considerably less large. If the validity of the law of exercise is assumed, i.e., that the strength of an associative link is proportional to the frequency of occurrence of the pair, then, given the fact that the most frequently occurring morphemes are members of the closed classes, it is inevitable that these morphemes should become the foci of associational links. From the law of exercise one would predict that the strongest associative bonds should form between closed-class morphemes, as, for instance, between prepositions and articles (e.g., *near the*, *of a*, *in some*), or between auxiliaries and verb endings (e.g., *is—ing*, *has—ed*, *has—en*); links somewhat less strong should occur between closed- and open-class morphemes—thus an association of some strength might be expected to be learned between the articles and virtually all the nouns in an English speaker's vocabulary, and between the auxiliary and verb endings and the verb stems. Paired-associate links of negligible strength would be expected to form between pairs of open-class words, except for a few pairs—few in proportion to the total number of possible pairs—which recur together frequently for ecological rather than grammatical reasons (e.g., *drive-car*, *drink-coffee*).[4]

Most cases of contingencies between positions can be schematized more or less as follows. One of two (or more) words, or classes of words may occupy the first position in a construction. Let us call these A′ and A″. These are followed by a word class, P, which is in turn followed by elements x and y, the choice of x or y being contingent on whether A′ or A″ occurs in first position. That is, if an A′ occurs then x occurs, if an A″ then y, giving grammatical sequences A′Px, A″Py; the elements x and y thus "agree" with the earlier part of the utterance. It is possible, of course, for x and y to precede P, in which case the formulae would read A′xP, A″yP, with the covarying elements contiguous. In terms of the theory one must assume that in the course of learning contingencies of this nature a paired-associate link forms between x and every A′, and between y and every A″. If A′ and A″ are members of a closed word class, as is often the case (e.g., pronouns each individually linked with particular verb endings x, y, . . .), the assumption seems to the writer reasonably plausible since the number of associations assumed is quite limited, and the amount of practice enormous. Frequently A′ and A″ are not completely different words but are distinguished only by accompanying closed-class elements. Thus A′ may take the form Af or fA and A″ the form Ag or gA, where f and g are closed-class morphemes, either affixes or separate elements like articles or auxiliaries. The formulae then take the form AfPx, AgPy (or fAPx, gAPy). Gender in French, and the singular-plural distinction in English and a large number of languages seem to be examples of this type.[5] The only associative linkages which need be assumed are between f and x, and g and y.

The theory has now developed all the ideas necessary for understanding grammatical frames (e.g., in English a gramatical frame consists of an arrangement of closed-class morphemes and dashes, such as *The—s—ly*, which completely determines the parts of speech going in each vacant position). If a part of a language fulfills the formulae fAPx, gAPy, and if it is assumed that the

---

[4] The recent finding (Glanzer, 1962) that closed-class words elicit a greater variety of responses than open-class words in free word association appears to support these contentions. However, it is not certain that free association data are germane, since there may be factors of set operative in free association experiments, which lead subjects to prefer responses based on meaning (e.g., perhaps, *black-white*) to responses that reflect directly learned verbal contingencies (e.g., perhaps, *black-board*).

[5] It is here assumed that the absence of an ending which is frequently present can itself serve as the focus of an association. Structural linguists frequently treat the absence of an element as itself an element; thus, in the same way that *boys* is analyzed as *boy* + -*s*, many grammarians analyze *boy* as *boy* + ø, where ø is the "zero ending" associated with the singular. The notion that the absence of a frequently present cue can itself serve as a cue does not seem objectionable psychologically. The English concord can thus be schematized as NøVs or NsVø (N = noun, V = verb, ø = zero ending); this exemplifies the text formula.

dependencies of fA and gA units on first position and of Px and Py units on second position are learned in addition to the paired associates f-x, g-y, then it is clear that the frames f——x, g——y will determine the parts of speech occupying the blanks.

From the assumption that children learn both positional regularities and paired associations between morphemes, it is possible to deduce the conditions under which overgeneralization would be expected to occur in the course of learning declensions and conjugations. Such errors would depend on the relative rates of learning positional regularities and associations. If the positional regularities are learned more rapidly, children should pass through a stage where "errors" such as *singed* and *broked* are common. The relative paucity of inflexions in English gives the English-speaking child less scope for errors of this nature than children learning some other languages; it would be interesting, for example, to know the extent and kinds of overgeneralizations that the elaborate case systems and conjugations of Russian or Finnish give rise to in the children of these countries. Guillaume (1927) provides some data on the development of the verb inflections in French. According to Guillaume, initially verbs tend not to be inflected: one form is used regardless of context. For example, in the case of the verb *tenir*, of which the three most used forms are *tenir*, *tenu*, and *tient* (or *tiens—tiens* and *tient* are, of course, phonetically identical), only *tient* may be used, e.g., *il a tient* instead of *il a tenu*. At a somewhat later stage the verb is inflected but overgeneralizations are frequent—Guillaume cites the infinitive *tiendre* (instead of *tenir*), the participle *éteindé* (instead of *éteint*), the imperfects *prendais*, *tiendais* (instead of *prenais*, *tenais*). Of particular interest is the fact that alternative incorrect instances of the same form are uttered in quick succession by the same child. Thus one child is reported as using both the participles *buvé* and *buvu* (instead of *bu*, from *boire*) indiscriminately at one period; similarly, both *ouvri* and *ouvert*, *pris* and *prendu*, are reported as occurring in the same or successive utterances. If positional regularities (e.g., learning to place *-é*, *-i*, or *-u* at the end of the verb stem) are learned more rapidly than paired-associates (e.g.,

associations of particular endings *-é*, *-i*, or *-u* with particular verb stems) are formed, then it would be predicted that such forms as *buvé* and *buvu* might both occur temporarily without a marked preference for one or the other being shown.[6]

If cases exist where associations are formed more rapidly than the positional regularities are learned, a different kind of error would be expected—one in which there is some inversion of the normal order of morphemes. Invented English examples might be *fall-downed*, or *hang-uping*.

The notion that associations form between pairs of morphemes may also provide an answer to the question raised earlier as to what makes the morphemes of a primary phrase go together as a unit. If the strength of an associational link between morphemes is a function of the proximity of the morphemes in the sentence as well as of the frequency of their joint occurrence, it would follow that in the great majority of utterances each open-class morpheme will be more strongly associated with the other morphemes of the primary phrase in which it occurs than with morphemes outside the phrase.

Conclusion

The preceding discussion indicates that the line of thought developed from the experi-

---

[6] It would probably be wrong to view the learning of conjugations as simply an associating of particular stems with particular endings. In the Indo-European languages conjugations tend to have a characteristic thematic stem vowel. Thus in French the stems of two conjugations end with a thematic *-e* or *-i* in many forms, and the "*-re*" verbs have a terminal consonant (cf. the futures *donn-e-r-ai*, *fin-i-r-ai*, *vend-ø-r-ai*). In Latin thematic long vowels *-ā*, *-ē*, *-i* were characteristic of three conjugations and in the remaining conjugation a consonantal (or short vowel) stem was thematic. It would follow from the general line of thought presented that these thematic vowels (or their absence) should permit a considerable economy in the number of associations learned, since often it need only be assumed that associations form between the radical and the thematic vowel on the one hand, and between the vowel and those endings specific to a conjugation on the other. In Latin the three long-vowel conjugations sometimes shared endings which were not possessed by the other conjugation, so that one might speculate that the length of the stem vowel itself may have been a focus for associations, permitting a further reduction in the total number of associations to be learned.

ments described certainly cannot provide a general theory of the learning of grammatical word order. However, the gross facts of English structure reviewed appear to be compatible with a modified version of the theory, restricted in scope. The necessary restrictions in scope are the limitation of the theory to the learning of the kernel grammar (although further study may permit extension to transformations), and the exclusion of the learning of contrasts between word orders.

As modified the theory proposes: (*a*) "What is learned" are the locations of units, and associations between pairs of morphemes. (*b*) The location learned is the location of a unit within the next-larger containing unit of a hierarchy of units. There are hierarchies at two levels: within sentences the units are primary phrases and sequences of primary phrases; within primary phrases the ultimate units are morphemes. (*c*) The learning of locations is a case of perceptual learning—a process of becoming familiar with the sounds of units in the temporal positions in which they recur.

REFERENCES

Bolinger, D. L. "Intonation and Grammar." *Language Learning*, VIII (1957), 31–38.

———. "A Theory of Pitch Accent in English." *Word*, XIV (1958), 109–49.

Braine, M. D. S. "The Ontogeny of English Phrase Structure: The first Phase." *Language*, XXXIX (1963), 1–13.

Brown, R. W. "Linguistic Determinism and the Part of Speech." *Journal of Abnormal and Social Psychology*, LV (1957), 1–5.

Chomsky, N. *Syntactic Structures*. The Hague: Mouton & Co., 1957.

Gibson, J. J., and Gibson, Eleanor J. "Perceptual Learning: Differentiation or Enrichment?" *Psychology Review*, LXII (1955), 32–41.

Glanzer, M. "Grammatical Category: A Rote Learning and Word Association Analysis." *Journal of Verbal Learning and Verbal Behavior*, I (1962), 31–41.

Guillaume, P. "Le développement des éléments formels dans le langage de l'enfant." *Journal de Psychologie*, XXIV (1927), 203–29.

Harris, Z. S. *Methods in Structural Linguistics*. Chicago: University of Chicago Press, 1951.

———. "Co-occurrence and Transformation in Linguistic Structure." *Language*, XXXIII (1957), 283–340.

Klein, S., and Simmons, R. F. "Automated Analysis and Coding of English Grammar for Information Processing Systems." *Sys. Developm. Corp. Rep.*, 1961, SP-490.

Miller, G. A. *Language and Communication*. New York: McGraw-Hill Book Company, 1951.

———, and Selfridge, J. A. "Verbal Context and the Recall of Meaningful Material." *American Journal of Psychology*, LXIII (1950), 176–85.

Trager, G. L., and Smith, H. L., Jr. "An Outline of English Structure." *Studies in Linguistics: Occasional Papers*, 1951, No. 3.

THOMAS G. BEVER, JERRY A. FODOR, AND WILLIAM WEKSEL

42   The following is a critique of Braine's preceding paper, Chapter 41. See the introduction to the latter.

Braine presents his counterarguments to the following paper in "On the Basis of Phrase Structure: A Reply to Bever, Fodor, and Weksel" (*loc. cit.*, LXXII, 483–92). Braine tries to defend his position and rejects the claim that his proposals are "inconsistent with the character of the verbal environment," and discusses the proposals about the learning of word classes, etc.

The discussion is continued in another paper by Bever, Fodor, and Weksel "Is Linguistics Empirical?" (*loc. cit.*, LXXII, 493–500), in which "the arguments for analyzing the English declarative as transformationally generated" are discussed at some length. (The latter two are not reprinted here, for considerations of space. Instead, a resumé of each follows Bever, *et al.*'s reply.)

A. B. A.

THEORETICAL NOTES ON THE ACQUISITION OF SYNTAX: A CRITIQUE OF "CONTEXTUAL GENERALIZATION"

It has been recently suggested that the child's assimilation of the syntax of simple sentences can be attributed to a process of "contextual generalization" whereby information about the ordinal position of words and phrases is transferred from sentences the child has observed to new sentences. The theoretical and experimental bases for this claim are examined in the present paper. It is argued that such a process could not, in principle, account for what children learn about the structure of or relations between the sentences of their language. It is further argued that the experiments which purportedly demonstrate the existence of contextual generalization are, in fact, equivocal.

INTRODUCTION

There is a wide gap between the view of language current in linguistics (cf. Chomsky, 1957; Fodor and Katz, 1964; Lees, 1960) and the view of the language-using organism implicit in psychological theories of learning. The reason for this is clear. Neither the methods nor the results of recent work on grammar are fully compatible with the meth-

Reprinted from Psychological Review *72.467–482 (1965) by permission of the authors and the American Psychological Association.*

This work was supported in part by the United States Army, Navy, and Air Force under Contract DA 36–039–AMC–03200 (E); in part by the National Science Foundation (Grant GP-2495); the National Institutes of Health (Grants MH-04747-04 and MPM-16, 760); the National Aeronautics and Space Administration (Ns G-496); the United States Air Force (ESD Contract AF 19 [628–2487]).

Thomas Bever is a Junior Fellow, Society of Fellows, Harvard University.

William Weksel was a National Science Foundation Postdoctoral Fellow during the preparation of this manuscript.

We wish to thank Margaret Bullowa and her staff for their kindness in making available to us the data discussed in Footnote 2.

odological and theoretical tenets prevalent in psychology.

The present paper examines the work of Braine (1963). This work has been selected for analysis because Braine attempts to assimilate insights provided by current linguistic theories while retaining an approach typical of psychological inquiries into syntax. The inadequacies of Braine's position thus suggest a number of respects in which such theories resist translation into the vocabulary of learning theory. In particular, since Braine's position differs only in details from that of such other learning theorists as Jenkins and Palermo (1964), the arguments we shall present apply to their work *mutatis mutandis*.

According to Braine, "the acquisition of grammatical structure, especially those aspects of grammatical structure which have to do with word order . . . [p. 241]" is to be explained by appeal to a process of *contextual generalization*. Contextual generalization is informally defined as a process whereby an individual who learns the position of a word or a phrase in the sentence he hears "tends to place this segment in the same position in other contexts [p. 243]." Thus, " 'What is learned' are primarily the proper locations of words in sentences. [p. 243]."

Braine clearly recognizes that the ability to deal with novel sentences constitutes a major part of the child's linguistic competence. It is thus central among the phenomena that a theory of language-learning must explain. Braine takes the ability to construct and comprehend novel sentences to be a special case of transfer of training based upon stimulus and response generalization. Specifically, contextual generalization is identified as a case of perceptual learning, "a process of auditory differentiation, or of becoming familiar with, the temporal positions of expressions in utterances [p. 245]."

ARGUMENTS FOR CONTEXTUAL GENERALIZATION

Braine notes the inadequacy of a theory of syntax acquisition based on associative relations between lexical items. Such a theory cannot account for the ability of speakers to recognize the grammatical structure of nonsense material. Thus, a nonsense syllable, *kivil*, is recognized as a nonce verb in:

1. People kivil every day.

That is, 1 is recognized as syntactically well formed despite the lack of associative connections between the words.

Such examples show that the speaker's ability to exploit syntactic relations does not depend upon forming associative bonds between lexical items. Therefore, Braine argues, the speaker's information about syntactic structure primarily concerns the grammatical properties of *locations* in sentences. Thus, the child learns such facts as: The first position in a simple English sentence is characteristically the noun position; the second position is characteristically occupied by a verb. Since the syntactic properties of a position do not, by definition, depend on the lexical item or phrase that appears in that position, novel material in a given location is perceived as having the grammatical properties characteristic of that location. Thus *kivil* is recognized as a verb in 1 because it appears in the position assigned the verbal element in such sentences as:

2. The boys eat the rabbits.
3. The boys do eat the rabbits.

For Braine, then, the syntactic properties of a segment are determined by the locations in which it occurs. A verb is defined as a word which characteristically appears in the second position in simple sentences, a noun is a word which characteristically appears in the first position in simple sentences, etc. To learn the syntactic properties of a word is primarily to learn the positions in which it can occur. In particular, given the positions a word can occupy in one sentence, we can often predict the positions which it may occupy in new sentences. From the fact that *eat* occupies the second position in 2, we can predict that it will occupy the homologous position in 4.

4. The wolves eat the rabbits.

Syntax assimilation thus consists of gen-

eralizing information about the positions in which a word is observed to occur. The correct use of a given word in a given position in new sentences is a consequence of such processes of generalization.

Braine holds that a description of word order acounts for much of the grammar of English and, consequently, that a theory which accounts for the learning of positions will have considerable explanatory power. Braine admits, however, that learning syntactic relations cannot consist solely of learning the appropriate relative positions of words and phrases. First, Braine points out, knowledge of relative positions would contribute little to the mastery of languages in which syntactic relations are expressed by inflection rather than order. Second, the notion of a position must be construed sufficiently abstractly so that a given sentential position can be occupied either by a word or by a phrase. (Notice, for example, that the "second" position in 3, i.e., the position functionally equivalent to the one occupied by "eat" in 2, is filled by the phrase "do eat.") Some explanation is required for the fact that phrases may exhibit positional privileges analogous to those exhibited by single words. In short, an explanation is needed of how phrases can act as syntactic units.

To accommodate inflection as a syntactic device and to account for the integrity of the phrase, Braine resorts to a limited associationism. He postulates associative bonds between "closed-class" morphemes (e.g., inflections) and "open-class" morphemes such as nouns and verbs. For example, Braine would presumably hold that the phoneme "s" at the end of a noun is associated with the lack of a phoneme "s" at the end of a following verb and conversely. Such associations hold for simple declarative sentences like:

5. The boy eats the rabbits.
6. The boys eat the rabbits.

Braine believes that the formation of associations, augmented by position learning, is adequate to explain how the syntax of simple declarative sentences is learned. In effect, Braine considers such sentences to be sequences of "primary phrases." Primary phrases are themselves sequences of open-

and closed-class morphemes connected by associative bonds. "The location learned is that of a unit within the next larger containing unit of a hierarchy of units. There are hierarchies at two levels: within sentences the units are primary phrases and sequences of primary phrases; within primary phrases the ultimate units are morphemes [p. 263]."

Braine is aware that the information that certain sequences of linguistic elements behave as units and that such units can appear only in specified positions in simple sentences does not exhaust the speaker's knowledge of syntax. There are many different kinds of sentences allowing nearly all possible orders of words and primary phrases. Thus, if we take into account *all* the types of sentences in which it may occur, there are indefinitely many permissible locations of a linguistic unit (see examples, sentences 35–41). A list of the positions available to a linguistic unit could at best specify its behavior in only a circumscribed part of the language. Yet it is only the learning of such a list that contextual generalization could explain.

Braine meets this objection by restricting the scope of his theory to the assimilation of the grammatical properties of simple declaratives. He maintains this restriction is not arbitrary since simple declaratives have psychological and linguistic characteristics which justify postulating special processes for their assimilation. Braine thinks simple declaratives may predominate in the child's verbal environment, thus forming the primary models from which the child's knowledge of his language is extrapolated. Second, Braine claims recent work in linguistics divides grammar into two parts.

According to Harris (1957) and Chomsky (1957), the grammar of a language can be hierarchized into an elementary part, called the "kernel" of the language, and a second part which consists of a set of transformational rules for deriving complex sentences from simple ones. The kernel grammar contains the definitions of the main parts of speech and describes rules for constructing simple declarative statements . . . [p. 257].

Thus, if we can explain the acquisition of simple declarative sentences, we have ac-

counted for the basic component of the grammar. The remaining portion—the complex sentences produced by transformation—is to be described as a set of *sublanguages*, one sublanguage for each type of sentence (passive, relative, question, etc.). Rather than attempting to study English in its full complexity, Braine concludes ". . . it seems . . . that it would be sound strategy to aim first at finding an explanation for the learning of the kernel of the language, i.e., for the learning of the structure of the simple declarative English sentence. This constitutes enough of a problem already [p. 342]."

Finally, Braine argues that perceptual learning, of which contextual generalization is a special case, is a primitive process which does not demand much in the way of intellectual capacity of the learner. Contextual generalization would therefore satisfy at least one requirement on any process involved in first-language learning, namely, that it "not require intellectual capacities obviously beyond the reach of the 2-year-old [p. 245]."

If the learning of syntax is the generalization of the ordinal positions in which linguistic units appear, it is evident that the initial stage must consist in the perceptual isolation of such units. Braine claims that an argument for the feasibility of contextual generalization is that the boundaries of such units can be identified with certain specifiable properties of the speech signal.

Braine proposes two sorts of cues the child could use to identify these boundaries. One is "intonation": The stress, rhythm, and pitch patterns of sentences are assumed to be acoustic features which communicate information about segmentation. The other is the position of closed-class morphemes which, Braine holds, tends to delimit phrases.

We now turn to a discussion of these arguments. We first consider the claim that simple declaratives ought to receive special treatment. Second, we investigate whether the linguistic character of simple declaratives can be selected by reference to the syntactic properties of sentential positions. Third, we ask how much of the relation between simple declaratives and other types of sentences can be expressed by such a specification. Fourth, we consider broader issues raised by Braine's treatment of inflection, intonation, and perceptual isolation of units. Finally, we discuss his experimental techniques and results.

THE ROLE OF DECLARATIVE SENTENCES

Because he believes that a theory of the simple declarative sentences explains the basic part of the grammar and that such sentences predominate in the child's linguistic environment, Braine holds an account of the learning of simple declaratives is important even if it does nothing else. We shall return to the question of the kernel grammar presently. Let us first consider the claim that the verbal environment of the child exhibits a preponderance of grammatical simple declaratives.

It is clear that normal speech among adults does not exhibit any statistical bias towards fully grammatical simple declarative sentences. On the contrary, adult speech is usually ungrammatical (cf. Maclay and Osgood, 1959), and there is little evidence that adults engage in a careful limitation of their linguistic output when conversing with children.[1] Moreover, the verbal environment of children includes utterances produced by adults conversing among themselves, utterances produced by siblings with little command of the language, utterances heard on radio and television, etc. These diverse sources presumably form a heterogeneous verbal environment.

Even if simplified speech predominates in the child's verbal environment, there is no reason to suppose that the environment is unusually rich in simple declaratives. Analyses we have made of the speech of mothers taped during conversations with their chil-

dren fail to support that hypothesis.[2] On the contrary, of a total of 432 utterances, 258 were fully grammatical. Of these, only 46 were simple declaratives.

Of course the character of the verbal environment plays a major role in language acquisition. It determines which language, vocabulary, style, and accent the child learns. *What is unknown, however, is which features of the verbal environment are critical for such learning.* There is, at present, no reason to believe that the learning of English is facilitated by a preponderance of simple declaratives in the child's sample of his language. Nor is there any reason to suppose that such a bias normally obtains.

We turn now to the question of whether the simple declarative has any formal or linguistic peculiarities to which its claim for special psycholinguistic status might be referred.

Braine makes a mistake that has unfortunately been common in psychological investigations concerned with generative grammar.[3] He supposes there exists a base or kernel grammar producing all and only simple declaratives and that the transformational operations producing complex sen-

---

[1] Brown and Bellugi (1964) do find a relatively large proportion of fully grammatical utterances in their recordings of mother's speech to children. They do *not*, however find that simple declaratives are preponderant among such utterances. On the contrary in the only sample of their data they present (a sample which they say is "rather representative"), only one of the six sentences produced by the mother is of the simple declarative type.

[2] The data were supplied by Margaret Bullowa and her staff at the Massachusetts Mental Health Center. The total represents 38 half hours of recorded conversation between three mothers and their children taped at ages ranging from 6 to 30 months. Six transcripts were selected for analysis, greater weight being given the recordings made at 20 months than those made at 6 months.

Neither our judgments of grammaticality nor sentential type were checked for interjudge reliability. While some degree of latitude may be involved in judgments of the former kind, the criteria for the latter are reasonably objective. It is clear that there is need for an extensive survey of the verbal environment of the child; the data we have cited are intended only as preliminary.

[3] For examples of discussions in which this mistake appears to have been made, see Miller (1962); Miller, Galanter, and Pribram (1960); Osgood (1963); and Mehler (1963). All these assume that linguistics assigns a privileged status to the simple declarative. For example, Miller's (1962) discovery that it takes less time to find the passive corresponding to an active than to find the passive corresponding to a question is *not* explained by appeal to the linguistic fact that the active is the underlying form in the production of the passive and the question. There is no such linguistic fact.

tences are defined over the declaratives generated by this base component. If this *were* the case, one might plausibly maintain that the status of the simple declarative as the underlying *linguistic* form justifies a parallel psycholinguistic precedence.

Braine is correct in asserting that there is a base form from which all syntactically related sentences are directly or indirectly derived. It is also true that base form is produced by a set of rules whose formal properties distinguish them from other rules in a generative grammar. *But it is not true that the base form is the simple declarative sentence.* The kernel grammar does *not* produce simple declarative sentences; it does not produce *any* sentences. Rather, the kernel grammar produces abstract structures that are transformed into a variety of different sentence types of which the simple declarative is one. In particular, the kernel sentence discussed by Chomsky (1957) should not be confused with these abstract structures. Kernel sentences differ from sentences of other types solely in that they are the consequence of applying only obligatory transformations to the kernel structure. Kernel sentences are thus in no sense the source for, or underlying form of, sentences of other syntactic types.[4]

Since the misunderstanding of the kernel notion has been widespread, it is worth indicating some of the linguistic considerations that militate against supposing the simple declarative to be the underlying form from which other sorts of sentences are derived. Consider the passive construction. We might attempt to derive *7b* from *7a* by a rule like that given in 8.

7a. The boy chases the dog.
7b. The dog is chased by the boy.
8. If NP_1 Verb NP_2 is a declarative sentence, and if NP_2 is the object of the verb, then NP_2 is Verbed by NP_1 is the corresponding passive.[5]

---

[4] That this has always been Chomsky's view is clear from a reading of *Syntactic Structures*. That Harris does not hold the simple declarative to be the base form follows from the fact that the notion of a derivation plays no role in Harris' theory. The mappings Harris (1957) employs in transformational analysis are characteristically symmetrical, hence there can be no questions of identifying an underlying syntactic form.

But now, consider 10, the result of applying 8 to 9:

9.   The boy chases the dogs.
10. *The dogs is chased by the boy.

a string which is not grammatical for many dialects since the number of the verb should be determined by the subject. To avoid 10, Rule 8 must be split into two rules:

8a. NP_1 V NP_2 + sg → NP_2 is V + ed by NP_1.
8b. NP_1 V NP_2 + pl → NP_2 + s are V + ed by NP_1.

However, consider 12 and 14, the result of of the application of 8a to 11 and 13 respectively.[6]

11. The boy is chasing the dog.
12. *The dog is is chasing ed by the boy.
13. The boy chased the dog.
14. *The dog is chased ed by the boy.

Just as the difference in the number of the object required us to adopt different passive rules for *7a* and 9, so two more rules, *8c* and *d*, will be required to passivize 11 and 15:

15. The boy is chasing the dogs.
8c. NP_1 is V ing NP_2 + sg → NP_2 + sg is being V ed by NP_1.
8d. NP_1 is V ing NP_2 + pl → NP_2 + pl are being V ed by NP_1.

and similarly for 13 and 16.

16. The boy chased the dogs.

---

[5] We shall adhere to the notational conventions employed by linguists. In particular, ungrammatical strings will be preceded by *. ø stands for the zero number of a linguistic class (the plural of the English word "sheep" is thus "sheep + ø"). The following abbreviations will also be employed: NP for Noun Phrase, T for Article, VP for Verb Phrase, S for Sentence, N for Noun, V for Verb, sg for the singular morpheme, pres for the present-tense morpheme, pl for the plural morpheme, Det for determiner. Be will be used to designate any inflection of the verb "to be."

[6] If *8a* can be allowed to interpret *is chasing* as a V at all, then it produces the incorrect form *12; if it cannot, then another new rule is required to produce 19 from 11. In all the examples in this paper, we do not claim to present the unique solutions and rules, either for those formulations which we show to be essentially incorrect or for those that are essentially correct. All the rules are considered out of the context of a presumed full grammar. *In* that context they might appear somewhat differently—but the distinctions and characteristics with which we are concerned will remain unchanged.

8e. NP_1 V + ed NP_2 + sg → NP_2 + sg was V + ed by NP_1.

8f. NP_1 V + ed NP_2 + pl → NP_2 + pl were V + ed by NP_2.

In general, if we derive passives from their corresponding actives, a different passive rule is required for each choice of object number and verb tense. For five tenses and two numbers there are at least 10 rules required to derive the simple passive from declarative sentences. Furthermore, even these 10 rules will not serve to derive the passive of more complicated sentences. For example, we will need special rules for:

16a. Does the boy chase the dog?
16b. Is the boy being chased by the dog?
17a. Why does the boy chase the dog?
17b. Why is the dog chased by the boy?

and so on.

In each of the cases we have discussed, the problem clearly arises from the attempt to derive the passive from its corresponding declarative. This difficulty would be avoided were it possible to define the transformation which rearranges the subject and object phrases so that it applies prior to the attachment of tense and number to the verb. In this way we specify the operations on the noun and verb relevant to passivization *without reference to the particular choice of tense and number they exhibit in a given sentence.* This rule is easily formulated:

18. NP_1 aux V NP_2 is rewritten as NP_2 aux be + Past part. V by NP_1.

However, it can be applied to generate all passives only if suitable abstract representations of sentences are provided as its domain. For example, the passive sentence, 19:

19. The dogs are being chased by the boy.

has, as its corresponding active, Sentence 15. Yet, if 19 is to be generated by an application of Rule 18, 15 cannot be its source, since 15 does not possess the formal properties required of strings in the domain of 18. No definite sense can therefore be given to the notion of applying 18 to 15. Rather, the source for 19 is the abstract illustrated in Figure 1.[7]

It can be demonstrated that derivations employing Rule 18 can account for the examples we have investigated so far. This means, in effect, that we have eliminated the proliferation of passive rules by insuring that inflections of number and tense are not specified by the passive rule. To do this, however, we have had to assume that the underlying form from which the passive derives is not a corresponding active but rather an abstract structure never realized in speech. Since analogous considerations show that the active itself is merely one of the deformations of this underlying structure, there would appear to be nothing in the linguistic theory of the derivation of English sentences which would justify assigning a special status to active declarative sentences.

CONTEXTUAL GENERALIZATION AND
THE LEARNING OF POSITION

Suppose, however, that we grant Braine's assumption that there is some point to a special theory of the psychological processes underlying the learning of the syntax of declaratives. We must ask how much of the character of such sentences emerges from an analysis of the order relations among their

---

[7] Of course, the result of 18's application to the structure in Figure 1 is *not* an actual sentence. The full derivation of Sentence 19 from the structure represented in Figure 1 is accomplished in at least three steps: (a) Rule 18 converts it into the string (constituent structure is not marked here) *the dog pl pl pres be + ing be + Past part. chase by the boy sg sg*; (b) an affix attachment rule (affix, V → V + affix) *then* applies to produce the string *the dog pl be + pl + pres be + ing chase + Past part. by the boy sg sg*; (c) morphophonemic "spelling" rules convert this into Sentence 19 (see the paragraph following 33 in this paper and Chomsky, 1957, for other examples of affix movement and sentence derivations). The concept of the abstract and concrete level in sentences is a formal representation of many intuitions: for example, the difference between "logical" and "apparent" grammatical relations, the description of relations among sentences, and so on (see Fodor and Katz, 1964, for various discussions). Notice that by having the affix attachment rule follow the passivization rule, 18, we avoid formally the multiplication of passive rules. Thus, this analysis is a formal account of the intuition that "passive" sentence is a unitary notion, and the intuition that it is the number of the apparent subject of the verb which determines verb number in English, not the number of the underlying or "logical" subject (see the section on inflection and Footnote 8 in this paper).

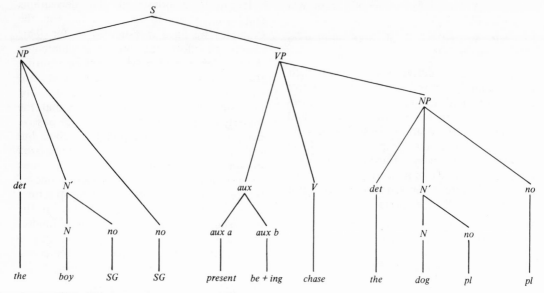

FIGURE 1. Tree diagram of the underlying (untransformed) structure of the sentence: "The boy is chasing the dog."

constituents. We shall see that very little of the speaker's knowledge of the syntactic structure of simple declaratives can be attributed to having learned such relations.

To see how little of the syntax of a simple declarative is expressed by order, it is only necessary to consider sentences whose grammatical structure is not so expressed. Thus a speaker who knows that 20 and 21 are sentences also knows that while 22 is perfectly good English, there is something wrong with the syntax of 23.

20. The kangaroo cost 10 dollars.
21. The child blew the kazoo.
22. The kazoo was blown by the child.
23. *Ten dollars was cost by the kangaroo.

This example is particularly embarrassing for Braine, since 20 and 23 exhibit precisely the sort of positional relations on the basis of which contextual generalization is supposed to operate. That is, since both "10 dollars" and "the kazoo" appear postverbally, and since "The kazzo" appears preverbally in 22, the operation of contextual generalization ought to permit the preverbal appearance of "Ten dollars" in 23. The ungrammaticality of 23 suggests that there must be a difference between "blow" and "cost." Though this difference is not revealed by their positional

privileges in simple declaratives, it is decisive for determining how passivization operates in sentences in which they occur.

A similar case is the following:

24. John phoned Jane up.
25. John phoned up Jane.
26. John phoned her up.
27. *John phoned up her.

Since "up" appears in the fourth and third positions respectively in 24 and 25, and since it appears in the fourth position in 26, Braine's theory predicts that place generalization requires its occurrence in 27. This prediction is incorrect. On the contrary, it is a necessary condition upon the grammaticality of sentences of the form:

28. John phoned up X.

that X not be a pronoun. Hence, if we are able to formulate the rule which permits 25 but precludes 27, we must take account not only of the ordinal positions of the words in those strings, *but also of the syntactic classes to which the words belong.*

These examples are a consequence of a quite general fact: *the types of expression that can appear at a given ordinal position in a simple declarative sentence are extremely heterogeneous.* This fact is of the utmost

270

importance for an evaluation of Braine's theory. For it entails that contextual generalization is an inadequate mechanism for extrapolating the grammatical regularities the child observes in his language. Many types of expression can appear at a given sentential position. Hence sentences exhibiting precisely the same ordinal relations among their segments may nevertheless be of different syntactic types. Since the operation of contextual generalization requires only that features of order be common to conditioned stimulus and generalized stimulus, it follows that we cannot infer that String S is a sentence whenever there exists a sentence, S', related to S in a way that satisfies the conditions for contextual generalization.

To put it slightly differently, the examples just discussed demonstrate that some of our information about the syntactic character of simple declaratives cannot be expressed in terms of location information; rules which determine the interrelations among simple declaratives and the relations between simple declaratives and other sorts of sentences distinguish between expressions that can appear in a given location.

The similarity betwen Braine's view and that of Jenkins and Palermo (1964) is most evident at this point. Jenkins and Palermo apparently hold that the syntactic structure of a sentence can be expressed by a sequence of markers representing the classes of which the words comprising the sentence are members. Thus, they remark that "... the ideas we want to present here are of two sorts: *sequence* and *class* [p. 164]" and that

> "Colorless green ideas sleep furiously" is a sentence in English not because it is true, or sensible, or interpretable by the listener, but because it is a "correct" assembly of classes appropriately modulated (*i.e.*, they are the right general classes of entries properly modified to take their places in the particular sequence). ... The critical question, then, is seen to be that of the organization of the elements into classes [p. 164].

It is thus evident that Jenkins and Palermo's view of syntax is simply a weaker version of Braine's. For while Jenkins and Palermo acknowledge only sequences of class markers (and inflection), Braine has noticed the necessity of providing some psychological

mechanism to account for the phrase structure of such sequences.

In short, there is no basis for Jenkins and Palermo's belief that the employment of mediational paradigms affords a breakthrough in the study of syntax assimilation. Though the formation of word classes can perhaps be accounted for by such paradigms, they throw no light whatever upon the assimilation of even such relatively superficial syntactic features as phrase structures. It goes without saying that appeals to them are utterly unilluminating on the question of how the child learns the deep syntactic structures with which this paper is primarily concerned.

THE DERIVATION OF ORDER

Thus far we have noted one sense in which order is a relatively unimportant feature of syntactic structure even in English where inflection is not widely used: Identity of order relations is compatible with considerable differences in syntactic form. There is a more important point which also stems from Braine's failure to distinguish between underlying and surface structure. Often a correct formulation of the rules determining syntactic structure requires distinguishing between the order of lexical items in the sentence and in the underlying representation from which the sentence is derived. While contextual generalization might conceivably account for learning the former, it is patent that it could not account for the learning of the latter.

For example, in our discussion of the passive we treated *be* + *ing* as a unit in the underlying representation of sentences like 15. There are intuitive and formal advantages to this treatment. It permits us to account for the intuition that *be* + *ing* functions as a semantic unit indicating a particular mode of the main verb. Moreover, treating these morphemes as a single item permits us to account for the fact that such strings as:

29a. *The man is chase the dog.
29b. *The man chasing the dog.

are not sentences: If *be* + *ing* is represented as a lexical unit, one of the morphemes comprising that unit cannot be selected without also selecting the other.

Cases in which simplicity of representation and linguistic intuition require an underlying order differing from the order of elements in the manifest sentence are found throughout English. Thus in sentences 24–27, the underlying form of the verb must be *phone + up*, since English restricts the particles that can accompany certain verbs. Thus we have no

30a.   *John phoned down the girl.
30b.   *John phoned the girl down.

Similarly, 31a, but not 31b, is grammatical.

31a.   They looked the house over.
31b.   *They looked the house in.

To account for such examples and for the fact that the verb-particle sequence forms a semantic unit, such sequences are recorded in the underlying form as *verb + particle*. But notice that, though the particle precedes the object in the *underlying* representation of 27, a mandatory transformation of that underlying structure permutes the particle and the object whenever the latter is a pronoun. Hence the underlying form of 27 has a different order from its manifest form. Moreover, this underlying order is *never* directly reflected in an actual sentence.

Finally, even the very simplest sentences derive from an underlying form in which the order of the elements differs from the manifest order. Consider:

32.   The child runs.

The terminal portion of the tree representing the underlying structure of this sentence is:

33.   Det N sg pres V.
       Øə/čaild/run.
       Øə/čayld/ranz

The tense marking (present) precedes the verb phrase in the underlying structure in order to permit a uniform treatment with more complicated sentences. In the manifest sentence, the tense marker is always attached to the first verbal element in the verb phrase whether that element is an auxiliary, modal, or compound verb. This is accomplished for complicated expansions of the auxiliary by a rule which permutes the tense marker with the adjacent verbal element to the right. If the tense and verb order for 32 were not as represented in 33, 32 would constitute an exception to this rule and would thus require

a complication of the grammar (cf. Chomsky, 1957, and Footnote 7).

This indirect relation between the order of elements in the underlying form and their order in the manifest sentence poses serious problems for *any* theory of syntax learning. It is clear that the child never encounters manifest models of the underlying sentence order. Adults do not utter such sequences as:

34.   Øə čaild s run.

We have seen, however, that in a formalization of English grammar 34 represents a step in the derivation of 32. Hence, if the child who learns English learns the rules governing the syntax, it follows that he *must learn to manipulate underlying structures, for which his verbal environment provides him with no explicit models.* It is evident that contextual generalization, simply because it *is* a variety of generalization, cannot account for such learning.

"SUBLANGUAGES"

We have seen that relatively little of the syntactic character of simple declarative sentences can be expressed in terms of the manifest order of their constituents. We now ask how much of the syntactic relations between simple declarative and other types of sentences can be expressed in those terms. We maintain that the behavior of a linguistic unit in complex sentences cannot be captured by a theory which represents its syntactic properties by a list of the positions it is capable of occupying. There are two reasons for this, one of which Braine acknowledges; the other has escaped him.

It is clearly possible to construct complicated sentences exhibiting almost any order of syntactic constituents. Thus in Sentence 15, Braine would presumably distinguish three major positions occupied, respectively, by *the boy*, *is chasing*, and *the dogs*. The relations between these three positions are, however, very flexible. Consider:

35.   The dogs are being chased by the boy.
36.   It is the dogs the boy is chasing.
37.   What is being chased by the boy are the dogs.
38.   What the boy is chasing are the dogs.
39.   It is the dogs that are being chased by the boy.

40. Chasing them is what the boy is doing to the dogs.
41. Chasing the dogs is what the boy is doing.

Far from it being the case, as Braine suggests, that transformation tends to produce relatively minor variations in order, examples 35–41 show that order is the syntactic property transformation is least likely to preserve.

Braine is aware that relative order is preserved only within sentences of the same syntactic type. This leads him to suggest that natural languages should be thought of as systems of "sublanguages," distinguished by a characteristic constituent order. This suggestion is defective in a number of ways. First, if sublanguages are specified solely by the ordinal relations of their constituents, there must be an infinity of sublanguages since sentences in a natural language may be arbitrarily long, and every pair of sentences which differ in length will ipso facto differ in constituent order at some level. It is thus logically impossible that the child should master his language by learning one sublanguage after another.

The preceding demonstrates what was shown above on purely syntactic grounds: The differences between types of sentences cannot, in general, be specified in terms of differences in constituent orders since sublanguages cannot be defined in those terms.

This can be seen most strikingly in the ambiguity of such sentences as:

42. The office of the president is vacant.

where the lexical items and order of constituents *at all levels* are the same on both readings despite the fact that any reasonable analysis of English into sublanguages must assign 42 to two sublanguages, because it can be questioned in two quite different ways (cf. 43 and 44):

43. Where is the office of the president?
44. Who held the office of the president?

There are other examples which illustrate the impossibility of exploiting constituent order to capture relations between syntactically different types of sentences: 45 is related to 46 rather than to 47 while the reverse holds for 48.

45. John is easy to please.
46. They please John.

47. John pleases them.
48. John is eager to please.

Since, however, the constituents of 45 and 48 are ordered in precisely the same way, we cannot appeal to order to explain the relations between the sublanguages these sentences belong to.

These examples reflect a fact that must be evident to anyone who has seriously considered the problem of describing the syntactic structure of a language like English: Very few of the interrelations between types of sentences are expressed by similarities and differences of manifest order. Rather, a theory which marks such interrelations must do so in terms of highly abstract constructs such as the phrase analyses and transformational histories underlying sentences. Linguistic evidence shows that no simpler apparatus explains intersentential relations that are intuitively evident to native speakers. It follows that Braine's attempt to specify sublanguages and their interrelations in terms of constituent order can be of no serious explanatory value.

INFLECTION

We now turn to some of the broader issues raised by Braine's theory. The first arises from difficulties implicit in Braine's assumption that the processes employed in learning order languages are different in kind from those employed in learning inflected languages.

The search for the mechanism of syntax acquisition is, presumably, a search for species-specific capacities common to all children. An adequate theory of syntax acquisition must explain the ability of a child to learn any language to which he happens to be exposed. It follows that a theory of language-learning which makes essential reference to linguistic features specific to a particular language or group of languages is necessarily suspect. However, one of Braine's arguments for contextual generalization rests on the fact that constituent order is a major device for expressing syntactic structure in English. It is thus notable that, whatever the relevance of word order to English, there exists a host of languages in which surface order is far less constrained (Russian and German, for example). The notion that contextual generalization is essential for the learning of syntax is thus incompatible with the assumption that the language-learning mechanisms are independent of the peculiarities of particular languages. Rather, Braine's position requires either that the child has different mechanisms with which to learn different languages (contextual generalization for English but not for Russian) or that he has a universal mechanism which, however, is biased to learning certain languages. The first of these suggestions is unparsimonious and not easily reconciled with the fact that languages *do* exhibit a number of important universal properties, suggesting a corresponding pretuning of the language-learning mechanisms (cf. Lenneberg, 1964). The second assumption is tantamount to the naïve view that some languages are "harder" than others. It can be maintained only in face of the fact that there exists no evidence that children find languages in which position is constrained easier to learn than languages in which it is not. Indeed, there exists no evidence that children find *any* natural language harder to learn than any other. (Compare the well-known differences in the assimilability of formally different types of writing systems.) In short, it is presumably the commonalities, not the differences, between natural languages that provide us with insight into the mechanisms underlying their assimilation.

In fact, the distinction between underlying and manifest sentence structure resolves the difficulty posed by the existence of inflection and order as alternative means for expression of syntactic relations. The difference between an "ordering" language and an "inflected" language *is one which concerns the manifest sentence only:* The structure of the underlying forms is similar in both types of languages as are the kinds of transformations which apply to the underlying representations.

In general the rules which determine inflection are formulated with reference to the order and function of elements in an underlying representation of a sentence. This underlying order may, of course, be deformed by the operation of later rules. For example, in Latin, the manifest sentences:

49a.   *Puer amat eam.*

49b.   *Eam amat puer.*
49c.   *Amat puer eam.*
49d.   *Puer eam amat.*
49e.   *Eam puer amat.*
49f.   *Amat eam puer.*

all share the same underlying form:

50.   *puer* + sg pres + *am ea* + *sg.*

ea has the accusative attached because it is in the object position in the underlying form, while *eo*, because it is in subject position, remains nominative. Subsequent transformations in Latin allow freedom of order in the manifest sentence, while preserving inflections of case and number attachment acquired in the underlying string.

The inflection of words in manifest sentences thus depends on the order of elements in their underlying representations. Inflection is *a direct reflection of the structural relations in the underlying form.* We have already seen that languages which constrain manifest order do so as a way of exhibiting underlying structural relations. Thus, the difference between inflecting and order language is a matter of how the underlying relations are reflected in the speech signal.[8]

In both cases, however, the same types of rules apply to abstract representations which underlie the manifest sentences. In both cases, it is primarily the assimilation of the rules for generating these underlying structures and for deforming them into manifest sentences that a theory of language-learning must explain. A theory which affords such an explanation would ipso facto provide a *uniform* treatment of the learning of inflected and uninflected languages.

PERCEPTUAL SEGMENTATION AND INTONATION

We have argued that the generalization of

---

[8] In fact, the most important difference between "ordering" and "inflecting" languages concerns the order in which syntactic rules are applied in generating sentences. Thus, derivations in "inflecting" languages tend to apply the rules which determine inflection (e.g., affix movement in Footnote 7) before the rules that rearrange constituents (e.g., passivization in Rule 18). In "order" languages the reverse is typically the case. "Order" languages express underlying relations in the order of elements in the manifest sentence.

We are indebted to M. D. S. Braine for pointing out an error in our original example from Latin.

position does not account for the learning of syntax. We now consider Braine's claim that the discrimination of acoustic properties of speech signals accounts for the learning of segmentation.

According to Braine, normal speech indicates its segmentation by stress, pitch, juncture, intonation pattern, etc. Braine reports brief experiments in which a nonsense utterance was spoken with differing stress patterns. Subjects were asked to respond with sentences which seemed grammatically similar. The major syntactic division in the response corresponded to the boundary following the stressed nonsense word. Braine concludes that stress and intonation are capable of transmitting structure.

Beyond doubt, extra stresses or artificially introduced pauses can induce structure in a random sequence. In natural speech, however, it is extremely difficult to determine the physical parameters which signal structural units. They cannot be simple pauses, for often large constituent breaks are not marked by pauses while relatively minor ones are coincident with large acoustic gaps. Physical intensity is directly related to "stress" only in the case of special emphasis, and "intonation" often does not correspond to the actual pitch of the voice fundamental. Indeed, it is the rule that the acoustic analogue of linguistic percepts is either found to be extremely complex or is not found at all. Though pauses, stress, sound units, intonations, etc., are *heard* as objective features of the flow of speech, it appears that these percepts are, in fact, the result of some elaborate manipulation of the acoustic data. In the case of stress and pauses in English it is clear that they are usually a function of the syntactic structures underlying the speech signal as well as its acoustics.[9]

If, however, such perceptual correlates of structure as stress, pause, and intonation have no simple acoustic analogues, it is pointless to argue that the child's learning of segmentation consists of the discrimination of stress, pause, and intonation. For the problem then arises of how the child *learns to hear* stress, pause, and intonation correctly. Insofar as perception of the correlates of segmentation is the result of complicated integrations of the acoustic signal with the syntax, the child cannot be capable of perceiving them before he has learned to analyze syntactic structure.

This difficulty raises doubts about the description of language learning according to which the child first isolates individual speech sounds and then groups them successively into words, phrases, and simple sentences. For example, it is widely accepted in the literature that the child effectively masters the intonation pattern of his language *before he has learned any words at all.*[10] Since intonation is intimately related to syntactic structure, this indicates that the order of assimilation of syntactic structures is unlikely to be the one mentioned above. Instead, it suggests that derived constituent structure may be among the earliest syntactic information assimilated.

In short, the correct interpretation may be not that the perceived location of pause, stress, and intonation are the child's clue to the analysis of structure, but rather that the prior analysis of structure is what determines where the child learns to hear pause, stress, and intonation. Nor is the possibility of some intermediate position excluded.

EXPERIMENTATION ON CONTEXTUAL GENERALIZATION

We have considered some inadequacies of explanations of syntax assimilation that appeal to contextual generalization. However, Braine has shown that subjects *can* learn miniature artificial languages whose constituents are nonsense words by position generalization. This may appear to provide a foundation for theories of language learning in which contextual generalization plays an important role. However, Braine's results are equivocal. A brief discussion of his experimental techniques is therefore in order.

There is some danger in applying results

---

[9] For a theoretical analysis of the relation between syntactic structure and stress see Chomsky and Miller (1963). Lieberman (1965) has shown experimentally that the perception of intonation and stress is dependent on a knowledge of the syntactic structure.

[10] See Jakobson (1941), Grégoire (1937), and McCarthy (1954). Jakobson has described this period of intonation imitation (around $1-1\frac{1}{2}$ years) as the period when the child "speaks without words."

garnered in the study of the learning of artificial languages by latency-aged children to the learning of first languages by preschoolers. First, it is possible that the psychological processes mediating the learning of first languages are pretuned for the assimilation of systems having quite specific formal properties. If this is correct, very little will be revealed about these processes by studying the assimilation of artificial languages whose structure is arbitrarily different from that of natural languages.

Second, as Thorpe (1961) has suggested, the learning of language may be one of the capacities for which

there ... exist specific brain mechanisms ready to be activated during and only during a particular period of the life span of the child and ... if they are not properly activated at the right time subsequent activation is difficult or impossible, resulting in permanent disabilities in later life [p. 200; cf. also Penfield and Roberts, 1959]. This speculation supports the widely held view that adults learn second languages in a manner essentially different from the way children learn first languages.

Braine has attempted to control for this source of error by replicating the simpler of his experiments with a population of 4-year-olds. The point is not however, that very young children may be incapable of contextual generalization. It is rather that there may be language-learning processes operative in younger children which do not occur in older ones. Braine controls for the former but not the latter of these possibilities.

We now consider the details of Braine's experiments. It is essential to Braine's argument to demonstrate the existence of contextual generalization among phrases as well as words. We have seen that Braine defines the notion of a position in such a way that it may be occupied by a word in one sentence and by a phrase in another.

Braine's experiments are thus divided into two groups. The first demonstrates contextual generalization in a language whose sentences are all of the type shown in Figure 2, where A and P are classes of single (nonsense) words, and a and p are items drawn from those classes.

Braine's second experiment purports to show that contextual generalization can also

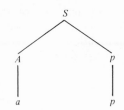

FIGURE 2. Tree diagram of the alleged structure of nonsense sentences in Braine's a + p language.

function when the constituents are phrases. Here Braine uses language in which sentences are said to be either of the type shown in Figures 3 or 4.

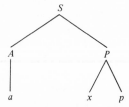

FIGURE 3. Tree diagram of the alleged structure of the nonsense sentences in Braine's a + xp language.

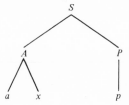

FIGURE 4. Tree diagram of the alleged structure of the nonsense sentences in Braine's ax + p language.

But Braine provides no support for the analyses of the String axp in Figures 3 and 4 beyond the remark that, in the situations where ax was intended to have phrase status, a and x were presented together, while in the situation where xp was intended to have phrase status, x and p were presented together.

In short, Braine's experimentation is at least compatible with the interpretation that what his subjects *learned* were strings with the structure exhibited in Figure 5. So long as this interpretation remains open, Braine can

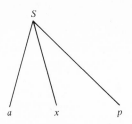

FIGURE 5. A possible alternative structure for sentences allegedly belonging either to a + xp or to ax + p languages.

hardly claim that his experiments demonstrate contextual generalization among phrase-length constituent.

In experiments with artificial languages consisting of a finite set of strings, it is extremely difficult to support claims about the psychological reality of abstract structures like phrases. In natural languages, appeals to the intuitions of speakers concerning the appropriate segmentation of sentences constrain phrase analyses to some extent. More important, formulation of the rules for transformation and stress imposes certain requirements upon the phrase-structure analysis since the phrase structure articulates the domain to which these rules apply. In the case of the artificial languages Braine studies, neither of these considerations holds. Speakers do not have structural intuitions about artificial language, and no language which consists of a finite set of strings requires phrase-structure rules in its grammar, for any such language can be enumerated by a simple list. If, therefore, it is suggested that Braine's subjects may not have analyzed the stimulus material in the way Braine wanted them to, it is difficult to see what reply he could make.

The difficulty may have stemmed from Braine's belief that the process responsible for the perceptual integrity of the phrase is association. On that view, copresentation of pairs of nonsense syllables would perhaps tend to establish such pairs as phrases. The fact that the pairs of items intended to be perceived as phrases were presented together would thus help to justify the analysis provided in Figures 3 and 4.

The claim that the integrity of the phrase is mediated by processes of association is,

however, totally untenable. Phrases in natural language can exhibit grammatical dependencies across strings of arbitrary length. It is thus inconceivable that the psychological unity of phrases could be attributed to associative bonds between the elements. Conversely, the suggestion that the basis of phrase integrity is associationistic in short phrases but that some different and unknown psychological mechanism operates in longer phrases is too evidently ad hoc to merit siderations.

REFERENCES

Braine, M. D. S. "On Learning the Grammatical Order of Words." *Psychological Review*, LXX (1963), 323–48.

Brown, R., and Bellugi, U. "Three Processes in the Child's Acquisition of the Syntax." *Harvard Educational Review*, XXXIV (1964), 133–51.

Chomsky, N. *Syntactic Structures*. The Hague: Mouton, 1957.

———, and Miller, G. "Introduction to the Formal Analysis of Natural Languages." In R. Luce, R. Bush, and E. Galanter, eds., *Handbook of Mathematical Psychology*. Vol. II. New York: John Wiley & Sons, Inc., 1963. pp. 269–323.

Fodor, J., and Katz, J., eds. "The Structure of Language." In *Readings in the Philosophy of Language*. Englewood Cliffs, N. J.: Prentice-Hall, Inc., 1964. pp. 479–518.

Grégoire, A. *L'Apprentissage du langage*. Liège, Belgium: l'Université de Liège, 1937.

Harris, Z. "Co-occurrence and Transformation in Linguistic Structure." *Language*, XXXIII (1957), 283–340.

Jakobson, R. *Kindersprache, Aphasie und allgemeine Lautgesetze*. Uppsala, Sweden: Uppsala Universität, 1941.

Jenkins, J., and Palermo, D. "Mediation Processes and the Acquisition of Linguistic Structure." In Ursula Bellugi and R. W. Brown, eds., *The Acquisition of Language*. Chicago: University of Chicago Press, 1964. pp. 141–69.

Lees, R. "The Grammar of English Nominalizations." *International Journal of American Linguistics*, XXVI (Pt. 2) (1960), 205–20.

Lenneberg, E. "The Capacity for Language Acquisition." In J. Fodor and J. Katz, eds.,

Readings in the Philosophy of Language. Englewood Cliffs, N. J.: Prentice-Hall, Inc., 1964. pp. 579–608.

Lieberman, P. "On the Acoustic Basis of the Perception of Intonation by Linguists." *Word*, XXI (1965), 40–54.

Maclay, H., and Osgood, C. "Heritation Phenomena in Spontaneous English Speech." *Word*, XV (1959), 19–44.

McCarthy, D. "Language Development in Children." In L. Carmichael, ed., *A Manual of Child Psychology.*, 2nd ed. New York: John Wiley & Sons, Inc., 1954. pp. 429–630.

Mehler, J. "Some Effects of Grammatical Transformations on the Recall of English Sentences." *Journal of Verbal Learning and Verbal Behavior*, II (1963), 346–51.

Miller, G. A. "Some Psychological Studies of Grammar." *American Psychologist*, XVII (1962), 748–62.

——, Galanter, E., and Pribram, K. H. *Plans and the Structure of Behavior*. New York: Holt, Rinehart & Winston, Inc., 1960.

Osgood, C. E. "On Understanding and Creating Sentences." *American Psychologist*, XVIII (1963), 735–51.

Penfield, W., and Roberts, L. *Speech and Brain Mechanisms*. Princeton: Princeton University Press, 1959.

Thorpe, W. H. "Sensitive Periods in the Learning of Animals and Men." In W. H. Thorpe and O. L. Zangwill, eds., *Current Problems in Animal Behavior*. Cambridge: Cambridge University Press, 1961. pp. 194–224.

MARTIN D. S. BRAINE

SUMMARY of
ON THE BASIS OF PHRASE STRUCTURE: A REPLY TO BEVER, FODOR, AND WEKSEL

43

"On Bever *et al.*'s central contention, the linguistic evidence seems insufficient to show that the order of elements in the simple declarative sentence is a deformation of the order in the underlying string: The deformation appears to be imposed by the choice of a particular phrase-structure model, rather than a fact about English. While undoubtedly insufficient and imprecise, the writer's proposals on grammar acquisition seem to have more potentialities than Bever *et al.* allow. Too little is known for it to be argued that they are inconsistent with the character of the verbal environment. Limitations of the proposals in respect to the learning of word classes and several other issues raised by Bever *et al.* are discussed."

THOMAS G. BEVER, JERRY A. FODOR, AND WILLIAM WEKSEL

SUMMARY of
IS LINGUISTICS EMPIRICAL?

44

"This paper continues the discussion of issues raised by Braine's theory of 'contextual generalization.' The arguments for analyzing the English declarative as transformationally generated are discussed at length. Broader issues about the nature of confirmation of claims made by grammars are also considered. It is argued that while the direct experimental verification of such claims is often not feasible, considerations of simplicity and generality can provide adequate grounds for their empirical confirmation or disconfirmation."

Note: It might be worthwhile for the reader to follow the full discussion in *Psychological Review*, LXXII (1965), 483–92 and 493–500. He may also want to read I. M. Schlesinger's paper "A Note on the Relationship between Psychological and Linguistic Theories," in *Foundations of Language*, III (1967), 397–402.

MARTIN D. S. BRAINE

45 As research went on in the past decade, linguists and psycholinguists became more and more concerned with the lower age groups and tried to analyze the first syntactic structures of the younger speakers. Several such studies are represented in this volume.

The present study by Braine attempts to interpret the structural characteristics of the first word combinations of three children followed from 18 months of age: According to Braine, the child learns that each of a small number of words belongs in a particular position in an utterance, and the complementary position is taken by any single-word utterance in his small vocabulary. Hence, the word combinations that are uttered have a characteristic structure containing two parts of speech: (1) the *pivot* which comprises the small number of words whose position has been learned, and (2) the X-class (a part of speech mainly in the residual sense) that consists of the entire vocabulary, except for some of the pivots.

As for utterances that are more complex and that deviate from the above pattern, Braine takes them to be early examples of construction belonging to the next phase of development.

Compare the other reading by Braine, "The Learning of Grammatical Order of Words," and the ensuing debate.

A. B. A.

THE ONTOGENY OF ENGLISH PHRASE STRUCTURE: THE FIRST PHASE

1.1

Students of infants and of language have long wondered over the fact that a structure of such enormous formal complexity as language is so readily learned by organisms whose available intellectual resources appear in other respects quite limited.[1] While a certain amount of work has been done on phonological development, and there has been much speculation about the acquisition of 'meanings,' development at the morphological and syntactic levels has been relatively

Reprinted from Language *39.1–13 (1963) by permission of the author and the Linguistic Society of America.*

[1] I am deeply indebted to Dr. and Mrs. Chaim Shatan, Dr. Dorothy Kipnis, and Mrs. Harold L. Williams, parents of the children, for their careful record keeping and continuous cooperation over a long period. The investigation was supported in part by USPHS small research grant M-5116(A) from the National Institute of Mental Health, Public Health Service.

little studied.[2] Yet it is perhaps the development at these levels that is the most striking
and puzzling.

Before the question *how* the child learns
can be broached, the question *what* the child
learns has to be answered. The question
'What is learned?' can be answered at two
levels. The first answer has to be a description
of the structure of the language at successive
stages of development, and the task is purely
one for structural linguistics. At a more inter-
pretative level, the question 'What is learned?'
is answered by a statement of the nature of
the stimulus attributes and relationships
which the child learns to distinguish; at this
level the task is as much psychological as
linguistic, and the answer should in some sense
'explain' why the grammar at a particular
stage has the structure that it has.

The present paper reports and attempts to
interpret the structural characteristics of the
first word combinations uttered by three
children followed by the writer from about
18 months of age. In the analysis of the data,
the structural features of the corpora will
first be described, then the sequence of
development, and finally, from the description
of structure an attempt will be made to infer
what was learned.

1.2
To provide a common time scale for each

---

[2] D. McCarthy, "Language Development in Children," in *Manual of Child Psychology*, ed. L. Carmichael (New York, 1954), reviews a number of studies
which employ traditional grammatical categories
instead of treating the child's speech as sui generis. Of
greater interest are a number of studies of children's
knowledge of English inflectional rules, reviewed by
J. Berko and R. W. Brown, "Psycholinguistic Research Methods," in *Handbook of Research Methods
in Child Development*, ed. P. H. Mussen (New York,
1960); but these studies use subjects at least three or
four years old, who have already mastered much of
English phrase structure. Some corpora of utterances
by children who seem somewhat more advanced than
those reported here have been recently discussed by
R. W. Brown and C. Fraser, "The Acquisition of
Syntax," in *Verbal Learning and Verbal Behavior*,
ed. C. N. Cofer, (New York, 1962), and also by W.
Miller and S. Ervin, "The Development of Grammar
in Child Language," in *The Acquisition of Language*,
Bellugi, U., and R. Brown, eds., *Monographs of the
Society for Research in Child Development*, XXIX
(1964), 9–34. Miller and Ervin's paper came to my
attention after this article was written; they note some
of the same phenomena discussed here. Their term
'operator' appears to correspond to my term 'pivot.'

child the month in which the first word
combination (i.e. utterance containing two
or more words) was uttered will be called the
'first month'; this month will be taken as the
starting point in all references to the time
of an event, e.g. 'first four months.' The
'first phase' in these children refers to the
first four or five months on this time scale,
and is defined statistically by a low rate of
increase in the number of word combinations.
In each child the number of different word
combinations at first increased slowly and
then showed a sudden upsurge around the
fifth or sixth month. For example, the
cumulative number of Gregory's recorded
different word combinations in successive
months was 14, 24, 54, 89, 350, 1400, 2500 +,
. . ., and undoubtedly the sampling was more
complete in the earlier than the later months.
In each child the upsurge in the number of
different word combinations in the fifth
and sixth months was accompanied by a
marked increase in the structural complexity
of utterances. The first phase appears to be
fairly well delineated, being characterized not
only by a particular temporal span and slow
increase in the number of word combinations,
but also by a typical and simple structural
property which it is the purpose of this paper
to describe.

2.   PROCEDURE

2.1.   *Gathering of the corpora*
In the case of two children, Gregory and
Andrew, the mother or both parents maintained a seriatim written record of their
child's spontaneous comprehensible utterances. A 'spontaneous' utterance was defined
as any utterance which was not a direct
imitation or repetition of something said by
another person in the previous few seconds. A
'comprehensible' utterance was defined as
any utterance which the parent could identify
with considerable confidence as an attempt
to say an English word or morpheme, or a
string of English words or morphemes.
The parents were instructed not to attempt
to represent pronunciation, but merely to
record in conventional spelling the word or
sequence of words they heard the child say.
In the case of word combinations the parents
also recorded a paraphrase into ordinary
English indicating what they understood by

the child's utterance. The written record of utterances was started when the child had an estimated vocabulary of 10–20 single-word utterances (i.e. before the first word combination appeared).[3]

In addition to listing the utterances, the parents also recorded how often each utterance occurred (up to five times). The measure of frequency was included to provide an internal check on the accuracy of the record; it was assumed that utterances heard several times would be less likely to be erroneously recorded than those heard only once. Since the few word combinations that occurred only once did not differ from the others in any discernible way, no distinction will be made when discussing the corpora between utterances occurring once and those occurring many times.

In the case of the third child, Steven, a similar written record was soon abandoned, primarily because a serious question arose whether certain sounds were properly identifiable as words. To resolve this question required investigation of phonetic regularities in Steven's speech. The entire corpus was therefore tape-recorded. The material discussed here was obtained in twelve play sessions of about four hours total duration, spaced over a four-week period during the fourth and fifth months. During the play sessions Steven's mother kept a running record of what she understood Steven to say; morpheme identifications were based on a comparison of her written record with the sounds on the tape, made in the light of what had been learned about the phonetic characteristics of Steven's speech.

The fact that the data on Steven were tape-recorded should not mislead the reader into thinking that the morpheme identifications are necessarily more reliable in his case. The major factor affecting the certainty with which a child's words can be identified is the clarity with which he speaks, and Gregory and Andrew spoke more clearly than Steven.

At the time of their first word combination two of the children were 19 months old and the third 20 months.[4]

2.2. 'Word' and 'word combination'

On the assumption that the morphological units of the child's speech might be longer, but would probably not be shorter than the morphemes of adult English, the following somewhat crude distributional criterion was adopted for a 'word' (or 'morpheme'—no distinction between 'word' and 'morpheme' will be made for the child's language). Those segments are considered 'words' which are the longest segments that cannot be divided into two or more parts of which both are English morphemes that occur in the corpus independently of the others. Thus *ice cream* and *all gone* are each classified as one word in Gregory's speech, since neither *ice* nor *cream*, nor *all* nor *gone*, occur in other contexts or alone. However, for Andrew *all gone* is classified as a combination of two words, since *gone* occurs by itself, and *all* occurs independently in *all wet, all dressed*, etc. In line with the criterion, the few expressions in which only one part occurs elsewhere (like English *cranberry*) are treated as single units.

In writing the children's utterances, the morphemic status will be indicated by spacing: where English words are run together (e.g., *howareyou*), they are not separate units by the above criterion.

---

[3] No tape recordings were made of Gregory and Andrew in the early months because of the uneconomically large number of hours spent in recording and listening that would have been required to obtain the small number of word combinations at the child's command. A few tape recordings were made in the fifth month, and after the sixth month a high proportion of each corpus was tape-recorded, the written record being eventually abandoned as no longer practicable. This later material is not discussed here. Comparison of the written record with tape recordings made at the same age revealed that constructions present in the one were always present in the other, and with about equal frequency, a fact which is evidence of the reliability of the written records.

[4] The procedure described leads to a lexical and not a phonemic representation of morphemes. With very young children there are reasons for not making a phonemic analysis preparatory to an investigation at the morphological and syntactic levels. For example, it is not easy to use the 21-month-old as an informant who gives same-different judgments to questions. Moreover, the contrasts that exist are not constant over time. The strong likelihood that a child may hear contrasts which he cannot produce not only means that partially separate analyses of receptive and productive functions would be necessary, but may also lead to a special situation in which phonemic strings would frequently have to be inferred from lexical ones.

3. GRAMMATICAL STRUCTURE

3.1. *Gregory*

Table 1 summarizes the 89 word combinations uttered by Gregory during the first four months. Over two-thirds contain one or another of a small group of words in first position. Thus, *byebye* occurs in 31 combinations, always in first position; *see* occurs in 15 combinations, always (except for the exclamatory *ohmy see*) in first position; similarly *allgone*, *big*, *my*, *pretty*, *more*, *hi*, and *nightnight* recur in first position in two or more combinations. These words will be called 'pivot' words, since the bulk of the word combinations appear to be formed by using them as pivots to which other words are attached as required. There is some communality among the words that follow the pivots: six of the words that follow *see* also occur after *byebye*; most or all of the words that follow *hi*, *my*, *big*, *pretty* are also to be found after *byebye*, and some after other pivot words. Although none of the five words that follow *allgone* occur after other pivots, this is probably accidental (cf. *allgone shoe* and *see sock*, *allgone lettuce* and *byebye celery*, *more melon*, *my milk*). The evidence suggests that the pivot words occupying utterance-initial position have essentially similar privileges of occurrence. Accordingly, there is a basis for defining two primitive word classes: a class of pivots (P) to which a few frequently occurring words belong, and a complementary class which has many members, few of which recur in more than one or two different combinations (49 different words follow pivots, 34 of which occur in only one combination). The latter class will be called the X-class.

All words which occur in the frame P(—) also occur as single-word utterances, whereas some of the pivots do not occur alone. There is, therefore, a basis for identifying the X-class with the class of single-word utterances.

Of the 89 word combinations, 64 are PX sequences. Five of the remaining combinations have a recurring element in utterance-final position: *do it*, *push it*, *close it*, etc. These appear to exemplify the same kind of pivotal construction as the previous combinations discussed, except that now the pivot is in the final position. *Do*, *push*, *close*, etc., all occur as single-word utterances; *it* does not occur by itself. These five combinations may therefore be classified as XP sequences. The remaining 20 combinations appear to have no determinable structure. Some of them are greetings or exclamations (e.g. *hi howareyou*), some are English compound words (e.g. *mail man*), others may well be early cases of later developing forms.

There is no overlap between the 49 words occurring in the frame P(—) and the five words occurring in (—)P. This lack of overlap may be accidental (the fact that the five words which follow *allgone* fail to occur following other first-position pivots has already been assumed to be accidental). However, it is primarily English nouns and adjectives that occur in the context P(—), whereas the words occurring in (—)P are all English verbs; Gregory may be adumbrating a substantive-verb distinction within the X-class. Using subscripts to denote subclasses, the structures employed by Gregory may be summarized as P_1X, XP_2, or, if one chooses to credit him with the substantive-verb distinction, P_1X_1, X_2P_2.

3.2. *Andrew*

Andrew's word combinations during the first five months are listed in Table 2. About half the combinations contain *all*, *I*, *see*,

TABLE 1. Gregory's word combinations, first four months.

14 combinations with *see* (—), e.g.	*byebye plane*
see boy	*byebye man*
see sock	*byebye hot*
see hot	
	hi plane
pretty boat	*hi mommy*
pretty fan	
	big boss
my mommy	*big boat*
my daddy	*big bus*
my milk	
	more taxi
do it	*more melon*
push it	
close it	*allgone shoe*
buzz it	*allgone vitamins*
move it	*allgone egg*
nightnight office	*allgone lettuce*
nightnight boat	*allgone watch*
31 combinations with *byebye* (—), e.g.	20 unclassified, e.g. *mommy sleep* *milk cup*, *ohmy see*

other, no, or *more* in utterance-initial position; the pivotal mode of construction seems quite comparable to Gregory's, although the individual words are not the same. However, while there was only one second-position pivot in Gregory's corpus, Andrew seems to have several, one of which is a phrase which itself has internal positional structure (*there,* preceded by *down, in, on,* or *up*).

There is some overlap between the sets of words that follow the various first-position pivots, e.g. *all fix* and *no fix, all wet* and *no wet, all shut* and *I shut, hi mama* and *no mama*;

TABLE 2. Andrew's word combinations, first five months.

Pivotal constructions

all broke	more loast
all buttoned	more walk
all clean	
all done	hi Calico
all dressed	hi mama
all dry	hi papa
all fix	
all gone	other bib
all messy	other bread
all shut	other milk
all through	other pants
all wet	other part
	other piece
I see	other pocket
I shut	other shirt
I sit	other shoe
	other side
no bed	
no down[a]	boot off
no fix	light off
no home	pants off
no mama[b]	shirt off
no more	shoe off
no pee	water off
no plug	
no water	airplane by[f]
no wet[c]	siren by
see baby	mail come
see pretty	mama come
see train	
	clock on there
more car[d]	up on there
more cereal	hot in there
more cookie	milk in there
more fish	light up there
more high[e]	fall down there
more hot	kitty down there
more juice	more down there
more read	sit down there
more sing	cover down there
	other cover down there

TABLE 2. (*Cont.*)

Other utterances

airplane all gone	what's that
Calico all gone	what's this
Calico all done[g]	mail man
salt all shut	mail car
all done milk	our car
all done now	our door
all gone juice	papa away
all gone outside[h]	
all gone pacifier	look at this
	outside more
byebye back	pants change
byebye Calico	dry pants
byebye car	off bib
byebye papa	down there
Calico byebye	up on there some more
papa byebye	

a 'Don't put me down.'
b 'I don't want to go to mama.'
c 'I'm not wet.'
d 'Drive around some more.'
e 'There's more up there.'
f 'A plane is flying past.'
g Said after the death of Calico the cat.
h Said when the door is shut: 'The outside is all gone.'

but these are the only examples (cf. *other bread* and *more toast; other milk, more juice, no water*). There is one case of overlap between the words preceding the second-position pivots: *light off* and *light up there.* More substantial overlap is present between the sets of words preceding second-position pivots and following first-position pivots: 9 of the 19 words that occur in the context (—)P also occur in the context P(—), e.g. *pants off* and *other pants, water off* and *no water, hot in there* and *more hot, sit down there* and *I sit.* Andrew's pivotal constructions may therefore be summarized by the formulae P_1X and XP_2. All words occurring in either P_1(—) or (—)P_2 also occur as single-word utterances; as with Gregory, the X-class may be identified with the class of single-word utterances.[5] But unlike Gregory, there is nothing to indicate that Andrew is

5 Some of the pivots (e.g. *more*) occur as single-word utterances, others (e.g. *all*) do not. Those that occur alone seem also to occur as X-words in word combinations (e.g. *no more, more down there*); they can therefore properly be regarded as belonging to both classes.

as yet developing anything like a substantive-verb contrast.

Of the 102 combinations, 73 are pivotal constructions. In a further 9 combinations a pivotal construction (*all* X) occurs as an immediate constituent of a longer utterance; these (and also *other cover down there*, listed among the pivotal constructions) seem to be early examples of more complex forms belonging to the next phase of development. The remaining 20 combinations have not been classified. Some of them may contain pivot words (e.g. *our car, our door*).[6]

3.3. *Steven*

Table 3 lists Steven's identifiable word combinations, recorded in twelve play sessions during the fourth and fifth months. The corpus was tape-recorded because the phonetic characteristics of Steven's speech made the morphemic status of parts of his utterances uncertain. In discussing these characteristics, phonetic symbols will be used. Since no phonemic analysis was made to determine what contrasts he controlled, these symbols are to be understood as identifications by English-speaking listeners; they provide only an approximate indication of the sounds. The lack of a phonemic analysis also makes it impossible to distinguish clearly between allophonic and allomorphic variation.

Steven's pronunciation is extremely variable —much more so than either Gregory's or Andrew's. In particular the last consonant of *that* and *it* takes a variety of forms: [t, d, h, ʔ, ð, tš, ts, z, tz]. Much of this variation is probably allophonic, but a terminal sibilant also appears occasionally after *here*

---

[6] In deciding whether utterances containing infrequently occuring words were pivotal constructions, the writer was sometimes guided by the child's subsequent development. For example, although *mail* occurs three times in first position (*mail man, mail car, mail come*), it is not classified as a pivot because there are no further cases of *mail* in first position in subsequent weeks; on the other hand, although *come* only recurs twice in final position, the subsequent uses of it in final position suggest that it is a pivot. Similarly, in Gregory's corpus (Table 1), although *more* and *pretty* only occur twice, they are regarded as pivots because they recur frequently in initial position before X-words in the next month of Gregory's development.

TABLE 3. Steven's word combinations, tape-recorded sample at end of fourth month.

Pivotal constructions

want baby	see record
want car	see Stevie
want do	
want get	whoa cards[c]
want glasses	whoa jeep
want head	
want high[a]	more ball
want horsie	more book
want jeep	there ball
want more	there book
want page	there doggie
want pon[b]	there doll
want purse	there high[d]
want ride	there momma
want up	there record
want byebye car	there trunk
	there byebye car
it ball	there daddy truck
it bang	there momma truck
it checker	
it daddy	beeppeep bang[e]
it Dennis	beeppeep car
it doggie	
it doll	that box
it fall	that Dennis
it horsie	that doll
it Kathy	that Tommy
it Lucy	that truck
it record	
it shock	here bed
it truck	here checker
	here doll
get ball	here truck
get Betty	
get doll	bunny do
	daddy do
see ball	momma do
see doll	(*want do*)

Other utterances

bunny do sleep	pon baby
Lucy do fun	pon Betty
want do pon[f]	sleepy bed
want drive car	eat breakfast
baby doll	two checker
Betty pon	Betty byebye car
byebye car	Lucy shutup Lucy shutup
Candy say	Lucy
find bear	

[a] 'Put it up there.'
[b] 'Put on' or 'up on' or both.
[c] 'The cards are falling.'
[d] 'It's up there.'
[e] 'The car that goes "beeppeep" is falling.'
[f] 'I want (you) to put (the jeep) on top.'

and *there*. Separate morphemic status is not assigned to the terminal sibilant, because forms with and without the sibilant are in free variation, and also because the terminal sibilant, present in the third and fourth months, disappears completely in the fifth and sixth months and reappears only when *is* occurs in other contexts in his speech. In addition to the allomorphs *it* ~ *its*, *here* ~ *heres*, etc., it is possible that *it* and *that* may not be independent morphemes, since there appear to be occasional intermediate forms, e.g. [het, ditz]. (In the latter case, Steven may be trying say *this*.) The general character of the combinations listed in Table 3 would not be altered by treating *it* and *that* as allomorphs.

From a grammatical point of view the most interesting phonological feature of Steven's speech is the periodic occurrence, at the beginning or in the middle of utterances, of either a front-central vowel, or, somewhat less often, of [d] or [t] followed by a front or central vowel. Steven's family usually identified these as English words—as *a* or *the* before nouns, as *I* before *want*, *see*, *get*, as *to* in such contexts as *want* (—) *do*, as *it* in context *want* (—) *high* or *want* (—) *up*, and as *is* or *of* in appropriate other contexts. Before *that*, *there*, *Lucy*, etc., these phonetic entities could not be interpreted. One or another of these elements is present in over 40 per cent of Steven's utterances. The tape recordings indicate that these elements occur before any word, that their phonetic shape is not affected by the class of the following morpheme and that utterances with and without them are in free variation. While it is quite likely that these elements are an interesting distillate of the unstressed and phonetically often obscure English articles, prepositions, and auxiliary verbs, there is no basis for giving them morphemic status at this stage of Steven's development (although it may be desirable at some later stage). The alternative course will be taken of regarding them as a periodic feature of the intonation pattern. Consistent with this decision is the fact that when these elements occur in utterances of three words or longer, they appear to separate immediate constituents; clearly defined junctures often appear at the same points. Thus, a vowel sometimes occurs at the marked point in *want* (—) *do* and *want* (—) *ride*, but in

want do pon and *want drive car*, the vowel seems to shift forward: *want do* (—) *pon*, *want drive* (—) *car*. Similarly there is a vowel at the marked point in *there* (—) *byebye car*, but never between *byebye* and *car*. Such marking of immediate constituents, however, has little relevance to the initial phase of development. Neither Gregory's speech nor Andrew's ever shows anything analogous to these elements.

Another feature of Steven's speech which is not present in either Gregory's or Andrew's at this stage is a generalized terminal vocative. No one listening to the play sessions has the least difficulty in distinguishing vocatives from other occurrences of proper names. Whether the intonational cues in Steven's speech alone would suffice to identify vocatives is not clear, since so many other cues are invariably present that it is difficult to find appropriate contrasts in the tape recordings. These terminal vocatives are omitted in Table 3. If none wishes to include them in Steven's grammar, one need only add a rule that, if 'S' is an utterance, then 'S, (proper name)' is also an utterance.

Table 3 indicates that Steven's word combinations have much the same structural features already described for Gregory and Andrew. Three-quarters of the combinations contain one or another of a small group of words (*want*, *get*, *it*, *there*, etc.) in utterance-initial position. Four combinations contain *do* in final position. In a further four combinations a pivotal construction is an immediate constituent of a longer utterance (*bunny do sleep*, etc.). The remaining combinations are not classified.

There is substantial overlap between the sets of words that follow the various first-position pivots. Five of the words that follow *want*, eight that follow *it*, three that follow *see*, and eight that follow *there* occur after more than one pivot: essentially similar privileges of occurrence are therefore indicated for the first-position pivots. Two of the words that precede *do* also occur after first-position pivots. The formulae P_1X and XP_2 again summarize the pivotal constructions. Words occurring in the contexts P_1(—) and (—)*do* also occur as single-word utterances; there is again ground for identifying the X-class with the single-word utterances.

In Steven's corpus there is much more overlap among the sets of X-words that are found each pivot than in Gregory's and Andrew's. No doubt this is because all Steven's utterances were recorded in special play sessions, so that there was greater constancy in the environmental stimuli eliciting Steven's utterances.

3.4. *The common structure of the three corpora*

The following structural properties appear to define the initial phase of development in these children.

(a) There are two word classes: pivots and X-words. The pivots are few in number; they tend to occur in several word combinations; and each is associated with a particular utterance position. Thus two subclasses are definable, P_1 associated with initial position, and P_2 with final position. The X-class is a large open class containing the child's entire vocabulary except for some of the pivots. X-words tend to recur in relatively few word combinations and do not appear to be tied to a particular utterance position; they occur alone or in the position complementary to that of the pivot word. One but only one of the children (Gregory) gives some evidence for a subdivision of the X-class.

(b) Single-word utterances are X. Multi-word utterances are either P_1X or XP_2, the former being much more frequent (for Gregory the formulae may be P_1X_1, X_2P_2).

The occasional utterances in the corpora that are more complex than the above (where a pivotal construction is an immediate constituent of a longer utterance) are taken to be early examples of constructions belonging to the next phase of development.

Structural formulae in linguistics can be construed in a weak or a strong sense. So far it has been asserted only that the sequences P_1X and XP_2 occur and are characteristic. Students of generative grammar, however, give a stronger interpretation to such formulae: the formula PX asserts that any P 'can' occur with any X. To construct and test a generative grammar it is necessary to have information not only about grammatical utterances, but also about ungrammatical ones. Information of the latter sort is difficult

enough to obtain with adult informants,[7] and seems clearly out of the question with children as young as these. Nevertheless, although it cannot be proved, it seems quite likely that the formulae P_1X and XP_2 are generative. The only alternative hypothesis is that, in the class of all grammatical sentences, some or all of the pivot words have unique sets of cooccurrents. By the fourth month both Gregory and Andrew had a recorded vocabulary of about 250 words, and internal evidence suggests that the true size may be two or three times as large.[8] If each set of X-words that occur with a given pivot is a random sample from this class (as the generative interpretation of the formulae implies), very little overlap between any pair of such sets would be expected; even taking into account the fact that some X-words occur much more frequently than others and would, therefore, be more likely to appear in any set taken at random, the amount of overlap to be expected is limited, and, though difficult to estimate, seems unlikely to be greater than that actually found in the corpora. There is, therefore, no reason to think that any of the pivot words have cooccurrents which are unique in any special way (with the possible exception of *it* in Gregory's speech).

An objection which has been raised against the assumption that any pivot can occur with any X-word is that it puts into the children's mouths some implausible expressions which seem highly foreign to English. For example,

---

[7] A. A. Hill, "Grammaticality," *Word*, XVII (1961), 1–10; H. Maclay and M. Sleator, "Responses to Language: Judgments of Grammaticalness," *International Journal of American Linguistics*, XXVI (1960), 275–82.

[8] By the end of the second month the recorded vocabulary was sufficiently large that the parents had difficulty in distinguishing which single-word utterances were new, and they recorded many fewer single-word utterances in the third and fourth months than in the second. However, during the first four months 150–200 words were recorded as having been uttered five times or more. There were probably many more less frequently occurring words which were not recorded. Even if the usual rank-frequency relation (Zipf's law, rf = K, in which the constant K approximates the total vocabulary, since it is the rank of the least frequently occurring word) fits the single-word utterances poorly, the total vocabulary must be very substantially greater than that recorded.

the formulae would allow Gregory to generate *more hot*, *big dirty*, *allgone hot*; Andrew to say *see read*, *other fix*, *I shirt*; and Steven to say *that do*, *there up*, *high do*. This objection is sometimes based on the idea that the children's utterances are a recall, or delayed imitation, of things they have heard adults say. As against this, there are a number of expressions in the corpora which are sufficiently strange to render it most unlikely that the children had heard them e.g. *see cold*, *byebye dirty*, *allgone lettuce*, *no down*, *more high*, *want do pon*, *there high*. In one child, not reported here, *the* was an early pivot word, yielding such utterances as *the byebye*, *the up*. Moreover, several 'strange' combinations, similar or identical to utterances generated by the formulae, appear in the fifth and sixth months; examples are *more wet*, *allgone sticky* (Gregory, after washing his hands), *other fix* (= 'fix the other one'), *more page* (= 'don't stop reading'), *see stand up* (= 'look at me standing up'), *this do* (= 'do this'). Manifestly, the strangeness of an utterance is no criterion of its grammaticality at this age.

3.5. *Continuity with later development*

What is here called the first phase of development has been defined by a certain time period (the first four or five months), a low rate of increase in the number of word combinations, and the presence of a characteristic structural feature (the pivotal construction). In order to justify treating a continuous development as composed of phases described separately, it seems appropriate to add some general remarks about the nature of the next phase.[9]

No claim is made that any discontinuity exists between phases. The pivotal type of construction continues long after the first five months, and new pivot words develop. However, several developments seem to occur more or less together around the fifth and sixth months. Forms in which pivotal constructions enter as immediate constituents have already been mentioned. The develop-

ment that has most impressed the writer is the appearance of an increasing number of utterances in which an X-word (e.g., an English noun) occupies both utterance positions. Examples are *man car* ('a man is in the car'), *car bridge* ('the car is under the bridge'), *coffee daddy* ('coffee for daddy'). These are not pivotal constructions,[10] but seem rather to exemplify a primitive sentence form, in which both components can be expanded by a $PX = X$ substitution rule, e.g., *man car* expanded to *other man#car*, *man#other car*. The large number of two-word utterances of this general type that appear around the sixth month give a random appearance to many word combinations in that phase of development. It may be this sentence form which has misled some observers into suggesting that children's first word combinations are for the most part mere juxtapositions of words without syntactic constraints.[11]

The development of this sentence form may explain the very sharp increase around the fifth or sixth month in the number of different word combinations uttered. Since the X-class is very large, the addition of an XX construction (or of any construction admitting a large open class in both positions) to the existing PX and XP constructions would at once greatly increase the number of word combinations that the grammar is capable of generating. The statistical change is, there-

---

[9] The next phase of development in these children will be fully discussed in a subsequent article. See also the longer discussions of children they have followed by Brown and Fraser, *op. cit.*, and Miller and Ervin, *op. cit.*

[10] They may form constructional homonyms with pivotal constructions, e.g. *bàby cháir* ('little chair': pivotal construction), usually without an intonation break, and *báby # cháir* ('the baby is in the chair'). The two constructions, however, certainly cannot always be distinguished from their intonation alone (# is used here and in the text as a general juncture symbol).

[11] Actually there are two parts to this assertion: (a) that the children learn the positions of certain words, and (b) that a sentence typically has just two positions—first and last. But (b) needs no discussion when utterances are just two words long. In experiments in children's learning of simple artificial languages, reported elsewhere (Braine, "On learning the grammatical order of words," *Psychological Review*, LXX (1963), 323–48), learning positions is explored when 'position' in a sentence is defined by successive fractionations, i.e., when a sentence has just two positions, each of which may be occupied by a word or a phrase, and when each constituent phrase in turn may be divided into two positions.

fore, explicable as a consequence of structural change.

4. SEQUENCE OF DEVELOPMENT

The order of appearance of the various word combinations shows a definite pattern. Gregory's third word combination was *see hat*; the next three were *see sock*, *see horsie*, and *see boy*; ten of his first 13 combinations contain *see* in first position. *Byebye plane*, the first word combination containing *byebye*, appeared in the third month; during the remainder of the month nine other combinations occurred containing *byebye* in first position. *Do it*, *push it*, and *close it* were all uttered at about the same time.

In the development of Gregory's language, it appears that from time to time a particular word is singled out, placed in a certain position, and combined with a number of other words in turn, often in quick succession. The words that are singled out in this way are of course the pivots. This sequence of development appears to be quite general. The majority of Steven's first word combinations contain *want* in first position. The same sequence occurs in Andrew's speech: *all* appeared in the first month, *other* did not appear until the third month and occurred in that month in five contexts; *no* and *there* appeared for the first time in the fourth month, both being quickly used in a number of different combinations. Less systematic observations on a number of other children suggest that this kind of development is quite typical of the initial stages of first-language learning (at least for the English language).

Throughout the first few months there is a large expansion of vocabulary. It seems clear that in this period the language expands rapidly in vocabulary by adding new members to the X-class, and that it develops structurally by singling out at intervals new pivot words.

Both functionally and developmentally, the distinction between open and closed word classes in the adult language (nouns, verbs, and adjectives vs. pronouns, prepositions, auxiliary verbs, etc.) seems quite parallel to that between X-words and pivots. The closed classes have relatively few members, and tend to serve in sentences as frames for the open-class words; historically their membership changes slowly. The pivots seem to play a similar role in utterances, also have few members, and add to their membership slowly.

5. WHAT IS LEARNED

It is suggested that a sufficient explanation of the structural features of the first phase is provided by the single assumption that the children have learned the positions of the pivot words, i.e. have learned that each of a small number of words 'belongs' or 'is right' in a particular one of two sentence positions. While the evidence provided by the corpora might suffice · without argument, it seems nevertheless desirable to make explicit the line of reasoning that leads to this inference.

In general, what a subject has learned is diagnosed from the generalizations that he makes. Thus, a naive rat, trained to jump for food towards an upright triangle in preference to a circle, will, when later confronted with a square and a circle, jump towards the square; but when the choices are an inverted triangle and a circle his jumps are randomly directed. The rat's generalizations provide information about what he must have learned in the original training: to jump towards something that an upright triangle shares with a square and does not share with an inverted triangle. Similarly, a child who has learned to indicate the past only by appending /ɨd/, /d/, or /t/ to verbs would be expected to construct by generalization 'incorrect' forms like *singed* and *breaked*, and to inflect nonsense words used as verbs in response to questions in appropriately designed experiments, e.g. *This man is ricking. He did the same thing yesterday. Yesterday he (—).*[12]

What generalization phenomena would be expected to follow from the learning merely of the position of a word? The principal expectation is that the word would be used freely in the position involved, i.e. there should be no restriction on the words appearing in the complementary position. Thus, if *a* is a word whose position (first position, say) has been learned, then the frame a (—) should admit any word in the vocabulary.

---

[12] J. Berko, "The child's learning of English morphology," *Word*, XIV (1958), 150–77.

If this condition does not hold, i.e. if there is some set of words k_1, k_2, k_3, etc., which occur in the frame a (—) and another set l_1, l_2, l_3, etc., which cannot occur in this frame, then either the position of a has not been learned (in which case there is some other explanation for the occurrence of ak_1, ak_2, etc.[13]), or something more has been learned over and above the learning of the position of a (which accounts for the exclusion of al_1, al_2, etc.[14]).

While a word whose position is learned would be expected to occur in that position with some regularity, the consistency with which a word occurs in a position is not by itself a useful criterion of whether its position has been learned. A word may occur consistently in a specific position without its position necessarily having been learned (e.g. *boat* in Gregory's corpus). Conversely, the fact that a word occurs in both positions is not necessarily a bar to the assumption that the child has learned that it is 'right' in one of these positions, since a word may generalize freely in one position and occur only in specific contexts in the other position (e.g. *more* in Andrew's corpus seems to occur freely when in first position, but in second position occurs only in *no more*, i.e. following a pivot). The inference that the position of a word has been learned must be based primarily on the degree to which the word is free from limitation to specific contexts when it appears in a particular position.

It is clear from the earlier discussion of the grammatical structure that the pivots and only these tend to recur in particular positions without limitations on their context. Frames P_1(—) and (—)P_2, which freely accept words in the vocabulary, are precisely the forms which would be expected if the children had learned the positions of a few words, and learned nothing else which would limit the occupancy of the complementary position.

6. CONCLUSION

The simplest account of the phenomena of the first phase of development seems to be as follows: out of the moderately large vocabulary at his disposal, the child learns, one at a time, that each of a small number of words belongs in a particular position in an utterance. He therefore places them there, and, since he has not learned anything else about what goes where in an utterance, the complementary position is taken by any single-word utterance in his vocabulary, the choice determined only by the physical and social stimuli that elicit the utterance. As a consequence of this learning, the word combinations that are uttered have a characteristic structure containing two parts of speech. One part of speech, here called pivot, comprises the small number of words whose position has been learned. The other, here called the X-class, is a part of speech mainly in a residual sense, and consists of the entire vocabulary, except for some of the pivots. During this first phase the language grows structurally by the formation of new pivot words, i.e. by the child's learning the position of new words. The language grows in vocabulary by adding to the X-class.

---

[13] For example, in the context (—) *boat*, Gregory places *byebye*, *pretty*, *nightnight*, and *big*. These are all pivots. Since the evidence indicates that not any word can precede *boat*, but only a small set, there is no basis for assuming that the position of *boat* has been learned. The occurrence of the specific utterances *byebye boat*, *pretty boat*, etc., can better be explained by assuming that the positions of *byebye*, *pretty*, etc. have been learned.

[14] For example, in the context (—) *it*, Gregory places *do*, *push*, *close*, *buzz*, *move*, and in the context P_1(—) he places such words as *boy*, *dirty*, *plane*, *hurt*, *mommy*, etc. If the occurrence of only verbs before *it* is not accidental, Gregory has not learned merely the position of *it*, but something more which limits its environment to English verbs.

46 This article is more or less a summary of the author's study (dissertation) on "A Descriptive Study of the Syntactic Structures in the Language of Children: Nursery School and First Grade," (Boston, 1961). The latter is evidently among the first studies by linguistically minded educators which were based on Noam Chomsky's novel transformational approach, as presented in his *Syntactic Structures* (1957). "The purpose of this study was to use an explanatory model of grammar, Chomsky's model of syntactic structures, to determine if it was capable of describing a children's grammar as a self-contained system and of indicating developmental trends."

Subsequent studies, inspired by the new transformational approach, were naturally more elaborate, as can be seen from the selections that follow. This study is of special significance because it is one of the first of its kind.

Later studies by Menyuk include *Sentences Children Use* (Cambridge, Massachusetts: The M. I. T. Press, 1968) and "The Role of Distinctive Features in Children's Acquisition of Phonology," *Journal of Speech and Hearing Research* XI (1968), 138–46.

A. B. A.

SYNTACTIC STRUCTURES IN THE LANGUAGE OF CHILDREN

Any technique used to describe a child's grammar must permit us to (a) examine language at particular times in its development as a self-contained system and (b) describe the changing processes of this system as the child matures. Such a technique is provided by a generative model of syntactic structures. Although a description of the syntactic structures in the child's language does not give a total account of his language development, it can go beyond the quantitative

Reprinted from Child Development *34.407–422 (1963), copyright 1963 by the Society for Research in Child Development, Inc., by permission of the author and the Society for Research in Child Development, Inc.*

Research Laboratory of Electronics, Linguistic Project, Massachusetts Institute of Technology, Cambridge, Massachusetts.

The investigation reported here was done in partial fulfillment of the requirements for the Ed. D. degree, Boston University, and was supported by a fellowship MF-8768 from the National Institute of Mental Health, Public Health Service. The author is indebted to Professor W. Prenovost of Boston University and Professor M. Halle of Massachusetts Institute of Technology for their critical assistance.

measure of percentages and proportion of adult usage and can encompass the interrelationship of various previously compartmentalized measures of grammar. It may, in addition, provide "a hypothesis concerning the specific nature of the innate intellectual equipment of the child" (Chomsky, 1961, p.36).

Chomsky (1957) gives us a technique for describing the rules or categories from which the child may generate the sentences in his language. This model of a grammar is analogous to a categorization theory of learning. The rules formulated for generating possible sentences in a language are the categories of grammatical structure in the language (the negative sentence, the imperative sentence, etc.). It is hypothesized that the attributes of a given category are memorized and the child can then produce new instances of the category. In using this technique to analyze the language of children, we may identify the grammatical categories of their language and determine which categories are acquired at an earlier or later age. In addition, this descriptive technique encompasses previously compartmentalized measures by allowing us to describe sequentially (a) the underlying structure of each sentence, (b) the structural changes necessary to derive other sentences from this basic sentence, and (c) the morphological changes which occur because of the previous sequences. In this way the child's grammar can be described as a structural whole rather than in segments.

Chomsky's model has not as yet been used to describe the grammar of children. It was for the purpose of exploring the efficacy of this technique for such a description that this study was undertaken.

TECHNIQUE

The generative model considers grammar as having a tripartite structure, namely, a phrase structure level, a transformation level, and a morphology level. Each of the three levels of grammar has a sequence of rules which generate the form of sentences within the level.[1]

The syntactic structures described at the phrase structure level are the parts of speech used to formulate simple-active-declarative sentences of the type "I play." Chomsky calls these sentences terminal strings (or sentences in a transitional state), and they form the basis for all other sentences.

The more complex sentences are formulated by a sequence of rules at the second level of the grammar which Chomsky has termed transformational rules. At this level of grammar the rules change the order of the symbols in the terminal string or allow symbols to be deleted or added. The transformational rules are of two kinds, optional and obligatory. The optional rules are chosen by the speaker. He can choose to formulate an affirmative sentence, a negative sentence, or an imperative sentence. Once having chosen a form, there is a set of obligatory rules which must be followed to produce sentences which will be accepted by the listener as grammatical. These sentences are of the type: "I did play" (affirmative), "I did not play" (negative), "Play" (imperative). The transformational rules carry strings with phrase structure into new strings to which the rules at the third level can apply. Transformations are derived from either one phase structure string (simple transformations) or from two or more phrase structure strings (general transformations).

At the third level of grammar there is a sequence of inflectional rules from which the actual sounds of speech are derived. These structures formulate, for example, the third person singular present of the verb and the past of the verb.

PROCEDURE

The population was composed of 48 private nursery school children and 48 first grade children.[2] There were 24 girls and 24 boys in the nursery school group and 25 boys and 23 girls in the first grade group. All the first grade children included in the sample had attended nursery school and kindergarten. The age range of the nursery school group was from 3 years, 1 month, to 4 years, 4 months, and the age range of the first grade group was from 5 years, 11 months, to 7 years, 1 month. There was no significant difference in the mean age of males and females in either group. The nursery school group's mean age was 3 years, 8 months, and the first grade group's mean age was 6 years, 5 months.

The population did not include children with a physical disability which impaired speech, or those with an IQ under 90 as measured by the Full Range Picture Vocabulary Test (Ammons). There was no significant difference between mean intelligence of nursery school children and first grade children or between males and females. Intragroup analyses comparing IQ of males and females within the two age levels also showed no significant differences. The nursery school children's mean IQ was 130.3 (SD = 11.2), and the first grade children's mean IQ was 132.0 (SD = 13.4).

Seventy-nine per cent of the nursery school children's parents were in the occupational categories of professional or semiprofessional and managerial, and 83 per cent of the first grade children's parents were in these same occupational categories. The remainder were in the occupational category of clerical, skilled trades, and retail business. Thus,

---

[1] Examples of the rules are given in the Appendix.

[2] Grateful acknowledgement is given to the children and teachers of the Young Israel and Beacon Nursery Schools and the first grade of the Edith C. Baker School in Brookline, Massachusetts.

parental occupation for all the children in both groups falls within the upper 24 per cent range of a middle-class population (*The Minnesota Scale for Paternal Occupation*).

Speech was tape recorded in three stimulus situations. The first situation was spontaneous speech responses to the projective test The Blacky Pictures (2). The second was conversation with an adult (the experimenter) generated by some of the questions suggested in the test manual and additional questions introduced by the experimenter. Each child was asked the same questions. The third situation was conversation with peers generated by role playing in a family setting. Each group was composed of three children (two girls and a boy or two boys and a girl). The situation was introduced in the following manner:

"You are going to pretend that you are a family. I have some things here which will help you to pretend." The play objects were then handed out. The children were then told, "Pretend that you've just gotten up in the morning and you're going to get ready for the day." The experimenter did not participate unless a question was directly asked, and then only a direct answer was given. The play situation was recorded for a period of 15 minutes.

The entire speech output of each child was recorded in a single day and was transcribed on the same day. Those children who produced less than 50 sentences were eliminated from the sample population. The mean number of sentences produced by nursery school children was 82.9 (SD = 16.7), and the mean number produced by first grade children was 05.7 (SD = 15.2). The t test showed that this difference was significant ($p < .01$). There was no significant difference in the mean number of sentences produced by males and females or children above and below the mean IQ within the two age levels or between them.

In addition to the above, the children were observed in their classrooms and written recordings were made of their speech. This was done for the purpose of cross validation, to determine if there were some syntactic structures which were used in the classroom situation and not in other situations. The children were observed in each classroom for a period of two hours. The language sample contained 8574 sentences obtained in the tape recorded situations and 1009 obtained in the classrooms.

The language sample of each child and of the classroom groups was analyzed using Chomsky's technique. A grammar was written which included all the rules used at both age levels to generate all the sentences obtained.[3] Using the chi square technique, comparisons of the number of children using structures which are grammatically acceptable were made between: (a) nursery school and first grade groups, (b) all males and females and males and females within the nursery school and first grade groups, and (c) all children above and below the mean IQ and children above and below the mean IQ within the nursery school and first grade groups. The same comparisons were made of the usage of structures which are grammatically unacceptable or, in other terms, restricted to a children's grammar.

RESULTS

At the phrase structure level of grammar (rules for simple-active-declarative sentences) and the morphology level of grammar (inflectional rules), all children used all the structures in a grammatically acceptable form. Therefore, no comparisons were made of the usage of these structures, but only of transformational rules where differences in usage were found. Simultaneously, structures restricted to a children's grammar were used by varying numbers of the children at all three levels of grammar, and therefore comparisons of the usage of all these structures were made. The rules described at the morphology level of the grammar in this study were limited to those structures in which forms restricted to a children's grammar occurred: third person singular and plural in the present tense of verbs, past tense of verbs, singular and plural of nouns, and possessive pronouns and adjectives. An example of each transformation

---

[3] The complete grammar is presented in the author's unpublished doctoral dissertation, A descriptive study of the syntactic structures in the language of children: nursery school and first grade, Boston University, 1961.

and each structure restricted to a children's grammar (taken from the children's language sample) is presented.

TRANSFORMATIONS

Simple Transformations
1. *Passive*—He was tied up by the man.
2. *Negation*—I am not.
3. *Question*—Is he sleeping?
4. *Contraction*—He'll choke.
5. *Inversion*—Now I have kittens.
6. *Relative question*—What is that?
7. *Imperative*—Don't use my brushes.
8. *Pronominalization*—There isn't any more.
9. *Separation*—He took it off.
10. *Got*—I've got a book.
11. *Auxiliary verb*
    a. *be*—He is not going to the movies.
    b. *have*—I've already been there.
12. *Do*—I did read the book.
13. *Possessive*—I'm writing daddy's name.
14. *Reflexive*—I cut myself.

Generalized Transformations
15. *Conjunction*—They will be over here and momma will be over there.
16. *Conjunction deletion*—I see lipstick and a comb.
17. *Conditional*—I'll give it to you if you need it.
18. *So*—He saw him so he hit him.
19. *Causal*—He won't eat the grass because they will cry.
20. *Pronoun in conjunction*—Blacky saw Tippy and he was mad.
21. *Adjective*—I have a pink dog.
22. *Relative clause*—I don't know what he's doing.
23. *Complement*
    a. *Infinitival*—I want to play.
    b. *Participial*—I like singing.
24. *Iteration*—You have to clean clothes to make them clean.
25. *Nominalization*—She does the shopping and cooking and baking.
26. *Nominal compound*—The baby carriage is here.

STRUCTURES RESTRICTED TO A CHILDREN'S GRAMMAR

Phrase Structure
1. *Verb phrase*
    a. *Omission*—The momma'll.
    b. *Redundancy*—He'll might get in jail.
    c. *Substitution*—Say the story.

2. *Noun phrase*
    a. *Omission*—Want it.
    b. *Redundancy*—She took it away the hat.
3. *Preposition*
    a. *Omission*—I want to go New York.
    b. *Redundancy*—You shop in over there.
    c. *Substitution*—Daddy took me at the train.
4. *Article*
    a. *Omission*—Giant wakes up.
    b. *Redundancy*—His name is a teddy bear.
    c. *Substitution*—I see a teeth.
5. *Particle*
    a. *Omission*—Put the hat.
    b. *Redundancy*—Take it in in there.

Transformations
6. *Double negation*—You can't put no more water in it.
7. *Contraction deletion*—They sleeping.
8. *Inversion restrictions*
    a. *Subject-object*—Brother and sisters I have.
    b. *Verb number*—There's three strings.
9. *No question*—What that is.
10. *There substitution*—It isn't any more snow.
11. *No separation*—You pick up it.
12. *Reflexive 3rd person*—He's licking hisself.
13. *Tense restriction*—They get mad and then they pushed him.
14. *Pronoun restriction*—Mommy was mad so he spanked Blacky.
15. *Adjective restriction*—I write that numbers.
16. *Relative pronoun restriction*—I see a dog what's white.

Morphology
17. *Verb form*
    a. *Omission*—He wash.
    b. *Redundancy*—He liketed it.
    c. *Substitution*—He growed.
18. *Noun form*
    a. *Omission*—I have two necklace.
    b. *Redundancy*—Where are the childrens?
    c. *Substitution*—We have childs in this school.
19. *Possessive*—Hims stomach hurt.

Comparison of the usage of transformations
Some transformations were used by signif-

icantly more of the first grade children than by the nursery children, whereas the inverse was never true. Evidence of this maturation in grammatical development is given in Table 1, where it is seen that the passive transformation, use of the auxiliary verb *have*, conjunctions with *if* and *so* as introductory segments, and the nominalization transformations were used by significantly more children in the first grade population than in the nursery school population. Figures of the significance of the differences are given in the last column of the table only when $p <$ .05.

TABLE 1. Comparison of the usage of transformations by nursery school and first grade children.

| | Number of children | | |
| | Nursery school N = 48 | First grade N = 48 | p* |
Transformations			
1. Passive	23	41	.05
2. Negation	48	48	
3. Question	44	48	
4. Contraction	48	48	
5. Inversion	45	48	
6. Relative question	47	47	
7. Imperative	35	42	
8. Pronominalization	16	26	
9. Separation	41	44	
10. Got	48	48	
11. Auxiliary			
a. be	48	48	
b. have	8	20	.05
12. Do	48	48	
13. Possessive	48	48	
14. Reflexive	29	44	
15. Conjunction	41	48	
16. Conjunction deletion	40	47	
17. If	12	30	.01
18. So	12	29	.01
19. Because	30	46	
20. Pronoun	48	48	
21. Adjective	48	48	
22. Relative clause	37	46	
23. Complement			
a. Infinitival	48	48	
b. Participial	19	31	
24. Iteration	5	13	
25. Nominalization	6	24	.01
26. Nominal compound	48	48	

*p values were obtained by chi square evaluations.

In Table 2 we see that many of the transformations which show significant maturation effects from nursery school to first grade have not yet been completely acquired by the first grade population. Although acquisition of the passive transformation has essentially been accomplished by the first grade, use of the auxiliary verb *have*, conjunctions with *if* and *so*, and the nominalization transformation still show significant departures from complete acquisition by the first grade group. This is also true of the pronominalization, participial complement, and iteration transformations. The latter two, namely participial complement and iteration, were used by more of the first grade children at a level approaching significance ($p <$ .10).

TABLE 2. Transformations used by significantly less than 100 per cent of first grade children.

| | First grade children N = 48 | | |
Transformations	Number	Per Cent	p
Pronominalization	26	54	.05
Auxiliary verb	20	42	.01
If	30	63	.05
So	29	60	.05
Participial complement	31	65	.05
Iteration	13	27	.01
Nominalization	24	50	.01

A chi square evaluation of the data considering the effects of IQ and sex upon transformation usage showed no significant difference in usage of transformations between males and females or between all children above and below the mean measured intelligence. Comparisons of the usage of transformations by males and females and by children above and below the mean measured intelligence within the nursery school and first grade levels were also made, and no significant differences were found. The results indicate that there is no difference between the sexes in the acquisition of syntactic structures. This is a finding noted in other studies using different means of describing children's grammar (Templin). Although no significant differences were found for those above versus those below the mean in intelli-

TABLE 3. Comparison of usage of structures restricted to children's grammar by nursery school and first grade children.

| | | Number of children | | |
		Nursery school N = 48	First grade N = 48	p
Structures				
1.	Verb phrase			
	a. Omission	5	0	
	b. Redundancy	5	3	
	c. Substitution	16	9	
2.	Noun phrase			
	a. Omission	19	19	
	b. Redundancy	24	40	.05
3.	Preposition			
	a. Omission	14	3	.05
	b. Redundancy	20	10	
	c. Substitution	16	8	
4.	Article			
	a. Omission	16	2	.01
	b. Redundancy	9	7	
	c. Substitution	4	2	
5.	Particle			
	a. Omission	9	2	
	b. Redundancy	2	1	
6.	Double negation	4	4	
7.	Contraction deletion	42	29	
8.	Inversion restrictions			
	a. Subject-object	8	7	
	b. Verb number	17	12	
9.	No question	18	2	.01
10.	There substitution	8	1	.05
11.	No separation	4	0	
12.	Reflexive 3rd person	10	8	
13.	Tense restriction	11	17	
14.	Pronoun restriction	12	11	
15.	Adjective restriction	15	2	.01
16.	Relative pronoun restriction	5	4	
17.	Verb form			
	a. Omission	29	20	
	b. Redundancy	16	7	
	c. Substitution	15	5	.05
18.	Noun form			
	a. Omission	10	6	
	b. Redundancy	9	4	
	c. Substitution	5	2	
19.	Possessive	7	0	.05

gence, the results should be viewed with some reservations since the comparison made was coarse and since all of those below the mean of this group were above average in intelligence.

Comparison of the usage of structures restricted to a children's grammar

As previously stated, all the rules found in phrase structure and the rules described at the morphology level of grammar were used by all the children in the sample population. Simultaneously, forms restricted to a children's grammar existed at all three levels. Therefore, comparisons were made of the usage of these unique forms at all three levels of the grammar.

The numbers of children in nursery school and first grade using the various unique structures are given in Table 3. The chi square technique with Yates' correction for small cells was used to compare these figures. There were significantly more children in the nursery school group who omitted prepositions and articles in phrase structure. Also, there were significantly more children in the nursery school group who could perform only the first steps in the following transformations: relative question, pronominalization, and adjective. That is, they could not bring them to correct completion. They could perform the optional steps in the transformation but, once having chosen a structure, they did not observe the additional obligatory restrictions. At the morphological level, there were significantly more children in the nursery school group who omitted the irregular past form of verbs and substituted regular past forms. In general, one can term all the unique forms noted here as omissions of restrictions which are obligatory once a structure has been optionally chosen.

Unique forms, however, occurred infrequently as compared to structures that follow the rules to completion. Table 4 shows the frequency of occurrence per sentence of the total number of restricted forms found in the

TABLE 4. Frequency of occurrence per sentence of total number of structures restricted to the children's grammar.

Structures	Nursery school	First grade
Omissions	.04	.02
Redundancies	.03	.04
Substitutions	.02	.01
Transformation restrictions	.07	.04

children's grammar. In this table all omissions, redundancies, and substitutions at
the phrase structure and morphology levels
are categorized together, as are all omissions
of restrictions on the transformation level.
There was no significant difference between
the two groups in the total numbers of the
various unique forms used. Contraction deletions accounted for .04 of the total per
sentence unique forms used at the nursery
school level and .02 at the first grade level.
It was the most frequent restricted form found
in the children's grammar. Contraction was
almost always chosen in using the auxiliary
verbs and modals, and this is consistent with
adult usage.

In addition to the trends noted above, significantly more first grade children used redundant noun phrases in their sentence formation.

Redundancies in other forms existed at the
phrase structure and morphology levels.
There seems to be a developmental trend
which resembles a damped oscillatory function rather than an asymptotic approach
toward a zero usage of restricted forms. At
the phrase structure and morphology levels
of the grammar, the children used rules with
omissions, then rules with redundancies
with decreasing maximum amplitude.

The decreasing amplitude indicates a gradual lessening in fluctuation toward a static
point which may be considered an adult
grammar. Since these restricted forms occurred with such infrequency in the language
sample, no quantitative statement about this
trend can be made. Figure 1 is a curve showing
the variation of the percentage of omission
minus the percentage of redundancy with

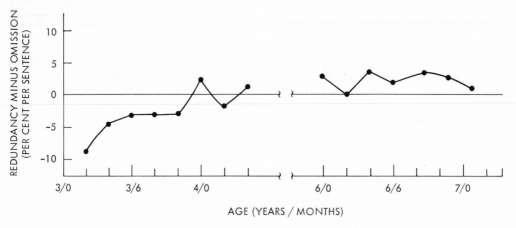

FIGURE 1.   Percentage of redundancy minus percentage of omission plotted at two-month intervals.

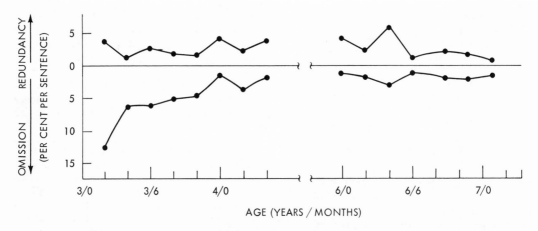

FIGURE 2.   Percentage of omission and percentage of redundancy plotted at two-month intervals.

age, and Figure 2 shows the variation of the percentage of omission and the percentage of redundancy separately.

Comparisons of the usage of structures restricted to the children's grammar were made between males and females and between children above and below the mean IQ. There were significantly more females in the total population who did not always use the pronoun restriction in conjunction and conjoining sentences ($p < .05$). There were no significant differences between males and females within the nursery school or within the first grade populations. In comparing the total population above and below the mean IQ, significantly more children below the mean substituted verb forms at the morphology level ($p < .05$). Within the nursery school population, significantly more children above the mean IQ used articles redundantly ($p < .05$). These measurements indicate that there is little significant difference between the sexes or between children above and below the mean IQ in the use of restricted forms. It should be noted, however, that in those instances in which significant differences occurred, the children above the mean IQ (at the nursery school level) used a redundant form, and the children below the mean omitted an obligatory rule. The previously stated reservations concerning the possible effect of intelligence on the usage of transformations apply to the usage of restricted forms as well.

DISCUSSION

The basic structures which generated all the sentences in the total language sample could be described within the framework of the Chomsky model. These syntactic structures include those found in both children's and adults' grammar and those which are restricted to a children's grammar. Thus, the technique is capable of describing a stage of development of children's grammar as a self-contained system.

All the basic structures used by adults to generate their sentences can be found in the grammar of the nursery school children. Mean sentence length has long been used as a valid quantitative measure of increased verbal maturity. In this study it was found that in the same stimulus situations the total sentence output increases significantly with age, and that as the child matures, syntactic structures are added to syntactic structures leading to increased length, but without adding to the basic structures used. For example, we find constructions such as conjunction plus conjunction plus conjunction ("I have a big, big teddy bear and I have a little doggie and he's named Blacky/Whitey and there's this big dog and he's named Peppermint"). The addition of structures to structures does not indicate that any different basic structures have been acquired.

In comparing the number of children in the nursery school group and in the first grade group who used each syntactic structure, it was found that most of the structures are used at an early age and are used consistently. If we look at the nature of the structures which are used by *all* of the children (for example, negation, contraction, auxilary *be*, etc.), it would seem that the theory of Piaget and others, which states that language is an expression of children's needs and is far from a purely imitative function even at a very early age, is a valid one. A need for social instrumentation and a method of categorizing the environment would motivate the usage of these structures. The particular constraints of the language shape the parameters of these structures. With those structures which show significant maturational changes in a comparison of nursery school and first grade children, there are indications that further significant changes occur beyond the 7-year level.

The structures which are restricted to a children's grammar occurred infrequently in the total language sample. It was found that significantly more children at the nursery school level omitted rules which are obligatory once a structure has been optionally chosen. In addition, at the phrase structure and morphology level, a damped oscillatory function was observed in the course of the maturational development toward a zero usage of restricted forms. The data is limited by the infrequency of occurrence of such forms. The possibility that such a function exists fits in well with an information theory conceptual framework. By using symbol patterns in a redundant fashion, we make it likely that an error will transform this pattern into some highly improbable pattern and thus enable us to detect a mistake. When the child begins to use the irregular form of verbs, for example, past experience tells him that the addition of "ed" is the rule for transforming present to past. If he is trying out a new verb in past form, he may use the regular past form and produce the verb "standed." He may then use the irregular past form plus the regular past to insure its "correctness." For example, he says "stooded." After repeated trials, he may then acquire the concept that past forms of some verbs do not require the regular inflectional ending, and he finally can produce "stood." All three stages of past tense verb formation exist in children's grammar.

One reservation to be kept in mind in looking at the results of comparisons of usage of all transformations is the presumption that *all* the transformations would be used by an adult in like stimulus situations.

SUMMARY

The purpose of this study was to use an explanatory model of grammar, Chomsky's model of syntactic structures, to determine if it was capable of describing a children's grammar as a self-contained system and of indicating developmental trends.

Language was elicited and tape-recorded in three stimulus situations: (a) spontaneous speech in response to The Blacky Pictures, (b) conversation with an adult (the experimenter), and (c) conversation with peers. For cross validation purposes, the language used in the classrooms of the sample population was transcribed. The language sample of each child and of the classroom groups was analyzed using Chomsky's technique.

It was found that the basic structures which generated all the sentences obtained could be described within the framework of the Chomsky model. A children's grammar was written which included all the rules used at both age levels to generate structures consistent with adult usage and those which, presumably, are not. All the basic structures used by adults to generate their sentences were found in the grammar of the nursery school group. In comparing the number of children at the two age levels who used these structures, it was found that most of the structures were used at an early age and used consistently. Structures which were still in the process of being acquired by the nursery school group were also still in the process of being acquired by the first grade group. Structures nonconsistent with adult usage occurred infrequently. Significantly more of the nursery school children omitted rules which are obligatory once a structure has been optionally chosen. There were few significant differences in the usage of all structures between males and females or between children above and below the mean IQ.

APPENDIX

The rules at the phrase structure level of the grammar are all of the type X becomes Y with the restrictions that only a single symbol can be replaced in a single rule and that X is not Y. The following is a partial listing of the rules:

X	becomes $\rightarrow$	Y
Sentence	$\rightarrow$ Noun phrase + Verb phrase + (Adverbial phrase)	
Noun phrase	$\rightarrow$ (Article) + Noun + (Prepositional phrase)	
Verb phrase	$\rightarrow$ Verb + (Noun phrase)	
Adverbial phrase	$\rightarrow$ Adverb	
Adverbial phrase	$\rightarrow$ Prepositional phrase	
Prepositional phrase	$\rightarrow$ Preposition + Noun phrase	
Article	$\rightarrow$ The, an, a	
Noun	$\rightarrow$ Man, ball, it, etc.	
Verb	$\rightarrow$ Hit, feel, etc.	
Preposition	$\rightarrow$ Of, for, in, etc.	

To derive the particular sentence "The man hit the ball," the following rules are used:

Sentence
Noun phrase + Verb phrase
Article + Noun + Verb phrase
Article + Noun + Verb + Noun phrase
Article + Noun + Verb + Article + Noun
The + Noun + Verb + Article + Noun
The + man + Verb + Article + Noun
The + man + hit + Article + Noun
The + man + hit + the + Noun
The + man + hit + the + ball

By repeating the rules, endless strings of

words may be derived. This is in keeping with the fact that no language places an upper limit on the length of sentences, although all actual sentences are finite.

The following are examples of some simple transformational rules which are used to derive various sentences from the single kernel sentence "The man hit the ball."

From phrase structure, where person, number, and tense are chosen, we derive the following form:

Sentence
Noun phrase + Verb phrase
Article Noun Verb + present
The   man   hit + present
Article + Noun + plural
the   ball   + plural

If we replace each symbol in this sample sentence with a number, transformations can be derived in the following manner:

Tranformations
1. Affirmation
    The man do hit + present
     1   2   3 4 +   5
                        the ball + plural
                         6   7 + 8
    Becomes→
    The man do + present hit
     1   2   3 +   5   4
                        the ball + plural
                         6   7 + 8
2. Question
    The man do + present hit
     1   2   3 +   5   4
                        the ball + plural
                         6   7 + 8→
    Do + present the man hit
    3 +   5   1   2 4
                        the ball + plural
                         6   7 + 8
3. Negative
    Do + present the man hit
    3 +   5   1   2 4
                        the ball + plural
                         6   7 + 8→
    Do + present not the man hit
    3 +   5   9   1   2 4
                        the ball + plural
                         6   7 + 8
4. Contraction
    Do + present not the man hit
    3 +   5   9   1   2 4
                        the ball + plural
                         6   7 + 8→

Do + present n't the man hit
3 +   5   9   1   2 4
                    the ball + plural
                     6   7 + 8

By one of the final obligatory transformations, the grammatical operators act upon the words in the sentence.

5. Affix
    Do + present n't the man hit
    3 +   5   9   1   2 4
                        the ball + plural
                         6   7 + 8→
    Present + do n't the man hit
    5   + 3 9 1   2 4
                        the plural + ball
                         6   8 + 7

The following are some examples of morphophonemic rules applied to the sentences obtained from transformational rules:

Morphophonemic Rules

                                        becomes
Third person singular present + hit → hits
Third person singular present + do → does
Plural + ball   → balls

From the above rules, the following sentences are derived:

1. The man does hit the balls.
2. Does the man hit the balls?
3. Does not the man hit the balls?
4. Doesn't the man hit the balls?

REFERENCES

Ammons, R. B., and Ammons, H. S. *Full Range Picture Vocabulary Test.* Psychological Test Specialists, 1958.

Blum, G. S. *The Blacky Pictures.* Psychological Corporation, 1950.

Chomsky, N. *Syntactic Structures.* The Hague: Mouton & Co., 1957.

———. "Explanatory Models in Linguistics." Department of Modern Languages, Massachusetts Institute of Technology, 1961. (Mimeo.)

Templin, M. C. *Certain Language Skills in Children.* University of Minnesota Press, 1957.

The Minnesota Scale for Paternal Occupation. Institute of Child Welfare, University of Minnesota, 1950.

47 Child bilingualism, the learning of two languages by small children, is a special facet of child language. No attempt is made in this volume to present excerpts from the few major studies devoted to this topic. Instead, a characterization of three of them is reproduced from Věroboj Vildomec, *Multilingualism* (1963), the only large study of the mastery of several languages, written by a polyglot and language teacher. It includes much discussion of bilingualism because there is very little early literature on multilingualism.

Michael West, whose work Vildomec cites, discusses bilingualism from the aspect of teaching English in Indian schools. The books and articles to which he refers are:

Jules Ronjat. *Le Développment du langage observé chez un enfant bilingue.* Paris, 1913.

Wilder Penfield. "A Consideration of the Neurophysiological Mechanisms of Speech and Some Educational Consequences." *Proceedings of the American Academy of Arts and Sciences*, LXXXII (1953), 201–14.

———. and Lamar Roberts. *Speech and Brain Mechanisms.* Princeton, 1959.

Michael West. *Bilingualism* (with special reference to Bengal). Calcutta, 1926.

———., "Bilingualism." *English Language Teaching*, XII (1958), 94–97.

Milivoïe Pavlovitch. *Le Langage enfantin; acquisition du serbe et du français par un enfant serbe.* Paris, 1920.

Werner F. Leopold. *Speech Development of a Bilingual Child; A Linguist's Record*, 4 vols. Evanston, 1939–49.

———. "Ein Kind lernt zwei Sprachen." *Sprachforum*, II (1957), 248–52.

Paul Christophersen. *Bilingualism* (inaugural lecture, Ibadan, Nigeria). London, 1948.

Robbins Burling. "Language Development of a Garo and English-Speaking Child." *Word*, XV (1959), 45–68. (Paper included in this volume).

For a detailed review by W. F. Leopold, cf. *Language*, XLI (1965), 100–105.

L^2 means second language, L^m mother tongue.

W. F. L.

MULTILINGUALISM

Three authors have written important works about their own children who acquired two languages simultaneously from the very beginning of their speech. The books of these authors deal mainly or entirely with preschool years and less thoroughly or not at all with speech at school age. One of the most interesting of these studies is that by J. Ronjat (1913) which covers up to the age of 4; 10 and deals with a case of complete

Reprinted from Věroboj Vildomec, General Linguistics and Psychology of Speech (*Leyden: A. W. Sythoff, 1963*), 25–26, by permission of the publisher.

bilingualism. Ronjat's method is: *one person —one language.* (A method which could be characterized by the words *one environment— one language* has been used recently by W. Penfield, 1952–1953, 207; cf. W. Penfield, L. Roberts, 1959, 253–54.) Ronjat's son Louis learned German from his mother and French from his father. The family resided in France. The results summarized on pp. 103–106 are: The pronunciation was from the very beginning that of a unilingual child in both languages; bilingualism did not lead to backwardness in speech; loans from one language into the other remained isolated; parallel development of phonetics, morphology, and syntax took place in both languages; the child soon became aware of his bilingualism and translated messages from one language into the other; he also acquired the abstract idea of language. These good results cannot be attributed, in the opinion of Ronjat, exclusively to his method although it is the safest and least tiring way. Later in life the languages became somewhat specialized. (The usefulness of the specialization of L^2 has been stressed recently by M. West, 1958, 97.) M. West (1926, 59–60) quotes a letter of Ronjat, dated 27th October, 1923, reporting that Louis Ronjat uses either language with equal facility in ordinary conversation; in technical matters, however, he prefers French—the school language, and for literary self-expression he uses German—the L^m.

M. Pavlovitch (1920) traces the speech development of his son Douchan acquiring simultaneously Serbian and French. His study would have been more interesting for our present purpose if he had not stopped when the child was two years of age; it would have been interesting, for instance, to compare the learning of declensions in the synthetic Serbian with that of the analytic French. In their results Pavlovitch and Ronjat are largely in agreement. Pavlovitch does not believe in heredity and says that if there is any, it is a predisposition of a more general than of a national character. His study contains many generalizations on bilingualism, although his child does not seem to have been really bilingual, and an extensive bibliography . . . .

The most thorough study of the speech of an individual bilingual child, and no doubt of any individual child, is that of W. F. Leopold (1939–1949; cf. 1956–1957). The incontestable advantage of this work is that it was written by a thorough linguist using systematically a phonetic transcription (the system of the International Phonetic Association). Another great advantage is that in his statistics he also takes into account the fact that many words were forgotten by the child . . . . The diary for Hildegard goes to the age of 15; 7, but the first two years are treated more thoroughly than the rest. Samples of the speech of Hildegard's younger sister Karla are also included. The two languages learnt by the girls are English (the family live in America) and German (the father's language). English is the language of environment except for stays in Germany. On the whole bilingualism is not so complete as in the case of Louis Ronjat, because the position of Hildegard's German is much weaker than that of her English. In the first two years of Hildegard's life bilingualism was important in vocabulary, in which German and English words were mixed. Otherwise there were only a few traces of the influence of bilingualism. Soon after her second birthday, Hildegard started to separate the languages from each other according to the person of the interlocutor. Later on, there was much influence of one language on the other in vocabulary, idiomatic phrases, and syntax; very little in sounds, morphology, and word formation. Her German was especially handicapped.

All three authors think that bilingualism did not harm the speech development or the general mental development of their children. W. F. Leopold (1939–1949, vol. III, 181, 182 and 187–88) seems even to have found some advantages for bilingualism in Hildegard's case:

The disregard for form in favor of content was probably furthered by bilingualism. . . . Bilingualism . . . helps to break down the intimate association between form and content. A bilingual child will pay more attention to things referred to, situations and actions described, and ideas expressed than to phonetic forms pronounced. . . . "Hildegard never clung to words, as monolingual children are often reported to do. She did not insist on the exact wording . . . I attribute this attitude of detachment from words confidently to bilingualism.

This opinion is shared by P. Christophersen (1948, 12), but opposed recently by R. Burling (1959, 67).

48 Bar-Adon has studied intensively the acquisition of Hebrew by the Israeli children. The study of Hebrew child language is particularly interesting since we have a case of the individual's language in the making within the community's "language in the making." Hebrew was revived around the turn of the century, and, from certain points of view, has been somewhat uncrystallized for quite a while, which permitted the young generation to create neologisms and new patterns on their own, often unheeded and undisturbed. Many of the "analogical" creations of the children, coincide with forms and patterns of earlier stages in Hebrew (which, as is known, has a long recorded history), and thus may be of special relevance for the study of processes in historical Hebrew as well.

The most comprehensive work on Hebrew child language was written by this author (in Hebrew, with English summary) in 1959: *Children's Hebrew in Israel*, 2 vols., Jerusalem. Another selection on "Primary Syntactic Structures in Hebrew Child Language" appears at the end of this volume. The latter study represents a revised approach by the author to processes of language acquisition within the generative-transformational framework.

W. F. L.

"ANALOGY" AND ANALOGIC CHANGE AS REFLECTED IN CONTEMPORARY HEBREW

It has been widely assumed, that languages are initially acquired, generation after generation,[1] by a kind of productive "imitation" (not reproduction!) which seems to play a particularly decisive role, in the acquisition of the phonological system (and to a great extent also in the lexicon). It is complemented by "analogy" and analogical creation (predominantly in morphology and syntax), as well as by some other processes or mechanisms.[2]

Even imitation (in opposition to "reproduction")[3] may be, or tends to be, different from the "original," in various ways, as well as selective—partly because of the ever-changing environment and range of persons "imitated."[4] However, "analogy" is still, by nature, a far more independent activity or

Reprinted from Horace G. Lunt, ed., Proceedings of the Ninth International Congress of Linguists (*The Hague: Mouton & Co., 1964*), 758–763, by permission of the publisher.

[1] There is a difference in "length" and density among the "generations." They are shorter and denser in the younger ages. The fact that children learn from other children carries important linguistic significance. For more details cf. Hockett's "Age Grading and Linguistic Continuity," *Language*, XXVI (1950), 449–57, and my "Linguistic Continuity and Contemporary Israeli Hebrew," 1961; part of it is summarized in my "The Evolution of Modern Hebrew," in J. Teller, *Acculturation and Integration* (New York: American Histadrut Cultural Exchange Institute, 1965), especially pp. 83–95.

[2] Cf. Leopold (1949), p. 79 and fn. 9 there. (For references see bibliography at the end of my paper.) Cf. his statements regarding imitation (156). Cf. Chomsky 1959, 42 f. There may be a *two-fold* distinction between the roles of *imitation* and *analogy*:

a. A kind of "vertical" distinction between the impact of *imitation* on the initial or basic acquisition of language by the child, and the subsequent development through *analogical* creativity. This is, in a way, a "diachronic" approach to linguistic processes, even throughout the development of an "idiolect"!

b. A "horizontal" distinction, i.e., between the role of *imitation* in certain areas of the language (e.g. phonology, lexicon), and that of *analogy*, say—in grammar (morphology, syntax). Both may operate simultaneously (although in different degrees) in "idiolect" and "dialect," thus calling for some "synchronic" approach. For Ullmann's comments cf. fn. 7 below.

[3] But like "borrowing," which for Bloomfield are identical. Cf. *Language* (1933), p. 365; also p. 476 f.

[4] *Ibid.*, p. 476. Cf. Leopold (1949), 156 (and his bibliogr. in fn. 69, 71). Cf. Hockett (1958), 321 f.

mechanism, which forges the subsequent development of the idiolect,[5] depending on the powers of abstracting, etc. It thus opens the way to constant variation and gradual changes in a language, even within the span of an "idiolect" and turns the optimum "static" state of synchronism or synchronic relationships into a relatively "mobile" one, and makes the so-called equilibrium of the language into a dynamic equilibrium, so to speak.

Linguistic changes are usually classified for analytical purposes, in accordance with the systems, or rather subsystems, categories, or other divisions and levels discernible in the language, e.g., phonetic,[6] phonemic, grammatical and morphophonemic, etc. However, the changes are mostly complex, interrelated, and they often involve several subsystems and processes simultaneously.[7]

As for the factors or mechanisms that are responsible for these changes there have been identified some minor ones (partly sporadic), such as metathesis, contamination, haplology, assimilation and dissimilation, as well as the major processes of sound change,[8] borrowing (i.e., external interference), and analogic creation.

We are here particularly concerned with the latter, and its implications and significance, especially in contemporary Hebrew.

Generally speaking, an inflected language provides greater challenge, or stimulus and opportunity, to the speakers to create or produce "analogically"—apparently, mainly to normalize or simplify patterns, or regularize paradigms.[9] Thus, morphology with its inflected paradigms will, probably, be most productive[10] in "analogy," and certainly—in a highly inflected language as Hebrew.

Modern Hebrew is an eclectic and still somewhat uncrystallized language, and will provide an even greater stimulus and opportunity to its speakers with highest analogic creativity in the domain of the *verb*, since the (possessive) declension of the noun has been in decline in the general "informal" speech, and has almost disappeared (except for specific cases) from the speech of the younger generation. (The reasons and circumstances of the changes are beyond the scope of this paper.)

The study of this half-century-old revived Hebrew speech may have a wider linguistic significance. It has been operating under tremendous, extraordinary, pressures of social, cultural and other demands, so that almost all linguistic processes have been intensively accelerated in meeting the new needs. The inherent capabilities and mechanisms of the language have been expanded, with very special and interesting manifestations in the speech of the younger generation, for whom Hebrew became for the first time again, in almost two millennia, a real *native* language. This process could be easily exposed to any kind of linguistic observation and follow-up, as if it were under laboratory conditions where you can "catch" fast developments with a "slow-motion" apparatus.

Thus the linguist could observe not only "analogic creation" in the making, but also the results: i.e., the analogic change, which usually occurs (seemingly suddenly) as soon as the innovations begin to replace the older forms (involving idiolect and dialect, or language).

---

[5] Hockett (1958) distinguishes between "linguistic phylogeny" (dialect, language) and "linguistic ontogeny" (idiolect), pp. 353 ff. The term "idiolect" was coined by Bernard Bloch (1948, p. 7). Cf. R. A. Hall (1951) p. 22. Following Herbert Spencer's definition of life one may say that "idiolect is a continual adjustment of the internal system to the external conditions" (this is true, in a way, regarding "language" too).

[6] Hockett (1958), 384–85 *et al.* differentiates between "sound change" and what he calls "sudden phonetic change." The latter has apparently developed from Bloomfield's "sudden sound-change" (1926), p. 164.

[7] Cf. Bloomfield (1933), regarding the replacement of OE *stanas* by the nominative-accusative form *stones*, which is now used for the whole plural, regardless of syntactic position. This "is part of a larger process, the loss of case inflection in the noun, which involved both phonetic and analogic changes" (410). Cf., however, Ullmann (1957) on the roles of sound laws vs. analogy as to the regularity in morphology: "synchronistically, analogy is a factor of regularity and sound laws factors of disruption; diachronistically, it is sound laws that work regularly and "analogy" that dislocates the pattern" (173).

[8] Hockett states that it is "one *kind* of phylogenetic change" as well as it must be recognized as one of the *mechanisms* involved in other kinds of phylogenetic change" (p. 388).

---

[9] Cf. Bloomfield (1933), 410. He identifies analogic change with "systematization" (p. 365).

[10] For "productivity" cf. Hoenigswald (1960), 59 ff.; Hockett (1958), 307 f., etc.

Under such a dynamism, which (as mentioned above) scarcely leaves an actual static status to synchronism, and in face of the intrinsic and intricate constant interactions between the language of the younger generation and that of the older, it seems somewhat difficult to adopt a rigid, formal distinction between "synchronic" and "diachronic" in both "idiolect" and "language."

Here we are confronted with what I am tempted to call codimensional situations, i.e., where "horizontal" and "vertical" or "space" and "time," respectively, do come in contact and "cross" each other.

It is very commonly said that analogy, by nature, disfavors irregularity and divergence,[11] in that it tends to regularize or normalize forms, patterns, or paradigms according to the commonest examples. Some would even expect it to be exclusively a kind of simplifying or economizing device, that reduces "irregularities," or the number of alternants or allomorphs, as in the case of CaCáCtem (/šamártem/) in contemporary Hebrew, for historical CǝCaCtém (/šǝmartém/), by "analogy" with CaCáCti (/šamárti/), etc. But "analogy" is in fact an unpredicted process or behavior (not yet fully explained psychologically), and hence it involves analogic patterning according to minor or rarer forms too. Thus it introduces conflicting analogies, "blends,"[12] *new* alternants, etc., e.g., historical /mak(k)ir/ is replaced by /mekir/, which in turn is incompatible with the other nonpast forms, like /tak(k)ir, nak(k)ir, lǝhak(k)ir/, etc.

To illustrate from the broader analogic creations let us take a glimpse, for instance, into the imperative. It has developed mainly along the following two lines:

(1) In "informal" speech, all over Israel, the normative forms of imperative have been replaced by the corresponding periphrastic forms of the second person of the future, e.g.: /telex vǝ-tašuv/, for /lex va-šuv/ "go

and return!", /titbayeš lxa/, for /hitbayeš lxa/, "be ashamed!". (One may say that there is now in those forms a semantic cofunctioning or hierarchy of functions of future and imperative, but this is immaterial here.)

There may possibly be several approaches or explanations to this phenomenon. (One of my informants, a teenager, "explains" that "it is unpleasant to command someone else"—therefore she uses the future forms for imperative too.) However, I believe that it can be best explained as an analogic creation connected with, or derived from, the "legitimate" negative forms for the imperative (as an apposition to them):

/al tavo/ > /ken tavo/ → /tavo/("come!")
/al tazuz/ > /ken tazuz/ → /tazuz/ ("move!"), etc.[13]

Needless to say, this is accepted most readily by the younger speakers, possibly because most of the commands to them are in the negative. For example, /al telex/, /al tazuz/ "don't go!", "don't move!", stimulate the responses /telex/, /tazuz/, with or without the emphatic /ken/ "yes," that naturally does not appear at all unless it is preceded by a negative challenge.

Such morphological innovations of course result in semantic changes too, for they alter the previous (morphosemantic) oppositions.[14]

(2) Also the formal-historical formation of the imperative has been "productive," especially in certain conjugations. Thus, for instance, we find practically all speakers use the pattern haCCiC for haCCeC (as in /halbiš/, /hagid/ "dress!," "say!", etc.,).

This is a product of proportions like tešev : šev "you will sit: sit!," t(ǝ)kabel: kabel "you will receive: receive! (masc. sing.)," and certainly of tagídi: (h)agídi "you will say: say! (fem. sing.)." Hence—tagid: (h)agid, talbiš: (h)albiš, as well as ta(ʿ)azvi: (ʿ)azvi for ʿizvi, "leave!", fem.), tišan : šan (for /yšan/ "sleep!"), tipol : pol (for /nfol/), and so on.

---

[11] Cf. Bloomfield's (1926) assumption H6: "Linguistic change may substitute sames for differents" and assumption H7: "Analogic change predominantly disfavors irregular glossemes and those which diverge from their fellows; it tends to disfavor them in inverse ratio to their frequency of occurrence."

[12] Cf. Hockett (1958), 433 etc.

[13] There is probably a grain of rebellion in this formation: notice the (optional) use of the superfluous emphatic /ken/ in the intermediary construction /ken tavo/ ("(do) not come" > "(do) *yes* come (= come indeed)" → "come!") which is very characteristic in contemporary Hebrew.

[14] This may imply changes in the syntactic structures too (thus posing new transformational problems, etc.), but this, again, is beyond our scope.

This process has affected much larger areas in the speech of the younger people, for whom it "generated" an over-all, "simple formula": *future* forms *minus* prefix = equals imperative (F—Pref = I).

This "formula" has produced very tangible changes in phonology and morphophonemics, as illustrated by such proportions as: *tištok*: *štok* "be quiet! (masc. sing.)", hence—*tištki*: *štki* (fem. sing), *tištku*: *štku* (pl.) (with initial 3-consonantal cluster, whereas historical Hebrew does not allow more than two), or *tispri*: *spri* (*adding* to the 3-consonantal cluster a change in the historical complementary distribution of the allophones [p ~ f]).

Such morphological changes do, indeed, very rapidly affect the existing "equilibrium" (relatively "dynamic" as it may be) and lead towards a reorganization of the sets of the "distinctive oppositions" (whether binary or otherwise) in all areas or levels of language.[15] We could go on and on like this, pointing out the various instances of analogical creations and comprehensive simplifications, levellings or normalizations (with extra productivity by the younger generation), within the verbal system, indeed in practically every category and paradigm. But, in keeping with our initial remarks, we prefer to classify here the analogical creation within the span of an "idiolect" in terms of *three* interrelated or "hierarchical" phases, connected with their time of appearance and duration:

(1) *Primary or initial creations* and replacements which appear at a very early age, soon after the child starts to "work" with the morphological patterns,[16] and which fade away around or before the age of seven.

Thus, analogies like /kibal /(for /kib(b)el/) "he received", following /kibálti/ "I received" etc. are very common until age 4–5; or /šatáti, šatáta/ "I drank, you drank", (for šatíti, etc.),

"normalizing" according to the predominant patterns of the "sound verb" (katálti, katálta) and others.

The most interesting analogy (which fades away by 6–7) is that of the pattern miCaCeC ("mikatel"), for the present form of the niph(al conjugation, for historical niCCaC (niktal), e.g.,/mikanes, mikanéset/ "entering" etc., for /nixnas/ etc., or /miza(h)er/ "being careful" for /nizhar/ and so on. Through this, the present of niph(al also integrates with the *nonpast* forms, in analogy with all the other so-called derived conjugations (excluding pa(al), thus creating a "unified" opposition of *past* vs. *nonpast* forms.

The residue of these "temporary" analogical creations and their impact on further developments deserve further investigation.

(2) *Secondary creations* take place in later stages. Many of them appear at school age, when the children are exposed to "grammar" (normative drill) and to correction by the teachers. Hence, part of them are rather hypercorrections, involving analogies with *minor* patterns, e.g.: /somáxat/ ("relying"—fem.) for /soméxet/; /mekir—mkirim/, for /mak(k)irim/ "knowing, recognizing", etc. Many of these innovations become part of the speech habits of the growing young adults.

(3) *Essential or permanent creations*, analogic creations that take place in childhood and last through adulthood, thus becoming part and parcel of the system of the idiolect, and, by multiplication, of the "language" as well. E.g. the second person plural of the past /katáltem/ or CaCáCtem (for kətaltém = CəCaCtém), /(h)evántem/ and /(h)ivántem/ for /havantém/ "you (pl.) understood" etc., with an obvious morphophonemic implication, i.e., that all the syllabic suffixes with initial consonant are now uniformly enclitic (or, in other words, that all the corresponding forms are now penultimate): CaCáCti,

---

[15] Creations made by the younger generation deserve special mention because: 1. They "grow" with the speakers, and gradually penetrate, as data show, into higher age-levels, thus anticipating, more or less, what will become general (historical) facts after a certain period. This is also implied by the processes of linguistic continuity (including crystallization of speech habits in puberty; free analogy; imitation of peers, etc.). 2. These native and seminative young speakers now constitute the major body of speakers for whom Hebrew is the primary or only native language.

[16] Leopold, for instance, states that the intellectual maturity needed for the first steps of abstraction or analogy in the realm of morphological patterns is normally not reached until the turn of the third year. He, however, mentions quite a few instances of awareness of morphological patterns in Hildegard's speech (p. 80 f.). Our data from Israeli children show that many reach this phase between 18–24 months. This is an interesting topic for a psycholinguistic study. Roger Brown has recently been conducting very important studies in this field.

CaCáCta ... CaCáCtem (!). Another example is the development in the imperative mentioned above: taCCiC and haCCiC for haCCeC etc. Further, the "regularization" of the past of pa'al conjugation—imposing the "katal" pattern and rejecting historical "katel" and "katol," e.g., /yašan/ for /yašen/ ("he slept"), /katánti/ for /katónti/ "I got small" (and among most younger speakers also /yaxálti/ "I could" for /yaxólti/). Or again, the "normalization" of the present there, by imposing the "kotel" pattern and rejecting the minor patterns of "katel", "katal", etc., which involves new oppositions between the past and the present in the minor patterns mentioned above). Or the "normalizations" in the pi'el conjugation like /pireš/ for /pereš/ or /peraš/ "he explained", and a whole host of changes and implications, that cannot even be hinted at in this brief presentation.

To sum up, "analogy" is at work throughout the development of the idiolect, on the background of the dialect. But whereas some analogical creations are confined within the younger age groups, fading away (or being again replaced by other forms) at a certain age, others acquire "tenure" or permanence, within a primary or a secondary phase.

We have glanced at analogic creation and analogic change-in-the-making in the speech of the younger generation, with some of the interactions between idiolect and language. The accelerated processes in contemporary Hebrew of successive analogical creation, replacement and change suggest that the formal division between synchronic and diachronic may require some "expansion", since there is "something" codimensional in between, especially in the crucial zone between idiolect and dialect.

It might be also worthwhile to mention that "analogy" or simplification, has affected the rules of "generation" in syntax, especially in adverbial clauses (temporal and locative) as well as in interrogative ones, but this constitutes a topic by itself.

BIBLIOGRAPHY

Bar-Adon, Aaron. *Children's Hebrew in Israel*, 2 vols. Mimeographed, Jerusalem, 1959 (in Hebrew, Summary in English). 549 pp.

———. "The Evolution of Modern Hebrew," in J. Teller, ed., *Acculturation and Integration* (New York: American Histadrut Cultural Exchange Institute, 1965), pp. 65–95.

———. *Linguistic Continuity and Contemporary Israeli Hebrew*, 1961 (paper read before the Linguistic Society of Michigan).

Blanc, Haim. "Hebrew in Israel: Trends and Problems." *The Middle East Journal*, XI (Autumn 1957), 397 ff.

Bloch, Bernard. "A Set of Postulates for Phonemic Analysis.," *Language*, XXIV (1948), 3–46, esp. p. 7.

Bloomfield, Leonard. *Language* (1933), esp. 275 f., 404 ff.

———. "A Set of Postulates for the Science of Language," *Language*, II (1926), 153–164, esp. 163–4; reprinted in M. Joos, ed., *Readings in Linguistics* [Part I] (New York: American Council of Learned Societies, 1957) [4th ed.: Chicago: University of Chicago Press, 1966], pp. 26–31.

Chomsky, Noam. Review of Skinner's *Verbal Behavior*. *Language*, XXXV (1959), 26–58 (esp. p. 42 f.).

———. *Syntactic Structures*. The Hague: Mouton, 1957.

Gleason, H. A. *An Introduction to Descriptive Linguistics*, rev. ed. (1961), esp. p. 391 ff.

Hall, Robert A. "Idiolect and Linguistic Super-Ego." *Studia Linguistica*, V (1951), esp. p. 22.

Harris, Zellig S. *Methods in Structural Linguistics*. Chicago, 1951. Esp. p. 299 ff.

Hockett, Charles F. *A Course in Modern Linguistics*. New York, 1958. Esp. 321 ff., 353 ff., 425 ff.

Hoenigswald, Henry M. *Language Change and Linguistic Reconstruction*. Chicago, 1960. Esp. p. 47, 59–64, 107 ff.

Jakobson, Roman, and Fant, C.G.M. and Halle, Morris. *Preliminaries to Speech Analysis*. Cambridge, Mass., 1952.

———., and Halle, Morris. *Fundamentals of Language*. The Hague: Mouton, 1956.

Leopold, Werner. *Speech Development of a Bilingual Child*, Vol. III. Evanston, 1949. Esp. p. 76 ff., 156 f.

De Saussure, F. *Course in General Linguistics*, Engl. Transl. New York, 1959. Esp. p. 22–23, 88 ff.

Ullmann, Stephen. *The Principles of Semantics*, 2nd ed. (1957). Esp. p. 172–73.

Whatmough, J. *Language: A Modern Synthesis*. New York, 1956.

49

This paper by Roger Brown and Ursula Bellugi-Klima is based on a longitudinal study of the development of syntax in two young children (18 months and 27 months). The authors discovered three processes in the child's acquisition of syntax: (1) imitation and reduction, (2) imitation with expansion, and (3) induction of latent structure, the latter being the most complex.

Roger Brown is a very familiar name in recent work on child language, and much credit for the renewed and extended interest in the study of child language in the 1960's is due to him. Brown, in collaboration with Ursula Bellugi-Klima, Colin Fraser, Jean Berko (Gleason), and others, has introduced novel psycholinguistic approaches to the study of language acquisition by children. He and his associates were also instrumental in adapting the emerging transformational approach to the study of child grammar, as well as in devising ingenious tests to study the child's processes of language acquisition, and in outlining interesting research methods. In this connection, we might refer the reader to the study on "Psycholinguistic Research Methods," by Jean Berko and Roger Brown, in *The Handbook of Research Methods in Child Psychology*, ed. P. H. Mussen (New York, 1961), pp. 517–57. Quite a few of his former associates and students are now active in other institutions. Brown is the author of *Words and Things* and numerous studies.

The widely used term "telegraphic speech" for brief constructions in early child language which sound like the telegraphic style, was first introduced in a paper by Brown and Fraser (cf. "The Acquisition of Syntax," in U. Bellugi and Roger Brown, eds., *The Acquisition of Language, Monographs of the Society for Research in Child Development*, XXIX (1964), 43–78).

Bellugi–Klima is a familiar name to students of child language. Her book *How Children Say No* is due in 1970 from M. I. T. Press. See also in this volume her paper written with E. Klima.

A. B. A.

THREE PROCESSES IN THE CHILD'S ACQUISITION OF SYNTAX

Some time in the second six months of life most children say a first intelligible word. A few months later most children are saying many words and some children go about the house all day long naming things (*table, doggie, ball*, etc.) and actions (*play, see, drop,* etc.) and an occasional quality (*blue, broke,*

Reprinted from Language and Learning (*a special issue of* Harvard Educational Review) *34.133–151 (Spring 1964) by permission of the authors and* Harvard Educational Review.

This investigation was supported in whole by Public Health Service Research Grant MH7088 from the National Institute of Mental Health.

bad, etc.). At about eighteen months children are likely to begin constructing two-word utterances; such a one, for instance, as *Push car.*

A construction such as *Push car* is not just two single-word utterances spoken in a certain order. As single word utterances (they are sometimes called holophrases) both *push* and *car* would have primary stresses and terminal intonation contours. When they are two words programmed as a single utterance the primary stress would fall on *car* and so would the highest level of pitch. *Push* would be subordinated to *car* by a lesser stress and a lower pitch; the unity of the whole would appear in the absence of a terminal contour between words and the presence of such a contour at the end of the full sequence.

By the age of thirty-six months some

children are so advanced in the construction process as to produce all of the major varieties of English simple sentences up to a length of ten or eleven words. For several years we have been studying the development of English syntax, of the sentence-constructing process, in children between eighteen and thirty-six months of age. Most recently we have made a longitudinal study of a boy and girl whom we shall call Adam and Eve. We began work with Adam and Eve in October of 1962 when Adam was twenty-seven months old and Eve eighteen months old. The two children were selected from some thirty whom we considered. They were selected primarily because their speech was exceptionally intelligible and becasue they talked a lot. We wanted to make it as easy as possible to transcribe accurately large quantities of child speech. Adam and Eve are the children of highly-educated parents, the fathers were graduate students at Harvard and the mothers are both college graduates. Both Adam and Eve were single children when we began the study. These facts must be remembered in generalizing the outcomes of the research.

While Adam is nine months older than Eve, his speech was only a little more advanced in October of 1962. The best single index of the level of speech development is the average length of utterance and in October, 1962, Adam's average was 1.84 morphemes and Eve's was 1.40 morphemes. The two children stayed fairly close together in the year that followed; in the records for the thirty-eighth week Adam's average was 3.55 and Eve's, 3.27. The processes we shall describe appeared in both children.

Every second week we visited each child for at least two hours and made a tape recording of everything said by the child as well as of everything said to the child. The mother was always present and most of the speech to the child is hers. Both mother and child became very accustomed to our presence and learned to continue their usual routine with us as the observers.

One of us always made a written transcription, on the scene, of the speech of mother and child with notes about important actions and objects of attention. From this transcription and the tape a final transcription was made and these transcriptions constitute the primary data of the study. For many purposes we require a "distributional analysis" of the speech of the child. To this end the child's utterances in a given transcription were cross classified and relisted under such headings as: "A + noun"; "Noun + verb"; "Verbs in the past"; "Utterances containing the pronoun *it*," etc. The categorized utterances expose the syntactic regularities of the child's speech.

Each week we met as a research seminar, with students of the psychology of language,[1] to discuss the state of the construction process in one of the two children as of that date. In these discussions small experiments were often suggested, experiments that had to be done within a few days if they were to be informative. At one time, for instance, we were uncertain whether Adam understood the semantic difference between putting a noun in subject position and putting it in object position. Consequently one of us paid an extra visit to Adam equipped with some toys. "Adam," we said, "show us the duck pushing the boat." And, when he had done so: "Now show us the boat pushing the duck."

Another week we noticed that Adam would sometimes pluralize nouns when they should have been pluralized and sometimes would not. We wondered if he could make grammatical judgments about the plural, if he could distinguish a correct form from an incorrect form. "Adam," we asked, "which is right, 'two shoes' or 'two shoe'?" His answer on that occasion, produced with explosive enthusiasm, was "Pop goes the weasel!" The two-year-old child does not make a perfectly docile experimental subject.

The dialogue between mother and child does not read like a transcribed dialogue between two adults. Table 1 offers a sample section from an early transcribed record. It has some interesting properties. The conversation is, in the first place, very much in the here and now. From the child there is no speech of the sort that Bloomfield called "displaced," speech about other times and other places. Adam's utterances in the early months were largely a coding of contempo-

[1] We are grateful for intellectual stimulation and lighthearted companionship to Dr. Jean Berko Gleason, Mr. Samuel Anderson, Mr. Colin Fraser, Dr. David McNeill, and Dr. Daniel Slobin.

raneous events and impulses. The mother's speech differs from the speech that adults use to one another in many ways. Her sentences are short and simple; for the most part they are the kinds of sentences that Adam will produce a year later.

Perhaps because they are short, the sentences of the mother are perfectly grammatical. The sentences adults use to one another, perhaps because they are longer and more complex, are very often not grammatical, not well formed. Here for instance is a rather representative example produced at a conference of psychologists and linguists: "As far as I know, no one yet has done the in a way obvious now and interesting problem of doing a in a sense a structural frequency study of the alternative syntactical in a given language, say, like English, the alternative possible structures, and how what their hierarchical probability of occurrence structure is."[2] It seems unlikely that a child could learn the patterns of English syntax from such speech. His introduction to English ordinarily comes in the form of a simplified, repetitive, and idealized dialect. It may be that such an introduction is necessary for the acquisition of syntax to be possible but we do not know that.

TABLE 1. A section from Adam's first record.

Adam	Mother
See truck, Mommy.	
See truck.	
	Did you see the truck?
No I see truck.	
	No, you didn't see it?
	There goes one.
There go one.	
	Yes, there goes one.
See a truck.	
See truck, Mommy.	
See truck.	
Truck.	
Put truck, Mommy.	
	Put the truck where?
Put truck window.	
	I think that one's too large to go in the window.

[2] H. Maclay and C. E. Osgood, "Hesitation Phenomena in Spontaneous English Speech," *Word*, XV (1959), 19–44.

In the course of the brief interchange of Table 1 Adam imitates his mother in saying: "There go one" immediately after she says "There goes one." The imitation is not perfect; Adam omits the inflection on the verb. His imitation is a reduction in that it omits something from the original. This kind of imitation with reduction is extremely common in the records of Adam and Eve and it is the first process we shall discuss.

IMITATION AND REDUCTION

Table 2 presents some model sentences spoken by the mothers and the imitations produced by Adam and Eve. These were selected from hundreds in the records in order to illustrate some general propositions. The first thing to notice is that the imitations preserve the word order of the model sentences. To be sure, words in the model are often missing from the imitation but the words preserved are in the order of the original. This is a fact that is so familiar and somehow reasonable that we did not at once recognize it as an empirical outcome rather than as a natural necessity. But of course it is not a necessity, the outcome could have been otherwise. For example, words could have been said back in the reverse of their original order, the most recent first. The preservation of order suggests that the model sentence is processed by the child as a total construction rather than as a list of words.

In English the order of words in a sentence is an important grammatical signal. Order is used to distinguish among subject, direct

TABLE 2. Some imitations produced by Adam and Eve.

Model Utterance	Child's Imitation
Tank car	Tank car
Wait a minute	Wait a minute
Daddy's brief case	Daddy brief case
Fraser will be unhappy	Fraser unhappy
He's going out	He go out
That's an old time train	Old time train
It's not the same dog as Pepper	Dog Pepper
No you can't write on Mr. Cromer's shoe	Write Cromer shoe

object, and indirect object and it is one of the marks of imperative and interrogative constructions. The fact that the child's first sentences preserve the word order of their models partially accounts for the ability of an adult to "understand" these sentences and so to feel that he is in communication with the child. It is conceivable that the child "intends" the meanings coded by his word orders and that, when he preserves the order of an adult sentence, he does so because he wants to say what the order says. It is also possible that he preserves word order just because his brain works that way and that he has no comprehension of the semantic contrasts involved. In some languages word order is not an important grammatical signal. In Latin, for instance, "Agricola amat puellam" has the same meaning as "Puellam amat agricola" and subject-object relations are signalled by case endings. We would be interested to know whether children who are exposed to languages that do not utilize word order as a major syntactic signal, preserve order as reliably as do children exposed to English.

The second thing to notice in Table 2 is the fact that when the models increase in length there is not a corresponding increase in the imitation. The imitations stay in the range of two to four morphemes which was the range characteristic of the children. at this time. The children were operating under some constraint of length or span. This is not a limitation of vocabulary; the children knew hundreds of words. Neither is it a constraint of immediate memory. We infer this from the fact that the average length of utterances produced spontaneously, where immediate memory is not involved, is about the same as the average length of utterances produced as immediate imitations. The constraint is a limitation on the length of utterance the children are able to program or plan.[3] This kind of narrow span limitation in children is characteristic of most or all of their intellectual operations. The limitation grows less restrictive with age as a conse-

quence, probably, of both neurological growth and of practice, but of course it is never lifted altogether.

A constraint on length compels the imitating child to omit some words or morphemes from the mother's longer sentences. Which forms are retained and which omitted? The selection is not random but highly systematic. Forms retained in the examples of Table 2 include: *Daddy, Fraser, Pepper,* and *Cromer; tank car, minute, briefcase, train, dog,* and *shoe; wait, go,* and *write; unhappy* and *old time.* For the most part they are nouns, verbs, and adjectives, though there are exceptions, as witness the initial pronoun *He* and the preposition *out* and the indefinite article *a.* Forms omitted in the samples of Table 2 include: the possessive inflection *-s,* the modal auxiliary *will,* the contraction of the auxiliary verb *is,* the progressive inflection *-ing,* the preposition *on,* the articles *the* and *an,* and the modal auxiliary *can.* It is possible to make a general characterization of the forms likely to be retained that distinguishes them as a total class from the forms likely to be omitted.

Forms likely to be retained are nouns and verbs and, less often, adjectives, and these are the three large and "open" parts-of-speech in English. The number of forms in any one of these parts-of-speech is extremely large and always growing. Words belonging to these classes are sometimes called "contentives" because they have semantic content. Forms likely to be omitted are inflections, auxiliary verbs, articles, prepositions, and conjunctions. These forms belong to syntactic classes that are small and closed. Any one class has few members and new members are not readily added. The omitted forms are the ones that linguists sometimes call "functors," their grammatical *functions* being more obvious than their semantic content.

Why should young children omit functors and retain contentives? There is more than one plausible answer. Nouns, verbs, and adjectives are words that make reference. One can conceive of teaching the meanings of these words by speaking them, one at a time, and pointing at things or actions or qualities. And of course parents do exactly that. These are the kinds of words that children have been encouraged to practice speak-

---

[3] Additional evidence of the constraint on sentence length may be found in R. Brown and C. Fraser, "The Acquisition of Syntax," in C. N. Cofer and Barbara Musgrave, eds., *Verbal Behavior and Learning* (New York: McGraw Hill Book Company, 1963).

ing one at a time. The child arrives at the age of sentence construction with a stock of well-practiced nouns, verbs, and adjectives. Is it not likely then that this prior practice causes him to retain the contentives from model sentences too long to be reproduced in full, that the child imitates those forms in the speech he hears which are already well developed in him as individual habits? There is probably some truth in this explanation but it is not the only determinant since children will often select for retention contentives that are relatively unfamiliar to them.

We adults sometimes operate under a constraint on length and the curious fact is that the English we produce in these circumstances bears a formal resemblance to the English produced by two-year-old children. When words cost money there is a premium on brevity or to put it otherwise, a constraint on length. The result is "telegraphic" English and telegraphic English is an English of nouns, verbs, and adjectives. One does not send a cable reading: "My car has broken down and I have lost my wallet; send money to me at the American Express in Paris" but rather "Car broken down; wallet lost; send money American Express Paris." The telegram omits: *my, has, and, I, have, my, to, me, at, the, in*. All of these are functors. We make the same kind of telegraphic reduction when time or fatigue constrain us to be brief, as witness any set of notes taken at a fast-moving lecture.

A telegraphic transformation of English generally communicates very well. It does so because it retains the high-information words and drops the low-information words. We are here using "information" in the sense of the mathematical theory of communication. The information carried by a word is inversely related to the chances of guessing it from context. From a given string of content words, missing functors can often be guessed but the message "my has and I have my to me at the in" will not serve to get money to Paris. Perhaps children are able to make a communication analysis of adult speech and so adapt in an optimal way to their limitation of span. There is, however, another way in which the adaptive outcome might be achieved.

If you say aloud the model sentences of Table 2 you will find that you place the heavier stresses, the primary and secondary stresses in the sentences, on contentives rather than on functors. In fact the heavier stresses fall, for the most part, on the words the child retains. We first realized that this was the case when we found that in transcribing tapes, the words of the mother that we could hear most clearly were usually the words that the child reproduced. We had trouble hearing the weakly stressed functors and, of course, the child usually failed to reproduce them. Differential stress may then be the cause of the child's differential retention. The outcome is a maximally informative reduction but the cause of this outcome need not be the making of an information analysis. The outcome may be an incidental consequence of the fact that English is a well-designed language that places its heavier stresses where they are needed, on contentives that cannot easily be guessed from context.

We are fairly sure that differential stress is one of the determinants of the child's telegraphic productions. For one thing, stress will also account for the way in which children reproduce polysyllabic words when the total is too much for them. Adam, for instance, gave us *'pression* for *expression* and Eve gave us *'raff* for *giraffe;* the more heavily-stressed syllables were the ones retained. In addition we have tried the effect of placing heavy stresses on functors which do not ordinarily receive such stresses. To Adam we said: "You say what I say" and then, speaking in a normal way at first: "The doggie will bite." Adam gave back: "Doggie bite." Then we stressed the auxiliary: "The doggie *will* bite" and, after a few trials, Adam made attempts at reproducing that auxiliary. A science fiction experiment comes to mind. If there were parents who stressed functors rather than contentives would they have children whose speech was a kind of "reciprocal telegraphic" made up of articles, prepositions, conjunctions, auxiliaries, and the like? Such children would be out of touch with the community as real children are not.

It may be that all the factors we have mentioned play some part in determining the child's selective imitations; the reference-making function of contentives, the fact that they are practiced as single words, the fact that they cannot be guessed from context, and the heavy stresses they receive. There are also other possible factors: for example, the left-to-right, earlier-to-later position of words in a sentence, but these make too long a story to tell here.[4] Whatever the causes, the first utterances produced as imitations of adult sentences are highly systematic reductions of their models. Furthermore, the telegraphic properties of these imitations appear also in the child's spontaneously produced utterances. When his speech is not modeled on an immediately prior adult sentence, it observes the same limitation on length and the same predilection for contentives as when it is modeled on an immediately prior sentence.

IMITATION WITH EXPANSION

In the course of the brief conversation set down in Table 1, Adam's mother at one point imitates Adam. The boy says: "There go one" and mother responds: "Yes, there goes one." She does not exactly reproduce the model sentence of the child but instead adds something to it or expands it. What she adds is a functor, the inflection for third-person on the verb, the very form that Adam had omitted when he imitated his mother.

One of the first things we noticed when we began to study child speech several years ago was the frequency with which adults imitated children. Indeed they seemed to imitate more often than did the children themselves. We later came to realize that adult imitations are seldom exact reproductions; they are usually expansions. The mothers of Adam and Eve responded to the speech of their children with expansions about thirty per cent of the time. We did it ourselves when we talked with the children. Indeed we found it very difficult to withhold expansions. A reduced or incomplete English sentence seems to constrain the English-speaking adult to expand it into the nearest properly formed complete sentence. Table 3 lists a few sample expansions from the hundreds in the records.

The first thing worthy of attention in the expansions of Table 3 is the fact that the words spoken by the mother preserve the

TABLE 3. Expansions of child speech produced by mothers.

Child	Mother
Baby highchair	Baby is in the highchair
Mommy eggnog	Mommy had her eggnog
Eve lunch	Eve is having lunch
Mommy sandwich	Mommy'll have a sandwich
Sat wall	He sat on the wall
Throw Daddy	Throw it to Daddy
Pick glove	Pick the glove up

order of the words in the child's sentences. To be sure, words and inflections are added but they are fitted in—before, and after and between the words the child used; they are not generally permitted to disturb the order of the child's words. It is as if these latter were taken as constants by the mother, constants to which some sentence had to be fitted. She acts as if she were assuming that the child means everything he says, all the words and also their order, but as if he might also mean more than he says. From the mother's point of view an expansion is a kind of communication check; it says in effect: "Is this what you mean?"

The second thing to notice about Table 3 is the character of the forms added to the child's utterances. They include the auxiliaries *is* and *will;* the prepositions *in, on, to,* and *up;* the verb forms *is, have, had,* and *having;* the articles *a* and *the;* the pronouns *her, he,* and *it.* For the most part, the words added are functors and functors are of course the words that the child omits in his reductions.

The interaction between mother and child is, much of the time, a cycle of reductions and expansions. There are two transformations involved. The reduction transformation has an almost completely specifiable and so mechanical character. One could program a machine to do it with the following instructions: "Retain contentives (or stressed forms) in the order given up to some limit of length." The expansion accomplished by Adam's mother when she added the third-person inflection to the verb and said "There goes one" is also a completely specifiable transformation. The instructions would read: "Retain the forms given in the order given and supply obligatory grammatical forms." To

---

[4] Brown and Fraser, *ibid.*

be sure this mother-machine would have to be supplied with the obligatory rules of English grammar but that could be done. However, the sentence "There goes one" is atypical in that it only adds a compulsory and redundant inflection. The expansions of Table 3 all add forms that are not grammatically compulsory or redundant and these expansions cannot be mechanically generated by grammatical rules alone.

In Table 3 the topmost four utterances produced by the child are all of the same grammatical type; all four consist of a proper noun followed by a common noun. However, the four are expanded in quite different ways. In particular the form of the verb changes: it is in the first case in the simple present tense; in the second case the simple past; in the third case the present progressive; in the last case the simple future. All of these are perfectly grammatical but they are different. The second set of child utterances is formally uniform in that each one consists of a verb followed by a noun. The expansions are again all grammatical but quite unlike, especially with regard to the preposition supplied. In general, then, there are radical changes in the mother's expansions when there are no changes in the formal character of the utterances expanded. It follows that the expansions cannot be produced simply by making grammatically compulsory additions to the child's utterances.

How does a mother decide on the correct expansion of one of her child's utterances? Consider the utterance "Eve lunch." So far as grammar is concerned this utterance could be appropriately expanded in any of a number of ways: "Eve is having lunch"; "Eve had lunch"; "Eve will have lunch"; Eve's lunch," etc. On the occasion when Eve produced the utterance, however, one expansion seemed more appropriate than any other. It was then the noon hour, Eve was sitting at the table with a plate of food before her, and her spoon and fingers were busy. In these circumstances "Eve lunch" had to mean "Eve is having lunch." A little later when the plate had been stacked in the sink and Eve was getting down from her chair the utterance "Eve lunch" would have suggested the expansion "Eve has had her lunch." Most expansions are not only responsive to the child's words but also to the circumstances attending their utterance.

What kind of instructions will generate the mother's expansions? The following are approximately correct: "Retain the words given in the order given and add those functors that will result in a well-formed simple sentence that is appropriate to the circumstances." These are not instructions that any machine could follow. A machine could act on the instructions only if it were provided with detailed specifications for judging appropriateness and no such specifications can, at present, be written. They exist, however, in implicit form in the brains of mothers and in the brains of all English-speaking adults and so judgments of appropriateness can be made by such adults.

The expansion encodes aspects of reality that are not coded by the child's telegraphic utterance. Functors have meaning but it is meaning that accrues to them in context rather than in isolation. The meanings that are added by functors seem to be nothing less than the basic terms in which we construe reality: the time of an action, whether it is ongoing or completed, whether it is presently relevant or not; the concept of possession and such relational concepts as are coded by *in*, *on*, *up*, *down*, and the like; the difference between a particular instance of a class ("Has anybody seen *the* paper?") and any instance of a class ("Has anybody seen *a* paper?"); the difference between extended substances given shape and size by an "accidental" container (*sand*, *water*, *syrup*, etc.) and countable "things" having a characteristic fixed shape and size (*a cup*, *a man*, *a tree*, etc.). It seems to us that a mother in expanding speech may be teaching more than grammar; she may be teaching something like a world-view.

As yet it has not been demonstrated that expansions are *necessary* for learning either grammar or a construction of reality. It has not even been demonstrated that expansions contribute to such learning. All we know is that some parents do expand and their children do learn. It is perfectly possible, however, that children can and do learn simply from hearing their parents or others make well-formed sentences in connection with various nonverbal circumstances. It may not be necessary or even helpful for these sentences to be expansions of utterances of the child. Only experiments contrasting expansion training with simple exposure to English will settle the matter. We hope to do such experiments.

There are, of course, reasons for expecting the expansion transformation to be an effective tutorial technique. By adding something to the words the child has just produced one confirms his response insofar as it is appropriate. In addition one takes him somewhat beyond that response but not greatly beyond it. One encodes additional meanings at a moment when he is most likely to be attending to the cues that can teach that meaning.

INDUCTION OF THE LATENT STRUCTURE

Adam, in the course of the conversation with his mother set down in Table 1, produced one utterance for which no adult is likely ever to have provided an exact model: "No I see truck." His mother elects to expand it as "No, you didn't see it" and this expansion suggests that the child might have created the utterance by reducing an adult model containing the form *didn't*. However, the mother's expansion in this case does some violence to Adam's original version. He did not say *no* as his mother said it, with primary stress and final contour; Adam's *no* had secondary stress and no final contour. It is not easy to imagine an adult model for this utterance. It seems more likely that the utterance was created by Adam as part of a continuing effort to discover the general rules for constructing English negatives.

In Table 4 we have listed some utterances produced by Adam or Eve for which it is difficult to imagine any adult model. It is

TABLE 4.   Utterances not likely to be imitations.

My Cromer suitcase
Two foot
A bags
A scissor
A this truck
You naughty are
Why it can't turn off?
Put on it
Cowboy did fighting me
Put a gas in

unlikely that any adult said any of these to Adam or Eve since they are very simple utterances and yet definitely ungrammatical. In addition it is difficult, by adding functors alone, to build any of them up to simple grammatical sentences. Consequently it does not seem likely that these utterances are reductions of adult originals. It is more likely that they are mistakes which externalize the child's search for the regularities of English syntax.

We have long realized that the occurrence of certain kinds of errors on the level of morphology (or word construction) reveals the child's effort to induce regularities from speech. So long as a child speaks correctly, or at any rate so long as he speaks as correctly as the adults he hears, there is no way to tell whether he is simply repeating what he has heard or whether he is actually constructing. However, when he says something like "I digged a hole" we can often be sure that he is constructing. We can be sure because it is unlikely that he would have heard *digged* from anyone and because we can see how, in processing words he has heard, he might have come by *digged*. It looks like an overgeneralization of the regular past inflection. The inductive operations of the child's mind are externalized in such a creation. Overgeneralizations on the level of syntax (or sentence construction) are more difficult to identify because there are so many ways of adding functors so as to build up conceivable models. But this is difficult to do for the examples of Table 4 and for several hundred other utterances in our records.

The processes of imitation and expansion are not sufficient to account for the degree of linguistic competence that children regularly acquire. These processes alone cannot teach more than the sum total of sentences that speakers of English have either modeled for a child to imitate or built up from a child's reductions. However, a child's linguistic competence extends far beyond this sum total of sentences. All children are able to understand and construct sentences they have never heard but which are nevertheless well-formed, well-formed in terms of general rules that are implicit in the sentences the child has heard. Somehow, then, every child processes the speech to which he is exposed so as to induce from it a latent structure. This latent rule structure is so general that a child can spin out its implications all his life long. It is both semantic and syntactic. The discovery of latent structure is the greatest of the processes involved in language acquisition and the most difficult to understand. We will provide an example of how the analysis can proceed by discussing the evolution in child speech of noun phrases.

A noun phrase in adult English includes a noun but also more than a noun. One variety consists of a noun with assorted modifiers: *The girl; The pretty girl; That pretty girl; My girl*, etc. All of these are constructions which have the same syntactic privileges as do nouns alone. One can use a noun phrase in isolation to name or request something; one can use it in sentences, in subject position or in object position or in predicate nominative position. All of these are slots that nouns alone can also fill. A larger construction having the same syntactic privileges as its "head" word is called in linguistics an "endocentric" construction and noun phrases are endocentric constructions.

For both Adam and Eve, in the early records, noun phrases usually occur as total independent utterances rather than as components of sentences. Table 5 presents an assortment of such utterances at Time 1. They consist in each case of some sort of modifier, just one, preceding a noun. The modifiers, or as they are sometimes called the "pivot" words, are a much smaller class than the noun class. Three students of child speech have independently discovered that this kind of construction is extremely common when children first begin to combine words.[5, 6, 7]

It is possible to generalize the cases of Table 5 into a simple implicit rule. The rule symbolized in Table 5 reads: "In order to form a noun phrase of this type, select first one word from the small class of modifiers

TABLE 5. Noun phrases in isolation and rule for generating noun phrases at Time I.

A coat
*A celery**
*A Becky**
*A hands**
The top
My Mommy
That Adam
My stool
That knee
More coffee
*More nut**
*Two sock**
Two shoes
*two tinker-toy**
Big boot
Poor man
Little top
Dirty knee

NP → M + N

M → *a, big, dirty, little, more, my, poor, that, the, two.*

N → *Adam, Becky, boot, coat, coffee, knee, man, Mommy, nut, sock, stool, tinker-toy, top,* and very many others.

*Ungrammatical for an adult.

and select, second, one word from the large class of nouns." This is a "generative" rule by which we mean it is a program that would actually serve to build constructions of the type in question. It is offered as a model of the mental mechanism by which Adam and Eve generated such utterances. Furthermore, judging from our work with other children and from the reports of Braine and of Miller and Ervin, the model describes a mechanism present in many children when their average utterance is approximately two morphemes long.

We have found that even in our earliest records the M + N construction is sometimes used as a component of larger constructions. For instance, Eve said: "Fix a Lassie" and "Turn the page" and "A horsie stuck" and Adam even said: "Adam wear a shirt." There are, at first, only a handful of these larger constructions but there are very many constructions in which single nouns occur in subject or in object position.

Let us look again at the utterances of Table 5 and the rule generalizing them. The class

[5] M. D. S. Braine, "The Ontogeny of English Phrase Structure: The First Phrase," *Language*, XXXIX (1963), 1–13.

[6] W. Miller and Susan Ervin, "The Development of Grammar in Child Language," in Ursula Bellugi and R. Brown, eds., *The Acquisition of Language, Child Development Monographs* (1964).

[7] Brown and Fraser, *op. cit.*

M does not correspond with any syntactic class of adult English. In the class M are articles, a possessive pronoun, a cardinal number, a demonstrative adjective or pronoun, a quantifier, and some descriptive adjectives —a mixed bag indeed. For adult English these words cannot belong to the same syntactic class because they have very different privileges of occurrence in sentences. For the children the words do seem to function as one class having the common privilege of occurrence before nouns.

If the initial words of the utterances in Table 5 are treated as one class M then many utterances are generated which an adult speaker would judge to be ungrammatical. Consider the indefinite article *a*. Adults use it only to modify common count nouns in the singular such as *coat*, *dog*, *cup*, etc. We would not say *a celery*, or a *cereal*, or *a dirt*; *celery*, *cereal*, and *dirt* are mass nouns. We would not say *a Becky* or *a Jimmy*; *Becky* and *Jimmy* are proper nouns. We would not say *a hands* or *a shoes*; *hands* and *shoes* are plural nouns. Adam and Eve, at first, did form ungrammatical combinations such as these.

The numeral *two* we use only with count nouns in the plural. We would not say *two sock* since *sock* is singular, nor *two water* since *water* is a mass noun. The word *more* we use before count nouns in the plural (*more nuts*) or mass nouns in the singular (*more coffee*). Adam and Eve made a number of combinations involving *two or more* that we would not make.

Given the initial very undiscriminating use of words in the class M it follows that one dimension of development must be a progressive differentiation of privileges, which means the division of M into smaller classes. There must also be subdivision of the noun class (N) for the reason that the privileges of occurrence of various kinds of modifiers must be described in terms of such subvarieties of N as the common noun and proper noun, the count noun and mass noun. There must eventually emerge a distinction between nouns singular and nouns plural since this distinction figures in the privileges of occurrence of the several sorts of modifiers.

Sixteen weeks after our first records from Adam and Eve (Time 2), the differentiation process had begun. By this time there were

distributional reasons for separating out articles (*a*, *the*) from demonstrative pronouns (*this*, *that*) and both of these from the residual class of modifiers. Some of the evidence for this conclusion appears in Table 6. In general one syntactic class is distinguished from another when the members of one class have combinational privileges not enjoyed by the members of the other. Consider, for example, the reasons for distinguishing articles (Art) from modifiers in general (M). Both articles and modifiers appeared in front of nouns in two-word utterances. However, in three-word utterances that were made up from the total pool of words and that had a noun in final position, the privileges of *a* and *the* were different from the privileges of all other modifiers. The articles occurred in initial position followed by a member of class M other than an article. No other modifier occurred in this first position; notice the "Not obtained" examples of Table 6A. If the children had produced utterances like those (for example, *blue a flower*, *your a car*) there would have been no difference in the privileges of occurrence of articles and modifiers and therefore no reason to separate out articles.

The record of Adam is especially instructive. He created such notably ungrammatical combinations as "a your car" and "a my pencil." It is very unlikely that adults provided models for these. They argue strongly that Adam regarded all the words in the residual M class as syntactic equivalents and so generated these very odd utterances in which possessive pronouns appear where descriptive adjectives would be more acceptable.

Table 6 also presents some of the evidence for distinguishing demonstrative pronouns (Dem) from articles and modifiers. (Table 6B). The pronouns occurred first and ahead of articles in three-and-four-word utterances—a position that neither articles nor modifiers ever filled. The sentences with demonstrative pronouns are recognizable as reductions which omit the copular verb *is*. Such sentences are not noun phrases in adult English and ultimately they will not function as noun phrases in the speech of the children, but for the present they are not distinguishable distributionally from noun phrases.

Recall now the generative formula of Table

TABLE 6.   Subdivision of the modifier class.

A.   Privileges peculiar to articles

Obtained	Not Obtained
A blue flower	Blue a flower
A nice nap	Nice a nap
A your car	Your a car
A my pencil	My a pencil

B.   Privileges peculiar to demonstrative pronouns

Obtained	Not Obtained
That my cup	My that cup
That a horse	A that horse
That a blue flower	A that blue flower
	Blue a that flower

TABLE 7.   Rules for generating noun phrases at Time 2.

$$NP_1 \rightarrow Dem + Art + M + N$$
$$NP_2 \rightarrow Art + M + N$$
$$NP_3 \rightarrow Dem + M + N$$
$$NP_4 \rightarrow Art + N$$
$$NP_5 \rightarrow M + N$$
$$NP_6 \rightarrow Dem + N$$
$$NP_7 \rightarrow Dem + Art + N$$
$$NP \rightarrow (Dem) + (Art) + (M) + N$$

(   ) means class within parentheses is optional

5 which constructs noun phrases by simply placing a modifier (M) before a noun (N). The differentiation of privileges illustrated in Table 6, and the syntactic classes this evidence motivates us to create, complicate the formula for generating noun phrases. In Table 7 we have written a single general formula for producing all noun phrases at Time 2 [NP → (Dem) + (Art) + (M) + N] and also the numerous more specific rules which are summarized by the general formula.

By the time of the thirteenth transcription, twenty-six weeks after we began our study, privileges of occurrence were much more finely differentiated and syntactic classes were consequently more numerous. From the distributional evidence we judged that Adam had made five classes of his original class M: articles, descriptive adjectives, possessive pronouns, demonstrative pronouns, and a residual class of modifiers. The generative rules of Table 7 had become inadequate; there were no longer, for instance, any combinations like "A your car." Eve had the same set except that she used two residual classes of modifiers. In addition nouns had begun to subdivide for both children. The usage of proper nouns had become clearly distinct from the usage of count nouns. For Eve the evidence justified separating count nouns from mass nouns, but for Adam it still did not. Both children by this time were frequently pluralizing nouns but as yet their syntactic control of the singular plural distinction was imperfect.

In summary, one major aspect of the development of general structure in child speech is progressive differentiation in the usage of words and therefore a progressive differentiation of syntactic classes. At the same time, however, there is an integrative process at work. From the first, an occasional noun phrase occurred as a component of some larger construction. At first these noun phrases were just two words long and the range of positions in which they could occur was small. With time the noun phrases grew longer, were more frequently used, and were used in a greater range of positions. The noun phrase structure as a whole, in all the permissible combinations of modifiers and nouns, was assuming the combinational privileges enjoyed by nouns in isolation.

In Table 8 we have set down some of the sentence positions in which both nouns and noun phrases occurred in the speech of Adam and Eve. It is the close match between the positions of nouns alone and of nouns with modifiers in the speech of Adam and Eve that justifies us in calling the longer constructions noun phrases. These longer constructions are, as they should be, endocentric; the head word alone has the same syntactic privileges as the head word with its modifiers. The continuing failure to find in noun phrase positions whole constructions of the type "That a blue flower" signals the fact that these constructions are telegraphic versions of predicate nominative sentences omitting the verb form *is*. Examples of the kind of construction not obtained are: "That (that a blue flower)"; "Where (that a blue flower)?"

For adults the noun phrase is a subwhole of the sentence, what linguists call an "immediate constituent." The noun phrase has a kind of

TABLE 8. Some privileges of the noun phrase.

Noun Positions	Noun Phrase Positions
That (flower)	That (a blue flower)
Where (ball) go?	Where (the puzzle) go?
Adam write (penguin)	Doggie eat (the breakfast)
(Horsie) stop	(A horsie) crying
Put (hat) on	Put (the red hat) on

TABLE 9. Pronouns replacing nouns or noun phrases and pronouns produced together with nouns or noun phrases.

Noun Phrases Replaced by Pronouns	Pronouns and Noun Phrases in Same Utterances
Hit ball	Mommy get it ladder
Get it	Mommy get it my ladder
Ball go?	Saw it ball
Go get it	Miss it garage
Made it	I miss it cowboy boot
Made a ship	I Adam drive that
	I Adam drive
Fix a tricycle	I Adam don't
Fix it	

psychological unity. There are signs that the noun phrase was also an immediate constituent for Adam and Eve. Consider the sentence using the separable verb *put on*. The noun phrase in "Put the red hat on" is, as a whole, fitted in between the verb and the particle even as is the noun alone in "Put hat on." What is more, however, the location of pauses in the longer sentence, on several occasions, suggested the psychological organization: "Put ... the red hat ... on" rather than "Put the red ... hat on" or "Put the ... red hat on." In addition to this evidence the use of pronouns suggests that the noun phrase is a psychological unit.

The unity of noun phrases in adult English is evidenced, in the first place, by the syntactic equivalence between such phrases and nouns alone. It is evidenced, in the second place, by the fact that pronouns are able to substitute for total noun phrases. In our immediately preceding sentence the pronoun "It" stands for the rather involved construction from the first sentence of this paragraph: "The unity of noun phrases in adult English." The words called "pronouns" in English would more aptly be called "pro-noun-phrases" since it is the phrase rather than the noun which they usually replace. One does not replace "unity" with "it" and say "The *it* of noun phrases in adult English." In the speech of Adam and Eve, too, the pronoun came to function as a replacement for the noun phrase. Some of the clearer cases appear in Table 9.

Adam characteristically externalizes more of his learning than does Eve and his record is especially instructive in connection with the learning of pronouns. In his first eight records, the first sixteen weeks of the study, Adam quite often produced sentences containing both the pronoun and the noun or noun phrase that the pronoun should have replaced. One can here see the equivalence in the process of establishment. First the substitute is produced and then, as if in explication, the form or forms that will eventually be replaced by the substitute. Adam spoke out his pronoun antecedents as chronological consequents. This is additional evidence of the unity of the noun phrase since the noun phrases *my ladder* and *cowboy boot* are linked with *it* in Adam's speech in just the same way as the nouns *ladder* and *ball*.

We have described three processes involved in the child's acquisition of syntax. It is clear that the last of these, the induction of latent structure, is by far the most complex. It looks as if this last process will put a serious strain on any learning theory thus far conceived by psychology. The very intricate simultaneous differentiation and integration that constitutes the evolution of the noun phrase is more reminiscent of the biological development of an embryo than it is of the acquisition of a conditional reflex.

50 This is a brief psycholinguistic treatment of the interesting problem of word-phrase relationship in children's language, as presented to nonspecialist readers of the magazine *Science*.

A group of 4–5 year old children was given the task of reversing the order of two-unit utterances, while a control group was asked to separate them. The children in the first group could easily reverse the order of unrelated items, but "had difficulty reversing utterances that formed common English sequences." The author suggests the following reasons for the difficulty: "(1) inability to separate English sequences into word units, and (2) semantic absurdity of reversed pairs."

No formal linguistic analysis is presented. It would be most interesting to conduct such an experiment on two-year olds. . . .

A. B. A.

CHILDREN'S LANGUAGE: WORD-PHRASE RELATIONSHIP

ABSTRACT: Unsystematic observations indicated that small children who could reverse the order of certain two-unit utterances had difficulty reversing utterances that formed common English sequences. Findings of this study indicate that the following factors are sources of difficulty in reversing pairs: (1) inability to separate English sequences into word units, and (2) semantic absurdity of reversed pairs.

A recent discussion of children's speech asserts that "the child's first two-word utterances are usually predicative statements painfully pieced together, with the words juxtaposed rather than connected."[1] This view suggests that the acquisition of language involves progressive addition of separate words into phrases and sentences. An oppos-

ing view suggests that the first multiple word utterances are learned as single units and only later differentiated into separate words. It has generally been assumed that children of 4 or 5 years of age who speak fluently can differentiate single words from multiple-word utterances. The demonstration that children have a tendency to define a single unknown word in terms of the entire context in which it occurs suggests, however, that each word is not endowed with a distinct meaning.[2] A recent Russian study cited by Ervin and Miller[3] reports that children who are asked to indicate the words in a sentence pick units longer than single words. The results of the experiment described here provide more direct evidence that preschool children have difficulty in dividing common word sequences into separate words.

The experiment was designed to determine the reliability of the following observation and to investigate its sources: pairs of digits were read to children and they were taught to say them in reverse order. This skill, easily acquired by most children between 4 and 5 years of age, could be transferred to pairs of letters and pairs of nouns. But when com-

Reprinted from Science *13.264–265 (Jan. 17, 1964) copyright 1964 by the American Association for the Advancement of Science, by permission of the author and the American Association for the Advancement of Science.*

Supported in part by grant No. MH 05120–03 from the National Institutes of Health to Harvard University. Center for Cognitive Studies, and in part by grant No. MH 06626–02 from the National Institutes of Health.

[1] J. Church, *Language and the Discovery of Reality* (New York: Random House, Inc., 1963), p. 63.

[2] H. Werner and E. Kaplan *Monographs of the Society for Research in Child Development,* XV (1950), 51.
[3] S. M. Ervin and W. R. Miller, in *Child Psychology,* 62nd Yearbook, National Society for the Study of Education, (Chicago: University of Chicago Press, 1963).

monly encountered "grammatical pairs" for example ("he went" or "pretty doll") were presented, these children had great difficulty in reversing them.

A group of children was set the task of reversing pairs in each of five different categories. Difficulty of two types of "nongrammatical pairs"—(1) letters and numbers, and (2) like parts of speech—was compared with that of three types of grammatical pairs: (3) commonly encountered pairs that did not form a grammatical sequence when reversed, (4) commonly encountered pairs that did form a grammatical sequence when reversed, and (5) anomalous pairs not commonly encountered (Table 1). Grammatical pairs were divided into these separate categories to permit further specification of sources of difficulty. Comparison of categories 3 and 4 made it possible to determine whether absurdity of solutions was a source of difficulty. Comparison of category 5 with categories 3 and 4 made it possible to determine whether all grammatical pairs were difficult, or only common English sequences.

The ability to separate the items making up a pair is prerequisite for reversing their order. That is, if one did not know where the first item ended and the second began, it would not be possible to say the second one first. In order to determine the extent to which difficulty of reversal results from inability to separate items, a second group of subjects was included. These subjects dealt with the same 15 pairs as the first group. Their task, rather than reversing the order of items in a pair, was to repeat the first item and await a tap before giving the second item.[4]

Sixty-six children between the ages of $4\frac{1}{2}$ and 5 years were included in the experiment, 33 in each group. Children were randomly assigned to one of the two groups. The 15 pairs of items were randomly ordered for each subject. Each subject was tested alone. A pair was presented, and, if the correct response was given, the experimenter said "fine" and continued with the next pair. If there was an incorrect response or no response in 20 seconds, the experimenter gave the answer: for group 1, saying the items in

[4] The crucial suggestion to include this group was made by George A. Miller.

TABLE 1. Pairs of items in each of the five categories described in the text.

Category	Pairs
1	5–2; D–S; 3–7
2	black–white; child–lady; foot–hand
3	man–runs; red–apple; she–went
4	I–do; you–are; it–its
5	table–goes; house–did; orange–cow

reverse order; for group 2, saying the first item, tapping, and then saying the final item.

Thirteen children in group 1 and ten children in group 2 were unable to do any pairs; three children in group 1 and four children in group 2 could do all pairs. Consideration of the relative difficulty of the different types of pairs was restricted to those subjects who had at least one pair correct and at least one error. The proportions of errors for the different categories in Table 2 were therefore based on 17 subjects for group 1 and 19 subjects for group 2. A separate Friedman two-way analysis of variance by ranks was done for each group. Differences between categories were highly significant in each case. Chi square for group 1 was 320 and for group 2 it was 353. Significance at .001 in each case required a chi square of only 18.5.

As in the observations that led to this experiment, group 1 had more difficulty reversing common English sequences than other pairs; the proportions of items missed in categories 3 and 4 were far greater than in categories 1 and 2. The anomalous pairs in category 5, however, were not much more difficult than pairs in categories 1 and 2. Thus, the fact that a pair forms a grammatical sequence seems to contribute relatively little to its difficulty if it is not a common English

TAALE 2. Proportion of errors in each of the five categories.

Category	Group 1	Group 2
1	0.20	0.14
2	.12	.14
3	.47	.30
4	.53	.49
5	.25	.18

sequence. From a consideration of group 1 alone, it would appear that the absurdity of a pair when reversed does not contribute to its difficulty; pairs that were grammatical when reversed (category 4) seemed about as difficult as those that were not (category 3). As we shall see, this conclusion is unjustified when group 2 is also considered.

In group 2, as in group 1, greatest difficulty was encountered in categories 3 and 4. The proportion of items missed in categories 1 and 2 was much lower. As in group 1, anomalous pairs were almost as easy as those in categories 1 and 2.

The similarity in pattern of error in groups 1 and 2 suggests that the ability to separate items in a pair is of primary importance in the ability to reverse them. In addition, it should be recalled that the number of complete failures and complete successes was very similar in the two groups. Further evidence of the overlap of the abilities to separate items and to reverse them was obtained by testing the 23 failures on the other task 1 week later. Of the 13 children who failed in group 1, two were able to do the task of group 2. Of the ten children who failed in group 2, one was able to do the task of group 1. All of these measures indicate that the task set group 2 was slightly easier than that set group 1. This would be expected, since

reversal of pairs is an additional operation after separation of the items in a pair.

Only in category 3 was reversal far more difficult than separation of items. This is the category in which group 1 had to transform common English sequences into absurd pairs. Thus absurdity of the resultant pair also seems to be a factor in the difficulty of reversing the order of items.

The experiment was not designed to distinguish the relative difficulty of separating different English sequences into their component words. It would be expected, however, that difficulty would vary in different sequences, and in fact, categories 3 and 4 were not equivalent. Very small children are taught certain words singly, particularly object names. Even certain verbs and adjectives may be taught separately. On the other hand, certain words are probably rarely used in isolation; examples would be forms of the verb "to be," and personal pronouns. The confusion of the small child as to exactly what is a single word might be expected to be greatest with sequences made up of words that have not been used in isolation. The attempt to find pairs that were grammatical when reversed (category 4) led to exclusive use of such words, and this could account for the fact that these were more difficult to separate than pairs in category 3.

WICK R. MILLER AND SUSAN M. ERVIN ∼∼∼∼∼∼∼∼∼∼∼

51 While Roger Brown, George A. Miller, Bellugi, McNeill, and others, were promoting developmental psycholinguistics (language acquistion in children) in the East, Susan Ervin (later Ervin-Tripp), Wick Miller, David Olmsted, Dan Slobin, C. Ferguson, and others, were active on the West Coast.

The present study on "The Development of Grammar in Child Language" was done by the linguist Wick Miller in collaboration with Susan Ervin. This collaboration produced another study: "Language Development" in H. W. Stevenson, ed., *Child Psychology, 62nd Yearbook of the National Society for the Study of Education, Part I* (Chicago, 1963).

As in most recent studies, these authors use Chomsky's transformational approach, although they were criticized by Chomsky himself on theoretical grounds (see the following selection), primarily for their oversimplification of the nature of grammatical description. Chomsky holds that a grammar should be a description of competence rather than performance.

This study is based on a longitudinal testing of 25 children, and on a more intensive text collection from a subgroup of five, since they were about two years old.

The authors' assumption (later rejected by Chomsky) was that "a person has two grammatical systems, one for encoding and another for decoding." They try to explore the first grammatical system, and to answer the question, "Is there any kind of system or pattern to the child's first sentences?" They speak of the positions of "operator" and "nonoperator" word clauses, but they are struck by the fact that "for most generalizations there were exceptions." Cf. Braine, "The Ontogeny of English Phrase Structure: The First Phase" in this volume. They discuss "the grammatical system with word class markers," as well as the problems of prosodic features (cf. Albright and Albright's reading in this volume), individual differences among the children's grammars, and developmental sequences of linguistic features.

As for transformations, they "were not found in the earliest linguistic system. The first to appear were nongeneralized." Also, "discourse agreement features are sequentially ordered."

Cf. Chomsky's formal comments in the next reading.

A. B. A.

THE DEVELOPMENT OF GRAMMAR IN CHILD LANGUAGE

Before describing the development of children's grammar, it is necessary to specify some of the properties of natural languages as used by adults. This is the model presented to the child and the eventual outcome of his development.

It is possible to analyze in all languages two types of constructs (or linguistic units): phonemes and morphemes. There are at least two corresponding systems which can be called the phonological and grammatical levels.[1] While this paper is concerned only with the grammatical level, certain properties of the phonological level will be briefly considered by way of contrast.

The phonetic substance, the raw material of language, can be analyzed into a finite set of mutually exclusive classes. The distinctive features by which the classes are contrasted are few in number. Each phonological system may be described in terms of different privileges of occurrence of the features or the sets of features called phonemes. Phonemes are grouped together into larger units in limited arrangements, and the groupings can be completely described by distributional statements. Thus it is possible to predict *all* possible phonemic shapes.[2] From the standpoint of the learner, the phonemic rules are given. Even nonsense words or coinages normally follow these rules. Imitation of sequences already heard is the normal mode of acquisition and use, and continues with the expansion of vocabulary.

If we turn to the grammatical level, we see many differences. Morphemes, like phonemes, can be grouped into a number of classes, but the nature of the classes is different. The classes can be divided into two groups, which following Fries (1952) we can call lexical and function classes. Lexical classes are large and open and the number of classes

Reprinted from Ursula Bellugi-Klima and Roger Brown, eds., Monographs of the Society for Research in Child Development, *Ser. No. 92, 29.9–34 (1964), Copyright 1964 by the Society for Research in Child Development, Inc., by permission of the authors and the Society for Research in Child Development, Inc.*

The project described in the paper is supported by a grant from the Department of Health, Education, and Welfare (M-3813) to the Institute of Human Development, University of California, Berkeley. Facilities have also been provided by the Center for Human Learning under support of the National Science Foundation.

[1] The term "level" has been used in a variety of ways in the linguistic literature. Our use of the term does not apply to the so-called levels within the syntactic system, or the distinction between morphology and syntax. As we use the term, the two levels correspond to what communication theorists call the channel and the message.

[2] Whorf (1940) has given a succinct statement for phonemic sequences in English monosyllables.

is small. English lexical classes include nouns, verbs, and adjectives. A lexical class can normally be divided into subclasses, e.g., English mass nouns, count nouns, proper nouns. In contrast, function classes are small and closed and the number of classes is larger. English function classes include prepositions, conjunctions, interrogatives, noun determiners, and auxiliaries. It is more often possible to point to a simple referent for members of lexical classes than for members of function classes. The contrast between lexical and function classes is often only a relative one, which may mean that it is not always a useful distinction to make in organizing a grammar.

The grammatical productivity of a language is infinite. A speaker can produce utterances which he has never heard before. Unless the words are nonsense or the sentence semantically aberrant, such utterances will be understood by the hearer. This property of grammars is in contrast to the phonological system. Any novel recombination of phonemes, while it may follow phonological distribution rules, is nonsense until or unless conventional meaning is assigned.

Every language has a major predication type formed by placing together two constructions. The predication is *exocentric*—that is, the resulting construction does not belong to the same class as either of the two constitutent constructions. In most languages at least one of the constituents of the predication is a member of a lexical class or an expansion of a lexical class, e.g., the English subject is composed of a noun or noun phrase. Most nonpredication constructions are *endocentric*, or expansions in which the head of the construction belongs to the same class as the resulting construction. An example is the noun phrase, *the three boys*, which is an expansion of the noun phrase, *three boys*.

The term *discourse agreement* is used to indicate formal relationships that cross sentence boundaries. They are of two kinds: (a) *class restrictions*, and (b) *verb restrictions*. The first ocur in answers to questions. A question has a formal structure, which normally restricts the formal structure possible in the response, and also a semantic content or a request for information. The comparison of two questions illustrates this point; on formal grounds we would expect the following answers:

A: *Where is Main Street? I don't know.* or *Straight ahead.*
B: *Can you tell me where Main Street is? No.* or *Yes.*

Obviously the responses to question B fail to meet the semantic requirements posed by the question. The two questions differ formally but are semantically equivalent.

In addition to "yes-no" questions, there are "or" questions and interrogative word questions. "Or" questions require a choice of an alternative if there is a falling intonation. The short response to interrogative word questions must be a word or phrase belonging to the same class as the interrogative word or words.

Verb restrictions involve the maintenance of tense or auxiliary features across sentence boundaries, and can be characterized as long components of a grammatical category. Compare the following set of sentences:

A: *This ice cream is good. Yes, it is.*
B: *This ice cream tastes good. Yes, it does.*

The initial sentences of A and B are semantically equivalent, but differ formally and require different responses. Verb restrictions can apply to successive utterances of the same or different speakers, but our attention will be focused on situations in which different speakers are involved, in particular when the second speaker is required to answer a "what—do" question.

In this paper we will distinguish three functional categories in the child's utterances. The first may be called *reference* (Skinner's *tacts*). It involves naming or describing and may be accompanied by pointing. Such behavior is initiated by the child and does not necessarily demand a response from another person. The second may be called *direction* (Skinner's *mands*) and demands verbal or active response from the hearer. Such utterances include commands and questions. It is often impossible to discriminate questions from reference utterances of the child. A third category may be called *responsive discourse* and includes informational responses. This category can be initiated by the interlocutor or the child, but we are primarily concerned with this category when initiated by the interlocutor.[3]

A person has two grammatical systems, one for encoding and another for decoding, or an active and passive grammatical system. For the adult, a single grammar can normally account for almost all of both systems. Quite clearly this is not the case with the child. We assume that a child must understand a grammatical pattern before he can produce it. Presumably the decoding and encoding systems at any point in time are not independent. It seems likely that rules could be found for the derivation of one from the other. Such a procedure might be a fruitful way to approach grammatical development. We have little evidence concerning the decoding system at this time.

THE RESEARCH PROJECT

The data mentioned in this paper were obtained in a project consisting of longitudinal testing of 25 children and more intensive text collection from a subgroup of five. Texts for four of the children were collected beginning when the children were about 2. The fifth child, Susan, was added when she was 1; 9. Text collection was scheduled to continue two years. The standardized tests collected from the larger group consisted of three tests: a plural test, a pronoun test, and two forms of a discourse agreement test. The children in the smaller sample were older than the other children in the group.

The texts were at first collected weekly, in sessions of 45 minutes, because of rapid change. As the rate of change decreased and the fluency of the children increased, the frequency of text collection was gradually reduced, until texts were collected at two-month intervals, in two or three sets of closely spaced interviews totaling four or five hours.

The texts were all tape recorded. The transcription was at first phonetic, but later it was made in the normal orthography marked for stress and intonation, with a phonetic transcription only for ambiguous material. The texts also included utterances of the investigator and pertinent contextual information.

The earliest texts were collected in unstructured interviews. As techniques which elicited certain types of utterances were noted, the investigator increasingly structured the interviews. For example, attempts to elicit negatives were made by putting clothes on the wrong doll or puzzle pieces in the wrong place. Doll clothing was used for eliciting possessives. To elicit an interrogative sentence, two dolls were "fed," and the child was told to "ask Joe what he wants to eat." Plurals were produced for nonsense objects made of play-doh. If one of the dolls was left behind, "because he is sick," the child was asked to talk on the toy telephone to find out how "Joe" was, another device for eliciting questions. Telephone conversations with the child tested his reliance on verbal rather than gestural cues. Techniques that were discovered in this way were incorporated where appropriate into tests for the larger group.

The plural test consisted of 17 items. In each case a toy object or picture was shown, its name elicited, and then two were shown. "Here are two what?" Thus the test did not give the children the option of using a syntactical plural signal rather than a morphological one. The items included certain pairs in which nonsense items (wooden constructions) were given names which had the same final consonant as a familiar word (*boy-kigh*, *block-bik*, *bed-pud*, *horse-tass*, *orange-bunge*). Irregulars were *foot*, *man*, and *house*. The singular of the regular and nonsense words was offered by the investigator if it was not offered by the child. In the case of *foot* and *man*, however, the singular was not offered by the investigator. This procedure was followed in order to determine which form, e.g., *foot* or *feet*, was used by the child as the singular. Testing was stopped on items after they had been contrasted for several months.

On the pronoun test, the child was questioned about pictures, the questions being designed to elicit sentences containing possessives and nominative pronouns varying in number and gender. In the test of discourse agreement, questions tested the class of responses, verb restrictions, comprehension of

---

[3] Linguists frequently distinguish three functions: referential, directive, and expressive; for a recent account see Hymes (1961, 1962), and Jakobson (1960).

subject-object distinctions ("Who is he feeding?" vs. "Who is feeding him?") and "why" questions. There were two matched forms alternated each month, using the same pictures.

THE FIRST GRAMMATICAL SYSTEM

The children in our project began forming primitive sentences of two or more words before their second birthday.[4] It is clear that the grammar of these sentences is not identical with the adult model. It is often striking that one can provide a translation of children's utterances into adult utterances by the addition of function words and inflectional affixes. It appears that the children select the stressed utterance segments, which usually carry the most information. Brown and Fraser have called this a "telegraphic" version of English.

Since children's language undergoes a constant process of change through imitation of adult models, it makes sense that it should be describable in terms of its relation to the adult model. There are, however, some utterances which cannot be described as telegraphic speech:

At 2; 3 Christy and her baby sister each had a balloon. The baby bit her balloon and broke it. Christy first said *Baby bite balloon*, then pointed to the unbroken balloon and said, *Baby other bite balloon no.*

Between 2; 1 and 2; 4 Lisa had a particular kind of construction which often generated sentences that had no adult analogue, e.g., *all-gone puzzle*.

A conversation between the investigator and Susan at 1; 10:

Susan: *Book read. Book read. Book read.*
Inv: *You want me to read book? OK.*
Susan: *Read book.*

The last example shows a correction by imitation in the direction of telegraphic speech. However, the child's original utterance either was an unpatterned error or represented a

productive pattern that deviated from the model.

Is there any kind of system or pattern to the child's first sentences? In attempting to answer this question we will examine some of the text material of Susan (1; 9 to 2; 0) and Christy (2; 0 to 2; 3).

Susan
Susan, according to her parents, started putting words together at 1; 8 to form multiword sentences. One-word sentences, however, predominated until 1; 9½. Thus, the system to be described represents the very beginning of the development of the grammatical level.

During this period the most common words in Susan's vocabulary were *off* and *on*. A consistent pattern emerges when the preceding words, classified as to part of speech in the model language, are charted, as in Table 1. The figures in the chart represent text occurrences, excluding obvious imitations and chain repetitions.

TABLE 1.   Antecedents of *off* and *on* (Susan 1; 9–2; 0).

	Noun	Verb	Other	Initial	Total
off	28	8	4	1	41
on	29	7	11	3	50

The words that preceded *off* and *on* showed a large amount of overlap, and can be combined into one list, in Table 2. Words marked with an asterisk were found only in sentences of more than two words. Other words have been found in two-word sentences. *This-one* is assumed to have been a unit in Susan's speech.

Most of Susan's sentences with *on* and *off* reflected model sentences with two-word verbs, but a few reflected the prepositional use. Susan used *off* and *on* in a construction which had the shape W + I; W stands for any word(s) and I stands for *off* or *on*. We can call this the particle construction. The W will be defined as the complement, the I as the particle. Most of the characteristics of the particle construction are illustrated in the following example taken from a text at 1; 10:

---

[4] We will use the term "word" rather than "morpheme" except when the distinction is necessary. A word class of the model language, as opposed to a word class of the child's language, is indicated by an abbreviation and a superscript "m," e.g., N[m] and Adj[m] indicate model language noun and adjective. Age is indicated by year and month, e.g., 2; 4 indicates 2 years and 4 months old.

TABLE 2.   Antecedent types for *off* and *on* (Suasn 1; 9–2; 0).

back	dress	Liz	shoe	that
bandage	dusting	one*	sit*	them*
blanket	fall	pants	snap*	this*
button	fix	paper	sock	this-one
came	flower	piece*	sweater	(neck) tie
chair	hair	salt	take*	
coat*	hat	scarf	(scotch) tape	
diaper	hold*	shirt	tear	

*These words were found only in sentences of more than two words.

Susan: *Hat off, hat off.*
Inv: *That's more than the hat off. The whole Santa's head* [of a toy Santa Claus] *came off.*
Susan: *Santa head off.* (Pause.) *Head on. Fix on, fix on.*

Class 1 words had a verbal force. Most of the examples of imitations were imitations of two-word verbs. She was able to construct sentences of this pattern that had no direct adult analogue, e.g., *fix on;* the adult would normally say something like *fix it* or *put it on.* This example also shows that *off* and *on* were opposites for Susan; this may help explain why these two particles were used so much more than other particles.

The particle complement was usually a N^m or noun phrase of the model language, but V^m was not uncommon: *White sweater off,* said while taking her sweater off; *white sweater on,* a request directed to her mother to put her white sweater on her; *salt on,* pretending to salt food; *scarf off,* said while taking her scarf off. The model language provides analogues in which the noun is the object: *I took my sweater off; put my white sweater on! I put the salt on; I took my scarf off.* There are also analogues in which the noun is the subject, but these seem less likely to have been the model for the child: *my sweater is off; my white sweater should be on; the salt is on; my scarf is off.* The fact that there were no sentences like *Susan off* or *Mommy on,* that is, transitive two-word verb sentences of the model analogue with the verb and object deleted, strengthens the view that the N^m usually represents the object of action. There were exceptions to this pattern, such as *chair off,* said while taking a teddy bear off a chair.

There were 12 sentences in which the complement was a two-word phrase:

White sweater on.
Blue sweater on.
Mommy sweater on.
Susan sweater on.
Susan coat on.
Bonnie coat on.
This dress off.
Put that on.
That came off.
Miller take off shoe sock.
Shouldn't take off shoe sock.
Let's take off shoe sock.

It will be seen that there was evidence for distinguishing two-word classes that reflected N^m and V^m. It was not clear if Adj^m should be grouped with N^m or kept distinct. Therefore the formulas $N^m + N^m$, $N^m + V^m$, or $V^m + N^m$, and perhaps also $Adj^m + N^m$ can be used to form expansions of the particle complement. The phrases that reflected auxiliary + verb, however, cannot be accounted for in this fashion. *Susan sweater on* and *Mommy sweater on* were ambiguous. In the first sentence a possessive relation was intended and a model analogue would be *Susan's sweater is on* or *Susan has her sweater on.* The second sentence was a request directed to her mother and a model analogue would be *Mommy, put my sweater on me.*

A rather neat pattern was found for the core of Susan's particle construction. There were, however, loose ends. In some sentences the particle was medial, and in a few it was initial:

Take off me (requesting help in taking her scarf off).
Sock off Liz (in imitation of *Let's take the shoes and socks off of Liz*).

Snap on off (said while playing with the snap of a doll's dress).

Want to hold on Liz.

Liz her hat back on (indicating she wanted to put Liz's hat on after it fell off).

This one blue one on.

Susan blue one sweater on (this and preceding sentence were used to indicate she wanted to wear her blue sweater).

On tight (putting her doll more securely on her Kiddy Kar so it would not fall off again).

Off of me (requesting help in taking her scarf off).

No recurrent pattern can be found for these sentences.

Other particles of the model language were common, but none were as common as *off* and *on*. *Up* occurred 15 times: three times after N^m, nine times after V^m, two times after other words, and once in initial position. There are a few examples that fit the pattern described for the particle construction: *sleeves up*, requesting the investigator to roll up her sleeves; *red shoe up*, leaning her shoes against the door sill, pointed up. *Up bed*, indicating she wanted the side of the crib raised, would be **bed up* if it followed the pattern of *off* and *on*. Several sentences were probably learned units, thus accounting for the larger number of V^m than N^m before the particle: *tear up; come up; Susan get up.*

The remaining model language particles were common as a whole, but no single particle was very frequent. A large number of the sentences followed the pattern of the particle construction, but there were a larger proportion of exceptions to the general pattern than were found with *off* and *on*. A good many exceptions seemed to reflect the prepositional uses of the words in the model language.

When Susan's linguistic system became more mature and more closely approximated the model, transitive sentences with two-word verbs were common. The elements that developed into the object and particle were represented at this stage. The verbs less frequently, and the subjects almost never were represented.

The words *this*, *this-one*, and *that* showed certain consistent features. We can designate these three words class 2. In initial position they formed the demonstrative construction. *This-one* had the phonological shape /disn/ or /disən/, and appeared to be a unit for Susan. The sequence /-n/ or /-ən/ was distinct from the vocabulary item /wən/ *one*. The demonstrative construction had less semantic consistency than the particle construction. It was usually used to identify an item: *this-one yellow, this book, this-one Joe, that bead.* But it could also be used to indicate location and action or quality (the last two are difficult to separate in Susan's speech): *this on top; this-one on; this-one tear.* The word classes of the model language that followed an initial class 2 word were also more variable, as shown in Table 3.

TABLE 3. Susan's demonstrative constructions (Susan 1; 9–2; 0).

	Second word				
First word	N^m	V^m	Adj^m	Class[1]	Other
this	9	1	1	3	2
this-one	3	3	2	3	4
that	9	1	1	6	6

Class 2 words were usually in initial position; class 1 words were usually in medial or final position. However the positional preference is more consistent for class 1 than for class 2.

A third class, labeled class 3, may be recognized, consisting of *a* (19 occurrences), *the* (nine occurrences), and *(an) other* (11 occurrences). Excluding some examples of *a* (discussed below), class 3 preceded a N^m or a noun phrase of the model language, except in: *a red* (in answer to *What kind of an apple is that?*); *is that the blue mine?; have another blue.* In addition *a* was found in a few sentences in medial position before words where *a* was inappropriate: *up bed, (side?) a bed*, requesting that the investigator raise the side of her crib; *this a Bonnie pants; have a pants; this-one a Joe?; I know a that; these a Liz pants; this a back on; this a Joe?; mine, all a mine.* Shortly before Susan said *have a pants*, she had said *here a lemon* in imitation of her mother's sentence *here's a lemon.* Sentence like *here's a lemon* and probably also phrases like *all of* (/ə/) *mine' piece of* (/ə/) *toast* provided the model for

Susan's pattern. The *a* seemed to have the function of dividing the sentence into two parts. This function was restricted to a two-month period from 1; 9½ to 1; 11½.

Eight words have been assigned to three classes. The remaining words in Susan's vocabulary were either less frequent or less consistent and cannot realistically be assigned to classes by the methods used for setting up classes 1, 2, and 3. Are we justified in lumping the remaining vocabulary items into one large undifferentiated class? If we group the remaining words into the word classes of the model language and examine only two-word sentences, we find that a certain pattern emerges. The results are given in Table 4. Sentences that included *I, me, mine* were excluded because these words came in late in the period and were replacing *Susan. What* is also excluded because it represented a late development. A number of other words were excluded either because they were rare and their class membership was difficult to assign, or because they appeared to belong to learned formulas. Prepositions and particles have been lumped into one class.

Class A reflected V^m. There was only one example of A + A (*want talk*). The most common patterns were A + B and B + A. There were only six examples of A + *it*, but these comprise all the examples of *it*. *It* seemed to function as a suffix for class A

words, and perhaps marked a subclass of A, words that reflected transitive verbs in the model. Class B reflected N^m and was common before classes A, B, and 1, and after class A. Class C, which reflected Adj^m, was not common. The words reflected a variety of subclasses in the model language. Classes B and C show similar patterns and we cannot be sure they represent two classes in Susan's speech. If N^m and Adj^m words belong to one class in Susan's linguistic system, we would expect to find examples of Adj^m + I, because the pattern N^m + I was so common. Class D represents locative adverbs, and class E prepositions and particles of the model. These two classes cannot be sustained by the evidence presented in the table. The words represented in D and E might be aligned in a different fashion but the evidence is too meager to group these words with confidence. There were not many examples of *more*, but the evidence seems to indicate that the word belongs to class 3.

Christy

A somewhat different pattern is found in Christy's grammatical development. The following paragraphs are based primarily on two-word sentences collected during 12 hours of recorded texts. The most common type of sentence began with *that*. The various initial elements of these sentences along with the following words are listed in Table 5.

TABLE 4.   Class contingencies in Susan's two-word sentences (1; 9–2; 0).

Second word	First word										
	1	2	3	A	B	C	D	E	*it*	*more*	Total
1	—	10	—	6	45	—	—	1	—	—	62
2	—	—	—	6	1	—	1	—	—	1	9
3	—	—	—	—	—	—	—	—	—	—	—
A	—	3	—	1	26	—	1	—	—	—	31
B	—	10	8	18	26	4	6	1	—	3	76
C	—	3	1	—	4	—	—	2	—	—	10
D	—	1	—	4	5	1	—	7	—	—	18
E	—	4	—	12	10	1	—	—	—	1	28
it	—	—	—	6	—	—	—	—	—	—	6
more	—	—	—	—	—	—	—	—	—	—	—
Total	—	31	9	53	117	6	8	11	—	5	240

Note.   Thirty-seven sentences that include the following words have been excluded: *night-night, I, me, my, mine, he, you, her, them, one, two, to, what, now, too, please, bye, like,* and *right* (in *right here*).

TABLE 5. Demonstrative sentences for Christy (2; 0–2; 3).

that	that's	this	thatsa	this a	thata	'sa
blue					blue	
broken			broken			
chicken	chicken					
dolly	dolly					
eye	eye					
elephant			elephant			
go		go				
hat	hat					
Joe	Joe					
pants	pants					
pretty			pretty			
truck	truck		truck	truck		truck
yellow	yellow					
			cup		cup	
airplane	bus	one	car	A	doggy	arm
blocks	milk		coffee		horse	baby
bowl	quack-quack		girl			block
cat			owl			boy
Christy's			pig			ear
Daddy's			plane			lion
dolly's						rabbit
fish						Wick
horsie						
huke*						
kitty						
neck						
pin						
pink						
po*						
Sarah						
turn						
yellow						

*Po and kuke were the names of two nonsense shapes of play-doh.

The lists may be pooled into one in view of the similarity of the lists and gradation of phonetic shapes represented by each category: /dæ, dæʔ, dæt, dæ, da, dat, dɔ, as, dæs, dædæ, dæda, dæa, æta, dætsa, dæsa, dæza, zæza, æza, sa, za, sæ, tsa/.

This and *this a* (found before *a, go, one,* and *truck*) and the variants of *that* may be pooled as class 1. The items in Table 5 and the items found after *this* (*a*) may be called class A. As a result of this classification, a construction can be identified which we may call the demonstrative construction: 1 + A ↓/↑ (the arrows indicate falling and rising intonation). There were 74 examples of such utterances.

Nineteen sentences began with *the* or *a*. The words which followed were *other,* or class A words. *The* and *a* never terminated a two-word sentence. These words have been designated class 2.

The words *in, on, out, away, over,* and *under* appeared in 16 sentences. They both preceded and followed class A and preceded class 1. There was one set which followed, but never preceded class A: *away, out;* others which preceded but never followed: *over, under;* and others of dual membership: *in, on.* The words which occurred in first position have been designated class D, and those in second position as class C. The decision to

TABLE 6. Class contingencies in Christy's two-word sentences (2; 0–2; 3).

Second Word	First word											
	1	2	3	A	B	C	D	where	what	(an) other	it	Total
1	—	—	—	—	2	—	1	—	1	1	—	5
2	—	—	—	—	—	—	—	—	—	—	—	—
3	—	—	—	3	5	—	5	—	—	—	—	13
A	74	18	9	41	5	—	3	10	—	8	—	168
B	2	—	—	10	2	—	—	1	—	—	—	15
C	—	—	—	4	2	—	—	—	—	—	—	6
D	—	—	—	—	—	—	—	—	—	—	—	—
where	—	—	—	—	—	—	—	—	—	—	—	—
what	—	—	—	—	—	—	—	—	—	—	—	—
(an) other	—	1	—	—	—	—	—	—	—	—	—	1
it	—	—	—	—	2	—	—	—	—	—	—	2
Total	76	19	9	58	18	—	9	11	1	9	—	210

Note. Nineteen sentences were omitted because they contained words of ambiguous class membership from the standpoint of the two-word sentence corpus: *his, walk, oh, no, else, my, right* (*right here*), *more, don't, two, both*.

split these words into two classes, in spite of the overlap in membership, is based on the presumed later evolution into prepositions and adverbs or two-word verb particles. The accent pattern for sentences containing these items was relatively consistent.[5] In 13 out of the 14 cases where the stress was recorded, it occurred on the second word, e.g., *on cóuch, clothes ón.*

In addition to preceding class 1 and class A, words in class C preceded *there* and *here*, e.g., *in thére* ↑. *There* and *here* may be designated as class 3. The words *where* and *what* occurred only in initial position. *Where* only occurred in sentences with falling pitch.

Class A was by far the largest class, both in terms of frequency and variety. Included are items which are N^m, V^m, and Adj^m. We may subdivide this category on certain distributional grounds. The sentences *see thís, hóld it, doed it,* and *óther this* were not paralleled by any instances in which N^m or Adj^m occurred in first position in the same frame, in spite of the fact that N^m was far more frequent than V^m. V^m never followed class 2, 3, or D. The pattern $1 + V^m$ was relatively infrequent compared to $A +$

V^m. V^m is designated class B, and the occurrences are shown in Table 6. If only two-word sentences are considered, the separation of class A and B is based on weaker evidence than the other class criteria, but it is quite likely that the analysis of longer sentences would confirm this division. On Table 5 the overlap was greatest between *that* and *that's*. If the words ending in *a* are viewed as in fact two words (*this a, that's a*), so that the sequences form three-word sentences, it may be seen that there are no cases of V^m in the last four columns, though three appear with *this* and *that*. Such sentences as *you hold this, make apple there,* and *take it off* suggest that the analysis of long sequences will require a separate class of verbs. In all cases except *apple eat* the semantic object followed the verb. The semantic actor normally preceded, except in *I carry Christy* which had two objects and *where go eye* and *where go toast, huh* which had an inversion regularly following *where*. There was insufficient evidence for further subdivision of class A.

Christy's grammar included an accentual system. The locative construction consisted of $A + Á$ or $A + \overset{3}{3}$. Sentences based on the possessive or adjectival analogue of the model consisted of $Á + A$: *baby róom* (in answer to *Where's the baby?*); *báby book*

---

[5] An accented word, defined for Christy's speech in the section on Prosody, is indicated by a primary stress mark.

TABLE 7. Classes in Christy's two-word sentences (2; 0–2; 3).

1	this, thisa, that, that's, that's a, 'sa, thata
2	a, the
3	here, there
A	arm, baby, bus, cat, Christy's, dolly, dolly's, fish, horsie, truck, pretty, yellow, etc.
B	come, doed, flying, go, goes, got, hold, see, sit, sleep, sleeping, turn, want, walking
C	away, in, on, out, way
D	in, on, over, under

(in answer to *Is that the baby's book?*); *bíg choochoo*. In a few cases, however, the second item was accented in sentences that had a possessive and adjectival analogue: *baby báll* (in answer to *Is that the baby's ball?*); *baby cár* (in answer to *Whose car is this?*); *a big wádi* (wadi = dog). The first example might reveal imitation of the investigator's stress. The accent pattern was not consistent in the possessive or adjectival construction, in contrast to the locative construction.

Discussion

The partial descriptions for Susan and Christy show that the two language systems were quite different in their details. Some of the differences could be ascribed to the age difference, but others were due to a difference in their language style. There were, however, certain characteristics that applied to the speech of all the children in the project except Harlan, who was beyond this phase of development from the beginning.

A few high frequency words tended to be restricted to a given position in the sentence and tended to define the meaning of the sentence as a whole. The use of these words marked the first step in developing the grammatical system of the model language. These words may be called operators. The classes of operators for Susan and Christy have been labeled with Roman numerals. The difference between operator classes and nonoperator classes is relative rather than absolute. The nonoperator words tend to be grouped into large classes, but the division between the classes is sometimes difficult to make. Part of this difficulty is probably the nature of the data. If a low

frequency word does not occur in enough different contexts, class assignments are difficult to make. But part of the difficulty may be the nature of the linguistic system of the child. The instability of class assignment is especially probable in a system based on order and not on additional markers. If a child has only heard a word from adults a few times, his sense of the meaning and the appropriate verbal contexts for that word may be easily changed by new experience. Thus, even though some regularity in order for two classes may exist, vacillation with regard to certain specific items may obscure that regularity. The method of classifying the child's words in part by pure distribution and in part by the word classes of the model language will not adequately account for all of the child's vocabulary, or vacillation of specific items. But the regularity displayed in the tables shows that this method yields information about structure.[6]

Operators are defined as those words having high frequency and few members in a class. These properties are found, in adult speech in function words. The children's operators tended to be derived from adult function words and to be precursors of the function words which characterized a later phase of their own development. The nonoperators were precursors of lexical words. There was some tendency for the most frequent models of operators to be words which could serve as substitutes for lexical classes and carry stress, i.e., pronouns (demonstratives) rather than pure noun determiners, particles of two-word verbs rather than pure prepositions.

If the child used the operators in constructions that had analogues in adult speech, adults reinforced the child's pattern and enabled him to approximate adult patterns more closely. If the operators or constructions did not reflect patterns in the model language, they dropped out. There was one clear example. From 2; 1 to 2; 4, Lisa used *byebye*, *no*, *all-gone*, *another*, and *please* as operators.

---

6 A grammar cannot be derived from the tables. The tables only show that the elements in the child's sentences are systematized. The best explanation for the systematization is that the child has word classes, classes that have at least some properties of word classes in adult speech. The tables do not tell what the classes are, but they do provide clues.

These words were used in a construction which consisted of an accented operator plus N^m: *nó toy*, indicating she did not want a particular toy any longer (contrast *no tóy?*, asking if there were any more toys). Many of the sentences can be related to the model only by reversing the order. Thus *all-gone puzzle* (the puzzles had just been put away) would normally be said by the adult as *The puzzle is all gone*, or some such sentence in which the word order is the reverse of Lisa's. It is always possible to find analogues that preserve the child's order, e.g., *It's all gone, the puzzle is* or *That which is all gone is the puzzle*. These are sentences the child is not likely to hear. This construction became less frequent and eventually disappeared.

Most of our analysis has been limited to two-word sentences, and the distinction between endocentric and exocentric constructions cannot apply. It seems clear, however, that this distinction will be needed to account for longer sentences. Most of the child's early constructions have exocentric models, and are probably to be considered exocentric in the child's system also. In addition, many phrases in longer sentences can probably be treated as expansions of single word classes. A characteristic feature of the children's speech was to take a construction that could be a complete predication for them and treat it as an expansion of one part of another construction. Thus the possessive construction in Christy's speech, Á + A, can be used as the demonstrative complement: *that Chrísty rabbit*. This kind of expansion seems to be typical in the early phases, and endocentric features of the model language were weakly represented in the children's language. There are certain problems to this kind of an analysis, however. In Christy's sentence *that one Joe*, *that one* can probably be treated as an expansion of the demonstrative, but in *–'s a one two* Christy was counting and *one two* appears to be an expansion of the complement. In *that this shoe*, *that* may be treated as the demonstrative, *this shoe* as the complement, and the complement also as a demonstrative construction. It is not certain, however, that such analysis can be formally sustained.

It seems surprising that the children's relatively systematic arrangement of classes could be sustained with so few overt markers. One explanation may be the relative semantic consistency of English lexical classes for the words in young children's vocabulary, a fact pointed out by Brown (1958, p. 247). He found experimentally that lexical items with class markers were systematically identified with certain types of referents (*ibid*, p. 251). Thus it may be that regularities of order are aided by the additional cue that is provided by semantic similarities between items in a class. We have very weak evidence on this point, from Harlan. The word *have* in English serves as a verb, but it does not have a meaning of action. Harlan had considerable difficulty in giving *have* the verb markers he used with other verbs. It might be objected that the difficulty stems from its use as an auxiliary, but this is a specialized use that had not yet (at 3; 1) appeared in Harlan's speech. Further, *do*, which was used by Harlan both as an auxiliary and main verb, was marked appropriately when *have* was not. Thus we have examples of past tense markers for many verbs, including *do*, at least six months before the past tense was marked for *have*, although contexts in which the past tense would have been appropriate for this verb did occur before that time. At 2; 7, after the regular testing of discourse agreement was begun, it was found that Harlan could answer a question about what someone was doing with an appropriate response. Notice that he did not say *having* in response to this question:

Inv: *What do you think Paul was doing with the hoe?*
Harlan: *Have.*
Inv: *Hm?*
Harlan: *Have it.*

This is not altogether a clear case, since the semantic peculiarity of *have* is reflected in its lower probability in the *-ing* form in adult usage.

The casual observer is often struck by what appears to be a complete lack of any system in the young child's first speech efforts. The composition of words into sentences appears to be random; any words can be juxtaposed. Our evidence shows this not to be the case. There was a complex system even at the earliest stages, even though it was a much simpler system than the extremely complex adult model. Are we justified in calling the kind of system that a young child has a formal grammar? This depends to a large extent on what a formal grammar is conceived to be.

From the standpoint of a linguist, a grammar can be conceived as a set of rules that will account for the sentences produced by the speaker and will not predict impossible sentences. Vocabulary items have to be assignable to word classes so that new sentences can be generated by operating with the grammar, Normally in natural languages many constructions have stateable and consistent semantic correlates, but it might be debated whether this is a necessary property.

It is obvious from the description of Susan's and Christy's speech that for most generalizations there were exceptions. Some sentences seemed to fall outside the system. Other sentences reversed the patterns that held in all other cases. It is sentences like *off of me; clean in, in clean* (in Susan's speech); and *I carry Christy; that one Joe; that one two* (counting); *where rattle Christy; big shoe red, red shoe big; apple more; more apple* (in Christy's speech) that cause problems. Almost any rule that allows these sequences allows others that seem impossible.

How shall we know what is impossible with a child? With adult informants, one can test a grammatical solution by eliciting paradigmatic material or by asking *Can you say . . . ?* This implies that a speaker can distinguish the grammatically impossible from the improbable; Maclay and Sleator (1960) have presented evidence that college rhetoric students could not make the distinction. Yet we do know that adults can correct their own grammatical mistakes. Harlan corrected grammatical errors in his speech. Was this simply recognition that the utterances were improbable?

There seem to be a number of views which could be defended as to whether a formal system existed for Susan and Christy. There were a few generalizations which could be made without exceptions, but these were weak in that they also predicted many sentences that did not appear and were im-

probable. It might be said that they were formal systems, but that they were undergoing change.

Alternatively, it could be said that the statistical tendencies and preferences were precursors of more stable and clearly defined classes. It might be argued that grammatical systems arise first in the child's exposure to differing probabilities in adult substitutions and sequences, which are reflected in a system of regularities which cannot be expressed by exceptionless rules.

THE GRAMMATICAL SYSTEM
WITH WORD CLASS MARKERS

Eventually lexical classes could be identified by markers and order, not simply order as in the earlier stage. Nouns were marked by the plural suffix and noun determiners, verbs by verbal suffixes and auxiliaries. At this time it is convenient to describe the child's grammatical system as a simplified grammar of the model, along with added grammatical rules to account for constructions that have no counterpart in the model language.

Most of the mistakes or deviations from the model can be classified as omissions (*I'll turn water off* for *I'll turn the water off*), overgeneralization of morphophonemic combinations (*foots* for *feet; a owl* for *an owl; breaked* for *broke*), the incorrect use of a function word with a subclass of a lexical class (using *a* with mass nouns and proper nouns), or doubly marked forms (adding the possessive suffix to a possessive pronoun, *mine's*). Except for the first kind, these mistakes point to the fact that classes were marked. The children seldom used a suffix or function word with the wrong lexical class, either at this stage or at the earlier stage when markers were not well developed; the only examples of this kind of mistake were provided by Susan: *I by-ed that* where the adult would say *I went by that*, and *stand up-ed* where the adult would say *stood up*. In the second example it could be argued that the *-ed* was not added to the wrong word class, but rather was added to the verb phrase instead of the verb.

Most of our discussion of this stage of development will be centered on the linguistic system of Harlan, who was at this stage of development at 2; 2 when we started working with him (the remaining children in the project entered this stage at 2; 6 or shortly thereafter).

At 2; 2, verbs in Harlan's system could be marked by the past tense suffix -ed, the progressive suffix -ing, the positive auxiliaries can, will, want, going, and the negative auxiliaries can't, won't, don't. The sentence: *I pushed it, I can push it* was typical. The markers were not always used, however:

Inv: *It popped.*
Harlan: (To his mother) *My balloon pop.*
Mother: *You popped it?*
Harlan: *I pop it.*

Harlan's parents reported that he had the past tense suffix a few weeks before we began working with him. At 2; 2 a few strong verbs were correctly used with the past tense: *My Daddy-O went to work; I made a somersault.* These forms varied with the base from:

Harlan: *I go boom boom* (past tense context).
Inv: *What'd you do?*
Harlan: *I went boom.*

Normally strong verbs were unmarked. The -ed form of the past tense was not added to such verbs until 2; 5: *I breaked that.*

At 2; 2 the progressive was simply the suffix -ing with no form of the verb *to be: Man talking on the telephone.* Thus the suffix had the same, or a very similar, distribution as the -ed suffix. At 2; 3, forms with *to be* were used sporadically: *Man's taking out the baloney. To be* was not consistently used until 2; 8.

Harlan grouped his auxiliaries into two sets, positive and negative. This resulted from his lack of negative transformations. In addition, he had two auxiliaries that are not in the model language, *want* and *going.* These words are analyzed as auxiliaries because they came directly before the verb without the infinitive marker *to: I want make two bowls; I going make a pig.*

At 2; 2 the most common noun markers were *the, a,* and the plural suffix -s. The markers were sometimes omitted in contexts where they should have been used: *I want the duck, I want the duck, I want duck.* Other words marked nouns, e.g., *some,* possessive pronouns, numerals, but they were less frequent.

At 2; 2 Harlan indicated the negative with a negative auxiliary, *not* or *isn't: I can't see the pig; That not go right; Isn't a boy. Isn't* was used primarily in one-word negations. It was not treated as a negative transformation of *is* as can be seen in: *That piece* (puzzle piece) *go right over there.* (Harlan tried the puzzle piece over there, and found it did not fit.) *Isn't.* Unfortunately our material does not allow us to say when the negative was first treated as a transformation, but the transformation pattern was present by at least 2; 8.

At 2; 2 *yes-no* questions were marked by the rising intonation. The following example at 2; 3 indicates that Harlan understood that some sort of inversion should take place:

Harlan: *Want d'you policeman?* /wan ǰuw pliysmæn ↑ /
Inv: *Hm?*
Harlan: *Want . . . want d'you policeman?* /want | want ǰuw pliysmæn ↑ /

We have noted that *want* was interpreted by Harlan as an auxiliary, and this may have had some influence on the inversion. But it is clear that Harlan did not understand the function of *do.* The interrogative inversion was used sporadically after this time, and became a productive pattern at 2; 8:

Inv: *You ask Liz what she wants, OK?*
Harlan: *D'you want honey, you do? OK.*

The elliptical transformation appeared quite suddenly at 2;7, and was common and productive at that time:

Inv: *Where's the deer going?*
Harlan: *Because he is.*

Inv: *How old are you?*
Harlan: *Because I am.*

Inv: *Why can't you do it with me?*
Harlan: *Because I can't.*

Inv: *When do you eat breakfast?*
Harlan: *Because I do.*

Inv: *How did the bird get there?*
Harlan: *Because he did.*

Inv: *You've seen this book before, Harlan.*
Harlan: *I have?*

Emphatic transformations occurred sporadically: *I did turn it off* (2; 3); *I did wake up* (2; 7).

The above paragraphs show that the verbal transformations involving *do* and other auxiliaries started to come in about 2; 3, and became an established feature in Harlan's grammar by 2; 8. (Transformations with interrogative words, not treated here, came in a little later; the sentences with interrogative words showed more complicated patterns of development.) The verb restrictions in discourse agreement patterns were fairly well controlled by 2;8.

There seemed to be a correlation between Harlan's grammatical development and the functional categories described in the introduction. After the development of the verbal transformations and the verb restrictions in discourse agreement, the functional category of responsive discourse was utilized. Since functional categories are more difficult to recognize than formal categories, and since most attention has been focused on the formal categories, this correlation may not be correct. It seems likely that language functions are correlated with grammatical development, whether or not the suggested correlation is correct.

The linguistic system of the child is very unstable. After the word classes are overtly marked, the instability is very noticeable, as the above sketch of Harlan's grammatical system shows. The formal patterns are not set, and the child frequently lapses back into older patterns. It takes a long time for the learned patterns to become automatic.

When the child is able to correct his mistakes, it indicates that he considers certain sentences to be ungrammatical. This is excellent proof that the child has a formal grammatical system. Harlan, the only child to exhibit this ability early, started correcting himself at 2; 9, soon after the appearance of verbal transformations and the development of verb restriction in discourse agreement.

PROSODIC FEATURES

Children are good mimics of prosodic features, particularly pitch, and they can give the impression of having the pitch-stress system under control. This may be true from a phonetic, perhaps even phonemic standpoint, but does not necessarily entail the use of the prosodic features in the grammatical system. The rising and falling intonations used to distinguish questions and statements were the only prosodic features consistently found in the linguistic system before the use of class markers. Even this contrast may be later than is generally recognized. The earliest and best record of this contrast is for Susan. In the early records for her at 1; 9, many sentences that ended in a level or rising pitch were interpreted as questions. The lack of a falling pitch was often the only indication that the sentence might be a question, and sometimes the context suggested that it was a statement. The adult (parent or investigator) always interpreted the sentence as a question and gave Susan an answer. Susan over 2 years old before the rising intonation consistently indicated a question. It may be that she learned the intonation by noting which sentences drew a response from the adult.

Prosodic features that had no analogue in the model language were sometimes used in the early period. Christy and Lisa had an accentual system based on pitch and stress. Each sentence had one accented word. The accented word received the last high pitch and/or strong stress. The pitch and stress of the preceding words were variable. Each construction in both children's linguistic system had a particular accent pattern, but the accent pattern was not always adhered to.

All of the children had primary and secondary stress, and a two-level pitch system at the time they developed a linguistic system with marked word classes. The two-level pitch system persisted well beyond this period, probably because two levels are sufficient to indicate most of the grammatical contrasts signaled by the English prosodic system.

INDIVIDUAL DIFFERENCES

We have noted that there were certain features common to the early development of the grammatical level for all the children. Each child had a set of operators, usually derived from function words of the model language, that served as a means of breaking into the model language system. The children did not have the same operators, however. These differences between the children in preferences were clear from the beginning and have persisted in differences in foci of development. It is possible that certain types of patterns or constructions are more compatible than others. Greenberg (1963) has pointed to correlated structures in languages and we might find some patterns in the individual differences between the children at various stages, but our evidence is scant at present.

Lisa had a particularly primitive phonological system. As a result, it was often difficult or impossible to understand her. In addition, final sibilants were absent for a considerable period and she was not able to mark the plural with the suffix -s. Instead she used a syntactic device: *one two shoe* meant *more than one shoe*. She later gave this up in favor of other number combinations. According to her mother, she would pick two numbers to indicate the plural, e.g., *eight four shoe*, and then after a few days she would pick another combination, e.g., *three five shoe*. She finally developed a final /θ/ and was able to say *shoeth*. There may be a relationship between Lisa's syntactic marking of the plural and her earlier use of an operator class which had no adult analogue. In addition, at a later stage of development Lisa seemed to develop some grammatical rules of her own, rules which had no counterpart in the model language.

There are some suggestions in our data that linguistic patterns correlate with some nonlinguistic behavior. Susan's favorite operators were *off* and *on*. Susan was a busy little girl who was always taking things off and putting them back on. Christy's favorite operator was *that*, and was used in the demonstrative construction to identify things. When the investigator arrived at Christy's house, she would run into the living room, sit down, and wait to be entertained—wait for the investigator to take toys out of his bag. Most of the children had a favorite toy and a favorite activity. Harlan had no favorite toy, but he had a favorite activity: talking. We found that if we could keep a conversation going he was less apt to throw things. Harlan had the most developed linguistic system of any of the children. He talked early and often. He also made more expressive

use of language than the other children: the diminutive baby talk suffix -*y* was productive by 2; 5; the expressive pitch pattern /312 ↑/ was in common use by 2; 2.

In the preceding sections we have described a technique in which the child develops the grammatical level by composing, by placing words together to form sentences. A less common technique consists of treating a polymorphemic sequence of the model language as a monomorphemic unit, and then at a later stage of development segmenting the sequence into its proper parts. It is our impression from parental reports that this is more common with second children than with the first born, but still never an important pattern; all of the children in the small group are first born. A third, closely allied technique is the learning, or imitating, of a sentence, understanding the meaning of most of the words and the meaning of the sentence as a whole, but not understanding the grammatical function of the elements. If a number of sentences of a similar pattern are learned, it might be possible for the child to come to recognize the grammatical function of the elements. This technique is rare, or perhaps nonexistent, because the child would probably have to learn by heart a large number of sentences before he happened to learn two that contrasted in the proper fashion. Christy had a number of sentences which appeared to have been memorized, e.g., *where are the shoe?* (2; 3). At this time neither *are* nor *is* were productive elements in Christy's speech, and there is no evidence that this or similar sentences were instrumental in her learning the copulative pattern.

DEVELOPMENTAL SEQUENCE

One of the purposes of this study is to describe developmental sequences of linguistic features. While the features studied are those of English, it would be valuable to be able to consider features inherent in any linguistic system. This is difficult to do until more is known about language universals and the prerequisites of language.

The relation between the time of mastery of skills may consist of co-occurrence or of necessary sequence. Sequential orders may arise either because one skill is dependent on the prior acquisition of another, because one is less often practiced, or because they differ in difficulty though are practiced equally. Many of the sequential findings of a normative sort have the third property. They occur because, on the average, it takes a different amount of practice to accomplish one task than another. We would like to separate the logically sequential features. These could be found best in an experimental transfer design, but, wherever in our data there are individual differences in acquisition patterns, some information about sequential dependence can be obtained from studying changes in individual systems rather than group averages.

Viewing the acquisition of phonological contrasts in terms of learning to distinguish features or properties rather than classes, Jakobson (1941) has proposed a developmental order for the phonological system of children. He has suggested that the child successively elaborates a phonological system approaching the adult's by binary division. If he begins with one feature or bundle of features for contrast, he can only have two classes; with two sets of independent features he may have four classes. Within each class he may have sounds which are in many respects phonetically different from the adult model.

Does anything of this sort happen in grammar? We have indicated that grammatical classes and grammatical markers do not have the structural properties of a matrix of features which phonemes have. The classes that are identified in grammatical analysis are not usually marked by features that can then be recombined to define another class. However, at various points in the grammatical system there are differing degrees of generalization possible. Proper, mass, and count nouns are contrasted by their occurrence with noun determiners, a function class that is unique to this system of classes. The learning of the morphophonemic series in the contrast plural/singular has greater generality. It can also serve in marking possessive nouns, and in marking third person singular verbs. An analogous series marks the regular past tense. At the level of grammatical transformations, a very broad transfer of skills is possible. We may seek for correlations between these related series. For example, though the contrasts plural/singular and possessive/nonpossessive may be acquired at different times for reasons which are semantic or based on frequency, if the contrasts of one are mastered, the other should be too. We have so far only one instance—Harlan—of mastery of both by a child in our study. He gave as productive forms *po-poez* for singular/plural at 2; 3 and *Joe-Joez* for possession at 2; 4½. At the latter date we find *nizz-nizzez* for singular/plural. But we do not find the possessive *Liz-Lizez* until 2; 7. *Joe* and *Liz* were the names of dolls which were used to elicit possession for body parts and clothing, so the opportunity for these contrasts was frequent. This slight evidence does not support the expectation that the morphophonemic contrasts would generalize.

If we turn back to the learing of division into word classes when it first appears, we are limited by the fact that we have only two types of information on which to base our judgment as to the productive operation of classes. One is rules of order with different words. The other is semantic consistency of constructions using these words. At the point at which we first analyzed the children's speech, there were already many classes discernible. Thus we cannot say that at the initial stage before word classes were defined by markers that there was evidence of a first division into two primordial classes which then were subdivided.

If the division into lexical classes is marked by affixes and function words later, then we may expect to find some of the divisions appearing only at the later stage. The division into mass, proper, and count nouns is possible at this point.

In addition to sequences that depend on the availability of markers, some depend on the availability of vocabulary. Thus the rules of order that apply to subclasses of adverbs only could appear after these words enter the vocabulary of children and co-occur in the same sentences.

The earliest forms of markers which we found were inconsistently used. They were the possessive suffix, the plural suffix, *the*, *and* and *-ing* which were used sporadically. If they were consistent as to class, though, even sporadic use could help identify a class. Thus the first use for these markers may be to identify lexical classes, rather than to distinguish subclasses within lexical classes or to identify constructions. *Want* and *going*, which were used by most of the children of the project as auxiliaries, marked verbs. On the whole, where suffixed and nonsuffixed forms existed, the children preferred the nonsuffixed forms rather than free variants. This was probably in part a phonological problem, since the children had less control of the final consonants than of the other parts of the phonological system.

At the point where subclasses begin to be distinguished so that markers are used as a consistent signal, it is possible to make some simple predictions. For cases with a semantic correlate, a child will first begin imitating forms correctly, and after using a certain number of contrasts correctly will generalize the contrast to new forms. Until enough instances are learned, there will presumably be a delay between these two points. Generalization to irregular cases should occur also; the preferred form for the singular of irregular nouns probably depends on the relative frequency of the singular and plural and relative case of pronunciation of the two. We already know from Berko's work (1958) that the plural of nouns with final fricatives, sibilants, and affricates tends to be late.

We have tested 25 children with systematic tests of familiar words, irregulars, and nonsense words with a technique similar to Berko's. Nearly always the contrast with familiar forms preceded the contrast with nonsense forms. Naturally, the familiar forms chosen give a rough estimate only We do not know whether it is the variety of types or the frequency of tokens showing contrasts which is crucial in determining the length of time before generalization occurs.

The average gap for *boy* vs. *kigh* was 2; 4 months; for *ball* vs. *kigh* was the same; for *block* vs. *bik* the gap was 1; 1 months; for *cup* vs. *bik* 1; 5 months. The cases were too few to estimate the gaps for the other contrasts. Thus the child who calls one cup by a different term than two cups might do the same with the nonsense toy *bik* in a month and a half. This analysis was not specific as to the phonological nature of the contrast.

Does the "concept" of plurality generalize; i.e., when one contrast occurs do the others occur soon after? There were artifacts in the restriction on age range provided by the time at which we stopped testing for this paper. For all items except those with fricative, affricate, or sibilant finals, the range between the first contrast to appear and the last was quite short—averaging $2\frac{1}{2}$ months including the nonsense items.

Two irregulars were used as tests for overextension: *foot* and *man*. Of the 15 children who produced a contrast, three said *feet-feets* and 11 said *foot-foots* about the same age as other stop plurals were produced. One child had *foot-footis* first. For 18 children, a contrast between *man* and a plural was offered. For all, the plural was at first *mans*. Two children showed irregular development that can be shown as follows:

Sarah

2; 4	bik-biks	tass-tassez	bunge-bunge	man-manz	foot-foots	box-box
2; 5	bik-biks	tass-tassez	bunge-bungez	man-manz	foot-footez	box-boxez
2; 6		tass-tassez	bunge-bungez	man-manz	foot-foots	box-boxez
2; 7	vik-biks	tass-tassez	bunge-bungez	man-man	foot-foots	box-bockez
2; 9	bik-biks	tass-tass	bunge-bunge	man-man	feet-feets	box-box
2; 10	bik-biks	tass-tass	bunge-bunge	man-man	foot-foots	box-box

Harlan

2; 8	bik-biks	tass-tassez	bunge-bungez	man-manz	foot-footez	box-box
2; 9	bik-biksez	tass-tassez	bunge-bungez	man-manzez	foot-footsez	box-boxez
2; 10	bik-biks	tass-tassez	bunge-bungez	man-manz	foot-footsez	box-boxez
2; 11		tath-tassez	bunge-bungez	man-men	foot-feet	box-boxez
3; 1	bik-biks	tass-tassez	bunge-bungez	man-manz	foot-feet	box-boxez

The vacillation in these series illustrates instability, regression, boredom, or, clearly with Harlan at 2; 9, playfulness. Harlan frequently invented games with language.

In sum, the acquisition of the plural contrast followed a simple pattern in most children from noncontrast to acquisition of particular instances of contrast, generalization several months, after acquisition of particular instances, and finally, differentiation of irregular forms.

In addition to inflectional suffixes, certain derivational suffixes are used to mark classes. For example, the diminutive or baby talk -*y* was used widely by the children in namnig animals—*doggy, horsey*—even when we tried to get them to use the nonsuffixed form for the purpose of testing plurality. However, the suffix was used productively by only one child, Harlan, who produced the following in an argument about a name at 2; 5½:

Inv: *Really. His name is Cootes. Bill Cootes.*
Harlan: *Billzy the Coooootsy.* (singing)

Transformations were not found in the earliest linguistic systems. The first to appear were simple (nongeneralized) transformations, such as the progressive (*be . . . -ing*), inversion of word order for questions, and the use of auxiliaries with *not*. There were some early interrogative inversions by Christy:

2.0   *Where's the arm?*
2.1   *Where go toast, huh?*
2.4   *Where belong shoe?*
2.5   *Where go button, Chrity, huh?*

Soon afterwards the coordinative transformation with *and* appeared. The two-part coordinative transformations (e.g., *both . . . and . . .*) and subordinative transformations have not appeared in our data yet.

Preliminary evidence suggests that discourse agreement features are sequentially ordered. We would expect discourse agreement features involving class restrictions to parallel the sequential development of the classes themselves. Appropriate answers to simple "who/ what" questions and "what . . . do" questions came early. Preliminary evidence indicates that the child's adverbs are learned in the order locative, temporal, manner; if true, it might be expected that discourse agreement would proceed in the order where, when, how. In a similar fashion the development of verb restrictions in discourse agreement should follow the development of verb structure.

BIBLIOGRAPHY

Berko, J., "The Child's Learning Of English Morphology," *Word*, XIV (1958), 150–77.

Brown, R. W., *Words and Things*. Glencoe, Illinois: The Free Press, 1958.

Fries, C. C., *The Structure of English*. New York: Harcourt, Brace & World, Inc., 1952.

Greenberg, J., "Some Universals of Grammer With Particular Reference to The Order of Meaningful Elements," *Universals of Language*, Cambridge, Mass.: The M.I.T. Press, 1963, pp. 58–90.

Hymes, Del H., "Functions of Speech: An Evolutionary Approach," in F. C. Gruber, ed., *Anthropology and Education*, (Philadelphia: University of Pennsylvania Press, 1961), pp. 55–83.

———. "The Ethnography of Speaking," in T. Gladwin and W. C. Sturtevant, eds., *Anthropology and Human Behavior* (Washington D.C.: Anthropological Society, 1962), 13–53.

Jakobson, Roman, "Linguistics and Poetics," in T. A. Sebeok, ed., *Style in Language* (Cambridge, Mass.: The M.I.T. Press, 1960), pp. 350–77.

Maclay, H., and M. Sleator, "Responses to Language: Judgements of Grammaticalness," *International Journal of American Linguistics* (1960), 275–82.

Whorf, B. L., "Linguistics as an Exact Science," reprinted in J. B. Carroll, ed., *Language, Thought and Reality* (New York: John Wiley & Sons, Inc., 1956), pp. 220–32.

52 The following selection is the "Formal Discussion" by Noam Chomsky of the preceding paper. The reader will find an introduction about Chomsky and his work at the head of Chapter 59, "Language and the Mind," in this volume.

A. B. A.

FORMAL DISCUSSION OF MILLER AND ERVIN'S THE DEVELOPMENT OF GRAMMAR IN CHILD LANGUAGE

My initial reaction to this paper was one of surprise that so much success could be attained in dealing with this question. It seems that the attempt to write a grammar for a child raises all of the unsolved problems of constructing a grammar for adult speech, multiplied by some rather large factor. To mention just the most obvious difficulty, since the language is constantly changing rather dramatically, it is impossible to use the one "method" available to linguists who attempt to go beyond surface description, namely, learning the language oneself. Clearly the general problem is at least as difficult, and, in fact, much more difficult than the problem of discovering the grammar of the language of a mature speaker, and this, I think, is a problem of much greater difficulty than is often realized. In fact, the only remarks I would like to make reflect an impression that underlying these descriptions of children's speech, laudible and interesting as they are, there is a somewhat oversimplified conception of the character of grammatical description, not unrelated, perhaps, to a similarly oversimplified view that is typical of much recent work on language in psychology and linguistics.

For one thing, it should be clearly recog-

nized that a grammar is not a description of the performance of the speaker, but rather of his linguistic competence, and that a description of competence and a description of performance are different things. To illustrate, consider a trivial example where one would want to distinguish between a description of competence and a description of performance. Suppose that we were to attempt to give an account of how a child learns to multiply (rather than how he acquires his language). A child who has succeeded in learning this has acquired a certain competence, and he will perform in certain ways that are clearly at variance with this competence. Once he has learned to multiply, the correct description of his competence is a statement, in one or another form, of some of the rules of arithmetic—i.e., a specification of the set of triples (x, y, z) such that z is the product of x and y. On the other hand, a description of the performance of either an adult or a child (or a real computer) would be something quite different. It might, for example, be a specification of a set of quadruples (x, y, z, w) such that w is the probability that, given x and y, the person will compute the product as z. This set of quadruples would incorporate information about memory span, characteristic errors, lapses of attention, etc., information which is relevant to a performance table but not, clearly, to an account of what the person has learned—what is the basic competence that he has acquired. A person might memorize the performance table and perform on various simple-minded tests exactly as the person who knows the rules of arithmetic, but this would not, of course, show that he knows these rules. It seems clear that the description which is of greatest psychological relevance is the account of compe-

Reprinted from Ursula Bellugi-Klima and Roger Brown, eds., Monographs of the Society for Research in Child Development, *Ser. No. 92, 29.35–39 (1964), copyright 1964 by the Society for Research in Child Development, Inc., by permission of the author and the Society for Research in Child Development, Inc.*

tence, not that of performance, both in the case of arithmetic and the case of language. The deeper question concerns the kinds of structures the person has succeeded in mastering and internalizing, whether or not he utilizes them, in practice, without interference from the many other factors that play a role in actual behavior. For anyone concerned with intellectual processes, or any question that goes beyond mere data arranging, it is the question of competence that is fundamental. Obviously one can find out about competence only by studying performance, but this study must be carried out in devious and clever ways, if any serious result is to be obtained.

These rather obvious comments apply directly to study of language, child or adult. Thus it is absurd to attempt to construct a grammar that describes observed linguistic behavior directly. The tape recordings of this conference give a totally false picture of the conceptions of linguistic structure of the various speakers. Nor is this in the least bit surprising. The speaker has represented in his brain a grammar that gives an ideal account of the structure of the sentences of his language, but, when actually faced with the task of speaking or "understanding," many other factors act upon his underlying linguistic competence to produce actual performance. He may be confused or have several things in mind, change his plans in midstream, etc. Since this is obviously the condition of most actual linguistic performance, a direct record—an actual corpus—is almost useless, as it stands, for linguistic analysis of any but the most superficial kind.

Similarly, it seems to me that, if anything far-reaching and real is to be discovered about the actual grammar of the child, then rather devious kinds of observations of his performance, his abilities, and his comprehension in many different kinds of circumstance will have to be obtained, so that a variety of evidence may be brought to bear on the attempt to determine what is in fact his underlying linguistic competence at each stage of development. Direct description of the child's actual verbal output is no more likely to provide an account of the real underlying competence in the case of child language than in the case of adult language,

ability to multiply, or any other nontrivial rule-governed behavior. Not that one shouldn't start here, perhaps, but surely one shouldn't end here, or take too seriously the results obtained by one or another sort of manipulation of data of texts produced under normal conditions.

It is suggested in this paper—and this is a view shared by many psychologists and linguists—that the relation between competence and performance is somehow a probabilistic one. That is, somehow the higher probabilities in actual output converge towards the actual underlying grammar, or something of the sort. I have never seen a coherent presentation of this position, but, even as a vague idea, it seems to me entirely implausible. In particular, it surely cannot be maintained that the child forms his conception of grammatical structure by just assuming that high probabilities correspond to "rules" and that low probabilities can be disregarded, in some manner. Most of what the child actually produces and hears (and this is true for the adult as well) is of extremely low probability. In fact, in the case of sentence structure, the notion of probability loses all meaning. Except for a ridiculously small number (e.g., conventionalized greetings, etc., which, in fact, often do not even observe grammatical rules), all actual sentences are of a probability so low as to be effectively zero, and the same is true of structures (if, by the "structure" of a sentence, we mean the sequence of categories to which its successive words or morphemes belong). In actual speech, the highest probability must be assigned to broken and interrupted fragments of sentences or to sentences which begin in one way and end in a different, totally incompatible way (surely the tapes of this meeting would be sufficient to demonstrate this). From such evidence it would be absurd to conclude that this represents in any sense the linguistic consciousness of the speakers, as have been noted above. In general, it is a mistake to assume that—past the very earliest stages—much of what the child acquires is acquired by imitation. This could not be true on the level of sentence formation, since most of what the child hears is new and most of what he produces, past the very earliest stages, is new.

In the papers that have been presented here —and again, this is not unrepresentative of psychology and linguistics—there has been talk about grammars for the decoder and grammars for the encoder. Again, there are several undemonstrated (and, to me, quite implausible) assumptions underlying the view that the speaker's behavior should be modeled by one sort of system, and the hearer's by another. I have never seen a precise characterization of a "grammar for the encoder" or a "grammar for the decoder" that was not convertible, by a notational change, into the other. Furthermore, this is not surprising. The grammars that linguists construct are, in fact, quite neutral as between speaker and hearer. The problems of constructing models of performance, for the speaker and hearer, incorporating these grammars, are rather similar. This of course bears again on the question of relation between competence and performance. That is, the grammar that represents the speaker's competence is, of course, involved in both his speaking and interpreting of speech, and there seems no reason to assume that there are two different underlying systems, one involved in speaking, one in "understanding." To gain some insight into this underlying system, studies of the speaker's actual output, as well as of his ability to understand and interpret, are essential. But again, it cannot be too strongly emphasized that the data obtained in such studies can only serve as the grounds for inference about what constitutes the linguistic consciousness that provides the basis for language use.

A few other minor remarks of this sort might be made to indicate areas in which experimental methods that go far beyond mere observation of speech in normal situations will be needed to shed some light on underlying competence. To take just one example, it is often remarked, and, in particular, it is remarked in this paper, that in the case of lexical items (as distinct from "function words," so-called) it is generally possible to assign referential meaning rather easily. Of course, as clearly stated in the paper, this is in part a matter of degree. However, I think that the notion that it is generally a straightforward matter in the case of lexical items is a faulty conclusion derived from concentration on atypical examples. Perhaps in the case of "green," "table," etc., it is not difficult to determine what is the "referential meaning." But consider, on the other hand, such words as "useful," where the meaning is clearly "relational"—the things in the world cannot be divided into those that are useful and those that are not. In fact, the meaning of "useful," like that of a function word, in some respects, must be described in partly relational terms. Or, to take a more complicated example, consider a word like "expect." A brief attempt to prescribe the behaviors or situations that make application of this word appropriate will quickly convince one that this is entirely the wrong approach and that "referential meaning" is simply the wrong concept in this case. I don't think that such examples are at all exotic. It may be that such atypical examples as "table" and "green" are relatively more frequent in the early stages of language learning (though this remains to be shown, just as it remains to be shown that determination of referential meaning in such cases is in some sense "primitive"), and, if true, this may be important. However, this is clearly not going to carry one very far.

Consider now a rather comparable phonetic example. One of the problems to be faced is that of characterizing the child's phonemic system. Phonemes are often defined by linguists as constituting a family of mutually exclusive classes of phones, and this is the definition adopted in this paper. If this were true, there would be, in this case, a fairly simple relation between performance (i.e., a sequence of phones) and the underlying abstract system (i.e., the phonemic representation of this sequence). One might hope that by some simple classification technique one might determine the phonemic system from the phonetic record or the phonemic constitution of an utterance from the sequence of its phones. There is, however, extremely strong evidence (so it seems to me, at least) that phonemes cannot be defined as classes of sounds at all (and certainly not as mutually exclusive classes) and that the relation between a phonemic system and the phonetic record (just as the relation between a phonemic representation of an utterance and its actual sound) is much more remote and complex. I do not want to try to give the evidence here; it is being presented elsewhere in fair detail. But I would like to reiterate, for what it is worth, my conviction that the evidence is extremely strong.

These two examples are randomly chosen illustrations of a general tendency to over-simplify drastically the facts of linguistic structure and to assume that the determination of competence can be derived from description of a corpus by some sort of sufficiently developed data-processing techniques. My feeling is that this is hopeless and that only experimentation of a fairly indirect and ingenious sort can provide evidence that is at all critical for formulating a true account of the child's grammar (as in the case of investigation of any other real system). Consequently, I would hope that some of the research in this area would be diverted from recording of texts towards attempting to tap the child's underlying abilities to use and comprehend sentences, to detect deviance and compensate for it, to apply rules in new situations, to form highly specific concepts from scattered bits of evidence, and so on. There are, after all, many ways in which such study can be approached. Thus, for example, the child's ability to repeat sentences and nonsentences, phonologically possible sequences and phonologically impossible ones, etc., might provide some evidence as to the underlying system that he is using. There is surely no doubt that the child's achievements in systematizing linguistic data, at every stage, go well beyond what he actually produces in normal speech. Thus it is striking that advances are generally "across the board." A child who does not produce initial s + consonant clusters may begin to produce them all, at approximately the same time, thus distinguishing for the first time between "cool" and "school," etc.—but characteristically will do this in just the right words, indicating that the correct phonemic representation of these words was present to the mind even at the stage where it did not appear in speech. Similarly, some of the data of Brown and Fraser seem to suggest that interrogatives, negatives, and other syntactically related forms appear and are distinguished from declaratives at approximately the same time, for some children. If so, this suggests that what has actually happened is that the hitherto latent system of verbal auxiliaries is now no longer suppressed in actual speech, as previously. Again, this can be investigated directly. Thus a child producing speech in a "telegraphic style" can be shown to have an underlying, fuller conception of sentence structure (unrealized in his speech, but actively involved in comprehension) if misplacement of the elements he does not produce leads to difficulties of comprehension, inability to repeat, etc., while correct placement gives utterances intelligible to him, and so on.

I would, finally, like to say that I don't intend these remarks as criticism of the present work, as it stands. It is clear from what has been presented already that quite a bit can be learned from observation of the spoken record. I make these remarks only to indicate a difficulty which I think is looming rather large and to which some serious attention will have to be given fairly soon.

DAN I. SLOBIN

53 Slobin belongs to the growing group of young psycholinguists who were trained or directly influenced by psycholinguists, such as George A. Miller and Roger Brown; linguists, such as Noam Chomsky, Morris Halle, J. J. Katz; and others in Cambridge, Massachusetts.

His doctoral dissertation, entitled *Grammatical Transformations in Childhood and Adulthood* (1963), was an important contribution. He then moved to

Berkeley, where he has been very actively engaged in independent psycholinguistic research, as well as in surveying and translating Russian studies on language acquisition.

His best known work is probably "The Acquisition of Russian as a Native Language," which first appeared in *The Genesis of Language* (F. Smith and G. A. Miller, eds., Cambridge: M. I. T. Press, 1966, pp. 129–48). Since it has been reprinted in various anthologies, we prefer to present here his less known, but most interesting study, "Grammatical Development in Russian-Speaking Children."

Among his studies are the following: "Imitation and Grammatical Development in Children," in N. S. Endler, et. al, eds., *Contemporary Issues in Developmental Psychology*, New York: Holt, Rinehart and Winston, 1968; and "Early Grammatical Development in Several Languages, with Special Attention to Soviet Research," Working Paper No. 11, Language-Behavior Research Laboratory, Berkeley: University of California, 1968.

A. B. A.

GRAMMATICAL DEVELOPMENT IN RUSSIAN-SPEAKING CHILDREN

The striking recent advances of developmental psycholinguistics have been based on careful study of the acquisition of English as a native language. The engrossing debate in regard to innate factors in language acquisition however (McNeill, in press) may be illuminated by cross-linguistic comparisons of child language. Unfortunately, extensive data on the acquisition of non-Indo-European languages are not yet available; there is, however, a sizeable Soviet body of literature which is worthy of the attention of American psycholinguists. Although Russian is also an Indo-European language, it is sufficiently different from English—most clearly in its highly inflectional grammatical structure—to serve as a useful contrast case to sharpen notions of universal aspects of language acquisition and linguistic competence.

In order to make the discussion intelligible to a non-Russian-speaking audience, a few words about the grammatical structure of the language are in order. Russian has three genders and six cases; nouns, adjectives, and

Reprinted from K. Riegel, ed., *The Development of Language Functions,* University of Michigan Language Development Program, Report No. 8, Ann Arbor, 1965, pp. 93–101, by permission of the author and the University of Michigan Press.

pronouns show gender, case, and number. Verbs are conjugated for person and number, and, in the past tense, also for gender of subject noun. Verbs are marked for tense (three tenses) and aspect (perfective-imperfective, and, for verbs of motion, also determinate-indeterminate). There are many participial forms. The morphology is highly productive, and freely-used suffixes of many sorts abound (e.g. diminuitive, augmentative, endearing, pejorative, agentive, and so on). Word order is much freer than in English.

The most careful and intensive longitudinal study of a child's language development ever published anywhere is probably the monumental work of Aleksandr N. Gvozdex (1961), a Soviet linguist and teacher. He kept a diary of the speech of his son, Zhenya, almost daily for the first few years of the child's life, and recorded his language extensively until the age of nine (1921–1929). The following discussion is based primarily on the speech of Zhenya, supplemented with data from psycholinguistic experiments with preschool children.

EARLY SYNTAX

The beginning stages of syntactic development look very much like those of English-speaking children described by Braine (1963a), Brown and Fraser (1963), and Miller and Ervin (1964). There is clearly a small class of "pivot words" (P) and a large open class of words (O), which can be combined into three types of two-word sentences: P + O, O + P, and O + O (McNeill, in press). Gvozdev argues that these sentences are constructed, rather than imitated or memorized as units, because most of the single words appear as separate utterances, and because the two-word combinations differ from adult sentences in form.

Two-word sentences appear at about 1,8; at first there are only a few such sentences, but they become the usual utterance type by 1,9. By 1,10 they are replaced in frequency by longer sentences. As has been noted by other investigators, new pivots are often playfully practiced, the child uttering long series of pivot sentences, holding the pivot constant and substituting a variety of words from the open class (cf. Weir, 1962). In line with American findings, membership in both pivot and open classes is heterogeneous from the point of view of part-of-speech membership in the adult language.

The first three-word sentence is a simple negation, which involves placing a negative element at the beginning of a sentence. This is the same initial negation form found by Bellugi (in press) though the adult model in Russian often involves a double negative. For example, the adult form *nyet nikavó*[1] ("not no-one"—i.e., "there is no one") is given by the child as *nyet kavó. Nyet, dam* is the child's equivalent of adult *nyet, nye dam* ("no, not I-will-give"). The same negative element, *nyet*, is used in all cases, even where the adult form would have only the single negative element *nye*: e.g. instead of *nye karmí* (don't feed), the child says *nyet kamlí*. Presumably, acoustic marking singles out *nyet*, rather than *nye*, as the primordial negative element. (It should also be noted that *nyet* is the independent negative element in Russian, analogous to English *no*.)

Another source of length is the addition of content words to short sentences. Gvozdev thinks that forms learned more recently appear later in sentences, and gives the example of elaboration of one-word utterances to two-word subject-object sentences, and, with the acquisition of new verbs, to

subject-object-verb sentences, although subject-verb-object order is dominant in Russian. For example, at the first stage the child may say *mama*; at the second, *mama niska* ("mama book"); and at the third *mama niska tsitats* ("mama book read"). (The forms are all unmarked in the child's system, and Russian does not use articles.) This subject-object-verb order is at first the dominant order in the child's speech, being replaced by subject-verb-object at about 1,11. (It is interesting to note that according to Greenberg [1963], it is apparently a linguistic universal that subject precede object in the dominant actor-action construction of a language, and that the two most common patterns are SVO and SOV.)

Word order is quite inflexible at each of the early stages of syntactic development. One might have predicted that Russian children, being exposed to a great variety of word orders, would first learn the morphological markers for such classes as subject, object, and verb, and combine them in any order. This is, however, hardly the case. Child grammar begins with unmarked forms —generally the noun in what corresponds to the nominative singular, the verb in its adult imperative or infinitive form, and so on. Morphology develops later than syntax, and word order is as inflexible for little Russian children as it is for Americans.

Arguments have been advanced by Braine (1963b) and by Jenkins and Palermo (1964) which rely upon the ordinal sequences of words in adult language to account for the order of elements in child sentences, and for the formation of word classes. Not only do the Soviet data cast doubt on these interpretations, but, as Bever, Fodor, and Weksel (1965) have pointed out, even in English, which does not make great use of inflection, order is not as important a feature of syntactic structure as might be imagined. It is certainly a much less important feature in Russian, thus lending further support to the critique developed by Bever et al. There must be something in LAD, the built-in "language acquisition device" discussed by McNeill (in press) and others, which favors beginning language with ordered sequences of unmarked classes, regardless of the degree of

---

[1] The transliteration is a very rough approximation to the sounds of Russian, and does not always match the Russian orthography.

correspondence of such a system with the input language.[2]

LATER SYNTAX

I have not yet examined Gvozdev's work to determine what happens to syntactic patterns after this early level; his classification of sentence types is not always the most useful, and extensive effort would be required— and should be expended—to reorganize his data for other sorts of analysis. He contends that by age three almost all of the complex and complex-subordinate sentence types of adult Russian are present, and that the child knows all of the generic grammatical categories (case, gender, tense, and so on) and has a good idea of their meanings. No new uses of grammatical cases enter after 3,9. By contrast, the learning of morphology and morphophonemics goes on for very much longer. It takes until seven or eight to sort out all of the proper conjugational and declensional suffixes and categories, stress and sound alternations, and the like. The Russian child does not fully master his morphology until he is several years older than the age at which the American child is believed to have essentially completed his primary grammatical learning. In this sense, then, it may be more difficult to learn to speak one language natively than another—though the basic learning is accomplished very rapidly.

(This point cannot be properly evaluated, however, until we have more information about the grammar of English-speaking children between the ages of five and eight.

---

[2] It may well be that order is important in the "base structure" of Russian, thus supporting McNeill's proposal (in press) that children "talk base strings directly." The most economical representation of an inflected language like Russian would order the language in the underlying representation. Inflections could then be added to the characteristic positions of parts of speech, and an additional rule or rules would then re-order this string. All of the world's languages make use of order in their grammatical structure, but not all languages have morphological systems. It would be reasonable, then, for LAD to assume the language to be ordered, to adopt a given order as a first guess, and later learn that it can be changed. This interpretation, of course, minimizes the contribution of the linguistic input, suggesting that it is more important in providing tests for hypotheses about the organization of language than it is in acting as an observation base for inference.

Full mastery of the auxiliary system, the subjunctive, and quantifiers, for example, is quite late in American children. It is not yet possible to adequately compare the lateness of such accomplishments with the lateness of other sorts of accomplishments in Russian. The unanswered question is whether the speech of a Russian seven year old is heard as more deviant from adult speech than is the speech of an American seven year old.)

MORPHOLOGY

Morphological markers enter when sentences increase from two to three or four words in length. All words are unmarked in Zhenya's speech until about 1,10, and then, in the one month between 1,11 and 2,0 there is a sudden emergence of contrasting morphological elements in various grammatical categories. In this one month, previously unmarked nouns are marked for: (1) number, (2) nominative, accusative, and genitive cases, and (3) past tense, and (4) present tense. Apparently once the principles of inflection and derivation are acquired—or, at any rate, the principle of suffixing—the principle is immediately applied over a wide range of types.

There are many other examples of simultaneous emergence of a grammatical principle in several domains. For example, gender agreement appeared simultaneously both in regard to adjective-noun agreement and noun-past tense of verb agreement. When a new grammatical case enters, it serves several functions at once. A variety of prepositions enter within a short period, and are combined with nouns in various grammatical cases. One is struck by the rapidity with which a principle is suddenly applied to an entire domain—and to the correct domain.

(Note, by the way, that the Russian child has no apparent difficulty in discovering morpheme boundaries. From the very beginning of inflections one sees a free use of word stems combined with a huge variety of bound morphemes. The word stem is clearly a psychologically real unit.)

Overregularizations are rampant in the child's learning of Russian morphology— small wonder, with the great variety of inflectional categories, and with the additional great variety of forms within each category, determined on the basis of both sound and grammatical relations. For example, not only must the child learn an instrumental case ending for each masculine, feminine, and neuter singular and plural noun and adjective, but within each of these sub-categories there are several different phonologically conditioned suffixes. The child's solution is to seize upon one suffix at first—probably the most frequent and/or most clearly marked acoustically—and use it for every instance of that particular grammatical category. Fox example, Gvozdev's son Zhenya at first used the suffix -om for all singular noun instrumental endings, although this suffix is used only for masculine and neuter singular nouns. This suffix, however, has only one other function—a masculine and neuter prepositional case ending for adjectives. The corresponding dominant feminine singular noun instrumental ending, -oi, on the other hand, serves a variety of functions, being an adjectival suffix for four cases in the feminine and one in the masculine. Thus, although feminine nouns are more frequent in Russian child speech, Zhenya initially used the suffix of fewer meanings—-om—for all instances of the instrumental case. This clarifies Gvozdev's statement that grammatical are acquired earlier than morphological details. The child already possesses the category of instrumental case—and marks it accordingly—but it will take several years, perhaps, before he learns to correctly mark every instance of the instrumental in accordance with gender and with morphophonemic principles.

Large-scale research with preschoolers (Zakharova, 1958) has similarly revealed early stereotyped case endings for each case in a child's repertoire. Like Zhenya, Zakharova's subjects used the suffix -om as a universal instrumental, and -u as a universal accusative. These endings are of high frequency, clearly marked acoustically in adult speech, and limited in the number of functions they perform.

Zakharova also found that, as gender comes to be more important in classifying nouns, other additional endings for each case enter. They do not, however, peacefully coexist with the already established endings. When a

child learns, for example, that -oi—the feminine noun singular instrumental ending—can also serve as a noun instrumental ending, he abandons the masculine and neuter instrumental, -om, which he has been using, and for a while uses -oi as a universal instrumental. Only later does -om re-enter to assume its place in standard Russian. Practice clearly does not insure the survival of a form in child speech—regardless of whether or not that form corresponds to adult usage (and, presumably, regardless of whether or not its usage by the child is "reinforced" by adults). (This is very similar to the development of the past tense in English, in which irregular strong forms, like did, are at first used correctly, only to be later driven out by over-generalizations from the regular weak forms, giving rise to transitory though persistent forms like doed.) Popova (1958) presents additional evidence of ontogenetic replacement of one suffix by another, finding that very young children overgeneralize the feminine past tense of the verb, and that older children overgeneralize the masculine.

As noted above, full mastery of the morphological system comes relatively late in Russian-speaking children. The distinction between mass and count nouns is not stabilized until age eight; the distinction between animate and inanimate nouns in the accusative is mastered only at four; gender agreement between nouns and verbs in the past comes at three, although agreement of number and person come a year earlier; declension of masculine and feminine nouns ending in palatalized consonants is not mastered until six or seven. Soviet psycholinguists interpret the order and rate of acquisition of morphological classes in terms of the relative semantic or conceptual difficulty of various classification criteria.

One line of evidence in this argument is the observation that lexical items referring to certain semantic categories appear at the same time as those categories become morphologically marked. For example, at 1,10, in Zhenya's speech, one finds the first use of the word mnogo (much, many) at the same time as the singular-plural distinction in noun markings. The words "right away" and "soon" enter at the same time as the future tense. And so on.

An attempt is made to set up the following order of acquisition of morphological class in reference to their meanings:

1. Those classes whose reference is clearly concrete emerge first. The first morphological distinction is number, at 1,10, followed shortly by diminuitive suffixing of nouns. The imperative, with its immediate, expressive character, also appears very early.

2. Classes based on relational semantic criteria—cases, tenses, and persons of the verb—emerge later than those with concrete reference.

3. The conditional is very late, not being used until 2,10, though its grammatical structure is exceedingly simple. Conditional subordinate clauses are also late, emerging at about 2, 8. In both cases, it seems to be the semantic or conceptual and not the grammatical aspect which is difficult for the child.

4. Noun endings indicating abstract categories of quality and action continue to be added until as late as seven. The only derivational noun suffixes learned before three are those of clearly concrete or emotive reference—diminuitive and augmentative, endearing and pejorative.

5. Grammatical gender is responsible for what is perhaps the most difficult and drawn-out linguistic learning of the Russian-speaking child, although it is almost always unequivocally marked phonetically. This is a category almost entirely in semantic correlates, and apparently such correlates are an important aid in learning form-class distinctions. At first the child uses the feminine past tense ending for almost all nouns, regardless of their gender markings—even he knows they are semantically masculine (e.g. *papa*). Later the child will use masculine past tense for many nouns which are semantically feminine. The verb inflection is simply not treated as having semantic content. Likewise, the child will first use one stereotyped case ending for all nouns in that case, regardless of their gender (even if can correctly identify gender-class membership on the basis of pronoun substitution and adjective agreement).

The semantic and conceptual aspects of grammatical classes thus clearly play an important role in determining the order of their development and subdivision.

REFERENCES

(More detailed discussion of Soviet psycholinguistics and Soviet child language can be found in Slobin [in press] and references cited therein.)

Bellugi, Ursula. "The Emergence of Inflections and Negation Systems in the Speech of Two Children." In T. Bever and W. Weksel, eds., *Studies in psycholinguistics*, (in press).

Bever, T., J. J. Fodor, and W. Weksel. "On the Acquisition of Syntax: A Critique of 'Contextual Generalization.'" *Psychology Review*, LXXII (1965), 467–82.

Braine, M. D. S. "The Ontogeny of English Phrase Structure: The First Phase." *Language*, XXXIX (1963a), 1–13.

Braine, M. D. S. "On Learning the Grammatical Order of Words." *Psychology Review*, LXX (1963b), 323–48.

Brown, R., and C. Fraser. "The Acquisition of Syntax." In C. N. Cofer and Barbara Musgrave, eds., *Verbal Behavior and Learning*. New York: McGraw-Hill Book Company, 1963, pp. 158–97.

Greenberg, J. H., ed. *Universals of Language*. Cambridge, Mass.: The M.I.T. Press, 1963.

Gvozdev, A. N. *Voprosy izucheniya detskoĭ rechi* [*Questions of the Study of Child Speech*]. Moscow: Akad. Pedag. Nauk RSFSR, 1961.

Jenkins, J. J., and D. S. Palermo. "Mediation Processes and the Acquisition of Linguistic Structure." *Monogr. Soc. Res. Child Develpm.*, XXIX (1964), 141–69.

McNeill, D. "Developmental Psycholinguistics." In T. Bever and W. Weksel, eds., *Studies in Psycholinguistics*, (forthcoming).

Miller, W., and Susan Ervin. "The Development of Grammar in Child Language." *Monogr. Soc. Res. Child Develpm.*, XXIX (1964), 9–34.

Popova, M. I. "Grammaticheskie elementy yazyka v rechi detei preddoshkol'nogo vozrasta" ["Grammatical Elements of Language in the Speech of Pre-preschool Children"]. *Vopr. Psikhol.*, IV (1958), 106–17.

Slobin, D. I. "The Acquisition of Russian as a Native Language." In T. Bever and W. Weksel, eds., *Studies in Psycholinguistics*, (forthcoming).

Slobin, D. I. "Soviet Psycholinguistics." In N. O'Connor, ed., *Present Day Russian Psychology*. Oxford University Press, Pergamon, (forthcoming).

Weir, Ruth. *Language in the Crib*. The Hague: Mouton & Co., 1962.

Zakharova, A. V. "Usvoenie doshkol'nikami padezhnykh form" ["Mastery by Preschoolers of Forms of Grammatical Case"]. *Dokl. Akad. Pedag. Nauk RSFSR*, III (1958), 81–84.

54 David McNeill is a very active and productive psycholinguist in the field of language acquisition, or, as he refers to it, "developmental psycholinguistics." His study under this title, "Developmental Psycholinguistics" has appeared in F. Smith and G. A. Miller, eds., *The Genesis of Language* (M. I. T. Press, 1966), pp. 15–84. It could not be included in this volume because of its size, but the reader is urged to read that interesting paper.

Another monograph-length work by McNeill, "The Development of Language," is about to appear in P. A. Mussen (ed.) *Carmichael's Manual of Child Psychology*.

The present paper, which was presented at the Edinburgh University Conference on Psycholinguistics (March, 1966), is concerned with the problems of the acquisition of abstract structures, the speed of acquisition by the child, and how these may be accounted for by Chomsky's and Katz's theory of innate ideas and linguistic universals. He then makes his own proposals, on the basis of language acquisition data of two Japanese children.

Note: This paper is formally discussed by Colin Fraser *et al.* in *Psycholinguistics Papers* (Edinburgh University Press, 1966), pp. 115–32.

See also the study by G. A. Miller and D. McNeill on "Psycholinguistics," in G. Lindzey and E. Aaronson, eds., *Handbook of Social Psychology*. Reading, Mass.: Addison-Wesley, 1969, Vol. III, pp. 666–794.

A. B. A.

THE CREATION OF
LANGUAGE BY CHILDREN

Superficial acquaintance with young children reveals one of the problems with which a theory of language acquisition must be concerned. At the age of eighteen months or so, children begin to form simple two- and three-word sentences. At four, they are able to produce sentences of almost every conceivable syntactic type. In approximately thirty months, therefore, language is acquired, at least that part of it having to do with syntax. The process of acquisition, as the title of this paper somewhat fancifully puts it, is one of invention. On the basis of a fundamental capacity for language, each generation creates language anew, and does so with astonishing speed.

A second problem for theories of language

acquisition concerns the nature of what is acquired. A transformational grammar entails a distinction between the superficial and underlying structure of sentences. The underlying structure must be so arranged that transformations can apply—a requirement which, in general, means that superficial and underlying structures differ. The linguistic information included in the underlying structure is essential for comprehending sentences; yet it is abstract information, never directly manifested in the surface form of speech. Somehow, children acquire such abstractions.

These problems are separate—the acquisition of abstract structures and the speed of acquisition, although an argument can be made that the solution to one is a solution to the other. More will be said on this below. But first, it is necessary to describe the general point of view to be explored here. As suggested in the first paragraph, this is that children are endowed with a biologically founded, inborn capacity for language acquisition. This hypothesis is not new. The

Reprinted from J. Loyns and R. J. Wales, eds., Psycholinguistics Paper (*Edinburgh: Edinburgh University Press, 1966*), *99–115, by permission of the author and publisher.*

existence of an inborn capacity for language was taken for granted during the nineteenth century. Horatio Hale, for example, in his Vice-Presidential address to the Anthropology Section of the American Association for the Advancement of Science in 1886 made large use of a presumed capacity for language in accounting for the origin of different linguistic stocks among Oregon and California Indians. Although seen as conservative, his theory was well received. However, stated so simply, the view that children are endowed with a capacity for language is not a particularly interesting hypothesis. It merely repeats the observation, apparently true, that man is alone among all animals in possessing language. To make the hypothesis interesting, it is necessary to show what some of the specific features of this capacity might be. On this, some definite suggestions can be made.

Chomsky (1965), Katz (1966), and others as well, have argued that the specific content of a child's capacity for language is manifested in the form of linguistic universals. These are features that define the general form of human language and so appear in natural languages everywhere, regardless of physical or cultural setting. A breif review of their argument will set the context for what follows.

One may think of the problem of language acquisition as being essentially the same as the problem faced by linguists in evaluating grammars written for particular languages. In constructing a grammar, a linguist hopes to reconstruct the tacit competence possessed by fluent speakers of the language. A child hopes to become such a speaker, so he, too, must reconstruct the competence of fluent speakers. In other words, he must formulate the grammar of the language to which he is exposed. One way a linguist has to evaluate the accuracy with which a grammar represents linguistic knowledge is to become a fluent speaker himself, and test the formulations of the grammar against his own intuitions. A child, however, cannot do this. He cannot evaluate the grammar that he supposes to underlie the language he overhears by becoming first a fluent speaker and then judging the grammar against his intuitions.

It is acquisition of the grammar in the first place that poses the problem. A child must evaluate proposed grammars in a different manner; and this, too, corresponds to a method of evaluation available to linguists.

In addition to testing a grammar against the intuitions of a native speaker, a linguist may use linguistic theory to select one grammar from a set of candidates, the selected grammar then representing the competence of native speakers. The selection is based on the existence of various linguistic universals. It is in this sense that linguistic theory is a hypothesis about the general form of human language. Evaluation conducted in this manner leads to what Chomsky (1965) calls 'explanatory adequacy.' Explanatory adequacy is obtained when linguistic theory gives a *principled* basis for accepting one way of representing the competence of the speakers of a language over other possible ways. A grammar descriptive of linguistic competence is explained when it can be derived from linguistic theory.

Language acquisition by children can be regarded in the same way. The terms of linguistic theory, if they were available to a child, would allow him to make a principled choice of the grammar by which to represent the competence of fluent speakers of the language to which he is exposed, and thus to become such a speaker himself. According to the argument advanced by Chomsky and Katz, this is precisely what a child does because linguistic theory describes his inborn capacity for language. An innate capacity for language, therefore, can be represented by the set of linguistically universal statements that are organized into linguistic theory. The acquisition of language can be regarded as the guided (principled) choice of a grammar, made on the basis of a child's innate capacity, a choice consistent with the evidence contained in the corpus of speech provided by the mature speakers to which a child is exposed.

Linguistic theory is under development and is far from complete. Linguists cannot yet make principled choices of grammars. Nonetheless, it is fairly clear what some of the universal statements in linguistic theory will be. They will include such matters as the formal distinction between rules of formation and transformation; the distinction between base and surface structure; the definitions of various grammatical relations, such as subject-predicate, main verb-object, and, possibly, modifier-head; plus many more. Some comment will be made below on each of these, particularly the last set—the basic grammatical relations. First, however, it is necessary to clarify two implications of these proposals of Chomsky and Katz. How does this theory account for the acquisition of abstract features, and how does it account for the speed of acquisition?

As to the first question, the answer is that it is badly put. The question should be instead: why do languages have abstract features at all? The answer to this revised question is quite simple: children place them there. It is possible for languages to contain abstract features because in each language these features correspond to aspects of children's capacity for language acquisition. Along with much else, the genersl notion of abstract phrase structures being transformed into surface structures is included in linguistic theory. This decision is independently motivated by many linguistic considerations, and does not depend on the effort to formulate a theory of language acquisition. The implication for language acquisition is that much of what children acquire consists of particular transformations, since most universal features of language are related to the base structure (Chomsky, 1965).

In answer to the second question—how to account for the speed of language acquisition—it is necessary to suppose that the features of language that correspond to the linguistic universals are among the first acquired. This hypothesis leads us to expect that children's first grammatical efforts will include the abstract features contained in linguistic theory. If it should be otherwise, an inborn capacity for language acquisition could *not* account for the speed of acquisition. However, if it should be the case the children display abstract features of language in their earliest grammatical productions, then one hypothesis—that these features reflect a child's biological endowment—can account for both the speed of acuisition and abstract-

ness of what is acquired. Some evidence in support of this hypothesis is presented in the next section.

THE BASIC GRAMMATICAL RELATIONS

The basic grammatical relations are the concepts of subject and predicate of a sentence; main verb and object of a verb phrase; and modifier and head of a noun phrase. They are defined in linguistic theory as configurations of the base structure of sentences (Katz and Postal, 1964; Chomsky, 1965). The subject of a sentence, for example, is the NP directly dominated by s in the base structure. The predicate of a sentence is the VP directly dominated by s (or, alternatively, dominated by Pred P—the difference will be ignored here, but see Chomsky, 1965, for discussion). The object of a verb phrase is the NP directly dominated by VP, whereas the main verb of a verb phrase is the V directly dominated by VP. Although not mentioned in the reference cited, the modifier of a noun phrase will be taken to be some kind of determiner directly dominated by NP, whereas the head of a noun phrase will be defined as the N directly dominated by NP. These definitions appear to be universal, which is to say that all languages appear to possess the configurations necessary to apply them, and so the definitions themselves are entered in linguistic theory. They may be written as follows, in a formulation that will become convenient later on:

Subject of   NP, s
Predicate of   VP, s
Main verb of   V, VP
Object of   NP, VP
Modifier of   D, NP
Head of   N, NP

The configurations to which these definitions apply are located in the base structure of sentences, not the surface structure, because of sentences like *John is easy to please* and *John is eager to please*, where the surface structures are the same, yet the word *John* stands in two different grammatical relations —object in the first, subject in the second. Thus, the definitions are 'abstract' in the sense used here.

The hypothesis given above—that abstract

features mentioned in linguistic theory will appear in children's earliest grammatical productions—requires that the basic grammatical relations will be honored in very early speech collected from children. One source of suport for this hypothesis comes from a child exposed to English, a little boy called Adam by Brown and Bellugi (1964).

At the time his speech was first recorded, Adam appeared to have three grammatical classes—verbs, nouns, and pivots. The evidence for distinguishing these classes was distributional. This is to say that English verbs had privileges of occurrence in Adam's speech different from those of English nouns. Adam's pivot class had a third privilege of occurrence, but it was grammatically heterogeneous from the point of view of English.

A little artihmetic shows that with three grammatical classes, N, V, and P, there are $(3)^2 = 9$ different possible sentence types two words long, and $(3)^3 = 27$ different possible sentence types three words long. If a child were combining words at random, all (or nearly all) these nine and twenty-seven different combinations should occur. However, not every combination is a manifestation of one or another basic grammatical relation. Only four of the nine two-word possibilities correspond to one or more of these relations, the remaining five being inadmissible from this point of view. An admissible combination would be N + V (e.g., *Adam run*), corresponding to the subject-predicate relation. An inadmissible combination would be P + P (e.g., *my that*). Among the three-word combinations, only eight manifest one or another basic grammatical relation, the remaining nineteen being inadmissible. An example of an admissible combination is V + N + N (e.g., *change Adam diaper*), corresponding to the verb-object relation, whereas an inadmissible combination would be V + V + N (e.g., *come eat pablum*).

Examples of every admissible combination were contained in the first three samples of Adam's speech that Brown and Bellugi collected. In itself, this result is not surprising. Altogether, some eight hours' recording were involved, and some 400 utterances from Adam. If the child were placing words together on some principle that allowed most of the possible combinations, those cor-

responding to the basic grammatical relations would be expected on grounds of the large sample size. However, all 400 of Adam's sentences were of the admissible type. There were no others. Thus, although *change Adam diaper* might have occurred, *come eat pablum* did not; for details, see McNeill (1966).

That this should be the outcome is certainly not obvious, *a priori*. In fact, one might have supposed that the result would have been different. Superficially, adult speech contains many examples of inadmissible sequences of Adam's grammatical classes. For example, the sentence type represented by *come and eat your pablum* is common enough. To judge from some of Braine's (1963a) experiments with artificial languages, people find it difficult to avoid acquiring patterns to which they are exposed, even when told that the patterns to not exemplify what they are to acquire. If we assume that the same sensitivity holds true of young children, then some explanation must be offered for the fact that Adam did not produce setences like *come eat pablum* after hearing examples like *come and eat your pablum* in parental speech. The explanation that suggests itself is that Adam was attempting to use only those sentence patterns that express the basic grammatical relations. An adult sentence like *come and eat pablum* did not serve as a model utterance becaue it does not directly manifest these relations, being instead a rather complex construction involving several transformations not yet part of the child's grammatical competence. In short, Adam may have been actively searching for ways to express the basic grammatical relations in his speech. As a result, his own earliest grammatical constructions were limited to direct expressions of these relations.

Thus, there is indication that children's earliest speech contains abstract linguistic features, in this case, the basic grammatical relations. The same conclusion is reached from an examination of the early speech of children acquiring Japanese.

I have recently begun collecting samples of speech from two children who live in Tokyo. Each child is visited twice monthly, in her home, where everything said to and by the child is tape recorded. Both girls are (at the present time: February 1966) approximately two years of age. Neither is especially gifted at Japanese; and from one exactly seventeen word-combinations have been recorded during the past three months. The second child, however, produces large quantities of patterned speech, and the evidence described below comes from her. In the interest of maintaining the tradition begun by Brown, she will be called Izanami, after the goddess of Japanese mythology who helped create the world.

In certain respects, Japancese is particularly revealing for the study of language acquisition. It contrasts with English in several ways, of which one is especially relevant to the question now under consideration. Japanese is a postpositional rather than a prepositional language. Very roughly, postpositions are comparable to prepositions in English (although not all English prepositions can be translated into Japanese postpositions, and conversely). Among the postpositions that have no English equivalent are two that obligatorily mark, in the surface structure of Japanese sentences, the grammatical subject of the sentence.

The two subject markers are *wa* and *ga*. Although both follow the subject NP of a sentence, they are not identical, and receive different analyses in a transformational grammar of Japanese (Kuroda, 1965). The differences between *wa* and *ga* will first be introduced by a few examples, then, following Kuroda, they will be characterized somewhat more systematically:

A man-ga is standing on the corner
The man-wa is standing on the corner
Man-wa is mortal

In answer to the question, 'which man is sick?', one would reply

That man-ga is sick

whereas in answer to the question, 'who is sick?', one could reply

That man-wa is sick

A person, naming some object, would say

This-wa is a digital computer,

whereas hearing someone refer to the vending machine in the corner as a computer, one could correct him by saying

This-ga is a digital computer.

The distributional similarity of *wa* and *ga*

is as close in Japanese as in these English examples, so that what is presented to a child in parental speech will not distinguish them. However, as the examples indicate, *wa* and *ga* play very different grammatical roles. Subjects of sentences that state general truths, subjects that have attributes given to them by the predicate, subjects that function like the logical premises of judgments, and words like *this* and *that* when they are used in definitions, all take *wa*. Quite often, *wa* can be translated into English with the expression 'as for . . . .' Thus, the examples given above can all be rendered:

As for that man, he is standing on the corner
As for man, he is mortal
As for that man, he is sick
As for this, it is a digital computer

In each case, an attribute—standing on the corner, mortality, computerhood—is judged applicable to the subject of the sentence. Kuroda calls this usage 'predicational judgment.' So much for *wa*.

The postposition *ga* differs from *wa* in two ways. That is to say, *ga* has two distinct senses, both different from *wa*. In one sense, *ga* is used in simple description. Instead of the predicate of the sentence being a property judged applicable to the subject, the subject and predicate stand in some roughly equal relation to one another. They are merely linked (see Weinreich, 1963, for a discussion of this relation). The connection is always felt to be momentary, as in *a man is standing on the street corner*. Typically, the subject of the sentence is a specific, yet indefinite noun, as in the example just cited. One does not attribute a property to an arbitrary member of the category, *man*. One merely observes what he is doing at the moment. The descriptive sense of *ga* reflects such momentary linkage.

The second use of *ga* excludes possibilities from a known set of alternatives. In this sense of *ga*, information is conveyed not only about the subject of the sentence, but also about the members of the set of alternatives not mentioned in the sentence. Thus, to use one of Kuroda's examples, if three people, John, Bill, and Tom are lying side by side in three beds, and a doctor arrives asking, 'Who is sick?', the answer *John-ga is sick* means not only that John is ill but, in addition, that Bill and Tom are well. Heavy stress often conveys this meaning in English— *Jóhn is sick.* The corresponding sentence with *wa* conveys information about John alone. If the reply is *John-wa is sick,* meaning 'as for John, he is sick,' nothing is learned about the state of health of Bill or Tom. The vaporous quality of much Japanese philosophy may exist because of this postposition, *wa.*

To turn now to the acquisition of Japanese: the proposal made before, and supported by the evidence of Adam's speech, strongly suggests that the postpositions *wa* and *ga* will appear early in Izanami's speech. This is because the subjects of adult sentences are consistently marked by *wa* and *ga,* which, in turn, relate to the base structure through fairly simple transformations. If Izanami is attempting to express the grammatical relation of subject in her sentences, she would have a basis for discovering and then using these transformations. If, on the other hand, she is not attempting to express the relation of subject, there would be no basis for her to formulate the transformation, so *wa* and *ga* should not appear.

What of the distinction between *wa* and *ga?* Izanami's mother uses *wa* twice as often as she uses *ga.* Presumably, this would favor acquisition of *wa.* Moreover, *wa* is involved whenever the mother introduces new vocabulary, describes permanent states and general truths, or attributes properties to objects. Some examples addressed to Izanami are *this-wa is a tape recorder* (pointing to it), *grandmother-wa lives in Kyoto,* and *papa-wa is big.* We can be certain that such sentences from Izanami's mother are understood, inasmuch as they are the principal means of introducing new vocabulary and information to the child, and there is no doubt that Izanami acquires both. Moreover, all these sentences involve a concrete object as the designated subject of the sentence (*this* accompanied by ostensive definition, *grandmother,* *papa*), as opposed to the *ga*-marked subject of a sentence, which is always an arbitrary member of a general category. For all these reasons, therefore, we might expect *wa* to appear.

The mother uses *ga* both in simple descriptions of transitory states and in the exclusion of alternatives from a known set. Some examples of the former are *you-ga sit well* (as Izanami manages not to topple over while sitting Japanese-style on the floor), and *yes, a bird-ga is on the fence;* whereas some examples of the latter are *which-ga do you want?* and *your other friends-ga want to play with you.* It is not clear what to expect Izanami to do with the descriptive *ga.* On the assumption, often made, that children develop grammatical relations by the labelling of enduring physical relations in the real world (e.g., the names of objects, or the relation of agent to action, as in the fact that people walk, children cry, houses stand, etc.), one would not expect *ga* to be acquired early. *Ga* is never used when these conditions prevail; *wa* is the required postposition. On the other hand, assuming that this kind of relation with the physical world is irrelevant to the acquisition of syntax, one would expect *ga* to appear as well as *wa.* The exclusive use of *ga,* because it requires a child to hold alternatives in mind and to exclude all but one, ought not to be acquired early.

The facts are as follows. Izanami uses only one of these postpositions, and it is *ga.* In eight hours of recorded speech, there were approximately 100 occurrences of *ga* and six occurrences of *wa.* All occurrences of *wa,* save one, were with the same word. Moreover, about one-quarter of the occurrences of *ga* were of the exclusive type, as in *this one-ga I like* and *the airplane-ga I prefer.*

In short, Izanami sharply distinguishes *wa* from *ga,* despite their distributional similarities in parental speech, selecting the descriptive use of *ga* as the principal concept to be encoded. It is clear from this fact alone that she is not working solely from the surface clues available to her, since on this basis *wa* and *ga* are virtually indistinguishable. *Ga* is included almost whenever called for in her speech, whereas *wa* is almost never supplied when required. *Ga* is never used in contexts calling for *wa.* Evidently, Izanami knows the transformation that introduces *ga.*

Izanami's sentences at the present stage of development are mostly two, three, and four morphemes long—which means that she is still in the earliest phase of producing patterned speech. Hence, there is strong support here for the proposal that children attempt to express the abstract relation 'subject of' in their most primitive grammatical efforts, which confirms what we have already seen in the speech of Adam.

The child's use of *ga* and her exclusion of *wa* clarifies the cognitive implications of the effort to express the grammatical relation of subject. The conceptual correlate of this relation is the linkage of subject and predicate as in momentary description. It is not the discovery of enduring relations between specific agents and actions in the physical world, nor the kind of relation involved in the application of names to objects. Izanami belies this hypothesis. Indeed, on Izanami's evidence, naming appears to be completely separate from grammatical development, since appellation in Japanese requires *wa*, which Izanami invariably omits, although naming of objects is common in her speech. If the development of appellation led to developments in grammar, Izanami's postposition would have to be *wa*.

The conceptual content of *wa* thus appears to lie outside a child's attempt to express the subject relation. It is important to note in this connection that Kuroda came to the same conclusion on completely independent grounds. The postposition *wa*, although it marks the subject of a sentence and never coexists with *ga*, nonetheless represents an essentially different concept that is added to the notion of grammatical subject. Accordingly, the situations that call for *wa* do not represent to a child the basic grammatical relation of subject (if by this, we now mean momentary description), even though it is a grammatical subject that should be marked. Hence, Izanami omits *ga* and ignores *wa*. This would seem to be very strong evidence of a child's impositions of conceptual constraints on to the speech he produces.

There remains the problem of Izanami's use of the exclusive *ga*. It appears to indicate that she can hold in mind several alternatives at once, select one of the set, and simultaneously exclude the rest. Presumably, children are not able to perform mental gymnastics of this order until they reach the age of seven or eight (Bruner and Olver, 1966), so its appearance in Izanami at the age of two occasions some surprise. It is possible, of course, that the linguistic evidence should be interpreted at face value. However, there is an alternative explanation. According to at least one Japanese informant (Nobuko B. McNeill), *ga* in its nondescriptive use not only encodes exclusion but also subjective certainty. Apparently one can easily tell the self-confident from the timorous in Japanese debates by noting who uses *ga* and who uses *wa*. The *ga*-sayers are the self-confident ones. The Japanese Milktoast prefers *wa*. All Izanami's uses of *ga* in its nondescriptive sense were statements of preference—*this one-ga I like, airplanes-ga I prefer*, and so on. If we can assume that a two-year-old knows what she likes, perhaps the apparently exclusive use of *ga* would be explained. Unfortunately, this account is *ad hoc* because there is no general reason to expect children to express subjective certainty through grammatical means.

In addition to the findings already cited from children acquiring Japanese and English, Slobin (1966) has presented evidence that children acquiring Russian also attempt to express abstract grammatical features in their earliest speech. Unlike adult Russian, where inflections carry information about the grammatical relations in sentences and word order is highly flexible, the earliest sentences of Russian children lack inflections and are composed in rigid order. This phenomenon can be explained if one assumes that Russian children attempt to express abstract structures but lack transformation rules of introducing inflections. Indeed, rigid word order is precisely what would be expected on the hypothesis that children include abstract features in their early speech, but must add to this inborn structure the particular transformations employed in their native language. As Slobin (1965) writes: "The most economical representation of an inflected language like Russian would order the language in the underlying representation. Inflections could then be added to the characteristic positions of parts of speech, and an additional rule or rules would then reorder this string."

The basis on which a child chooses to build sentence order may depend on what he believes to be the local manifestation of the basic grammatical relations. For the Russian child described by Slobin, sentences were produced in the order subject-object-verb, whereas the statistically predominant order in parental speech was subject-verb-object. There are several ways in which such a difference could arise. In general, the attempt to express the basic grammatical relations means producing sentences with an underlying structure of the type conventionally represented by labelled brackets or tree diagrams. The attempt to express the basic grammatical relations does not, however, determine the order in which constituents will appear (and, indeed, this is one of the idiosyncratic aspects of language). Linguistic theory can offer no guidance to a child at this point, so order must be discovered from parental speech. In the case of the Russian child described by Slobin, it is possible that occasional appearances of s o v sentences in parental speech led him to conclude that s o v is the preferred order in Russian. But deviant orders can arise in other ways as well. Consider, for example, the English sentence fragment, *hit the ball*. In fact, it is a verb phrase, manifesting the verb-object relation. However, to a child who expects the basic grammatical relations to hold in parental speech but does not yet know the order of constituents in English, the fragment *hit the ball* is ambiguous. Depending on a child's interpretation of the meaning of the fragment, it can be taken to manifest either the verb-object relation or the subject-predicate relation. If he thinks the fragment means 'the ball hit something,' then he must analyze it as corresponding to the relation of subject-predicate. Such a child would be expected to produce sentences backwards for a time. As a matter of fact, reversal of constituents occurs in the early speech of children. One of Braine's (1963*b*) subjects, for example, produced sentences like *allgone shoe*, *allgone lettuce*, which are inversions of the corresponding sentences in adult English (*the shoe is allgone*, *the lettuce is allgone*). It is possible that the Russian child's s o v order also arose from such initial 'ambiguities' in parental speech.

We have seen three indications that children include abstract linguistic features in their early speech. In every case, the abstract feature appears to have been one or another basic grammatical relation. Since the evidence comes from children acquiring three very different languages, it appears that children do identical things in the face of radically different conditions of learning. The proposal that linguistic theory represents children's inborn capacity for language accordingly gains empirical support.

Other abstract features that appear early in children's speech can be briefly mentioned, also. In particular, the forms underlying negation (Bellugi, 1964; summarized in McNeill, 1966) and interrogation (Bellugi, 1965) appear early and can be taken as evidence in favour of the proposal. In general, one would expect that the capacity for language acquisition is very rich, governing many (if not all) abstract aspects of language. Future observations of children developing linguistic competence will provide opportunities to evaluate this expectation.

One characteristic of children's early speech is the appearance of the so-called 'Pivot-Open' construction. The terminology, Pivot (P) and Open (o), was introduced by Braine (1963*b*) to describe the primitive grammatical classes that he had observed in children's speech. Others have observed a similar division of children's vocabulary (Brown and Fraser, 1964; Miller and Ervin, 1964). The P-class typically has a fixed position with respect to the o-class, sometimes before and sometimes after, although more often before; it always contains few members compared to the o-class; and each member is generally used with relatively higher frequency than individual words in the o-class. Most new vocabulary enters the o-class, whereas the P-class is relatively closed. All these are stable characteristics of the P-O distinction.

Many workers in the area of language acquisition have assumed that this distinction marks the beginning of a child's grammatical system, subsequent developments arising from the opposition of P and o. However, the proposal considered in this paper—that children attempt to express the basic grammatical relations—suggests a different interpretation. The P-O distinction may merely be a by-product of deeper grammatical developments. To justify such a reinterpretation, however, it is necessary to consider additional characteristic of P and o classes.

P and o classes are usually heterogeneous

from the point of view of adult grammar, often containing words from several adult grammatical classes. The P class of Brown's subject, Adam, contained articles demonstratives (*this*, *that*), possessives (*my*, *your*), various adjectives, and the words *other* and *two*. The O class of one of Ervin's subject contained nouns, verbs, and adjectives. Such heterogeneity appears to be the rule, and it raises a puzzling problem. Although heterogeneous, these classes appear to be *generically appropriate*. Adam illustrates this nicely. His P-class included both the articles, all the demonstratives and possessives at his command, and all the adjectives in his vocabulary at the time, even though he was not yet distinguishing these various adult classes. Somehow, Adam placed words from these classes in his P-class before he recognized the grammatical distinctions on which the adult classes are based. Adam must have been sensitive to something held in common by these several adult classes.

One explanation is that Adam classified words according to a set of gross grammatical categories, this set in turn belonging to a hierarchy of categories. The upper levels of the presumed hierarchy would be the result of obliterating distinctions drawn at lower levels (Chomsky, 1964b). The lowest level of all in the hierarchy would be the classes of adult grammar. The upper levels, on the other hand, might be linguistically universal. Accordingly, the grammatical categories of all natural languages would be subclasses of the same set of gross categories, and Adam's generic P-class could then be one of the generic classes taken from the upper regions of this universal hierachy (McNeill, 1966).

It is conceivable that this view is correct. However, an analysis of Izanami's speech throws it into serious doubt. It is the effort to accommodate her grammar and Adam's within one consistent scheme that leads to a reinterpretation of the P-O distinction. If Izanami possesses P and O-classes (and it is not certain that she does), they would be as follows:

Pivot	Open
this	*lady*
this-one	*baby*

that-one	*cat*
good	*mommy*
not (adj)	*milk*
hurtful (adj)	*school*
dirty	*hold*
pretty	*look*
little	*good*
	happy
	beautiful
.	.
.	.
.	.

Izanami's and Adam's P-classes overlap wherever possible. Japanese has no articles, and possessives are themselves constructions, so neither is expected to appear in Izanami's P-class. But her P-class does contain demonstratives and adjectives, as does Adam's, which appears to support the notion of a universal hierachy of categories. However, note Izanami's O-class: it, too, contains adjectives, which means that neither her P nor her O-class is generically appropriate. It will be impossible for Izanami to develop the adult class of adjectives in the way that Adam did, by subdividing the P-class. Izanami will have to recombine P and O-classes in order to obtain a single class of adjectives.

What is needed is a theory broad enough to explain both Adam and Izanami, both generic and nongeneric classification. The proposal already discussed—that the basic grammatical relations are part of a child's capacity for language—provides such a theory. In order to apply the definitions of the basic grammatical relations, it is necessary to assume that the information symbolized as NP, VP, D, N, and V is also available to a child. The definitions provided above indicated this. Accordingly, the evidence from Izanami and Adam in support of the proposal that these relations are part of the capacity for language is likewise in support of the proposal that the information contained in the definition of these relations is part of the capacity for language.

The suggestion here is that children sort words, not according to a hierarchy of categories, but according to where they occur in sentences that manifest one or another basic grammatical relation. Words are classified in terms of which symbol (NP, VP, D, etc.)

forms the context of the word sorted. If children do this, they would, in effect, be using the basic grammatical relations as a source of basic grammatical features.

There are six possible features, the six symbols included in the definitions of the basic grammatical relations. Presumably all six are available to a child. Two are used here to illustrate how classification might proceed. Whenever a child observes a word in parental speech fulfilling the definition of a *modifier*, the word is tagged (—N); on the other hand, whenever he observes a word fulfilling the definition of a *predicate*, it is tagged (NP—). A given child may use only one of these features, or he may use both. If both are used, they may be applied disjunctively or conjunctively—disjunctively when every word is given only one feature or the other, conjunctively when some words are given both features. The following would be the result:

Either feature applied alone would lead to a generically appropriate class. Adam's P-class, for example, would result from using (—N) alone, since *this, that, a, the, two, my, your*, and various adjectives all fulfil the definition of modifier in parental speech. Applying both features disjunctively would lead to the cross classification that Izanami displayed—some adjectives would be tagged (—N) whereas others would be tagged (NP—). Hence, some would be used in one position in sentences, some in the other position. Moreover, some adjectives, those that happened to be classified (NP—), would fall together with nouns and verbs, both of which would also be classified (NP—). Verbs, nouns, and adjectives are exactly the contents of Izanami's O-class. Finally, applying the two features conjunctively would yield a separate class of adjectives for both Adam and Izanami.

If this is what children do, the implications for the status of the P-O distinction are not encouraging. P-O ceases to be a basic step in the acquisition of grammar. Instead, it is a superficial characteristic of children's sentences, derived from the effort to assign features to words. The statistical imbalance between P and O that Braine observed, which is used to define the two classes, simply reflects the fact that parental speech presents relatively few words fulfilling the definition of a modi-

fier. Words classified (—N), therefore, occur with high frequency in a child's speech and the set of words so classified expands only slowly. Words classified by features other than (—N) would appear in speech as O-words of various types, the latter classification being based on their greater numerosity and smaller frequency.

A CODA

If we accept the proposal that linguistic theory describes children's inborn capacity for language, a further question may be (and often is) asked. The question concerns the specificity of this capacity. There is occasionally a feeling that if children should possess specific capacities, the capacities must be specific to something other than language. A common suggestion is that children have a specific capacity to process data in wonderful ways, one outcome of which is linguistic competence (cf. some of the discussion contained in Smith and Miller, 1966). The assumption implicit in these suggestions is that a capacity not specific to language will be simpler than one specific to language. The assumption is probably false and certainly it is unjustified. There remains, nonetheless, a question as to the extent that language rests on specific abilities, and something should be said on the implications of assuming that these abilities are not unique.

The argument will be that if the abilities underlying language are not specific to language, then cognition generally must have properties matched by the universal aspects of language. At the very least, cognition must possess the universal features of the base structure, plus the notion of a transformation rule.

In grammar, transformations relate the surface structure of sentences to the underlying base structure. An infinite variety of surface types is reduced to a finite variety of base types. The implication of assuming that the capacity for language is a general ability, not one specific to language, is that there is a set of general principles of cognition whereby superficial complexity and diversity are traded off against abstract simplicity and uniformity. In this sense, transformational grammar may provide a model of cognition in general, differing from a theory of cognition primarily in the terminology used.

It follows from this proposal that the variety of abstract types available to cognition is strictly limited—it is to this limited set that all superficial diversity is reduced. Among the abstract types included, however, presumably there would be fundamental methods of combining concepts, corresponding to the basic grammatical relations. The basic grammatical relation, in fact, would be special cases of such fundamental methods of combination.

The present proposal is, of course, highly programmatic. Its only merit is to make reasonable the suggestion that language acquisition rests on more general cognitive abilities. Although programmatic, the proposal is open to empirical tests of various kinds. Suggested cognitive abilities can be rejected by showing that they do not appear in nonlinguistic cognitive development at the time that they appear linguistic development. It would be important to know, for example, if Piaget's (1952) examples of sensori-motor and preoperational development could be interpreted as the unfolding of a transformational system. It should be noted in passing that there is no justification for supposing that linguistic development is more rapid than cognitive development, previous claims notwithstanding (as in McNeill, 1966). Without an analysis of the system acquired in cognitive development that is comparable to the linguistic analysis of syntax, a comparison of the speed of cognitive and linguistic development is simply not possible. That cognitive development apparently continues until the age of twelve, whereas linguistic development is apparently complete by the age of four, may only mean that the acquisition of a system of general knowledge is three times as complex as the acquisition of English.

REFERENCES

Bellugi, Ursula and Roger Brown, eds., *The Acquisition of Language* (Monographs of the Society for Research in Child Development, 92). Lafayette, Ind.: Child Development Publications, 1964.

Braine, Martin, D. S., "On Learning the Grammatical Order of Words," *Psychological Review*, LXX (1963a), 323–348.

———, "The Ontogeny of English Phrase Structure: The First Phase." *Language*, XXXIX (1963b), 1–13.

Brown, Roger and Ursula Bellugi. "Three Processes in the Child's Acquisition of Syntax," *Language and Learning*-Special Issue of *Harvard Educational Review*, XXXIV, Spring 1964, pp. 133–51.

Brown, Roger, and C. Fraser, "The Acquisition of Syntax." In Bellugi and Brown (1964), pp. 43–79.

Bruner, J. S., and R. Olver, eds., *Studies of Cognitive Growth*. New York: John Wiley & Sons, Inc., 1966.

Chomsky, Noam, "Degrees of Grammaticalness." In Jerrold A. Fodor, and J. J. Katz, eds., *The Structure of Language: Readings in the Philosophy of Language* (Englewood Cliffs, New Jersey: Prentice Hall, Inc., (1964b).

———, *Aspects of the Theory of Syntax*. Cambridge, Mass.: The M.I.T. Press, 1965.

Katz, Jerrold J., *Philosophy of Language*. New York: Harper and Row, Publishers, 1966.

———, and P. M. Postal, *An Integrated Theory of Linguistic Description*. Cambridge, Mass.: The M.I.T. Press, 1964.

Kuroda, S.-Y., *Generative Grammatical Studies in Japanese* (doctoral dissertation, M.I.T.). 1965.

McNeill, David, "Developmental Psycholinguistics." In F. Smith and G. A. Miller, eds. (1966), pp. 15–84.

Miller, Wick, and Susan Ervin, "The Development of Grammar in Child Language." In Bellugi and Brown, eds. (1964), pp. 9–34.

Piaget, Jean, *The Origins of Intelligence in Children*. New York: International University Press, 1952.

Slobin, Dan I., *"Grammatical Developments in Russian-Speaking Children*, Center for Human Growth and Development, The University of Michigan, Report No. 8 (1965).

———, "The Acquisition of Russian as a Native Leanguage." In Smith and Miller (1966), pp. 129–148.

Smith, Frank, and George A. Miller, *The Genesis of Language: A Psycholinguistic Approach*. Cambridge, Mass.: The M.I.T. Press, 1966.

Weinreich, Uriel, "On the Semantic Structure of Language." In Joseph Greenberg, ed., *Universals of Language* (Cambridge, Mass.: The M.I.T. Press, 1963).

D. L. OLMSTED

55

Olmsted is an anthropological linguist. He attempts to present a theory of his own on the child's acquisition of the phonology of his native language. Olmsted states that his theory "predicts learning, measured by correct pronunciation of phones, as a function of ease of perception. The general prediction is that the more discriminable phones are learned earlier and the less discriminable ones later." The author also tries to compare it with some previous suggestions, but without any detailed discussion.

C.f. the more recent study by D. B. Peizer and Olmsted on "Modules of Grammar Acquisition, in *Language*, XLV (1969), pp. 60–96.

A. B. A.

A THEORY OF THE CHILD'S LEARNING OF PHONOLOGY

Introduction. This paper presents a theory of the child's acquisition of the phonology of his native language. The theory predicts learning, measured by correct pronunciation of phones, as a function of ease of perception. The general prediction is that the more discriminable phones are learned earlier and the less discriminable ones later. Finally, the theory is compared with some previous suggestions in this field.[1]

Postulate 1. At about the age of six

Reprinted from Language *42.531–535 (1966) by permission of the author and the Linguistic Society of America.*

[1] These formulations have been much improved by vigorous criticism from participants in the class in psycholinguistics at the Linguistic Institute 1962, University of Washington, particularly James J. Asher, David McNeill, Agnes Niyekawa, Anita Marten, W. Ballantyne, J. Connors, C. Davis, G. Drachman, N. Pitaro, and C. Yakulic. I am also indebted to Frank A. Logan, Susan Ervin, Jarivs Bastian, and George. A. Miller for their helpful criticisms of a version circulated in dittoed form. An earlier version of the paper was read before the Linguistic Society at its annual meeting in 1962, and presented as a lecture before the linguistic group at the Moscow State University in 1963, where it provoked a vigorous discussion. I wish to thank Serge von Oettingen, Y. S. Stepanov, and Urie Bronfenbrenner for suggestions regarding the translation into Russian of certain technical terms in linguistics and psychology.

months, the child has learned to distinguish cries of distress (made by himself or others) from the general impression made by the vocal activity involved in ordinary speech. [In what follows, brackets enclose comments not properly part of the deductive chain.]

Definition. 'Audible vocal activity' excludes cries of distress [which are part, not of the phonology of any language, but of a vocal-gestural system that is probably largely innate].

Postulate 2. The sound of the human voice has, when the child reaches the age of six months, acquired secondary reinforcing properties.[2]

Corollary. Therefore the child is motivated to engage in audible vocal activity.

Postulate 3. The child's vocal activity is only partially reinforcing to himself, since it is sometimes masked by noise.

Postulate 4. The positive effects of the child's vocal activity are counteracted to the extent that such vocal activity is paired, by chance, with noxious stimuli.

[2] Cf. O. Hobart Mowrer, *Learning Theory and the Symbolic Processes* (New York, 1960); N. E. Miller and John Dollard, *Social Learning and Imitation* (New Haven, 1941).

Postulate 5. Other things equal, stretches of adult speech uttered in the child's presence are, as a function of their frequency of presentation, accompanied by reinforcement.

Postulate 6. Such stretches of speech thus gain secondary reinforcing properties in proportion to their frequency.

Postulate 7. The prepotency (probability of occurrence in the child's vocal activity) of such stretches is thus a function of their frequency of presentation. [Can we, as a result, do without a special theory of imitation for these responses?]

Postulate 8. Speech consists of phones.

Theorem. Adult speech presented to the child contains the phones of the language in about the same proportions as they occur in ordinary adult speech.

(Partial) definition. Phones consist of articulatory components.

Postulate 9. These components have characteristic acoustic qualities.[3]

Postulate 10. These acoustic qualities contribute differentially to the discriminability of phones.[4]

Corollary. Some components are more discriminable than others.

Postulate 11. Each phone is a unique combination of components. [This is not the usual unique-in-time-and-space postulate.

Each phone, as defined here, is a *class* of unique events, each of which is indistinguishable from the others with respect to the components that define it.]

Definition. Components are not necessarily coterminous with phones.

Postulate 12. The acoustic qualities of a component during a phone are not independent in discriminability of the influence of the other components with which it is associated in this and neighboring phones. [This postulate can also be a theorem.]

Postulate 13. Some phones are more discriminable than others in a given context. [Here a postulate, this statement can be and has been a theorem, as in the experiment by Miller and Nicely.]

Definition. Learning a phone has been accomplished when the child pronounces it correctly in context, as judged by the adult native speaker. [The theory is about learning to speak (dependent variable) as a function of perception (independent variable); thus we want a measure of learning that can be judged fairly directly from overt responses.]

Postulate 14. The learning of complex responses is a function of the extent and accuracy of feedback cues from the subject's own behavior.

Definition. Cues from articulatory activity include kinesthetic feedback and auditory feedback.

Postulate 15. Auditory cues can be compared with previously heard correct pronunciations of adults.

Postulate 16. Auditory cues are the source of the feedback that is most effective in influencing the learning of phones and components.

Postulate 17. The conditions under which talk is directed at the child vary constantly, there being sometimes steady partially masking noise, and sometimes loud interruptions at various frequencies.

---

[3] It is not asserted that acoustic qualities are produced by characteristic articulations; there is considerable evidence that this is not the case. Even the present postulate may be overturned by experiment; nevertheless, it is probably accurate by and large, and reasonable for the moment, though it is recognized that further work may require a complex restatement of it.

[4] Here and in what follows, I lean heavily upon the work of George A. Miller and Patricia E. Nicely, "An Analysis of Perceptual Confusions among Some English Consonants," *Journal of the Acoustical Society of America*, XXVII (1955), 338–52. Reprinted in Sol Saporta, ed., *Psycholinguistics: A Book of Readings* (New York, 1961).

Postulate 18.   While such interference never, for the physiologically normal, results in failure of language-learning, it gives an advantage (higher probability of being learned earlier) to those phones whose components are more easily discriminable.

Postulate 19.   The more easily discriminable components in English are voicing and nasality, followed at some distance by friction and duration, with place of articulation bringing up the rear.[5]

Postulate 20.   As the the child starts to learn meaningful speech, his utterances are, in most cases, identifiable as attempts to say some combination of morphs that are part of adult language in his speech community.

Definition.   In those identifiable attempts, phones not identical (in components and their number and arrangements, though not necessarily in absolute acoustic terms) with the corresponding adult phones are errors.

Postulate 21.   While we cannot predict individual errors, partly because of the variations in noise level, we are able to predict, in general, the direction of error, as follows.

Theorem.   At any stage before the phones of the language are learned to asymptote, there are more errors based on place of articulation than on friction or duration.

Theorem.   At any stage before the phones of the language are learned to asymptote, there are more errors based on place, friction, or duration than on voicing or nasality.

Theorem.   At any stage before the phones of the language are learned to asymptote, there are about as many errors based on voicing as on nasality. [These theorems should be testable, possibly with the help of con-

fusion matrices of the sort developed by Miller and Nicely, *Journal of the Acoustical Society of America*, XXVII (1955), 338–52.]

Theorem.   At any stage before learning to asymptote, correct responses are learned more rapidly to the extent that more discriminable components are involved in their production.

Corollary.   Phones of low discriminability will be learned late. [This is accomplished because, by that time, the child has learned enough context made up of more discriminable phones to aid him in two ways: (1) The child, knowing context, can 'direct attention' to less discriminable phones, which, in context, carry too little information to make communication fail; thus 'paying attention' is reinforced, even if the phone is not discriminated. (2) As a result, the child may learn the effects of a phone on its more discriminable neighbors at a time when it is nondiscriminable or badly discriminated as a result of noise or chance factors of articulation (full mouth etc.)]

One earlier[6] theory of the acquisition of phonology is essentially a gestalt theory, asserting as it does that the child learns phonology by learning oppositions or phonemic contrasts at the time when he is selecting from the babbling inventory those contrasts which exist in the adult language and suppressing all others. The present theory takes a different view; it assumes that a contrast can only be learned *after* the child has learned to recognize and pronounce at least three phones (contrast demands that phones x and y occur contrastively in some environment z: $xz \neq yz$ seems to be a minimal statement of the requirements of an opposition), and that therefore some of the interesting parts of the learning process have already taken place before opposition learning is possible. Moreover, the earlier theory virtually ignores the babbling stage, one which poses intriguing problems for any theory of language acquisition. Why, for example, should responses present in the

---

[5] It is possible, though not certain, that this order of discriminability is universal and not limited to English. The principal evidence for English is the experiment by Miller and Nicely. *Friction* is used here for their *affrication*.

[6] First set forth in Roman Jakobson, *Kindersprache, Aphasie und allgemeine Lantgeseize* (Uppsala, 1941).

hierarchy of the child be lost and have to be relearned?[7] Are certain early sounds (those of the cooing stage) accidental by-products of innate mechanisms, whose force is lost as the infant emerges from the first weeks of life, so that the sounds have to be 'relearned' later?

More important, there are crucial difficulties involved in any attempt to test, replicably, *any* theory of the learning of oppositions. The difficulties are those of sampling, loss of interesting learning data, and interpretive troubles; they are discussed more fully in what follows.

If the object of a child-language study is the recording of the sequence of learning oppositions, then problems of sampling are acute. The observer must spend large amounts of time observing and analyzing the child's speech, since a single occurrence of a phone in the text would not be a guarantee that an opposition was present. Even then, moreover, it is possible that items showing the crucial opposition would be absent from the sample of a particular month, particularly when the opposition is first being established and is perhaps confined to a small number of utterances.

Recording the introduction of oppositions has also tended to suppress information about the first learning of phones, since most investigators taking this approach have waited until an opposition is fairly consistently maintained before marking it as present. The resulting records give the impression that such contrasts are learned all in one jump, whereas investigators of child language indicate in their footnotes that in fact phones appear sporadically, and sometimes in free variation with others better established, before they are stabilized as part of the system of items in contrast.

The difficulties of interpretation center about failure to distinguish various tasks in the acquisition of phonology: learning responses (articulations), learning the perceptual system of the language (characteristic cues from neighboring phones), learning social uses of articulation and perception of the language (phonemic system). By concentrating on the latter, the traditional theory has led its testers to overlook interesting information on the learning of the more elementary and earlier systems which are necessary conditions of the acquisition of the phonemic system. For example, in attempting to evaluate the order in which oppositions are acquired, they have had recourse to some notions about difficulty of articulation with little empirical support.

The present theory has several advantages: it concentrates upon the earlier, logically preceding system; uses the contributions of studies on learning, perception, and phonology in a single formulation; reduces sampling difficulties; intoduces a measure of the amount of difficulty in learning a phone (compounded of its perceptual difficulties, which can be measured elsewhere, rather than of its presumed articulatory intricacy); enjoys ease of testability by scoring the child's responses as errors compared with adult usage, instead of having, in testing the older theory, to make a phonemic analysis of the rudimentary system without being sure that all relevant material is in the corpus.

Of these advantages,[8] probably the foremost is ease of testability. A sample can be recorded at any time between the age when

---

[7] Werner F. Leopold, "Patterning in Children's Language-Learning," in Saporta, ed., *op. cit.* See also Leopold's *Bibliography of Child Language* (Evanston, 1952), and his great pioneering work, *Speech Development of a Bilingual Child* (Evanston, 1939–49; 4 vols.).

[8] An incidental by-product of the present theory is a possible explanation of certain puzzling phenomena from the babbling and cooing periods. It has been reported (cf. Leopold, *op. cit.*) that certain sounds pronounceable as early as the second or third month of life later drop out of the child's repertoire. Since the amount of vocalization is not decreasing, this apparent loss of responses poses a difficult problem for students of the subject. It is possible that velar consonants and high-back vowels are incidental by-products of the innate mechanisms of sucking and crying during the first few months of life and that they are articulated quite well at a time when the perceptual apparatus of the child is insufficiently developed to permit the kind of auditory feedback necessary to 'fix' the response in the hierarchy. Thus the necessity to relearn these phones later, when the auditory, perceptual and cerebral development has proceeded to the point where it is possible. In any event, the production of [k] before [i] is perhaps so different a task from the cooing [k] before [u], that there is little or no transfer of response availability.

the child first attempts recognizable meaningful utterances and the age when he has learned the phonological system completely. The theory predicts, for example, that the percentage of errors based on nasalization will be less, *at any age*, than the percentage of errors based on place of articulation, when percentage is calculated in relation to phones (of the relevant type) *attempted*. A project designed to test these hypotheses on a sample of 100 children is now under way. Any interested linguist can test the theory for himself relatively easily; communication of the results is solicited.

JEFFREY S. GRUBER

56

Gruber may be considered representative of the recent generation of young linguists and psycholinguists, whose primary interest is the study of child language, usually from a transformational point of view, and who had direct contact with linguists of the M.I.T. school like Noam Chomsky, Morris Halle, Edward Klima, and others.

The material for this study, like that for several other studies on child language which were done around Cambridge, comes from the longitudinal data collected, on tapes and sound-films, by M. Bullowa, M.D., under a National Institute of Health Grant "Development from Vocal to Verbal Behavior in Children."

This paper deals with certain aspects of syntax of *one* child, who at a certain stage of his language development did not manifest the subject-predicate constructions of mature language. Nouns that *appeared* to be used as the subjects of subject-predicate constructions acted as the *topics* of topic-comment constructions, like those that sometimes occur in adult English.

Gruber proposes that "a child learning a language for the first time, first produces sentences without subjects. Then he uses the innately known topic-comment construction to compose richer sentences. Later, if he is learning English, he comes to give this construction its special characteristics, ultimately arriving at the subject-predicate constructions."

TOPICALIZATION

IN CHILD LANGUAGE

1. SURVEY

In this paper we will analyze certain aspects of the syntax of one child who was acquiring English.[1] We will try to show that this child did not at one stage manifest the subject-predicate construction for his sentences in the way that adult English speakers do. Even though nouns *appeared* to be used as the subjects of subject-predicate constructions, further analysis of the data disclosed that these nouns act as the topics of topic-comment constructions. Such topic-comment constructions appear at times in

---

Reprinted from Foundations of Language *3.37–65 (1967) by permission of the author.*

This work was supported in part by the Joint Services Electronics Program under Contract DA 36–039–AMC–03200(E); and in part by the National Science Foundation (Grant GK-835), the National Institutes of Health (Grant 2PO1MH-04737-06), the National Aeronautics and Space Administration (Grant NsG-496), and the U.S. Air Force (ESD Contract AF19-(628)-2487), and also NIH (Grant 2-T01 HD 00111-01).

I am indebted to M. Bullowa and W. Browne for having helped me with the manuscript, and to N. Chomsky and E. Klima for their comments and criticisms contributing to the theoretical considerations in this paper. I am especially grateful to M. Halle, whose patient perusal and discussion of this paper with me much improved its content.

[1] Material for this study comes from the longitudinal data collected by M. Bullowa, M.D., under NIH Grant MH 04300–01–04, "Development from Vocal to Verbal Behavior in Children."

adult English speech. For instance, in the sentence "salt, I taste it in this food," "salt" is the topic, and "I taste it in this food" is the comment. This sentence would have the tree structure shown in Figure 1.

In this figure an ordinary English sentence, showing a subject-predicate construction, is dominated by S'. This S', which in turn is immediately dominated by S, is the comment. The NP immediately dominated by S is the topic. On the other hand, the NP and VP immediately dominated by S' are the subject and predicate of the comment, respectively. In the comment, the NP with the same referent as the topic is represented by the pronoun *it*.

We shall say that the topic NP, dominated by S, is cogenerated with the comment S', also dominated by S. Saying that NP and S' are cogenerated merely indicates that they are dominated by the same S in the surface structure. We say nothing as yet about the way in which this cogeneration is to be effected. S' will be the symbol used to indicate a comment clause when it is necessary to distinguish the node dominating such a clause from the node dominating the sentence as a whole.

While such constructions as these seem somewhat accessory to the adult grammar of English, they were essential to the child's grammar at the stage under study. Moreover, this type of construction was absent in our data for the speech of the child's exclusively English-speaking parents. The child could thus have had no model for these constructions, and they must therefore represent independent creations of his own (based perhaps on creative interpretations of adult speech).[2]

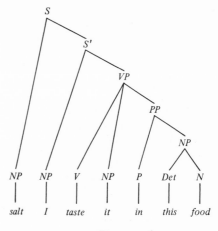

FIGURE 1

Topic-comment constructions exist as an essential part of the adult grammar in many languages, such as Chinese and Japanese. In these languages, a topic noun phrase, in addition to being part of the syntactic construction outlined previously, has a specific semantic interpretation, further differentiating it from the subject noun phrase.[3] We have found no evidence that the child's constructions possess any special interpretation when compared with the subject-predicate construction, although it is possible that they do. We relate the topic-comment constructions of the child to those noted in Chinese and Japanese, nonetheless, because the syntactic form of both of these constructions is very similar, and because they both appear to play essential parts in their respective grammars.

The precise formalization[4] of these topic-comment constructions will be discussed below. Because of thier ultimate similarity to the subject-predicate construction in English, we will suggest that the subject-predicate is merely a special case of the topic-

---

[2] It has been suggested that the child in the process of acquiring his mother tongue utilizes an innate knowledge of the structure of language (Chomsky, N., "The Logical Basis of Linguistic Theory," *Proceedings of the Ninth International Congress of Linguists, Cambridge, Mass., 1962* (The Hague; Mouton, 1964); Lenneberg, E., "A Biological Perspective of Language," in *New Directions in the Study of Language*, E. Lenneberg, ed., (Cambridge, Mass.: MIT Press, 1964). The existence of such innate knowledge implies the existence of language universals. All human languages must be similar to each other in the sense that each is a particular development of that sort of linguistic system for which the child is predisposed. We here seek to discover language universals by studying language acquisition.

---

[3] S.-Y. Kuroda, "Generative Grammatical Studies in the Japanese Language," MIT PhD. Thesis, June, 1965.

[4] The formal tools used will be those that have been developed through work in the field of generative grammar (N. Chomsky, *Aspects of the Theory of Syntax*, [Cambridge, Mass.: MIT Press, 1965]). A generative grammar is an attempt to formalize precisely the infinite set of sentences grammatical in a given language, specifying explicitly what is left to intuition in traditional grammars.

comment construction. If this is the case, i.e., if the topic-comment construction is a logically more fundamental construction than the subject-predicate construction, so that the former underlies the latter, this would provide a possible explanation for the child's independent creation of it. The spontaneous creation of the topic-comment construction could then be attributable to the innate capabilities of the child, to his innate "knowledge" of language.

This child, Mackie,[5] produced sentences which suggested a topic-comment interpretation when a little over two years of age, at least between 790 and 881 days, the period studied. The major evidence appeared in the differences between Mackie's treatment of pronouns and of nouns when used as apparent subject of the sentence.

In this paper we will tentatively employ the term *subject* to refer to the noun or pronoun immediately preceding the verb in Mackie's sentences, either in the surface structure or on an underlying level. In general, such terms from traditional grammar as noun, pronoun, verb, etc., will be used to refer to syntactic categories as one would use them in describing adult English. How far these usages should be regarded as adequate or significant definitions for the grammar which Mackie has internalized will become apparent by the end of this paper.

One of the most noticeable characteristics of Mackie's speech at this stage is that most of his sentences have either a pronominal subject or no subject expressed at all. A noun appears as subject only rarely. Nouns

as objects of verbs or of prepositions are frequent, however. Of 297 instances of nouns used by Mackie, only 11 times was a noun used in the preverbal position that we call subject position in English. In 61 cases the noun seemed to be used as the object of a verb or a preposition, and the remaining 225 cases consisted of nouns used in isolated noun phrases, in the position following the copula, or in an ambiguous usage. While the noun often appeared following the copula, as in "that's a truck," the subject of the copula was always a pronoun.

The parents, too, seldom used nouns as subjects during the recorded observations. This fact would seem to suggest that the same explanation is possible for the disuse of nouns by the child as by his parents: namely, that given the concrete referential situations about which they are most likely to speak, pronouns are merely more convenient to use than nouns. However, as we shall see below, there is good reason to reject this as an explanation for the child's speech. A more satisfactory interpretation of the evidence is that the child, in his grammar, generates a "subject" noun is a quite different way from a "subject" pronoun. Hence our evidence has significance for the internalized grammar of the child, not just for his behavior in a given situation.

2. TOPICALIZATION IN SENTENCES WITH INTERROGATIVE PRONOUNS

Consider first how Mackie forms questions with interrogative pronouns (e.g., *where*, *what*, *why*, etc.) preposed to the sentence. During this period we find the following such questions (this is an exhaustive list):[6]

1a. what do wheel?
 b. what does the truck?
 c. where went the wheel?
 d. where's the a a truck?
 e. where's the wheel?

---

[5] Mackie was recorded for a half-hour weekly, from birth until approximately 30 months of age. The recording was resumed at 34 months of age. The recorded observations consist primarily of interactions between the child subject and those in his environment with minimal interaction between the observers and the subject family. Two tracks of magnetic tape at $7\frac{1}{2}$ ips and 16 mm. black and white two-frame-per-second film are taken at each observation. One tape track records the subjects' vocalizations and environmental sounds; the other records description of ongoing behavior and interaction whispered into a shielded microphone and a patterned timing signal. (M. Bullowa, L. G. Jones, and T. G. Bever, "The Development from Vocal to Verbal Behavior in Children," *Monographs of the Society for Research in Child Development*, Serial No. 92, XXIX [1964], No. 1).

[6] Transcription of the child's utterances were made to approximate morphemes of adult English as closely as possible. When, for example, *where's* is transcribed, we do not necessarily imply that this is indeed a contraction in Mackie's language derived from *where is*, but only that Mackie's utterance seemed to come close to this English word in sound. If an utterance is repeated more than once in the corpus, the number of times is indicated by a numeral followed by a "×".

f.   where's the man?
g.   what is this?
h.   who's that?
i.   why it go?
j.   where it is? (4×)

We see that such questions with an apparent noun subject have the normal order of subject followed by main verb inverted, as in examples 1a–f. (We will regard sentences 1g and 1h in the same way, allowing *this* and *that* to be considered like nouns.) However, when a pronoun such as *it* was subject, there was no apparent inversion, as in examples 1i–j.

In the English grammar of adults, sentences with an interrogative pronoun preposed have inversion of the auxiliary verb and the subject. This is acounted for by the following transformational rule, in which $Q + NP$ represents an interrogative pronoun, NP the subject noun phrase, Aux the auxiliary verb, and X the rest of the sentence:

Tr-1:   Q + NP   NP   Aux   X
         1   2   3   4 → 1 3 2 4

Mackie's sentences in 1, therefore, deviate from those of his parents in two ways.

First of all, in an adult English grammar, the inversion transformation Tr-1 applies without regard to whether the subject NP is a noun or a pronoun. NP may refer to either. Hence an adult grammar yields inversions in both utterances "where is it?" and "where is John?" For the child, however, we do not obtain "where is it?", but rather 1j "where it is?" The inversion transformation would apply only in the case that the subject of the underlying sentence is a noun, for we do obtain "where's the man?", and similar sentences, 1d–h.

Secondly, for the grammar of an adult English speaker, the inversion transformation never applies to main verbs. We do not obtain such a sentence as "where went the wheel?" in adult English. But in the child's speech, we find just this sentence and others similar to it, sentences 1a–c. The child's transformation therefore would have to apply to main verbs if and only if the verb has a noun subject. This would give us 1a–c, but not sentences of the type "why go it?" with a pronoun subject. Instead we obtain "why it go?" 1i, without inversion. Finally,

for the adult, inversion *always*, applies to the copula of interrogative sentences, e.g., "where is it?" and "where is the man?" But for the child this transformation would have to be restricted to the copula *be* when *be* has a noun subject.

A transformational rule with the above specifications is possible. Its form would be that of Tr-2:

Tr-2:   Q + NP   (Det +)N   V   X
         1   2   3   4 → 1 3 2 4

Such a transformation, used by the child, would have no model in the questions presented to him by the adult. The environments of its application would be broader for the types of verb to which it applies and more restricted for the types of subject. it is difficult to imagine how such a highly specific transformational rule Tr-2 could have been arrived at by the child, who would have been presented with evidence for a transformational rule of quite different specifications, Tr-1.

However, we might attempt to account for the child's application of the inversion transformation to all verbs, including main verbs, as a type of overgeneralization. It is true that the auxiliary verb is not yet manifested in the child's grammar. Consequently, he would not be expected to make the distinction between main verbs and auxiliary verbs. It might be reasonable therefore to suggest that the child's inversions shown in 1a–fare manifestations of an inversion transformation which, applying indiscriminately to all verbs, is a rough precursor of the adult transformational inversion which applies only to auxiliary verbs.

But if we assume that the child at the period under discussion has internalized an inversion transformation such as Tr-2, especially if it is a precursor of the adult transformation, then we would expect it to remain in some form as a part of his grammar at subsequent stages of development. However, this is not the case. A sampling eight months later showed no inversion whatever for such questions as above. Questions with interrogative pronouns and apparent noun subjects at the later period have the form seen in the following examples.

2a. where this guy goes?
  b. what that guy do?

It would only increase the mystery to say that the child could have learned to use an inversion transformation at one time and ceased to use it at a later time.

Postulating a transformational inversion for the child in questions with interrogative pronouns is unsatisfactory on still further grounds. Klima and Bellugi[7] have observed a stage in the development of child language (presumably after the period under discussion) at which there is inversion in questions answerable by *yes* or *no* and also pre-position of interrogative pronouns, but at this stage there appears to be a performance limitation barring the two transformations from applying together.

Inversions for questions answerable by *yes* or *no* are accounted for in adult grammar by a transformational rule similar to Tr-1. Instead of there being an interrogative pronoun $Q + NP$ as the necessary condition for such a transformation, there is only the underlying question marker Q, which is generated at the beginning of the sentence and later deleted.[8] Hence, for the adult, an inversion transformation applies for all instances of Q (either Q itself or $Q + NP$). We replace rule Tr-1 by the modified form Tr-3.

Tr-3: Q(+ NP) NP Aux X
         1   2   3   4 → 1 3 2 4

This will yield in the adult grammar sentences such as "is the toy a truck?" in which Q exists alone at the beginning of the underlying sentence; as well as sentences such as "where is the truck?", in which $Q + NP$ is at the beginning.

An interrogative pronoun is generated at the beginning of a sentence by a pre-position transformation that removes a noun phrase from its ordinary position in a sentence and unites it to the question marker at the beginning of the sentence (forming $Q + NP$). This transformation is as follows:

___ [7] E. Klima, and U. Bellugi, "Syntactic Regularities in Children's Speech," *Proceedings of the Psycholinguistic Conference, Edinburgh, 1966.*

[8] J. Katz, and P. Postal, *An Integrated Theory of Linguistic Descriptions*, Research Monograph No. 26 (Cambridge, Mass.: MIT Press, 1964), pp. 79–116.

Tr-4: Q   X   NP   Y
       1   2   3   4 → 1 + 3 2 ∅ 4

For example, from an underlying tree structure such as Figure 2, we obtain the following tree structure, applying only Tr-4 (see Figure 3). Subsequent application of Tr-3 in the adult grammar yields the surface tree of adult English (see Figure 4).

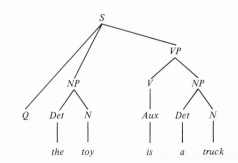

FIGURE 2

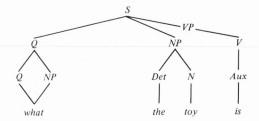

FIGURE 3

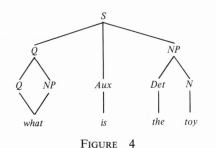

FIGURE 4

At the stage which Klima and Bellugi report, the child has apparently internalized Tr-3 and Tr-4. One obtains, using only Tr-3, sentences of the type "is the toy a truck?" Also, one obtains, using only Tr-4, "what the toy is?" But one does not obtain sentences such as in Figure 4, "what is the toy?", in which both Tr-3 and Tr-4 must apply to the same tree.

The period we are discussing, however, is

different from that just presented, since both apparent inversion, Tr-3, and pre-position of interrogative pronouns, Tr-4, sometimes occur together in our period. Also there does not seem to be true inversion, Tr-3, applying alone in the case of yes-no questions. We only have apparent inversion in the appearance of *do* or *does* before the subject.

3a. does it work?
 b. do I make this way?

No other auxiliary appeared before the subject to yield such sentences as "is it a dog?", "is he running?", or "has he a book?" In addition, we have no examples of the auxiliary *do* appearing after an interrogative pronoun during the period studied.

In cases when *does* or *do* does not appear, the question marker is manifested only by a rising intonation in the child's speech, and not by any sort of inversion, as may occur in adult speech. For example, each of the following utterances was distinguished as a question by a rising intonation:

4a. you fight?
 b. see it?
 c. you fix it?
 d. me show you?
 e. go round?
 f. that go?
 g. that broke?
 h. that truck?
 i. that's a train?
 j. it's wagon?

It would be unwarranted to postulate an inversion, Tr-3, operating only in such cases as 3a and 3b. Moreover, before inversion appears with other auxiliaries or in other instances of yes-no questions, or before other auxiliaries appear at all, it would be best to consider this *do(es)*, not as an auxiliary, but as a question marker. In other words, *do(es)* is itself an optional phonological materialization of the question marker Q assumed always to underlie yes-no questions, but which is never so manifested in adult English. We can then avoid requiring inversion to occur. Against this is the apparent agreement that seems to exist between *do(es)* and the subject, *does* occurring with the third person singular and *do* with all other pronouns. There were no examples with *do(es)* with noun subjects. This agreement, however,

does not imply that the word which agrees with the subject is necessarily a verb. In Mackie's speech, verbs cannot be so characterized, since there is no consistent agreement between the verb and its subject. Although it is possible that *do(es)* is a verb here, we will assume it is not a verb, and that there is no inversion.

At the stage under discussion then, inversion, Tr-3, does not occur alone as a transformation. Consequently it would be a complication to assume that inversion occurs only when pre-position of an interrogative pronoun, Tr-4, also occurs. Moreover, such a situation would not fit in consistently with the subsequent stage which Klima and Bellugi report, at which inversion, Tr-3, occurs in addition to pre-position, Tr-4, but at which these two transformations still cannot occur together.

If we do not account for the peculiar inversion of word order by an inversion transformation, to what then do we attribute the phenomenon we have been discussing?

We propose that the appearance of a noun as the subject of a sentence such as "where went the wheel?" is due to the cogeneration of a clause generated without an overtly manifested subject, together with a noun phrase. That is, we will generate the comment clause and the topic noun phrase of a topic-comment construction. Just how the cogeneration of such a noun phrase is to be formulated will be discussed in Section 6. It has been indicated, however, that most of Mackie's sentences at this time have subjects manifested only by pronouns or not manifested at all. Both "where it went?" and "where went?" occur, the latter having no subject expressed. These would have tree structures derived from the underlying tree structures (Figures 5 and 6) respectively:

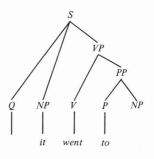

FIGURE 5

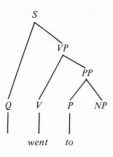

FIGURE 6

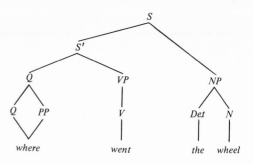

FIGURE 9

The pre-position transformation Tr-4 may effect the pre-posing of prepositional phrases, PP (as well as noun phrases, NP), after which a preposition such as *to* may no longer appear in the output. Hence, after application of Tr-4, we obtain the derived trees of Figures 7 and 8.

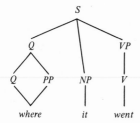

FIGURE 7

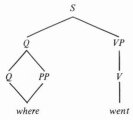

FIGURE 8

Generating the clause of Figure 8, "where went?", with a noun phrase such as "the wheel" following it, we obtain "where went the wheel?" which would then have the tree structure given in Figure 9, according to our hypothesis.

The obvious selectional restrictions between the cogenerated noun phrase, e.g., "the wheel," and the verb, e.g. "went," will be treated in Section 7.

Questions of the form

5.   the wheel where went?

formed by generating the two elements mentioned above in the opposite order did not occur, however, although we might expect such a question to occur. Its non-occurrence could be attributed to a limitation on the number of noun phrases generated at the same side of the comment clause. In such interrogative sentences as those above there is already an interrogative pronoun attached to the beginning of the sentence by Tr-4, which may eliminate the possibility of another noun phrase being attached there. We shall mention this problem again in Section 6.

The nonoccurrence of "where the wheel went?" at this stage will be accounted for by allowing only pronouns as subjects (alternating with no subject expressed at all). Such sentences are exemplified by the trees of Figures 5 and 6. Otherwise such a sentence could be generated merely by moving "where" in "the wheel went where?" to the head of the sentence as in adult grammar. On the other hand, the occurrence of "where it went?" is readily accounted for in the child's grammar. But since the categorization of *it* (or *he, I,* or *she,* for example) will be such as not to allow it to be used as topic, i.e., generated at the beginning or end of S', we can explain the nonoccurrence of "where went it?"

Thus the phenomenon described above can be explained by assuming that the child utilizes at this stage some notion of topicalization, whereby he can state the topic before or after the sentence, in much the same way as is found in languages such as Chinese and Japanese. Topicalization, we recapitulate, means that some major constituent of a sentence, such as a noun phrase, which is identical with (or has the same referent as) a constituent in the given sentence, may be generated before or after this sentence. In the given sentence, then, this noun phrase is represented by a pronoun or by nothing at all. The cogenerated constituent is called the topic, and the given sentence is called the comment.

3. TOPICALIZATION WITH NOUNS IN SENTENCES WITHOUT INTERROGATIVES

If this is the correct interpretation of the apparent inversion presented, we should expect to find evidence of topicalization in the child's declarative sentences. Topic-comment constructions indeed seem to appear overtly in the sentences:

6a. it broken, wheels
 b. car, it broken

In these constructions the topic is after the comment clause and before *it* respectively. The subjects are manifested by pronouns in the comment clauses. The topic has the same referent as the subject pronoun. Sentences 6a and 6b have tree structures as in Figures 10 and 11 respectively:

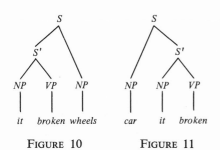

FIGURE 10   FIGURE 11

The topic noun phrase may in other instances have the same referent as the object of the verb. And further still, it may relate to some noun phrase by a relation of possession rather than by identity of reference. In 7a–c, we have the topic referring to the object. In 7b–c, we have the topic related to the noun in the comment clause as possessor to the thing possessed.

7a. those other, put them?
 b. car, he take the wheel
 c. he take the wheels, fire engine

For sentences 7b–c, approximate paraphrases in adult English would be "as for the car, he took its wheel," and "as for the fire engine, he took its wheels."

For 7c, interpretations other than topicalization are possible. For example, paraphrasing it as "he took the wheel off the fire engine," we would consider the omission of the preposition *off* as a factor in its generation; with the paraphrase "he took the wheels of the fire engine," we would have genitive construction. But the word order in the child's grammar for a genitive construction is "fire engine wheels," omitting '*s*. Also, positive evidence leads us to believe 7c is a topic-comment construction. Sentences 7b and 7c both occurred during the same period of communication and interaction between Mackie and his father, the falling intonation characteristic of declarative sentences is manifested independently in both "he take the wheels" and "fire engine," and there is a short but distinct pause between the two parts.

We should also expect there to be declarative topic-comment constructions in which the subject of the comment clause, rather than being manifested by a pronoun, is not manifested at all. Indeed, these would be just those rare cases of a noun apparently used as the subject of a declarative sentence. Thus, with ∅ representing the absent subject, we have from an underlying

8a. girl, ∅ go away

which has the tree structure as given in Figure 12, the resulting sentence

8b. girl go away.

8b would have the tree structure of Figure 13 if this were an ordinary subject predicate construction. Compare Figures 12 and 13.

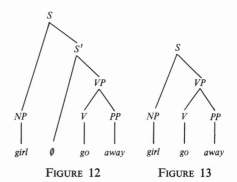

FIGURE 12   FIGURE 13

Figure 12 is entirely parallel to Figure 11 above, differing in whether or not the subject is generated. This sentence, which actually occurred, would have as paraphrase something like "as for the girl, she went away." On the same day the utterance

9a.   go way wheels

was observed, which we may take to be of the same structure, coming from

9b.   ∅ go way, wheels

where the topic appears after the comment clause. 9b would have the tree structure of Figure 14.

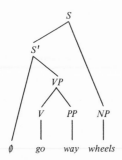

FIGURE 14

This figure is entirely parallel to Figure 10, except that the subject is again not manifest. Similarly we have both of the following:

10a.   choo choo over there
   b.   over there train

in which we have comment clauses with absent subjects, and with topics before and after the comment clauses respectively.

That the position of the topic before or after the comment clause is perfectly arbitrary is demonstrated by the occurrence of the four sentences of 8, 9, and 10, on the same day.

Are all occurrences of nouns apparently used as subjects really topics at this stage? If they are not subjects, one would have no reason to expect any greater number of occurrences of the noun before the comment or predicate than after it. Indeed there is very nearly an equal distribution. The following sentences, together with those of 8-10, exhaust the cases of possible topicalization, where nouns are generated as topics to declarative comment clauses with subjects absent.

Topic after the comment

11a.   all broken wheel
   b.   break pumpkin
   c.   in there wheels
   d.   in there baby
   e.   there's the man
   f.   there's the truck
   g.   there's the wheel
   h.   go truck
   i.   go in there train

Topic before the comment

12a.   dump truck all fixed
   b.   other wheel broke
   c.   truck broke
   d.   wheel in there
   e.   pony in there
   f.   motor in the car
   g.   fire truck there
   h.   Mama goes
   i.   wheels move
   j.   the wheel fall on

In some of the sentences above there is a short but significant pause indicating the juncture between the sentence and the topic. This is clearly the case in 10b, "over there train," as well as in 12g, "fire truck there," and 11h, "go truck." A clear juncture is not always discernible, however, although the mere potentiality of a juncture could indicate a topic-comment construction.

It was difficult to discern whether 12f was really "motor in the car" or "motor in there, car." In the case of the latter, we would have "car" as topic following the sentence, relating to "motor" or "there."

A number of the sentences of 11 and 12 may have analyses alternative to topicalization. The sentences beginning with "there's the" (11e–g) may have an analysis for the child distinct from the one given above, since these are acceptable constructions in adult grammar and persist in later stages after other instances of topicalization have disappeared. (The same applies to the interrogative sentences beginning with "where's the," previously mentioned, examples 1d–f.) These sentences may, for example, have the same analysis as for the adult, being caused by an inversion transformation applying to sentences of the type "the wheel is there." It is doubtful that the child derives them in this way, however, since this requires the generation of nouns in subject position. Alternatively, the sentences may be generated in a fashion completely parallel to nominal or copular sentences of the type "that's a wheel." Then "there" would be the same type of introductory pronoun as "that" above.

The sentence "there the wheel in there," and others like it, occur in the child's speech, and are not cases of topicalization since no noun phrase occurs either at the beginning or at the end of the sentences. If *in there* can be omitted from this construction, then we would have a sentence such as 11e–g. However, it is also possible that some of the sentences of 12, such as "wheel in there" with apparent topic before the comment clause, have a similar origin; that is, the sentence "there wheel in there," with "there" omitted. Consequently some of the sentences of 11, and some of those of 12, may in fact be formed by means other than topicalization.

It is true that in adult English discourse topicalization as here described sometimes occurs. For example, in the course of conversation it is natural to say such a sentence as "the house we saw yeasterday, the Smiths have decided to buy it." However, in the speech of Mackie's parents such a construction is apparently a rare occurrence, if it occurs at all. There were, in fact, during the period studied, no clear cases of such topicalization in their recorded discourse, a good deal of which has been collected along with Mackie's productions. The sentences which most nearly approximated it in our sample were either affirmations of Mackie's naming some object or they were ellipses of a common type. For example, when Mackie pointed out an object, saying "the boy," his father affirmed this, saying "Boy. See the boy up there?" In another instance, Mackie's mother asked him "what is it? A pumpkin?", which question is an ellipsis of "What is it? Is it a pumpkin?" Mackie's adoption of the topic-comment construction as an essential part of his grammar therefore cannot be attributed to imitation of his parents' speech. It seems to have been an independent innovation.

4. TOPICALIZATION WITH PRONOUNS

There is no evidence to suggest that Mackie used pronouns such as *he, she, it, I,* as topics. Whereas there were instances of verbs fol-

lowed by noun subjects, there were no instances of verbs followed by the above pronoun subjects. As was seen in Section 2, the same situation obtained in interrogative sentences in which nouns but not pronouns appeared after the verb. With declarative sentences also, it is unlikely that there is an inversion transformation reordering subject and verb; in such a case, the transformation would hold only if the subject were a noun. Now however, we can understand the distinction in the uses of nouns and the above pronouns in terms of topicalization, by saying that nouns may be used as topics, while such pronouns may not be.

While it appears that the pronouns above cannot ever be used as topics, this is not the case for pronouns such as *me, him, them,* those commonly used as objects. Thus there is a distinction between Mackie's use of so-called case-marked and unmarked pronouns.[9] Mackie was found to use both marked (*me, him, them*) and unmarked pronouns (*I, he, it*) as apparent subjects of copular sentences. Thus to express "he is a dog," Mackie might say "he dog," or "he's dog," or "he's a dog," as well as "he is a dog." Or he might use the so-called marked form, as in "him dog." However, in all circumstances where Mackie used the marked form, the copula was absent. During this period, Mackie was found to say the following copular sentences beginning with a marked pronoun. This list is exhaustive:

13a. him bear
  b. him bad dog
  c. them eyes
  d. me no bear

But there were no examples of sentences of the form "him's a bad dog" or "him is a bad dog."

We shall interpret the sentences of 13 as manifesting the topic-comment construction. If we say that the case-marked pronouns apparently used here as subjects are really topics, then to avoid generating "him's a bear" we need only avoid generating the copula in sentences in which the subject is not manifested. This must be done in any case, since there are no such sentences as "is a

[9] E. Klima, "Relatedness between Grammatical Systems," *Language*, XL (1964), 1–21.

bear." If the subject pronoun is absent, so is the copula; hence the absence of the copula in "him bear" could be attributed to the absence of the subject pronoun, in which case the pronoun "him" would be the topic.

To be more explicit, "he's a bear" would have the ordinary tree structure of adult English, namely as in Figure 15. On the other hand "him's a bear" does not occur. That is the tree structure of Figure 16, with *him* the topic does not occur. Figure 16 does not occur since its postulated subtree, namely Figure 17, does not occur.

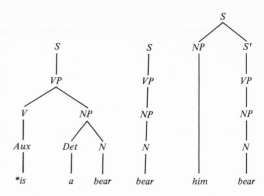

FIGURE 17   FIGURE 18   FIGURE 19

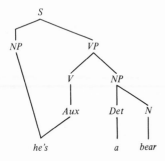

FIGURE 15

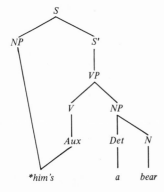

FIGURE 16

What does occur is the isolated noun phrase, "bear," which, if we treat it as a variant of "he's a bear" with the subject and copula absent, will have the tree structure of Figure 18. If Figure 18 is a subtree of a topic-comment construction in which "him is the topic, we would have sentence 13a, whose tree is given in Figure 19.

The case-marked pronouns also appear as the subjects of noncopular sentences. In the subject position we have either marked or unmarked pronouns:

Unmarked

14a. I wanna
   b. he take the wheel, fire engine
   c. I show you?
   d. I write
   e. I see the tree
   f. he bites anyone

Marked

15a. me wanna truck
   b. me take the wheel
   c. me show you?
   d. me draw
   e. him go right back
   f. no him no bite

That the cases of marked pronouns as subjects are instances of topicalization is supported by the contrast in intonation pattern between such instances as 14c and 15c. In 14c, as expected for questions, there is a continuous rise starting from the first morpheme "I." However, in 15c, there is a fall in pitch on the first morpheme "me" followed by the expected interrogative rise for the rest of the sentence. In other words, for 15c, "me" has the intonation of a declarative sentence, and stands separated from the rest of the sentence. Such a break seems to be impossible if the subject position is occupied by an unmarked pronoun, which cannot be a topic. However, the declarative intonation on the topic is not obligatory, since later repetitions of "me show you?" have a continuous rise.

There were two occurrences of case-marked pronouns used as topic after the comment clause. One of these was a sequence of copula type sentences like those given in 13:

16.　car them them car

If we consider the string composed of the first two morphemes as a unit, then it appears that we have a sequence of comment followed by topic. Actually, however, except for the fact that nouns proper are more commonly used as the object of the copula than are case-marked pronouns, we have no reason to say which of these morphemes is topic and which is comment.

The other instance of a pronoun appearing as topic after the comment was the utterance:

17.　catch me

This sentence did not have the meaning which normal English word order would suggest. The meaning apparently was "I can catch it." This can be seen from the behavioral context in which 17 appeared. Mackie and his father were playing at tossing things to each other. After Mackie said the above, his father responded with "can you catch the pumpkin?" Then Mackie repeated what he himself had just said, with the topic preceding the sentence this time. He said "me caught it," followed by "me catch it." The sort of ambiguous construction we have in sentence 17, is just what one would expect in the case of topicalization with a transitive verb.

We must seek to explain the distributional differences between case-marked and unmarked pronouns. It appears from the foregoing that the case-marked pronouns have the same distribution as nouns do while the unmarked pronouns are restricted to pre-verbal or precopular position. The former can be used as topics, while the latter cannot.

Suppose that the case-marked pronouns are categorized in the child's grammar precisely like nouns while the unmarked pronouns are not so categorized. There is further evidence to support this view. In the following utterance the marked pronoun *him* appears to be used as the noun head of a noun-phrase.

18.　he's a bad him

Moreover while both case-marked and unmarked pronouns appear in subject position, in other positions, such as in isolation, or as the objects of verbs or of prepositions, only the case-marked pronouns appear. This distribution has been observed by others (Klima, personal communication).

Such a distribution can also be very simply interpreted if we assume that the unmarked pronouns cannot be treated like nouns (or noun-phrases), while the marked ones must be so treated. Then, for example, *him* is allowed in apparent subject position, as the topic noun-phrase, while it is not possible to get *he* as the object noun-phrase. We will say that in isolation, as topics, or as the objects of verbs or prepositions, we have only noun-phrases. Conversely, as subjects we only have the unmarked pronouns. All noun-phrases and case-marked pronouns which appear to be subjects are identified as topics. The noun-phrase itself does not occupy subject position.

We will later face the question why the case-marked pronoun is categorized as a noun while the unmarked pronoun does not come to be categorized in this way by the child.

5.　FORMALIZATION OF SENTENCE TYPES

Let us now consider the formal generation of these strings. The copular sentence could be derived by the rules:

R-1　S　→ (Pro) NP
R-2　Pro → he, she, they, I, we, you, it, this, that
R-3　NP → (Det) N, him, me, them, you, this, that, etc.

The constituent *Pro* is optional, since the subject is often absent. We shall not discuss the nature of *Det*, the determiner, which is of independent interest. Note that we are treating case-marked pronouns as instances of the noun-phrase, NP. Perhaps to treat them as instances of the noun would be more precise (cf. ex. 18). The essential thing is that these case-marked pronouns be classified with noun-phrases, which are free in their occurrence, as opposed to the unmarked pronouns, *Pro*, which are much more restricted and are not included among possible elements of the noun-phrase. The elements dominated by *Pro* are just those which occupy subject position quite generally, and serve no other purpose.

The copula ('s, is, 'm, etc.,) could be inserted by a transformational rule. It never occurs except when *Pro* is present, and its form is determined by the form of *Pro*. Thus, for example, 's is used for *he* and *it*. Such a transformational rule would be:

$$\text{R-4 (optional)} \quad \# \# \quad \underset{1}{\text{Pro}} \quad \underset{2}{\text{NP}} \quad \# \# \quad \to 1 + \begin{Bmatrix} \text{'s} \\ \text{'m} \\ \text{'r} \\ \text{is} \end{Bmatrix} 2$$

There is no evidence to suggest the copula is independent of the pronoun. By inserting the copula by a transformation we are essentially treating the sequence of *Pro* followed by the copula as an optional spelling of *Pro*. That is, *he's* is another form of *he*, *I'm* is another form of *I*, etc. In fact, the spelling of *Pro* as *Pro* + *copula* is possible even when followed by a verb phrase, VP, as in ordinary noncopular sentences. These would be utterances of the form "*I'm go*" and "*he's put*," which are observable in our data and reported by others.[10] Such utterances have been thought of as instances of the child's rendition of the progressive aspect. That is, the child says the above instead of "I'm going" or "he's putting," leaving off the *ing* ending of the progressive from the verb. However, an alternate interpretation, proposed here, is that the child says the above instead of "I go" and "he put."

Instead of having both the rewriting rule for *Pro* (R-2) and the transformational insertion of the copular elements with environmental restrictions (R-4), we can combine the two in a new rule for rewriting *Pro*, in which the elements rewritten have optional spellings. This would be:

R-5

$$\text{Pro} \to \begin{Bmatrix} \text{that} \\ \text{this} \\ \text{he} \\ \text{it} \\ \text{she} \end{Bmatrix} (+ \begin{Bmatrix} \text{'s} \\ \text{is} \end{Bmatrix}), \begin{Bmatrix} \text{they} \\ \text{we} \\ \text{you} \end{Bmatrix} (+ \text{'re}), \text{I}(+ \text{'m})$$

---

[10] E. Klima, personal communication; also R. H. Weir, *Language in the Crib*, Janua Linguarum, Series Major, XIV (The Hague: Mouton, 1962).

There will be no copula when we have a case-marked pronoun in place of *Pro*, since the presence of a copula, being an optional spelling of *Pro*, depends on the presence of *Pro*. We are treating case-marked pronouns not as elements of *Pro*, but as nouns. How the case-marked pronouns (and the nouns) can be generated in subject position will be treated when the mechanics of topicalization is discussed below (Section 6).

To account also for the ordinary noncopular sentences we extend R-1 into:

$$\text{R-6} \quad \text{S} \to (\text{Pro}) \begin{Bmatrix} \text{NP} \\ \text{VP} \end{Bmatrix}$$

followed by the expansion of VP into its many forms, one of which is

R-7 VP → V NP

in which NP, as has been said, will include, for example, *him*, but not *he*.

6. FORMALIZATION OF TOPICALIZATION

We can formalize the generation of topic-comment expressions in several ways. One way is to say that a topic-comment expression consists of the juxtaposition of two types of sentence: the free noun-phrase, as generated by choosing NP in R-6 without Pro, and a sentence of any type generated by R-6. In other words, topicalization can be treated as some sort of conjunction between two underlying sentences. The relation of identity or possession called for between the topic and some element in the comment clause, has already been described.

Alternatively, we can generate topic-comment expressions by specifying a rule whose right side elements consist of a noun phrase (NP) and a sentence (S') of any type generated by R-6; the topic and the comment respectively. These right side elements must be order free with respect to one another. This would be a rule such as:

R-8 S → NP S'

The order has to be free since both orders occur.

A third possibility is to have a rule establishing order of the form:

R-9 $S \rightarrow S'\ NP$

followed by an optional transformation preposing the NP:

R-10 $S'\ NP$
$1\ \ 2 \rightarrow 2\ 1$

A fourth possible hypothesis for the mechanism of topicalization is that some noun-phrase of the sentence is extraposed either before or after the sentence. According to this hypothesis nouns would have to be generated in subject position and would then be extraposable. We might still maintain that the unmarked pronouns are not categorized as nouns by the child, while marked pronouns are, since only nouns, including marked pronouns, would be extraposable.

The first formulation (juxtaposition of two sentence types) has the advantage over all the others of accounting for certain intonation patterns sometimes occurring in topic-comment constructions: at times the topic is uttered with a declarative intonation independent of the rest of the sentence. For example, the topic may have a declarative intonation while the comment clause has an interrogative intonation. Furthermore, identifying the topic with an isolated noun-phrase is supported by the fact it is just those pronouns which cannot occur in isolation (*he*, *she*, *it*, *I*, etc.), which also do not occur as topics. We cannot explain the disuse of these pronouns as topics by saying that they have alternate forms when used as topic, since *it*, unlike *he*, has no alternate form.

The second formulation is unsatisfactory in that a rule such as R-8, with free order, is a type of rule never before used in phrase-structure grammars. Phrase-structure rules which establish order among the right side elements have always been found necessary, since a particular order has always been assumed to be basic. There is, however, no certainty in this assumption.

In the third and fourth formulations, one could account for the absence of "the wheel where went," by limiting the application of the relevant preposing transformations to one application of either of them. To get this sentence, first "where" and then "the wheel" would have to have been moved to the head of the sentence, two preposings. In the third formulation, one could restrict rule R-10, a rule similar to Tr-4, from applying when Tr-4 does, so that only "where went the wheel?" would be obtained, provided preposing the interrogative pronoun Tr-4 were obligatory.

The fourth formulation, however, would allow the utterance "where the wheel went?", sentences of which type have not been found in the corpus investigated. We would have the added specification that extraposition to the end of the sentence is obligatory for the subject when an interrogative pronoun is preposed.

The first three formulations postulate an underlying form to characterize the topic-comment construction, whereas the fourth characterizes topicalization as a process. Formulating topicalization as a process of extraposition would automatically establish the identity relation between the topic and some noun-phrase within the comment clause. However, it would not account for the suspected instances of topicalization in which the relation between the topic and the noun-phrase within the comment clause is one of possession rather than of identity.

Taking the process of extraposition as our formulation of topicalization means that in some instances noun-phrases must be generated as subjects so that they could then be extraposed. But this would amount to abandoning the idea, which we have labored to demonstrate, that noun-phrase subjects are really not generated in S by the child. Nouns would be generated as subjects on a par with nouns generated anywhere else. We are postulating, however, that at this early stage of development of language, the sentence structure and the processes of its generation are simpler than those of the adult. Saying that subject position is restricted to morphemes categorized as *Pro* implies a simplicity of structure which will be discussed below; and postulating that topicalization is really the cogeneration of a noun phrase and a sentence seems to be simpler and more basic than postulating extraposition.

Extraposition in the child's grammar would make the process of generation of sentences more complex than in adult grammar, since subject noun-phrases would have to be generated before extraposition occurred. Consequently the child would have an additional rule in his grammar, extraposition, compared to the rules which the adult has as an intrinsic part of his grammar. If topicalization were extraposition, one would expect Mackie's present stage to be preceded by a period in which subjects were generated, this being followed by the addition of topicalization by extraposition as a new rule to the grammar. However, the preceding stage is probably one in which neither subjects nor topics are generated, judging from other reports (see below).

Our main reason in the formalization of topicalization for favoring an underlying form over a process is that it is then possible, as we shall see, to understand why case-marked pronouns are considered nouns, and unmarked pronouns are not; in addition, by this means light can be shed on the very essence of the subject-predicate construction itself, and its origin.

7. SUBJECTLESS SENTENCES

Thus far we have surmised that the child, at the stage of development under discussion, generates sentences in which only an unmarked pronoun, not a noun-phrase, can serve as subject (rule R-6). But is the element *Pro* to be considered a subject in the same sense as the term would be used in describing adult English?

Since the term subject is universally defined for adult grammars as the noun-phrase immediately dominated by an S node, usually the highest node of the sentence, and since the element *Pro* is emphatically not a noun-phrase, the element *Pro* cannot be a subject with the same definition as for adult English.

There are, however, further considerations which lead to the conclusion that it would be unwise to consider *Pro* even as a rough precursor to the adult subject. Note that if we combine the topic noun-phrase, NP, with the comment clause, S', we have the sequence *NP S'*. Expanding S, here S', by R-6, we have the sequence *NP Pro VP*. Thus if the whole sequence is thought of as being dominated by S, then we could characterize this eventual stage of development by the rule "S → NP

Pro VP." Since *Pro* may be absent, this rule is sometimes identical to "S → NP VP." It is this rule, with an NP in subject position, which the child will ultimately have to arrive at. But if topicalization and Rule R-6 together reduce to the rule "S → NP VP," we cannot regard *Pro* as the precursor of the subject NP, since the topic is. Hence the node labelled *Pro* should not be considered a rudimentary subject at all, but rather some sort of introductory word to verbs. It is more or less a verbal article, or perhaps on a par with an inflectional affix of a verb.

It is reasonable to reformulate Mackie's grammar in accordance with the above. Let us emphasize the fact that *Pro* is not the subject by removing it from the right side of R-6 and specifying it as a feature of the verb. Then instead of R-6 we would have simply:

R-6′   S → VP

After R-7 has applied we could expand V into a set of features by R-11:

$$\text{R-11} \quad V \rightarrow \begin{bmatrix} \text{PRO} \\ \begin{Bmatrix} V' \\ \text{COP} \end{Bmatrix} \end{bmatrix}$$

The notation signifies that every verb is specified for a value of the feature PRO plus either V′ or COP. The features implied in PRO, V′, and COP would then be optionally manifested before the verb, constituting the same variety of spellings as for *Pro* generated by R-5. The feature COP (for the copula) has a zero manifestation. It means that a copula is implied, and not some other type of verb, V′ which is generally manifested.

In this way we treat the elements of *Pro* as features of the verb, not as a noun phrase. To maintain that *Pro* is not a subject noun-phrase, we must favor for our formulation cogeneration of an underlying NP outside of S over extraposition of some NP in S (e.g., the subject). Note, however, that although the element *Pro* is not a noun-phrase, it must have referential qualities, since the cogenerated topic noun-phrase must be identical to it in reference.

Figure 12, in accordance with our new formulation, would become the tree structure of Figure 20.

If we had chosen to spell out the appropriate features of PRO we would obtain the sentence of Figure 21:

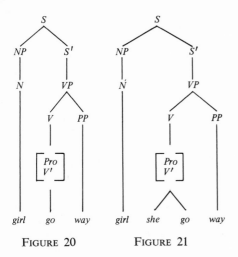

FIGURE 20   FIGURE 21

Note that now all our topic-comment sentences are structurally similar to subject-predicate sentences, even when a pronoun appears as subject, since the pronoun is now a part of the verb phrase.

Given that *Pro* is not a subject noun-phrase, we can now understand why the case marked pronouns are treated as nouns, while the unmarked pronouns are not. That a pronoun such as *him* is treated as a noun-phrase is quite a reasonable generalization for the child to have made. For *he*, however, the child does not make this generalization. *He*, the unmarked pronoun, is presented to the child only in the subject position. Since by R-6' the child does not generate noun-phrases in the subject position, he will not recognize *he* as a noun-phrase. Rather he will assume *he* (or its optional spelling *he's*) to be a preverbal introductory particle or an inflection of the verb.

Thus, we surmise that the child constructs, instead of subject-predicate relations, what could be called predicate sentences as characterized by R-6'. A predicate sentence would be one that describes a situation without specifying any element of that situation as the thing which the sentence is about. It would be a subjectless or topicless sentence. (Consider, for example, the English sentence "there's a man in the room," as a possible predicate sentence.)

The existence of subjectless sentences at some stage in the acquisition of language has further implications. Let us touch upon the relationship between the child's use of pronouns and their usage in some adult dialects of English. It is true that in some adult dialects the marked pronoun can appear in subject position in certain contexts. For example, in some subdialects of English the marked pronoun will appear as subject if not immediately preceding the verb. In such a dialect one would have "they read books" with the unmarked pronoun; but one would also have "them two read books," with the marked pronoun, when the marked pronoun is separated from the verb by some morpheme, such as the numeral "two." Moreover, there is the tendency in modern English dialects to use the marked pronoun in isolation, rather than the unmarked form. In answer to the question "who's there?", one would reply "me," rather than "I," even though the full form of the answer is "I am here," and not "me am here" or "me is here." In other words, there is a drift in English-speaking communities toward a grammar in which the pronoun, once used only as object, has come to be used in additional contexts. This same drift has been manifested in French to an even greater degree than in English. In French, for example, sentences paralleling exs. 13 are now acceptable adult forms.

One might propose to explain the child's use of pronouns by saying that in learning English he has been exposed to a dialect such as those above and apprehended the distinction in the usage of pronouns employed in it. To some degree this may be true. However, in the dialect of Mackie's parents there did not seem to be any instances of case-marked pronouns used in subject position. In addition, the distinction employed in adult grammars is in general more subtle than that manifested by the child: for example, *them* may be used as subject, but only if it does not immediately precede the verb. But more importantly, we are led to refrain from resting on this conclusion by looking at the situation in another way: on the basis of the manner in which the child acquires language we can explain precisely the historical drift described in the previous paragraph.

We propose that for a child learning English, the form of the pronoun which is used for the object of the verb or of the preposition is the form which he first recognizes as a noun phrase. Until much later he does not recognize the form used for the subject, *Pro*, as any more than an introductory particle or a verbal inflection, since he does not recognize the subject or unmarked form as a noun-phrase. To the extent that the child's first hypotheses regarding his mother tongue persist uncorrected into adulthood, the marked pronoun will be the form used with the same generality with which the noun phrase is used; and to the same extent, the unmarked pronoun will be the form restricted to positions immediately preceding the verb. In other words, the marked, or more highly specialized, pronoun in the adult grammar will become the unmarked one, or more highly generalized one in the child's grammar and vice versa.

This explanation is consonant with the hypothesis that linguistic changes occur by means of innovations occurring during the child's acquisition of language.

One would expect that such an historical drift in the use of pronouns would be universal among languages at certain stages. The form of the pronoun used as the subject becomes more and more restricted in this usage, more and more bound to the verb as an inflection; while the form used in the verb phrase becomes used in wider and wider circumstances. The speculated universality of this sort of drift rests on the universality of the child's failure to generate nounphrase subjects in his early grammars.

8. SIGNIFICANCE OF TOPICALIZATION

Let us compare the topic-comment construction with the pivot + open-class construction discussed by Braine[11] and others. According to Braine, the child's first two-word utterances are constructed by the concatenation of an element of a small, closed class of words, called the pivot class, with an element of the open class, usually a noun. It often

11 M. Braine, "The Ontogeny of English Phrase Structure: The First Phase," *Language*, XXXIX (1963), 1–13.

happens that a pivot-class word appears before an open-class word, a noun, as for example in "all-gone shoe." Here, just as in the case of Mackie's speech, the order is the reverse of what would be possible for an adult, who would say "the shoe is all-gone." We might seek to explain the position of apparent subjects after the predicate in 11 by analyzing these sentences as pivot + open-class constructions.

However, the situation must be different for Mackie, whose stage of language development is beyond the two-word sentence stage referred to by Braine. Note that while Braine says that his pivot + open-class construction may deviate from the order expected on the basis of adult grammar, it also appears that a given element of the pivot class has a fixed position, either before or after the open-class word. This is not true, for example, for *go way* and *over there* in our material, both of which appear both before and after a noun (exs. 8b, 9a, and 10a, b). Hence Braine's phenomenon, which is of earlier appearance, is different from the phenomenon here presented.

In his review of current results[12] and speculations on the development of language, D. McNeill[13] specifies, among others, two rules which are present in the early grammars of children, presumably at a stage prior to the stage at which we are describing Mackie. (Mackie's speech prior to this period has not yet been investigated.) These rules are, as specified by McNeill:

12 M. Braine, *loc. cit.*; R. Brown, "The Acquisition of Language," *Disorders of Communication*, XLII (1964); R. Brown, and C. Fraser, "The Acquisition of Syntax," in *Verbal Behavior and Learning*, C. N. Cofer and B. S. Musgrave, eds., (New York; McGraw Hill, Book Company, 1963); R. Brown, and C. Fraser, "The Acquisition of Syntax," in *The Acquisition of Language*. U. Bellugi and R. Brown, eds., *Monographs of the Society for Research in Child Development*, Series No. 92, XXIX (1964), 79–92; R. Brown, and U. Bellugi, "Three Processes in the Child's Acquisition of Syntax," *Harvard Educational Review*, XXXIV (1964), 133–51; S. Ervin, "Imitation and Structural Change in Children's Language," in *New Directions in the Study of Language*, E. Lenneberg, ed., (Cambridge, Mass.; MIT Press, 1964).

13 D. McNeill, "Developmental Psycholinguistics," Center for Cognitive Studies, Harvard University (mimeographed). [It later appeared in Frank Smith and George A. Miller, eds., *The Genesis of Language: A Psycholinguistic Approach* (Cambridge, Mass.: The M.I.T. Press, 1966), pp. 15–84].

McN r-1   S   → (P) + NP

NP   → $\begin{Bmatrix} (P) + N \\ N + N \end{Bmatrix}$

McN r-2   S   → Pred-P

Pred-P → (V) + NP

NP   → $\begin{Bmatrix} (P) + N \\ N + N \end{Bmatrix}$

Here we have the usual symbols, except that P stands for a pivot-class word. *Pred-P* stands for "Predicate Phrase," and V stands for a main verb, such as *go*, *put*, etc. P is a word like *that* or *he*, used in rule McN r-1 to yield sentences like "that a man" and "he dog" and hence is like our *Pro*. The expansion of NP is the same for both rules. Note then that we can reformulate McN r-1 and McN r-2. Except for the expansion of NP, they together generate the same strings as the following set of rules:

McN r-3   S   → VP

McN r-4   VP → (V) NP

McN r-5   V   → $\begin{Bmatrix} V \\ P \end{Bmatrix}$

McNeill observes that the child's sentences do not consist of a subject NP followed by a predicate VP. These are subjectless sentences. The pronominal elements in the class designated by P, while perhaps confusable with subjects, as our *Pro* is, are more like introductory words or affixes. These comprise a small closed class of morphemes, as opposed to the large open classes, such as N and V. At this stage there seems to be an association between the pivot class, P, and the verb, V.

McN r-3 is identical to our R-6′, and McN r-4 is similar to R-7. McN r-5 can be interpreted as generating verbal features, as does our R-11. The only difference is in the ultimate manifestation of these features. For McN r-5 either the verbal features (V) or the features of *Pro* (here P), but not both, can be manifested. For Mackie's speech for rule R-11 either the verbal features or those of *Pro* or both may be manifested, the features of *Pro* being spelled out to the left of V.

We contend that at Mackie's stage of development the elements dominated by *P* in McNeill's notation (namely, those we have dominated by *Pro* in our notation) are still categorized in the same way as pivot-class words. They are not to be regarded as noun-phrase subjects. Rather they are a part of the verb.

Thus the child's first grammars generate subjectless sentences. A similar phenomenon seems to occur in Japanese. In a recent talk[14] D. McNeill pointed out that a Japanese child learning his mother tongue very seldom used the phrase post-position *wa*[3]. This particle is used to indicate a topicalized noun-phrase, the topic of the sentence. The noun-phrase followed by *wa* is placed at the beginning as the topic. What McNeill has observed may be an example of the very same fact observed with Mackie. At some stage of development Japanese children learning Japanese produce topicless predicates just as English-learning children produce subjectless predicates.

If at an early stage the child produces sentences composed of nouns in isolation, or produces subjectless sentences, how then does the subject-predicate construction ultimately arise as the child reaches adult competence? McNeill recognizes his two rules given above as the two halves of sentence structure which need to be combined together to yield the form of adult sentences. He speculates that the combining of these rules is precisely what happens.

This sort of development is just what we have found. The cogeneration of a noun-phrase with a predicate sentence characterizes topicalization here described. It would seem then that the topic-comment relation is the precursor of the subject-predicate relation.

The case of the Japanese children described above seems to suggest that the notions of "subject" and "topic" may be essentially the same thing. The relations of *subject-predicate* and *topic-comment* may refer to the same underlying psychological reality. In fact, the similarity of these notions to the more general relation of *figure-ground*, which is perhaps more immediately relevant to other psychological phenomena, has been suggested (M. Bullowa, personal communication).

---

[14] D. McNeill, "Some Universals of Language Acquisition," Harvard Center for Cognitive Studies Colloquium, Cambridge, Mass., January 20, 1966.

Topic-comment constructions seem to evolve into subject-predicate constructions, the notion of subject being a special case of the notion of topic. The peculiar feature of the subject, perhaps, is that the subject is the obligatory, most deeply embedded topic of the sentence in a language which is so structured as to have it. Languages with topicalization such as Japanese, may topicalize several times in one sentence. English has one and only one topic, namely the subject, unless the passive sentence represents topicalization of some other noun phrase in addition.

The stage of development of Mackie's grammatical skills discussed in this paper seems to be a transitional one. It is the stage presumably after he would generate the pivot + open-class constructions that Braine shows, and after the period when subjectless predicates alone are generated. But it is before the period when he constructs English sentences in accordance with the subject predicate relation. The topic-comment construction characterizes this intermediate stage.

It is due to the independence of topicalization from normal English structure that sentences were produced sufficiently strange in appearance to spark an investigation of their nature; but it is due also to this very independence or universality of topicalization that it is reasonably successful as a means of communication between the child and his parents. The parents can interpret the child's utterances in terms of the subject-predicate constructions which adult speakers generate. The child can interpret the parents' subjectpredicate constructions in terms of his own topic-comment constructions, of which the subject-predicate construction is a special case.

We speculate that a child learning a language for the first time first produces sentences without subjects. Then he uses the innately known topic-comment construction to compose richer sentences. Later, if he is learning English, he comes to give this construction its special characteristics, ultimately arriving at the subject-predicate construction.

ROGER BROWN, COURTNEY CAZDEN, AND URSULA BELLUGI-KLIMA

57 Here is another sample of the recent psycholinguistic work done by Roger Brown and his associates, in which they examine the effect on the child's development of grammatical knowledge of two aspects of the speech he hears: variation in the frequency with which particular constructions are modeled and variation in the frequency of particular parent responses—expansions, expressions of approval and disapprovel, and occasional questions. (Cf. Cazden's doctoral dissertation on "Environmental Assistance to the Child's Acquisition of Grammar," Harvard University, 1965.)

The heroes of this study, Adam, Eve, and Sarah, are already familiar characters in the literature. See Selection 49 above.   A. B. A.

THE CHILD'S GRAMMAR
FROM I TO III

A group of us at Harvard are engaged in a longitudinal study of the development of grammar in three preschool children. One of the children, Eve, is the daughter of a graduate student. Another, Adam, is the son of a minister who lives in Boston. The third, Sarah, is the daughter of a man who works as a clerk in Somerville. The parents of the

Reprinted from John P. Hill, ed., Minnesota Symposia on Child Development, *Vol. 2* pp. 28–73. (*Minneapolis: University of Minnesota Press, 1968*), © copyright 1968 University of Minnesota, by permission of

University of Minnesota Press.

This research was supported by Public Health Service Research Grant MH-7088 from the National Institute of Mental Health.

first two children have college educations; Sarah's parents have high school degrees. The principal data of the study are transcriptions of the spontaneous speech of the child and his mother (occasionally also the father) in conversation at home. For each child we have at least two hours of speech for every month that he has been studied; sometimes as much as six hours. Sarah's records are entirely transcribed in a phonetic notation that includes stress and intonation. The other children's records are not in phonetic notation except at a few points where some particular hypothesis made the notation necessary.

Figure 1 identifies an initial developmental period which has been the focus of our analyses thus far. The initial period has been defined in terms of the means and ranges of utterance length, terms external to the grammar. The period begins, for all three children, when the mean was 1.75 morphemes and ends when the mean was 4.0 morphemes. The longest utterance at the lower bound of the interval was 4 morphemes; at the upper bound, 13. Mean length of utterance is useful as a rough term of reference for developmental level in this early period but it grows more variable and less useful with age.

As can be seen from Figure 1 the children were not the same chronological age when the study began: Eve was 18 months; Adam and Sarah were 27 months. We selected these three children from some 30 considered on the basis of matched initial performance rather than age. At the end of the period for analysis Eve was 28 months, Adam 42 months, and Sarah 48 months. In terms of the utterance length the rates of development of the three children may be ordered; Eve, Adam, Sarah.

The research is directed at two general questions: (1) What does the child know of the structure of English at successive points in his development? (2) By what processes does he acquire his knowledge? The most explicit, comprehensive, and systematic from in which adult knowledge of grammar has been represented is the generative transformational grammar (Chomsky, 1957; 1965). A generative grammar is a rule system that derives an infinite set of well-formed sentences and assigns them correct structur dalescriptions. The most demanding form in which

to pose the question of the child's knowledge of structure at any time is to ask for a generative grammar that represents his knowledge. We are attempting to write such grammars for the three children at each of five points in the intial developmental period. These points are marked with lines and Roman numerals in Figure 1; they fall at nearly equal intervals across the period. For the grammars we make detailed distributional analyses of 700 utterances from each child.

A complete annotated grammar is between 50 and 100 pages long and so none is presented here. We do, however, present portions of a single grammar, the one written for Adam at III, to illustrate the kinds of knowledge such a grammar is designed to represent. Then, using Adam III as a kind of temporary terminus we provide a descriptive overview of developments in the first period. Following this we offer more detailed discussions of two specific developments: segmentation into morphemes and the construction of "Wh" questions. Finally we review what we have learned about the role of "training variables" in grammar acquisition.

A PORTION OF ADAM III

The sentence *Where those dogs goed* was not actually created by Adam in III; it is a composite that illustrates more of the interesting features of his grammar than does any single sentence he actually formed. Let us follow through the derivation of this composite sentence using the grammar constructed for Adam at III.

The grammar is a set of mechanical procedures or algorithms for generating sentences and assigning structural descriptions to them. The "generation" in question is "logical" rather than "psychological" in the sense that the grammar does not constitute a model of practical processes by which sentences might actually be produced or understood. The grammar is psychological in that it is supposed to *represent* Adam's knowledge about the organization of sentences and it is presumed that this knowledge somehow enters into actual production and comprehension.

The structure of grammatical knowledge is not given in any direct and simple way in

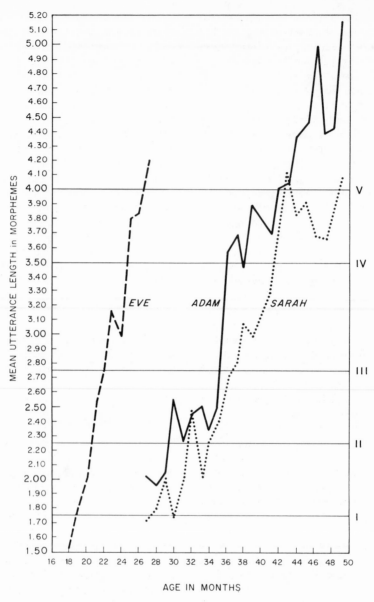

FIGURE 1

spontaneous speech. It is worked out from spontaneous speech by a process of inference that is far from being either mechanical or certainly correct. The process is something like trying to fit together the pieces of an immense jigsaw puzzle and something like the process of trying to decipher an unknown Minoan script and not at all like the process of doing experiments in a psychological laboratory. We operate on the general assumption that the child's terminal state of knowledge is of the sort represented by current transformational grammars (e.g., Chomsky, 1965; Katz and Postal, 1964; Klima, 1964). However, we do not simply attribute to each sentence that the child produces the analysis that would be appropriate to that sentence if it were produced by an adult; if we were to do that, the inquiry would be largely vacuous. Insofar as the child's particular sentence—and all related sentences—depart from adult forms the grammar is tailored to the departures. The most informative departures are analogical errors of commission such as *goed* in the sample sentence. Harder to interpret, but still important, are errors of omission such as the absence of auxiliary *did* from the sample sentence. Omissions in a sentence are at least easy to detect but omissions in the distributional range of a form are harder to detect and harder to interpret since it is necessary to weigh the probability that an omission is simply a consequence of the size of the sample that has been taken. Finally all the errors that occur must be considered in comparison with conceivable errors that do not occur. Even this full procedure will not render the construction completely determinate in all respects. The indeterminacies are tentatively resolved by assigning the usual adult representation insofar as that representation does not depend on forms that have never appeared in the child's speech. We shall be able to illustrate most aspects of this process in what follows.

The phrase-structure level
A phrase-structure rule in adult grammar rewrites a single symbol into symbol(s) distinct from the one rewritten. Roughly speaking, the phrase structure represents the adult's sense of hierarchical grouping in a sentence; the feeling we have that a sentence "cracks" or "breaks up" into natural major constituents which in turn break up into natural smaller constituents. It also represents such basic sentence relations as are called in traditional grammar subject of a sentence, predicate of a sentence, object of a verb, and so forth. The phrase structure includes everything essential for a complete semantic interpretation but it does not necessarily order elements as they are ordered in the ultimate surface structure.

Each derivation begins with the symbol S for *sentence*, not because Adam is supposed to have a generic intention to compose a sentence which precedes the composition of any particular sentence, but because the grammar is a kind of extended definition of the meaning of *sentence*. The first rule of the phrase structure rewrites S into Nominal and

Predicate and a set of abstract morphemes symbolized as imp, wh, and neg. These last three represent the germs from which, respectively, imperatives, interrogatives, and negatives can be developed. The abstract morphemes do not stand for any particular words but provide the occasion in adult grammar for transformations which result in a great variety of imperative, interrogative, and negative expressions. The abstract morphemes are in parentheses to indicate optionality; sentences need not be either imperative, interrogative, or negative. In the derivation of a declarative affirmative sentence none of the abstract morphemes is selected. The imp and wh symbols are in brackets to indicate that the symbols are mutually exclusive; a sentence is not simultaneously imperative and interrogative.

The second rule of the phrase structure makes a fundamental division among predicates. The symbol Cop (for *copula*) expands either as a form of *be* or as β which ultimately has no phonological representation (Adam produces sentences like *That my book* which should contain a *be* form but do not). Sentences with Cop are sometimes called equational sentences. The verb (or its absence) is followed in such sentences by a noun phrase (NP) functioning as predicate nominative or an adverbial or a descriptive adjective (included in Det which means *determiner*). Sample sentences are: *That's a clock; Doggie is here; Doggie big*. The main verb (MV) form of the predicate may, if the verb is a transitive, be followed by a NP functioning as direct object which may in turn be followed by some sort of adverbial (Adverb). Intransitive verbs take adverbials but not direct objects.

In rule 4 the auxiliary (Aux) is introduced and in rule 5 it is rewritten. These rules are somewhat different from the rules that represent adult use of the adult auxiliary. What kinds of distributional facts about Adam's speech suggest the rules we have written? Adam's Aux is introduced into MV but not Cop; the adult auxiliary would be introduced into both. The adult rule represents the fact that adults combine *be* forms with past (e.g., *was*) and with auxiliary verbs (e.g., *I want to be*) and with progressive (B + ing) aspect (e.g., *He is*

FIGURE 2:   Phrase structure rules and derivation.

Rules of the phrase structure	Derivation of "Where those dogs goed?"
1. S → ([imp/wh]) (neg) Nominal–Predicate	wh–Nominal–Predicate
2. Predicate → [MV/Cop]	wh–Nominal–MV
3. MV → Vb (Comp)	wh–Nominal–Vb–Comp
4. Vb → (Aux) V (Prt)	wh–Nominal–Aux–V–Comp
5. Aux → [V^c/B + ing/Past]	wh–Nominal–Past–V–Comp
6. Comp → [Adverb/Nominal (Adverb)]	wh–Nominal–Past–V–Adverb
7. Cop → B–Pred	
8. B → [be/β]	
9. Pred → [Det/Nominal/Adverb]	
10. Adverb → [Loc/Adv/Prep Phr]	wh–Nominal–Past–V–Loc
11. Loc → [somewhere/Adv/Prep Phr]	wh–Nominal–Past–V–somewhere
12. Prep Phr → Prp [Nominal/Adv]	
13. Nominal → [something/NP]	wh–NP–Past–V–somewhere
14. NP → (Det) N	wh–Det–N–Past–V–somewhere

KEY

Symbols do not all have exact equivalents in the terminology of traditional grammar so translations are only suggestive. The exact sense of each symbol is given by the grammar itself.

( ): optionality
[x/y]: mutual exclusivity
   of x and y
Adv: adverb
Adverb: adverbial
Aux: auxiliary
B: *be* or *β*
B + ing: progressive aspect
β: should contain *be* form but
   does not
Comp: complement
Cop: copula
Det: determiner or descriptive
   adjective
imp: imperative
Loc: locative adverbial

MV: main verb
N: noun
neg: negative
NP: noun phrase
Past: past tense
Pred: predicate adjectival,
   nominal, or adverbial
Prp: preposition
Prep Phr: prepositional
   phrase
Prt: particle
S: sentence
V^c: catenative verb
V: verb
Vb: verbal
wh: interrogative

being good) as well as combining main verbs with these operations. Adam, on the other hand, never combined *be* with auxiliary operations. The division between equational and main verb sentences lies deep in Adam's grammar just because he includes Aux in the one and not the other.

In rule 5 Aux is rewritten as three consti-tuents: catenative verbs (V^c) such as *wanna*, *gonna*, and *hafta;* the progressive aspect (B + ing) which produces such forms as *walking* and *eating;* the Past morpheme which produces such forms as *walked* and also *feeled.* Why are the three constituents collected together and placed before the V? The descrip-tion does not accord with the surface characteristics of Adam's relevant sentences, for, although the catenatives do precede verbs on the surface, the progressive and past inflections are affixed to the ends of verbs. At a later point in the grammar, in the transformational component, there has to be a rule that transposes stems and affixes so as to produce the correct surface order. In that case why set them wrong in the first place? For several reasons. In the first place, as a means of representing the relation of mutual exclusion which obtains among the three auxiliary elements in Adam's speech. He never combines two or more auxiliaries to say such things as *I was eating* or *I wanted to eat*, though adults of course do. Deeper motivation for the Aux constituent derives from the requirements of the transformational component. In the construction of imperatives, for example, Adam never uses an auxiliary. He says *Please read* but not the likes of *Please reading* or *Please wanna read* or *Please readed*. It is convenient to be able to exclude all of the possibilities at once by forbidding the use of all auxiliaries in imperatives and for that you need an Aux constituent. Behind the convenience, of course, is the fact that catenative verbs, progressives, and pasts are distributed in sentences as if they were, on some level, one thing.

These are some of the considerations that shape the form of the first five rules. How does one use the rules to construct a derivation? The derivation of a sentence is, essentially, the pathway through the rules that will yield the sentence. There must be such a pathway for every sentence and none for nonsentences. One constructs a derivation by applying the rules to successive strings, making those (permitted) choices which will in the end produce the intended sentence. The first step of the derivation in Figure 2 might be read, "the symbol S is rewritten, by Rule 1 as: 'wh-Nominal-Predicate.'" Since the intended sentence is to be an interrogative, wh is chosen from among the optional abstract morphemes. The intended sentence is to contain a main verb (*go*) and so MV is selected by Rule 2. The sentence will also contain a locative and since these develop out of the complement ("Comp") that constituent must be added

by Rule 3. There is to be a Past auxiliary and Rules 4 and 5 accomplish its selection.

And so the derivation proceeds. The last line, sometimes called the "preterminal" string, still does not look much like the sentence *Where those dogs goed?* Instead of the interrogative word *where* we have the abstract interrogative morpheme wh and the locative "somewhere." This last is not the word *somewhere* but is rather a kind of dummy element standing for an unknown, or unspecified, locative. The *where* interrogative will be derived by transformation from the wh element and the dummy locative. The preterminal string contains, in place of the lexical items *those*, *dog*, and *go*, symbols for the categories (or parts of speech) to which these items respectively belong: "Det," "N," and "V." In the next level of the grammar the category symbols will be replaced by appropriate lexical items and the result will be a terminal string: "wh-those-dog-Past-go-somewhere."

The subcategorization level

If determiners, nouns, and verbs from the lexicon were allowed freely to replace the category symbols Det, N, and V in the preterminal string underlying the sample sentence the results would often be ungrammatical. In addition to *those dogs go* we might have *a dogs go* and *those Adam go* and *the stone knows* and what not. There are, in English, restrictions on the co-occurrence of lexical items which forbid many of the combinations that the phrase structure rules alone permit. These restrictions have traditionally been formulated in terms of lexical subcategories. For example, among nouns, those that may take determiners are said to belong to the common noun subcategory and *dog* is one such. Nouns that may not take determiners are called proper nouns such as *Adam*. Nouns are also subcategorized on other principles; count nouns (including *dog*) may be pluralized whereas mass nouns (e.g., *air*) may not. How is subcategorization to be represented in the present grammar? We will illustrate the general character of the rules with reference to one constituent of the sample sentence, the subject Nominal which is represented in the preterminal string as Det-N and is to be represented in the surface sentence as *those dogs*.

Each entry in the lexicon of the language is going to be assigned certain syntactic features (such as + ct for count nouns) which represent certain distributional potentialities of the lexical items. In addition, the lexical category symbols which we find in the last line of the phrase-structure derivation—such as Det and N and V are going to expand into complex symbols which also contain syntactic features. The complete complex symbol will be a kind of grappling hook with a set of syntactic features constituting a particular sort of denticulate surface shaped to retrieve the right kind of item from the lexicon.

The complex symbol is, first of all, marked with the name of the major category (e.g., + N). In the lexicon all nouns (for instance *dog* in Figure 3) are assumed to be similarly marked. Now we have the first level of subcategorization, sometimes called strict subcategorization. This involves the assignment to each complex symbol of syntactic features which are simply, its frames or contexts, stated in terms of category symbols. It is as if one were to scan the preterminal string and take note of the fact that each category occurs in the context of certain other categories and then enter those category contexts which restrict the selection of lexical items. In our own example the symbol N occurs in the context Det—. When, therefore, N is replaced by a particular noun from the lexicon that noun must be of the sort that may be preceded by a determiner; in fact by a common noun and not a proper noun. The facts can be expressed by assigning the complex symbol for N the contextual feature [+Det—] and by assigning all common nouns in the lexicon including *dog* this same feature and by adopting a replacement rule which allows the complex symbol for N to be replaced by only those lexical items having matching syntactic features.

From Rule 14 of the phrase structure we know that, *in general*, which means across all sentences, determiners are optional before nouns. In the particular sentence under derivation, however, there is to be a determiner before the noun, and that fact must enter into the derivation. The need for specifi-

cation of a contextual feature arises only but always where there is, in the phrase structure, an optional environment for a lexical category. Contextual features are needed at several points in Adam's grammar. By assigning verbs the contextual features + ___NP and − ___NP, for instance, it is possible to retrieve transitive verbs when they are required and intransitives when they are required.

At the next level in the expansion of the complex symbol, syntactic features are added which are not defined in terms of the categories of the preterminal string. In the case of the nouns in a sentence the syntactic features are context-free,—that is, they are selected without reference to other complex symbols in the sentence. The syntactic features added to the symbols for determiners and verbs are context-sensitive, which means they are selected with reference to markers already added to nouns. Such rules are sometimes called selection rules. By this arrangement other words are made to agree with nouns rather than nouns with them. For English, in general, and also for Adam III, the "selectional dominance" of the noun is not just a convention but is rather a representation of certain facts about sentences.

The symbol N in our present derivation acquires the marker + ct rather than − ct and the marker + no rather than − no. It is then equipped to retrieve a count noun from the lexicon, a noun marked + ct as *dog* is in Figure 3. Lexical entries for nouns will not be marked + no but, rather, ± no, to indicate that they may be pluralized, or else − no to indicate that, like *air*, they may not be pluralized. It is just these markers, and in addition a marker that indicates whether a noun is human (+ hum) or not, that are needed for nouns in Adm III.

The symbol Det acquires syntactic features in a context-sensitive manner, taking its lead, as it were, from the head word in the noun phrase. Since that head word, the N, has the features + ct and + no the determiner to accompany it must have features which comprise a matrix to the noun's patrix. Det requires the features [−[+ ct]N] and [−[+ no]N]; the features require that the determiner drawn from the lexicon be one

FIGURE 3: Subcategorization Rules and Derivation.

Subcategorization Rules

LEXICAL CATEGORY	CATEGORICAL CONTEXTS	OTHER SYNTACTIC FEATURES
N → [+ N][a]	N → [+ Det___]; [− Det___]	N → [+ ct]; [− ct]
		N → [+ no]; [− no]
Det → [+ Det][b]		Det → [___[+ ct]N]; [___[− ct]N]
		Det → [___[+ no]N]; [___[− no]N]

Derivation

Preterminal string............. wh–Det–N–Past–V–somewhere

Complex symbol expansion .... N → [+ N, + Det___, + ct, + no]
Det → [+ Det, ___[+ ct]N, ___[+ no]N]

Replacement by lexical items .... *dog,* [+ N, + Det___, + ct, + no]
those, [+ Det, ___[+ ct]N, ___[+ no]N]

[a] Lexical entry: *dog,* [+ N, + Det___, + ct, ± no]
[b] Lexical entry: *those,* [+ Det, ___[+ ct]N, ___[+ no]N]

that is able to modify count nouns in the plural.

The fully expanded complex symbols for our sentence (there would be one for V as well as N and Det) serve to select lexical entries. The general lexical rule (which need not be stated since it constitutes part of the definition of derivation) is: Where a complex symbol is not distinct from a lexical entry the latter can replace the former. The lexical entry for *dog* is one of those common count nouns that can replace the symbol for N in the present derivation, and *those* is among the entries that can replace the symbol for Det. These processes are illustrated in Figure 3 which includes the rules and derivation.

The transformational level

The phrase structure and subcategorization levels together comprise what has been called the base structure of a grammar. In a derivation the base structure yields a structured string of morphemes such as wh— [those dog]Nominal [Past–go]vb—somewhere; this string contains only some of its labeled bracketings. Transformational rules map such underlying strings into new structured strings which are closer to actual sentences. Transformations delete, substitute, and permute elements—as phrase structure rules cannot. Roughly speaking, transfor-

mations represent the feeling native speakers have that the members of a certain set of sentences are related to their counterparts in another set by a single function.

Adam III includes 24 transformational rules. Some of the grammatical functions they perform are: agreement in person and number for subject and verb; agreement in number for subject and predicate nominative; creation of such elliptical possessives as *yours* and *mines;* and deletion of subject *you* from imperatives. In the derivation of our sample sentence, transformations are needed to transpose an affix and stem and to incorporate *somewhere* into wh. The rules and the steps in the derivation appear in Figure 4. A transformational rule describes the structure of the kind of string to which it is applicable; there will generally be an indefinite number of strings which satisfy that structural description. In an actual derivation it is a particular string that is transformed.

The morphophonemic level

Rules on this level really belong to the phonological component but to bring the derivation of our composite sentence to a recognizable form we need to use two of them. They are:

XV.   wh + somewhere → *where*
XXIV. [X]v + Past → X + *-ed*

FIGURE 4:   Transformation rules and derivation.

XIV.   Wh incorporation for MV sentences:
        wh — Nominal — Verb (Nominal)
        — somewhere *implies* wh + somewhere
        — Nominal — Verb (Nominal)
XIX.   Affixation of Past*:
        $X^1 - [Past]_{Aux} - V - X^2$
        implies $X^1 - V + Past - X^2$

Derivation

Base.   wh — [those dog]$_{Nominal}$ [Past — go]$_{Verb}$
          somewhere
XIV.   wh + somehwere — those — dog
         — Past — go
XIX.   wh + somewhere — those — dog
         — go + Past

The numbers assigned the rules are those they carry
in the full grammar.
*X^1 and X^2 simply stand for any other sentence
constituents.

Rule XXIV results in the erroneous form
goed. The occurrence of this error marks the
absence from Adam III of the adult morphophonemic rule:

$[go]_V$ + Past → *went*

In terms of the conventions with which we
are working, then, the error in question is a
superficial one. It can be corrected by adding a
single rule which does not disturb the remainder of the grammar in any way.

Now that we have a general picture of the
children's competence at III let us characterize in a general way developments between
I and III.

OVERVIEW OF DEVELOPMENTS
BETWEEN I AND III

Figure 1 indicates that there are large differences in rate of linguistic development among
Adam, Eve, and Sarah but the order of events
is, for these three unacquainted children,
strikingly uniform. So much so that it is
possible to describe developments between
I and III in a way that is true of all. This is
not so say that there are no differences among
the children. One that is especially consistent
and interesting concerns the rate of production of ungrammatical and anomolous forms.

Adam produced these at about four times the
rate of either girl. Adam spoke of "talking
crackers," said his nose could "see" and
addressed the microphone as if it were a
person, and said, *Its went* and *Why I can't
do that* and *That a my book*. The girls were
more literal and, except for telegraphic
omissions, more often grammatical. From
other data we have seen and from what
parents tell us there is evidently great individual
variation among children on this dimension;
probably it explains the very different notions
of language development that particular
psychologists derive from their own children.
When the girls made errors they were the
same kinds of errors that Adam made. For
that reason we have assumed that the induction and hypothesis testing involved is common to the three and simply more copiously
externalized by Adam. He gives us a richer
"print out" and so we more often cite evidence
from his records than from the records of Eve
and Sarah.

Sentence types

From I to III the children seem to be working
chiefly on simple sentences. This is not to say
that all or even most of the children's *utterances* were complete simple sentences. It is
rather to say that the most complex constructions they produced were simple sentences;
that they never (or almost never) conjoined
or embedded simple sentences. We do not
find the likes of *John and Mary laughed* or
The man you saw is here or *I want you to eat*.

In saying that the children from I to III
seemed to be working on the structure of
simple sentences it is necessary to make
explicit the fact that we do ot intend to make
two related but stronger claims. We do not
claim that in I and III the children learned
nothing about conjoining and embedding;
it is possible, after all, that some restriction
on performance prevented them from revealing in spontaneous speech all that they
had learned. Nor do we say that the children's
knowledge of the simple sentence was complete before they started to embed and con-
join; that is clearly untrue. In III there were
a few instances of embedding; and at that
point all three children still had a great deal
to learn about simple sentences. Auxiliary

elements were only occurring singly; there were no combinations. There were no passives and only the simplest reflexes of negativity. There were no tag questions and indeed well-formed *Yes-No* questions of all kinds were missing. Clearly embedding and conjoining do not wait upon the development of complete knowledge of simple sentences.

What sorts of simple sentences were the children working on from I to III? Declarative-affirmative sentences, of course, but we shall leave till last the description of these since most of the knowledge involved is not specific to them but is common to all sentences. In addition to declarative-affirmative sentences the children were working on negatives, imperatives, and interrogatives. We saw in Adam III that these are developed, in transformational grammar, from the abstract morphemes neg, imp, and wh. From the beginning of our records, from I that is, the children gave evidence of understanding the meaning of these morphemes. What they lacked was the transformational rules which develop surface structures expressing these morphemes. These rules were entirely lacking in I. In III there were 8–12 transformational rules serving this purpose. This is still only a fraction of the adult rules and some of the child's rules at III were not proper adult rules at all.

René Spitz (1957) says that the child begins at about 15 months to shake his head as an intentional negative signal usually having the sense of resistance to some attempt to influence him. In I we find this signal and also the word *no* used to resist imperatives and to answer *Yes-No* questions. We also find *no* added initially to several sorts of utterance: *No fall, No put, No picture in there*, etc., and this seems to be the child's own invention. In II and III the *no* forms were supplemented by *can't won't*, and *don't*. It seems unlikely to us that these were related transformationally, as they are in the adult language, to *can, will*, and *do*—unlikely for the reason that the affirmative modal auxiliaries had not appeared at this time. The forms seemed simply to be a set of preverbal forms introduced by obligatory transformation when the neg morpheme was in the base structure of a sentence with a main verb.

Imperative sentences in adult grammar are derived by transformation out of underlying strings containing the morpheme *imp* and having *you* as subject and *will* as auxiliary. This analysis is motivated by such adult sentences as: *Go chase yourself* and *Come here, will you?* Neither reflexives (*yourself*) nor tags (*will you*) occurred in early child speech and so the facts justifying the adult analysis were lacking. In the recording sessions at home one could often be quite sure that a child's sentence had an imperative meaning but there was nothing in the surface form of his imperative sentences that could serve as a reliable sign of this meaning. To be sure, such sentences were often produced without explicit subject, as are adult imperatives, but the children also very often omitted the subjects of sentences clearly intended to be declaratives. What happened between I and III was that the subjectless sentence came to be ever more nearly restricted to the imperative but it was not exclusively imperative even in III. In addition, there were a few words the child learned to use after I (especially *please* and *gimme*) which may be confidently interpreted as imperative markers.

Very few of the linguistic reflexes of imperativity developed, then, in this first period but from the start in I there were indications that the child understood the imperative meaning. This evidence on the responsive side lay in the child's compliance with or (at least as often) resistance to the force of a parental imperative. On the performance side it lay in the child's occasional persistence in using certain constructions again and again to accomplish some effect in a resistant adult.

Interrogatives are of two basic types: *Yes-No* questions and *Wh* questions. We shall leave for a later section the description of *Wh* questions. From I to III the child's *Yes-No* questions were identifiable by rising intonation but not, consistently, by any other feature. It was as if he asked "Yes or No?" by speaking any sentence or sentence fragment with questioning intonation. Well-formed *Yes-No* questions, with the subject and the first member of the auxiliary transposed, appeared later than III.

The grammatical structure of declarative-affirmative simple sentences is almost entirely represented by the base component of a grammar, the phrase-structure and subcategorization rules. All of this structure is relevant also to negatives, imperatives, and interrogatives but these latter include something more—rules in the transformational component. There are several kinds of knowledge represented by the base component: relations within a sentence, a hierarchy of constituents, and subcategorization or co-occurrence restrictions. We shall say something about each of them.

Basic sentence relations

The basic relations are those called subject of the sentence, predicate of the sentence, and object of the verb. So far as our materials permit us to judge, the child's knowledge of these relations which, in English, are chiefly expressed by order undergoes no development. He seems to express the relations he means to express from the very start. At any rate there are very few detectable errors in all the records. In most utterances it is clear that the intended subject and object are the constituents found in subject and object position. For instance: *I dump trash out, I making coffee, You need some paper.* It is unlikely that the child intended to convey the reversed relations: *Trash dump me out, Coffee making me, Some paper need you.* There are in the records a handful of exceptions in which the intended object seems to be in subject position: *Paper find, Daddy suitcase go get it, Paper write.* But these are the only exceptions in thousands of well-ordered sentences.

The precision with which the child expresses basic sentence relations is an imprtant fact since these relations are probably linguistic universals and so the relations themselves may be preformed organizations in the human brain. Perhaps subject and object relations are to the child what nut-burying is to the squirrel, an innate pattern requiring only a releaser to set it in operation. Perhaps, but we shall not want to draw that conclusion until we have more data. The children we have studied scrupulously preserve sentence word order not only with respect to basic relations but also with respect to the order of articles,

adjectives, auxiliary verbs, and adverbs and all other words. In imitation tasks they omit words buts eldom confuse order. This may be a general feature of imitation in children or perhaps only a feature of the imitation of speech. The accurate expression of sentence relations by children learning English may, therefore, be a kind of incidental consequence of the fact that English expresses these relations by word order. We should like to know how well the relations are expressed by children learning a language that expresses subject and object relations by case endings (see Slobin, 1966, for some evidence concerning Russian).

Constituents

The Aux is a constituent that developed in the period from I to III. In I all main verbs occurred in unmarked generic form. In II and III a set of operations on the verb developed, the same set in all three children: the progressive, the past, and a set of semiauxiliary verbs we call catenatives. Most prominent among these latter are *gonna, wanna,* and *hafta.* The three operations on the verb are represented as a constituent Aux for reasons already described.

The NP is a constituent that was present even in I but which underwent consolidation and elaboration between I and III. The constituent status of the NP even in I is attested to by the fact that the children quite consistently responded to questions in *Who* or *What* with some sort of NP. This equivalence in the exchanges of discourse is evidence that the many particular NP's were organized together. In adult speech the NP has four principal functions in simple sentences: in equational sentences it serves as subject and as predicate nominative; in main verb sentences as subject and direct object. For the children the NP had these four functions from the start. At any rate some sort of NP served each function but, whereas an adult will use every sort of NP in all positions, in the children's speech at I each position seemed to require a somewhat different formula for the NP. Subjects of equational sentences were often impersonal pronouns (especially *that* and *it*) but predicate nominatives never were. Subjects of main verbs were almost always names of persons or animals whereas direct objects were almost always names of inanimate things. Subject NP's in both kinds of sentence, at I, never consisted of more than one morpheme—a simple pronoun or noun. Object and predicate nominative NP's at I were, on the other hand, somewhat more complex; they might consist of two nouns (e.g., *Adam book*) or a determiner and noun (e.g., *my book*). If we write a grammar that stays close to the sentences actually obtained at I we must include four distinct versions of NP, which makes a fragmentary grammar strangely unlike the adult form. One of the things that happened between I and III was that the four NP came to resemble one another closely enough so that a single NP symbol, that is rewritten by a single set of rules, could be entered in all four positions. In addition, the NP grew in complexity in all positions.

There are, finally, constituents which had still not developed by III. These include the adverbials "Time" and "Manner." There were occasional time and manner expressions in the children's speech by III but they were few. Most importantly˙ the children at III were not giving grammatically appropriate answers to time (*When*) and manner (*How*) questions. Of the adverbials, the locative is by far the first to develop. It is clearly present even in I.

Strict subcategorization
The progressive inflection (*-ing*) emerged for all three children between I and III. In adult English this inflection is not used with all verbs. So-called "process" verbs, like *sing*, *walk*, *eat*, etc, freely take the progressive whereas "state" verbs like *need, equal, know*, and *like* do not. To say *I am singing the song* is quite correct but *I am knowing the song* is strange. The process-state subcategorization of verbs can be represented, in an English grammar, in the expansion of the complex symbol for "V." A choice is made between two features which represent contexts at the level of the phrase structure; the features are: $[+[be + ing]\_\_\_]$; $[-[be + ing]\_\_\_]$.[1]

---

[1] The form be + ing refers to English grammar, whereas the form used earlier, B + ing, refers specifically to the grammar of the children in this study.

These features are entered also in relevant verbs in the lexicon. The interesting fact is that these rules were already needed for the children's grammar at III because the children observed the subcategories and made no mistakes of the type: *I liking candy* or *I wanting a book*. Such mistakes were not simply absent from the samples used for the grammars; they were absent from all of the data over the full range from I to V.

David McNeill has recently (1965) argued that children must have innate knowledge of a hierarchy of subcategories corresponding to whatever hierarchy may prove to be a linguistic universal. The complete absence of subcategorization errors in connection with the progressive inflection seems to provide a certain support for McNeill's position or, at any rate, does so if the following interpretation of his position is acceptable.

If we ask what could possibly be universal and so innate about the process-state distinction the answer must surely be the underlying semantic principle. The distributional facts, such as the rule for *-ing*, are known to be specific to particular languages. How could an innate process-state distinction forestall inflectional errors? Something like this would have to be true: As the meaning of each new verb were learned, verbs like *walk*, *eat*, *need*, and *like*, the semantic entry would have to include all innate subcategorization features as well as individual elements of meaning. In short, *walk* would from the first be tagged as a "process" and *need* as a "state."

When at a later time the child attended to distributional facts peculiar to English, such as the fact that some verbs were inflected with *-ing* and some not, he would have a set of ready hypotheses to explain the cleavage. He would test to see whether it was governed by one or another of the preestablished, universal subcategorizations. And of course the process-state subcategorization defines the proper dotted line for *-ing*. It is somewhat as if a child in learning to recognize coins kept track of all the attributes that are ever significant in a coinage system—color, weight, size, design, texture, etc. Then when he first encountered the distributional facts of monetary exchange, such as the fact that two coins of one kind equal one of another, he would quickly see which of the perceptual attributes he had been keeping track of were useful.

The absence of error in connection with a semantically principled subcategorization is one prediction of the "innateness" hypothesis and this prediction is confirmed in the case of the progressive. However, one easily thinks of other predictions that are not confirmed. The division of nouns into mass and count subcategories is semantically based and as likely to be universal as the process-state division but the children were, at V, still making some errors in their use of the noun subcategories. Some subcategorizations in English are unprincipled (i.e., they have no semantic base); for example, the verb subcategories that take regular and irregular inflections for Past. Not surprisingly children make many mistakes in cases like these, where rote learning of the subcategory membership of each verb is really the only possibility. In fact, errors in this connection are often heard in the elementary school years. The errors are to be expected. But if the children have innate subcategories should they not, on first encountering unprincipled cleavages, act as if they expected one or another of the innate principles to govern the cleavage? On first encountering the fact that some verbs take -ed and some do not, a child ought to test the hypothesis that all of the former verbs might be processes and the latter states, the hypothesis that the former might be transitives and the latter intransitives, etc. There is no trace of anything of the kind in our data.

The full story is too long to tell but our present best guess is that the absence of error with -ing is not to be attributed to innate subcategorization. And, in general, we have not found any reason to believe that subcategories are innate other than the usual reason—it is awfully difficult to figure out how they are learned.

Noncategorical syntactic features
Plural number in English is marked by inflection of the noun and this inflection, like the progressive, was entirely absent in I and often present by III. The expression of number in English is vastly more complicated than the expression of something like progressive aspect. For example, there must be agreement in number between a head noun and its determiners, between a subject noun and a predicate nominal and between a pronoun and its antecedent noun. Number and person together, as features of a subject noun, determine the form of the verb: *walks* or *walk; is* or *are*. In Adam III number is introduced in the base structure in the form of two context-free syntactic markers in the complex symbol for the noun: [+no] and [−no]. There are related markers for the complex symbol of Det and for many lexical items. There are three transformations and several morphophonemic rules.

The development of number in the three children illustrates nicely the difference between deep and superficial acquisition of a grammatical feature. In terms of chronological age, Eve began to inflect nouns some 14 months earlier than did Sarah. However, when Eve first used plurals she made many mistakes in all aspects of number agreement whereas Sarah, from the start, made almost no mistakes. What this means is that in Eve's grammar number first appears as a low-level morphophonemic rule which, in effect, says that nouns have an optional pronunciation with a terminal sibilant. The introduction of this rule leaves the rest of Eve's grammar undisturbed. For Sarah, number enters in the base structure and effects complex changes in the total grammar. So we see that Eve was not always so far in advance of Sarah as the simple mean length of utterance index would alone indicate. And we see that acquisitions which may look alike if we only examine certain words or endings may look very unlike when the total distributional pattern is examined.

In summary of this overview it is correct to say that the child's early grammar comprises a base structure that is not very different from that of the adult grammar and a syntactic transformational component that is rudimentary in III and almost totally absent in I. This is not the same as saying that children directly speak base-structure sentences. It is not clear what that could mean since morphophonemic and phonetic rules are required to make sentences of the underlying strings. But the underlying strings themselves seem to be chiefly those that can be generated by the base.

We proceed now to a more detailed discussion of two problems in the early period.

SEGMENTATION INTO MORPHEMES

In order to learn grammar a child must segment the speech he hears into morphemes because morphemes are the ultimate units of grammatical rules. There are short-run regularities which can be formulated in terms of smaller units, the segmental phonemes, but the longer-run regularities which render an infinitite number of meanings constructible and interpretable cannot be formulated in terms of phonemes.

It may be useful to imagine an erroneous segmentation into morphemes and what its consequences would be. Consider the following set of utterances that a child might easily hear:

My book.   *Your book.*
My bike.   *Your bike.*
My birthday.   *Your birthday.*

If we let a slash mark represent a morpheme cut, then the segmentation below is an erroneous one:

Myb | ook   *Yourb | ook*
Myb | ike   *Yourb | ike*
Myb | irthday   *Yourb | irthday*

These morphemes are odd in printed form but they represent sound combinations that are, in terms of English phonology, easily pronounceable; think of *scribe* and *orb*, *Ike* and *oops*.

Suppose the child who has segmented in the above fashion, goes on to store the contexts of each morpheme to the (unintentional and unconscious) end of discovering general and meaningful construction rules. The result may be represented in part as:

$$\begin{bmatrix} \underline{\quad}ook \\ \underline{\quad}ike \\ \underline{\quad}irthday \end{bmatrix}_{myb} \quad \begin{bmatrix} \underline{\quad}ook \\ \underline{\quad}ike \\ \underline{\quad}irthday \end{bmatrix}_{yourb}$$

$$\begin{bmatrix} myb\underline{\quad} \\ yourb\underline{\quad} \end{bmatrix}_{ook} \quad \begin{bmatrix} myb\underline{\quad} \\ yourb\underline{\quad} \end{bmatrix}_{ike}$$

Myb and *yourb* have identical context entries which are distinct from the entries for *ook* and *ike;* these latter two being themselves identical. In these circumstances it would be reasonable to infer the existence of two morpheme classes ($C_1 \rightarrow$ *myb, yourb;* $C_2 \rightarrow$ *ook, ike, irthday*) and of a construction signifying possession which is created by selecting class members in proper sequence (C_1–C_2). These inferences founded on a mistaken segmentation do not lead anywhere. For the small set of utterances that preserve the artificial co-occurrence of certain morphemes and a subsequent /b/ phoneme the segmentation would appear to work. Given *my b/rake* and *my b/and* the child could construct *your b/rake* and *your b/and* with approximately correct meaning. However, outside this artificial range his false morphemes would not work. He would not hear *the ook, the ike, the irthday,* Nor would he hear *myb pencil, myb doggie, yourb Mommy.* And he would find unanalyzable such new possessives as: *my pencil, my doggie, my Mommy, your pencil, your doggie.*

Compare the results of a correct segmentation. The context entries would look like this:

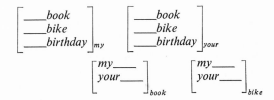

One morpheme class would represent a start on possessive pronouns and the other a start on count nouns. A construction rule written in terms of these classes correctly anticipates *your brake* from the occurrence of *my brake; my band* from *your band* and so on in an indefinite number of cases. Furthermore, the tentative morphemes *book, bike, birthday, my,* and *your* will recur with approximately the same meaning in such new constructions as *the book, my old hat,* and *your good friend.* A correct segmentation is repeatedly confirmed by its continuing ability to unlock regularities and structural meanings. An erroneous segmentation is a false trail winding off into the desert.

Judging from our materials and from what we know of the materials of others, morpheme segmentation errors such as *myb pencil* or *the ook* are not common. It is easy to overlook the segmentation problem in child speech because there is so little evidence that it exists. The evidence we found in the fine structure of our data makes us think that segmentation is a real problem in the sense that it is something a child learns but that it is a problem for which he has highly effective solution procedures.

For example, Adam produced in an early record the sentence *It's big*. What was the status in Adam's grammar of the form *'s* (or *is*)? In adult grammar *is* is a morpheme distinct from such other morphemes as *it* and *big* and organized closely with *am* and *are* as forms (allomorphs) of the verb *be*. We find in Adam's records certain errors of commission which suggest that *is* was differently organized for him. He produces hundreds of well-formed equational sentences with *it* as subject but he also produced a large number of odd ones. The following are representative:

It's fell (sample 14)
It's hurts (sample 17)
It's has wheels (sample 21)
It's went on the top (sample 22)

The form *is* has no place in these sentences and seems to have been imported into them as an on-hanger of *it*. Perhaps, then, the adult polymorphic form *its* was a single unanalyzed morpheme for Adam. How does this hypothesis fare when tested against all the relevant evidence?

Suppose the hypothesis were wrong and that Adam was, in fact, learning to organize *is* in the correct, adult way. What errors ought he then to have made? Since *is*, as a form of *be*, is closely related to *am* and *are* we should expect the several forms to have occasionally displaced one another in Adam's sentences through disregard of the features of the subject noun phrase that are supposed to select them. There ought to have been such errors as: *I is*, *we is*, *I are*, and *he am*. There were not any such in Adam's early records, and that fact supports the conclusion that *is* was not at first organized as a form of *be*.

In certain contexts *is* is obligatory: (1) in such reduced equational sentences as *it big*; (2) in sentences with a verb inflected for progressive aspect such as *it going*. When Adam began sometimes to produce an audible *is* in such contexts he did not, for many months, always do so. It is quite usual to find on the same page of a protocol otherwise

identical sentences with and without *is*. Of course, adults too do not always sound all their segmental phonemes, but this particular reduction, from *it's* to *it*, is not one that adults make. Its occurrence in Adam suggests that for him *it's* and *it* were just varying pronunciations of one morpheme.

The range of *is* in Adam's speech in the early records was restricted in an important way. The word *it* is, of course, an impersonal pronoun and as such it subsitutes for impersonal noun phrases. When such noun phrases themselves occur as subjects of equational sentences and with verbs inflected for progressive aspect, an adult uses *is;* for example, *The top is big; The top is spinning*. In such cases during the many months when we believe *it-s* was organized as a single morpheme, Adam always failed to produce *is*. That is what should happen if our hypothesis is correct. If, on the contrary, *is* were a separate morpheme the difference between its invariable absence with noun phrase subjects and its only occasional absence with *it* as subject would be unaccountable.

There is another revealing restriction of range. If *it's* were simply a variant of *it* then it ought to have occurred sometimes in all of the sentence positions that *it* ever fills. As the third column of Table 1 shows, *it* was an object of a verb more often than it was a subject. An adult would never use *it's* as a pronoun object but our hypothesis about *it's* predicts such errors for Adam. If *it's* was a simple variant of *it*, he ought to have formed such sentences as *get it's* and *put it's there*. As column 3 of Table 1 shows he never made such errors.

The forms *it* and *it's* were in perfect complementary distribution. This is not a phonologically conditioned complementary distribution of the kind that obtains for the several forms of the regular plural inflection in English. In the phonologically conditioned case the several forms are perfectly predictable and so the variation among them is always redundant and the descriptive linguist (e.g., Harris, 1942; Hockett, 1947; Gleason, 1961; Nida, 1948) considers the froms to be allomorphs of one morpheme. The complementary distribution that obtains for *it* and *it's* seems to be conditioned by grammatical role (sentence subject vs. verb object) and in such cases the linguist does not necessarily conclude that the forms are allomorphs or variant forms.

Many languages use inflectional forms to signal the role of a word in a larger construction. When nouns are involved (the most familiar instance) we speak of cases. Subject and object case (or nominative and accusative) are marked in Sanskrit, Latin, Greek, Finnish, and very many other languages (Gleason, 1961). In English, nouns are not inflected for case; nominative and accusative forms are distinguished by word order (e.g., *John saw Mary* vs. *Mary saw John*). However, Adam used *it* and *it's* as if *'s* or *is* were a nominative case ending. If *it* and *it's* were organized in this way then *is* was a separate morpheme and we are incorrect in suggesting that *it's* was a single form, a variant of *it*. The possibility is an interesting one. With case being a common syntactic device in the languages of the world it is reasonable to suppose that it should be among the hypotheses about linguistic structure that the human mind would be disposed to entertain and test (Chomsky, 1965; Fodor, 1966). Much of the distributional data available to Adam would seem to have confirmed this hypothesis and so he might reasonably have organized the facts about *it* and *it's* in this way until a greater mass of data motivated reorganization. However, for various reasons which cannot be detailed here, it is quite clear that Adam's *is* was not functioning as a case ending. The conclusion that best fits all the evidence is that *it* and *its* were allomorphs of a single morpheme, their occurrence being conditioned by grammatical role.

Errors of segmentation were rare in Adam Eve, and Sarah but *it's* was not the only case. The clearer instances[2] include: *I'm,*

that-a, drop-it, get-it, put-it, want-to, have-to, going-to, another-one, what-that, and *let-me.* These pairs have two characteristics which, taken together, distinguish them from pairs that were not mistakenly analyzed. The first characteristic is a phonetic one. Pairs like *its, wanna, lemme, put-it,* and indeed all pairs in the set, are regularly run together by adults as if they were in fact single words (Heffner, 1949). This is to say that the morpheme boundary is not in these pairs marked in any way whatever. The pairs all lack the open juncture phoneme ($/+/$) which marks the majority of morpheme boundaries in English. Perhaps then children are able usually to avoid segmentation errors because they regularly "cut" the stream of speech at just those points where $/+/$ occurs. This, however, is not a simple claim.

How are children able to recognize $/+/$? It is not a phonetically simple feature. To be sure, detectable pauses in a sentence, when they occur, usually occur at morpheme boundaries, and pause is usually considered one of the phonemic manifestations of $/+/$. The difficulty is that pause is only an intermittent feature. How is $/+/$ identified more generally?

Consider the following pairs: *nitrate* and *night-rate; slyness* and *minus; mark it* and *market.* There need be no actual pause in either member of a pair but still there is a difference one can hear; a difference in the amount of aspiration on the $/t/$; a difference in the duration of the vowel $/ay/$; a difference in the release of $/k/$. For each pair there is a phoneme that takes two somewhat different forms. In order to be able to classify the related but different sounds as single phonemes and so simplify description the linguist creates the junctural phoneme $/+/$ and assigns to it the phonetic features distinguishing a pair (Harris, 1951). The phonemic transcriptions will then look like this:

/nayt + reyt/	/slay + nɨs/	/mark + ət/
/naytreyt/	/maynis/	/markət/

It follows that the phonetic values of $/+/$ are a disjunctive set and they are in fact elaborately so. It follows also that $/+/$ is not itself a segment at all since aspiration, duration, and the like have no existence apart from particular vowels and consonants.

---

[2] Brown and Bellugi (1964) previously interpreted some portions of the relevant evidence in other ways. For instance, errors like *That a my boot* and *That a your car* were thought to indicate that Adam had adopted a mistaken rule permitting articles to precede every sort of nominal other than pronouns. Errors like *drop it book* and *get it pencil* suggested that Adam, in learning to substitute pronouns for noun phrases, was making both explicit. In certain points of detail, previously overlooked, the present view that *that-a* and *drop-it* and *get-it* were all unanalyzed single morphemes, provides a closer fit to the data than do the previous interpretations.

TABLE 1. The forms *it* and *it's* in early Adam samples.

Samples	Sentences with it as subject requiring is as verb (e.g., it's big; it's going).		Sentences with it as subject forbidding is as verb (e.g., it hurts; it went).		Sentences with it as object forbidding is to occur (e.g., get it, put it there).	
	is *absent*	is *present*	is *absent*	is *present*	is *absent*	is *present*
5–7	—	1	—	—	73	—
8–10	—	2	1	—	106	—
11–13	—	4	2	—	89	—
14–16	4	6	8	2	94	—
17–19	3	33	2	10	132	—
20–22	3	54	—	18	112	—

The open juncture, in short, is an invention of linguistic science designed to simplify language description. How could a child possibly learn to recognize /+/ and use it to segment the speech he hears?

The /t/ one hears in *night rate* occurs also at the ends of words (e.g., *night* or *right*) and so can occur terminally in complete utterances whereas the /t/ of *nitrate* is never terminal. Similarly the /ay/ of *slyness* may be terminal (as in *sly* or *die*) but the /ay/ of *minus* may not. And, in general, that form of a phoneme which is found within utterances at morpheme boundaries is found also in final position in total utterances, but the form found within utterances internal to a morpheme, is never final utterance in a total utterance. A child might learn that. He might learn to give special status to utterance-internal consonants or vowels which assumed the forms they ordinarily assumed in utterance-final position. In fact, he might learn to make morpheme cuts at just these points and to make contextual entries in terms of the resultant units.

When a child first begins to produce polymorphemic utterances he has for some time been producing single-morpheme utterances. Let us suppose that he has made independent entries for all of these—both the one-morpheme utterances like *dog* and the polymorphemic utterances like *my dog*. At this point the polymorphemic utterances might simply have the status for him of longer words. Suppose now that an internal analysis routine is activated which involves retrieving two entries at a time and comparing them, phonemically, from left to right. Suppose,

further, that he returns to storage pairs that are distinct in their very first phoneme but retains for further analysis pairs that start out identically. Let him then make a tentative morphemic cut at the first point of phonemic divergence in the pair. Let him finally look up the resulting segments to see if there are already independent entries for them—as there usually would be if they were morphemes—and mark as morphemes just those segments having prior entries. If he picked a pair like br/eak and br/ing, he would cut them as indicated but would find no prior entries for any of the segments and so would not mark them as morphemes. However, a pair like *my/dog* and *my/cat* would yield segments having prior entries. A child who started in this way might soon discover that cuts yielding morphemes by his original criteria regularly coincided with terminal-type vowels and consonants (or one might say with /+/). Thereafter he could make segmentation cuts wherever terminal phonemes occurred without regard to either identical sequences or prior entries. By this account the value of /+/ is discovered from its correlation with more primitive criteria. It is possible, however, that the terminal vowels and consonants are themselves the most primitive criterion of morpheme segmentation.

Although errors of segmentation seem only to occur across boundaries which are not marked with open juncture in adult speech it is far from being the case that every such unmarked boundary will give rise to an error of segmentation. Adults will run together *Pop's here* as well as *It's here*. But Adam organized *is* as a feature in the pronunciation not of any noun but only of the pronoun *it*. Probably the important factor here is the second characteristic which helps to define the pairs erroneously organized as single morphemes. Each such pair was characterized by a high transition probability in the speech the mothers addressed to their children. After the first member, the second was more frequent by far than any other morpheme. Nouns like *Pop* or *Adam* sometimes appeared as subjects of equational sentences but they also often appeared as subjects of main verbs, too often apparently for Adam to make the mistake of thinking *is* belonged to the nouns. *It*, on the other hand, appeared hundreds of times a day as subject of equational sentences but was very seldom, surprisingly seldom, the subject of any other verb. The high transitions in these pairs have nothing to do with grammar of course but are simply accidental statistical features of mother-child interaction. They demonstrate that bias in the language sample to which a child is exposed can, in an extreme case, result in a partially erroneous formulation of the underlying grammar.

It is important to make it perfectly clear that the evidence for segmentation errors is not simply or even primarily phonetic. We are not relying on the fact that Adam's version of *its* often sounded like *iss* or that his rendering of *want to* sounded like *wanna*. The important evidence is distributional; the fact that Adam said *Its hurts*, for instance, and that he said *I want to play* but never *I want you to play*. When at length the children corrected their few segmentation errors and reconstrued the forms of *be* and articles the evidence was again distributional and in some cases quite dramatically clear. In the case of Adam's *a*, for instance, the form appeared for 19 samples in only a restricted portion of its proper range—chiefly with *that* as pronoun subject.[3] Then, in samples 20 and 21, the full range quite suddenly filled out and *a* appeared with noun phrases in isolation, noun phrases

functioning as subjects of sentences, noun phrases in locative questions, etc. We do not yet know what it is that causes reconstruction of forms at one time rather than another.

TRANSFORMATIONS IN *WH* QUESTIONS

Wh questions are those using an interrogative word from the set *Who, Whom, What, Where, When, Why,* and *How*. Contemporary generative grammars of English (e.g., Katz and Postal, 1964; Klima, 1964) do not all derive *Wh* questions in just the same way but they all do utilize transformational rules to represent the systematic relations between these questions and the declaratives that answer them. *Wh* questions begin to appear in good quantity and variety at Level III; indeed the composite sentence, derived with rules from Adam III, was such a question. We want to ask here whether there is, in the form of these questions, evidence which directly supports the notion that the child acquires implicit knowledge of the sort represented by the transformational rules of the adult grammar. The brief discussion here is drawn from a full research report (Brown, 1966) which presents the evidence for all *Wh* questions in all the protocols from I through V.

Table 2(a) sets out some adult questions and answers in such a way as to expose the systematic relations existing among them. Consider first the two middle columns. Each question in "normal" form stands by the side of a semantically equivalent, but less frequent, "occasional" form in which the *Wh* word is in final position and is to be spoken with heavy stress and rising intonation. If someone said: "John will read the telephone book," one might respond "John will read what?" and this response is an occasional form. The occasional form for the subject nominal—the first entry—is unlike the others in the column in that the *Wh* word appears initially, its normal position.

The occasional forms (except the subject nominal) are all related to their normal counterparts by the same function. In describing the function let us take the occasional form as the base or starting point. The nor-

---

[3] The form appeared also with a few strictly transitive verbs in which, as in *that*, it seems to have been a feature of pronunciation. Representative errors are: *have a two minute, get a one.*

TABLE 2. Systematic relations among questions and answers.

a) Constituents, questions and answers

Constituents to be specified	Normal questions[a]	Occasional questions[a] [b]	Possible answers[a]
Subject nominal	"*Who* will read the book?"	"*Who* will read the book?"	"*John* will read the book."
Object nominal	"*What* will John read?"	"*John* will read what?"	"John will read *the book*."
Predicate nominal	"*What* is that?"	"*That* is what?"	"That is *a book*."
Predicate	"*What* will John do?"	"John will *do what*?"	"*John* will read the book."
Locative adverbial	"*Where* will John read?"	"John will read *where*?"	"John will read *in the library*."
Time adverbial	"*When* will John read?"	"John will read *when*?"	"John will read *this evening*."
Manner adverbial	"*How* will John read?"	"John will read *how*?"	"John will read *slowly*."

indicates heavy stress and rising intonation.

b) The derivation of normal questions

Base	John — will — read — something
Preposition and *wh* incorporation	wh + something — John — will — read
Transposition	wh + something — will — John — read
Morphophonemic	what — will — John — read

[a] *Wh* words and substitutes for them are italicized.
[b] Words with all letters capitalized receive heavy stress and rising intonation.

mal form can be created from the occasional in two steps. The first would move the *Wh* word from final position to initial position; we call this preposing. The second step would interchange the subject of the sentence and the auxiliary; we may call this transposing. The same two steps will generate all the questions of the second column from their respective counterparts in the first column. Essentially these two steps are the transformational rules used in adult grammar to derive *Wh* questions. The main difference is that normal questions are not derived from actual occasional questions but from underlying strings which are similar to the occasionals.

Consider now the sentences of the last column which are examples of well-formed answers to the questions standing opposite them. Question and answer differ in the words that are italicized in each case and only in these words. The italicized words in the answers may be said to stand in place of the italicized *Wh* words—in the *exact* place, the very sentence locus of the *Wh* word, for the occasional questions. The normal questions, we know, shift the place of the *Wh* word. The material italicized in the answer is the material most directly responsive to the question. Indeed it is the only essential part of the answer. "What will John read?" "*The book.*" "When will John read?" "*This evening.*" In fact, each interrogative word is a kind of algebraic "x" standing in the place of a particular constituent of the sentence, the constituent identified in the left column of Table 2(a). The *Wh* word asks for specification of that constituent. It marks the spot where information is to be poured into the sentence and the form of the *Wh* word—whether *who, what, where,* or *when*—indicates the sort of information required.

A transformational grammar of adult English can represent the systematic relations of Table 2(a) in the following way. Associated with each of the sentence constituents involved there is a stand-in element symbolized as "someone," "something," "somewhere," "sometime," and "somehow." The derivation of a *Wh* question begins in the phrase structure with the selection of the interrogative morpheme wh. Then, from the

constituent which is to be specified in a well-formed answer, the stand-in element is selected rather than some particular NP or Loc or whatever. The phrase structure derivation terminates in an underlying string which is just like the string for the occasional question except that the stand-in element stands where the interrogative words stand in the occasional questions of Table 2. In the derivation of normal questions a first transformation preposes the dummy element and incorporates it into wh and a second transformation transposes the order of the subject NP and the first member of the auxiliary. A morphophonemic rule rewrites the wh + stand-in component as the appropriate interrogative word: wh + something as *what*; wh + someone as *who*; wh + somewhere as *where*, etc. The derivation rules and sample strings are represented in Table 2(b).

Production of a hypothetical intermediate
The composite sentence derived by Adam III was *Where those dogs goed?* and not *Where did those dogs go?* How is Adam's form related to the derivation of the normal adult form? It is a sentence that would be produced by the rules of Table 2(b) if the second transformation, the one that transposes subject and auxiliary were simply omitted, if the morphophonemic rules followed upon the preposing transformation alone. In short, Adam seems to have given phonetic form to a structure that is generated by the adult grammar as a hypothetical intermediate, a structure not actualized as a question by adults. The composite form is, in this respect, representative of all Adam's *Wh* questions in III and for many months after III. Eve and Sarah both also constructed these preposed *Wh* questions though not in such quantity as did Adam. Table 3 represents the relation between the children's version of various *Wh* questions and the two varieties of well-formed adult questions.

A transformation in discourse
The derivation rules loosely described in Table 2(b) and presented in explicit form in Adam III presuppose the establishment of such major sentence constituents as NP and

TABLE 3.   The child's *Wh* question as a hypothetical intermediate in adult grammar.

Occasional questions	Child's questions[a]	Normal questions[b]
"Who will read the book?"	"Who will read the book?"	"Who will read the book?"
"John will read what?"	"What John will read?"	"What will John read?"
"That is what?"	"What that is?"	"What is that?"
"John will do what?"	"What John will do?"	"What will John do?"
"John will read where?"	"Where John will read?"	"Where will John read?"

[a] Derivable from occasional questions by preposing.
[b] Derivable from occasional questions by preposing and transposing.

Loc since the dummy elements are associated with these constituents. We have seen in our Overview that there was good evidence of the existence of these constituents from early in the records. The most persuasive evidence was the children's ability to answer *Who* and *What* questions with noun phrases and *Where* questions with locatives. We also reported in the Overview that time and manner adverbials did not seem to be organized as constituents in I to III since the children did not make grammatically appropriate answers to *When* and *How* questions. If the responsive constituents were not organized as such then *When* and *How* questions could not be derived in the children's grammar by the kinds of rules we have proposed. It is consistent, therefore, to find that Adam in III was still not making *When* and *How* questions.

In another respect Adam's performance in III seems not to have been consistent with the rules. He produced a large number of *Why* and *Why not* questions. But in all of the prior 16 samples he had only once answered a *Why* question in a way that could possibly be considered appropriate. In this case, then, we seem to have the question construction occurring before there is any evidence on the responsive side that the relevant grammatical organization exists.[4] We have also, incidentally, a demonstration that, in language development, comprehension need not always precede production.

---

[4] Adult *why* questions cannot be derived in a way that is directly parallel to other *Wh* questions. We have not gone into the details because they do not alter the fact that Adam produced such questions when his responses gave no evidence that he could analyze them correctly with respect either to grammar or semantics.

When we look at Adam's *Why* and *Why not* questions in their actual discourse setting we find something unexpected and interesting. They were often closely related to an immediately antecedent declarative from his mother. Table 4 contains a set of mother's declaratives on the left and Adam's *Why* responses on the right. Some of the differences between members of these pairs are not peculiar to *Why* questions. For instance, the telegraphic reduction process that eliminates *was*, *-ing*, and *a* from the adult sentence is quite general in child speech. Setting aside such nonspecific differences we may say that Adam's questions are a simple function of his mother's antecedent declaratives: the word *why* is placed in front of the declarative. In Table 4 we have also a set of questions in *Why not* and these too have apparent bases in the mother's speech. Setting aside a few details, what happens is that the words *Why not* are added in initial position to mother's negative declaratives. In creating these questions Adam seems to have been operating with a rule very like the preposing transformation.

Where did Adam's *Why* and *Why not* transformations come from? Once in a long while his mother produced a *Why* question as a direct follow-up of a declarative repeating in her *Why* question the proposition expressed in the declarative. Probably Adam was attempting to imitate this performance. But his imitation did not come out right. Suppose the antecedent declarative were "He can't dance." Mother would follow this with "Why can't he dance?" Adam's version, on the other hand, would be "Why he can't dance?" Mother not only preposed *Why*, she also transposed the subject and

TABLE 4.   *Why* and *Why not* questions from Adam 17–19 with apparent bases.

Mother's Declaratives	Adam's Why *Questions*
"He was playing a little tune."	"Why he play little tune?"
"I see a seal."	"Why you see seal?"
"You bent that game."	"Why me bent that game?"
"Well, because she wanted to."	"Why she want to?"
"I think it's resting now."	"Why it's resting now?"

Mother's Declaratives	Adam's Why not *Questions*
"I guess I'm not looking in the right place."	"Why not you looking right place?"
"Because you weren't careful."	"Why not me careful?"
"I don't see any."	"Why not you see any?"
"You can't dance."	"Why not me can't dance?"
"You're going to have to buy another one and give it to Ursula because you're breaking that one."	"Why not me break that one?"

auxiliary in the manner of the adult grammar. Adam only preposed. Probably he copied according to his present understanding—as children also do when they pretend to drive a car or read a newspaper. Perhaps his imitation took the form it did because that form was close to the general operation that Adam was using with his other *Wh* questions.

So we do have some evidence that the knowledge represented by transformation rules in the derivation of *Wh* questions was learned by the children. They did not simply start to produce well-formed questions at a given point in time. All three children first produced a simpler form that would result from the application of just one of the two transformations required. And Adam—always the one to make interesting errors—also created *Why* questions in circumstances that suggest the application of the same single transformation to declarative bases supplied by his mother.

THE ROLE OF TRAINING VARIABLES

Whatever the processes by which children acquire grammar, their primary data come from the speech they hear. Part of our work has consisted of attempts to isolate antecedents in the child's linguistic environment which may affect the rate or quality of the child's development. By antecedents we do not mean global variables like social class,

but specific features of parent speech and parent-child interaction.

We have learned something about the effects of two aspects of variation in the speech to which a child is exposed: variation in the frequency with which particular constructions are produced or "modeled," and variation in the frequency with which particular reactions are made to a child's utterances. The reactions we have studied are expansions, occasional forms of *Wh* questions, and expressions of approval and disapproval.

The work has progressed through three phases: first, discovery of relationships between parent speech and rate of language development in our three subjects; second, a manipulative experiment with different subjects to test a hypothesis derived from those observation; and third, more detailed analyses of relationships within our longitudinal data. We will describe these phases in turn.

Preliminary observation and an experiment
When we began work several years ago one of the first things we noticed was the frequency with which parents responded to the young child's telegraphic utterance[5] by echo-

---

[5] We have not in this paper discussed the telegraphic aspect of the child's early sentences since that was a major topic of such earlier papers as Brown and Fraser (1963) and Brown and Bellugi (1964). In I, II, and III, however, the speech of the three children was extremely telegraphic, as the data in Table 7 indicate.

ing what the child said and filling in the missing functors. If the child said *Eve lunch* or *Throw Daddy*, the parent often responded with the nearest complete sentence appropriate in the particular situation—*Eve is having lunch* or *Throw it to Daddy*. Brown and Bellugi (1964) called such responses expansions and suggested that they might provide optimal data for the acquisition of grammar. It was not their intention to suggest that the child learned grammar by storing the expanded versions of his telegraphic utterances, since he could not in this way learn more than the finite set of sentences he had at some time attempted to produce. Brown and Bellugi recognized that expansions were only data, and that grammatical knowledge was a general rule system somehow derived from data. They argued, however, that the data provided by expansions were maximally relevant and seemed to be delivered with ideal timing.

At the same time, we have always realized that the relevance and timing of particular forms of interaction may have no importance for the acquisition of grammar. It is quite possible that the adult need do nothing but "model" the language in the sense of providing samples of well-formed speech. When evidence is limited to natural observations, it is not possible to separate the effect of expansions from the effect of the amount of well-formed speech that the child hears. The mothers of Adam and Eve responded to the speech of their children with expansions about 30 per cent of the time. Sarah's over-all language development was slower, and her mother expanded fewer of Sarah's utterances. But Sarah's mother also talked less to her child in general. In our samples of three parents, expansion rate and general volubility varied together, and their effects on language acquisition could not be teased apart.

A manipulative experiment was designed to separate these two aspects of the child's language environment and compare their effects (Cazden, 1965). The subjects were twelve Negro children, aged 28–38 months. They were all attending a private day-care center in Boston where thirty children under $3\frac{1}{2}$ years were cared for by one adult. Four matched trios were formed on the basis of

the child's chronological age, talkativeness, and initial level of language development as judged by his mean length of utterance during an orientation period. Within each trio the children were randomly assigned to one of three treatment groups: expansion, modeling, or control.

The expansion group received 40 minutes per day of intensive and deliberate expansions. The modeling group received exposure to an equal number of well-formed sentences that were not expansions. One of two tutors, trained for this research, talked with each child in these two groups in an individual play session every school day for three months. The sessions were held in two small rooms in the center normally used only at nap time. We equipped both rooms with toys and books selected to stimulate conversation. The play sessions were monitored at regular intervals during the three-month period to ensure the separation of the critical interaction variables. Children in the control group received no treatment, but they were brought into the treatment rooms every few days so that they stayed familiar with the materials and the tutors.

Tape recordings were made of each child's speech at the beginning, middle, and end of the three-month period. The tapes were transcribed by a secretary who was trained by a linguist on our staff and who was ignorant of the treatment assignment of the children. The transcriptions were then coded according to strict rules. The dependent variables were six measures of language development. One was a test of the child's ability to repeat sentences; five measured aspects of the child's spontaneous speech—mean length of utterance in morphemes, noun phrase index, verb complexity, copula index, and sentence-type index. The last four indexes were devised for this research.

Two statistical analyses were used to test the hypothesis that expansions would be the more effective treatment. First, the six dependent variables were considered separately. A two-way analysis of variance (treatment × tutor) was computed for the posttest scores on each measure separately, with the pretest scores on that same measure as a covariance control. Then, in order to compare the children on their over-all growth on the six measures considered together, growth was operationally defined as the sum of the child's six gain score ranks, and Friedman's nonparametric two-way analysis of variance was used to test the significance of group differences. In neither analysis was there any evidence that expansions aid the acquisition of grammar. Contrary to our hypothesis, modeling was the more effective treatment.

Before speculating on possible explanations for these results, we need to examine what happens when forms of interaction which naturally co-occur are experimentally separated. Originally, we assumed that modeling without expansion had no positive features of its own. But this turns out not to be the case. If a child says *Dog bark* when a dog is indeed barking, the expanding adult says *Yes, the dog is barking*. The nonexpanding adult who desires to maintain a reasonable discourse sequence—as our tutors did—has to contribute a related idea: *Yes, he's mad at the kitty*, or *Yes, but he won't bite*. Thus a treatment which focuses on grammatical structure confines the adult to expanded echoes of the child and limits the ideas to the child's presumed meaning, whereas a treatment that focuses on the idea extends that idea beyond the presumed meaning of the child and introduces more varied words and grammatical elements to express those related ideas. In natural conversation, parents often provide both grammatical expansions and semantic extensions. Our tutors were asked not to do this in order to keep the distinctions between the experimental treatments as sharp as possible.

Three reasons can be suggested for the results. Cazden originally proposed that richness of verbal stimulation might be more important than the grammatical contingency of the adult response. If we consider the learning of syntactic rules to be akin to concept formation, then learning may be aided by variation in noncriterial attributes—for instance, the particular noun stem in the case of inflection for plurality. If the process of first-language learning is akin to scientific theory construction in which hypotheses are tested against available data, then a meager set of data may be disadvantageous. We have seen that bias in the mother-to-child

sampling of the possibilities of English grammar caused Adam to make the segmentation error revealed in such a sentence as: *It's fell*.

Miller and McNeill (1968) suggest an alternative explanation. When an adult attempts to expand a child's telegraphic utterances far more often than parents spontaneously do, some of the expansions probably misinterpret the child's intended meaning. Instead of facilitating the acquisition of grammar, such erroneous expansions may mislead the child and interfere with his learning.

Still a third explanation is possible, separately or in conjunction with either of the previous two. Artificial elevation of the expansion rate may depress attentional processes in the child. We know from many current studies of child development that stimuli of a certain degree of novelty—not too familiar and not too strange—command the greatest attention. The acquisition of language should be facilitated by those environmental events which enhance the child's attention to the adult's utterance and to relevant features of the verbal and nonverbal context in which it is spoken. In these particular experimental treatments a better degree of novelty may have been attained in the modeling treatment. We do not consider this experiment conclusive evidence. All we can say is that the benefits of expansions remain unproved.

Training variables in the longitudinal data
In the last two years we have gone back to the longitudinal data on Adam, Eve, and Sarah to look more carefully for evidence of the effects of parental speech. In selecting dependent variables, we have learned to reject measures of the child's performance in favor of better indicators of the child's grammatical knowledge, and we have substantive findings on the independent variables of expansions and modeling, occasional questions, and expressions of approval and disapproval.

Grammatical knowledge versus performance　In certain facts concerning construction frequency there lies a major trap for the student of child speech who is interested in the development of knowledge of grammar. The first fact is that in mother-to-child speech the various constructions that English grammar permits are of grossly unequal frequency. The second fact is that the frequencies are astonishly stable across the three mothers in our study. The third fact is that frequencies in child speech, within the limits of the child's competence, tend to match adult frequencies. We have examined frequencies on many levels, from major sentence types all the way down to the several allomorphs of *be*, and the story is always the same: rank order correlations among the mothers and between each mother and her child range from .65 to .90.

Some of the stable inequalities one might have guessed: active affirmative-declarative sentences are much more common than negatives or *Yes-No* interrogatives or *Wh* interrogatives, and well-formed passives are almost nonexistent. Others are easy to understand but are not likely to have occurred to anyone who has not counted: the impersonal pronouns *it*, *this*, and *that* as sentence subjects almost always have their allomorph of *be* (*is*) as verb, whereas the personal pronouns *I*, *you*, *he*, etc. as subjects have a main verb much more often than an allomorph of *be*; *Where* questions are very much more frequent than *When* or *How* or *Why* questions; catenative semi-auxiliaries like *wanna* and *gonna* are much more frequent than the modal auxiliaries *will* or *can*, and *may* and *must* are seldom heard; the progressive inflection *-ing* is much more frequent than the regular past *-ed*, and irregular pasts (e.g., *ran*, *saw*, *did*) are more frequent than regular pasts; and so on. The important general fact is that there seems to be something like a standard frequency profile for mother-to-child English, a profile that children match within their competence at any given time, and in this profile great inequalities exist even among very simple and familiar constructions.

Consider two examples in detail: major sentence types and expressions of possession. If we set an arbitrary frequency in child speech as a criterion of emergence, for instance the occurrence of three instances of a given sentence type in each of three consecutive samples of 700 utterances, we find a high rank order correlation between parental frequencies and order of emergence in the child for 24 types of sentence—affirmatives, decla-

ratives, negatives, yes-no interrogatives, and *Wh* interrogatives using, respectively, lexical verbs or *have* or *be* or *will* or *can* or *may*. Lexical and *be*-verbs in declarative sentences are the most common in all three mothers, and they appear first in the speech of all three children. But suppose we entertain the extreme hypothesis that all 24 verbs enter the child's competence simultaneously. Because the probability that a given construction will attain an arbitrary criterion varies with its standard frequency in mother-to-child English, and because these frequencies are grossly unequal, lexical and *be*-verbs would appear first on a strict probability basis. The student of child speech might then conclude that the hypothesis of simultaneous development was false when it could indeed still be true. Highly stable orders of construction emergence, in terms of an arbitrary frequency criterion, are not inconsistent with the possibility that the children in question know how to form all the constructions from the start but produce them with unequal frequency.

The same misleading performance match appears when we relate individual differences in construction frequencies among the children to differences in their mother's speech. For instance, one of the first individual differences we noted was Eve's tendency to use N + N constructions far more often than Adam or Sarah did. At I, the frequencies of N + N in 700 utterances were: Eve–66; Adam–40; Sarah–10, of which 8 were imitations. In looking for an explanation, we thought it possible that the speech of the three mothers might differ in the frequency with which sentences were spoken from which N + N constructions might be telegraphically derived. The best match to the rank order of the children was the particular subset of parental N + N constructions which express possession such as *Daddy's chair*. In the first 1253 utterances of each mother, these frequencies were: Eve's mother–31; Adam's mother–24; Sarah's mother–only 6. This is an extremely interesting relationship. One can hypothesize that territoriality and property rights are more important in homes where father is a graduate student, and that this is related to the child's tendency to use the N + N construction. But it is not sufficient evidence that greater frequency in parent speech produces earlier learning in the child. It is the antecedents of grammatical *knowledge* we are seeking, not influences or performance.

There are various ways out of the trap, all involving the utilization of data that are better indices of knowledge or competence than is an arbitrary frequency of production. One can consider child frequencies against a background of known stable adult frequencies and so set frequency criteria that are not entirely arbitrary; one can consider frequencies of forms in contexts that make them obligatory; one can consider the pattern of omissions in the total distributional range of a form; one can consider the adequacy of the child's responses to adult questions and assertions; above all one can utilize the child's analogical errors of commission. In analyses of the relation of child speech to parental speech, the frequency of forms in contexts that make them obligatory has proven an especially useful measure. Each of these contexts in the child's speech can be considered a learning trial, and we can compute the proportion of times in which the child performs appropriately as that proportion changes over time.

Further evidence on expansions and modeling Because we considered the manipulative experiment inconclusive, we have probed further into the effect of expansions and modeling on the growth of specific aspects of grammatical knowledge in our three subjects. We have charted the emergence of prepositions in Eve's speech, and of appropriate answers to four kinds of *Wh*

questions and five noun and verb inflections in all three children.

Table 5 presents the data for the emergence of Eve's prepositions. Two findings are of interest. First, for any given preposition, both the frequency with which it is modeled and the frequency (but not proportion) of expansions is strongly related to the point at which that preposition is regularly supplied by the child in all the phrases requiring it. In samples 1–6, Eve's mother uses *in* and *on* approximately three times as often as she uses *with*, *of*, *for*, or *to*. In samples 7–12, Eve supplies *in* and *on* correctly at least 90 per cent of the time while the proportion correct for each of the other four prepositions is between .67–.77.

Second, there is no relation at all between modeling frequency of particular phrases— *in there* versus *in the wastebasket*— and the point at which the child produces that phrase with the preposition in place. A given preposition pops into all the phrases requiring it at about the same time, and it does not matter whether the particular phrase has been often modeled by the mother or not. This is a good example of how parent speech aids the induction of general rules and does not provide models for imitation as such.

With *Wh* questions, we can determine what proportion of a given type elicits semantically and grammatically appropriate answers from the child. Four *Wh*-adverbial questions are rather well matched in grammatical (though probably not semantic) complexity, but they differ greatly in parental frequency. For all three mothers at II, the order of frequency is locatives first (about $\frac{3}{4}$ of the total), than causal,

TABLE 5. Eve's performance in supplying various prepositions in Samples 7–12 compared with Eve's mother's modeling frequencies and expansions in Samples 1–6.

Preposition	Mother's modeling frequencies 1–6	Mother's proportion of expansions 1–6	Proportion correct in Eve 7–12
On	157	.57(25/44)	.90(82/92)
In	142	.61(20/33)	.92(147/159)
With	54	.64(7/11)	.67(29/43)
Of	33	.50(1/2)	.70(14/20)
For	32	.40(2/5)	.69(11/16)
To	31	.00(0/3)	.78(7/9)

TABLE 6. Four kinds of adverbial questions: parent frequencies at II and appropriate responses from the child at V.

Question	Frequency of questions across mothers	Proportion of appropriate responses across children
Locative	228	.64 (29/45)
Explanation	29	.40 (14/35)
Manner	18	.11 (1/9)
Time	7	.50 (1/2)

manner, and time. In other words: *where, why, how,* and *when.* This rank order matches the rank order of proportion of appropriate responses from the children at V except for time questions for which the data are too few to be reliable. Pooled data for the three mothers and children are presented in Table 6.

Before turning to the emergence of inflections, another comment on method is in order. For relating child behavior to parent behavior in a sample of more than one child, two approaches are possible. The child's language can be related to antecedents in his parent's speech, and this relationship then compared across the dyads. No direct comparison of the children is made. The preceding analyses of 24 verb forms, prepositions, and answers to *Wh* questions were of this type. Alternatively, differences in the language of the children can be related to differences in the language of their parents. The preceding analysis of N + N constructions was of this type. Here direct comparison of the children is required, and the experimenter faces the question of a metric for that comparison. We have analyzed the emergence of inflections in both ways.

The five regular inflections which emerge between I and V are the plural and possessive inflections on the noun, and the present progressive, regular past, and present indicative inflections on the verb. For this analysis we used as a criterion of emergence the first sample of three, such that, in all three, the child supplies the inflection in at least 90 per cent of the contexts in which they are clearly required. The charting of this aspect of development is a lengthy story in itself and will be reported in detail elsewhere. We shall describe here only the data for the correlations between the sequence of emergence and three features of the child's linguistic environment: the proportion of times in which his omitted inflections are expanded by the parent during the entire period I–V, the absolute frequency of those expansions, and the frequency with which the inflections are modeled in four samples of 700 parent utterances which immediately precede Levels II, III, IV, and V of the children's speech.

First we computed rank order correlations for each child separately. For all three children, order of emergence within each child's language system is more strongly related to the frequency with which the inflection is modeled by the parent than it is to the proportion or frequency of expansions. The only statistically significant positive correlation is with frequency of modeling for Sarah— $\rho = .90$ (p< .05).

We have also looked for relationships between differences among the children and differences among their parents. It is here that a metric for comparing the children is required. In the above analysis N + N constructions, the three children were compared at II. The metric, therefore, was mean length of utterance. A more conventional metric is age. We have analyzed individual differences in the order of emergence of inflections on both bases of comparison. The contrast in outcomes is itself informative.

When we compare the children on the basis of age, the order of development is what one would expect from Figure 1: Eve way out in front, Adam second, and Sarah third. But when we ignore age and compare the children on the basis of mean length, the rank order of the children changes sharply. At II, when all three children have a mean length of 2.25 morphemes, only Sarah has reached the 90 per cent criterion on any inflection (plurality). By IV, when mean length has increased to 3.50 morphemes, she has reached criterion on five inflections, Eve has achieved four, and Adam two. Data tabulated independently for percent of missing functors (everything except nouns, verbs, adjectives, and adverbs) at II and V yield the same relationship. These data are presented in Table 7.

Looked at in this way, the relative position of Eve and Sarah is reversed. At any given

TABLE 7. Percent functors missing at II and V.

	II	V
Eve	.81	.43
Adam	.83	.20
Sarah	.74	.15

mean length value for utterances, Sarah is handling inflections and functors in general more successfully than Eve. Conversely, since Eve's speech contains proportionately more content words than Sarah's, her utterances are more informative. Eve had undoubtedly caught up in the provision of functors by the time she reached Sarah's age, probably well before. The point is that Sarah is less behind in the provision of obligatory functors than in what she is trying to say.

Table 8 shows the relationship between order of emergence of the five inflections on these two bases of comparison (age and mean length) and proportion and frequency of expansions and frequency of modeling in parent speech. Order of emergence is given in summed ranks which range from 5 to 15—first to last of the three children on the five inflections combined.

As one would expect from the previous discussion of mother-child communication patterns, the difference in modeling frequency among the parents is small. But the difference in proportion and frequency of expansions is considerable. Sarah's telegraphic utterances which omit inflections are followed much less frequently by a parent utterance which includes the appropriate inflection than is the case for Adam and Eve. This we expected from our observation of differential expansion rates at the beginning of our work. What is surprising is the negative relation between expansion rate and order of emergence in terms of mean length of utter-

ance. Sarah receives the lowest density of expansions, yet her language system is relatively the most advanced in the provision of inflections. It is hard to reconcile this finding with our original hypothesis that expansions should provide the most usable information for the acquisition of all types of functors.

Expressions of approval and disapproval. It might be supposed that syntactically correct utterances come to prevail over those that are incorrect through the operation of positive reinforcement and punishment on the part of adults. Because events subsequent to a child's speech are infinitely various, one can never be sure that there is no event which functions as a reinforcer or punishment. In practice, however, we know that certain events are likely to function this way, such as signs of approval or disapproval. The proposition "Syntactically correct utterances come to prevail over syntactically incorrect utterances through the selective administration of signs of approval and disapproval" is a testable one.

The proposition cannot be true for the natural case of parents and children at home unless parental approval and disapproval are in fact appropriately contingent on syntactical correctness. If the reactions *are* appropriately contingent, then they may or may not have the effects proposed. For this analysis we worked with samples II and V. The general plan was to contrast the syntactic correctness of the population of utterances followed by a sign of approval—*That's right*, *Very good*, or just *Yes*—with the population of utterances followed by a sign of disapproval—*That's wrong* or *No*. The results are simply stated: there is not a shred of evidence that approval and disapproval are contingent on syntactic correctness.

TABLE 8. Emergence of inflections and two features of parent speech.

	Summed ranks of order of emergence in terms of age	Summed ranks of order of emergence in terms of mean length	Proportion of parental expansions	Frequency of parental models
Eve	5	11	.45(191/427)	499
Adam	12.5	12	.51(348/679)	576
Sarah	12.5	7	.29(86/294)	471

What circumstances did govern approval and disapproval directed at child utterances by parents? Gross errors of word choice were sometimes corrected, as when Eve said *What the guy idea*. Once in a while an error of pronunciation was noticed and corrected. Most commonly, however, the grounds on which an utterance was approved or disapproved in Levels I through V, were not strictly linguistic at all. When Eve expressed the opinion that her mother was a girl by saying *He a girl* mother answered *That's right*. The child's utterance was ungrammatical but mother did not respond to that fact; instead she responded to the truth value of the proposition the child intended to express. In general the parents fit propositions to the child's utterances, however incomplete or distorted the utterances, and then approved or not according to the correspondence between proposition and reality. Thus *Her curl my hair* was approved because mother was, in fact, curling Eve's hair. However, Sarah's grammatically impeccable *There's the animal farmhouse* was disapproved because the building was a lighthouse and Adam's *Walt Disney comes on, on Tuesday* was disapproved because Walt Disney came on, on some other day. It seems, then, to be truth value rather than syntactic well-formedness that chiefly governs explicit verbal reinforcement by parents—which renders mildly paradoxical the fact that the usual product of such a training schedule is an adult whose speech is highly grammatical but not notably truthful.

Interaction routines with occasional questions In describing the systematic relations that underlie the grammar of *Wh* questions we introduced in Table 2 the forms called occasional questions. We introduced them because we believe they are a great help in making those relations clear in explicit form to adults. We naturally wonder, therefore, whether the occasionals also help to make the relations clear in implicit form to children. The mothers of Adam, Eve, and Sarah produced such questions in two circumstances which may be represented as follows:

I. Say Constituent Again.

1) Child: "I want milk." Mother: "You want what?" Child: "Milk."
2) Child: "Put milk in glass." Mother: "Put milk where?" Child: "In glass."

II. Constituent Prompt.

1) Mother: "What do you want?" Child: (No answer.) Mother: "You want what?"
2) Mother: "Where will I put it?" Child: (No answer.) Mother: "I will put it where?"

The first sort of interaction occurred when mother found a part of a child's utterance unintelligible. She then repeated what she had understood and replaced the constituent which was the locus of unintelligibility with the right kind of *Wh* word. Since the *Wh* word appeared in the sentence position of a constituent (found wholly or partially unintelligible) the result was an occasional question. The occasion was unintelligibility in a constituent and the response, on the child's part, was repetition of the constituent displaced. The mother's question is essentially a request to "say the constituent again" and that is the name we have given to this kind of interaction. What should exchanges of this type be able to teach the child? Perhaps the membership of each type of sentence constituent. Members of NP for instance are just those terms, of whatever complexity, that can be replaced by *what*.

The second type of interaction was initiated by the mother. She asked a question in the normal form, for example "What do you want?" and received no answer. She then reformulated the question as "You want what?" which is, incidentally, an occasional question. She was, in effect, turning the question into a sentence completion item and since the mothers typically resorted to this prompting form when the normal form had failed they must have felt that it was easier to process. In our materials the occasional form was, in fact, more likely to elicit an appropriate answer than was the normal form. What should exchanges of this type be able to teach the child? Fundamentally, the equivalence of particular normal and occasional questions—equivalents are just those questions that replace one another when no answer is forthcoming.

A large amount of structural information is revealed with unusual clarity in these two interactions because of the use of the occasional question. It must be possible to discover the systematic relations that underlie the grammar of *Wh* questions without the benefit of the occasional question since many children who learn English do not have attentive mothers around to echo them and prompt them. However, it may be easier to discover the relations if the middle term is often heard. It may be accidental but, in our records the occasional form was used much more frequently by the mothers of the two children whose grammatical understanding developed more rapidly: Adam and Eve. In samples of 7000 parental utterances, Adam's mother produced occasional questions at the rate of 1 in 57 utterances; Eve's mother at the rate of 1 in 80; Sarah's mother at the rate of only 1 in 146.

Whether or not the occasional questions prove to be helpful for the discovery of *Wh* grammar, it seems likely that the many kinds of grammatical exchange occurring in discourse will prove to be the richest data available to the child in his search for a grammar. It may be as difficult to derive a grammar from unconnected static sentences as it would be to derive the invariance of quantity and number from simply looking at liquids in containers and objects in space. The changes produced by pouring back and forth, by gathering together and spreading apart, are the data which most strongly suggest the conservation of quantity and number. We suspect that the changes sentences undergo as they shuttle between persons in conversation are, similarly, the data that must clearly expose the underlying structure of language.

SUMMARY

We have examined the effect on the child's development of grammatical knowledge of two aspects of the speech he hears: variation in the frequency with which particular constructions are modeled, and variation in the frequency of particular parental responses—expansions, expressions of approval and disapproval, and occasional questions. There is a small amount of evidence that modeling frequency does affect the acquisition of knowledge. With regard to the parental responses of expansion and approval-disapproval, the present evidence is that neither has any effect on the development of grammatical knowledge. The role of occasional questions is still unknown. Our own interest in isolated training variables is giving way to an interest in the structural information latent in various forms of linguistic interaction. Perhaps we shall someday find that home linguistic environments do vary significantly in structural richness but that any single form of response is unreliable index of this variation even as age-of-weaning has proved an unreliable index of something more important—general child-rearing attitudes.

REFERENCES

Brown, R. "The Development of *Wh* Questions in Child Speech." *Journal of Verbal Learning and Verbal Behavior*, VII (1968), 279–90.

———, and Bellugi, Ursula. "Three Processes in the Child's Acquisition of Syntax." *Harvard Educational Review*, XXXIV (1964), 133–51.

———, and Fraser, C. "The Acquisition of Syntax." In C. N. Cofer and Barbara S. Musgrave, eds., *Verbal Behavior and Learning*. New York: McGraw-Hill Book Company, 1963.

Cazden, Courtney B. "Environmental Assistance to the Child's Acquisition of Grammar." Unpublished doctoral dissertation, Harvard University, 1965.

Chomsky, N. *Aspects of the Theory of Syntax*. Cambridge, Mass.: The M.I.T. Press, 1965.

———. *Syntactic Structures*. The Hague: Mouton, 1957.

Fodor, J. A. "How to Learn to Talk: Some Simple Ways." In F. Smith and G. A. Miller, eds. *The Genesis of Language*. Cambridge, Mass.: The M. I. T. Press, 1966.

Gleason, H. A. *An Introduction to Descriptive Linguistics*, rev. ed. New York: Holt, Rinehart, & Winston, Inc., 1961.

Harris, Z. S. *Methods in Structural Linguistics*. Chicago: University of Chicago Press, 1951.

———. "Morpheme Alternates in Linguistic Analysis." *Language*, XVIII (1942), 169–80.

Heffner, R. M. S. *General Phonetics*. Madison: University of Wisconsin Press, 1949.

Hockett, C. F. "Problems of Morphemic Analysis." *Language*, XXIII (1947), 321–43.

Katz, J. J., and Postal, P. M. *An Integrated Theory of Linguistic Descriptions.* Cambridge, Mass.: The M.I.T. Press, 1964.

Klima, E. S. "Negation in English." In J. A. Fodor and J. J. Katz, eds., *The Structure of Language: Readings in the Philosophy of Language.* Englewood Cliffs, N. J.: Prentice-Hall, Inc., 1964.

McNeill, D. "Developmental Psycholinguistics." In F. Smith and G. A. Miller, eds., *The Genesis of Language.* Cambridge, Mass.: The M.I.T. Press, 1966.

Miller, G. A., and McNeill, D. "Psycholinguistics." In G. Lindzey and E. Aronson, eds., *Handbook of Social Psychology*, 2nd ed., Vol. III. Reading, Mass.: Addison-Wesley, 1968/69.

Nida, E. S. "The Identification of Morphemes." *Language*, XXIV (1948), 414–41.

Slobin, D. I. "The Acquisition of Russian as a Native Language." In F. Smith and G. A. Miller, eds., *The Genesis of Language.* Cambridge, Mass.: The M.I.T. Press, 1966.

Spitz, R. A. *No and Yes: On the Genesis of Human Communication.* New York: International University Press, 1957.

EDWARD S. KLIMA AND URSULA BELLUGI-KLIMA

58 Here is a study on "Syntactic Regularities in the Speech of Children" which was done by Edward Klima, a familiar name in current transformational linguistics, and by the psycholinguist Ursula Bellugi-Klima who does not need any further introduction here (cf. our introduction to her other work "Three Processes in the Child's Acquisition of Syntax," in collaboration with Roger Brown. Selection No. 49. See also No. 57).

This paper is a completely revised version of a paper which they presented at the Edinburgh University Conference on Psycholinguistics (March, 1966) and which originally appeared in *Psycholinguistics Papers*, ed. J. Lyons and R. J. Wales (Edinburgh University Press, 1966). The student may want to read this paper in conjunction with Edward Klima's work "Negation in English," in *The Structure of Language*, ed. J. J. Fodor and J. A. Katz (Englewood Cliffs, N. J.: Prentice-Hall, 1964) pp. 246–323.

It sheds new light on some of the problems which have been discussed in other selections, as the student will be glad to learn.   A. B. A.

SYNTACTIC REGULARITIES IN THE SPEECH OF CHILDREN

What we have set as our goal is the grammatical capacity of children—a part of their general linguistic competence.[1] The question of course is how to arrive at this competence. The utterances produced—which might seem to be a direct access to competence—cannot give the total answer. There is really no way to determine which of the child's utterances are grammatically nondeviant in terms of his own grammar. And even if the grammatically nondeviant utterances could be reliably determined, they could only give hints as to the total grammatical capacity of the child, which includes not only what has been produced (or understood) but also what could be produced (or understood). The situation

Reprinted from J. Lyons and R. J. Wales, eds., Psycholinguistics Papers (Edinburgh: Edinburgh University Press, 1966), 183–208, by permission of the authors and Edinburgh University Press.

[1] This work was supported in part by The Joint Services Electronics Project under contract BA 36–039–AMC–03200 (E), in part by the National Science Foundation Grant GP-2495, The National Institute of Health Grant MH 0473–05, The National Aeronautics and Space Administration Grant NSG-496, The U.S. Air Force ESD contract AF 19 (628–2487), and Public Health Service Research Grant MH 7088–04 from the National Institute of Health.

is the same as that involved in describing our own adult grammar if we limited ourselves to what had been uttered over some short period of time and faithfully gave equal weight to everything uttered, no matter how it actually came out. What is actually done, in analyzing the adult language, is to select. Sentences are selected which are felt intuitively to be most free of deviances, and then one goes beyond the mere corpus to develop a more structured theory that excludes sentences which are wrong grammatically (i.e., present clear deviances) and that explains the status of the other cases. The range of difficulties that face the analyst in describing the language of children on the basis of their utterances should be illuminated by examining a sketch of grammatical structure in adult English.

Approaching the grammar of child language from the other direction answers certain of the problems—that is, from the point of view of the child's ability to understand sentences. Sentences the child understands describe the scope of his grammar more accurately than those he produces, just as with the adult. But if the child's "understanding" of adult sentences is examined, there is some evidence to suggest that the child comprehends sentences according to his existing grammar. Where comprehension involves syntactic characteristics not present in the child's utterances it seems that this does not represent a relatively rich grammar coupled with a much poorer production device, but rather a limited grammar coupled with a liberal perceptual device that sifts out or by-passes unfamiliar material. As an example, with children whose speech did not contain passives, we tested comprehension of the passive construction, using pairs of pictures. One picture showed a cat being chased by a dog, and another a dog being chased by a cat. When the children were asked to show "The cat is being chased by the dog," a number of them pointed to the picture of the cat chasing the dog.[2] This suggests that these children may have been processing the passive sentences as if they were active sentences, i.e.,

in terms of usual subject–verb–object relations, sifting out the unknown material, specifically the passive auxiliary and the agentive preposition. We plan in the future to use as much information on comprehension of syntax as possible in investigating the grammar of children.

A striking characteristic of the language-acquisition situation is the fact that the particular linguistic ability that develops in the individual child as he gradually masters his native language is grossly underdetermined by the utterances he hears. Not only does he understand, produce, and recognize as perfectly normal countless sentences he has never heard, but he will recognize as deviant in some way or other countless utterances that he has heard produced during his linguistically formative years. The child will recognize as deviant all the various slips of the tongue, false starts, interrupted completions, and noises that are present in our everyday utterances. Given the external characteristics of language acquisition, the psycholinguist asks: How do any two children—to say nothing of those of a whole speech community—arrive at anywhere near the same language? How does a particular language—each time it is acquired by a child—keep from changing radically? Since language does not change radically in this situation, there must surely be some general principles at work, and it is the principles underlying language acquisition which we want eventually to illuminate.

But first, prior questions must be investigated. If one looks closely at the development of speech in children who have heard totally independent language environments during the early period of language acquisition, it may well be that each will follow an independent path in his grammatical growth and syntactic patterns. And if the limitations on what the child produces have little relationship to his grammatical capacity, one would not expect that a study of children's speech would reveal regularities in the order of appearance of structures across children. We propose to investigate the development of negative and interrogative structures in the speech of three children in order to examine some of these aspects of language development.

---

[2] Colin Fraser, Ursula Bellugi, and Roger Brown, "Control of Grammar in Imitation, Comprehension, and Production," *Journal of Verbal Learning and Verbal Behavior*, II (1963), 121–35.

THE LANGUAGE ACQUISITION PROJECT

We have as data for this research a developmental study of three children, whom we have called Adam, Eve, and Sarah in previous reports with Professor Brown and his associates. Each child was followed by a different investigator. Tape recordings of mother-child interchanges were made regularly in the children's homes.

The families were totally unacquainted and independent of one another, and each child heard a different set of sentences as 'input.' The children were beginning to string words together in struotured utterances when we began the study. One child was 18 months old, another 26 months, and the third was 27 months old; however, all three were at approximately the same stage of language development.

For each child, then, there are two to four sessions of the speech of the mother and child per month as data. These sessions were tape-recorded and later transcribed together with a written record made at the time of the recording which includes some aspects of the situation which relate to the meaning of the interchange. In order to describe stages in development we picked two end points in terms of mean utterance length. The first stage is from the first month of study for each child; i.e., the mean utterance length is about 1.75 morphemes. The last is from the month in which the mean utterance lengths approach 3.5 morphemes for each of the three children; and the second stage is between the two. (See Figure 1.)

Each period represents several thousand child utterances. From the total speech we isolated the negative statements and the questions for analysis, and we have suggested outlines for a study of the development of these systems in the children's speech. We have used the children's utterances and evidence about the children's understanding of these constructions in the language of others, in attempting to consider the children's developing grammatical capacities.

NEGATION IN ENGLISH

To begin, let us touch on some of the linguistic facts about the terminal state toward which the children are progressing, that is, the syntax of English negatives and interrogatives. We shall consider *Neg* as a formant which combines with parts of the sentence to constitute negation in the sentence. Among the realizations of *Neg* are the negative particle *not* and its contracted form *n't* (e.g., "It isn't true"), and a small set of negative words including the negative pronouns *nobody* and *nothing* ("Nobody came"), the negative determiner *no* (e.g., "No students passed"), the negative adverbs *never*, *nowhere*. Although there are many complexities in the total picture of negation in adult English that do not occur at all in the early periods, the basic facts about negation in simple sentences are all relevant—in particular the form and position of the negative formant.

Negation and auxiliary verbs

The negative particle *not* appears most simply in conjunction with the auxiliary verbs in English and is generally contracted with them in a speech. Consider first the modal auxiliaries (M) (*will, can, may, must, could, would, shall, should,* etc.) and notice that the negative particle is located after the first auxiliary verb of the sentence if there is one. Compare these sets of affirmative and negative sentences:

The man will finish today.	The man won't finish today.
The baby can sit up.	The baby can't sit up.
He will have been doing it.	He won't have been doing it.

In sentences in which *be* comes first in the verb phrase (whether as progressive (*be-PrP*) or passive (*be-PP*) auxiliary) or as main verb, the negative particle follows *be*, as it follows *have* when the latter is auxiliary for the perfect (*have-PP*) and occurs first in the verb phrase, and also, restrictedly, when *have* is the main verb:

They are coming here.	They aren't coming here.
Her face is red.	Her face isn't red.
I have done it.	I haven't done it.
I have time for that.	I haven't any time for that.

In each, the contraction of the negative element with the auxiliary is optional. One can say either: *They can not go,* or *They can't*

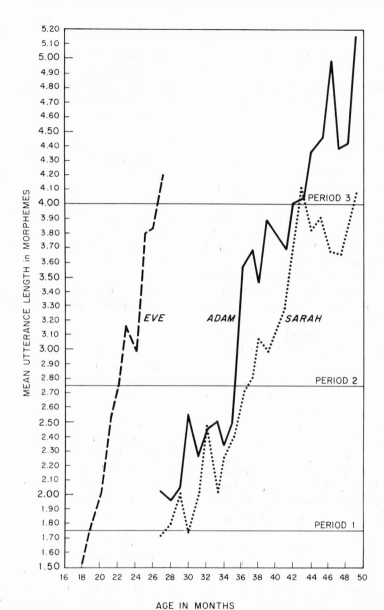

FIGURE 1. Age in months.

go, although the latter seems more frequent in informal speech.

The negative element is not attached to other main verbs, nor does it stand in place of an auxiliary; thus we do not say *I want'nt it, or *I not want it, but rather I don't want it.[3] The auxiliary verb do occurs in negative sentences with the particle not where the affirmative version of a sentence does not have an auxiliary verb, and not only carries the negative particle but also the tense marker (T). He made it is the affirmative sentence corresponding to He didn't make it. Thus auxiliary do is left unspoken in affirmative declaratives and imperatives—except under special conditions as in "Do be quiet" and "He did so leave."

Negative imperative

We analyze negative imperatives as having auxiliary do followed by the negative formant,

---

[3] An asterisk preceding an utterance means that this is not a grammatical sentence of English.

then optionally *you* (or an indefinite *anybody*), then the imperative modal auxiliary (IMP) (which in certain circumstances is realized as *will* or *can*) and finally the main verb:

Don't be late, will you!
Don't you do that again.
Don't anybody move.

Negation and indefiniteness

Special cases aside, sentences of standard English permit only one negative formant per main verb. The presence of such a negative formant provides an appropriate condition for the occurrence of one or more indefinites (indef) (*any, anybody, anything, anywhere, ever*) as subject, object, or other complements to the main verb in the same environments in which indeterminates (indet) (*some, somebody, something, somewhere, once*) occur in the corresponding affirmative declaratives and imperatives. Compare the following sets:

You have *some* milk.	You haven't *any* milk.
Give me *some* more.	Don't give me *any* more.
I want *something*	I don't want *anything*.
Somebody left *something*.	*Nobody* left *anything*.

We shall describe this negative coloring as the conversion of indeterminates into indefinites in the context of a negative formant. However, no indefinites may precede the form representing the final realization of the negative formant, whether this form is the negative particle *not/n't* or a negative word (e.g., *nobody*). Thus "Nobody left anthing" is grammatical but not "*Anybody left nothing." Note particularly in this respect the special form of active-passive pairs:

Nobody saw anything new.
Nothing new was seen by anybody.

and not "*Anything new was seen ·by nobody," which would be predicted by the identity, otherwise holding, between object of the active and subject of the passive, on the one hand, and subject of the active and agent of the passive, on the other. We capture this fact by assuming that the negative formant combines with an indefinite (or the first of several indefinites) which is then realized as a negative word (*any* as *no*, *anybody* as *nobody*, etc.), obligatorily if the indefinite precedes the main verb and all its auxil-

iaries; otherwise, optionally. Compare the single possibility: "Nobody saw him," with the alternates of its corresponding passive "He wasn't seen by anyone," and "He was seen by nobody."

Negation not included in this study

The sections described above cover the problems which arise in relation to negatives in the children's speech as far as we have considered it in this study. Symptomatic of sentence negation in adult English is the possible occurrence of an either-clause (*I didn't like it and he didn't either*); the negative appositive tag (*I don't like dogs, not even little ones*); and the question tag without not (*He's not going, is he?*). None of those occur in the children's speech in these early stages. Affixal negation does not occur either (*unfortunately, impossible, unmade*), nor do inherently negative words like *doubt, reluctant*.

This discussion comprises part of what we mean by the negative system, and the auxiliary system in adult English; that is, the occurrences and nonoccurrences involving those parts of the grammar. We will try to capture the nature of these systems by a set of rules something like those on the following pages, although undoubtedly as more is learned about grammatical systems in general and about English in particular, the form of these rules will be different. We feel that in their present state they do at least capture the spirit of this part of the grammar in a way that is compatible with other aspects of the grammar of English. One can think of the rules as giving some verifiable substance to our claim that these occurrences and nonoccurrences fit together in some systematic way.

RULES FOR NEGATION IN ADULT ENGLISH

The verb phrase with its auxiliaries has at one level in its derivation the following possible forms:

$$[\text{T--}do]_{\text{Aux}_1} \ (Neg) \ \left[\begin{Bmatrix} \text{IMP} \\ \text{M} \end{Bmatrix} \ (have\text{-}PP) \right.$$

$$\left. (be\text{-}PrP) \ (be\text{-}PP) \right]_{\text{Aux}_2} \left[\begin{Bmatrix} \text{V} \\ be \\ have \end{Bmatrix} (\text{NP}) \ldots \right]_{\text{VP}}$$

or, after contraction of *not* to *n't*:

$$[\text{T--}do \ (Neg)]_{\text{Aux}_1} \ \text{etc.}$$

This represents the underlying structure after certain transformations (the details of which are not important in this study) have already operated; for example, the positioning of the negative formant, the occurrence of the passive auxiliary.

Transformations:

I. Replacement of *do*

$$T - do - (Neg) - \begin{Bmatrix} M \\ have \\ be \end{Bmatrix}$$

$$\Rightarrow T - \begin{Bmatrix} M \\ have \\ be \end{Bmatrix} - (Neg) - \phi$$

II. Negative Coloring
   1. $X^1 - Indet - X^2 - Neg - X^3$
       $\Rightarrow X^1 - Indef - X^2 - Neg - X^3$
   2. $X^1 - Neg - X^2 - Indet - X^3$
       $\Rightarrow X^1 - Neg - X^2 - Indef - X^3$
   (If *Neg* is treated as occurring initially in the underlying string, then a simpler formulation is possible.)

III. Formation of Negative Words
   1. Obligatory
       $X^1 - Indef - X^2 - Neg - X^3$
       $\Rightarrow X^1 - Neg + Indef - X^2 - \phi - X^3$
   2. Optional
       $X^1 - Neg - X^2 - Indef - X^3$
       $\Rightarrow X^1 - \phi - X^2 - Neg + Indef - X^3$

IV. *Do* Deletion
   $T - do - V \Rightarrow T - \phi - V$
   or, expanded to include imperatives as approximately:

$$T - do - (IMP) \begin{Bmatrix} V \\ be \\ have \end{Bmatrix}$$

$$\Rightarrow T - \phi - (IMP) - \begin{Bmatrix} V \\ be \\ have \end{Bmatrix}$$

NEGATION IN CHILDREN'S SPEECH

What it is that the child learns in becoming a mature speaker of the language is, of course, the whole system which we have tried to capture by the rules above, and certainly not those particular tentative rules. It should be understood that when we write rules for the child grammar it is just a rough attempt to give substance to our feeling about, and general observations demonstrating, the regularity in the syntax of children's speech.

We have intentionally allowed ourselves much freedom in the formulation of these rules. Even within this freedom we feel that at the very earliest stages, perhaps we fitted the language unjustifiably to what we assume to be the underlying structure of adult language. These rules reflect, but certainly do not describe completely, the utterances produced by the child. Whenever possible we took into consideration comprehension of utterances; but comprehension, like speech, only reflects grammatical capacity. Our aim in both cases is to find basic regularities.

One of the ultimate objectives in describing such regularities is to discover—given the child's own linguistic abilities as they have developed at some particular stage and given the utterances that he hears—what system or possible systems the child will ascribe to the language. We are interested in the basis for particular constructions, notably those that characterize the language of all three children.

Not very much is known about how people understand a particulr sentence or what goes into producing one; but something is known about the systematicity of adult language. It has seemed to us that the language of children has its own systematicity, and that the sentences of children are not just an imperfect copy of those of an adult.

Are there hazards in considering the grammar of a childs language from the point of view of his speech? Of course there are many. One possibility is that the limitations on what is produced have nothing at all to do with the grammar but have to do with factors of memory, immediate requirements of explicitness, and the like. However, if this were the case, one would not expect the order of appearance of certain structures, and in particular certain systematic 'mistakes,' to be regular across children. We want to emphasize here that we are not dealing with the expression of semantic concepts on the part of the child, or of basic grammatical notions like subject function and transitivity; rather we are concerned with the way he handles lower-level syntactic phenomena like position, permutability, and the like.

Period 1

The sentences we want to describe from period 1, are taken from the protocols of all three children:

No heavy
No want stand head

No more sharpen it
No Fraser drink all tea
More . . . no
No singing song
No the sun shining
No money
No sit there
No play that
No fall!

Unless otherwise noted, the sentences included in this study represent large numbers of like utterances in the children's speech, and are not to be considered isolated examples but rather reflections of recurrent structures occurring in the children's spontaneous speech. Notice that there are no negatives within the utterances, nor are there auxiliary verbs. The element which signals negation is *no* or *not*, and this element either precedes or follows the rest of the utterance.

Let us refer to the elements from *sharpen it, more, the sun shining*, in the above sentences as the Nucleus. Notice incidentally that there seems to be limited structure to the Nucleus. The sentences consist largely of nouns and verbs without indication of tense or number. Inflections, prepositions, articles, adjectives, adverbs, auxiliary verbs rarely occur. The negation system at period 1 can be considered as follows:

(1) $\left[\begin{Bmatrix} no \\ not \end{Bmatrix} - \text{Nucleus}\right]_s$ or $[\text{Nucleus} - no]_s$

At this stage, there is no clear evidence that the child even understands the negative embedded in the auxiliary of adult speech, without at least some reinforcement. During this early period, the mothers often reinforce their negative statements as in, *No, you can't have that*, to insure the children's comprehension of the negative impace of the sentence. What is interesting in the speech of the child at this stage is that he employs extremely limited means for negative sentences in his own speech, and the same system is repeated in all three subjects. In subsequent periods there may indeed be an initial sentence adverb *no*, but this initial element is not a sufficient or even necessary part of sentence negation.

The rule for negation that we have given serves many negative functions in the child's speech at period 1.

Adult: *Get in your high chair with your bib, and I'll give you your cheese.*
Childl *No bibby.*
Adult: *Oh, you don't want your bibby?*

Adult: *Well, is the sun shining?*
Child: *No the sun shining.*
Adult: *Oh, the sun's not shining?*

(An adult leans over to talk to the child. Child looks up and puts up a hand in warning.)
Child: *No fall!*

Period 2
Some of the sentences we want to describe, again from all three children, are as follows:

I can't catch you.
I can't see you.
We can't talk.
You can't dance.
I don't sit on Cromer coffee.
I don't want it.
I don't like him.
I don't know his name.
No . . . Rusty hat.
Book say no.
Touch the snow no.

Don't leave me.
Don't wait for me . . . come in.
Don't wake me up . . . again.

That not 'O,' that blue.
That no fish school.
That no Mommy.
There no squirrels.

He no bite you.
I no want envelope.
I no taste them.

A characteristic of child language is the residue of elements of previous systems, and the sentences produced might well be described as a coexistence of the rules at period 1, and a new system. Let us begin with a basic structure something like:

(2) S → NP – (*Neg*) – VP

where the formant *Neg* has as possible lexical representatives *can't, don't, not*, and occasionally *no*. The auxiliary verbs can be thought of as occurring in the speech of the children only when accompanied by *Neg*, since it is a fact that the auxiliary verbs do not occur in questions or declarative utterances at this stage. They occur only in negative sentences, and in these limited forms. This first rule can be related to the shape of sentences by the following rules:

(3) $\text{Neg} \rightarrow \begin{Bmatrix} no \\ not \\ V^{neg} \end{Bmatrix}$

(4) $V^{neg} \rightarrow \begin{Bmatrix} can't \\ don't \end{Bmatrix}$

where the particular selection of the negative is determined by the Main Verb with *don't* and *can't* restricted to occurrence before instances of nonprogressive main verbs.

Two auxiliary verbs appear in the negative form, *don't* and *can't*. These are considered as lexical representations of V^{neg} since there are no occurrences of *I can do it, Can I have it?, He shouldn't have it, They aren't going*, etc., but only instances of the sort described above. The negative element is also found within the sentence, but not connected to an auxiliary verb, as in *He no bite you*.

There a number of sentences with *no* or *not* followed by a predicate. There is a limited class of subjects in this set. The negative imperative has appeared in the speech of all three children, in the form: *Don't leave me*. In the previous stage the imperative form was presumably *No fall*. There is at this stage an affirmative imperative as well, as in *Come here* and *Do it*. There are hardly any sentences with indefinite determiners or pronouns, but there are by now personal and impersonal pronouns, possessive pronouns, articles, and adjectives.

It is clear that the child understands the negative embedded in the auxiliary of the sentence by this stage. For example:

Mother: Oh, we don't have any bread.
Child: We have buy some.

Mother: He doesn't have a ball.
Child: Why not he have ball?

There is also evidence that the child uses negatives to contradict a previous preposition either expressed or implied by this stage, as in:

Mother: Did you play in the snow?
Child: No, play sunshine.

Mother: You told me to sit on it.
Child: No, you sit *there*.

Period 3

A sample of the setences to be described, again from all three children:

Paul can't have one.
I can't see it.
This can't stick.
We can't make another broom.

I didn't did it.
Because I don't want somebody to wake me up.
I don't want cover on it.
I don't . . . have some . . . too much.
You don't want some supper.
You didn't caught me.
You didn't eat supper with us.
I didn't see something.
Paul didn't laugh.
I didn't caught it.

I gave him some so he won't cry.
'Cause he won't talk.
Donna won't let go.

No, I don't have a book.
No, it isn't.
That was not me.
I am not a doctor.
This not ice cream.
This no good.
They not hot.
Paul not tired.
It's not cold.

I not crying.
That not turning.
He not taking the walls down.

Don't put the two wings on.
Don't kick my box.
Don't touch the fish.

I not hurt him.
I not see you anymore.
Ask me if I not made mistake.

In the speech of the children, the modal auxiliaries and *do* and *be* now appear in declarative sentences and questions, as well as in negative sentences; so we can now begin with a basic structure like:

(5) $\text{S} \rightarrow \text{NP} - \text{Aux} - \text{VP}$

and suggest some rules as follows:

(6)   Aux $\rightarrow$ T $-$ V^{aux} $-$ (*Neg*)

(7)   V^{aux} $-$ $\begin{Bmatrix} do \\ can \\ be \\ will \end{Bmatrix}$

where *be* is restricted to predicate and progressive and is optional; *can* and *do* are restricted to nonprogressive main verbs.

Transformations:
I. Optional *be* Deletion
    NP $-$ *be* $\Rightarrow$ NP
II. *Do* Deletion
    do $-$ V $\Rightarrow$ V

In the speech of the children at this stage the negative auxiliary verbs are now no longer limited to *don't* and *can't* and the auxiliary verbs now appear in declarative sentences and questions, so that the auxiliary verbs can be considered as separate from the negative element of the sentence.

Indeterminates now start appearing in the children's speech, in affirmative utterances as *I want some supper* or *I see something*. The children's negative sentences have the form, *I don't want some supper* and *I didn't see something*. The negative versions are clearly not imitations of adult sentences, and indicate that the complex relationship of negative and indefinite has not yet been established. Examples of indefinite coloring are rare, and do not appear with any regularity until subsequent stages.

RULES FOR NEGATION IN CHILDREN'S SPEECH

Period 1

(1) $\left[\begin{Bmatrix} no \\ not \end{Bmatrix} - \text{Nucleus} \right]_s$ or [Nucleus $-$ *no*]$_s$

Period 2

(2) S $\Rightarrow$ NP $-$ (*Neg*) $-$ VP

(3) *Neg* $\Rightarrow$ $\begin{Bmatrix} no \\ not \\ V^{neg} \end{Bmatrix}$

(4) V^{neg} $\Rightarrow$ $\begin{Bmatrix} can't \\ don't \end{Bmatrix}$

where the particular selection of the negative is determined by the main verb with *don't* and *can't* restricted to occurrence before instances of nonprogressive main verbs.

Period 3

(5) S $\Rightarrow$ NP $-$ Aux $-$ VP

(6) Aux $\Rightarrow$ T $-$ V^{aux} $-$ (*Neg*)

(7) V^{aux} $\Rightarrow$ $\begin{Bmatrix} do \\ can \\ will \\ be \end{Bmatrix}$

where *be* is restricted to predicate and progressive, *can* and *do* to nonprogressive main verbs.

Transformations:
I. Optional *be* Deletion
    NP $-$ *be* $\Rightarrow$ NP
II. *Do* Deletion
    do $-$ V $\Rightarrow$ V

INTERROGATIVES IN ENGLISH

For questions in adult English, we represent the interrogative nature of the sentence by the formant Q, with which may be associated: (a) interrogative words (represented here by *wh* + *indet* in various functions, ultimately realized as *what, who, which, where, how, why*); or (b) the sentence as whole in the form of a *yes/no* question represented here by *wh* preceding the major parts of the sentence, i.e., Q–*wh*–NP–Aux–VP. In direct *yes/no* questions, *wh* has no lexical realization, whereas in the corresponding indirect questions it is realized as *whether*. Compare "Will John leave?" with "They wonder *whether* John will leave." In adult English, either the whole sentence may be questioned (a *yes/no* question) or one or more parts may be questioned (an interrogative word question).

If Q and either an interrogative word (*wh* + indet) or the *wh* of *yes/no* questions precede the entire subject noun phrase of the sentence, then that noun phrase and the first auxiliary verb are inverted. If the interrogative word is part of the subject, then there is no inversion. Thus, "What will that person make?" and "Will that person make something?" but no inversion in "Which person will make something?" Auxiliary *do* is unspoken, unless some element (e.g., the subject because of inversion) intervenes between *do* and the main verb. (Recall that in negation, the negative particle also had the effect of preserving the otherwise unspoken auxiliary *do*.)

Rules for questions in adult English
S $\rightarrow$ Q $-$ *wh* $-$ NP $-$ Aux $-$ VP
VP $\rightarrow$ (as on page 416)

NP → {. . . wh + indet (provided that Q, but not Q – wh, introduces S)}

Transformation:

I. Replacement of *do*

$$T - do - (Neg) - \begin{Bmatrix} M \\ have \\ be \end{Bmatrix} \Rightarrow T \begin{Bmatrix} M \\ have \\ be \end{Bmatrix}$$

II. Interrogative Preposing (optional)

$Q - X^1 - wh + indet - X^2 \Rightarrow$
$Q - wh + indet - X^1 - X^2$

III. Interrogative Inversion

$Q - wh \ (+ \ indet) - NP - Aux_1 - X \Rightarrow$
$Q - wh \ (+ \ indet) - Aux_1 - NP - X$

IV. *Do* Deletion

$T - do - V \Rightarrow T - \varnothing - V$

QUESTIONS IN CHILDREN'S SPEECH

Period 1

The questions to consider, from all three children, are:

Fraser water?
Mommy eggnog?
See hole?
I ride train?
Have some?
Sit Chair?
No ear?
Ball go?

Who that?
Why?
What(s) that?
What doing?
What cowboy doing?

Where Ann pencil?
Where Mama boot?
Where kitty?
Where milk go?
Where horse go?

Again, one can consider the elements *Fraser water, Mommy eggnog, Ann pencil, milk go*, in the above questions as the Nucleus. As with the negative, in period 1 there is very limited structure to the Nucleus, which consists primarily of nouns and verbs without indication of tense and number.

The questions without an interrogative word can be thought of as Q *yes/no*–Nucleus, where the *yes/no* marker is expressed as rising intonation. There are no other identifying characteristics of *yes/no* questions in adult English, since there are no auxiliaries, and there is no form of subject-verb inversion.

From the context of mother-child interchange, it seems that these rising intonation sentences are frequently responded to by the adult as if they were *yes/no* questions. The formulation suggested is:

(8) S → Q$^{yes/no}$ – Nucleus

The *wh* questions can be described as a list which includes only a few routines that vary little across the three children. The most common questions are some version of *What's that?* and *Where NP (go)?* and *What NP doing?* It is not at all clear that the *What* in *What cowboy doing?* has any relationship to a grammatical object of the verb do (that is, that it is a special case of Q Nucleus where the particular interrogative occurs as the object of *do*). What might be said, with reservation, is that, indeed, there is a relationship in the child's speech between sentences like *go NP* and *Where NP go?* but that the special interrogative form is bound to the particular word *go* and does not at all have the generality of the adult structure. Paraphrases of the above questions for the child might be: "I want to know the name of that thing"; "I want to know what you call that action;" and "I want to know the location of that (previously present) object." One might tentatively suggest a formulation as follows:

(9) S → Q^{what} – NP – (*doing*)
(10) S → Q^{where} – NP – (*go*)

Let us take as an example the interrogative word questions in which the object of a verb is the missing constituent and has been replaced by a preposed *what*. If one looks at the set of these questions, which the mother asks the child in the course of the samples of speech, one finds that at period 1 the child generally does not respond or responds inappropriately, as in:

Mother: *Well, did you hit?*
Child: *Hit.*

Mother: *What did you do?*
Child: *Head.*

At this stage, then, the children are producing questions that only superficially resemble these questions in which the object of a verb has been questioned and preposed, and they do not understand this construction when they hear it.

Period 2

Some of the questions to consider are:

See my doggie?
Dat black too?
Mom pinch finger?
You want eat?
I have it?

Where my mitten?
Where baby Sarah rattle?
Where me sleep?

What book name?
What me think?
What the dollie have?
What soldier marching?

Why you smiling?
Why you waking me up?
Why not he eat?
Why not me sleeping?
Why not . . . me can't dance?
Why not me drink it?
You can't fix it?
This can't write a flower?

There is some development in the superficial structure of the sentences since period 1. Notably, pronouns have developed, articles and modifiers are more often present, some inflections (present progressive and plurals) occur, and the verb phrase may include a prepositional phrase or preverb. There are no modal auxiliaries in affirmative sentences, and only two negative modal forms (*don't* and *can't*). There are few indeterminates or indefinities.

There seems to be a gradual development of rules and not necessarily the wholescale replacement of one total system by another. Constituent questioning is developing. Although the interrogative word *what* appears in sentences which have a missing object, there are nonetheless occurrences of that interrogative without those conditions. It is perhaps premature to associate this word in each case with a specific deleted constituent of the sentence. But certainly there is already some association of what will be referred to as a zero interrogative constituent and the interrogative introducers *what*, *where*, and *why*. That is, in period 2 Q^{what} (perhaps also Q^{where}) has begun in its function of requesting the information that would

be supplied by a specific syntactic constituent of the sentence (the object of a verb) and the questioned constituent is left blank. We suggest that the child's question "What the dollie have?" may well have some such structure as:

$$Q^{what} - the\ dollie_{NP}\ [[have]_V\ [\varnothing]_{NP}]_{VP}$$

and that already there is a general relationship between introductory *what* and the occurrence, *without* an expressed object noun phrase, of any verb like *have*. In period 2, there is still no inversion of subject and verb in *yes/no* questions.

By this stage there are appropriate answers to most questions. The responses reflect that the child understands that the object of a verb or preposition is being questioned:

Mother: *What d'you need?*
Child: *Need some chocolate.*

Mother: *Who are you peeking at?*
Child: *Peeking at Ursula.*

Mother: *What d'you hear?*
Child: *Hear a duck.*

We suggest for Period 2:

(11) $S \rightarrow \begin{Bmatrix} Q^{yes/no} \\ Q^{what} \\ Q^{where} \\ Q^{why} \end{Bmatrix}$ – Nucleus

(12)   Nucleus $\rightarrow$ NP – V – (NP)

(13)   NP $\rightarrow \begin{Bmatrix} \cdots \\ \varnothing\ /\ \text{if the sentence is introduced} \\ \text{by } Q^{what} \end{Bmatrix}$

Period 3

The questions to consider are:

Does the kitty stand up?
Does lions walk?
Is Mommy talking to Robin's grandmother?
Did I saw that in my book?
Oh, did I caught it?
Are you going to make it with him?
Will you help me?
Can I have a piece of paper?

Where small trailer he should pull?
Where the other Joe will drive?
Where I should put it when I make it up?
Where's his other eye?
Where my spoon goed?

What I did yesterday?
What he can ride in?
What you had?

What did you doed?
Sue, what you have in you mouth?
Why the Christmas tree going?
Why he don't know how to pretend?
Why kitty can't stand up?
Why Paul caught it?

Which way they should go?
How he can be a doctor?
How they can't talk?
How that opened?

Can't it be a bigger truck?
Can't you work this thing?

Between the previous stage and this one many parts of the children's grammar have undergone developments. There is now a class of verbal forms that inverts with the subject in certain interrogatives (*yes/no* questions) and may take the negative particle with it. One particular verb, *do*, occurs only in its function as a helping verb in inverted questions and negatives, seldom in interrogative word questions. At this point, the system that has been developed bears striking similarities to the adult pattern. Notice, however, that the auxiliary verbs are not inverted with the subject noun phrase in interrogative word questions. There are other aspects that set this child's system apart from the adult language, namely the child does not produce the full set of sequences of the adult auxiliary system. In the adult system, the possible sequences are (M) (*have*-pp) (*be*-prp); that is, any combination of these, but always in that order, where tense appears always on the first, or if none of these are present, then with the main verb. The children, at this stage, do not produce any combinations of auxiliaries.

Considerable development is found in the children's grammar by this stage. In addition to the noun and verb inflections appearing in the previous stage, one finds possessive markers, third person singular present indicative, and the regular past indicator. The sentences are no longer limited to simple English sentences. There is considerable development in complexity, and we find relative clauses and other clauses present for the

first time: *You have two things that turn around; I told you I know how to put the train together; I gon' get my chopper for chopping down cows and trees; Let's go upstairs and take it from him because it's mine;*

Let us begin with the same basic structure as for negatives at stage 3:

(14) $S \rightarrow (Q(wh))\ NP - Aux - VP$

(15) $Aux \rightarrow T - V^{aux} - (Neg)$

(16) $V^{aux} \rightarrow \begin{Bmatrix} can \\ do \\ will \\ be \end{Bmatrix}$

(17) $NP \rightarrow \begin{Bmatrix} wh + \text{indet} \\ \ldots \end{Bmatrix}$

Transformations:

I. Interrogative Word Preposing
$Q - X^1 - wh + \text{indet} - X^2 \Rightarrow$
$Q - wh + \text{indet} - X^1 - X^2$

II. Interrogative Inversion (Characterizing only *yes-no* questions)
$Q - wh - NP - Aux - X \Rightarrow$
$Q - wh - Aux - NP - X$

III. *Do* Deletion
$do - V \Rightarrow V$

In *yes-no* questions, we have noted that the children invert the auxiliary component with the subject noun phrase appropriately. Affirmative sentences generally have an auxiliary. In interrogative word questions, however, the auxiliary is generally not inverted. The auxiliary form of *be* is optional at this stage, and the auxiliary *do* is not present in the final shape of most of the interrogative word questions.

RULES FOR QUESTIONS IN CHILDREN'S SPEECH

Period 1
(8) S: $Q^{yes/no} - \text{Nucleus}$
(9) $\rightarrow Q^{what} - NP - (doing)$
(10) $\rightarrow Q^{where} - NP - (go)$

Period 2

(11) $S \rightarrow \begin{Bmatrix} Q^{yes/no} \\ Q^{what} \\ Q^{where} \\ Q^{why} \end{Bmatrix} - \text{Nucleus}$

(12) $\text{Nucleus} \rightarrow NP - V - (NP)$

(13) $NP \rightarrow \begin{Bmatrix} \ldots \\ \varnothing \end{Bmatrix}$ / if the sentence is introduced by Q^{what}.

Period 3
(14) $S \rightarrow (Q(wh)) - NP - Aux - VP$
Transformations (as on this page)
I. Interrogative Word Preposing

II.   Interrogative Inversion
(Only for *yes-no* questions)
III.   *Do* Deletion

SUMMARY

The speech of the three children consists primarily of a small set of words strung together at the earliest stage we have investigated in two-and three-word sentences. Among the early systematic aspects of child speech in its step-by-step approximation to the adult system are the following: in the early period the negatives and an ever-growing class of interrogative introducers occur first in the sentence, as sentence modifiers in the basic framework. The association of the interrogative word with other constituents of the sentence is very limited at first, restricted at the beginning to a complement of one or two particular verbs (e.g., *go* in *Where* NP *go*). Only later does the association apply to whole categories, such that the proposing of *wh* + prefixed elements can be spoken of with any generality. The auxiliary verb emerges first (anticipated perhaps by the optional occurrence of the copula *be*) always associated with negatives (as *can't*, *don't*). Not until afterwards do the modal auxiliary verbs and *do* appear inverted with the subject, and then only in the *yes/no* questions (ie., the question not introduced by an interrogative word). At the same time, the modal auxiliary verbs, but not *do*, finally emerge indepenent of interrogatives and negatives.

Not until the next stage does the inversion of auxiliary verbs extend to questions introduced by an interrogative word. Negation is embedded in the auxiliary verbs by this third stage, but the complex relation of negative and indefinite is not established yet. We have attempted to capture the regularities which we found in the speech of the three children in the rules which we have suggested for negatives and interrogatives.

SYMBOLS

S	sentence
Neg	negative formant
Q	interrogative formant
X	variable
Det	determiner
Aux	auxiliary verb
IMP	imperative modal auxiliary
MV	main verb
NP	noun phrase
VP	verb phrase
indet	indeterminate
indef	indefinite
T	tense marker
wh	interrogative word
have-PP	perfect
be-PrP	progressive
M	modal auxiliary verbs
+	incorporated with
( )	symbol enclosed is optional
[ ]subscript	node dominating enclosed constituent
{ }	choose one of list
∅	null

NOAM CHOMSKY

59

Noam Chomsky is Professor of Linguistics at the Massachusetts Institute of Technology. He has been instrumental in the development of transformational generative grammar and has published extensively on linguistics and the philosophy (and psychology) of language. His publications include the following books: *The Logical Structure of Linguistic Theory* (1955), *Syntactic Structures* (1957), *Current Issues in Linguistic Theory* (1964), *Aspects of the Theory of Syntax* (1965), *Cartesian Linguistics* (1966), and in collaboration with Morris Halle, *The Sound Pattern of English* (1968). He has also published numerous articles.

His small book *Syntactic Structures* (1957) is considered by many as an epoch-making study, and within a few years, through his publications and teaching, the generative transformational approach has become prevalent in linguistics; it has also affected psycholinguistics, and the study of child language in particular. Its impact is apparent in most child-language studies of this decade, although Chomsky has addressed himself to the problem of language acquisition only marginally, especially in his "Formal Discussion" of Miller and Ervin's paper "The Development of Grammar in Child Language" (1964) (see Selection 52) and in the first chapter of his *Aspects of the Theory of Syntax* (1965). He subsequently touched upon it in his chapter on "The Formal Nature of Language," which constitutes an Appendix to Eric Lenneberg's *Biological Foundations of Language* (New York and London: John Wiley and Sons, Inc., 1967), 397–442. More recently he devoted special attention to the problems of language acquisition in his *Language and Mind* (New York: Harcourt, Brace and World, Inc., 1968, VII + 88 pp.), and in "Language and the Mind," *Psychology Today*, 1968, I (9), 48–51, 66–68, which follows.

Chomsky's revolutionary ideas, further developed and elaborated in the past decade by himself and other scholars, have fertilized both linguistic and psychological (also philosophical) theories about the nature of language, its acquisition, its structure, and its description. In recent years they have permeated almost the entire literature of these fields.

The new ideas and concepts, briefly expounded by Chomsky in the following reading, concern a generative grammar, a system of rules underlying speech production and its interpretation. It is also a "transformational" grammar, involving concepts of linguistic competence and performance, surface structure and deep structure, base rules and transformational rules. Chomsky's renewed and intensified rationalist approach makes use of innate ideas, universals of language, and models of language acquisition—in opposition to the rather prevalent empiricist and behaviorist theories. All of these concepts have brought about a series of reevaluations, not only among linguists but also among psychologists. Chomsky's ideas apply especially to psycholinguist studies of language acquisition, as part of acquisition of knowledge in general, problems of psychological validity of grammatical concepts, of the psychological reality of linguistic descriptions, and of related problems (some of them are already incorporated in the present volume). One of the earliest examples of the utilization of the generative-grammar approach by a psychologist (psycholinguist) is the paper, "Some Psychological Studies of Grammar" *American Psychologist*, *XVII*, 1962, 748–762, by George A. Miller, who has contributed other important studies to the general field of psycholinguistics.

As for a selection from Chomsky's works, it was rather difficult to find a self-contained study of adequate length that concentrates on language acquisition. The only reading that meets those criteria is his article on "Language and the Mind" which we present here. We must, however, point out that it is a somewhat popularized article and does not fully demonstrate Chomsky's rigor and subtlety. We therefore recommend that the readers acquaint themselves with the above-mentioned works, and with the bibliographies therein. It is certainly essential for all students who are interested in independent research. Those who are unable to read much are urged to read at least the first chapter of *Aspects of the Theory of Syntax*. A. B. A.

LANGUAGE AND THE MIND

How does the mind work? To answer this question we must look at some of the work performed by the mind. One of its main functions is the acquisition of knowledge. The

two major factors in acquisition of knowledge, perception and learning, have been the subject of study and speculation for centuries. It would not, I think, be misleading to characterize the major positions that have developed as outgrowths of classical rationalism and empiricism. The rationalist theories are marked by the importance they assign to *intrinsic* structures in mental operations—to central processes and organizing principles in perception, and to innate ideas and principles in learning. The empiricist approach, in contrast, has stressed the role of experience and control by environmental factors.

The classical empiricist view is that sensory images are transmitted to the brain as impressions, They remain as ideas that will be associated in various ways, depending on the fortuitous character of experience. In this view a language is merely a collection of words, phrases, and sentences, a habit system, acquired accidentally and extrinsically. In the formulation of Williard Quine, knowledge of a language (and, in fact, knowledge in general) can be represented as "a fabric of sentences variously associated to one another and to nonverbal stimuli by the mechanism of conditioned response." Acquisition of knowledge is only a matter of the gradual construction of this fabric. When sensory experience is interpreted, the already established network may be activated in some fashion. In its essentials, this view has been predominant in modern behavioral science, and it has been accepted with little question by many philosophers as well.

The classical rationalist view is quite different. In this view the mind contains a system of "common notions" that enable it to interpret the scattered and incoherent data of sense in terms of objects and their relations, cause and effect, whole and part, symmetry, gestalt properties, functions, and so on. Sensation, providing only fleeting and meaningless images, is degenerate and particular. Knowledge, much of it beyond immediate awareness, is rich in structure, involves universals, and is highly organized. The innate general principles that underlie and organize this knowledge, according to Leibniz, "enter into our thoughts, of which they form the soul and the connection . . . although we do not at all think of them."

This "active" rationalist view of the acquisition of knowledge persisted through the romantic period in its essentials. With respect to language, it achieves its most illuminating expression in the profound investigations of Wilhelm von Humboldt. His theory of speech perception supposes a generative system of rules that underlies speech production as well as its interpretation. The system is generative in that it makes infinite use of finite means. He regards a language as a structure of forms and concepts based on a system of rules that determine their interrelations, arrangement, and organization. But these finite materials can be combined to make a never-ending product.

In the rationalist and romantic tradition of linguistic theory, the normal use of language is regarded as characteristically innovative. We construct sentences that are entirely new to us. There is no substantive notion of "analogy" or "generalization" that accounts for this creative aspect of language use. It is equally erroneous to describe language as a "habit structure" or as a network of associated responses. The innovative element in normal use of language quickly exceeds the bounds of such marginal principles as analogy or generalization (under any substantive interpretation of these notions). It is important to emphasize this fact because the insight has been lost under the impact of the behaviorist assumptions that have dominated speculation and research in the twentieth century.

In Humboldt's view, acquisition of language is largely a matter of maturation of an innate language capacity. The maturation is guided by internal factors, by an innate "form of language" that is sharpened, differentiated, and given its specific realization through experience. Language is thus a kind of latent structure in the human mind, developed and fixed by exposure to specific linguistic experience. Humboldt believes that all languages will be found to be very similar in their grammatical form, similar not on the surface but in their deeper inner structures. The innate organizing principles severely limit the class of possible languages, and these principles determine the properties of the language that is learned in the normal way.

The active and passive views of perception and learning have elaborated with varying degrees of clarity since the seventeenth century. These views can be confronted with empirical evidence in a variety of ways. Some recent work in psychology and neurophysiology is highly suggestive in this regard. There is evidence for the existence of central processes in perception, specifically for control over the functioning of sensory neurons by the brain-stem reticular system. Behavioral counterparts of this central control have been under investigation for several years. Furthermore, there is evidence for innate organization of the perceptual system of a highly specific sort at every level of biological organization. Studies of the visual system of the frog, the discovery of specialized cells responding to angle and motion in the lower cortical centers of cats and rabbits, and the somewhat comparable investigations of the auditory system of frogs—all are relevant to the classical questions of intrinsic structure mentioned earlier. These studies suggest that there are highly organized, innately determined perceptual systems that are adapted closely to the animal's "life space" and that provide the basis for what we might call "acquisition of knowledge." Also relevant are certain behavioral studies of human infants, for example those showing the preference for faces over other complex stimuli.

These and other studies make it reasonable to inquire into the possibility that complex intellectual structures are determined narrowly by innate mental organization. What is perceived may be determined by mental processes of considerable depth. As far as language learning is concerned, it seems to me that a rather convincing argument can be made for the view that certain principles intrinsic to the mind provide invariant structures that are a precondition for linguistic experience. In the course of this article I would like to sketch some of the ways such conclusions might be clarified and firmly established.

There are several ways linguistic evidence can be used to reveal properties of human perception and learning. In this section we consider one research strategy that might take us nearer to this goal.

Let us say that in interpreting a certain physical stimulus a person constructs a "percept." This percept represents some of his conclusions (in general, unconscious) about the stimulus. To the extent that we can characterize such percepts, we can go on to investigate the mechanisms that relate stimulus and percept. Imagine a model of perception that takes stimuli as inputs and arrives at percepts as "outputs." The model might contain a system of beliefs, strategies for interpreting stimuli, and other factors, such as

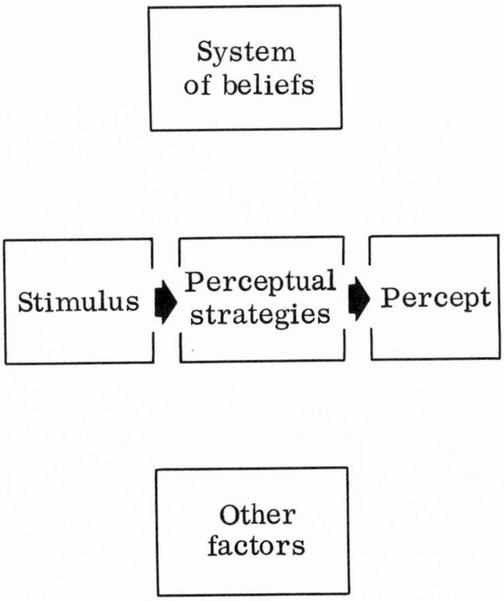

FIGURE 1. Each physical stimulus, after interpretation by the mental processes, will result in a percept.

the organization of memory. We would then have a perceptual model that might be represented graphically, as in Figure 1.

Consider next the system of beliefs that is a component of the perceptual model. How was this acquired? To study this problem, we must investigate a second model, which takes certain data as input and gives as "output" (again, internally represented) the system of beliefs operating in the perceptual model. This second model, a model of learning, would have its own intrinsic structure, as did the first. This structure might consist of conditions on the nature of the system of beliefs that can be acquired, of innate inductive strategies, and again, of other factors such as the organization of memory (see Figure 2).

Under further conditions, which are interesting but not relevant here, we can take these perceptual and learning models as theories of the acquisition of knowledge, rather than of belief. How then would the models apply to language? The input stimulus to the perceptual model is a speech signal, and the percept is a representation of the utterance that the hearer takes the signal to be and of the interpretation he assigns to it.

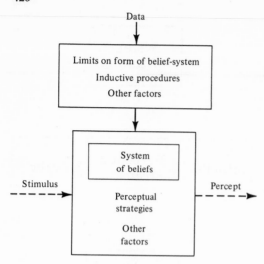

Data

Limits on form of belief-system

Inductive procedures

Other factors

System
of beliefs

Stimulus   Percept

Perceptual
strategies

Other
factors

FIGURE 2.   One's system of beliefs, a part of the perception model, is acquired from data as shown above.

We can think of the percept as the structural description of a linguistic expression which contains certain phonetic, semantic, and syntactic information. Most interesting is the syntactic information, which best can be discussed by examining a few typical cases.

The following three sentences seem to be the same syntactic structure.

(1)   I told John to leave
(2)   I expected John to leave
(3)   I persuaded John to leave

Each contains the subject *I*, and the predicate of each consists of a verb (*told, expected, persuaded*), a noun phrase (*John*), and an embedded predicate phrase (*to leave*). This similarity is only superficial, however—a similarity in what we may call the "surface structure" of these sentences, which differ in important ways when we consider them with somewhat greater care.

The differences can be seen when the sentences are paraphrased or subjected to certain grammatical operations, such as the conversion from active to passive forms. For example, in normal conversation the sentence "I told John to leave" can be roughly paraphrased as:

(1a)   What I told John was to leave

But the other two sentences cannot be paraphrased as:

(2a)   *What I expected John was to leave
(3a)   *What I persuaded John was to leave

Sentence (2) can be paraphrased as:

(2b)   It was expected by me that John would leave

But the other two sentences cannot undergo a corresponding formal operation, yielding:

(1b)   *It was told by me that John would leave

or

(3b)   *It was persuaded by me that John would leave

Sentences (2) and (3) differ more subtly. In (3) *John* is the direct object of *persuade*, but in (2) *John* is not the direct object of *expect*. We can show this by using these verbs in slightly more complex sentences:

(4)   I expected the doctor to examine John
(5)   I persuaded the doctor to examine John

If we replace the embedded proposition *the doctor to examine John* with its passive form *John to be examined by the doctor*, the change to the passive does not, in itself, change the meaning. We can accept as paraphrases "I expected the doctor to examine John" and

(4a)   I expected John to be examined by the doctor

But we cannot accept as paraphrases "I persuaded the doctor to examine John" and

(5a)   I persuaded John to be examined by the doctor

The parts of these sentences differ in their grammatical functions. In "I persuaded John to leave" *John* is both the object of *persuade* and the subject of *leave*. These facts must be represented in the percept since they are known, intuitively, to the hearer of the speech signal. No special training or instruction is necessary to enable the native speaker to understand these examples, to know which are "wrong" and which "right," although they may all be quite new to him. They are interpreted by the native speaker instantaneously and uniformly, in accordance with structural principles that are known tacitly, intuitively, and unconsciously.

These examples illustrate two significant points. First, the surface structure of a sentence, its organization into various phrases, may not reveal or immediately reflect its deep syntactic structure. The deep structure is not represented directly in the form of the speech signal; it is abstract. Second, the rules that determine deep and surface structure and their interrelation in particular cases must themselves be highly abstract. They are surely remote from consciousness, and in all likelihood they cannot be brought to consciousness.

A study of such examples, examples characteristic of all human languages that have been carefully studied, constitutes the first stage of the linguistic investigation outlined above, namely the study of the percept. The percept contains phonetic and semantic information related through the medium of syntactic structure. There are two aspects to this syntactic structure. It consists of a surface directly related to the phonetic form, and a deep structure that underlies the semantic interpretation. The deep structure is represented in the mind and rarely is indicated directly in the physical signal.

A language, then, involves a set of semantic-phonetic percepts, of sound-meaning correlations, the correlations being determined by the kind of intervening syntactic structure just illustrated. The English language correlates sound and meaning in one way, Japanese in another, and so on. But the general properties of percepts, their forms and mechanisms, are remarkably similar for all languages that have been carefully studied.

Returning to our models of perception and learning, we can now take up the problem of formulating the system of beliefs that is a central component in perceptual processes. In the case of language, the "system of beliefs" would now be called the "generative grammar," the system of rules that specifies the sound-meaning correlation and generates the class of structural descriptions (percepts) that constitute the language in question. The generative grammar, then, represents the speaker-hearer's knowledge of his language. We can use the term *grammar of a language* ambiguously, as referring not only to the speaker's internalized, subconscious knowledge but to the professional linguist's representation of this internalized and intuitive system of rules as well.

How is this generative grammar acquired? Or, using our learning model, what is the internal structure of the device that could develop a generative grammar?

We can think of every normal human's internalized grammar as, in effect, a theory of his language. This theory provides a sound-meaning correlation for an infinite number of sentences. It provides an infinite set of structural descriptions; each contains a surface structure that determines phonetic form and a deep structure that determines semantic content.

In formal terms, then, we can describe the child's acquisition of language as a kind of theory construction. The child discovers the theory of his language with only small amounts of data from that language. Not only does his "theory of the language" have an enormous predictive scope, but it also enables the child to reject a great deal of the very data on which the theory has been constructed. Normal speech consists, in large part, of fragments, false starts, blends, and other distortions of the underlying idealized forms. Nevertheless, as is evident from a study of the mature use of language, what the child learns is the underlying ideal theory. This is a remarkable fact. We must also bear in mind that the child constructs this ideal theory without explicit instruction, that he acquires this knowledge at a time when he is not capable of complex intellectual achievements in many other domains, and that this achievement is relatively independent of intelligence or the particular course of experience. These are facts that a theory of learning must face.

A scientist who approaches phenomena of this sort without prejudice or dogma would conclude that the acquired knowledge must be determined in a rather specific way by intrinsic properties of mental organization. He would then set himself the task of discovering the innate ideas and principles that make such acquisition of knowledge possible.

It is unimaginable that a highly specific, abstract, and tightly organized language comes by accident into the mind of every four-year-old child. If there were not an innate restriction on the form of grammar, then the child could employ innumerable theories to account for his linguistic experience, and no one system, or even small class of systems, would be found exclusively acceptable or even preferable. The child could not possibly acquire knowledge of a language. This restriction on the form of grammar is a precondition for linguistic experience, and it is surely the critical factor in determining the course and result of language learning. The child cannot know at birth which language he is going to learn. But he must "know" that its grammar must be of a predetermined form that excludes many imaginable languages.

The child's task is to select the appropriate hypothesis from this restricted class. Having selected it, he can confirm his choice with the evidence further available to him. But neither the evidence nor any process of induction (in any well-defined sense) could in themselves have led to this choice. Once the hypothesis is sufficiently well confirmed, the child knows the language defined by this hypothesis; consequently, his knowledge extends vastly beyond his linguistic experience, and he can reject much of this experience as imperfect, as resulting from the interaction of many factors, only one of which is the ideal grammar that determines a sound-meaning connection for an infinite class of linguistic expressions. Along such lines as these one might outline a theory to explain the acquisition of language.

As has been pointed out, both the form and meaning of a sentence are determined by syntactic structures that are not represented directly in the signal and that are related to the signal only at a distance, through a long sequence of interpretive rules. This property

of abstractness in grammatical structure is of primary importance, and it is on this property that our inferences about mental processes are based. Let us examine this abstractness a little more closely.

Not many years ago, the process of sentence interpretation might have been described approximately along the following lines. A speech signal is received and segmented into successive units (overlapping at the borders). These units are analyzed in terms of their invariant phonetic properties and assigned to "phonemes." The sequence of phonemes, so constructed, is then segmented into minimal grammatically functioning units (morphemes and words). These are again categorized. Successive operations of segmentation and classification will lead to what I have called "surface structure"—an analysis of a sentence into phrases, which can be represented as a proper bracketing of the sentence, with the bracketed units assigned to various categories, as in Figure 3. Each segment—phonetic, syntactic or semantic—would be identified in terms of certain invariant properties. This would be an exhaustive analysis of the structure of the sentence.

With such a conception of language structure, it made good sense to look forward hopefully to certain engineering applications of linguistics—for example, to voice-operated typewriters capable of segmenting an expression into its successive phonetic units and identifying these, so that speech could be converted to some form of phonetic writing in a mechanical way; to mechanical analysis of sentence structure by fairly straightforward

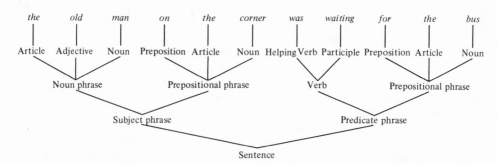

FIGURE 3.   A type of sentence analysis now abandoned as inadequate at every level is this labeled bracketing which analyzes the sentence by successive division into larger units with each unit assigned to its own category.

and well-understood computational techniques; and perhaps even beyond to such projects as machine translation. But these hopes have by now been largely abandoned with the realization that this conception of grammatical structure is inadequate at every level, semantic, phonetic, and syntactic. Most important, at the level of syntactic organization, the surface structure indicates semantically significant relations only in extremely simple cases. In general, the deeper aspects of syntactic organization are representable by labeled bracketing, but of a very different sort from that seen in surface structure.

There is evidence of various sorts, both from phonetics and from experimental psychology, that labeled bracketing is an adequate representation of surface structure. It would go beyond the bounds of this paper to survey the phonetic evidence. A good deal of it is presented in a forthcoming book, *Sound Pattern of English*, by myself and Morris Halle. Similarly, very interesting experimental work by Jerry Fodor and his colleagues, based on earlier observations by D. E. Broadbent and Peter Ladefoged, has shown that the disruption of a speech signal (for example, by a superimposed click) tends to be perceived at the boundaries of phrases rather than at the point where the disruption actually occurred, and that in many cases the bracketing of surface structure can be read directly from the data on perceptual displacement. I think the evidence is rather good that labeled bracketing serves to represent the surface structure that is related to the perceived form of physical signals.

Deep structures are related to surface structures by a sequence of certain formal operations, operations now generally called "grammatical transformations." At the levels of sound, meaning, and syntax, the significant structural features of sentences are highly abstract. For this reason they cannot be recovered by elementary data-processing techniques. This fact lies behind the search for central processes in speech perception and the search for intrinsic, innate structure as the basis for language learning.

How can we represent deep structure? To answer this question we must consider the grammatical transformations that link surface structure to the underlying deep structure that is not always apparent.

Consider, for example, the operations of passivization and interrogation. In the sentences (1) John was examined by the doctor, and (2) did the doctor examine John, both have a deep structure similar to paraphrase of Sentence 1, (3) the doctor examined John. The same network of grammatical relations determines the semantic interpretation in each case. Thus two of the grammatical transformations of English must be the operations of passivization and interrogation that form such surface structures as Sentences (1) and (2) from a deeper structure which in its essentials also underlies Sentence (3). Since the transformations ultimately produce surface structures, they must produce labeled bracketings (see Figure 3). But notice that these operations can apply in sequence: we can form the passive question "was John examined by the doctor" by passivization followed by interrogation. Since the result of passivization is a labeled bracketing, it follows that the interrogative transformation operates on a labeled bracketing and forms a new labeled bracketing. Thus a transformation such as interrogation maps a labeled bracketing into a labeled bracketing.

By similar argument, we can show that all grammatical transformations are structure-dependent mappings of this sort and that the deep structures which underlie all sentences must themselves be labeled bracketings. Of course, the labeled bracketing that constitutes deep structure will in general be quite different from that representing the surface structure of a sentence. Our argument is somewhat oversimplified, but it is roughly correct. When made precise and fully accurate it strongly supports the view that deep structures, like surface structures, are formally to be taken as labeled bracketings, and that grammatical transformations are mappings of such structures onto other similar structures.

Recent studies have sought to explore the ways in which grammatical structure of the sort just described enters into mental operations. Much of this work has been based on a proposal formulated by George Miller as a first approximation, namely, that the amount of memory used to store a sentence should reflect the number of transformations used in deriving it. For example, H. B. Savin and E. Perchonock investigated this assumption in the following way: they presented to subjects a sentence followed by a sequence of unrelated words. They then determined the number of these unrelated words recalled when the subject attempted to repeat the sentence and the sequence of words. The more words recalled, the less memory used to store the sentence. The fewer words recalled, the more memory used to store the sentence. The results showed a remarkable correlation of amount of memory and number of transformations in certain simple cases. In fact, in their experimental material, shorter sentences with more transformations took up more "space in memory" than longer sentences that involved fewer transformations.

Savin has extended this work and has shown that the effects of deep structure and surface structure can be differentiated by a similar technique. He considered paired sentences with approximately the same deep structure but with one of the pair being more complex in surface structure. He showed that, under the experimental conditions just described, the paired sentences were indistinguishable. But if the sequence of unrelated words precedes, rather than follows, the sentence being tested, then the more complex (in surface structure) of the pair is more difficult to repeat correctly than the simpler member. Savin's very plausible inference is that sentences are coded in memory in terms of deep structure. When the unrelated words precede the test sentence, these words use up a certain amount of short-term memory, and the sentence that is more complex in surface structure cannot be analyzed with the amount of memory remaining. But if the test sentence precedes the unrelated words, it is, once understood, stored in terms of deep structure, which is about the same in both cases. Therefore the same amount of memory remains, in the paired cases, for recall of the following words. This is a beautiful example of the way creative experimental studies can interweave with theoretical work in the study of language and of mental processes.

In speaking of mental processes we have returned to our original problem. We can now see why it is reasonable to maintain that the linguistic evidence supports an "active" theory of acquisition of knowledge. The study of sentences and of speech perception, it seems to me, leads to a perceptual theory of a classical rationalist sort. Representative of this school, among others, were the seventeenth-century Cambridge Platonists, who developed the idea that our perception is guided by notions that originate from the mind and that provide the framework for the interpretation of sensory stimuli. It is not sufficient to suggest that this framework is a store of "neural models" or "schemata" which are in some manner applied to perception (as is postulated in some current theories of perception). We must go well beyond this assumption and return to the view of Wilhelm von Humboldt, who attributed to the mind a system of rules that generates such models and schemata under the stimulation of the senses. The system of rules itself determines the content of the percept that is formed.

We can offer more than this vague and metaphoric account. A generative grammar and an associated theory of speech perception provide a concrete example of the rules that operate and of the mental objects that they construct and manipulate. Physiology cannot yet explain the physical mechanisms that affect these abstract functions. But neither physiology nor psychology provides evidence that calls this account into question or that suggests an alternative. As mentioned earlier, the most exciting current work in the physiology of perception shows that even the peripheral systems analyze stimuli into the complex properties of objects, and that central processes may significantly affect the information transmitted by the receptor organs.

The study of language, it seems to me, offers strong empirical evidence that empiricist theories of learning are quite inadequate. Serious efforts have been made in recent years to develop principles of induction, generalization, and data analysis that would account for knowledge of a language. These efforts have been a total failure. The methods and principles fail not for any superficial reason such as lack of time or data. They fail because they are intrinsically incapable of giving rise to the system of rules that underlies the normal use of language. What evidence is now available supports the view that all human languages share deep-seated properties of organization and structure. These properties—these linguistic universals—can be plausibly assumed to be an innate mental endowment rather than the result of learning. If this is true, then the study of language sheds light on certain long-standing issues in the theory of knowledge. Once again I see little reason to doubt that what is true of language is true of other forms of human knowledge as well.

There is one further question that might be raised at this point. How does the human mind come to have the innate properties that underlie acquisition of knowledge? Here linguistic evidence obviously provides no information at all. The process by which the human mind has achieved its present state of complexity and its particular form of innate organization are a complete mystery, as much of a mystery as the analogous questions that can be asked about the processes leading to the physical and mental organization of any other complex organism. It is perfectly safe to attribute this to evolution, so long as we bear in mind that there is no substance to this assertion—it amounts to nothing more than the belief that there is surely some naturalistic explanation for these phenomena.

There are, however, important aspects of the problem of language and mind that can be studied sensibly within the limitations of present understanding and technique. I think that, for the moment, the most productive investigations are those dealing with the nature of particular grammars and with the universal conditions met by all human languages. I have tried to suggest how one can move, in successive steps of increasing abstractness, from the study of percepts to the study of grammar and perceptual mechanisms, and from the study of grammar to the study of universal grammar and the mechanisms of learning.

In this area of convergence of linguistics, psychology, and philosophy, we can look forward to much exciting work in coming years.

AARON BAR-ADON〰〰〰〰〰〰〰〰〰〰

60

The author (see Introduction to Chapter 48) discusses syntactic structure and word order in the first phase of the development of syntax in young children. Theories about innate ideas, linguistic competence, and some universals in language acquisition are studied, and findings in several languages are compared, while the focus is on the primary syntactic structures in Hebrew child language.

Initially, the child develops a simple grammatical system whose overt manifestation is the so-called telegraphic speech (close to "speaking" base structures?), with a few grammatical categories, simple hierarchical rules, etc.

The early syntactic structures of children seem to be universally close to each other (like the base structures); hence, a basic initial division of Sentence into Implicator and Explicator is proposed. Evidently, child language should not be studied merely as a reduction of adult language, but rather as an illustration of the child's developing linguistic theory.

The author also examines the holophrastic stage and attempts to explain how the environment understands the child's "imperfect" sentences, in conjunction with discussing Noam Chomsky's idea of degrees of grammaticalness.

A. B. A.

PRIMARY SYNTACTIC STRUCTURES IN HEBREW CHILD LANGUAGE

0. This paper is a preliminary discussion of word order and syntactic structure in the first phase of the development of syntax in the language of children, focusing on Hebrew-speaking children in Israel.[1] This phase begins with the child's first use of syntactic combinations and usually continues through most of the ensuing year. Students of child language, from both the linguistic and psychological points of view, have lately devoted special attention to the initial stages of language acquisition. [In the following pages we will try to bring to bear some of the Hebrew findings.]

1.11. We are interested in the entire process of language acquisition by the child. Actually, we are interested in more than describing the linguistic *performance* of the child, i.e., his concrete utterances, we are interested in what is behind this external manifestation. We are interested in the linguistic *competence* the child acquires while he is evolving a grammatical theory.

The study of the difference between performance and competence in child language is not a simple matter, since it is hardly possible to ask the little child questions pertaining to grammaticality, or to acceptability of an utterance. It is also difficult to discover, through other acceptable experiments such as analysis of imitation and comprehension of adult sentences, the linguistic *intuition* of the young child. Some more intricate psycholinguistic methods of experimentation are,

however, being considered now. As we shall see later, children themselves often provide various clues for detecting their inner syntactic structures. (See 8.51.)

1.12. As soon as the child produces his first utterances, with syntactic combinations of two or more morphemes, or words (for convenience sake we will use the term "word"), rather than the strict "single-word" utterances, we may start a syntactic analysis and an attempt to study his internalized grammatical system. Theoretically, we may start it with the strictly single-word-utterance stage, assuming that this is the "sentential" structure according to the child's concept at that stage (one can even discern various functions within the single-word sentence), but this is obviously more speculative, and we will return to this problem later.

1.21. Meaningful speech starts around the age of one year. Some children may start somewhat earlier, others may do so several months later, while still others may begin appreciably later, for a variety of reasons. It is interesting that some of the latter may start right away with more advanced sentence structures, having used this latent period to better internalize the system, to better refine the theory, the [abstract] concepts and rules of sentence. Indeed, some of these children, during the longer pre-sentence or pre-combinatory period, do mature mentally a little more, and thus may be able to handle more abstract concepts, recognize more complex constructions (essentially a matter of abstraction), and therefore may also be able to produce, from the inception of their speech production, longer and more complex sentences. Naturally, such a longer incubation period of language in highly intelligent children deserves special study.

A preliminary abstract of this paper was presented in Hebrew at the Fourth World Congress of Jewish Studies, at the Hebrew University, Jerusalem, 1965. Cf. proceedings in *PAPERS: Fourth World Congress of Jewish Studies*, Vol. II, 1968, 123–128.

*I wish to thank The University of Texas' U.R.I. and the American Council of Learned Societies for making it possible for me to carry out this research.

[1] On the revival of Hebrew and its emergence as a modern living language around the turn of the century, and the role of the Israeli children in the processes of its nativization, see Aaron Bar-Adon (1959), (1965), and (forthcoming).

1.22. At any rate, two to three years from that turning point in speech development, whenever it takes place in the individual cases, most children will have mastered the basic structures of the language of their surroundings (home, speech community) both passively and actively. And by the age of six, when they are ready to enter the first grade, practically all normal children are already familiar also with the main transformations of their native language, although some of them may still have difficulties, especially with the negative, the passive, and of course with complex embeddings. Most of the latter may be connected with mental or intellectual maturation, rather than pure grammatical ability, even if it is innate.

1.23. It is, indeed, remarkable how fast and how independently[2] the little child manages to perform this enormous mental task of language acquisition, even before he is capable of carrying out other complex mental or intellectual tasks. In a way, it does not seem to depend on intelligence solely, since unintelligent children and even children with various retardations also manage to acquire language, although it is limited to a certain degree.[3] Evidently, the child should be credited with a capacity for analysis and internalization, since he obviously does not learn by rote and merely duplicate the sentences he has heard, but rather he seems to be

extracting the rules of the language he is exposed to and creating for himself a set of rules, a grammatical system, as it is apparent from his speech. One might conceive of this system as a theory that the child makes up about the internal system possessed by the speakers around him. This competence is not limited to the actual corpus of sentences that he possesses or has been exposed to, but it goes beyond it, enabling him to recognize, comprehend, and adequately produce himself an infinite set of completely new sentences. Moreover, he also learns to recognize, sift,[4] and disregard poor examples of adult speech such as deviant, incomplete, and disorganized sentences. His theory is based on an "ideal grammar" that allows almost only well-formed sentences to be considered and generated.

1.24. The child in the process of language acquisition is often compared to the professional linguist who tries to discover the structure of a language and to describe it. But what the linguist does explicitly, in formal terms, the child does implicitly. Yet, as it has been pointed out, the child too must be working very systematically, even when unconsciously, in order to accomplish the enormous task of mastering such a complex system as that of a natural language, and within several years only.

1.31. The question of whether language rules are acquired solely through experience on the basis of induction and association, as claimed by the empiricists and behaviorists, or whether the child is born endowed with innate ideas concerning language and language acquisition, as proposed by the rationalists —this question cannot, naturally, be treated in detail within this limited framework. It should be mentioned, however, that the question has lately attracted the attention of linguists, especially those of the generative-transformational school. It was introduced by Noam Chomsky and developed by other colleagues as well.

---

[2] It is true, even if one includes the first year of life and exposure to language, and allows for a greater part of the pre-school years, as claimed by some scholars, e.g., Colin Fraser, in his Discussion of D. McNeill's paper "The Creation of Language by Children," (in *Psycholinguistic Papers*, J. Lyons and R. J. Wales, eds., Edinburgh: Edinburgh University Press, 1966, 115 f.). Students of child language often emphasize the absence of explicit formal teaching of a first language or of instructing the child how to construct the grammar. Any help that a child receives from his adult environment is only of secondary relevance to his own independent process of language acquisition. On the other hand, the child seems to be endowed, as will be discussed later, with some innate capacity for language acquisition, coupled with an intuition about certain "linguistic universals" that provide him with what one might call an "image of human language," which in turn must be restricted to a rather limited set of options. Otherwise we might end up with a Babel of speech. It follows that the language model of the environment, e.g., that of his home, is crucial for the child in determining the structure of his particular target language. See also discussion on "The Role of Parental Speech in Language Acquisition" within David McNeill's comprehensive paper "Developmental Psycholinguistics," *The Genesis of Language*, eds. Frank Smith and G. H. Miller, (Cambridge, Mass: The M.I.T. Press, 1966), 65 f. See Lenneberg (1964), (1966), (1967).

[3] See Lenneberg (1967), pp. 304–326.

[4] I like the term "sifting" introduced by Edward S. and Ursula B. Klima in their paper "Syntactic Regularities in the Speech of Children" in *Psycholinguistic Papers*, (see f.n. 2), p. 183 f. A revised version appears in our *Child Language: A Book of Readings*.

I will only mention at this point that soon after this agelong controversy had been reopened by Chomsky within linguistic circles, Jerrold Katz devoted a special study to it, *Innate Ideas* (which appeared first in mimeographed form in 1965),[5] in which he presented interesting arguments, based partly on Chomsky's views on this problem,[6] and in line with classical rationalistic conceptions.

1.32. It seems to me that the more one deals with the study of the earlier stages of child language, the more he is inclined to accept a view that the child is indeed endowed with some built-in or innate capacity for perceiving and acquiring knowledge in an organized way—for abstraction, for learning a system for internalizing a theory of rules and generalizations. And in the particular case of language this applies to the capacity to form concepts about utterances and sentences, and to perceive the relation between sound and meaning (the phonetic-semantic correlation, which may be of a more universal nature) and its association with a particular syntactic system. Once mastered, these concepts will serve him henceforth also for recognizing, predicting, and generating constructions beyond the concrete model or the actual experience he has had. An almost

inescapable conclusion is that the notion of innate ideas about language in general (without predisposition to any particular one) implies the existence of some language universals or linguistic universals.

1.33. The study of linguistic universals, i.e., the essential properties of natural language,[7] has lately attracted many a linguist, but nothing is conclusive at present. Yet, it seems quite reasonable to assume that some basic universals of language (whatever they are) will be inherently associated with an innate ideas endowment. Thus, equipped with a general capacity for acquiring knowledge of various kinds including the learning of a linguistic system in the abstract, and with certain tools such as universal guidelines and restrictions on the nature of grammar, the child is capable of constructing a theory, indeed an "ideal" theory (one which disregards deviant examples) of the underlying rules of the particular language that he will happen to be exposed to at this early stage. In other words, the child comes equipped with the basic tools for fast acquisition of a language, any language, without a preconceived preference about what will become his native language. The selection of a language will be determined when he falls into the particular home and environment that he happens to be born into.

1.34. It is an established fact, and I have had the opportunity myself to observe several cases of it, that children from one speech community and language family who are raised from infancy by foster parents from a different speech community and language family, acquire the language of their new parents and environment without any outlandish residue whatsoever.

1.35. I am therefore willing to accept in broad lines a theory such as the one presented by Chomsky and Katz (and followed by scholars like David McNeill and others) about a continuous three-stage process of

---

[5] It was later incorporated in his book *The Philosophy of Language*, N. Y., Harper & Row (1966). See especially pp. 240–283, and note the cross references. Cf. Lenneberg (1964); (1967) 220–23, 393–94.

[6] Especially in his book *Aspects of the Theory of Syntax* (Cambridge, Mass: The M.I.T. Press, 1965). See particularly the first chapter. See also his formal comments on a paper by Wick Miller and Susan Ervin [-Tripp] in a conference on "Language Acquisition," in which he also introduced the distinction between "competence" and "performance," in Ursula Bellugi and Roger Brown (eds.), *The Acquisition of Language*. Monographs of The Society for Research in Child Development, Serial No. 92, 1964, Vol. XXIX, No. 1, pp. 35–39. Further material by Chomsky may be found in his subsequent works, e.g., *Cartesian Linguistics*, New York, Harper and Row (1966), esp. pp. 59–73; "The Formal Nature of Language" which is an Appendix in Lenneberg's *Biological Foundations of Language* (1967); in *Language and Mind*, New York, Harcourt, Brace & World, Inc. (1968) (VII + 88 pp.); and in "Language and the Mind," in *Psychology Today* of February 1968, pp. 48–51, 66–68. Also in N. Chomsky and M. Halle *The Sound Pattern of English*, New York, Harper & Row, 1968. Cf. also J. J. Katz, op. cit., pp. 275–76.

[7] Cf. Chomsky and Halle (1968), p. 4. Re theory: cf. J. Bar-Hillel, Review of P. Garvin, in *Foundations of Language* III (1967), 420 f.

hypothesis construction, verification, and evaluation,[8] or a process of implicit theory construction. The child hears sentences of a certain language. Equipped with an abstraction capacity, necessary for acquiring complex knowledge, he formulates for himself hypotheses about the rules of that language and makes predictions about subsequent sentences involving other experiences with the use of the language. He checks and examines his predictions, eliminates the wrong hypotheses and evaluates the others, the correct ones, by means of a simplicity principle. And so on.

1.36. Presumably, these manipulations are carried out unconsciously, as is the general learning process. Yet, one might bring evidence for certain conscious activity as well, for instance the child's common rhetorical questions, where the child poses a question and then answering himself (see examples (17)–(19) below), or in presleep soliloquies, such as those studied by Ruth Weir. It is quite possible that in such cases, the child plays not only with contents and semantics, but with grammatical structure as well: he may be testing hypotheses in a more or less organized, conscious way. Moreover, it is also possible that when the child asks his environment questions about the obvious, he is testing at the same time hypotheses through those invited reactions of the mature speakers.[9] In other words, he initiates questions whose answers will furnish him with clues for his hypotheses. It sounds somewhat tricky, but there is no doubt that quite a bit of ingenuity is demonstrated by children in the process of language acquisition. The

process goes on until the child matures linguistically.[10]

This theory will also explain the presence, or coexistence, of forms that sound irregular, even in terms of the child's own grammar, in the various stages of his linguistic development. But this is all in broad lines. Naturally, things are not so simple in their details. At any rate, our Hebrew evidence taken from small children who started producing syntactic constructions very early,[11] at about one year of age, seems to be providing support to this approach.

1.4. After a period, which usually lasts several months, of one-word utterances (basically referential?), the child switches to producing short sentences, which seem to be mostly two-word sentences, but not necessarily always so. Obviously, there is no rule that the child should start with one-word utterances, then switch first to two-word sentences, then gradually to three-word sentences, then four, etc., as some people may be inclined to believe. It is not uncommon for a child to come up with three-or-more-word sentences from the very beginning.[12] Yet it seems to be true that most of the sentences produced by children at that *initial* combinatory ("syntactic") stage are two-word sentences, although three-word sentences are quite common, too, and that the average length of sentences grows with the age, experience, and mental maturation of the child.[13]

2.1. We have tried to present briefly some new approaches to the study of child language. Now, let us encounter some concrete instances.

---

[8] Cf. Chomsky's "A Review of B. F. Skinner's *Verbal Behavior, Language*, 35 (1959), 42–44, 55–58, (Repr. in *Fodor & Katz*, eds.), *The Structure of Language: Readings in the Philosophy of Language*, Prentice-Hall, Inc., 1964. Cf. also, J. J. Katz, *Philosophy of Language*, p. 275.

[9] I might mention in this context that Roger Brown has noted (in a private communication) that, for instance, questions of the type *Where NP*? are "usually rhetorical as object named will be present but other person is to point at it." The same applies to questions like *What that*?, which are "part of a basic set of referential operations," rather than real *wh* questions as they are for the adults.

[10] It is worthwhile emphasizing that the child reaches linguistic maturity before maturing in most other areas!

[11] It is my impression that the younger the children are, the more illuminating their evidence is.

[12] Professor Noam Chomsky of M.I.T. has told me that his daughter, Avi, has uttered, around the age of 18 months, and within the "two-word-stage" the following seven-word sentence: *Avi see man going bye-bye in car*, i.e., "Avi sees a man going bye-bye in a car." Some children skip the one-word stage after having only babbled!

[13] Psychologists tend to consider the mean sentence-length an "index" for the rate of the child's mental development and maturation.

For example, the majority of the first Hebrew sentences of the children that I studied through follow-ups (especially the two children whom we will call here Gil and Gila) were indeed two-word sentences,[14] while fewer sentences at that initial stage, but certainly not a small minority, were longer.[15] Gila, who started with syntactic combinations just before the end of her first year, provided the following examples:

Words with stress on the ultimate syllable are not marked for stress. Only the penultimate stress is indicated by ´.

(1)	*ába ba*	"Daddy come (came)."
(2)	*ba ába*	"Came (come) Daddy."
(3)	*ze*[16] *búba*	"This[16] [is a] doll."
(4)	*ze búba íza*[16]	"This [is] Dolly Iza (Aliza)."
(5)	*ma ze?*[17]	"What [is] this?"
(6)	*ába, bo*[18]	"Daddy, come!"
(7)	*bo, ába*	"Come, Daddy!"
(8)	*dóda, bo*[18]	"Aunty, come!"
(9)	*bo*[18]*, dóda*	"Come, Aunty!"
(10)	*dóda, bóyi*	"Aunty, come!"
(11)	*ába, akum*[19]	"Daddy, get up!"
(12)	*búba, kuki*[20]	"Dolly, [sing] kuki!"
(13)	*búba kan*[21]	"Dolly here."
(14)	*ába to[v]*	"Daddy good."

(15)	*búba tova*[22]	"Dolly good." (f.s.)
(16)	*kóva búba*[23]	"Hat dolly."

2.22. And with rhetorical questions and answers:

(17)	*mi kóki?*[17]*—ine kóki*	"Who [is] Kóki?— here's Kóki."
(18)	*éyfo ába?—ába po*[22]	"Where [is] Daddy? —Daddy is here."
(19)	*bi ba?*[23]*—ába ba. Ken, ába ba*	"Who came? Daddy came." "Yes, Daddy came."

2.23. However, already in the first two months of that stage we have also recorded utterances like:

(20)	*ze búba íza*[16]	"This [is] Dolly Iza (Aliza)."
(21)	*ine búba íza*	"Here [is] (behold) Dolly Iza."
(22)	*mi ze ba?*	"Who [is] this (that) came?"
(23)	*besa adáyim*[24]	"Egg [is in] hands."
(24)	*ába, bo lali*[25]	"Daddy, come to me!"

---

[14] In some of the following two-word sentences, one of the elements is a vocative or address (e.g., *aba, ...!* or *..., aba!*), but the other element is asually an imperative. One may say that, in addition to the VP, and NP, the pronoun-subject *you*, is included.

[15] To be sure, we are using here only a small sampling, not the entire corpus of either child. We have a *very* detailed record of their speech development from their first word until the age of six (extending over thousands of pages each).

[16] In standard Hebrew *zot buba aliza* "This (fem.) Dolly Aliza." She also uses the masculine demonstrative *ze* at this stage instead of the feminine *zot*. See Sentences (20), (43), and (44). If this is indeed an answer to a possible question like *ma ze?* "What [is] this?" as in Sentence (5), then *ze* is understandable here too.

[17] A brief discussion of the use of interrogatives in Hebrew child language follows in Section 2.3.

[18] She uses here the masculine form *bo* for the feminine form *bói*, but in (10) she already uses *bóyi*.

[19] Either for *ába, lakum* "Daddy, to get up!" or for *ába, takum* "Daddy get up!" (a common use of Fut. 2 m.s. for formal Imperative *kum*).

[20] Addressing her older sister, whom she called *búba* ("Dolly") and asking her to sing for her the song about the *kukiya* (cuckoo bird).

[21] Even at this stage she already knows the synonyms *po* and *kan* "here," e.g., *búba kan* "Dolly here," and *ába po* "Daddy here."

[22] It is interesting that she knew here to use the feminine form *tova* "good." (*tov* + fem ⇒ *tov* + *a* ⇒ *tova*) although in the previous sentence she failed to realize the final *v*. She has *gender* in her competence!

[23] This was said under the following circumstances: she pointed at the hat of an embroidered doll on her pillow and asked me *ma ze*? "What's this?" I said *ze kóva šel búba* "This [is] a hat of dolly," and she repeated *kóva búba* "hat dolly," This occurred at the end of her fourteenth month.

[23a] *bi ba?* for *mi ba* as in (17) and in (22) where we have a clear *mi* ("who"). She apparently started with *b* instead of *m* inder the impact of the following *ba*, since she does definitely have an *m* in her inventory at this stage; furthermore, the word *mi* ("who") appears by itself several times in its normal form even in our present sampling. See Section 2.3 regarding the general problem of the use of interrogatives in Hebrew child language.

[24] *besa adáyim* for *be(y)ca* (= [*beytsa*]) *bayadáyim* "An egg [is] in the hands." She said it when her father showed her an egg he was holding in his hand.

[25] *lali*, an interesting novel construction, which, like many other "deviate" forms, indicates that the child has indeed internalized the system, although her theory has led her this time to a "normalization" of a pattern that may not have been in use in the standard language. In this particular use of *lali* the following inductive process may have taken place. Having often heard forms like *lax* "to you" (fem. singular), *lánu* "to us," *laxem* "to you" (pl, masc.), *lahem* "to them" (masc.), she derived *lali* "to me," which is actually tautological, since *li* consists of the elements *l(ə)* "to" + *-i* "me." The fact is that she knows the conventional form *li* as well, and uses it in (25) and (34).

(25) *íma, sim li*[26]   "Mommy, put
                              (masc.!) for me."
(26) *búba íza kan*   "Dolly Iza (Aliza)
                              [is] here."
(27) *kóki, búba íza kan*   "Kóki, Dolly Iza
                              [is] here."
(28) *ine búba íza sam*[27] "Behold, Dolly Iza
                              [is] there."
(29) *búba, bói ada*[28]   "Dolly, come to girl."
(30) *bo e yeadim*[29]   "Come to children!"
(31) *ába, íma, bo búba*   "Daddy, Mommy,
     éza[30]   come to Dolly Eza
                             (= Iza, Aliza)!"
(32) *at ro'a agala?*   "Do you (f.s.) see
                             [a] wagon?"
(33) *at bagala?*[31]   "[Are] you in
                             wagon?"
(34) *uga atet li ába*[32]   "Cake to give to me
                             Daddy."

2.231. The circumstances of the last sentence were as follows: Her father said, *Carix latet lah uga*, "[It is] necessary to give (to) her cake," and she immediately re-

sponded, *uga atet li ába*, "Cake [to] give (to) me Daddy." *Atet* is obviously a reduced form of *latet*, i.e., without the element *lə/la*, "to." (Gila's brother, Gil, uses in example 64 what amounts to the bare Infinitive Construct). But her entire sentence is not a mere reduction of her father's sentence. Notice the following differences: she changes the word order of the corresponding phrase "[Someone] to give (to) her cake" ([S]-V-Indirect O-O) to "Cake [to] give (to) me Daddy" (O-V-Ind. O + S); to suit her "direct speech" she changed *lah* "to her" to *li* "to me," and finally added *ába* "Daddy" as Subject.

As for forms such as (*a*)*tet* (see examples 34 and 64), which look like Infinitives stripped of the prefix *lə/la*, "to" (often coinciding with the classical Infinitive Construct), they may serve as general verbals, before finer distinctions of tense and aspect, person, number and gender develop. Earlier studies of child language wondered about the starting point of the child's verbal system, mainly about whether it is the Imperative or the Infinitive. Our Hebrew findings show that it is mostly closer to the base of the Non-Past forms, the ones that are in widest use in the communication of the child with the environment.[32]

2.241. Each new combination or construction seems to have a day or period when they are especially dear and popular with the child, out of sheer liking, or just for the sake of "practice." The "day" of the phrase *bo* [*h*]*éna* "come here!" (technically masculine) arrived when Gila was in her fourteenth month, i.e., after a period of two months of producing syntactic combinations, and we recorded her following discourse (monologue):

(35) *ába, bo éna*[33]   "Daddy, come here!"
(36) *ába, bo éna*   "Daddy, come here!"

There is also a slight possibility of a merger of *elay* "unto me" with *li* "to me," i.e., *elay* + *li* → *lali*(?), but the preposition *el* "unto" has not yet appeared in this stage (see footnote 29).

[26] In standard Hebrew the corresponding forms wil be *íma sími li*, i.e., with the feminine form of the verb "put!" *sími* rather than the masculime *sim*. Gila does not yet consistently make the distinction between masculine and feminine forms and she makes quite a few mistakes. The masculine singular forms seem to prevail. This also applies to the plural, as in (31). Still, it is amazing how she manages to make the distinction in so many cases, inserting feminine forms in sentences (10), (15), (29), and others. The same applies to her brother Gil who knows how to make many distinctions, although he often fails to do so, but for him it is "ladies first." See footnote 35 and Section 2.41.

[27] She still realizes /š/ as [s]; she does not have yet the distinction [s]-[š] and pronounces *šam* as [sam].

[28] *buba, bói ada* as compared with standard *buba bói el* [*ha*]*yalda*, "Dolly, come to [the] Girl." As mentioned above, she calls her sister *búba* "Dolly" and by *yalda* [*ada*] "girl" she means herself. She calls her sister to come to her.

[29] *bo e yeadim* for standard *bo el* [*ha*]*yəladim* "come to [the] children." In *e* we do apparently have here a kernel of the preposition *el* "unto," but this seems to be an isolated instance at this stage.

[30] The standard form is *ába, íma bó*[*u*] [*el*] *búba*[*al*]-*iza*. She uses the verb *bo* in singular, rather than the plural *bóu*, omits the preposition *el* and contracts *aliza* to *iza/eza*.

[31] It is not clear whether *bagala* stands for the definite "in the wagon" *bə* + *ha* + *agala* ⇒ *b a agala* ⇒ *bagala* or for the indefinite *bəagala* "in a wagon."

[32] For details see Aaron Bar-Adon (1959), I, Section 0.62 and II, Section 5.02. Also footnote 40 below, and 9.222.

[33] See Ruth Weir's *Language in the Crib*, The Hague, Mouton & Co., 1962. Weir refers to such sequences, or discourse constructions, as "break downs" (vs. "build-ups" and "completions"). See her interesting analyses, p. 81 ff., and Roman Jakobson's foreword, "Antony's Contribution to Linguistic Theory," op. cit., pp. 18–20. Note that utterances (35)–(38) are alike in mature speech.

(37) *bo éna*   "Come here!"
(38) *éna*   "Here."
(39) *bá'i*[34]   "Come!"

From the discourse it seems obvious that she knows how to separate *bo [h]éna* "come here" into two constituents. Yet, it is not clear in the following example, whether the locational phrase "to Dolly Iza" is really meant to be an apposition to "here," or whether "Come here!" serves as an idiomatic phrase:

(40) *ába bo éna búba*   "Daddy, come here
      íza   [to] Dolly Iza."

And when she was 14 months old, she also started as follows:

(41) *kóva búba ína*   "Hat Dolly [R]ina."

Then, after a short interval, she continued with this long monologue:

(42) *búba ína kóva*   "Dolly Rina hat."
(43) *búba ína ze*   "Dolly Rina this."
(44) *búba kóva ze*   "Dolly hat this."
(45) *íne búba ína af*   "Here Dolly Rina
                            nose."

From the same period we have also recorded:

(46) *íne pe búba*   "Here mouth Dolly."
(47) *íne af búba*   "Here nose Dolly."

If we compare (45) with (47) we may paraphrase (45) as "Here (behold)—Dolly Rina has a nose," and (47) as "Here [is] (behold) nose [of] Dolly." The change in word order between (41) and (42) will be discussed below. To be sure, the Hebrew word order is retained in the English translation throughout, and the missing elements can be easily made up in both by the reader.

Also in our sampling are included, at random, several interrogative sentences like (5) *ma ze*? "What [is] this" and (17) *mi kóki*? *ine kóki* "Who [is] Kóki? Here [is] Kóki." See also examples (19), (22), and (63). It was not our intention to deal at this time with this challenging problem, which has recently drawn, with regard to English, the attention of scholars like U. Bellugi-Klima, E. Klima, R. Brown, and others (see References). We might only mention in

passing that even these scanty examples show the ability of both children to make the distinction between *mi* and *ma* "who" and "what," animate and inanimate.

Roger Brown indicated in a personal communication that in English, children at first do not seem to control this distinction, and that the only English *wh* questions at this time, which are not really *wh* questions but part of a basic set of referential operations, would be *what that*? (A request to name the object denoted) and *where NP*? (This is usually rhetorical, since the object named will be present but the other person is to point at it). I suppose it may be true for many Hebrew-speaking children as well, but apparently it is not universal.

Our subjects, Gila and Gil, did, of course, ask very frequently, while pointing with their fingers, like most (all?) children *ma ze*? and *máze*? "What [is] that?" and "Whatsthat?" but they obviously did also make use of *ma* "what" and *mi* "who" in other combinations, even within the first two to three months of their syntactic development. This was in the fourteenth month in the case of Gila, and the seventeenth of Gil. It is interesting though that in (17) *mi* "who" apparently serves for *eyfo* "where," if we take the answer *ine kóki* "Here's Kóki" as a clue.

2.31 Here are a few examples from Gil, who was about a year-and-a-half younger than his sister, and who started making up sentences in his fourteenth month, many of which start with a vocative:

(48) *day, ába?*   "Enough, Daddy?"
(49) *ába, day!*   "Daddy, enough!"
(50) *kxi ze*[35]   "Take (feminine) this!"
(51) *kúku, ába*   "Kuku (= peek-a-boo),
                         Daddy!"
(52) *ába, kúku*   "Daddy, kuku (peek-a-
                         boo)!"
(53) *íma, kxi (khi)*   "Mommy, take
                         (feminine)!"

---

[34] *bá'i* is evidently a merger of *ba* "comes" (present) / "came," and *bó'i* "come!" (imperative feminine).

[35] He uses here the feminine form *kxi* "take" (to fem.), even to *ába* rather than the masculine *kax* (to masc.), and sometimes even speaks of himself in the feminine, being surrounded by two older sisters, a mother, and a grandmother. However, in (55) we hear *kax* "take!" (masc.) when he talks to his father, as compared with *kxi* "take!" (fem.) to his mother in (53).

(54)	*ába, kxi*[35]	"Daddy, take (feminine!)!"
(55)	*ába, kax*	"Daddy, take!"
(56)	*tírí, ima*	"See (fem.), Mommy!"
(57)	*ába, tere*[36]	"Daddy, see (masc.)!"
(58)	*ma kara, ába?*	"What happened, Daddy?"
(59)	*alom, pápta*[37]	"Shalom (Hi), Grandma."
(60)	*íne iparon*	"Here's a pencil."
(61)	*lo roce*[38]	"[I] don't want."

2.32. And soon we also hear longer combinations from him:

(62)	*ába, ten li*	"Daddy, give me!"
(63)	*ma ta se?*[39]	"What you do?"
(64)	*lo roce tet*[40]	"Don't want give."

2.41. Here may be an appropriate place to say a few words about some of the selectional rules used by Gil and Gila at this stage, i.e., what restrictions are imposed by them on co-occurrence of lexical items in a sentence or a string of words.

As we shall see later, richly inflected languages, Hebrew being one of them, are more flexible in terms of word order. This greater

---

[36] *teré*, for *tiré* (more formal: *tir'é*). This use of the future tense "you will see!" for the formal imperative is very common in Israeli speech. Gil certainly used it in an idiomatic way, rather than as a reference to the future. His first real use of the Future was at the age of 20½ months.

[37] *alóm*, *pápta* for the standard *šalóm*, *sábta* (or formal: *sávta*). Phonological perfection is by no means a condition for manipulating the syntactic and semantic components.

[38] *lo roce* "don't want" for *ani lo roce* "I don't want." This omission of the pronoun *ani* "I" is quite common in informal speech of Israeli youth—naturally, when rejecting requests for doing something that they do not like to do. . . .

[39] *ma ta se* for the formal *ma ata ose*? (Informally, speakers often pronounce *ma ta* for *ma 'ata*) "What [do] you do?" (The auxiliary [do] is redundant in Hebrew!)

[40] *lo roce tet* for formal *ani lo roce latet*, "I don't want to give." The Pronoun "*ani*," as mentioned in footnote 38, is sometimes omitted in the general speech of the youth. See footnote 32. The full form of the infinitive is *latet*. It is made up of the prepositional element *lə/la* "to" and the "infinitive construct" (which is not used by itself in modern Hebrew, unlike Biblical Hebrew) *tet* "give, giving." See below regarding the omission of secondary elements in child language (the "telegraphic speech"). Interestingly enough, young Israeli children will sometimes come up with forms that may have occurred only in Biblical or Mishnaic Hebrew.

---

freedom is considered to be of some advantage for the young learner, but it may also work in the opposite direction. Similarly, one would infer that the richer a language is in terms of selectional features, i.e., the more restrictions are imposed on co-occurrence of lexical items, the more chances there will be for children to differ in their matching of related items (to mismatch items or "err" from the adults' point of view).

2.421. For example, Hebrew, more than English, maintains a very strict distinction of Gender (Masculine and Feminine; no Neuter) and Number (Singular and Plural; Dual is limited to certain instances and behaves like the Plural) throughout the Noun and Adjective (also the numerals 1–19, and the units 3–9 beyond 20 differ for masculine and feminine), as well as the Verb, where the person-distinction is added as well. An agreement in terms of Gender and Number, and Person wherever applicable, prevails between the NP that functions as the Subject of the sentence and its VP which functions as the Predicate, when the latter is a Verb, Adjective, Pronoun, Demonstrative, but not a Noun. To be sure, the selection is made according to the gender of the NP that functions as Subject of the sentence (sentences with Extrapositions may need special treatment).

2.422. This means that in sentences (8), (9), (25), (39), (50), and (54) both children violated the selectional rules of Gender. This may also apply to (43) and (44), if we take *ze* "this" to be the Predicate, although in many other cases they knew very well how to apply them. As a matter of fact, I was surprised to find out that in the majority of the cases they *did* know how to make the distinction between Masculine and Feminine and to match a masculine Subject with a masculine Predicate, and a feminine Subject with a feminine Predicate, as in (1), (2), (6), (7), (10), (11), (14), (15), (19,) (24), (29), (30), (33), (33), (35), (36), (37), (40), (53), (55), (56), (57), (61), (62), (63), and (64). In other words, (8), (9), (25), (39), (50), and (54) are deviant forms even in terms of the child's own grammar. In (8), (9), and (25) the Verb is feminine and does not agree with the masculine Subject, but in (50) and (54) a feminine Verb is used for a masculine Subject. It will take the child several years to *master* all the selectional rules.[41] Even in kindergarten one will still hear some deviant selections, but they will be gradually diminishing, as is the case in English-speaking children who, as R. Brown points out, "are often still making errors of gender in pronouns at 3 and 4 years."

2.431. Let us see first how Gender in general is determined in Noun and Adjective:

sus "horse"	*susa* "mare"
talmid "male student"	*talmida* "female student"
yéled "a boy"	*yalda* "a girl"
moré "male teacher"	*mora* "female teacher"
tov "good (masc.)"	*tova* "good (fem.)"
yafé "beautiful (masc.)"	*yafa* "beautiful (fem.)"

It is easy to see that the Masculine is unmarked (has Ø ending), while the Feminine in all the examples is signalled by the -*a* ending, which happens to be the most common Feminine marker in the Noun and Adjective. Less frequent feminine endings are -*et*, -*it*, and -*at*. The latter is common in construct state and inflections. One rule for Feminine is therefore quite simple:

Masc + -*á#* ⇒ Fem

2.432. As mentioned above, Hebrew has no Neuter Gender, hence all Nouns, whether

---

[41] By the way, a careful study of the language of the older children and of young native Israeli adults will show a certain residue of "deviant" forms that in some cases look like "corrections" of historical inconsistencies in Hebrew grammar. This will be very apparent in Gender within the cardinal numbers, especially 3–10, 11–19 and the units 3–9 beyond twenty, where the formal (historical) masculine numbers have the typical feminine endings, and vice versa. *šaloš* "three" (with reference to fem. ! ! !), vs. *šaloša* "three" (masc. ! ! !). The children have a problem with these inconsistent forms (a similar problem exists in Arabic), and naturally try to "normalize" them. Normalizations of this type are continued by many mature native speakers of Hebrew, and this is one of the ways that Israeli children have affected the development of Modern Hebrew speech since its revival at the turn of the century. For details see Bar-Adon (1959), (1964), (1965) and (forthcoming).

animate or inanimate [±Animate] are classified as either Masc. or Fem. In the case of the inanimate the Gender will obviously be determined on a formal basis, i.e., whether the ending is Ø or -*á*; if it is -*á*, then it is, usually treated as Feminine, and if it is Ø it is usually Masculine (there are a few exceptions in each), and the selectional rules will be applied accordingly, as Adjective and Verb (and Non-Verbal, Adjectival, Predicates) are concerned. For example:

1a. *yéled* "a boy," *yéled tov* "a good boy," *yéled nafal* "a boy fell"
1b. *yalda* "a girl," *yalda tova* "a good (f.) girl," *yalda nafla* "a girl fell (f.)"
2a. *sus* "a horse," *sus tov* "a good horse," *sus nafal* "a horse fell"
2b. *susa* "a mare," *susa tova* "a good (f.) mare," *susa nafla* "a mare fell (f.)"
3a. *séfer* "a book," *séfer tov* "a good book," *séfer nafal* "a book fell"
3b. *uga* "a cake," *uga tova* "a good (f.) cake," *uga nafla* "a cake fell"

Note that the Verb has various suffixes for signalling the Feminine, and there is no need for us to go further into it here.

2.44. Returning to the earlier stage which concerns us here, one will ask, how do the young children discern Gender and what determines their selections? I suspect that their distinctions and selections are made by considerations that are essentially similar to those of adults, although on a somewhat impressionistic basis. There is no doubt that from a very early stage of their mental development, certainly within the single-word stage, they develop a perceptual distinction between male and female. For instance, they will recognize and often refer to any male as *ába* "Daddy," and any female as *íma* "Mommy." Then they will probably add to the distinction, or replace it with *dod-dóda* "Uncle-Aunt," perhaps also with *sába-sábta* "grandfather-grandmother," using it to refer to any old man or woman, respectively, and so on. They will manifest this recognition in real life and in pictures as well. They recognize, for instance, "Human" and distinguish "Male" from "Female" in humans by the natural gender, in animals by a combination of gender with form, and in inanimate objects by the form. One might say that they seem to develop a certain idea about lexical categories, as well as about subcategorization rules and distinctive features (of the type [αF], where α = + or −), such as the [syntactic] features of [± Human], [± Masculine], and about selectional rules. I am not so sure about the extent of the use of [± Animate] at this stage, or if we ought to judge by the selectional rules employed. Note the following sentence said by one of the children while pulling up his slipping pants:

(64a) *bo, bo sáyim* "come, come (sing.) pants!"

The sentence is used for the "standard" *bó'u, bó'u, mixnasáyim*, with a violation of the selectional restrictions of Number [agreement] (the verbs are in Singular while the noun is Plural), and of animateness. On the other hand, it is amazing how the child knows to make the utmost use of a limited vocabulary.

2.451. As for Number and the reference to Plural, we might return to sentence (31) in which the verb "come" is the Singular *bo* rather than the Plural *bó'u* referring to both Daddy and Mommy!
Similarly, we recorded the following word-string of a girl who was showing her socks:

(64b) *abáyim [nə]kiya* "socks clean (f.s.)"

She uses this for the formal *garbáyim nəkiyim* "socks clean" (m. pl.), although most speakers would use the feminine plural *nəkiyot* in informal speech.

2.452. The children were obviously slow in acquiring the Plural distinction, i.e., in applying the selectional restriction of Number with respect to plural. As for the Determiner, there were no cases of its use with the Article. We may therefore say that both children did not have the feature [± definite] at this stage, and naturally no selectional restrictions should be expected in this area. (For the impact of the dominant Gender of the environment, see footnotes 26 and 35. The dominance of the womenfolk was obvious in the case of Gil, and this is an interesting factor.)

2.51. It is quite obvious from the examples of the children's speech that the medium

or framework of syntactic relations is indeed most important for the semantic interpretation, while the full grammatical apparatus, which is said to supply in adults' grammar "the input for the phonological interpretation," is later inlaid and perfected by the child.

2.52. I assume you were not confronted with any special difficulties in the identification and interpretation of the preceding speech samples of the "telegraphic speech" type.[42] This speech retains certain general features of the adult language—primary distinctions, relations and functions—that are gradually refined with the child's linguistic development. They make it possible for the environmental audience to understand and communicate with the child. (See our explanations below, especially 3.13–3.17 and in 11.4.) I further assume that you guessed the (41), *kóva búba ína* "hat Doly Rina," means that the hat in question belongs to Dolly Rina, is Dolly Rina's (for [*ha*] *kova* [*hu*] or [*ze*] *kova* "This [is] a hat") [*šel*] *búba rina* meaning "[The] hat [he = is] [of] Dolly Rina," (see sentence (16) and footnote 23), while the following sentence, (42), *búba ína kóva* "Dolly Rina hat" tells that Dolly Rina has a hat, perhaps instead of [*lə*]⌢ (or in the definite: [*la*])⌢ *búba rina* [*yeš*] *kóva*, i.e., "[to] Dolly Rina [there is] a hat." In essence, they mean the same, both evidently having the same underlying structure. They may also correspond to *búba rína—*[*yeš*] [*lah*] *kóva*, "Dolly Rina—[there is] [to her] a hat," a kind of extraposition, which, by the way becomes quite common in a subsequent stage as will be expounded later. If we take a subsequent structure (65!) as a clue, we might be more convinced that (42) is indeed a paraphrase of (41), only in the reversed order of the two major constituents (see discussion there). In that case, apparently, word order is not significant; it may be merely a stylistic inversion in the surface structure.

3.1. How does the environmental audi-

---

[42] This term has been recently introduced into the literature on child language by Roger Brown of Harvard and his associates. See uses in Jakobson (1941 [1968]).

ence understand this "telegraphic speech"? Let us mention here briefly a few cues.

3.11a.   First, the word order is most often (although not always, and not by all children) retained as in the model or the target language. Hence *kóva búba ína* "hat Dolly Rina" will correspond, as mentioned above, to mature *[ha]kóva [hu] šel búba rína*, "[The] hat is of (belongs to) Dolly Rina," or "This is a hat of Dolly Rina," as in (16), while the differently ordered sentence, which is made up of the same three elements, *búba-ína-kóva* "Dolly-Rina-hat," will evidently relate that *lə/labúba rína yeš kóva*, or *búba rína-yeš lah kóva*, "Dolly Rina has a hat." On the surface, they sound different, but basically they are the same, and may be paraphrased in the same manner. Since the child does not use transformations at this stage, not even the "Copula" transformation (I believe this applies to English as well, where not only "be" but also "have" is deleted from the basic [base?] structures of the child), three overtly different sentences like the following,

a.   Dan is a boy   *dan˙yéled*
b.   Dan has a boy   *lədan yeš yéled/dan yeš lo yéled*
c.   [This is] Dan's   *[ze (hu)] hayéled šel*
     boy/The boy of Dan   *dan*

will have the same basic representation in child language (and in "Deep Structure"?):

d.   Dan boy   *dan yéled*

Evidently "This boy is Dan" *hayéled haze hu dan* will be represented by "boy Dan" *yéled dan*. (See also our discussion below about "Implicator" and "Explicator.")

3.12b.   Second, the child's intonation contours are basically the same as the adult's. The deletions are of the weaker-stressed and lower-pitched elements—often but not always! (See below).

3.13c.   Third, and this is a very important matter that has not yet been fully investigated: there seems to be a parallelism between the child's "imperfect" sentences in the early stages of his speech development and the adult's semi-grammatical sentences. This is the general phenomenon of "degrees of grammaticalness or grammaticality" (or, from the other end, the "degree of deviance") with respect to a well-formed sentence. The native speaker-hearer will evidently assign semantic interpretation not only to strictly well-formed, grammatical sentences, but also to semi-grammatical ones. This refers to sentences with a certain relaxation of, or deviance from "selectional rules" (including various subdivisions), or from strict "subcategorization rules," or violation of constraints on "lexical categories," and the like.

3.14.   This phenomenon, according to Chomsky,[43] is accounted for by supplementing the generative grammar, which is by nature restricted to well-formed sentences, with a "hierarchy of categories" of various levels that

---

[43] See, for instance, N. Chomsky, *Aspects of the Theory of Syntax* (1965), pp. 148–153, and his bibliography in footnote 4. For the differentation between "acceptability" (which belongs to performance) and the more abstract "grammaticalness" (within competence) see Chomsky, op. cit., pp. 10–12. For a later exposition, with application to child language see D. McNeill, "Developmental Psycholinguistics," pp. 32–37 (see footnote 2 above). In an earlier treatment, "Some Methodological Remarks on Generative Grammar," *Word*, XVII, 1961, pp. 219–239 (part was reprinted as "Degrees of Grammaticalness," in Fodor and Katz, pp. 384–389), Chomsky poses the critical question: "By what mechanism can a grammar assign to an arbitrary phone sequence a structural description that indicates its degree of grammaticalness, the degree of its deviation from grammatical regularities, and the manner of its deviation?" (p. 386). He then tries to answer it on a formal basis, and he summarizes as follows: "Without going into details, it is obvious how . . . a degree of grammaticalness can be assigned to any sequence of formatives when the generative grammar is supplemented by a hierarchy of categories [and subcategories]. The degree of grammaticalness is a measure of the remoteness of an utterance from the general set of perfectly well-formed sentences, and the common representing category sequence will indicate in what respects the utterance in question is deviant," (p. 387). It is then suggested that "a generative grammar supplemented by a hierarchy of categories can assign a degree of grammaticalness to each sequence of formatives" (p. 388); or that by use of alternative suggestions "the generative grammar itself may impose degrees of grammaticalness on utterances that are not directly generated, through the intermediary of the category hierarchy projected from the set of generated sentences." (p. 389). See also Miller and Chomsky, "Finitary Models of Language Users," *Handbook of Mathematical Psychology*, II, ed. Luce et al., 1963, esp. pp. 443–449.

gradually increase in distinctiveness and refinement. This allows us to impose interpretations on semi-grammatical sentences, compare them with each other on a detailed reliable basis, and determine their relative closeness to, or remoteness from, a well-formed sentence, according to the levels in the hierarchy of categories and subcategories they have in common. This is presumably how our linguistic competence operates. Obviously, the more levels the sentence in question has in common with the compared well-formed sentence, the closer it is to well-formedness, also to interpretability and acceptability. In other words, a deviating sentence will be tolerated and interpreted by the native speaker-hearer, as long as it is within the hierarchy of categories, in such a way that it has certain levels in common with a formally generated sentence, or is not too far from a well-formed sentence. Such a sentence will be only moderately violating the category restrictions, while at the same time preserving its most crucial distinctions and features, thus making it possible for the native speaker-hearer to interpret and accept them somehow.

One would indeed speculate that the more the "hierarchy of categories" can be subdivided into levels and better defined and further refined, and the more the semantic features can be classified and specified—the more helpful and revealing it will be not only for the study of adults' linguistic competence, but also for the study of language acquisition in general. It will be revealing in particular for the relation and interaction between the so-called "telegraphic speech" of the child and the "generative grammar" of the native speakers around him, with their intuitions about well-formed sentences, and their flexible competence that allows for certain deviations from common speech patterns. It seems that different individuals will allow for certain different deviations. I wonder how the "bare" deep structure constructions will sound to most innocent speakers. Some of them will probably sound like child language.

3.15. There is also the interesting phenomenon of individuals closest to a young child best understanding his "deficient"

utterances, i.e., they do best in imposing semantic interpretations on the utterances they hear. They are probably trying harder to analyze the structures and subcategorize the formatives in great detail, and thus are able to discover more semantic association and overlapping. It seems to me that this interaction also plays a very important role in the process of the child's acquisition of language.

3.16. In this respect, I believe, on the basis of my observations, that the impact of other children, especially slightly older siblings and somewhat older colleagues, wherever they are available, is of no less importance than that of the parents. Children seem to possess a special sense for "speech analysis" of their younger siblings or friends, and often they interpret the child's speech to adults, sometimes even to his parents. If the child's "deficient" utterance is somehow interpreted, it draws a meaningful response, naturally, with a better formed sentence, and often with an expansion[44] of the child's sentence that in turn provides the "erring" child with a clue for re-examining his theory or "improving" his generative grammar so that it is in line with that of the mature environment. One might say that the peculiar *analyticity* of children (the fact that a four-year-old can interpret his two-year-old fellow amazingly) may stem from their chronological closeness to the mentality and strategy of early-stage language formation, and from a special speech perception that may be sharpest at that time, but there are probably other reasons, too—the flexibility of their intuitions about deviant and well-formed sentences, and perhaps a special ability to trace back the "sifting" done by the younger child, or even to operate on deep structure. But this problem, which deserves a detailed treatment, obviously cannot be further discussed here.

3.17. To return to our topic, it seems that the average early-stage child language sentence lies, from the point of view of the mature speakers, within the boundaries of such an intermediate level or tolerable

---

[44] See Brown & Bellugi (1964), 140 f.; and McNeill (1966), 65 f., 70 f.

"degree of grammaticalness" (which advances and improves with the growth of the child), that a semantic interpretation can be imposed without special trouble. Therefore, a sentence like *búba ína kóva* "Dolly Rina hat" is immediately interpreted by the listener to mean "Dolly Rina has a hat," while *kóva búba ína* "hat Dolly Rina" is interpreted as "The hat is Dolly Rina's," or "The hat belongs to Dolly Rina," and *búba bói ada* (for *yalda*) "Dolly, come girl" will be interpreted as "Dolly, come to the girl," (referring to herself) and so on.

3.2.   Why *mostly* (although not absolutely) a short two-word sentence at the beginning!

Some scholars have tried to relate it to the short memory span of children at that tender age. Observing the rather lengthy and fluent monologues of such young children, (for instance, the one about Dolly Rina and the hat), I doubt whether it is indeed the memory span that limits the sentence span. One will notice that the vocabulary during this stage is not so small either and in many cases is quite appreciable, sometimes consisting of hundreds of words. This indicates a retention or memory capacity that again makes a two-word limitation inconceivable. Besides, the child does not learn by heart a list, or a corpus, of utterances that he just reproduces or imitates but, as it has been stated, he learns to apply his innate ideas about learning a complex system like a language and its universals concerning "Sentence" and its general properties, basic grammatical relations (e.g., subject vs. predicate, etc., within the deep structure of sentences), to the particular language he hears, and he derives a theory about its construction rules. Thus, from the finite elements and rules before him, the child creates for himself a generative grammar through trial and error. Often the child may come up with unconventional forms, such as (in English) "he hitted" for "he hit" or "oxes" for "oxen," similarly in Hebrew *aba'im* "fathers" for the formal *avot*, or *išot* "women" for *našim*. But those "faulty" constructions are actually the best positive indication that the child has assimilated the system, internalized the rules, and has started generating constructions independently. The child usually derives and applies first the rules with the broadest generalization or greatest distribution (e.g., the regular plural), and then adds to them the necessary restrictions, transformations, and the like.

I would therefore be more inclined to accept, though in part, an explanation such as the one by Brown and Bellugi that states, "The constraint is a limitation on the length of utterance the children are able to program or plan," which is "characteristic of most or all of their intellectual operations."[45] This is only a partial explanation. Obviously, what is most difficult for the young child is the degree of complexity and the number of transformational operations involved in the longer more complex sentences. Actually, when one goes beyond the two or three word sentence, he is almost right away confronted with some transformations. The child hears them and probably perceives them too (as his reactions indicate), but he sticks primarily to the bare base-structures, sifting and leaving out transformations, relations, etc. One might also add the impact of the child's limited range of interest. It is quite possible that it is also affected by the fundamental binary concept, which the child at this stage seems to be adapting to the basic sentence structure. (See our exposition in Section 11 regarding an Implicator-Explicator structure.)

3.3.   Synchronically, as it is known, each stage in the development of the child's language should be treated as a discrete entity deserving individual analysis. On the other hand, child language is in a constant process of development, accompanied by what I am inclined to call a "dynamic equilibrium" or "mobile equilibrium."[46] On this subject, and on the subject of the generic relation between child language and adult

---

[45] Roger Brown and Ursula Bellugi-Klima "Three Processes in the Child's Acquisition of Syntax," *Harvard Educational Review*, [A special Issue on "Language and Learning"], XXXIV (1964), p. 137. They add that "the limitation grows less restrictive with age as a consequence, probably, of both neurological growth and of practice, but of course it is never lifted altogether," (ibid).

[46] For details see Aaron Bar-Adon, "Analogy and Analogic Change as Reflected in Contemporary Hebrew," *Proceedings of the Ninth International Congress of Linguists*, ed. H. G. Lunt, Mouton & Co., The Hague, 1964, p. 758 f.

language, one may ask: what is the nature, or what are the characteristics of the child's brief (abbreviated?) sentences with respect to the model Sentences of the adults that the child hears around him, and will master by himself by the end of his linguistic development?

As mentioned above, the child's speech may be seen from a certain point of view as a "telegraphic speech." Even our few examples show clearly that during his speech at this stage, the child employs only the principal elements: he retains the major part of the "contents words," or "contentives," especially nouns and verbs and some adjectives, but tends to omit "function words," or "functors," especially prepositions, adverbs, conjunctions, determiners, certain inflection affixes, etc. And from a parallel intonational point of view: the child tends to retain the words or formatives with the primary stress and high pitch (which are usually coupled with the contentives), while omitting the weaker-stressed and lower-pitched words (again, usually the "function words"). As we shall see later, the original word-order and intonation are generally retained.

There are other factors besides heavy stress that also promote the retention of the contentives. Naturally, there is the inherent exclusive semantic importance of the contentives—they are hard to guess from the context when they are omitted—while the functors can be supplemented or guessed with greater ease, as we could see in the examples. Some students of child language also add the use of contentives in the single-word utterances and in the preceding preliminary stage, the frequent "practice" with them in isolation (which children indeed like to do).

It seems to me that in this respect, Hebrew does not differ, for instance, from English, and it may be that this phenomenon is within the range of universal rules that may operate in all natural languages—the perhaps universal concepts of grammatical classes, hierarchical rules, basic grammatical relations, and so on.

3.4. The term "telegraphic speech" may be somewhat misleading if one identifies the "contracted" speech of the young child with the style of the telegrams of adults.

That style is a mere reduction from the normal, adult style. It preserves the contentives while omitting formatives of secondary importance, especially the functors, but it does observe the basic grammatical rules. However, in the "telegraphic speech" of the child not all the sentences are necessarily a reduction from mature sentences. It is easy to see that during this stage the child produces or generates unique sentences that have no "father" or "brother" in adult language. They are generated according to the child's *own* concept of "Sentence," his *own* grammatical theory, which has been developing independently.

It is possible to see in the child's "telegraphic speech" a system in which the child often formulates the minimal base structures of the type of sentences that he has internalized. It is also possible to see in this "contracted" speech something similar to "transformations" of contraction or deletion, as some do, although not quite. It seems that the most promising hypothesis is to conceive of the internalized grammar of the child in the initial phase as a simple grammar, with very simple grammatical classes and categories, rules and relations. As proposed by Chomsky and others, in mature language syntactic structures are believed to have two aspects: a concrete, or physical, or overt one, and an abstract, or covert, or inner one. Or, as it is usually said, they have a surface structure (the physical shape) and a "deep structure" (the abstract form). The surface-structure is related to the phonetic form in representation of speech, while the deep structure underlies the semantic interpretation more in the abstract and provides the meaning. Thus, the correlation between sound and meaning, between the phonetic and sematic counterparts, is mediated through and determined by syntactic structures of a certain complexity. Evidently, only in very simple structures is there a direct correlation between the surface structure and the semantic interpretation. In all other cases the semantic interpretation of the surface structure is underlaid by the abstract deep structure, often in a complex way and through a series of "grammatical transformations" in it that produces the physical surface structure as we hear it and perceive it.

3.41. This will probably explain why we are tempted to say that those little tots, especially in the early phases of their speech development, may be overtly using "deep structures," or that they may be "speaking" more or less "base structures," or intermediate underlying structures like the base structures that are generated directly by the base rules, or "intermediate underlying structures" like those that are assumed to underlie the surface structures of our ordinary mature speech. Naturally, they do so before acquiring and implementing the use of transformations, which affect the base structures and which, as mentioned above, are in little use during the initial stages of language acquisition.

4.1. This infrequent use of transformations in the inititial stages occurs not only in a language like Hebrew, which normally has non-verbal predicate constructions (e.g., *aba po* "Daddy [is] here," used in both child and mature language), but also in English, in which the normal pattern of *mature* language is "Daddy is here." Thus, we hear both in Hebrew and English child language predicates consisting of only a Nominal, or an Adjective, or a Demonstrative, or a Possessive Pronoun, or a brief Prepositional Phrase or a Locational Phrase—*without* a Copula. It is also not uncommon at this stage to hear sentences consisting of such a predicate only, without an overt subject constituent. E.g., *ze!* "this!," *po* "here," *day!* "enough!," *buba* "Dolly," and others.

4.2. The base rules for these simple sentences, with allowance for some expansion in brackets, looks as follows:[47]

(1)   S → (NP) + [Aux] + VP
(2)   NP → (Det)N

---

[47] See Chomsky, *Aspects* (1965), 106 f., and Bach's modifications in "*Have* and *Be* in English Syntax," *Language*, Vol. XLIII (1967), pp. 462–485, see esp. 473 f: A general application of this approach to Hebrew is being developed by Y. Hayon in his doctoral dissertation on "Relativization in Hebrew: A Transformational Approach" (The University of Texas, 1968/9). Some of his ideas are useful for our case as well.

(3) $VP \rightarrow (V(\text{Prep-Phrase}) [\text{Manner}]) \begin{Bmatrix} \text{Predicate} \\ \text{(NP)} \end{Bmatrix}$

(4) $\text{Predicate} \rightarrow \begin{Bmatrix} \text{NP} \\ \text{Adjective}^{48} \\ \text{Place} \\ \text{Prep-Phrase} \end{Bmatrix}$

4.21. Naturally, such a derivation for child language is simpler than the parallel ones suggested by either Chomsky or Bach with respect to mature English and which can with relatively small modifications be applied to mature Hebrew as well (see note 47). For instance, we don't have here a "Time" constituent because it is not very meaningful at *this* stage. The child's awareness of and reference to Time (and Tense) develops somewhat later. So there is no need, for the time being, of an Auxiliary (Aux) and rules of the sort

$$\text{Aux} \rightarrow \text{Tense}; \quad \text{Tense} \rightarrow \begin{Bmatrix} \text{Past} \\ \text{Future} \end{Bmatrix}$$

relating to such non-verbal predicates until a later stage. For the same reason it will be superfluous to expand here our rule to the following ones used by Chomsky (Aspects, 106) and adopted by others:

(1)   S → NP⌃Predicate-Phrase
(2)   Predicate-Phrase → Aux⌃VP (Place) (Time)

4.22. The predicative Prepositional-Phrase (Prep-Phrase) constituent is, however, present from the early stages of Hebrew child language. Accounting for it is important not only for Hebrew child language but also for mature Hebrew, as well as for early child constructions in English and quite a few other languages. Furthermore, it may be useful also for the description of mature English (deep structure) if one subscribes to the theory that Copula is not generated by the base rules but inserted by transformations.

4.3. Here are some typical phrase markers of that stage:

---

[48] The status of "Adjective" in deep structure has been debated in the literature lately; some consider it a Nominal, others feel that it behaves like a Verbal. A recent summary of the two opposing views is included in R. A. Jacobs and P. S. Rosenbaum, *English Transformational Grammar*, 1968, esp. pp. 63 f. One does not necessarily have to accept their solution for the case of Hebrew.

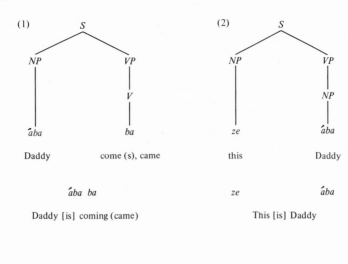

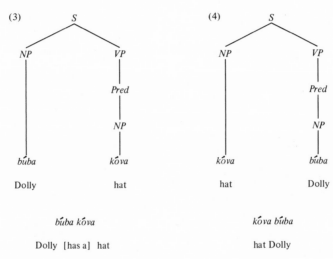

FIGURE 1

Referring to (4),

kóva búba = kóva [šel] búba
           = kóva [yeš lə] ⌢ búba
hat Dolly = hat [of] Dolly
           = hat [there is to] Dolly

(See discussion of Possessive and Genitive constructions below.)

4.4. I believe that the non-verbal predicative constructions of early child language of the aforementioned types are also significant for the general problem of the status of Copula. By their very structure, they provide further support to the thesis that Copula, in general (and in the case of English not only *Be* but also *Have*), is not necessarily part of the base structure or generated by the base-rules, but is inserted by the proper transformations (see note 41).

4.41. The *Have* constructions in Hebrew are quite different from their English counterparts. Whereas in English the *Have* "possessive phrases" are of the type

Subject—*Have*—Object, or
$NP_{[s]}$—*Have*—$NP_{[o]}$,

in Hebrew they are basically expressed by

$NP_{[s]}$—*lə*-$NP_{[o]}$, or Subject—*lə*-Object,

i.e., the predicate is expressed by the preposi-

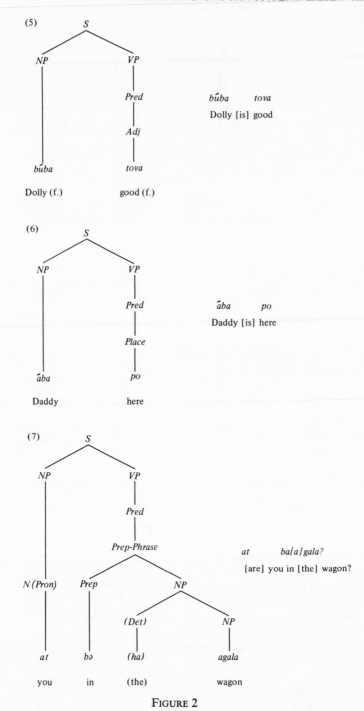

FIGURE 2

tion (Posses.) *lə-* "to, for" followed by an NP, e.g.: *ková lədan* "[A] hat [there is] to Dan."

If this NP is a pronoun, then it will be transformed morphophonemically into the common possessive pronomial suffixes that will combine with the *lə-*, i.e., we will have the inflexion of *lə-*. For example, if *ani* is "I", and *ata* "you" masc. sing., then "to me" and "to you" (corresponding to "I have," "you have") will become:

lə- + *ani* ⇒ *lə-* + *-i* ⇒ *li*
lə- + *ata* ⇒ *lə-* + *-xa* ⇒ *ləxa*, etc.

Hence:

buba li "A doll to me" (i.e., "I have a doll," "A doll belongs to me.")
buba ləxa "A doll to you" (m.s.), (i.e., "A doll belongs to you.")

Notice that the English paraphrase of "NP [belongs] *to* NP" is somewhat closer to representing the Hebrew (see details below).

4.42.   In the surface structure, the morpheme *yeš* "[there] exist[s]" appears between the Subject and the Predicate, or it may appear elsewhere, mostly initially. I suppose it will be best to consider it as a mere "Existence Indicator" (or marker) and to treat it as another Copula-element inserted by (optional) transformational rules whenever applicable, e.g.:

buba [yeš] li "A doll exists to me" ("I have a doll.")
buba [yeš] ləxa "A doll exists to you" (m.s.), "you have a doll."
buba [yeš] lədan "A doll exists to Dan" ("Dan has a doll.")

or, as it appears most often in the surface structure, in the word order:

[yeš] li buba, etc., and
lədan yeš buba, etc.

4.5.   Let us have a closer look at those structures in general Hebrew (for other details see Hayon, op. cit.).

4.51.   In a way, one might conceive of *yeš* as an allomorph of the tri-consonantal "root" or ("discontinuous morpheme") *h-y-y* "Be," while being limited to the Present and denoting "being" or "existence" in the *absolute* which we will mark by E (one may choose ∃), in the form of:

S → NP + E (or: E + NP?)
E → *yeš* (in the Present which is the unmarked Tense)

Note that NP + *yeš* is often inverted by the speakers to

yeš + NP, as in the famous Biblical phrase:
yeš elóah "Exists [there is] a God," or the com-

monly used phrase, also with and by children:
yeš xašmal "[There] is electricity," when the light is on.

4.511.   In certain cases, especially when the NP (Subject) is a Pronoun, *yeš* will be inflected, e.g., *yeš* + *ani* ⇒ *yešni* for the first person, *yeš* + *hi* ⇒ *yešnah* for third person feminine, etc.:

omrim yeš/yéšnah érec ... "They say [there] exists a land ..."
xoševni(/xošváni) uvxen yešni "Cogito ergo sum," i.e., Descartes' famous postulate, "I think, therefore I exist."

4.512.   The negative in the Present (which is unmarked for Tense!) is expressed by the Negation morpheme *eyn* that will occupy the same locus in the sentence, e.g.:

eyn érec "Not [exist] land" ("There does not exist a land.")
eyn xašmal "Not [exist] electricity" (There is not electricity.")

Roughly: S → Neg + NP,   (from   NP + Neg?), where Neg → *eyn* (or: Neg͡Existence ⇒ Neg + *yeš* ⇒ *eyn*).

4.52.   In the Past and Future ("Tense"):

xašmal haya/yihye "Electricity [there] was/will be," or as it mostly appears in the reversed word order:
haya/yihye xašmal

4.521.   The derivation will look like this:

S → NP + Tense͡*h-y-y*
where:

Tense → $\begin{Bmatrix} \text{Past} \\ \text{Future} \end{Bmatrix}$

4.522.   I suppose we could shorten it, on an ad hoc basis into:

S → NP + Tense
Tense → $\begin{Bmatrix} \text{Past} \\ \text{Future} \end{Bmatrix}$ *h-y-y*

4.53.   And in the Negative:

lo haya/yihye xašmal, from
xašmal lo haya/yihye "Electricity not was/will be"

4.531. And the derivation will have the form:

S → NP + Neg + Tense⌢h-y-y (or: with Neg initially)

Neg → lo/-Tense, where

Tense → $\begin{Bmatrix} \text{Past} \\ \text{Future} \end{Bmatrix}$

4.532. Based on 4.522 we might formulate the derivation as:

S → NP + Neg Tense

Neg → lo/-Tense, where (roughly)

Tense → $\begin{Bmatrix} \text{Past} \\ \text{Future} \end{Bmatrix}$ h-y-y

4.533. These were the absolute-existence constructions which actually correspond to the English *Be*-Existence, as main verb, rather than to *Have*, although the same word *yeš* is used in the Present (the unmarked

Tense) for both *Be*-Existence and *Have*-Possession predicates. As noted, with Tense (Past or Future) there is a switch in either case to *h-y-y* inflected in the appropriate tense and according to the Person-Number-Gender of the Subject.

4.6. In the Possession-Predicates, which in Hebrew are actually instances of a Prep (osition)-Phrase Predicate as compared with the English *Have*-Possession Predicate, we have as mentioned above, two types (if we desire to separate Pron from N, which will prove useful in the discussion of child language structures below), both of which may include an optional affirmative[49] *yeš*, or the negative *eyn*, or Tense *h-y-y*. For convenience we will mention here only the most common structures, some of which may not be exactly in the assumed word-order of the deep structure:

$$\text{NP} + le\text{-NP}$$

I

NP + lə-N, etc.

(1) *kóva [yeš] lədan / lədan [yeš] kóva*
"A hat [is] to Dan" (Dan has a hat)

(2) *kóva eyn lədan / lədan eyn kóva*
"Don doesn't have a hat"

(3) *kóva [haya/yihye] lədan / lədan [haya/yihye] kóva*
"Dan had/will have a hat"

(4) *kóva [lo] [haya/yihye] lə dan / lə dan [lo] [haya/yihye] kóva*
"Dan did/will not have a hat"

II

NP + lə-Pron, etc.

kóva [yeš] li / li [yeš] kóva
"A hat is to me" (I have a hat)

kóva eyn li / eyn li kóva
"I don't have a hat"

kóva [haya/yihye] li / [haya/yihye] li kóva

"I had/will have a hat"

kóva [lo] [haya/yihye] li / [lo] [haya/yihye] li kóva
"I did/will not have a hat"

4.7. In mature Hebrew, sentences of those types will have the following derivation (we will mark here Existence [in the present] by the symbol E; unmarked Tense is Present):

S → NP + (Neg) $\begin{Bmatrix} \text{(E)} \\ \text{(Tense)} \end{Bmatrix}$ + lə⌢NP

$\left(\text{NP} → \begin{Bmatrix} \text{N} \\ \text{Pron} \end{Bmatrix} \right)$

(E → yeš)

Tense → $\begin{Bmatrix} \text{Past} \\ \text{Future} \end{Bmatrix}$ h-y-y

Neg → $\begin{Bmatrix} eyn/\text{-E} \\ lo /\text{-} \begin{Bmatrix} \text{Past} \\ \text{Fut} \end{Bmatrix} h\text{-}y\text{-}y \end{Bmatrix}$

or shorter:

Neg → $\begin{Bmatrix} eyn/\text{-E} \\ lo/ \text{-Tense} \end{Bmatrix}$

---

[49] One might even go farther and say that the *yeš* is an affirmative-*emphatic element*, as in the use of *ken* "yes," in situations like those listed in column 3. They are quite common among the younger generation when making a strong counter statement.

(1)	*Positive*	*Negative*	*Emphatic-Affir-mative*
	ze tov	*ze lo tov*	*ze ken tov!*
	This [is] "good"	"This [is] not good!"	"This [is] *yeš* good!"
(2)	*hu ba*	*hu lo ba*	*hu ken ba!*
	"He came"	"He [did] not come"	"He *yeš* came!"

4.71. Strictly speaking, *yeš*, like Copula, is not part of the base structure but is inserted transformationally, and if we want to be more elaborate, we may develop an optional *yeš* insertion rule such as the following (somewhat simplified) rule:

[₅ X NP Y Predicate Z]₅
 1 2 3   4   5 ⇒ 1 2 3⌢*yeš* 4 5

This rule applies only when 3 is unmarked for Tense. Remember that the Present is the unmarked Tense, while Tense refers to Past or Future.

4.72. If, however, the use of Tense is included, then the rule will change to:

[₅ X NP Tense Predicate Z]₅
 1 2 3   4   5 ⇒ 1 2 3⌢*h-y-y* 4 5

When Tense is included then the insertion of *h-y-y* is necessary. The morphophonemic rules will then provide the appropriate forms (conjugations) of the verb, in accordance with the selected tense and the Person-Number-Gender to conform with those forms of the NP that function as the Subject of the sentence.

4.73. The rules for the insertion of Copula (which in the case of Hebrew is usually a pronoun) wherever applicable, and the rules for Aux → Tense⌢*h-y-y* when desired are essentially the same.

4.74. Let us now return to the main problem, i.e., how does it look in child language in the early stages?

4.741. In sentences of type I, which in mature Hebrew have the pattern NP + (Neg) $\begin{Bmatrix} (yeš) \\ (Tense) \end{Bmatrix}$ + *lə*⌢NP, with the latter NP appearing as N, the middle constituents are actually redundant for the young speakers. There is not yet any real reference to time (no "Tense"); *yeš* and also *h-y-y* are treated like the Copula elements, i.e., they are not generated by the base rules. And since transformations are rarely used at that stage, the entire constituent is not represented. As for *lə-*, since prepositions in general are of secondary import and therefore not yet used,

the *lə-* will not appear either. The initial bi-constituent structure will therefore be [₅ NP + NP]₅

4.742. As for sentences of type II, where the second NP is a (possessive) Pronoun, i.e., *lə-* is inflected, it is even rarer to see the whole constituent, since inflections (also of secondary significance) are not present at that stage. Even the independent pronouns are not too common yet, although some children may start using them rather early. In such cases, one may hear direct juxtapositions of elements or intermediate combinations of forms that reflect intermediate steps in the morphophonemic changes. For example, in mature Hebrew *li* "to me" goes through the following steps:

$$lə + \text{"speaker"} \Rightarrow \frac{lə\text{-} + ani}{\text{to} + \text{I}}$$
$$\Rightarrow \frac{lə\text{-} + \text{-}i}{\text{to} + \text{me}} \Rightarrow \frac{li}{\text{to me}}$$

4.743. The children at this stage, if they make such connections at all, still use pretransformational concatenations or juxtapositions such as *lə*⌢*ani* "to I", in some cases more than *li* "to me." Thus they will mostly wind up with the binary construction:

$$S \rightarrow NP_1 + NP_2$$

or to include Negation:

$$S \rightarrow (\text{Neg}) \, NP_1 + NP_2, \text{ where Neg} \rightarrow \begin{Bmatrix} lo \\ eyn \end{Bmatrix}$$

That is, Neg at this stage may be either *lo* or *eyn*. Also, without context restriction, its place in the sentence is rather flexible. But this should be further studied.

4.8. All *yeš* constructions, including those denoting existence in the absolute, seem to be taken by the young speakers as some kind of Copula and are omitted in the early stages. Hence the [NP + *yeš*]₅ type (or with order reversed, [*yeš* + NP]₅) appears as [NP]₅, and the [NP + *yeš* + *lə*⌢NP]₅ type appears as [NP₁ + NP₂]₅. This may also explain why even in the two-and-more-word stage there are still many *one-word* sentences used, especially in pointing out existence of objects.

4.9.   Thus, we may say that in the strictly one-word phase, when a child says with falling intonation [*buba*]ₛ "Doll", or [NP]ₛ in general, that this is a condensed holophrastic manifestation of, say, [*yeš buba*]ₛ "There exists a Doll," or of [*yeš* NP]ₛ. The existence is thus implied, taken for granted, and only the other constituent that explicates it (the "Explicator" as we will call it later) is actually mentioned.

5.   More on the one-word sentence:

5.1.   We may even say that the holophrastic "nucleus" may correspond to, or represent, almost any constituent in the mature language and thus express various relations in the abstract. It will usually focus on that constituent carrying the least predictable or most important information, either as a Subject (as in the preceding example), or as a Predicate, as when the child says *tov* "Good" while petting someone, or *xam* "Hot" or *kar* "Cold" while touching something or just referring to something that is or was in his past experience and was associated with those attributes or properties.[50] By the same token, it may focus on a Locative or Adverbial of Place— e.g., [*po!*]ₛ "Here!" which is derived from varied constructions such as [NP *po*]ₛ "NP [is] here," [*sim* NP *po*]ₛ "Put NP here!" etc. It may concentrate on a Direct Object—e.g., [*máyim!*]ₛ "Water!" i.e., "I want water," or "Give me the water!" or the like. Similarly, it may represent a Prepositional Phrase such as [*dan*]ₛ "Dan" for, say, "This is Dan's."[51] With such a view in mind, there is indeed good reason to refer to the single-word period in the development of language as the "holophrastic" period, which deserves very careful study.

5.2.   It is not our purpose here to exhaust the problems of the holophrastic stage, but in the framework of our general discussion I should like to present a thesis that might prove useful in analyzing the holophrastic structures, and perhaps also some of the subsequent ones such as the Extraposition type, which will be discussed later.

5.21.   Let us assume that each statement uttered by the speaker is a kind of a *response*, an *answer* to a *question*, whether this question is overt or covert, explicit or implicit, actual or rhetorical, e.g., [*ze mi?*]ₛ "That [is] *who*?"— a brief answer is [*dan!*]ₛ "*Dan!*"; an elaborate is [*ze dan*]ₛ "That [is] *Dan*," where the interrogative *Who* and its correlate *Dan* substitute for each other. Both of them constitute the Predicate of a non-verbal sentence, which in turn means that the one-word answer [*dan!*]ₛ also contains the Predicate. By the same token, a question like [*dan oxel ma?*]ₛ "Dan is eating *what?*" will have the one-word answer [*tapúax*]ₛ "[An] apple," or the full sentence *dan oxel tapúax* "Dan is eating [an] apple." The question focuses on the (direct) Object, and therefore the one-word sentence [*tapúax*]ₛ "Apple" represents a direct Object. The same holds true for all other constituents.

5.22.   We are not concerned here with the structure or development of the *Wh* questions in child language. Roger Brown has written, for English, a detailed study on "The Development of Wh Questions in Child Speech,"[52] and noted two intermediate steps between the statement (the possible answer) and the normal question—i.e., (a) a question in which the *Wh* is placed in the same locus as the constituent it substitutes for (Brown calls it the "occasional question," though I prefer to call it the *underlying question*), and (b) the child's question. Thus, between the normal question (3) "What will John read?" and the answer "John will read the book," Brown inserts an "occasional question," (1) "John will read whát," which he considers the "Base," and the child's question (2) "What John will read?"

---

[50] An interesting perceptual case is the following. Gila was given for the first time a plate made of clear plastic. Her immediate reaction was: *máyim* "water."

[51] See Werner F. Leopold, "Patterning in Child Language Learning," *Language Learning*, Vols. 1 and 2 (1953–54), 10; and Philip Lieberman, *Intonation, Perception and Language* (Cambridge, Mass: The M.I.T. Press, 1967), especially pp. 44 f. See also Lieberman's bibliography on intonation and related problems.

---

[52] The *Journal of Verbal Learning and Verbal Behavior*, VII (1968), pp. 279–290.

which he considers "a hypothetical intermediate in adult grammar." In (1) there is a heavy stress and rising intonation on the *Wh* element. In (2) a "preposing" of the *Wh* takes place, and in (3) a "transposing" step interchanges the Subject and the Auxiliary verb. One might say, in a more general way, that in child English we have a single-word transposition whereas in mature English we have a double transposition.[53] In Hebrew there is generally no need for a second transposition in (3) in which case the order in (3) is the same as in (2), except for structures in formal Hebrew starting with an Adverbial of Time or Place and whose Tense is

Past or Future. This means that in simple structures like the above examples, the child's question will be either like (1) or like (3). For example, for the statement *dan oxel tapúax* "Dan is eating an apple" the questions will be (1) *dan oxel ma?* "Dan is eating what?" and (2) and (3) *ma dan oxel?* "What Dan eats?" The short answer will be the holophrastic [*tapúax!*]ₛ "Apple!"—the type of utterance that interested us in a few paragraphs above.

5.3. The following table will illustrate the correlation between the possible single-

The Child's Wh Questions in Hebrew with English Correspondences[54]

Underlying Question	Child's Question	Adult Question	Short Answer	Full Answer
(1) *ze mi?* This [is] *who?*	*ze mi/mi ze?* /*Who* this [is]?	*mi ze?* *Who* is this?	*dan.* Dan.	*ze dan.* This [is] *Dan.*
(2) *ze ma?* This [is] *what?*	*ze ma/ma ze?* /*What* this [is]	*ma ze?* *What* is this?	*léxem* Bread.	*ze léxem.* This is *bread.*
(3) *mi oxel?* *Who* is eating?	*mi oxel?* *Who* is eating?	*mi oxel?* *Who* is eating?	*dan.* Dan.	*dan oxel.* *Dan* is eating.
(4) *dan ose ma?* Dan is *doing* what?	*ma dan ose?* *What* Dan [is] doing?	*ma dan ose?* *What* [is] Dan doing?	*oxel.* Eating.	*dan oxel.* Dan is *eating.*
(5) *dan oxel ma?* Dan is eating *what?*	*ma dan oxel?* *What* Dan [is] eating?	*ma dan oxel?* *What* [is] Dan eating?	*léxem* Bread	*dan oxel léxem.* Dan is eating *bread.*
(6) *dan oxel eyfo?* Dan is eating *where?*	*dan oxel eyfo/eyfo dan oxel?* *Where* Dan [is] eating?	*eyfo dan oxel?*[55] *Where* [is] Dan eating?	*po!* Here!	*dan oxel po.* Dan is eating *here.*
(7) *dan oxel eyx?* Dan is eating *how?*	*eyx dan oxel?* *How* Dan [is] eating?	*eyx dan oxel?* *How* [is] Dan eating?	*yafe.* Nicely.	*dan oxel yafe.* Dan is eating *nicely.*

word-sentence statements (answers) and the full, well-formed ones. This will suggest, at least theoretically, that the child's single-word

utterances are instances of column 4, "Full Answer." If this is the case, we may then very

---

[53] In *An Introduction to Descriptive Linguistics*, rev. ed. (New York: Holt, Rinehart and Winston, 1961), p. 177, H. A. Gleason made a somewhat similar observation regarding the single-word transposition in the colloquial usage "Who is John writing to?" and the formal "To whom is John writing?"

[54] The English correspondences are based on R. Brown's findings; ibid.

[55] As mentioned above, in the Past ("ate" = *axal*) the formal question is ordered *eyfo axal dan?* "Where ate Dan?" This has greater correspondence to the reordering in English, but the children stick to the one-word transposition (or preposing) *eyfo dan axal?* The same applies to questions on Place and Manner.

well attribute to the child, even at that early, holophrastic stage, a certain degree of awareness of syntactic constituents, relations, and functions.

Sentences of the types (1) through (6) are common from the very beginning. This includes instances of Nominal (including Prep-Phrases for Hebrew) and Verbal Predicates (1), (2), and (4); of Subject (3); of Object (5); and of Locative (6). The Adverbials of Manner (7) appear slightly later. Subsequently, Adverbials of Time and Cause will develop, whereas Purpose will come much later. Again, the last analysis may shed some new light on the problem of the holophrastic structures, but is not meant to be exhaustive in any way.

6.1. This analysis may also help us in explaining a somewhat later phenomenon in child syntax, the *Extraposition* structures, which are rather frequent in the subsequent stage or stages of the developing child's speech, although they are infrequent in mature language, both Hebrew and English.[56] Take, for example, the following [composite] sentences:

(1) *dan—hu gadol.* "Dan—he [is] big" (vs. regular *dan gadol* "Dan [is] big").

(2) *dan—hu yošev po.* "Dan—he [is] sitting here"

(vs. regular *dan yošev po* "Dan is sitting here").

(3) *dan—kóva yeš lo/dan—yeš lo kóva.* "Dan —a hat [there] is to him/Dan—[there] is to him a hat" (i.e., "Dan—he has a hat") vs. the regular *kóva yeš lədan/lədan yeš kóva* "A hat [there] is (exists) to Dan."

(4) *dan—hakóva šelo po.* "Dan—the hat of his (= his hat) [is] here," vs. the regular *hakóva šel dan po* "The hat of Dan (= Dan's hat) [is] here."

6.2. The above examples will have the Phrase-markers (1′) through (4′) respectively.

Note: This is apparently the underlying structure of (3), and Transformational Rules will map the underlying structure onto a derived surface structure, such as *dan—yeš lo kóva*, as follows: (1) A pronominalization rule will convert *dan* of s′ into the pronoun *hu* "he," and morphophonemic rules will then convert *lə- + hu ⇒ lə- + -o ⇒ lo*; i.e., "to + he ⇒ to him." (2) *yeš* will be inserted by the appropriate *yeš* transformation, as mentioned above. If the child does not make full use of transformations and insertions at this stage, his basic structure will evidently boil down to something like *dan—kova* "Dan—hat."

6.3. We will notice in (4′) that the possessive construction [*kóva*] *šelo* "his [hat]" is conceived here as originating from a relative clause that is embedded in an NP that contains another NP. (See Jacobs and Rosenbaum [1968] 199–211, 231, and see Section 7 below.) I agree with Jacobs and Rosenbaum that genitive [and possessive] constructions originate as relative clauses. The case of Hebrew will only support it, since, as it is known, *šel* is a later development of the Relativizer *ašer*,[57] or its contracted form *še-*

---

56 See J. S. Gruber, "Topicalization in Child Language," *Foundations of Language*, III (1967), pp. 37–65, esp. p. 38. One may say that a sentence like (1) *dan hu gadol* "Dan, he is big" stands for something like "[Speaking of] Dan, he is big," or "[Referring to] Dan, he...," or "[As for] Dan, he...," or in an expanded form "[I am speaking of] Dan—he is...," or even "[I want to tell you about] Dan—he...." These are Extrapositions of the type that one would perhaps refer to as "Topicalizations" or "Implicatorizations." Various other types of Extrapositions, in a more general sense of the term, have recently been discussed in the literature. See for instance the analyses of Extraposition Transformations in embedded (nominal) complementations in English in Rosenbaum (1967), and briefly also in Jacobs and Rosenbaum (1968), esp. pp. 171 f. These are obviously beyond our present scope but may be interesting for comparison in the analysis of subsequent stages. As for Hebrew, see Uzzi Ornan (1967). He is certainly right that Extraposition can apply to the Subject constituent, as in our Sentence (1), or to any other constituent! Another treatment with a further classification is included in Rubenstein (1968).

---

57 In Hebrew the Relativizer is not a Pronoun, as it is in English and many other languages, including a Semitic language like Arabic. See the brief (incomplete) summary of previous views in Ornan (1965), pp. 77 f. and his (fragmentary!) summary of the development of *šel* in Hebrew (op. cit., p. 25), a fact that was discussed in detail by N. H. Tur-Sinai, M. H. Segal, H.B. Rosen, Y. Peretz (1967, p. 151; see his bibl.), and recently by Y. Hayon, op. cit. Identity of an element for relativization and possession exists also in Aramaic.

(1′)

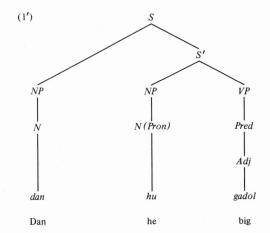

(2′)

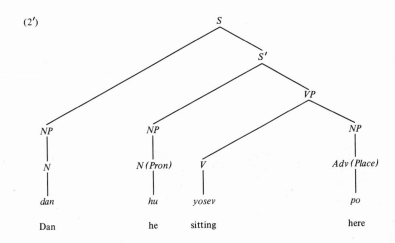

(3′)

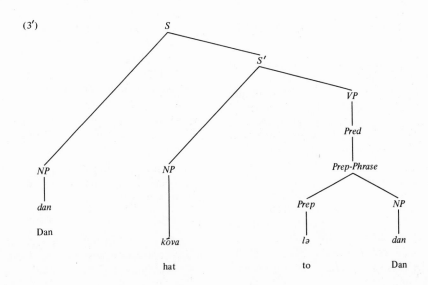

(4')

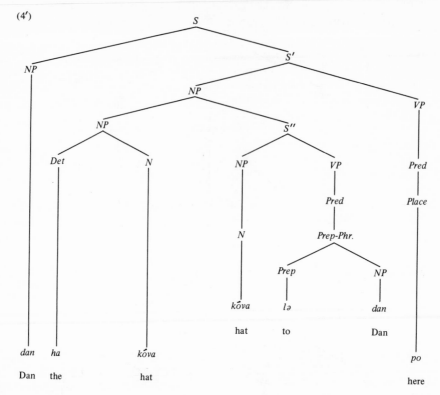

plus the preposition *lə-* "to" (belonging to): *ašer lə-* ⇒ *šeˆlə-* ⇒ *šel(-)*. Then, through the appropriate transformations, *dan* of S″ will be pronominalized and then converted by morphophonemic rules into *lo* "to him," as in Sentence (3), and the relativizer *še-* will be preposed while *kóva* of S″ will be deleted. We will leave further discussion of these constructions, which are typical for a subsequent stage, to a special treatment of that stage.

6.4. On this basis, it is quite possible that utterances like *búba ína kóva* "Dolly Rina hat" do not necessarily reflect the structure *ləbuba rina [yeš] kova* "To Dolly Rina [there is] a hat" (from *kova [yeš] ləbuba rina* "A hat [there is] to Dolly Rina") which is the common manifestation of overt

S → NP + [*yeš*] + *lə*ˆNP,

but may be also an illustration (reflection? forerunner?) of the Extraposition type. In that case it would stand for something like *(ha)buba rina—yeš lah kova* "(The) Dolly Rina—[There] is to her a hat," whose Phrasemarker is similar to that of No. (3) above.

Represented by the pronoun (pronominal suffix) *-ah* of *lah* (= *lə-* + *ah*, from *lə* + *hi* "to + she") in the right hand phrase, the extraposed element *buba rina* "Dolly Rina" now occupies the position of Subject in the expanded (complex) sentence, both [psycho] logically and formally, while the rest serves as the Predicate Phrase. And if in children's speech the copulative element *yeš* "there exists, there is," and the prepositional phrase *lah* "to her," which includes the pronominalization of *buba rina*, are omitted (the former because it is not part of the base rules, and the latter because it is a "secondary element") the remaining constituent *kóva* is obviously the Predicate and the Explicator. The two usually coincide. (See Section 11.)

7. An interesting development within that early period may be witnessed in the following sentence:

(65) *še[l] ába kóva* "Of Daddy hat"

In terms of structure, a new element is added corresponding to the formative *šel* "of, belonging to," articulated at this time as [*še*]. It is quite possible that it serves as a general "copulative" element denoting "relation to, belonging," which is an internal development in the child's own grammatical system with a certain complex set of relations to mature language, rather than a mere imitation of adult language. There is evidently no one-to-one relationship. It is obviously a step beyond the short construction that lacks this element, i.e., *ába kóva* "Daddy hat," which is taken to mean either [*lə*] *ába* [*yeš*] *kóva* "To Daddy [there is] a hat," like (42) above, or [*ha*]*kóva* [*hu*] [*šel*] *ába* "[The] hat [he = is] of Daddy" (i.e., "The hat is Daddy's," similar to (41) or (16) above in reverse order, all paraphrases having the same underlying structure), or speculated to be a contracted Extraposition. (See Section 6.3.)

At any rate, the present construction (65) [*šel⌢*NP + NP]ₛ may provide some support to the last interpretation if we take its intermediate underlying structure to be [PN + šel⌢NP]ₛ, and of (41)[+16] to be that of (42). Naturally, it is not impossible that *kóva* was added after the essential constituent had been said, in which case we take it as "performance," not "competence." (One might suggest that we take it as a sort of "cleft sentence" in the sense of "What to Daddy is a hat," but this is highly speculative.)

7.1. It is apparent from the preceding that there are quite a few common features to Hebrew and English *child language*, and that the initial structures of the child's syntax are quite similar in the two languages. A similar resemblance between Russian and English was pointed out in 1966 by Slobin.[58] When children's speech in other languages is studied and analyzed, certain general patterns and linguistic universals will evolve. One thing seems, however, quite clear—the earlier, "primitive" stages of children's speech are closer to each other in different languages than the full adult languages, that their *basic* structures are "more universal." With the growing refinement in the acquired languages

comes further differentiation between structures of languages.

7.2. Child language(s) could serve as the basis for a reinforced search for *basic* "linguistic universals." From this point of view, child language should not be studied as a "reduction" of mature language, but as an illustration of the growing linguistic competence, of the developing linguistic theory. This study should then start from where these universals start, from the "primitive hypothesis" about the holophrastic "sentence" that consists of the "punch word" (it may correspond to various constituents, as mentioned above) through the simple constructions, like the above examples, with the broadest common base rules (and notions about abstract underlying "deep structures," and appropriate permutations or reorderings), onto the developing branchings, embeddings, and transformations, where the diversified languages start differing more substantially from each other. This dividing line may also be the first limit of "linguistic universals."

To put it differently, if we want to think in terms of syntactic rules represented by a [deep structure] phrase-marker, the higher nodes will represent those grammatical elements that are common to children's speech all over. One will locate there the most universal categories (the members of each of which are functionally the same), functions and relations. As we go down the nodes, or down the rules and derivations, we follow the hierarchy of categories: we proceed from the most inclusive to the more differentiated, more individual, more exclusive, refining categories, functional elements, and relations. The child starts with S, which may be realized as a single word, and develops it to an Implicator-Explicator type (see Section 11), or, if you wish, to S → NP + VP, but the internal subdivision of any of these components will occur in a subsequent stage of the child's linguistic development. When transformational rules are combined with those of the abstract deep structures (the base component), mapping them into related concrete surface structures, the division between individual languages becomes more apparent and more complete.

To be sure, transformations in themselves,

---

[58] He states (in 1967, pp. 132–33) that "the beginning stages of syntactic development [in Russian-speaking children] look very much like those of English-speaking children described by Braine (1963a, *Ontogeny*...), Brown and Fraser (1963), and Miller and Ervin (1964)."

i.e., the transformational capacity, are part of an innate capacity. They are "biologically given," as phrased by Lenneberg,[59] but the specific ones that are applied to one language or another are, like the grammars of individual languages, instances of an indefinite number of possibilities within the given class.

8. *On word-order.* Several studies on child language[60] have pointed out the general correlation between the [overt] word order in children's "telegraphic speech" and that of mature language, the former omitting certain elements like the functors that carry a relatively lower semantic load and a weaker stress. It is readily observable in actual spontaneous speech, and it has been examined in various tests of imitation of longer sentences by young children. The patterns of "sifting" were found to be quite similar, but with certain variations.

8.1. It is often pointed out that, for example, in English the order S-V-O (Subject-Verb-Object) is retained, because that order by itself is in English a syntactic signal, but we may still wonder whether the elements that are retained in free speech or in imitation tests do really have a one-to-one relationship to mature language (or whether they indeed are always preserved in that order).

8.11. In this context, an interesting question was raised by students of English child language, who "would be interested to know whether children who are exposed to languages that do not utilize word order as a major syntactic signal, preserve order as reliably as do children exposed to English" (see footnote 45), i.e., what do children do in languages in which word order is more flexible and less significant?

On the subject of word order, it should be noted that (a) it plays a significant role in

determining the grammatical relations defined by surface structure, but it does not seem to have great significance in determining grammatical relations in deep structures,[61] although this, in turn, does not mean that there is no inherent organization or definite abstract ordering in the deep structures (or the "semantic representations"). Also it should be noted that (b) even in English, word order is not always as crucial as one might be led to think (see Bever, Fodor and Weksel's (1965) arguments against Braine's (1963b) views, and Braine's (1965) reply).

8.12. Hebrew is certainly a good example of a richly inflected language with a relatively high flexibility of word-order, but it should be made very clear that this is only a *relative* flexibility and that Hebrew has very definite restrictions of its own. Furthermore, there does not seem to be any known natural language with a completely "free word order," where no grammatical transformations are needed, and where the rule for realizing underlying abstract structures, or abstract representations, is utterly simple. In other words, there seems to be an internal organization, an underlying word order, in all languages (presumably assigned by the categorical rules that normally define the system of grammatical relations), so that not each free permutation of the words of any sentence in a language will be a paraphrase of the respective original sentence as in set-systems. Hebrew is obviously no exception to this rule.

8.13. In many cases, what may seem like "free" reordering within a string will turn out to be, on closer examination, affected by contextual or semantic considerations (not excluding emphasis), coupled with necessary shifts and transformations. There seems to be some division of tasks between grammatical transformations (which cannot evidently cover the entire range of stylistic inversions) and stylistic reordering. Highly inflected languages will tolerate more stylistic reordering than the uninflected or less inflected ones, but even the former will tolerate such stylistic inversions or reorderings only to a point short of ambiguity, where grammatical

---

[59] Lenneberg (1967, pp. 325–26) states that, "The transformations of grammar are biologically specialized transformations, applicable to acoustic patterns that have in man the function of communication. This type of transformational capacity is clearly biologically given, but the specific transformations as they occur in one or another language are just some of the infinitely possible ones."

[60] See Brown and Bellugi [= Klima] (1964), pp. 133–41.

[61] See Chomsky, *Aspects* (1965), p. 221.

rules will come in and generate corresponding structures independently.

It is indeed possible "that there are several underlying generalizations that determine when such reordering is permissible, and what its semantic functions are. . . ."[62] This is a most intriguing problem that has been studied very little so far, but we cannot go here into further theoretical aspects of word order and its universal implications.

8.2.   Let us return to the sentences of Gila and her brother, Gil, who as indicated, started "syntaxing" and "sentencizing" at a very tender age (especially Gila!), before most other faculties had a chance to develop significantly. And by the way, it seems to me that such conditions may be optimal for studying the theory of language acquisition and the structure of language, (i.e., deep structure/semantic representation). Obviously such early speakers, who start producing syntactic combinations in their twelfth month and evidently start comprehending them even earlier, have a very short period of exposure to the language of their environment, or for that matter, a short time to develop other mental faculties. So, in whatever linguistic structures they develop at this stage they may be manifesting something closer to the "origin" or "source" of the human linguistic capacity.[63]

---

[62] *Ibid*, pp. 126–27.

[63] It may be completely subjective, and I don't know yet what concrete implications can be derived from the study of the *early* language learner, but this problem certainly deserves a special study. I might add parenthetically that *most* children studied in the literature on child language started making syntactic combinations at a relatively much later age (beyond eighteen months). It is probably just a coincidence that most of the young Hebrew speakers that I studied were early combiners (after all these were only several dozen). Theoretically, I can hardly believe that the structure of a language should have any effect on the timing of the beginning of meaningful speech and syntactic combinations, since it would affect the basic idea of "innate ideas," but it may deserve a special study too. There is, however, an understandable difference between richly and poorly inflected languages in the subsequent full mastery of morphology and morphophonemics. This is pointed out by Slobin (1966, pp. 135–36) in a comparison of Russian with English.

8.21.   It might seem that in short sentences of the early stage there is not much room for significant changes from the "model" or the input language, but actually there are quite a few possibilities for deviant combinations that the children I studied did *not* take advantage of. I am referring to combinations like *ze ine ába* "This behold Daddy" (but *ine ze ába* "Behold this Daddy"), or for instance *ba mi ze?* "Come who this?" or *ze ba mi* "This come who?," or the like, but *mi ze ba?* "Who this came?," etc. The same applies, and even more so, to the longer utterances. An inherent order of derivation seems to prevail everywhere, often more than required in normal Hebrew speech. (See our conclusions in Section 9.1.)

8.22.   It does not mean that such sentences are not possible during this stage, and certainly many detailed follow-ups and analyses are needed in order to establish reliable patterns, but we did not find them in the language of those children that we followed very consistently and very carefully for hours day after day over six years, and I believe it is not only a matter of observable performance. I suppose such sentences were not generated by the children's *rules*, and to the extent that they may have been produced without our noticing it (which is possible, too), they would obviously be considered deviant and ungrammatical by the children's grammar itself. And this is of course a very important point.

8.23.   Similar findings for Russian-speaking children were reported by the famous Russian student of child language, Alexander N. Gvozdev, and then analyzed and expounded by Dan Slobin.[64] They noted that early Russian child language is more inflexible than mature Russian, which as it is known, does have a quite flexible word order. The initial stages were presented by Slobin in terms of Pivot words (P) and Open Class words (O). Then in the three-word stage, the order was found to be S-O-V, although the dominant order in Russian is S-V-O, but a little later towards the end of the child Zhenya's second year, it changed to S-V-O.

---

[64] Dan Slobin (1966), pp. 132–35.

And Slobin concludes: "Word order is as inflexible for little Russian children as it is for Americans."[65]

8.3. It is easy to see that:

(1) The little novice speaker of even a highly inflected language does not make use of the morphological device of inflections. Therefore he is in exactly the same situation as the child speaking a poorly inflected language. Both will usually stick to a specific word order.

(2) The child's speech does indeed usually start with more or less unmarked classes, even in highly inflected languages. To the extent that order in early child language differs from that of mature language, it might be worthwhile looking into the possibility that the former represents a "basic" order of deep structure and semantic representation. Inflections are considered secondary elements and are added later, at which time certain reorderings may be applied.

(3) The dominant word order in mature language, even in languages theoretically quite free in their order, seems to have a definite impact on the child's grammar, although the child's grammar is by itself generative, not imitated.[66] (See Section 8.6.)

8.4. There are, however, very interesting reports about consistent but more or less free juxtaposition of words among certain children[67] who evidently constitute a small minority. Such cases may carry the seed for most important refinements in the general theory of language acquisition. But the fact remains that the majority of the children, regardless of their various idiosyncrasies, develop common patterns of language-in-the-making. This makes it possible for linguistic systems (languages) to continue

over the generations, usually with relatively minor changes from one generation to the other. Otherwise, linguistic continuity would not be possible at all. Naturally, the accumulation of many minor changes over many generations and centuries may add up to significant changes, but this is part of the normal evolution and processes of continuity[68] of language, with the participation and indeed contribution of children to it.

8.5. At the age of sixteen months we recorded the following sentence by Gila (in which there already is an embedding of a reduced relative clause in-the-making)

(66) *ni la tadégel axéla*   "Give (fem.) to her O.M. (Object Marker) the flag [of] Raxéla."

This corresponds to the mature Hebrew *tni la[h] et hadégel (/tadégel) šel Raxéla;* i.e., the difference is mainly in the presence or absence of the possessive preposition *šel* "of, belonging to" (which, as mentioned above, includes a relativization element and implies relativization). *Tadégel* is a fluent realization of *et + ha⌐dégel,* i.e., the Accusative Particle, or Object Marker (O.M.) *et +* the article *ha (et + ha ⇒ ta),* and the noun *dégel* "flag." This form *tadégel* is quite common in the rapid speech of many native speakers, especially the youth and young adults. By the way, in "give her" she was referring to herself (= give me).

8.51. The O.M. (*et*) in its abbreviated form *t-* appears already in the fourth month of Gila's speech experience, but not always does it combine with a Direct Object. Sometimes it may combine with what corresponds to a Subject in mature language. Nevertheless, towards the end of that month we have very convincing evidence of awareness of the Object, based on a usage that Gila could by no means have picked up from adult speech. Her older sister wanted a piece of chewing-gum, but without actually mentioning it in

---

[65] Slobin, (1966), p. 134.

[66] Roman Jakobson's formula is "the child creates as he borrows," (1941 [1968], p. 14).

[67] For instance, Roger Brown told me (in a private communication) about a study on three Finnish speaking children done by his student M.B. Two of them preserve word order, but one varies it rather freely. Even in cases where the children evidently mean to imitate an adult, the one little boy often changes the order, which is a very rare phenomenon in English. This boy is not consistently using word order to distinguish Subject from Object, as one would expect, especially if one accepts the notion that "basic Sentence relations are innate." Braine "On learning . . . ," 1963b, 338) cites the case of Gregory's partial flexibility of VS rather than of SV order.

[68] On processes of linguistic continuity in modern Hebrew see Aaron Bar-Adon (1959), (1965), and (forthcoming). Cf. Charles F. Hockett, "Age Grading and Linguistic Continuity," *Language,* XXVI (1950), pp. 449–57.

the presence of little Gila, she said to her father *ten ləima o li*, "Give to Mom or to me." Gila heard it and understood that her sister was speaking about giving something to Mom. Since the sentence started with an imperative, "give!" the Subject was understood; it was followed by the Indirect Object *ləima* "to Mom," and what was missing here was evidently the *Direct Object* of the transitive verb *ten* "give!" So Gila took the element *o li* "to me" in the original sentence to be that Direct Object (see the parallel to Sample 66!), and she urged her father:

(67) *ten ta-oli*   "Give O.M. the *oli*"

Notice that she not only applied the abbreviated Accusative or Object Marker *'t-/ta*, but it is possible that she also knowingly switched from the "indefinite" form *o li* (which she took to be a noun, and in that case an indefinite one) to a definite one, which is implied in *ta-oli* (*'t + ha ⇒ ta*).

8.52. It is hard to think of a more ingenious artificial way of testing the child's linguistic competence and his rules about sentence structure, about what elements or constituents should be there, and in what order.

8.53. In this example it is also clear that while allowing for a flexible arrangement of Indirect and Direct Object when she produced the sentence herself, she put the Direct Object immediately after the verb. One may, of course, say that there was no other choice in this two-word (+ "you" implied) sentence, and if we look back at sentence (66), we will see that she used there both an Indirect and a Direct Object, but this is immaterial. She obviously knows how to use both and is flexible about their internal order, both in comprehension and production, as the mature speakers around her are.

8.54. To be sure, in sentences of this kind, in which artificial ("nonsense?") elements appear by design or by chance, one can best detect the child's linguistic competence and his internalized linguistic theory. It is certainly not less informative than, say, presenting questions to adult speakers about grammaticality and the like.

8.6. Word order in Hebrew is indeed much more flexible than in English, and "theoretically" (if all layers and styles of Hebrew are taken into consideration), it appears to be very flexible in a great many constructions. But in effect this freedom of reordering is restricted as mentioned above, and is limited to a large extent by the most acceptable usages, which exclude cases of ambiguity. As it is known, acceptability and grammaticality do not necessarily coincide. A sentence may be grammatical but not acceptable and vice versa. As mentioned above, contextual and semantic variations may also play a role in restricting flexibility. In other words, it is not only a matter of stylistic reordering (performance), but also of grammatical transformations (competence), and vice versa.

8.61. For practical purposes, let us assume that the most common acceptable form should be considered the "dominant," or "standard" form for comparison with the child's speech. The child hears in most cases a particular syntactic order, and according to this he creates his theory about the syntactic rules that govern certain types of sentences. These rules generate his grammatical sentences, while others will naturally be deviant or ungrammatical. The bulk of the child's sentences will follow his own grammar of a given time. But, as mentioned above, his entire grammar, before it reaches a certain point of stability and perfectness after several years of experience with the language, is in a constant flux. It is in what we called a "mobile equilibrium," still open on the one hand to constructions derived from some past rules that do not fit the new system very well, and on the other hand, to new rules that are forerunners of a new stage but do not yet comprise his entire theory. The inconsistency will naturally differ from one individual child to another and from one transition period to another. And of course we must not deny the *child* what we allow mature speakers, their slips, faulty starts, and other deviant sentences that we "do not count" in the analysis of their linguistic competence. The child certainly deserves more allowance on this score. This will apply to syntactic structures in the strict sense, and to word order as well. See, for instance, the parallelism in Sentences (26), (27), (28).

The greatest flexibility of order in child language is displayed in short sentences—here mature language also leaves much freedom for the speaker—i.e., in sentences like (1)/(2), (6)/(7), (8)/(9), (41)/(42), (48)/(49), (51)/(52), and (56)/(57).

We will not attempt here to make an exhaustive list of word order patterns, but will try to sum up a few that represent at least part of the above mentioned samples.

I   VERBAL SENTENCES

A. *Two-word Sentences*
  (a) Flexible (interchangeable) order:

1. S-V/V-S	1, 19/2
2. Voc-V_I/V_I-Voc	6/7, 9/9, 56/57

  (b) Inflexible order:

1. V-Loc	35, 36, 37
2. V_I-O	50, 67

B. *Three (-or-more)-word Sentences*
  (a) Flexible order:

S-V-O/O-V⌒Ind O-S	32/34 (see 9.222)

  (b) Inflexible order:

(Voc)-[S]V_I $\begin{cases}\text{(Ind)O}\\ \text{Loc}\\ \text{PP}\end{cases}$	62, (67) 35, 36, 40 24, 25, 29–31
([S]V_I-Ind O-O	66

C. *Negation* (Inflexible?)

[S]-lo⌒V-(O)	61, 62

D. *Wh Questions* (Inflexible?)

(Voc)-Wh-(*ze*)-(S)-V	17a, 18a, 19a, 22, 58, 63

The Voc may come finally instead of initially.

II   NON-VERBAL SENTENCES

A. *Two-word Sentences (S-P)*
  (a) Flexible order:

1. $N_1 + N_2$/$N_2 + N_1$	16, 41/42
2. Dem(*ze*)-N/N-Dem(*ze*)	3, (4)/(43)
3. (Voc + AM/AM + Voc	(48/49)

  (b) Inflexible:

1. Dem(*ine*) + N	17b, (21), 60
2. N + Adj	14, 15
3. N + Loc	13, 18b, 23, (33)
4. (N + PP	(23), (33)

B. *Three (-or more)-word Sentences*
  (a) Flexible:

Dem(*ze*) + N(+N)/N(+N) + Dem(*ze*)	4, 20/43, 44

  (b) Inflexible:

1. Dem(*ine*) + N + N	45, 46, 47
2. N(+N) + Loc	27, 28

[This will obviously soon change.]

9.   WORD ORDER IN THE FIRST SYNTACTIC PHASE

We will use the following symbols: S = Subject, V = Verb, O = [Direct] Object, Ind. O = Indirect Object, Voc = Vocative, O.M. = Object (= Accusative) Marker, [S]V_I = Verb in Imperative with S implied, Loc = Locative or Locational Adverbial, PP = Prepositional Phrase, N = Noun, Adj = Adjective, Dem(*ze*) = Demonstrative *ze* "this," Dem (*ine*) = Demonstrative *ine* "behold." Wh refers here to the interrogatives *mi* "who," *ma* "what," *eyfo* "where."

P = Predicate, AT = Adverbial of Time, AM = Adverbial of Manner, [ ] = implied, ( ) = "optional," / = interchangeable. Numbers refer to the numbers of the sample sentences above. (Generally, O may include complements, etc.).

9.1. *Partial Conclusions*: (1) We can see here a variety of combinations with established word orders. (2) In a way, the children whose language is analyzed here seem to stick to a relatively rigid word order, actually more than is required in mature Hebrew, and this is very interesting. Evidently, some (if not most) of the children impose on themselves very definite rules once they have established their theory about the system, as we discussed in 8.22–8.3 above.

9.2. Our random sampling of Gil and Gila's sentences may not be sufficient for determining the basic, deep (internal, inherent, and underlying) word order in their speech, but we don't have the space for presenting a full corpus. Besides, one of the major problems in determining the inherent word order at such an early stage is the fact that children then do not usually utilize the various distinctions that help the linguist to determine the basic, deep word order of the related mature language. This will apply to distinctions [in Hebrew] such as Definite vs. Indefinite (marked vs. unmarked) "Nominative" vs. "Accusative" or Subject vs. [Direct] Object (unmarked vs. marked), use of prepositions, adverbs, and the like.

9.21. However, a certain trend can be recognized even in this small sampling. It seems to agree generally with that of the fuller corpora of the speech of these children and of others that I followed. It also agrees with what I believe is the basic word order in modern Hebrew speech.

9.22. I hope to be able to explore this problem in greater detail elsewhere, and I will make here only a few tentative statements without discussion at this time.

9.221. (1). The basic order in (mature) modern Hebrew speech is evidently S-O-V.

In Greenberg's lists of "basic data on the 30-language sampling" for his Universals of Grammar,[69] Hebrew is listed as type I, a language with V-S-O order. He probably had Biblical Hebrew in mind, not modern Hebrew speech. Also, Greenberg evidently based his entire theory on surface structure, although with some insights about deeper structures. There is no point in examining here other aspects of Universal order.

9.222. (2). The basic order in the idiolects of the children that I studied seems to be S-O-V, too.

This does not mean that we won't hear different orderings, but we will say that such cases are permutations of the underlying, deep order and that they require adequate descriptions and interpretations. Thus, for example, we may have to interpret sentence (34) *uga atet li aba* "Cake to give to me Daddy" as either a surface structure of O-V-Ind O-S, or as a paraphrase of a complex sentence such as "this is the cake which Daddy gave me."

In that case, we have to assume the embedding of a relative clause, "[which] Daddy gave me." This is not impossible at all, in view of the advanced nature of this sentence, the use of *li* "to me," and the length and complexity of the sentence. (See 11.2.) Fuller discussion should be postponed to the next stage.

9.223. (3). Normally, the Indirect Object seems to precede the Direct object, and according to 9.222 this will apply to the "relative clause" in Sentence (34) as well.

9.3. This would be an appropriate place to analyze the children's prosody, especially *intonation*, but I am afraid I am not yet ready for it. It requires a special study based on additional material and a more elaborate theory than currently available. As for the general problem, it has been pointed out that normal children do absorb simple melodies at a very tender age, and they also seem to be adequately impressed by the intonation of the speech around them. Indeed, even during the

---

[69] Greenberg, ed. (1963), pp. 86–87.

babbling stage we may detect something similar to "intonation drill." Some scholars have even thought that this is all that babbling is about. Intonation was considered for quite a while the major vehicle for acquisition of syntax, but lately various doubts have been raised about this thesis. Indeed, the whole problem of prosody needs further study.[70]

10. Let us return to the syntactic analysis. We have encountered the children's various constructions, i.e., the one-word utterance of the N type, and the expanded NP; the non-verbal predicative utterances, the so-called equational sentences without the display of Copula; and the verbal sentences, although mostly without "secondary" constituents, as mentioned above.

10.1 A few years ago, several students of child language pointed out that from a distributional point of view some of the words the child uses belong to a small class of words whose frequency is much greater than that of other words in his vocabulary. Although the second class is much richer lexically and is more open to absorbing new elements, the frequency of its items is much less, and some of them may appear only once during that stage.

10.2. Martin Braine[71] tried to interpret the structural characteristics of the early word-combinations of three children who were followed from the age of eighteen months. He suggested that the child learns that each

---

[70] For an interesting discussion of prosody see Braine (1968, Mimeo), Section 2.12. Cf. P. Lieberman (1967), pp. 38–47.
[71] Martin D. S. Braine "The Ontogeny of English Phrase Structure: The First Phase," *Language*, XXXIX (1963), 1–13. See also his article "On Learning the Grammatical Order of Words," *Psychological Review*, LXX (1963), 323–48, and the interesting ensuring controversy with Bever, Fodor and Weksel: "On the Acquisition of Syntax: A Critique of 'Contextual Generalization,'" *Psychological Review*, LXXII (1965), 467–82; the counterattack by Braine "On the Basis of Phrase Structure: A Reply to Bever, Fodor and Weksel" (op. cit., pp. 483–92); and another reply by Bever-Fodor-Weksel, "Is Linguistics Empirical?" (op. cit., pp. 493–500). In this context we also should mention, among others, Brown and Fraser (1963), Miller and Ervin (1964), and Gvozdev, too, as mentioned in 8.23 above.

of a small number of words belongs in a particular position in an utterance, while a complementary position can be taken by any other word in the child's relatively small vocabulary. Hence the structure that he considers characteristic consists of two parts of speech: (1) the *Pivot* which comprises the small number of words whose position has been learned, and (2) the X-Class (a part of speech mainly in the residual sense, later referred to in the literature as the Open Class) which consists of the entire vocabulary except for some of the pivots. Braine also suggested that words that are combined with the pivot may also occur as single-word utterances, but the pivot words may not occur alone.

10.3. This interesting study was very helpful in attracting the attention of students of child language to the early stage of language development, even though not everybody agreed with him. I should like to make only one comment. The imbalanced division into the two classes in Braine's interpretation seems somewhat oversimplified. An exceedingly large proportion of phrases that did not fit the system were left aside, even if we take into consideration the fact that certain ones belong to the next phase. The fact that the child inserts into both positions meaningful words that combine into "grammatical" sentences (certainly according to the child's own grammar at that stage) and that the child utters for his necessary communication, does undoubtedly show that this speech is not something like a mere arbitrary play with structures. The child does first learn a framework of syntactic-semantic relations rather than inlaying lexical items. And indeed, we have seen sentences in which the two kinds of constituents may change their positions, contrary to what is implied in Braine's division. For example, see Sentences (4), (20)/(43), (44), (41)/(42), and perhaps even (18a)/(18b), and (19a)/(19b). This may apply even to cases like (1)/(2), etc. Furthermore, Sentences (38) and (39) demonstrate that either element may occur alone and constitue a single-word utterance.

10.31. Although such findings do not seem to support Braine's thesis, it is true that the child does devote time and effort exercising and examining various constructions and combinations by means of repetition, substitution, and the like. This is demonstrated in a most interesting way in Ruth Weir's *Language in the Crib* (1963), a study about the pre-sleep soliloquies of her two-and-a-half-year old son. This little boy, who evidently started combining later than our subjects, devised for himself various drills:

what color—what color glass . . .
not the yellow blanket—the white . . .
it's not black, it's yellow . . . not yellow—red . . .

But all these combinations are very meaningful communicative constructions. Compare Gila's drills by means of rhetorical questions:

(a)   While presenting a hair band (at the age of thirteen months), she says:
    (68)   *seé. ma ze?—seé. ine see* (corresponding to mature *séret. ma ze?—séret.* [*h*] *ine séret*)
       "[A] band. What's this? [A] band. Here's (behold) a band."
(b)   See samples (17), (18), (19) above.
(c)   While pointing at a button (*kaftor*) [pronounced by her as *to*]:
    (69)   *ma ze? ine to, ima.*
       "What's this? Here's (behold) a [but]ton, Mom."

11.   It seems to me that already at the very beginning of the child's syntactic-semantic experience, at the stage when he uses structures that may sound like the underlying base structures themselves (almost with a direct correlation between sound and meaning, as mentioned above), the child discovers a simple binary division between the elements of the sentence (and primarily from a *semantic* point of view). One element, which I propose to call [for lack of a better term] the "*Implicator*," is the implied element in the sentence that the child starts from when he comes to communicate his thought [or to formulate his "base question" as suggested earlier]. The other one is the "*Explicator*," the element that explicates, introduces the novelty, and is the focus of a relevant Wh question. As such it also usually (although not always) attracts the heaviest stress.

11.1.   Let us see a few examples. If we compare sentences (3), (4), and (20), *ze*

búba ina "This is Dolly Rina"—we changed the doll's name from *iza* "Aliza" to *ina* "Rina" as in (43)—with sentence (43) *búba ina ze* "Dolly Rina this," we will notice several things:

(a) Sentences (4) and (20) may answer a question, e.g., *ma ze?* "what's this?" while the child points at an object, which becomes thus implied and represented by the demonstrative. If the object happens to be Dolly Rina, the answer will be *ze búba ina* "This [is] Dolly Rina." This will also explain why the masculine *ze* will often appear in such sentences even in mature Hebrew. But Sentence (43) probably really answers a different question, *mi búba ina?* "Who is Dolly Rina?" Here "Dolly Rina" and the fact that there is such a doll are taken for granted; only the question is *who* or *which* one it is. The answer, of course, will put the emphasis on *ze* "this," i.e., "*This* is the one." Such an answer with *ze* "this" in *initial* position will have an "emphatic" stress on *ze!*.

11.21.   This assumption is well supported by a quick examination of the monologue in Sentences (42)–(45). Gila starts out looking at her Dolly Rina and notices that it has a hat. She "asks" herself, say, "What does Dolly Rina have?" and the answer is then, "Dolly Rina [has a] hat." So she asks rhetorically, "But who (or which) is Dolly Rina?" and she answers in (43) *buba ina zé* "Dolly Rina is this!" And for a summary of the elements of this "drill" monologue, she then answers a combined question like "Which is Dolly's hat?" by saying (44) *buba kova ze* "Dolly hat this," again with an emphatic stress on *ze*.

11.22.   Notice the development of (42)–(45):

(42)	*búba ína kóva*	Dolly Rina [has] hat.
(43)	*búba ína ze*	Dolly Rina [is] this.
(44)	*búba kóva ze*	Dolly [has] hat [is] this.

Looking at this sequence one cannot help thinking that these are not three isolated sentences, but that here might be the origin of an embedding of a "relative clause," that, say, (42) is to be embedded into (43) resulting in (44) which should be paraphrased as "Dolly [Rina] which has a hat is this." If this interpretation is acceptable, then we are witnessing here a unique case of relativization

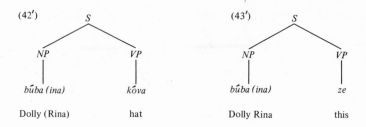

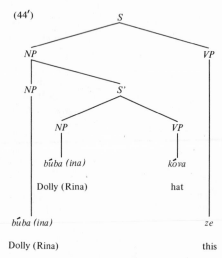

FIGURE 3

in the making—rather, the underlying, deep structure of relativization.

11.23. This can be roughly illustrated in the diagrams above.

11.3. Let us return to our suggestions in 11.1 and see how this is reflected in terms of prosodic features. The intonation/stress patterns of those sentences (assuming that 1, 2, 3 will represent three levels of stressing or pitch levels, i.e., lower, normal and higher levels respectively) will be:

	2 (1) 3			(1) (2) 3
(20)	*ze búba ína.*	vs.	(43)	*búba ína ze!*

It is apparent that in (20) the demonstrative *ze* is the Implicator and *búba ína* is the Explicator, while in (43) it is reversed, i.e., *ze* is the Explicator and *búba ína* is the Implicator. In other words, the same lexical items can serve as Implicator in one combination and as Explicator in another. They do not necessarily belong to one position.

11.31. In such cases, the function of the Implicator will coincide with that of the Subject of the Sentence, and that of the Explicator, with the function of the Predicate. Both of them can easily change tasks in a Non-Verbal sentence.

11.4. Can the same be said for sentences with Verbal Predicates like (1)/(2), i.e., is there an identical coincidence of Implicator-Subject and Explicator-Predicate there too? Presumably yes, if the permutation of NP and VP only rearranges the elements overtly without changing their basic order, functions, or relations. Otherwise it would imply that phrases other than NP's can occur as Subjects within the underlying deep structure. As mentioned above, what counts is the deep order of elements and relations. It seems that the usual (basic?) order is Implicator-Explicator. As noted above, this may change in some of the Wh questions, also in emphasis, and the like.

11.41. One may, of course, say that at the early stage there is no clear distinction between Nouns and Verbs and Adverbs, etc., and that any part of speech can constitute either an Implicator or an Explicator. Maybe so. But then there is no problem.

11.42. On the other hand, one may argue that the relation Subject-Predicate (both designating grammatical functions, as distinct from notions like NP and VP which designate grammatical categories) is a fundamental grammatical relation of deep structure, whereas that of the corresponding Implicator-Explicator is the basic grammatical relation of surface structure. As a matter of fact, such arguments were presented by Chomsky in connection with a Topic-Comment theory.[72]

But I think that (a) the Implicator-Explicator distinction is deeper and more comprehensive than that of Topic-Comment. In effect, topic-comment constructions should constitute one specific type of construction, with special emphasis on the Extrapositions and Topicalizations mentioned above.[73] (b) Although for very simple structures and for this stage in particular, it is often difficult to set a clear demarcation line between competence and performance, deep structure and surface structure, this division seems to be a very basic one with regard to deep structure, at least for the early stage. As such it may belong to the top of the hierarchy of categories and ensuing relations or, as mentioned above, it may be at the higher nodes of a general Phrase-marker, developing as follows:

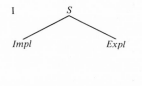
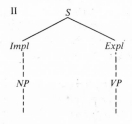

FIGURE 4

And the NP in turn will function as Subject, and the VP as Predicate, etc. (Perhaps a Predicate-Phrase node should be inserted between Expl and VP.) As such it may belong to the linguistic universals and thus be part of the child's innate endowment.

11.5. The Implicator-Explicator division is based on an assumption that the child wants to *communicate* with his environment from the very beginning. His first unit of communication is S, which is mostly (but not universally, since some children start with longer sentences) expressed by a single-word sentence, and we do not refer to naming only. The rest of his meaning is implied and expected to be understood. The environment, however, seems to experience some difficulty in interpreting such "stripped" sentences, which are in a way even more abstract than "deep

structures," and sometimes misinterpret them to the child's disappointment. Through their "expansions" of the child's sentences the adults try to show him the way to improve and expand his sentences. The child may become aware of it and add a slight refinement, e.g., by mentioning the implied element, the Implicator, as well. His initial rule is then:

S → (Impl) + Expl

The Implicator may not be mentioned, but the Explicator, which carries the important, novel, explicit information, is always there. (See 5.21–5.3 above.)

As the child goes on with the process of language acquisition, he continues developing his grammatical theory in general and his notion of S in particular, introducing further refinements in its constituents, stage after stage. Pretty soon he will start adding trans-

---

[72] Chomsky, *Aspects* (1965), p. 221.

[73] For the special application of these to child language see Gruber, 1967.

formational rules to his base structures and will try to perfect his phonology.

12. To sum up:

In the initial syntactic stage, the child develops a simple grammatical system whose overt manifestation is the so-called "telegraphic speech." Even the brief sentences of this stage, which are close to "speaking" base structures (see again Section 11), manifest the thesis of innate [linguistic] ideas and language universals, and may reveal the child's linguistic competence and his developing grammatical theory. On the holophrastic aspects see Section 5.

At this stage the child seems to possess only a few grammatical categories with simple hierarchical rules, which in turn reflect mainly the basic grammatical relations. In comparison with adult language, word order is pretty much "preserved" in child language; the contentives are essentially preserved while the functors are disregarded. They are of secondary importance for the understanding of the sentence and are also characterized by lower stress.

Chomsky's idea about relative degrees of grammaticalness may be helpful in explaining one of the ways in which the child is understood by his environment. Our observation that slightly older children best understand their younger peers deserves special attention too.

Initial syntactic structures in children's languages seem to be universally close to each other, while in the full languages they are very diversified. But this fact should not surprise us, since the children's [overt] sentences are close and often identical to the base structures, and the essential structures of the base are presumably common to all natural languages. Also, studying the developments and stages in the refinements in syntactic structures (and in the notion of Sentence) may be significant for determining limitations on linguistic universals (see 7.2). Child language should not be studied merely as a "reduction" of mature language, but rather as an illustration of the child's developing linguistic theory.

Word order in Hebrew child language is another interesting problem of general appeal, especially in view of the fact that Hebrew has a relatively flexible word order,

but children seem to be more inflexible than adults. Hebrew word order is compared with findings about English and Russian children's speech in Sections 8 and 9.

The internal, crude, but basic division of Sentence is a binary one of Implicator and Explicator, characteristic of the children's syntax in the first phase of their syntactic development. Transformations and transpositions may not appear at the very beginning, but they will appear at subsequent stages; however, see the unique case of "raw" relativization in 11.2. It seems that the question "transformation" precedes other "transformations" in child language, but usually it is *not* accompanied at the beginning by structural changes, by transpositions, either in Hebrew (even mature contemporary speakers do not usually observe the classical system that includes transpositions; see 5.22), or in English,[74] although in mature English various structural changes take place in such sentences. Extraposition structures may be posited even for the early stage (see section 6), but a full discussion of them should be postponed to the next stage.

Some of the early speakers that I studied, especially Gila and Gil, started quite early with the use of transformations as well, and their development is very interesting, but this stage will have to be dealt with elsewhere.

REFERENCES

Bach, Emmon. "*Have* and *Be* in English Syntax," *Language*, Vol. XLIII (1967), 462–485.

Bar-Adon, Aaron. *Children's Hebrew in Israel*, 2 Volumes (in Hebrew, summary in English), Jerusalem (1959).

———. "Analogy and Analogic Change as Reflected in Contemporary Hebrew," *Proceedings of the Ninth International Congress of Linguists*, ed. H. G. Lunt, The Hague, Mouton & Co., 1964, 758–763.

———. "The Evolution of Modern Hebrew" in *Acculturation and Integration*, New York, Histadrut Cultural Exchange Institute, 65–95 (1965).

———. "Processes of Nativization in Contem-

---

[74] For instance the little girl, Dawn, of Austin, Texas, asks during this early stage *Where they are?* compared with the mature "*Where are they?*"

porary Hebrew," in *The Revival of Modern Hebrew*, ed. Aaron Bar-Adon (forthcoming).

Bar-Adon, A., and Leopold, W. F. *Child Language: A Book of Readings*, Englewood Cliffs, N.J., Prentice-Hall, Inc. (in press).

Bellugi, Ursula, and Brown, Roger (eds.). *The Acquisition of Language*, Monographs of the Society for Research in Child Development, 1964, XXIX, No. 1.

Bever, T. G., Fodor, T. A., and Weksel, W. "On the Acquisition of Syntax: A Critique of (Contextual Generalizations,)" *Psychological Review*, LXXII (1965), 467–482; also "Is Linguistics Empirical?" 493–500.

Braine, M. D. S. "The Ontogeny of English Phrase Structure: The First Phase," *Language*, XXXIV (1963a), 1–13.

——. "On Learning the Grammatical Order of Words," *Psychological Review*, LXX (1963b), 323–348.

——. "On the Basis of Phrase Structure: A Reply to Bever, Fodor and Weksel," *Psychological Review*, LXXII (1965), 483–492.

——. "The Acquisition of Language in Infant and Child," Mimeo (1968).

Brown, Roger. "The Development of Wh Questions in Child Speech," *Journal of Verbal Learning and Verbal Behavior*, VII (1968), 279–290.

Brown, R., and Bellugi, U. "Three Processes in The Child's Acquisition of Syntax," *Harvard Educational Review*, XXXIV (1964), No. 2 (A Special Issue on Language and Learning), 133–151.

Brown, Roger and Fraser, Colin. "The Acquisition of Syntax," in *Verbal Behavior and Learning*, C. N. Cofer and B. S. Musgrave, eds., New York, McGraw-Hill Book Company, 1963. (Reprinted in Bellugi and Brown [1964], 43–79.)

Chomsky, Noam. "A Review of B. F. Skinner's *Verbal Behavior*," *Language* (1959), 26–58 (esp. 42–44, 55–58). Reprinted in Fodor and Katz, eds. (1964), 547–578.

——. (1964a) "Formal Discussion" of Miller and Ervin (1964), in Bellugi and Brown, eds. (1964), 35–39.

——. (1964b) "Degrees of Grammaticalness," in Fodor and Katz (1964), 384–389. Reprinted in part from Chomsky's "Some Methodological Remarks on Generative Grammar," *Word*, 17 (1961), 219–239.

——. *Aspects of the Theory of Syntax*, Cambridge, Mass., The M.I.T. Press, 1965.

——. *Cartesian Linguistics*, New York, Harper & Row, 1966, esp. pp. 59–73.

——. "The Formal Nature of Language," Appendix A in E. Lennelberg (1967), 397–442.

——. "Language and the Mind," *Psychology Today*, I (9), February 1968, 48–51, 66–68.

——. *Language and Mind*, New York, Harcourt, Brace and World, Inc., 1968.

Chomsky, N., and Halle, M. *The Sound Pattern of English*, New York, Harper & Row, 1968.

Fodor, J. A. and Katz, J. J. (eds.), *The Structure of Language: Readings in the Philosophy of Language*, Englewood Cliffs, N. J., Prentice-Hall, 1964.

Greenberg, Joseph H. "Some Universals of Grammar with Particular Reference to the Order of Meaningful Elements," in Joseph H. Greenberg (Ed.), *Universals of Language*, Cambridge, Mass., The M.I.T. Press, 1963, 58–90.

Gruber, Jeffrey S. "Topicalization in Child Language," *Foundations of Language*, III (1967), 37–65.

Hayon, Yehiel. *Relativization in Hebrew; A Transformational Approach*, Ph. D. Dissertation at the University of Texas, Austin, Texas, 1969.

Jacobs, R. A. and Rosenbaum, P. S. *English Transformational Grammar*, Waltham, Mass., Blaisdell Publishing Co., 1968.

Jakobson, Roman "Antony's Contribution to Linguistic Theory," in Weir, 1962, 18–22.

——. (1941 [1968]) *Kindersprache, Aphasie und allgemeine Lantgesetze*, Uppsala, 1941. English Translation by A. R. Keiler [used here]: *Child Language, Aphasia and Phonological Universals*, The Hague, Mouton & Co. (1968).

Katz, J. J. *The Philosophy of Language*, New York, Harper & Row, 1966, esp. pp. 240–283.

Klima, E. and Bellugi-Klima, U. "Syntactic Regularities in the Speech of Children," in Lyons & Wales (eds.), 1966, 183–208. Revised version in Bar-Adon and Leopold, (eds.) (in press).

Lenneberg, Eric H. "The Capacity for Language Acquisition," in Fodor and Katz (1964), 579–603.

——. "The Natural History of Language," in Smith and Miller (1966), pp. 219–252 (with discussion by R. A. Chase, et al, 253–271).

―――. *Biological Foundations of Language*, New York, John Wiley and Sons, Inc. 1967.

Leopold, W. F. *Speech Development of a Bilingual Child; A Linguist's Record*, Vols. 1–4, Evanston, Ill., Northwestern University Press, 1939–49.

―――. "Patterning in Child Language Learning," *Language Learning*, V, Nos. 1 and 2 (1953–54), 1–14.

Lieberman, Philip. *Intonation, Perception, and Language*, Cambridge, Mass., The M.I.T. Press, 1967.

McNeill, David. (1966a) "Developmental Psycholinguistics," in Smith and Miller (1966), pp. 15–84.

―――. (1966b) "The Creation of Language by Children," in Lyons and Wales (eds.) (1966), pp. 99–115.

Miller, G. A., and Chomsky, N. "Finitary Models of Language Users," *Handbook of Mathematical Psychology*, II, ed. Luce et al, 1963, esp. pp. 443–449.

Miller, Wick and Ervin, Susan. "The Development of Grammar in Child Language," in Bellugi and Brown (eds.) (1964), pp. 9–34.

Ornan, Uzzi *Taḥbir ha'ivrit haḥadaša*, Jerusalem, Akademon, 1965 (in Hebrew).

―――. *"Pirkey Yiḥud"* ("Extraposition Sections"), *Ma'alot*, VII, Nos. 1–2, October 1967, 46–59 (in Hebrew).

Peretz, Y. The Relative Clause, Tel Aviv, Dvir, 1967.

Rosenbaum, Peter S. *The Grammar of English Predicate Complement Constructions*, Cambridge, Mass., The M.I.T. Press, 1967.

Rubinstein, E. *The Nominal Sentence* [in Contemporary Hebrew], Israel, Hakibbutz Hameuchad, 1968.

Slobin, Dan I. "The Acquisition of Russian as a Native Language," in Smith and Miller (1966), 129–148. (Cf. the general discussion, 149–152.)

Smith, Frank and Miller, George A., eds. *The Genesis of Language: A Psycholinguistic Approach*, Cambridge, Mass., The M.I.T. Press, 1966.

Weir, Ruth. *Language in the Crib*, The Hague, Mouton & Co., 1962.

TOPICS FOR REPORTS, TERM PAPERS, AND MAJOR RESEARCH PROJECTS

> This list of topics, like the original idea for this reader, is a by-product of the graduate course on child language that was conducted by the author in 1963–64 at the University of Texas, Department of Linguistics.
>
> It should be taken merely as a suggestive list, and it is hoped that it might be of some use to instructors and students in the selection of topics for either minor or major research projects.

1. *Development of Grammatical Patterns in Child Language.*

   What are the processes and stages in the development of grammatical patterns in child language. Are there any general (universal?) trends, e.g. in terms of order or sequence of acquisition of certain patterns, transitions, and the like among various children?

2. *Test of the Child's Control of the Linguistic Rules by Nonsense Forms.*

   Instructions: Construct a set of adequate tests for eliciting the child's knowledge of the system. Try to elicit new formulations by the child with special emphasis on either phonology or grammar (morphology and/or syntax), semantics, or on all of them. You may experiment with individual children or with groups. Describe your procedure and findings. Compare the latter with reports in the literature. Conclude.

3. *Systematic Errors by Children as Evidence of the Child's Implicit Knowledge of the Language System (Its Regularities and General Rules).*

4. *"Grammaticality" and Child Language.*

   Compare a system of child language (of one individual or of a group) with that of the adult community. What are the differences, if any, in terms of "grammaticality"? What areas, if any, are most susceptible to "modifications"?

5. *Judgment of "Grammaticality" by Children.*

   Instructions: Devise an empirical test to investigate the reaction of children with respect to "grammaticality."

6. *Transformational Grammar and the Linguistic Processes in the Development of Language in Children.*

   What is the relationship between the implicit development of grammatical patterns in child language, and the explicit transformational approach of the linguist. (Does a child acquire a set of "transformational rules" which generate his sentences?)

7. *Transformational Grammar and Child Linguistics.*

8. *"Psycholinguistics" and "Child Linguistics."*

Describe and analyze the application of recent psycholinguistic methods to the study of child language.

9. *The History of Child-Language Study: Trends and Methods.*

10. *The Theory of "Linguistic Relativity" and the Processes of Language Acquisition by Children.*

    Note: For earlier bibliography, consult J. B. Carroll. "Linguistic Relativity, Contrastive Linguistics, and Language Learning," *International Review of Applied Linguistics in Language Teaching,* I (1963), 1–20.

11. *Bilingualism in Child Language.*

    a. Give a summary of the findings in the literature on bilingualism in children. What are the implications?
    b. Report a case study of a bilingual child (or a group of children).

12. *Preverbal Vocalization Developments in Infants.*

    A summary of the literature (if possible, some experimental test).

13. *Acquisition of Stress and Intonation by Infants.*

14. *Intonation and Syntax in the Linguistic Development of Children.*

    What are the relationships between intonation patterns and syntactic structures in child language?—intonation as "forerunner" of syntactic developments (language without words"?)? Intonation as "carrier" of syntax? Or what?

15. *Patterns of Substitution in Children's Phonology.*

    What are the relations between the adult's system and the child's system? Can definite rules of substitution be derived? (Try to analyze it from both directions—of child language as well as adult language.)

16. *On the Role of Anticipation in the Children's Substitution Methods.*

    (Scan the various diaries and case studies.)

17. *Child Language and "Baby Language" (as employed by adults):*

    Describe the various cultures, as compared with the respective child language on the one hand and adult language on the other. (Cf. studies by Austerlitz, Cassagrande, Ferguson, *et al.*)

    Robert Austerlitz. "Gilyak Nursery Words." *Word,* XII (1956), 260–79.
    Joseph B. Cassagrande. "Comanche Baby Language." *International Journal of American Linguistics,* XIV (1948), 11–14.
    C. A. Ferguson. "Arabic Baby Talk." In *For Roman Jakobson,* ed. M. Halle *et al.* (The Hague, 1956), pp. 121–28.

18. *Reduplication in Child Language.*

19. *Imitation, Selection, and Analogy in the Development of Child Language.*
     A review of the literature and critical analysis.

20. *Linguistic Changes in the Course of the Child's Acquisition of Language and their Implications (if any?) for the Study of Linguistic Change in General.*

21. *On the Acquisition of the Morphological Patterns by Children.*
     a. Analysis of available studies.
     b. Try to devise a test for the study of the child's acquisition of passive and active morphological awareness and control. (Experiment, if possible.)

22. *On the Acquisition of Syntax by Children.*
     a. Analysis of available reports in the literature on child language.
     b. Try to devise a test for the study of the child's passive and active control of syntax. (Experiment, if possible.)

23. *Prosodic Features in the Development of Child Language.*

24. *Lexical Studies:*
     a. Lexical patterning in child language.
     b. On the lexical study of child language.
     c. A critical analysis and review of the literature.

35. *On Semantic Structures in Child Language.*

26. *Application of Theories and Findings on Child Linguistics to Second Language Teaching.*

27. *Is Special Redefinition of Grammatical Units (Phoneme, Morpheme, Sentence, Sequences, Parts of Speech, etc.) Necessary or Unnecessary for the Analysis of Child Language?*

28. *The Child's Early Phrase Structures and His Self-Devised Presleep Soliloquies ("Drills"), and Some of Their Implications, e.g.:*
     a. For language teaching in pathological cases.
     b. For second language teaching.

29. *Child Linguistics and General Linguistics.*
     a. Child linguistics as a branch of general linguistics.
     b. Contributions of child linguistics to the general linguistic theory.

30. *Statistical Linguistics and the Study of Child Language.*

31. *Jakobson's Six Functions of Language as Reflected in Child Language.*

32. *The Process of Language Acquisition and the Theory of Distinctive Features:*
    a. The system of distinctive features.
    b. Patterns of development in child language.
    c. Are distinctive features necessarily binary?

33. *Experimental Study of the Development of Distinctive Features in the Process of Acquisition of Phonology in Children.*

34. *A Theory and a Method for Economical Teaching of the Phonology of a Language to Infants, Based on the Distinctive Features.*

    Instructions: Try to devise a theory and a method for the actual teaching of English phonology to infants in the most economical way, based on the theory of distinctive features (cf. the reports on experiments of this sort which were conducted in Russia). To what extent is it feasible?

35. *The "First Word" or the First Systematic Contrast?*

    Analysis of theories and methods of child-language study.

36. *"Telegraphic Style" in Child Language and Its Grammatical (Syntactic and Morphological) as Well as Phonological Implications.*

37. *Parts of Speech and Their Functions in Early Child Language.*

    Order of reference to nouns, adjectives, verbs, etc.; tense and aspect in the verb, etc.

38. *Communication and Egocentric Speech in Child Language.*

39. *Artificially Constructed Vocal Stimuli for Identifying the Actual Cues Used by Children in their First Language Acquisition.*

40. *On Detection (or Diagnosis) of Speech Sound Retardation in Early Childhood.*

    Cf. O. C. Irwin, "Phonetical Description of Speech Development Childhood," in Louise Kaiser, ed., *Manual of Phonetics* (Amsterdam, 1957), pp. 404–25. See the questions posed on p. 404, and the answers to them in the course of the presentation.

41. *Derivation and Compounding of New Words in Child Language.*

42. *On the Role of Visual Imitation in the Acquistion of Early Phonemic Inventories in Child Language.*

    Note: This may be connected with the following topic:

43. *Processes of Language Acquisition in Blind Children as Compared with those of Normal Children.*

    Note: The objectives of this study are:
    a. To discover the differences in the pattern of language acquisition in both groups.

       b.   Hence: to determine the role of the *visual clues* as compared with the acoustic clues. Cf. the preceeding topic.

44. *Child Language and Linguistic Continuity.*

45. *Hierarchic Structures in Child Vocabulary.*

46. *Semantic Learning in Children.*

Cf. W. Leopold, *Speech Development of a Bilingual Child*, Vol. III, 592–643.

47. *Patterns of Word-Association in Children's Languages as Compared with Those of Adults.*

Are there some universal trends in this respect?

48. *The Transition from the "One Word" Phase to the "Two Word" and Multi-word Phases in the Child's Syntax.*

49. *Competence and Performance in Child Language.*

50. *Language Universals in "Child Language."*

51. *The Acquisition of Complex Syntactic Structures in Children.*

Note: Consult now Carol Chomsky, *The Acquisition of Syntax in Children from 5 to 10.* Cambridge, Mass.: M. I. T. Press, 1969.

A. B. A.